WE ARE ONE!

MELVIN I. UROFSKY is professor of history and chairman of the Department of History at Virginia Commonwealth University in Richmond. He has also taught at the State University of New York at Albany, and at Ohio State University. He is the author of *American Zionism from Herzl to the Holocaust; Big Steel and the Wilson Administration: A Study in Business-Government Relations; a Mind of One Piece: Brandeis and American Reform;* editor of *Why Teachers Strike; Perspectives on Urban America;* and coeditor of *Letters of Louis D. Brandeis.*

We Are One!

American Jewry
and Israel

MELVIN I. UROFSKY

ANCHOR PRESS/DOUBLEDAY   GARDEN CITY, NEW YORK   1978

Acknowledgments are made to the following for their kind permission to reprint these poems:

"Israel," by Karl Shapiro. From *Selected Poems* by Karl Shapiro. Reprinted by permission of Random House, Inc. © 1948 by the author.

"Masada," by Stanley Cooperman. From *Cannibals* by Stanley Cooperman. Reprinted by permission of Oberon Press, © 1972 by the author.

ISBN: 0-385-07580-4
Library of Congress Catalog Card Number 77–12878
Copyright © 1978 by Melvin Urofsky

For Jerome Eckstein and Sally Lawrence

"Ah," my father murmured. Then he said quietly. "Reuven, listen to me. The Talmud says that a person should do two things for himself. One is to acquire a teacher. Do you remember the other?"

"Choose a friend," I said.

—Chaim Potok, *The Chosen*

CONTENTS

Illustrations

Introduction

In the Preface to *American Zionism from Herzl to the Holocaust*, I wrote that "the problems and achievements of American Zionism since 1942, and the relation of American Jewry to Israel, form a separate and unified story, but one which must be told at another time." This book is an attempt to tell that story, to examine the complex set of relationships which form the unique bonds between the world's two largest Jewish communities. In some ways, it is a successor volume to *American Zionism* and takes up where that book left off, with the Biltmore conference of 1942, an event which closed out "the apprentice years" of American Zionism.

But as I researched this study, interviewed dozens of people both in the United States and Israel, and grew more familiar with contemporary conditions, it became apparent that attempts to limit the story to Zionist activities alone would yield at best only a partial and distorted view of the subject. From 1942 to 1948, American Zionism and its leaders did occupy the center stage in the fight to create an autonomous Jewish homeland in Palestine, to establish a refuge for that pitifully small number who escaped the destruction of the Holocaust. The recognized leaders of American Jewry were all Zionists or, as in the case of Henry Monsky of B'nai B'rith and Joseph Proskauer of the American Jewish Committee, men who came to accept the Zionist program on pragmatic if not ideological grounds. Without taking anything away from the *Yishuv* in Palestine, which had rebuilt the land and then paid

in blood and fire for its independence, the establishment of the Third
Jewish Commonwealth marked a triumph for American Zionism, both
in terms of its political struggles with the American government and in
the United Nations, and in proselytizing the American Jewish community.

After 1948, however, American Zionism as an organized movement
faded in power and influence, both as a result of Israeli maneuvering
and of its own narrow vision. The Jewish state, far more than a Zionist
creation, became the cherished inheritance of nearly all Diaspora Jews.
Support of Israel gradually developed into the least common denominator of Jewish identity, the one sure sign that an American Jew still
retained allegiance to the Jewish people. Now, not only organized
Zionists but all of American Jewry rallied to Israel in times of crisis,
supported the Jewish state by means of political pressure and financial
contributions, accepted Israeli culture and artifacts as an integral part
of American Jewish life, and brought Israel to the very center of its
group consciousness.

Yet in doing so, the various components of American Jewry confronted a number of difficult questions about relations to the state,
about the meaning and importance of Israel in American Jewish life,
about responsibilities between the two communities, and about possible
conflicts between identification and obligations as Jews and as Americans. Some groups found little trouble in answering these questions to
their own satisfaction; others found the questions difficult and the possible answers even more disturbing. In essence, this book is a study of
those questions and answers. It is not a "finished portrait," not only because history does not provide final answers, but also because we are
looking at a process and not a static situation. I hope that the pages
which follow will shed some light on that process.

As with the earlier book, this study has a definite orientation: It is
written from the vantage point of American Jewry—its attitudes, its
achievements, its problems, and its changing condition. My main proposal is that relations between American Jewry and Israel are composed
not only of ties that bind, but of differences that sunder as well. Many
people see the Israeli-American Jewish nexus as fairly simple and
straightforward; it is anything but that. If one accepts the analogy of
the Jewish people as an extended family, then relations among parts are
as ambivalent as those of any large and contentious family—loving, hating, cajoling, supportive, cantankerous, simple, and complex. Indeed,

were it anything else, there would be no need for this book. The very complexity of these relations, to me at least, make a fascinating if at times frustrating subject.

American Jews are constantly faced with a number of situations in which they must play different roles. They are *Americans,* with all the challenges and privileges that implies, and they are *Jews,* carrying the burdens and obligations, the joys and beauties, of four thousand years of known history. In general, no contradiction exists between these two demands, but rather an infinite number of options when confronting specific issues. For example, intermarriage between Jews and non-Jews is of concern to American Jews as Jews, who see it as threatening the survival of the community. Yet to American Jews as Americans, it is a mark of acceptance within the general society. At most times, support of Israel within the Jewish community has been matched with a generally sympathetic attitude by the United States government and American society as a whole. Yet there have been times, such as in 1956 and 1973, when American Jews had to oppose their government's policy. As Jews, the community has had to deal with the traditional idea of *galut,* of exile outside of *Eretz Yisrael,* but as Americans, nearly all Jews consider the United States a second Zion. And then, both as Americans and as Jews, especially those belonging to the Conservative and Reform movements, they have had to deal with an established Israeli rabbinate which runs counter to American ideas of pluralism.

These problems are part of the process of interaction not only between American Jewry and Israel, but also of the acculturation of American Jews within American society. The nature and history and situation of the American Jewish community and of its many components are integral to the study of relations between it and Israel. It is a drama with many acts yet to play.

                                    *   *   *

The preface to Marvin and Bernard Kalb's *Kissinger* includes a marvelous line: "Needless to say, all errors are my brother's." Would that I could say the same. Despite the help of many people, in the end all errors of fact or of judgment are mine. Nonetheless, I want to thank the many men and women who, in one way or another, made it possible and pleasant for me to complete this study.

A number of people were kind enough to spend time with me explaining their own role in the American-Israeli relationship or sharing their knowledge and insight about current conditions and problems. In the United States, these included: Howard Adelson, president of the United Zionist Revisionists of America; Morris Amitai of AIPAC; Samuel Cohen, former executive director of the American Zionist Federation and now director of the Jewish National Fund in America; Carmella Carr, executive director of the AZF; Dr. Judith Abarbanel Diesendruck of the World Zionist Organization's academic desk; Professor Leo Diesendruck, chairman of the executive committee of the AZF; Nahum Goldmann, president of the World Jewish Congress; Itzhak Hamlin of the WZO American Section; Charlotte Jacobson, chairman of the WZO American Section; I. L. Kenen, former director of AIPAC; the late Judge Louis Levinthal, former president of the Zionist Organization of America; Mel Parness, executive secretary of B'nai Zion; the late Shad Polier of the American Jewish Congress; Rabbi David Polish, former president of the Central Conference of American Rabbis and chairman of the AZF Ideological Commission; Rabbi Emanuel Rackman, now president of Bar-Ilan University; Faye Schenk, president of the AZF; Ralph Stern, president of the Young Leadership Cabinet of the United Jewish Appeal; and Jacques Torczyner, former president of the ZOA and currently a member of the WZO American Section.

In Israel I spoke with Yehuda Avner, then assistant to the Prime Minister; Rabbi Morton Berman, former executive with the Keren Hayesod; Zelig Chinitz, executive director of the United Israel Appeal; Reuven Dafneh, head of the North American Desk in the Foreign Ministry; Professor Moshe Davis, head of the Institute for Contemporary Jewry at Hebrew University; Hon. Eliahu Elath, former Israeli ambassador to the United States; Professor Daniel J. Elazar of Temple and Bar-Ilan Universities; Professor Evyatar Friesel of Hebrew University; Professor Lloyd Gartner of Tel-Aviv University; Rabbi Israel Goldstein, former president of the ZOA and of the Jewish National Fund; Professor Aryeh Goren of Hebrew University; Hon. Moshe Kol, former Minister of Tourism; Natanel Lorch, secretary to the Knesset; Arthur Lourie of the Foreign Ministry; Hon. Golda Meir, former Prime Minister of Israel; the late Julian Meltzer of Yad Weizmann; Professor Meyer Passow of Bar-Ilan University; Professor Natan Rotenstreich of Hebrew University; the late Ezra Shapiro, head of the Keren Hayesod; Colonel Dov Shefi, chief military legal officer for the administered territories; Avraham Shenker, director of the WZO Organization and Education Department; the late Meyer Weisgal, chancellor of the Weizmann Institute; and the late Zvi Yaron, editor of the WZO's *Forum* and a member of the Israeli Zionist Ideological Commission.

I am especially indebted to the late Rose Halprin, past president of Hadassah, and Emanuel Neumann, past president of the ZOA, both of whom spent many hours with me patiently explaining the byzantine workings of the Zionist movement and recalling many fascinating events in long and crowded lives.

One of the great satisfactions of the historical profession is the give and take among colleagues, by which process one's errors may be found and corrected, and one's arguments refined and focused. The following friends read all or part of the manuscript, and I am indebted to them for their kind words and valuable suggestions: Howard Adelson of the City College of New York; Judy Diesendruck of the WZO; Leo Diesendruck of the AZF; Henry Feingold of Baruch College; Ben Halpern of Brandeis University; Menahem Kelner of the University of Virginia; Susan Kennedy, Edward Kopf, and Robert Talbert of Virginia Commonwealth University; Monty Penkower of Touro College; Rabbi David Polish; Ralph and Frances Stern; Jacques Torczyner of the WZO American Section; and Carl Hermann Voss of the Ecumenical Institute at Tantor, Jerusalem.

I am especially indebted to the comments of David W. Levy of the University of Oklahoma and Jerome Eckstein of the State University of New York at Albany. With great wisdom, patience, and above all humor, they helped me—indeed, forced me—to rethink many of my points in order to avoid ambiguity and confusion. Their labors have again confirmed the depths of our friendship. I am also indebted to my son, Philip E. Urofsky, who read and commented on the manuscript, not only for his comments but also for the *nachas* he gave me in doing so.

Research is done in libraries and archives and repositories, and the historian's work can be made immeasurably easier if he is fortunate enough to work with knowledgeable and co-operative staffs. Much of my manuscript research took place at three archives, and their staffs went out of their way to make my visits there pleasant as well as fruitful. My thanks, and respect, to Sylvia Landress, head of the Zionist Archives and Library in New York, and to her associates, Esther Togman and Rebecca Sherman; to Dr. Michael Heymann, director of the Central Zionist Archives, Jerusalem, and his colleague, Dr. I. Phillipp;

and especially to Nehama A. Chalom, curator of the Weizmann Library in Rehovoth, and to her staff, Rhonda Epstein and Shoshana Kafri. Dr. Abraham Alsberg, the Israeli State Archivist, kindly granted me permission to examine papers within the thirty-year restricted period.

I am also grateful to Miriam Leikind of the Silver Archives in Cleveland; Vera Prousnitz of the Goldstein Archives in Jerusalem; Fannie Zelcer of the American Jewish Archives; and Bernard Wax and Nathan Kaganoff of the American Jewish Historical Society. Israel Goldstein, Morton Berman, and the late Meyer Weisgal kindly opened their private papers to me, and Myer Feldman allowed me to read his oral history memoir in the Kennedy Library. Rachel Gershuni was invaluable as a research assistant in Jerusalem, and Geoffrey Wigoder of the Oral History Program at the Institute of Contemporary Jewry went out of his way to facilitate transcription of my tapes and provide access to the Institute's holdings. Helen Rivkind of the Jerusalem office of the American Professors for Peace in the Middle East proved of great assistance in arranging several of my interviews.

I cannot say enough of the assistance and support I received from my colleagues at Virginia Commonwealth University. My secretary, Betty Leviner, typed endless notes and manuscript copy, and so ran my office to give me the time to do my research. Parts of the manuscript were also typed by Janet Good and Suzette Poupore. Jane Westenberger, Janet Howell, and Eileen Meagher of the Interlibrary Loan Office cheerfully processed and conscientiously tracked down each of many, many requests.

The actual writing of the manuscript was greatly facilitated by the National Endowment for the Humanities, which awarded me a senior research fellowship during 1976–77. Dean Paul D. Minton and Associate Dean Albert M. Lyles, whose support and encouragement have been constant since I first came to Virginia Commonwealth University, went out of their way to help arrange a year's leave of absence so I could accept the fellowship.

My editor and friend Loretta A. Barrett has worked with me on this book for what seems to both of us a very long time. To her, and to all of these people, my sincere appreciation and the hope that this work will justify their assistance and confidence.

Last but certainly not least, my thanks to my wife, Susan, and my sons Philip and Robert for their encouragement in the project, their toleration of my idiosyncrasies during research and writing, and for their occasional outbursts of exasperation, which always helped me to regain a better perspective of what is important in life.

Richmond, Virginia

DECISION AT BILTMORE

It was a cool spring day in New York, May 10—Mother's Day—1942, with a faint chance of showers later in the afternoon. The day before, Alsab had won the fifty-second running of the Preakness Stakes in the record time of 1:57; New York led Cleveland by one game in the American League, while Brooklyn held a two-game edge over Pittsburgh in the National League. Leon Henderson, head of the Office of Price Administration, warned that there could be further rationing problems, and rayon stockings went on sale for a dollar a pair at Arnold Constable's. Reports were coming in of a major American naval victory over the Japanese in the Coral Sea, and the War Department released the information that German submarines had sunk three American ships in the Gulf of Mexico. Book stores were featuring Ludwig Lewisohn's translation of Franz Werfel's classic *The Song of Bernadette*, while moviegoers saw Abbott and Costello in *Rio Rita*, Veronica Lake and Alan Ladd in *This Gun for Hire*, Charlie Chaplin in *The Gold Rush*, or Mickey Rooney in *The Courtship of Andy Hardy*. Hitler still held a firm grip on the Continent, but RAF bombers had inflicted heavy damage on the German seaplane works at Warnemuende. On Broadway, the marquees listed a number of long-running hits, including *Arsenic and Old Lace*, *Life with Father*, *Blithe Spirit*, and *Lady in the Dark*, which starred Gertrude Lawrence.

Few of the more than six hundred men and women in the grand ballroom of the Hotel Biltmore that afternoon, however, paid more than passing attention to any of these items, with the exception of the war news and the disturbing rumors of mass murders of Jews by the Nazis. The plight of European Jewry had become the main concern of Jewish organizations all over the country, and the Emergency Committee for Zionist Affairs, representing the four largest American Zionist groups—the Zionist Organization of America, Hadassah, Mizrachi (religious Zionists), and Poale Zion (Labor Zionists)—had called this extraordinary conference to develop a unified strategy which, hopefully, would win the support not only of the five million Jews in the United States, but which would also be accepted by the leaders of the Allied governments.

But as they waited for the chairman to call the conference to order, they undoubtedly also thought of the problems confronting them—the failure of Great Britain to keep the promise of the Balfour Declaration, the tensions between the *Yishuv* (the Jewish settlement in Palestine) and the Arab population of the Holy Land, the internal differences within the Zionist movement over its goals, and the deep divisions in the American Jewish community over the entire question of Jewish nationalism.

*   *   *

Ever since Theodor Herzl had sounded the call in 1897 for Jews to re-establish themselves in their ancient homeland in Palestine, the Zionists had worked to bring about the ancient dream of redemption. A major step closer to this goal came in 1917, when the British, seeking to win over Jewish opinion during World War I, promised in the Balfour Declaration to help establish a Jewish homeland in Palestine after the end of hostilities. At the 1920 San Remo conference, the victorious Allies awarded a mandate over the former Turkish territory to Great Britain, and had written the Balfour promise into its Preamble. Buoyed up by this triumph, hundreds of thousands of Jews moved over the next two decades to join the *Yishuv*; there they cultivated the desert, built a modern city in place of sand dunes, and introduced up-to-date agricultural and industrial methods as well as modern health and sanitary techniques. In all of these endeavors, the members of the *Yishuv* received material aid from Jews in the Diaspora through a variety of Zionist, and some non-Zionist, funds and agencies.

But as the *Yishuv* prospered, it faced the problem of a growing Arab nationalism, which resented the establishment of a Jewish center in the midst of Arab lands. The fact that the Jews brought the benefits of modern medicine and agriculture to Arab peasants, or that they provided new water supplies to Arab villages, made no difference to militant Arabs, who opposed not only the Zionist program, but British rule as well.[1] From time to time Arab leaders incited bloody riots against the Jews in Palestine, and each time they discovered that the British, instead of bringing force to bear against the troublemakers, tried to placate them. As a result, Arab demands grew by leaps and bounds, and the British, attempting to appease the Arabs, practically forsook their earlier promises to the Jews.

By 1939 the Zionist Organization had grown disenchanted with its former British friends. A number of Zionist groups began discussing ways of fighting the British, for Hitler had created a situation in Germany that made a haven for oppressed Jews an absolute necessity. The advent of war, however, mooted the issue; Hitler had to be defeated first, but Jews must still be permitted to come to *Eretz Yisrael*. Palestinian Jews accordingly joined British fighting forces on the one hand, while on the other they established an elaborate system of illegal immigration to bring in refugees from the Nazi terror.[2] The war also shifted the main center of Zionist activity from Europe to the United States, which until 1941 remained out of the fighting. American Jewry was the wealthiest and most powerful Jewish community in the world, but it stood deeply divided on the question of Zionism and the future of Palestine. It would be fair to say that most of America's five million Jews had been indifferent to Zionism until the late 1930s. They and their parents had chosen to leave Europe and come to the United States rather than go to Palestine. Here they had found liberty and opportunity without the legal and social restrictions which were Europe's feudal heritage. While most immigrants never rose above the level of factory worker or small shopkeeper, they saw their children go to college and become professionals—doctors, lawyers, teachers—with status and prosperity far beyond the dreams of European Jews. While many of them retained some emotional ties to the millennial dream of Jewish restoration in Palestine, it played little part in their daily lives. They made token donations to Zionist funds, but few joined the movement or actively supported its projects.

Hitler changed this situation by making Jews acutely sensitive to the need for a refuge. Even those opposed to Jewish nationalism recognized that there must be some place which would accept persecuted Jews.

The United States, wracked by the Depression, refused to allow in new immigrants while millions of its own citizens remained unemployed. An international conference at Evian in France produced pious platitudes about the poor suffering Jews, but not one major country offered to take in more than a token handful of refugees. When Golda Meyerson (later Meir) left Evian, she told reporters: "There is only one thing I hope to see before I die, and that is that my people should not need expressions of sympathy anymore." The *Yishuv* alone wanted to take in persecuted German Jews, but the British would not even allow Palestine to appear on the Evian agenda for fear of offending Arab feelings.[3]

The plight of European Jewry did lead American philanthropic agencies to join together in the United Jewish Appeal, but from the beginning the umbrella organization was torn by internal dissent about whether or nor Palestine was the best solution for the refugees. Anti-Zionist leaders feared that a Jewish homeland would raise political questions about their loyalty to the United States. How, they asked, could an American citizen be loyal both to the United States and to a foreign Jewish state? What would happen were the United States and the Jewish state ever to come into conflict, perhaps even be on opposing sides during a war? Would their true allegiance to America be recognized by their non-Jewish fellow citizens, or would they be ostracized, as had German Americans during 1917 and 1918? They had chosen who and what they wanted to be—Americans who practiced the Jewish religion—and the whole idea of Zionism, of Jewish nationalism, threatened their status. American Zionists had resolved this issue for themselves years earlier through the famous Brandeis synthesis, which saw assistance in creating a democratic Jewish society in Palestine as supportive of the broader principles of American freedom and social justice.[4] But for Jews who placed a high value upon assimilation into the gentile society (while nominally remaining Jews), Jewish nationalism remained a frightening specter.

This latter group included many influential and wealthy persons, and they controlled the purse strings of the UJA. From 1938 to 1940, they cut down the percentage of funds allocated to Palestine from UJA collections from 35 to 20 per cent. Louis Lipsky, chairman of the American Jewish Congress governing council, charged that behind the scenes a "struggle was carried on to subordinate the ideals and objectives of the Zionist movement to the aims and desires of a small but

influential group of Jews who are anxious to keep American Jewish life
loyal to isolationist, assimilationist ideals, who are always limiting the
Jewish interest, always avoiding Jewish identification, always seeking
to have Jewish life adjust itself to the fears and negations arising out of
an everlasting apology for Jewish existence."[5] By 1941 the Zionists were
ready to walk out of the UJA, and announced that unless they received
at least 50 per cent of all local welfare fund collections, they would
mount an independent campaign. Henry Monsky, president of the
150,000-member fraternal order of B'nai B'rith, declared that whether
American Jews were Zionist or not, they had the duty to oppose Hitler
by rebuilding Palestine. Even the previously anti-Zionist Central Conference of American Rabbis decided that Zionism and Reform Judaism
were compatible, and called upon "all Jewry to aid in [Palestine's] upbuilding as a Jewish homeland by endeavoring to make it not only a
haven of refuge for the oppressed but also a center of Jewish cultural
and spiritual life."[6]

With European Jewry being decimated, the World Zionist Organization had no choice but to transfer many of its activities to the United
States. The president of the WZO, Chaim Weizmann, pleaded with
the Americans to forget past differences, so as "to stand together in
these hours of trial, to create a real *union sacré,* and to do your utmost
to save whatever remnant of our people may be rescuable from the
wreckage."[7]

Old enmities, however, like old habits, frequently die hard. The
"differences" mentioned by Weizmann dated back more than two decades and represented fundamental cleavages between American and
European Zionist philosophies, as well as numerous bitter political battles between the two sides. For the Europeans, Zionism was the first
step of the messianic redemption, and they imbued the movement with
a strong tone of religiosity, which appeared not only in the pious modes
of the Mizrachi but even in the supposed secularism of Poale Zion.
Moreover, the Europeans saw Zionism as a means of saving Jews from
anti-Semitism, and therefore demanded an "ingathering of the exiles"
with the true Zionist literally and figuratively ascending unto Zion,
making *aliyah* in returning to Judaism's ancient homeland. There, and
only there, could Jews lead free lives both as Jews and as human
beings.

American Jews tended to look at Zionism in a more pragmatic and
secular manner. They too saw Palestine as a refuge from persecution,

but they did not see themselves as among the persecuted. They certainly did not accept the demand that they should leave America and make *aliyah* to Palestine. The Brandeis synthesis specifically rejected any obligation of *aliyah* for American Jews; here, safe in a land of freedom, they would provide emotional, political, and financial support to help Jews fleeing from anti-Semitism in Europe and elsewhere to build a new home for themselves in Palestine. While Brandeis did not oppose Americans who wanted to move to Palestine, and indeed encouraged them to do so, he and his followers emphatically rejected the notion that the majority of American Jews had an obligation to emigrate to the Holy Land.

These philosophical differences had erupted in a series of political battles between Brandeis' followers and the Weizmann faction, led in the United States by Louis Lipsky. The latter group had gained control of the ZOA in 1921, but had been unable to provide leadership for the cause, and had been ousted in 1930. Weizmann's attempts to place his followers in key positions on the Emergency Committee only angered the Americans, and a series of articles in *The New Palestine,* the main journal of the American movement, hammered away at the need for a strong and independent stand by American Zionists.[8]

American Zionists, as well as non-Zionist Jews, also saw themselves first as Americans and second as Jews and Zionists, and this had made many of them reluctant to push for increased American aid to Great Britain, which from September 1939 until December 1941 carried the brunt of the battle against fascism. They were well aware that the majority of Americans did not want to get involved in a "European" war, and had worried that isolationist groups would cry: "See, the Jews are dragging us into the war; Jews want American boys to die for them." David Ben-Gurion believed that most American Jews shared the attitude of one man he had met who said: "We Jews are a minority here. If I stand up and demand American aid for Britain, people will say after the war the 'dirty Jews got us into it,' that 'it was a Jewish war,' that 'it was for their sakes that our sons died in battle.' "[9]

The major problem confronting the Zionists, however, involved the lack of a precise definition of just what the movement wanted. Later events have obscured the fact that up until the late 1930s, with the exception of the militant Revisionists led by Vladimir Jabotinsky, few Zionists identified an autonomous state as the end goal of the movement. Granted, Herzl's manifesto, which created modern political Zionism, had been titled *Der Judenstaat* (The Jewish State). But prior to British perfidy in the White Papers of 1930 and 1939, most Jewish leaders expressed their goal as the creation of a homeland in Palestine, one which might remain indefinitely a British protectorate. In part, they avoided the term "state" to avoid upsetting their non-Zionist allies who, while committed to a cultural or religious center in the Holy Land, feared the implication of a political entity. On a more practical plane, few thought the *Yishuv* would ever achieve the population and economic stability necessary to maintain a viable state.

A survey of the Zionist press in the decade prior to the Biltmore conference indicated that the term "Jewish State" had almost disappeared from common usage.[10] American Jews, who always emphasized short-term, practical goals, were primarily concerned that Jews would have a place to go, a refuge from persecution, and they cared little what form such a haven would take. The rise of Hitler together with Britain's retreat from the Balfour pledge caused a painful rethinking of Zionist means and goals. As early as 1932, the brilliant young Labor Zionist theoretician Chaim Arlosoroff, and others predicted that a gradual "evolutionary" or "organic" progression would not work; as the forces opposing Zionism gained strength, the movement would have to gamble and force Great Britain's hand in order to gain control of its own destiny. Few Zionists grasped this point as early as Arlosoroff did, but by the late thirties a number of Zionist leaders understood, or feared, that gradualism would not succeed with a Britain bent on appeasing the Arabs in order to safeguard oil supplies and to keep the Arab world out of the Axis orbit.[11]

The main protagonists in this debate were Chaim Weizmann, the longtime president of the World Zionist Organization, and David Ben-Gurion, the fiery young chairman of the Jewish Agency Executive in Palestine. Weizmann, born in 1874, had been raised in the intensely Jewish and Zionist atmosphere of a Russian *shtetl*. He later studied chemistry in Germany and eventually settled in England, where he developed a number of important processes in synthesizing petroleum products. His scientific work gained him access to important government leaders and influential members of British society, to whom he preached the Zionist message. His greatest triumph had been the Balfour Declaration, which propelled him to the leadership of the movement. As president of the WZO he had led the fight against the

Brandeis group in 1921 and had traveled endlessly collecting funds to further Zionist work in Palestine.

But Weizmann's success with the British in the First World War, his acceptance by British society, and his familiarity and love of British customs had also warped his view toward the nation which held the mandate over Palestine. While he opposed the various British measures to limit the size of Palestine or to restrict Jewish immigration, he could not oppose England itself. He could not conceive of a future for Palestine separate from the destiny of Great Britain and the Commonwealth. Even when he finally endorsed the idea of statehood, he did so in moderate terms, and insisted that the only way the Zionist Organization could succeed was through close co-operation with and reliance upon Britain.[12] Nothing should be done which might harm close relations between the Jewish homeland and England.

David Ben-Gurion, on the other hand, had no reason to trust the English or to desire close ties with them. Born in Poland in 1886, he had immigrated to Palestine at the age of twenty and had quickly risen to become one of the leaders of Poale Zion there. He helped to found the Histadrut, the General Federation of Labor, and from that power base went on to become chairman of the Jewish Agency Executive in Palestine, second in influence within the Zionist movement only to Weizmann. Ben-Gurion's experience in Palestine taught him that the Jews could rely only upon themselves, not upon anyone else, and certainly not upon Great Britain. Where Weizmann was willing to mute Zionist demands during the war, Ben-Gurion had declared that the battle against Hitler would not halt Jewish opposition to the 1939 White Paper, which restricted Jewish immigration to Palestine. "We shall oppose the White Paper as though there were no Hitler," he announced, "and we shall oppose Hitler as if there were no White Paper." Shortly after the outbreak of the war, he had told a secret meeting of the leaders of the Haganah, the Jewish defense force in Palestine: "We must clarify to ourselves the path we must follow and the goal toward which we must strive. The First World War in 1914–18 brought us the Balfour Declaration; this time we must bring to pass a Jewish State."[13]

Ben-Gurion and other Zionist leaders reached this conclusion hesitantly. They did not object to statehood *per se,* but feared that their hand was being forced prematurely. Jews still did not have a majority in Palestine, the supposed *sine qua non* for autonomy, and while the *Yishuv* had made great strides in developing industry and agriculture,

Palestine's economy was far from self-sufficient. But the callous disregard of Jewish suffering by the "enlightened" countries overrode all other considerations. The Jews must have a place to go, one which they would control. In the summer of 1941 Berl Katznelson, the influential Labor Zionist leader and editor of *Davar*, put it quite bluntly: "If it were possible to have a regime that assures free mass immigration and colonization in Palestine, the existence of a Jewish state as such would become of secondary importance. But our experience in recent years should have taught us that in the present period of world history, there is only one type of regime that can guarantee these conditions, and that is a Jewish state."[14]

Although American Zionists for the most part tended to be more militant in their attitude toward Great Britain and the need for an autonomous Jewish homeland, they too underwent a similar struggle between those committed to moderation and those who agreed with Ben-Gurion that only through Jewish self-effort would a state be achieved. The leading American Zionist following Brandeis' death in 1941 was his disciple and colleague, Rabbi Stephen S. Wise, who had been one of the first Jews in America to recognize and call attention to the Nazi menace. Wise's service in Zionist ranks dated back to the days of Herzl and the founding of the Federation of American Zionists in 1897, and he had done much to make the movement an acceptable part of American Jewish life. A leading figure in civic and industrial reform as well as in Jewish affairs, Wise knew and was known by many government officials, including President Franklin D. Roosevelt. Wise trusted Roosevelt, and in order not to embarrass the British during the war acceded to the President's request that Zionist demands be deferred until after the war.

Such an approach had no appeal to Abba Hillel Silver, rabbi of the prestigious Congregation Tifereth Israel in Cleveland, or to his long-time friend Emanuel Neumann, whose genius for public relations would be an important factor in Zionist work during and after the war. Silver distrusted Roosevelt and the British, and was keenly aware of how often international promises to the Jews had been broken. "Put not your faith in princes," he declared, and he wanted American Zionism to exert constant pressure on the American and British governments to grant Zionist demands regarding Palestine, especially the right of the Zionist movement to control immigration into the country. In January 1941, Silver, who like Wise was a brilliant orator, became the first American Jewish leader to openly advocate a Jewish state. Only the large-scale resettlement of Jews in Palestine after the war, with the aim of an autonomous Jewish state, would solve the Jewish problem.

The issue, though, was far from decided when the Biltmore conference convened in May 1942. The audacity of the demand and recognition of the many barriers which would have to be surmounted before it could be achieved made many of the delegates wonder if the question of statehood should even be raised.

*   *   *

The milling and confusion in the ballroom ended when Stephen Wise called the conference to order, and in his opening remarks set the tone which would dominate the proceedings: "This nationwide emergency Zionist conference has been assembled in order that unity . . . may come to obtain in the councils of the Zionist movement. We are met together in order that all American Zionists, irrespective of party sectarianism, undivided in resolution, we may be enabled to win over an ever larger number of American Jews, indeed all American Jews, to the support of the Zionist cause."[15] Speaker after speaker, representing the different factions and parties within the movement, rose in the next two days to echo Wise's call for unity.

But if all factions agreed on the necessity for unity and action, the nature of that action still raised a number of questions. Chaim Weizmann recognized not only that the American groups wanted to adopt a militant program, but also that implicitly they were attacking the policy of co-operation he had followed with the mandatory power for more than two decades. Sadly he admitted that the British had not kept their word in Palestine, that had the spirit of the mandate been upheld, tens of thousands of Jews might have been saved. But the old man's devotion to Britain could not be quenched; he still grieved over the death of his son Michael, an RAF pilot, only three months before. He pleaded with the assembly not to make this a Jewish war against Britain, but to fight alongside the brave English people in their battle against Hitler's tyranny. Although the audience, profoundly moved by Weizmann's talk, applauded him at length, the delegates then proceeded to ignore nearly all of his recommendations.

The most pressing problem facing the conference was the salvation of those European Jews who would survive the war. Weizmann feared that at least a quarter of the Jews in eastern and southeastern Europe would be dead at the end of the war. Not for another year would evidence of Hitler's "Final Solution" reach the West and confirm the rumors of the mass liquidation of European Jewry. Those who could flee the Nazis now, and those who would survive, where would they find refuge? To the Zionists, and to many non-Zionists as well, there could be but one answer: Palestine. But as long as the British ruled there, Ben-Gurion argued, as long as the White Paper remained the official policy of His Majesty's Government, there would be no haven in Palestine for persecuted Jews. Both the British and the White Paper would have to go.

At Biltmore, Ben-Gurion was still willing to leave the formulation of "detailed plans" until after the war, but he laid down three principles he considered essential: reaffirmation of the Balfour pledge to establish a Jewish homeland, Jewish control of immigration and internal affairs in Palestine, and complete equality of all the inhabitants of Palestine— Jew and Arab. If anyone missed the implications, Ben-Gurion spelled them out: "Zionism in action means nation-building, state-building." The *Yishuv* would bear the brunt of the effort, but the Jews in Palestine would be supported by their brethren all over the world. "A Jewish Palestine will arise," he declared. "It will redeem forever our suffering and do justice to our national genius. It will be the pride of every Jew in the Diaspora, and command the respect of every people on earth."

The militants, led by Ben-Gurion and Silver, easily had their way. Those urging caution, or patience, or continued reliance on Great Britain, had to admit that such policies in the past had yielded nothing but a ban on further immigration into Palestine at the moment when open doors were most desperately needed. In a ringing resolution, the conference demanded "that the gates of Palestine be opened; that the Jewish Agency be vested with control of immigration into Palestine and with the necessary authority for upbuilding the country, including the development of its uncultivated lands; and that Palestine be established as a Jewish commonwealth integrated in the structure of the new democratic world. Then and only then will the age-old wrongs of the Jewish people be righted."

The conference ended on the same note as it had begun—a call for unity. In an emotional final session, the delegates unanimously endorsed the Biltmore Declaration, and the various factions publicly made peace with one another. Clasping hands, men and women rose to sing the Zionist anthem, *Hatikvah* (The Hope).

*   *   *

Historians and Zionist partisans have endlessly debated Biltmore and its significance, and whether the conference marked a radical turn in Zionist policy or ideology.[16] Some of these questions may never be answered, but certain things are clear about the effect Biltmore had.

First, the conference marked the emergence of David Ben-Gurion as the dominant figure in the Zionist movement. Emanuel Neumann has summed this up best: "The question was not who wrote [the declaration]. The question was whose spirit prevailed at the Biltmore conference. With regard to that, I have little doubt that it was Ben-Gurion's spirit that prevailed and that inspired us. He was much more explicit on the subject of our demand for a Jewish State. Weizmann was not opposed to it. . . . But it wasn't his banner as it was in the case of Ben-Gurion, who made it his."[17]

Second, the declaration had enormous psychological impact. In 1942, American Zionism suffered from a severe sense of helplessness. The British had behaved treacherously, and in the White Paper of 1939 had seemingly put an end to the Zionist dream of a Jewish homeland. For nearly a decade Hitler had been persecuting European Jewry and now had plunged the entire world into a devastating war, whose primary victim would be the Jewish people. America—indeed, the entire free world—had failed to open its doors to Jewish refugees. In the face of endless calamities, the normal tasks and controversies of Jewish communal life seemed trivial and irrelevant. How to help? What to do? Those were the important questions. Biltmore provided an anchor, a specific task, a goal that spoke not only to the frustrations but also to the aspirations of American Zionists. It also, at least temporarily, gave the various Zionist factions a common theme around which they could unite.

Did Biltmore affect Zionist history? Did it speed or hinder the realization of a Jewish state? Joseph Proskauer, head of the American Jewish Committee, believed then and later that the declaration was ill-timed, and some historians have agreed with him. Howard Morley Sachar, for example, considered "political manifestos . . . altogether ill-suited to [the Jews'] current plight," while Ben Halpern noted that the program contained internal contradictions. The demands of the conference could only be met through the willingness of the Mandatory to reverse its policy of the previous decade; if Great Britain had been even slightly willing to do any of these things, there would have been no need for a Biltmore Declaration at all.[18]

But political manifestos may serve a number of purposes—legal, political, or propagandistic—as did the manifesto adopted by the American Continental Congress in July 1776. Biltmore came to mean many things, both within and outside the Zionist movement. Jewish leaders as early as 1942 were staking out a Jewish claim in the postwar world, a claim to a Jewish homeland. Time and again, they would refer to Biltmore not only as indicative of their goal, but also as a justification for it. Over the next three years, the Zionist organizations would secure hundreds of petitions and statements endorsing Biltmore, until the document eventually assumed a quasilegal status of its own.

Within the movement, Biltmore can be seen as a major step on the road to statehood. It defined an *Endziel*, an "end goal," around which all factions could rally, a "maximum objective" upon which there was near-unanimous agreement. Before that "maximum objective" could be realized, however, American Zionism would have to conquer its own internal factionalization, and even more important, overcome rather substantial opposition within the American Jewish community.

Part One

The Return to Zion

And I will turn the captivity of My people Israel,
And they shall build the waste cities, and inhabit them;
And they shall plant vineyards, and drink the wine thereof;
They shall also make gardens, and eat the fruit of them.
And I will plant them upon their land,
And they shall no more be plucked up
Out of their land which I have given them,
Saith the Lord thy God.

Amos 9:14–15

Chapter 1

UNITY AND ACTION

Even before the Biltmore conference, Zionist leaders had initiated a series of meetings with non-Zionist groups, seeking some accommodation which would lead to a united American Jewry. News from Europe of Hitler's massacres reinforced the conclusion that only the American Jewish community would have the material and political strength to fight for Jewish rights during and after the war. Only American Jewry could provide the leverage to force open Palestine for the survivors of the Nazi madness. But to achieve this power, American Jewry and the rest of the nation in effect had to be "Zionized."

The two leading non-Zionist groups in the United States were the fraternal order of B'nai B'rith, with about 150,000 members, and the prestigious American Jewish Committee. Originally founded in 1906, the Committee had from the start been dominated by the wealthy German-Jewish elite; through its access to the large Jewish fortunes and its control of the Joint Distribution Committee, it had been the main source of funds to help overseas Jewish communities since the early days of the First World War. Although originally anti-Zionist, under the leadership of Louis Marshall the Committee gradually came to support rebuilding Palestine for religious and cultural reasons, but shunned any nationalistic overtones in that work; it endorsed *Zion*, but not *Zionism*. In 1929, Marshall, who enjoyed immense prestige in the community, led prominent non-Zionists into an agreement with Chaim Weizmann and the World Zionist Organization to create the enlarged Jewish

Agency for Palestine, with membership divided evenly between the two groups.[1] Marshall's sudden death a few weeks after this agreement, and the lackluster leadership of his successor, Felix Warburg, prevented the Agency from ever developing into the true partnership envisioned by Marshall and Weizmann.

Because of the Agency's failure to link the non-Zionists closely with the rebuilding of Palestine, non-Zionist and even anti-Zionist attitudes increased within the American Jewish Committee during the 1930s. Although no longer exerting the influence it had three decades earlier, the Committee still enjoyed extensive contacts with high government and business leaders, and had access to wealthier Jews. If the Committee could be persuaded to support a Palestinian homeland, without the implications of Zionist nationalism, then there might emerge a unified American Jewry to support Zionist claims to free immigration into Palestine after the war.

When Chaim Weizmann visited the United States in the spring of 1941, he informally contacted Sol Strook, the president of the Committee, "to see whether common grounds for united action could not be found." Strook invited several of his colleagues to join the discussions, and eventually the Committee itself formally endorsed the negotiations. After Strook's death, his successor, Maurice Wertheim, who was personally sympathetic to much of the Zionist program, took over the discussions, and representatives from the Zionist Emergency Committee, the American Jewish Congress, B'nai B'rith, and the Jewish Labor Committee periodically joined in the talks.[2]

By February 1942, the negotiations centered on the issues of Jewish civil rights in the Diaspora, open immigration into Palestine and the creation of a Jewish commonwealth there, and the possibility of raising a Jewish "army" to fight with the Allies. On the first question the Committee had long been committed to the proposition that the civil and political rights of Jews everywhere were inviolate, and that nothing should be done in Palestine that might affect those rights elsewhere. Wertheim agreed in principle on the right of free immigration, but differed with the Zionists over the rationale; at the beginning of the talks he was not yet ready to envision a Jewish state.[3] On the army issue, confusion gripped both sides. The Zionists, especially members of the *Yishuv*, wanted to pressure the British into allowing Palestinian Jews, as well as those who had escaped from Nazi Europe, to form their own brigades within the British Army. This would give the Jews a greater claim to inclusion at the peace table on the grounds that they, as a distinct group, had fought with the Allied forces. The British opposed the scheme, not only because it would alienate the Arabs, but also because they feared that at the end of the war there would be a well-trained and well-armed body of Jews in Palestine. The Committee hesitated to endorse any scheme which might embarrass the British in their time of trial, and within Zionist ranks many shared the Committee's sentiments.

When David Ben-Gurion arrived in the United States in February 1942, he immediately injected himself into the discussions, much to Weizmann's chagrin.[4] But Ben-Gurion and Wertheim took a liking to each other, and the Palestinian leader realized that Wertheim might be prepared to go farther than he had indicated, and might take the American Jewish Committee with him. At a meeting of the Zionist Emergency Committee, Ben-Gurion explained that it would be fruitless to attempt to get the American Jewish Committee to endorse the Biltmore plan; there need not be full agreement so long as the two sides accepted the minimal political points essential to the Zionist plan.[5]

On June 4, at Wertheim's home in Cos Cob, Connecticut, he and Ben-Gurion initialed the "Cos Cob formula." In it the Zionists and the American Jewish Committee agreed to act in common "for the fulfillment of the original purposes of the Balfour Declaration whereby through unrestricted Jewish immigration and large-scale colonization under a regime designed for this purpose, Jews may constitute a majority in Palestine and establish an autonomous commonwealth." In a Jewish Palestine, all the inhabitants would enjoy complete equality of rights, and its establishment would not affect the rights of Jews in any other country.[6] This statement did not go as far as the Biltmore program, for it represented considerable concessions on both sides.[7] The non-Zionists accepted the need for a Jewish commonwealth; the Zionists, by affirming that the state would not affect Jewish rights outside Palestine, in effect renounced the idea that Jews formed a separate Diaspora nationality. They also made a major concession in agreeing to delay statehood until there was a Jewish majority in Palestine, since the Biltmore program called for immediate autonomy. Both sides thought it best to drop the army idea.

Originally, the formula was to have been kept secret until it could be presented to the full Committee, but the contents leaked out. Immediately the anti-Zionists on the Committee sprang into action to defeat the agreement. The chief opponent of the formula, and at that time a strong anti-Zionist, was Judge Joseph M. Proskauer, the senior partner in a prestigious New York law firm, who took great pride in the fact that his father had fought with the Confederacy in the Civil War.[8] As early as April, when he realized that Wertheim might be willing to endorse the commonwealth idea, Proskauer had set himself firmly against it. "The time has come," he declared, "when the American Jewish Committee has got to fish or cut bait on Zionism. . . . I find there is a rising tide, not of non-Zionism, but of anti-Zionism, and it has got to have expression." He believed that the establishment of a Jewish commonwealth, in Palestine or any place, would be a Jewish catastrophe, since it would, he contended, adversely affect Jewish rights in the United States and elsewhere.[9] Proskauer threatened to bolt the Committee and to take his fellow anti-Zionists with him if Wertheim persisted in pushing the agreement. Rather than split the Committee, Wertheim withdrew the Cos Cob formula; shortly thereafter, pleading reasons of health, he resigned from the presidency.[10]

The failure of this first attempt to reach common ground with the non-Zionists had not been unanticipated. Of all the Jewish groups in this country, none proclaimed allegiance to American values more loudly than did the American Jewish Committee, yet none was more fearful of democracy within Jewish life, nor clung more tenaciously to the bugaboo of dual loyalty.[11] Having failed to win the Committee over by direct means, the Zionists, if they were to secure a united Jewry, would have to bypass the Committee and isolate it. This process had already begun. Even while Ben-Gurion negotiated with Wertheim, the Zionists approached the other important non-Zionist body, the B'nai B'rith, in hope it would join the drive to unite American Jewry.

*   *   *

The B'nai B'rith was founded in 1843 as a fraternal organization of German-American Jews, but it later welcomed eastern European Jews as well, and by 1940 this latter group comprised the bulk of B'nai B'rith's large membership. In 1916, when the Zionists clashed with the American Jewish Committee over creating a Jewish congress, B'nai B'rith leaders tried to moderate between the two factions; throughout the 1920s and 1930s, the organization had carefully avoided those political issues which divided Zionist and anti-Zionist. Although recognized as a non-Zionist body and considered neutral, the B'nai B'rith actually harbored much pro-Zionist sentiment. Above all, its leaders believed in the necessity for unity among American Jewry.

The president of B'nai B'rith, Henry Monsky, had been exploring a variety of options, to achieve that unity when he met with Chaim Weizmann, Stephen Wise, Louis Lipsky, and others at the St. Regis Hotel in New York in May 1941. Although they adopted no specific plans, the Zionist leaders evidently encouraged Monsky to continue his search for unity without committing himself to anything specifically Zionist in nature.[12] They remembered that the B'nai B'rith had sided with the Zionists in the congress fight in 1916, and sensed that Monsky, who was deeply affected by the tragedy in Europe, would ultimately, of his own accord, adopt the Zionist program. In the meantime, however, they merely urged Monsky to continue his quest for a suitable format in which the various factions could be united.

Once Proskauer torpedoed the Cos Cob formula, B'nai B'rith remained the only non-Zionist group of any stature willing to co-operate with the Zionists, and by the fall of 1942 the Zionists were meeting regularly with Monsky. The plan they agreed upon called for B'nai B'rith to sponsor a major conference of American Jewry, similar to the American Jewish Congress in 1916. Nahum Goldmann predicted that the same results would be achieved—namely, a large enough percentage of American Jewry would endorse the conference, leaving the American Jewish Committee one of two alternatives: either to join, as they had in 1916, or to be isolated from the community and be rendered impotent.[13] Despite some qualms among Zionist leaders about allowing Monsky to take the initiative in this matter, Goldmann, Wise, and Lipsky insisted that only the B'nai B'rith president had the prestige to do the job. They also knew that Monsky, an able, hard-working executive, had resented his exclusion from the negotiations with the American Jewish Committee and that he now saw an opportunity to wrest leadership in American Jewry away from the Committee.[14]

On January 6, 1943, Monsky sent out a letter to thirty-four national Jewish organizations, inviting them to send delegates to a meeting at the Hotel William Penn in Pittsburgh on January 23 and 24. The purpose of the gathering, he explained, was to seek agreement on the role the American Jewish community would play in representing Jewish demands after the war. "American Jewry," he wrote, "must be ready to voice the judgment of American Jews along with that of the other Jewish communities of the free countries with respect to the the the postwar status of Jews and the upbuilding of a Jewish Palestine."[15] Of the thirty-four groups invited, thirty-two accepted and sent from one to three representatives each, making a total of seventy-eight men and women who gathered in Pittsburgh on the twenty-third. Only the Jewish Labor Committee, which also harbored a large anti-Zionist bloc, and the American Jewish Committee refused to attend.

To allow full freedom of opinion, Monsky, who chaired the Pittsburgh meeting, ruled that votes cast by individual delegates for or against any resolution would not be binding on their respective organization, which would then be free to accept or reject the results. With very little difference of opinion, the assemblage agreed that it would be fatal for world Jewry if the American community failed to prepare itself during the war for the peace negotiations afterward. Preparation, however, required unity of purpose, and that could only be achieved through the calling of a truly representative body. Remembering how a quarter century earlier the American Jewish Committee had tried to limit the scope of the American Jewish Congress, the Zionists secured approval of two significant items. One forbade the executive to limit freedom of speech or action at the proposed Jewish assembly, and the other put the question of Palestine on the agenda.[16] Before adjourning, the delegates elected an executive committee, with Monsky as temporary chairman, to serve until the full assembly could meet.

The executive committee held its first session within hours after the delegates departed. By February 1 it had established headquarters in New York and titled itself the Executive Committee for the Organization of the American Jewish Assembly. A few days later it mailed out detailed proposals for electing representatives to the Assembly, together with a copy of the various items adopted in Pittsburgh, to nearly every Jewish organization in the country, including many that had not been represented at the preliminary meeting, and asked them to co-operate. By the end of the month, over twenty national Jewish bodies had ratified the proposal and stood ready to join in the call for the conference.[17]

The American Jewish Committee, and particularly its newly elected president, Judge Proskauer, were furious. The Committee had made a concerted effort to get Monsky to postpone the Pittsburgh session. By not attending, the Committee had not only lost the initiative, but had allowed the Zionists to tailor the agenda to suit their program. As

Nahum Goldmann later noted: "It was the mistake of their life not to have participated, because with them absent we took over the real leadership. Had they been there, they would have organized a non-Zionist bloc and even the B'nai B'rith would not have gone along with us 100 per cent as they did."[18]

The Committee, fearing that it would be outmaneuvered unless it acted quickly, issued a statement of its own, calling for an international trusteeship over Palestine which would protect the rights of Jews to immigration, safeguard the civil and religious rights of all the inhabitants, and prepare the country for independence at some indeterminate time. The document drafted by Proskauer reaffirmed as an eternal verity that the Jews of the United States were American citizens, and "there can be no political identification of Jews outside of Palestine with whatever government may there be instituted."[19]

What Proskauer expected from this document is hard to say. Perhaps he hoped that the prestige of the Committee, and what he saw as the essential common sense of the statement, would re-establish the Committee's leadership in the Jewish community. Almost certainly he was unprepared for the flood of derision which greeted it. Harry Friedenwald, an elder statesman of American Jewry, resigned from the Committee in protest, to the great applause of the Zionists.[20] One typical editorial in the Jewish press declared that "every word and phrase [of the Committee statement] reflects a point of view which is diametrically opposed to the positions taken and maintained by the creative forces in American Jewish life during the past fifty years."[21]

Proskauer's anti-Zionism was now sadly out of tune with the sentiment of the overwhelming majority of American Jews, even those Jews who did not consider themselves Zionists. Proskauer moved in a limited and rarefied sphere, where he met people who for the most part thought as he did, and he mistook their opinions for that of American Jewry as a whole. However, by early 1943, American Jews had begun to discern the true nature of Hitler's "Final Solution," and they saw the Zionist program, with its call for free immigration into Palestine, not only as desirable, but also as the *only* solution to the problem. Proskauer completely failed to gauge the emotions and attitudes of his fellow Jews, who were no longer willing to leave the destiny of world Jewry in the hands of an elite which still believed in the court Jew mentality of politely begging favors from the great powers.[22]

As a matter of course, the Assembly executive committee reinvited the American Jewish Committee to join in, but there were some within the Committee who supported Proskauer's decision to boycott the Assembly. The Committee's executive secretary, Morris D. Waldman, although not personally opposed to a Jewish state in Palestine, resented what he saw as Zionist encroachments upon the diplomatic areas that had long been the Committee's domain. He labeled the Assembly a Zionist trick, calling Henry Monsky a "Zionist stooge." If the Committee participated, he warned Proskauer, it would be outnumbered thirty to one and would be nothing more than a tail to the Zionist kite.[23]

But Proskauer, like Louis Marshall and Cyrus Adler a generation earlier, realized that boycotting the Assembly would cost the Committee much of its influence with American Jewry. Moreover, moderate forces within the Committee as well as Zionist leaders urged Proskauer not to bring down the shame for rupturing American Jewish unity on his head.[24] Acting on his own, he decided to accept the invitation, but only if Monsky and his colleagues agreed to certain conditions. At first Proskauer tried to limit the Assembly to a mere advisory session. Rebuffed there, the Committee requested the new organization be called "the American Jewish Conference" (evidently "assembly," for some reason, smacked of disloyalty), with each organization and individual retaining freedom of action regardless of the vote of the Conference.[25] The Monsky group regarded the change of name as a minor matter and recognized that the Conference would, in any event, have no power other than moral suasion to enforce its decisions. They therefore acceded to the requests and co-opted Proskauer to the executive; little did he realize what was in store for him.

*   *   *

To ensure that the Conference would be as representative as possible of American Jewry, the executive committee devised an elaborate system of allotting delegates to both national and local groups. A total of 64 nationwide organizations, such as Hadassah, B'nai B'rith, the American Jewish Congress, and others, received 125 delegate seats. In addition, elections took place in 78 communities and 58 regions, covering all 48 states and the District of Columbia. Each local group was entitled to one elector for the first 50 members, and then one more for each additional 75. All told, 1.5 million Jews in 8,486 local groups chose 22,500 electors, who then selected 379 delegates. Undoubtedly the American

Jewish Conference was the most representative gathering of American Jewry ever to take place.

To ensure order within the Conference, each delegate had to affiliate with one of nine blocs: American Jewish Congress, B'nai B'rith, Conservative Religious, General Zionists (including the ZOA and Hadassah), Jewish Labor Committee, Labor Zionists, Reform Religious, Orthodox Religious, and "Designation Reserved." A delegate could thus align himself with a pro-Zionist group, or one of several neutral blocs. The problem, as the non-Zionists saw it, was that the Zionist organizations had stacked the deck. In the local elections the Zionists, using their enormous membership, had selected delegates not only in their own blocs, but also among many of the neutral ones as well. Nahum Goldmann estimated that as many as 80 to 85 per cent of the delegates would be Zionists.[26] The American Jewish Committee, which had a small national membership, could only muster the three delegates assigned to it.

The first session of the American Jewish Conference opened solemnly at the Waldorf-Astoria in New York on August 29, 1943. Henry Monsky greeted the 504 delegates with the same Hebrew phrase that Nathan Straus had used in opening the American Jewish Congress in Philadelphia 25 years earlier: *"Hineh mah tov u'mah na'im, shevet achim gam ya'had."* (Behold how good and pleasant it is for brethren to dwell together in unity.) Monsky praised the democratic nature of the assembly and warned that American Jews would no longer allow any self-appointed elites to speak for them. But his theme was unity: "Our people's salvation depends upon a united front. With magnificent fortitude have the Jews in the stricken lands manifested once again the will of Israel to survive. Their fight is our fight. Their struggle is our struggle. Their ultimate fate may in large measure determine our fate. The doctrine of isolation in matters of Jewish interest is fatal to our cause. We are an integral group, call it what you will—religious or national— it matters not, for we do have a common inheritance, a common history, a common religion, common traditions, and a common cause, and we must strive for a common basis of action."[27]

In order to achieve that unity, Monsky and his colleagues committed what would prove to be a major error. Instead of electing a single person as president, they decided upon a presidium representing all groups. A number of delegates tried to create a movement to draft Stephen Wise as president; but the elderly leader of American Jewry had borne enough honors and burdens in his life, and much to Monsky's gratification, refused to allow his name to be considered. Instead Wise, with a number of others, including Joseph Proskauer, joined the presidium.[28]

The major issue at the Conference would be Palestine, and here a number of conflicting pressures were building. The State Department, which had reacted negatively to the Biltmore program, tried at first to have the Conference delayed, much as the American Jewish Congress had been postponed at Woodrow Wilson's request until after the First World War. The State Department warned against any actions which would embarrass Great Britain, and threatened to issue a joint Anglo-American statement "urging their citizens to refrain from a public debate of the Palestine issue in the interest of the war effort." When the Zionists remained firm in their plans, the American Jewish Committee proposed a series of measures which would either dilute any Palestine statement, or more effectively, bar it from the Conference agenda, and here the Committee unexpectedly found a weakness in the Zionist front.[29]

Although the more militant Zionist leaders, such as Ben-Gurion, Silver, and Neumann, stood solidly on the Biltmore program, a number of their colleagues doubted its acceptability to American Jewry as a whole. They did not oppose the call for the creation of a Jewish state in Palestine; rather they questioned the means of securing general approval. Rabbis James G. Heller and Barnett Brickner, for example, were willing to sign a resolution adopted by the Union of American Hebrew Congregations in June 1943 which endorsed a Jewish state, but followed the American Jewish Committee recommendation that a Jewish majority in Palestine be achieved first. In defending their action before the Emergency Committee, Heller averred that the Reform body had come much closer to Zionist aims than ever before, and that for the Zionists blindly to demand nothing less than Biltmore would only alienate potential allies.[30]

Heller was not alone in this view. Nahum Goldmann, who tried to be acceptable to militants and moderates alike, had suggested for some time that the Biltmore program not be pushed at the Conference. Even though the Emergency Committee planned to make the demand for a state the basis of its proposals to the Conference,[31] Goldmann quietly contacted the American Jewish Committee and suggested that a compromise might be possible. If the Committee would back the Zionist demand for unlimited immigration into Palestine, then the Zionists would not push the issue of statehood.[32] Since the Committee no longer opposed a Jewish state "on principle," but only saw the Biltmore program as "untimely," Proskauer offered to co-operate with the Zionists at the Conference in "other areas" of common Jewish concern. Agreement was seemingly reached whereby the statehood issue would not come before the plenum but would be deferred until a later session. Even Stephen Wise, who had fought so long for a state, agreed to the compromise as the price for what he hoped would be unity within American Jewry.[33]

When Emanuel Neumann heard that the presidium would prevent a Palestine resolution from reaching the floor, he hastened to Abba Hillel Silver's room to see if this were true. Silver, who was to chair the Palestine committee of the Conference, dejectedly confirmed the rumor; all the Zionist work in arranging the Conference would be lost. Neumann demanded that Silver address the Conference, and once he got the reluctant Silver to agree, hurried off to find some bloc that would yield time to the Cleveland rabbi.[34] Through a parliamentary maneuver, Neumann arranged for Silver to gain the rostrum under the sponsorship of Stephen Wise's own group, the American Jewish Congress.

It was one of the master orator's greatest speeches. "Why," he asked, "has there arisen among us today this mortal fear of the term 'Jewish Commonwealth,' which both British and American statesmen took in their stride, and which our own fellow Jews of both camps endorsed a quarter of a century ago? Why are anti-Zionists, or non-Zionists, or neutrals—why are they determined to excise that phrase and, I suspect in some instances, the hopes?" The opponents of the phrase, he charged, had never really reconciled themselves either to the Balfour Declaration or to the Mandate; all that Palestine meant to them was a country of possible Jewish immigration, like any other country in the world. "Once having made this monumental concession that Jews have a right to go to Palestine, and that that right should not be restricted, they feel justified in asking Zionists to make a little concession of their own, just a little concession, namely, to surrender that for which they and their fathers hoped and prayed throughout the centuries, and which is already in the process of fulfillment—a Jewish commonwealth in Palestine."

What was at stake, Silver explained, was not a phrase, or even a question of timing, but rather the salvation of a people fighting for its life. "How long is this crucifixion of Israel to last? From the infested, typhus-ridden ghetto of Warsaw; from the death block of Nazi-occupied lands where myriads of our people are awaiting execution by the slow or quick method; from a hundred concentration camps which befoul the map of Europe; from the pitiful bands of our wandering ghosts over the entire face of the earth, comes the cry: Enough! There must be a final end to all this, a sure and certain end."

As to unity among Jewry, Silver found it strange that "If I agree with certain people, that is unity. If I ask them to agree with me, that is disunity. Unity," he thundered, "calls for the realization of the national restoration of Palestine. . . . We cannot truly rescue the Jews of Europe unless we have free immigration into Palestine. We cannot have free immigration into Palestine unless our political rights are recognized there. Our political rights cannot be recognized there unless our historic connection with the country is acknowledged and our right to rebuild our national home is reaffirmed. These are inseparable links in the chain. The whole chain breaks if one of the links is missing."[35]

As he read the Palestine Committee's resolution, which fully endorsed the Biltmore program, the cheering assembly rose to its feet and burst into *Hatikvah,* the Zionist anthem. Even those members of the presidium who had been willing to compromise on the issue now realized that the Jewish people, as represented in the Conference, were far more militant than some of their purported leaders. Henry Monsky declared that "this resolution when adopted will become a historic document, vital to the fate and destiny of the people of Israel. The time has come now not for speeches but for consecrated action. Therefore, I claim the privilege, one that I shall cherish for the rest of my life, of seconding the motion."[36]

Not all of the delegates were so moved. Proskauer, feeling betrayed at the failure of the Zionist leaders to keep Palestine off the agenda, rose to say that he now appreciated the feelings which must have affected Daniel as he entered the lions' den. He offered, as a substitute motion, the earlier American Jewish Committee statement calling for open immigration and a trusteeship, and in the name of unity, pleaded with the delegates to adopt it.[37]

But if Proskauer sought unity, he found it in the opposing vote of the Conference. Of the 504 delegates, 480 cast their ballots in favor of the original resolution; when the chairman called for nays, only four cards were raised, three of them by the Committee delegates. Herman Shulman of the ZOA urged Proskauer to see for himself where the people stood, and begged the Committee president to assume his rightful place with the leaders of American Jewry. "There is a case to be presented, Judge Proskauer, a very good case. Take it, Judge Proskauer! But take it as it is now written—and, as I said before, as it has been implemented by the sweat and blood of our people." As it turned out, Proskauer would eventually take up his people's case, but as the American Jewish Conference prepared to adjourn, he was far from ready to do so. In fact, within two months, the Committee would nearly shatter the sense of unity and high morale that prevailed at the conclusion of the Conference.

For the next few weeks, speaker after speaker, paper after paper, basked in the warm glow of unity, which everyone saw as the result of the Conference. In their goodwill, the Zionists even praised Judge Proskauer for his open-mindedness, and for not walking out of the Conference, as many people had expected him to do.[38]

Proskauer, together with Morris Waldman, wanted to walk out, believing that Wise and Goldmann had not kept their word. But they decided to make their protest, then wait until the executive committee of the American Jewish Committee met to decide whether to stay in the Conference. Nevertheless, when Proskauer announced the secession of the Committee on October 24, it was without having submitted the issue to the total Committee membership, though the annual meeting was less than three months away. If Proskauer had felt like Daniel before, this time there would be no friendly presidium to hold back the lions.

The only group to applaud the secession was the uncompromisingly anti-Zionist American Council for Judaism. The Zionists were vehement in their denunciation of the Committee's "isolationist" and "Jewishly destructive" act. Within the Emergency Council, Abba Silver lumped together the battle against the Committee and the British White Paper, and said that now it had to be a fight to the finish. He called for an all-out attack on the Committee in synagogue pulpits, from speaker platforms, in newspapers, and on the radio, to make sure that everyone, Jew and non-Jew alike, recognized that the American Jewish Committee spoke only for itself and not for American Jewry. *The New Palestine* editorialized that the Committee had chosen to isolate itself from the community. "Theirs is a self-imposed *herem* [excommunication], and surely they have, by their action, earned the right to the epithet of 'isolationists' in the widest sense of the term."[39]

The non-Zionist Jewish press also joined in the denunciation, and many Jews withdrew their support from the Committee. In the three months following Proskauer's announcement, four members of the executive committee and forty-five members of the general council resigned in a much-publicized protest. In addition, ten of the eighteen national organizations affiliated with the Committee severed their ties, while dozens of resolutions of protest showered down on the New York office from resentful local chapters.[40]

The actual damage to Jewish unity by the Committee's withdrawal was minimal; in fact, in view of the general damnation of the Committee, it may have strenghtened the Zionist hand. Every one of the sixty-three remaining organizations reaffirmed its ties to the Conference. Moreover, those who formerly believed that American Jewry as a whole did not support the Biltmore program now recognized that the resolutions adopted at the Biltmore in 1942 and at the Waldorf-Astoria a year later did indeed reflect the sentiment of American Jewry. By walking out, the American Jewish Committee endowed the Zionist program with a measure of communal approval it had never before enjoyed. Much of that approval, however, must also be credited to the energetic campaign by the Zionists to win America's support for a Jewish homeland in Palestine.

*   *   *

Louis E. Levinthal, president of the Zionist Organization of America, published a "Credo" in 1943 summing up his philosophy as a Zionist. He wrote: "I am confident that we can win the support of the overwhelming majority of American Jewry—those Jews who are not ashamed of their Jewish identity and who have faith in the Jewish future. I am sure, too, that we can obtain the endorsement of all true Americans, regardless of creed or race or nationality. For I have faith in the stability of American democracy and in the sincerity of the allegiance of American citizens to the ideals and aspirations of our beloved country."[41] This statement aptly summarized two of the main foci of Zionist activity during the war years: "Zionizing" the bulk of American Jewry, and beyond that, winning over the sympathy and support of Christian America for the Zionist goal of a postwar Jewish homeland in Palestine.

By the time the American Jewish Conference met, a number of developments had primed American Jews, both Zionists and non-Zionists, to assume the responsibilities of speaking for, and in whatever ways possible, caring for, world Jewry. Salo Baron, the noted historian, summed up this attitude: "If during the First World War American Jewry came to maturity, the Second War has placed in its hand undisputed leadership of world Jewry, with all the challenges and responsibilities which it entails." Even before the rumors of mass exterminations were confirmed, American Jews *knew* that the end of the war would see European Jewry a shadow of its former strength. Just as in the First World War, much of the fiercest fighting on the eastern front raged in areas of heavy Jewish population; pre-1939 policies left little doubt that Jews in Nazi-occupied Europe would face terrible hardships, though not until the end of the war would the full extent of the Holocaust be known. But by 1942 much of American Jewry realized that it would have to take up the burden of maintaining Jewish life.[42]

But it is one thing to be prepared emotionally to act; it is something else to convert that willingness into action. Between 1942 and 1945, the Zionists provided the nucleus around which this psychological tension could coalesce. The president of the ZOA accurately predicted in October 1942 that "the Jews of America sense the temper of the time, and will not endorse halfway measures or halfhearted efforts. I am convinced that they are prepared to follow those who speak and act boldly."[43] At Biltmore, in a simple and direct form, the Zionists gave American Jewry an understandable rallying point, one confirmed sixteen months later at the American Jewish Conference: an autonomous Jewish homeland would succor the survivors of Hitler's evilness and which in the future would always offer a haven to the persecuted. Zionism meant much more than statehood, and this was realized by its opponents. But because anti-Zionists and non-Zionists conceded the need for open immigration into Palestine, because they admitted the terrible dangers facing European Jewry, their concern with the implications of Jewish nationalism made no impression. To many, the American Jewish Committee seemed to be responding to Jewish agony with a "Yes, but . . . ," and they had no patience with the "buts."[44]

This common faith in Palestine, which by the end of the war was shared by nine of every ten Jews, was reinforced by a belief that the time had come for American Jewry to act as a community to support such goals. In cities and towns across the land, various Jewish philanthropies had, over the previous two decades, learned to co-operate in joint planning and fund-raising operations, and had taken the first steps toward co-ordination on a national level. Having learned that co-operation worked locally, communal leaders demanded that the major overseas groups, primarily the Joint Distribution Committee, controlled by the non-Zionist American Jewish Committee, and the Zionists, cease their bickering and work together. In 1941, on the eve of American entry into the war, the Joint Distribution Committee and the Zionists had reached organizational agreement; as the war years passed and Zionism gained in local support, the United Jewish Appeal became a truly nationwide effort which devoted more and more of its proceeds to work in Palestine. The Zionists now had the upper hand, and did not have to mask their goal of statehood, as they had in the 1920s, to gain the aid of non-Zionist wealth. Perhaps more importantly, the pattern of unity in philanthropy might lead to unified political activity.[45]

Still another factor that helped win community support could be found in a resurgence of the old Brandeisian dictum on the compatibility of Zionism and Americanism. Prior to Pearl Harbor, many Jews had been fearful of calling too loudly for American aid to the Allies, lest they be accused of trying to involve the United States in a war to save Jews. Even after this country entered the war, some Zionists felt that their activity would have to be suspended for the duration of the war. But all Americans now shared the same desire as the Jews, namely the rapid and total defeat of fascism, and the Zionist leaders wisely decided that by throwing their organization into war work as well as Zionist work, they could increase the attractiveness of their cause. The Zionists worked energetically in each of the war bond drives, and earned a special commendation from the Treasury Department for their performance. In the fourth Liberty Bond drive, the ZOA alone accepted a quota of $25 million and raised more than $68 million.[46]

In this setting, American Zionism unleashed organizational and propaganda drives unparalleled in its history. Between 1942 and 1945, membership in the Zionist Organization of America, the dominant political group within the Emergency Council, increased from 49,952, to 136,630, while Hadassah, the leading women's organization, saw its roster grow from 86,329 to 142,665. The Labor Zionists, consisting of Poale Zion (men) and Pioneer Women, grew from 22,500 to 36,000, while the religious bloc of Mizrachi, Hapoel Hamizrachi, and Mizrachi women moved up from 69,000 to 86,500. All told, the number of

enrolled Zionists in the major groups increased by 56 per cent, to a total
of over 400,000. In addition, there were numerous smaller groups, such
as the Revisionists, B'nai Zion, and Junior Hadassah, whose member-
ship lists brought the total enrolled Zionist population in the United
States to approximately 500,000 in 1945, the largest it had ever been.[47]
Nor is there any question that hundreds of thousands of other Jews
who did not pay their *shekel* (annual dues) to join a specifically
"Zionist" organization shared Zionist sentiments. The fraternal order of
B'nai B'rith, with about 150,000 members, while nominally non-
Zionist, had under Henry Monsky's leadership moved to support the
Zionist program. The American Jewish Conference, representing 1.5
million Jews directly and another million indirectly, had overwhelm-
ingly endorsed the Biltmore platform.

Zionist strength stretched beyond the numbers on its rosters. The
Emergency Committee for Zionist Affairs (reorganized in 1943 as the
American Zionist Emergency Council) assumed the immense task of
spreading the Zionist message in every town and city in the land. To
this end, it established 76 state and regional branches, with over 400
local committees. Hundreds of books, articles, pamphlets, and radio programs were prepared and distributed to public libraries, chaplains, community centers, schools and colleges, ministers, writers, and influential
citizens. Pro-Zionist books, often written by non-Jews, such as Sumner
Welles' *Palestine's Rightful Destiny* and Norman MacLean's *His Terrible Swift Sword*, received Zionist subsidies, with special arrangements
made with the publishers for free distribution to important individuals
or groups. A number of academic studies were commissioned, all designed to refute the British contention that Palestine could not be further developed to absorb additional immigrants. One of these, Walter
Clay Lowdermilk's *Palestine, Land of Promise*, published in 1944, won
great popularity as a best seller. Lowdermilk, a soil conservationist in
the Department of Agriculture, had prepared a government study in
the late 1930s extolling the achievements of the *Yishuv* in reclaiming
the barren areas of Palestine. He also devised a plan for a Jordan Valley Authority, which he predicted would multiply the agricultural and
industrial potential of Palestine, making it capable of supporting several
million people.

The total number of written materials generated by the various
Zionist groups easily ran into the millions. In 1943–44, the ZOA alone
distributed over a million leaflets and pamphlets. Each month the

Emergency Council published a political bulletin, *Palestine,* which went to over 16,000 educational, political, and religious leaders across the country. While one can always question the efficacy of such propaganda campaigns, the fact remains that throughout the war period American citizens were inundated with reminders of the Zionist program, all designed not only to reveal the plight of European Jewry, but also to enhance the belief that Zionism enjoyed wide public support. One piece, for example, compiled by the Zionist Organization of America, contained sympathetic statements from congressmen and senators endorsing a Jewish homeland in Palestine and opposing the 1939 White Paper. Of the 535 members of the 78th Congress, 411 backed the Zionist call for American action to sanction a Jewish commonwealth. Representatives of every state in the Union, accounting for 86 per cent of the Senate and 75 per cent of the House, contributed statements to the ZOA.

Nor was Zionist propaganda limited to printed works. The Emergency Council orchestrated an extensive campaign of personal contacts. According to one commentator: "Utterly devoted and tireless bands of local Zionists of all parties hounded local editors for favorable comment, arranged forums for the Zionist case in churches, schools, and civic groups, solicited statements from political candidates, sent deputations at their own expense to Washington to interview congressmen and senators, and at critical junctures flooded the White House, the State Department, and congressional offices with literally thousands upon thousands of letters and telegrams." In order to demonstrate how widespread public support was for the Zionist program, the various Zionist groups organized massive petition and letter-writing campaigns. President Roosevelt received one such petition in January 1945 seconding the Biltmore program and signed by more than 150 college presidents and deans and 1,800 faculty members drawn from 250 colleges and universities in 45 states. A total of 41 state legislatures and hundreds of municipalities, representing more than 90 per cent of the nation's population, approved pro-Zionist resolutions. Schoolchildren in both Jewish and non-Jewish religious and Sunday schools were given form letters or postcards and asked to send them to their senators, representatives, and the President. In 1944, when the Emergency Council stepped up its campaign to abrogate the White Paper, over 12,000 letters and telegrams were dispatched from Meriden, Connecticut, to the President and the Secretary of State, although the entire Jewish population of that city did not exceed 1,500 people. Insofar as public sentiment might sway official policy, the Zionists left no stone unturned to ensure that public officials recognized that the American people favored the cause of a Jewish homeland in Palestine.[48]

                    *   *   *

The Zionists, throughout the war period, carefully cultivated Christian America. From a standpoint of practical politics alone, the Zionists recognized that only if the larger community supported their aims would they be able to influence governmental policy. A minority, no matter how efficacious its propaganda or skillful its public relations, no matter how many important contacts it has made, cannot affect American foreign policy unless it either neutralizes the majority or wins it over to active support of the cause.

There had always been so-called Christian Zionists, those who supported or worked for or prayed for the return of Jews to Palestine. For some Protestant millennial sects, the second coming of Christ required the early return of Jews to Zion. Some Christians saw Zionism as a humane antidote to persecution, while some anti-Semites saw the movement as a means to rid Europe (or America) of Jews and the Jewish problem. But there were many who believed in the necessity of Jews having a home of their own. The Zionists had tapped this vein of Christian sentiment as early as 1930, when Judge Julian Mack and the Reverend Charles Edward Russell had created the Pro-Palestine Federation of America to enlist Christian clergymen in support of Zionism. Another Christian group, the American Palestine Committee, began to function in 1932, with senators, congressmen, and other dignitaries among its sponsors. But for the most part, Zionists had failed to exploit potential Christian support during the 1930s, despite the obvious willingness of some Christian friends to oppose both fascism and the White Paper. Emanuel Neumann charged that "we Zionists have isolated ourselves from the vital current of American life and American thought. We have withdrawn into our shell."[49] The Zionists could no longer afford to hide in that shell.

One obvious place to seek non-Jewish support was in American labor. Jews had been active in the union movement, and had created some of the most powerful and vital labor organizations in the country within the garment trades. As early as 1923, American Jewish trade unionists began working in support of Histadrut, the General Federation of Jewish Labor in Palestine. The *Gewerkschaften* campaign in support of Histadrut had become an annual fund-raising event within the Jewish unions, and Histadrut had gradually come to the attention of non-Jewish labor chiefs. Even though William Green, president of the American Federation of Labor, and Philip Murray, head of the Congress of Industrial Organizations, were not on speaking terms for several years, they still would share platforms in support of Histadrut and Zionism. Because the Jewish Labor Committee, which represented a number of primarily Jewish labor groups, refused to endorse the Biltmore program, the Emergency Council created its own umbrella vehicle to co-ordinate labor support, the American Jewish Trade Union Committee for Palestine, with Max Zaritsky, president of the Hatters Union, as chairman, and both Green and Murray as honorary chairmen. On the Committee letterhead were listed as honorary vice chairmen the names of nearly every important labor leader in the country. Both the AFL and the CIO passed strong resolutions in support of a Jewish commonwealth in Palestine, and Zaritsky could tell the House Committee on Foreign Affairs that "American organized labor—12 million strong—reservedly and unequivocally supports the aspiration of the Jewish people for the establishment of their homeland in Palestine."[50]

Although a few clergymen had opposed Hitler from the beginning, the bulk of Christian America had been indifferent to the Jewish plight. In a Roper poll in 1938, 95 per cent of the sample disapproved of Hitler, but less than 9 per cent favored admitting more refugees into the United States. Even after *Kristallnacht* in November 1938, when the Nazis destroyed thousands of synagogues and Jewish businesses in Germany, 77 per cent answering a Gallup poll opposed letting more Jews into this country. A few months later, the editors of *Fortune*, reviewing these and similar surveys, asked: "Would Herr Hitler and his German-American Bunds be safe in the joyful conclusion that Americans don't like the Jews much better than do the Nazis?" An editorial in the *Christian Century* shortly after Hitler had come to power candidly admitted: "The Christian mind has never allowed itself to feel the same human concern for Jewish sufferings that it has felt for the cruelties visited upon Armenians, the Boers, the people of India, American slaves, or the Congo blacks under Leopold imperialism. Christian indifference to Jewish suffering has for centuries been rationalized by the terrible belief that such sufferings were the judgment of God upon the Jewish people for their rejection of Jesus."[51]

This attitude persisted well into the war, and even after the war, despite the growing knowledge of Hitler's "Final Solution." When the American rabbinate called for a day of fasting and prayer on December 2, 1942, to mark the anguish of European Jewry, there was little support from church groups. As Hayim Greenberg, editor of the *Jewish Frontier*, wrote, the American Jew "felt singularly alone. As he witnessed the apathy of vast America to this crime against mankind . . . he felt outraged and bereft—excluded from the human family whose members share in each other's fate."[52] The anti-Semitism built into Christian theology for nineteen centuries could not be expunged overnight, but it outraged Jews that Christian leaders, supposedly speaking for a religion of love and compassion, could find no room in their hearts to seek solace for the Jews. The anti-Zionist Federal Council of Churches did not even admit that "something like a policy of deliberate extermination of the Jews in Europe is being carried out" until December 1942, and in May 1943 finally held a day of compassion for European Jewry. Although the Council called the event a success, at least one minister termed it "a complete fiasco."[53]

The Zionists recognized that those who might be described as "theological anti-Semites" would not be won over, but they also believed that millions of decent, humane Christians, appalled by Nazi savagery, could become potent allies in the Zionist cause. At Biltmore, Abba Hillel Silver had declared: "We must make [the Christians] understand that we Jews stand to come out of this war, even after an Allied victory, defeated, unrequited, and betrayed. We must make them understand what has been the basic fact in the Jewish tragedy right through the ages, the fact of our national homelessness, of our abnormal political status in the world, and that after the Second World War . . . the ultimate solution of the Jewish problem must finally be sounded, and the ultimate solution is the establishment of a Jewish nation in Palestine."[54]

To win Christian support, the Zionists created two organizations: the American Palestine Committee and the Christian Council on Palestine. Emanuel Neumann was the guiding genius in establishing the American Palestine Committee, which was really a revivified version of the earlier Pro-Palestine Federation. Neumann, with the encouragement of Justice Brandeis, had begun work on this project in early 1941, and by April had secured Democratic Senator Robert Wagner as chairman and Republican Senator Charles F. McNary as cochairman.

From its beginning, the Committee had a distinguished roster; its seven hundred founding members included 67 United States senators, 143 congressmen, and 22 governors, as well as "distinguished jurists, educators, clergymen, publishers, editors, writers, and civic leaders," all of whom had access to influential members of government and industry. Fields workers, salaried by an annual subsidy of more than $70,000 from the Zionist Emergency Council, fanned out across the nation and built 75 local chapters, with some 15,000 members. Local ZOA and Emergency Council chapters were directed to provide their Christian Zionist allies with funds, clerical services, and moral support, so that the American Palestine Committee could "crystallize the sympathy of Christian America for our cause, that it may be of service as the opportunity arises. Sympathy is like any other force: It is effective only when properly channeled."[55]

The Christian Council on Palestine began operations in December 1942, with Henry A. Atkinson as chairman and Carl Hermann Voss as executive secretary. It grew from 400 clergy at its inception to about 3,000 by the end of the war, when it merged with the Committee into the American Christian Palestine Committee. The majority of the Council could be described as humane Christians, appalled at the suffering of the Jews, but it included many philo-Semites as well. Voss, for example, was a disciple and admirer of Stephen Wise, and once described Wise as having more "Christian charity" than any Christian Voss had ever met.[56]

Both Christian groups received subsidies from the Zionist Emergency Council and supported large-scale distributions of pro-Zionist materials, written primarily by and for non-Jews. However, both groups also resented the Emergency Council often acting in their names without prior consultation, though this problem was solved in 1944 with the granting of greater autonomy to the executive directors, Voss of the Council and Howard M. LeSourd of the Committee.[57]

The Emergency Council had originally hoped that some 50,000 Christians would join pro-Zionist organizations; less than 20,000 actually did. But the importance of the two groups cannot be measured just in terms of numbers. The American Palestine Committee provided the Zionists with influential non-Jewish allies who could open doors which would otherwise have remained closed to them; similarly, the Christian Council approached clergy all over the country and appealed to them for support of Zionist aims in Palestine on *Christian* grounds, an argument which would have been poorly received had it come directly from the Zionists. The effectiveness of the two Christian groups can be seen in the 1944 campaign to repeal the White Paper. More than 3,000 non-Jewish organizations, including unions, Rotary, Elks, churches, Lions, and the Grange, to name but a few, passed pro-Zionist resolutions and sent petitions, letters, and telegrams to Washington in favor of a Jewish state in Palestine.[58] These groups had been reached by speakers from the American Palestine Committee and the Christian Council, who could enter into many places where Jews were still unfamiliar and often unwelcome figures.

Just as important, the support of these Christians redeemed the gentiles, at least in part, in Jewish eyes. Despite the indifference of the majority to the terrible carnage in Europe, some men and women, other than Jews, cared about what happened. The empathy of men like John Haynes Holmes and Reinhold Niebuhr could not be, and was not, dismissed as hypocrisy, and did much to offset the blatant callousness and anti-Semitism of many members of the Federal Council of Churches. Without the support engendered by the Christian committees, it is doubtful if the Zionists would have been able to secure adoption by both major parties of pro-Zionist planks in their 1944 platforms.

*   *   *

It would appear that American Zionists and their supporters accomplished a great deal during the war years, and indeed they did. They neutralized much of the anti-Zionist sentiment within the Jewish community and won the endorsement of American Jewry for a Palestinian homeland. Through a superb propaganda campaign, orchestrated by Jewish and Christian groups, they made their case known to almost all Americans. Yet the real extent of their success would not be recognized until after the war. For the most part, American Zionist leaders then considered the period from 1942 to 1945 a disaster, and saw the many problems and catastrophes surrounding them as far outweighing the seemingly minor accomplishments. For despite growing support for a Palestinian homeland, the American government did all it could to undermine Zionist work, while in Europe, the long night of death settled on six million Jews. In the light of these frustrations, the unity created at Biltmore and the American Jewish Conference nearly disintegrated.

Chapter 2

UNBEARABLE BURDENS

On July 31, 1941, as German armored units sliced eastward into the most heavily Jewish areas of Russia, Hermann Göring, acting on Hitler's orders, directed Reinhardt Heydrich, chief of the *Sicherheitsdienst* (SD), to "make all necessary preparation with regard to organizational and financial matters for bringing about a complete solution of the Jewish question in the German sphere of influence in Europe." With the dispatch of that order, the Nazis shifted their policy from one of expelling Jews from the Third Reich, with its attendant slaughter of those who could not be evicted, to an intense concentration on the planned extermination of European Jewry. Seven months later, in the pleasant Berlin suburb of Wannsee, Heydrich convened a meeting of some fifteen agency heads and there put the finishing touches on the "Final Solution" of the Jewish problem: Jews of the conquered territories would be transported to the eastern front for slave labor, to be killed when they could no longer work; Jews unfit to labor for the glory of the Reich—the sick, the elderly, and the infirm—would be deported to special camps for "elimination."[1] For the next three years, the Nazis carried out this policy, building an elaborate system of death camps which murdered six million Jews. The dream that Hitler articulated in *Mein Kampf*, to create a Europe free of Jews, had been virtually realized by the time the Allies finally smashed the German war machine.

The first unconfirmed reports of mass killings were made by the German novelist and expatriate, Thomas Mann, in his BBC broadcasts in December 1941. On July 9, 1942, Stanislaw Mikolajczyk, a member of the Polish government-in-exile, announced to the press that the Nazis were systematically destroying the Jews of Poland and had already butchered more than seven hundred thousand men, women, and children. Although Jewish officials had been aware for some time that Hitler was killing Jews, they refused to believe that the Nazis planned to exterminate an entire people. Yitzhak Gruenbaum of the Jewish Agency discounted stories of mass murders, as did Leon Kubowitzki of the World Jewish Congress, who said that "such things do not happen in the twentieth century." The editors of the militant *Jewish Frontier* also dismissed rumors of a Nazi extermination plan as "the macabre fantasy of a lunatic sadist." In an interview more than thirty years later, Judge Louis Levinthal recalled that it simply seemed unbelievable: "It was incredible to me that these atrocities were taking place. I honestly didn't believe it. I thought it was propaganda, exaggerated, and apparently a lot of others felt the same way."[2]

Within a short time, however, evidence confirmed rumor as truth. Gerhard Riegner, representing the World Jewish Congress in Geneva, learned in early 1942 about the Wannsee meeting, as well as details concerning the use of Zyklon B gas and the mass shootings of Russian Jews by special Nazi squads. Riegner gathered corroborative material from refugees fleeing Germany, and in August 1942 compiled a report for Stephen Wise, president of the Congress. He gave one copy to Howard Elting, Jr., the American vice consul in Geneva, asking him to notify the United States government and to transmit the report to Rabbi Wise. Through the British consul, Riegner sent a second copy to Wise by way of Sidney Silverman, a Labour representative in Parliament and chairman of the British section of the World Jewish Congress.

Wise received the report, not from his own State Department, but through the British Foreign Office, which routinely forwarded the message. Elting's superior believed the report to be an inflammatory pack of lies. In Washington the State Department's Division of European Affairs suppressed Riegner's story because of the "fantastic nature of the allegations," and decided not to inform Rabbi Wise "in view of the apparently unsubstantiated nature of the information." But Wise already had the document in hand, and in great agitation hurried to present it to Sumner Welles, who as Under Secretary of State had approved its suppression. Welles asked Wise not to say anything until the

State Department could verify the information, and Wise reluctantly agreed.[3]

For the next three months one report after another arrived testifying to Nazi atrocities, and Hitler himself took no pains to hide his intent, predicting in one tirade after another "that the war can end only . . . by the disappearance of Jews from Europe. . . . This war will see the annihilation of Jewry." In September, Wise personally received further reports gruesomely detailing how one hundred thousand Jews in Warsaw had been massacred and their corpses used to make soaps and fertilizers.[4] By November even the skeptics in the State Department could no longer prevent news of the "Final Solution" from leaking out. On November 25, Sumner Welles informed Wise that State now possessed information which "confirms and justifies your deepest fears," and authorized the rabbi to release the documents.

The report of the planned genocide of European Jews stunned their American brethren, who now knew what they had only feared—that Hitler's rantings were much more than threats. The first reaction was one of grief and fury. Grief that, as Chaim Weizmann later wrote, "we shall be left in Europe with one huge cemetery of everything Jewish that had been built up over the last thousand years."[5] Sorrow over the destruction of a creative society that in many ways surpassed the rabbinic flowering of the seventeenth and eighteenth centuries.[6] Sorrow, too, that the dreams of emancipation and assimilation had been savagely shattered, especially in a land where Jews had declared themselves to be above all else good and patriotic Germans.

The fury exploded in the only way open to American Jewry, a series of mass demonstrations against the Nazi regime and a demand for some action to stop Hitler from carrying out his insane plan. Petitions were circulated urging that the Jews of Palestine be permitted to form their own army, that Palestine be opened to refugees, that something, *anything*, be done. But nothing was, and there has been continuous criticism, much of it justifiably bitter, about the indifference of Western society during the Holocaust.

As early as 1943 Chaim Weizmann predicted that future historians would be unable to understand "the apathy of the civilized world in the face of this immense, systematic carnage of human beings whose sole guilt was membership in the people which gave the commandments of the moral law to mankind. He will not be able to understand why the conscience of the world had to be prodded, why sympathies had to be stirred."[7] One explanation of the general indifference to the suffering has been that the very enormity of the crime precluded belief. As late as December 1944, two years after the State Department had confirmed details of the "Final Solution," the majority of Americans refused to believe that a whole people could be wiped out, despite the fact that in November 1944 the War Refugee Board had reported that more than 2.5 million people had been killed at concentration camps in Poland.[8] Still another theory portrays the Western world as a silent accomplice, appalled by the methods but not necessarily unhappy over the results. In his diary, Nazi propaganda chief Josef Goebbels wrote: "At bottom I believe that both the English and the Americans are happy that we are exterminating the Jewish riffraff." Richard Rubenstein, who has written extensively on the moral implications of the Holocaust, concludes, "the more one studies the literature of the period, the more difficult it is to avoid the conclusion that Goebbels was right."[9]

But while apathy among the general populace might be attributed to disbelief or a latent anti-Semitism, what can be said about the charges that American Jewry knew what was happening and still did nothing? As early as 1943, Hayim Greenberg, a veteran Labor Zionist leader, in a moving article entitled "Bankruptcy," called upon world Jewry to pray for an American Jewish community seized by moral bankruptcy, obtuseness, and callousness, a community doing nothing to save Hitler's victims.[10] More recently Meir Kahane has charged that the "Jewish oligarchy was seized by a deadly paralysis and a moral numbness that led them to watch haplessly and quietly as a third of the Jewish people was slaughtered."[11] Elie Wiesel, who has done much to interpret the Holocaust to this generation, wonders "if we had acted and responded with more genuine concern then, with more *ahavat israel* [love of Israel], perhaps the executioner would not have dared to destroy the remaining. . . . One of the reasons why the killers' program was so magically successful was that the rescue of European Jewry was not the first or even the second priority of our Jewish leaders. What went wrong with the Jewish heart? What went wrong with the Jewish conscience? What paralyzed the one and stifled the other."[12] Wiesel's accusations are echoed in several scholarly works, most notably Saul S. Friedman's *No Haven for the Oppressed*, which not only charges American Jewish leaders with impotence and silence, but also denounces them for complicity in a State Department policy of covering over news of Nazi atrocities.[13]

But what were American Jews to do? Were they to bring more pressure on their government to accept additional refugees? Were they to propose plans for bombing the rail lines leading to the death camps; or to call for retributive bombings to discourage Axis satellites from aiding in the further roundup of Jews; or to hold mass meetings to focus attention on the massacres in Europe; or to propose temporary havens for refugees? All this they did, working to influence the government and to rescue as many Jews as possible from Hitler's crematoria.[14] Are American Jewish leaders blamed for not caring, or for being unable to produce results? Reviewing the literature on this subject, one suspects that the overwhelming evil of genocide, the enormity of the crime, has distorted the sense of balance necessary to distinguish what *ought* to have happened from what actually *could* have been accomplished. In much of this writing is the tacit assumption that American Jews could have greatly affected the actions and policies of the Roosevelt administration, and by so doing have saved innumerable Jews in Europe. But is this a justifiable assumption? In their attempts to bring more refugees into the United States, American Jews were thwarted by anti-Semitism in the State Department, which controlled the issuance of entry visas. In their efforts to force the rescission of the White Paper, American Zionists found themselves confronted by both the State and War departments, which feared the effects such actions would have on the Arabs and on Middle Eastern oil supplies. And their appeals to the President met with constant sympathy and expressions of support but with absolutely no concrete results.

*   *   *

As American Jews tried to exert either political pressure or moral suasion on behalf of Hitler's victims, they discovered three bases of power in Washington which were able to help: Congress, the White House, and the State Department. They also discovered that in the complex administrative and political relationships of America at war, those advocating change faced much greater obstacles than those seeking to preserve the status quo. In the name of the "war effort," obstructionists could prevent major policy shifts which affected either European Jewry or the Middle East; failing that, they could retard or nullify implementation of policy decisions. Time and again American Jewish leaders were told that their request could not be granted because it would impede the fight against the Axis. Since Jews, above all else, wanted a quick end to the war, they lacked the leverage to counter such arguments. While the British and Americans assiduously wooed the Arabs, they knew that Jews in England or America or Palestine would not defect to the fascists. Given this situation, the sphere of activity in which American Jewry could be effective in exerting political pressure was narrowed.

In general, Jewish leaders, especially the Zionists, found Congress most sympathetic to their pleas for abrogation of the White Paper and the establishment of a homeland in Palestine. Numerous members of both parties in the House and the Senate joined the American Palestine Committee, and it was relatively easy to reach a congressman who had a pro-Zionist delegation in his district. The Emergency Committee's propaganda campaign to win non-Jewish support paid off most in Congress, where members by nature count heads; their tallies told them that their constituents favored the Zionist program. Moreover, in 1922 Congress had passed a resolution in favor of a Jewish homeland in Palestine.[15] As far as individual senators or representatives were concerned, support of a Jewish Palestine could do nothing but win them votes, both Jewish and non-Jewish, without alienating any important blocs.

On the other hand, the campaign to admit more refugees ran aground on the same political tallies; Congress knew that the majority of Americans opposed further immigration, even for those fleeing the Nazi terrors. The war saw a sharp upsurge in ethnic tensions, with repeated outbreaks of violence in New York, Detroit, Los Angeles, and elsewhere. The animus against Jews, while small in comparison with antiblack sentiment, still rose. One half of the people polled in a 1943 survey believed that Jews held too much influence over American business, and the fear of a full-scale outbreak of anti-Semitism led Rabbi Abba Hillel Silver to charge that the Old World style of Jew hatred had come to America to stay.[16] In such a mood, it is little wonder that most people opposed letting in refugees, and even the most humane congressman, unless he had a large bloc of Jewish voters in his district, was not eager to defy this attitude.

One can also understand how the State Department, with its middle-level bureaucrats, could not only block the entry of additional refugees, but also utilize red tape to make sure that even permissible quotas remained unfilled. Despite protests by Jewish groups against the anti-refugee and anti-Semitic attitude of State Department officials, the lat-

ter recognized that on this issue both public and congressional sentiment favored restriction. Despite the attacks of some Jewish
congressmen, notably Emanuel Celler, the State Department's policy
remained unchanged through the worst years of the Holocaust. The
Near Eastern Division especially opposed Zionist plans in Palestine,
and by adroit maneuvering and waving of the "war effort" banner,
defused pro-Zionist sentiment in the Congress sufficiently to prevent
passage of any strong measures either criticizing the White Paper or
calling for a Jewish homeland in Palestine.

The real tragedy is that the one man capable of leading Congress
and of overriding State Department obstructionism did not do either.
Perhaps it is unfair to blame Franklin D. Roosevelt for ignoring the
Jews of Europe, burdened as he was by the immense problems of governing the United States and leading the United nations to victory
over the Axis, pressures which eventually took their toll on April 12,
1945. But if there has been one President in this century with whom
American Jewry has identified, to whom it gave its heart both politically and emotionally, that was Franklin Roosevelt. During the 1930s
he had opened the doors of government service to Jews on a large scale
for the first time, and men like Felix Frankfurter, Samuel Rosenman,
Henry Morgenthau, Jr., and Ben Cohen held positions of influence and
power in the New Deal. Most important, the masses of Jews loved and
trusted him; they wrote him personal letters, sent religious calendars
and talismans, and planted trees in his honor in Palestine. At election
time, heavily Jewish districts would sometimes give him pluralities of
over 90 per cent, a situation which led Republican Congressman Jonah
J. Goldstein to pun: "The Jews have three *velten* [worlds]: *die velt*
[this world], *yene velt* [the next world], and *Roosevelt*." At his
death, no community in the country mourned for him as did American
Jewry; throughout the land synagogues echoed with the biblical lamen-
tation, "Know ye not that there is a prince and a great man fallen this
day in Israel!"[17]

Certainly Zionist leaders believed that in Roosevelt they had a
friend in power. During the 1930s, Louis Brandeis, Felix Frankfurter,
Stephen Wise, and other Zionists had direct and easy access to the
White House. The President personally intervened to prevent the British from closing off Jewish immigration into Palestine following the
1936 riots; three years later Roosevelt delayed but was unable to stop issuance of the White Paper.[18] During the war years Roosevelt saw

Zionist leaders on numerous occasions and always left them with the belief that he supported their program; the reports they wrote afterward are replete with joyful expressions of the President's backing. Ben-Gurion in mid-1942 declared that "the highest authorities were approached and . . . we have on our side the goodwill of the President of the United States." Chaim Weizmann described Roosevelt's attitude a year later as "completely affirmative," and in 1944, Stephen Wise, Meyer Weisgal, and the editors of *The New Palestine* all found reason to praise Roosevelt as being "strongly with us." At Roosevelt's death Zionist leaders were near-unanimous in praising him as a friend of their cause, and in Palestine flags flew at half mast in mourning.[19]

Yet on the two major issues of concern to American Jewry—European refugees and a Palestinian homeland—Franklin Roosevelt did practically nothing.

*   *   *

The failure of the United States—indeed, of the Western democracies—to deal with the refugee crisis has been well documented,[20] but a brief review of the situation can clarify the frustration felt by American Jewry during the war years. Even before the war, an international conference on refugees at Evian, France, had shown that Jews fleeing Hitler would not be welcomed elsewhere. James G. McDonald, the former League of Nations High Commissioner for Refugees, worked valiantly to help the persecuted, only to be ignored by Germany and rebuffed by the other countries. Bitterly but accurately he assessed the situation: "The world has become disagreeably conscious of the Jews; they are considered a drug on the market."[21]

Despite America's tradition as a haven for the oppressed, the nation built by immigrants closed its doors in the 1920s. During the Depression, economic considerations dampened humanitarian concerns; with millions of Americans unemployed, there was little enthusiasm for bringing in additional men and women—foreigners—to compete in the job market. Even children, the most innocent victims of the Nazis, were not welcome. When Congress considered legislation in early 1939 to admit ten thousand German refugee children, public sentiment ran more than two to one against it; polls testing support for liberalization of the immigration laws found upward to 85 per cent opposed.[22] Following a historic pattern, the economic and social dislocations of the thirties had stirred up latent prejudices against all minorities, and Hitler's virulent anti-Semitism found strong echoes in this country among the followers of Father Charles G. Coughlin, William Dudley Pelley, George W. Christians, Harry A. Jung, and other would-be *fuehrers*.[23] During the war years, despite the growing awareness of Nazi atrocities, antiminority sentiment increased, and while it affected a number of groups, Jews felt it most acutely. Chaim Weizmann, visiting the United States in early 1943, told Felix Frankfurter how shocked he was at the degree of anti-Semitism he saw in the United States. "Hitler has won," Weizmann concluded, "insofar as his campaign against the Jews is concerned."[24]

Tragically, this hostility against aliens resonated most strongly in those offices of the State Department charged with handling visa applications. By July 1941 public protests were heard about the mistreatment of Jewish refugees at key consulates in Lisbon, Berlin, and Zurich. Refugees were denied visas unless they could get police reports of good conduct, a near-impossible condition in the Third Reich. In Lisbon the consul refused to issue replacement visas to applicants whose original documents had expired because they could not get to an American consulate in time. Delay, according to Henry Feingold, became "the order of the day, as consuls, aware of the unsympathetic attitude of their superiors toward refugees, outdid themselves in an effort to build up a good record" of blocking visa applications. As late as 1944 the State Department continued to thwart immigration, even when directed to other countries. The Nazies offered to exchange a group of rabbis, 238 in all, from Auschwitz for disabled German prisoners of war held in Texas. All obtained passports for various Latin American countries, but by the time the consuls and their supervisors approved the paperwork, all 238 had been shipped to the gas chambers at Birkenau.[25]

Feingold, who has written the most balanced book on the refugee crisis, identifies the responsible government official in this bureaucratic dance of death as Breckinridge Long, Jr., who was appointed Assistant Secretary of State for Special Problems in January 1940, ostensibly to facilitate refugee attempts to find asylum. Instead, Long, a veteran foreign service official, used his experience and expertise in manipulating red tape to choke off the flow of refugees into the United States. Long is a classic case of old-line gentry confused and alienated in a world of change, seeking a scapegoat upon which to blame his troubles. A descendant of the Breckinridges of Kentucky and the Longs of North

Carolina, he saw "his people" as the real Americans, rather than the "foreigners" crowding into New York with unpatriotic ideas. Extremely anti-Semitic, he identified Jews as communists and shared Hitler's Jewish phobia. After reading *Mein Kampf*, he declared it "eloquent in opposition to Jewry and to Jews as exponents of Communism and chaos." His diary reveals a paranoid personality, one who believed himself destined to fight a long list of "enemies," both of himself and of America.[26] In his crusade against Jewish refugees, Long brought to bear a singleness of purpose, knowledge of the inner workings of government, and influential friends in both the White House and in Congress. Martin Dies, chairman of the House Committee on Un-American Activities, gave him access to committee files and worked closely with him to kill legislation for refugee relief. At the White House Edwin M. ("Pa") Watson kept Long advised of the work of refugee advocates, and at Long's behest would often block requests for appointments with the President from leaders in the rescue work such as James G. McDonald and Stephen S. Wise. Long had two additional factors working on his side: the passive attitude of Secretary of State Cordell Hull and the conflicting pressures within the Jewish community.

Hull, a soft-spoken lawyer from Tennessee devoted to the cause of peace, was the wrong person to head the State Department during wartime. A man of goodwill, he sympathized with the Jewish plight, and on several occasions pledged he would do all he could to help. In his memoirs, he recalled that "President Roosevelt and I had many conferences on the subject of Hitler's attempt to exterminate the Jews. We eagerly studied all ideas and information that might be in the least helpful in relieving their inconceivable situation."[27] But Hull hesitated to act, afraid perhaps that the fact he had married a Jew would open him to criticism of favoritism for "his own." Hull also lacked initiative and tended to rely on the reports and advice of his subordinates, and at that time practically no Jews, and very few Jewish sympathizers, worked at State. As a result, Hull found himself dependent on men like Breckinridge Long for assessments of the situation, and Long, to use Emanuel Celler's phrase, had a "heartbeat muffled in protocol."

Furthermore, Long recognized that the situation within the Jewish community prevented any concerted effort or agreement on a single plan: "The Jewish organizations are all divided amid controversies . . . there is no cohesion nor any sympathetic collaboration—rather rivalry, jealousy, and antagonism." Although the Zionists had been able to fire enthusiasm in the community for a Jewish homeland, so long as the British enforced the White Paper Palestine could not answer the terrible needs of a people one step away from death. Without Palestine, American Jewry had no firm options to offer; they could merely propose a variety of settlement arrangements, international rescue funds, and methods to permit additional refugees into the United States. Typically, when Stephen Wise spoke to Roosevelt in December 1942, the document Wise presented on behalf of a number of Jewish organizations contained a stark and somber indictment of the Nazi program, but lacked any specific plans for dealing with the refugees, since the different groups could not agree on one.[28]

The most serious charge in this area is that the Zionists deliberately sabotaged any plan that did not make Palestine the primary haven for Jewish refugees. A proposal for "free ports" in Palestine, to temporarily hold refugees until after the war, drew the scathing denunciation of Israel Goldstein, who opposed "selling the Jewish birthright for a mess of publicity. As well might one ask for temporary shelter in one's own home. Not free ports in Palestine but Palestine in its entirety as a free port for the Jewish people is our slogan."[29] George Backer, of the Joint Distribution Committee, who attended the special conference in Bermuda in 1943 to deal with the refugees, charged that the Zionists undermined efforts to find other places for the Jews by insisting that only Palestine would be acceptable. Backer believed that other options existed, and told an interviewer that "if the Zionists had helped in leadership perhaps tens of thousands could have been saved." When Sol Bloom also suggested alternate resettlement schemes, he came under fire from Zionist leaders. During maneuvers for a congressional resolution in 1944, according to Henry Feingold, "Zionists were more interested in having the White Paper revoked than in circumventing its effects by means of temporary havens."[30]

One can question the assumption beneath the charges against American Jews that had they only been able to unite, they could have done something to save thousands, perhaps millions, of lives. One reason that American Jewry could not unite is that no feasible solution offered itself. What proposal could a united Jewry have made? Would the doors of Palestine have been opened any sooner if all of America's five million Jews had called for it? The British fought every attempt to admit more Jews into Palestine, and in the end, only a civil war drove the British from the Holy Land. Would more refugees have been accepted into the United States? David Wyman, a critic of American policy during this period, notes that from 1933 to 1945 approximately a quarter of a million refugees from fascism reached safety in the United States. However, prior to 1938 the quota for German immigration was never filled, and not because of the State Department; German Jews refused to believe that Hitler meant what he said. Even if the Department had allowed the quotas from 1938 through 1941 to be used completely, an additional fifty thousand people at most would have been permitted to enter.[31] From 1942 to the end of the war, these quotas remained unused, and Congress refused to sanction any proposal to apply the German quotas to refugees isolated in neutral countries. Given such difficulties, it is hard to believe that even a concerted effort by American Jewry would have had significant results.

No country wanted to take in Jews, a fact recognized most clearly by the Zionists.[32] The Bermuda conference of 1943 was exactly what its critics said: a piece of window dressing where American and British delegates, safe from the activities of Jewish pressure groups, could utter empty pieties and do nothing. The British would not allow Palestine on the agenda, and for all the grand talk of resettlement elsewhere, no one could propose any scheme which would have accommodated more than a token handful of refugees. Emanuel Celler bitterly summed up the results of Bermuda as "a diplomatic mockery of compassionate sentiments and a betrayal of human instincts and ideals." Of the twenty-eight nations fighting Hitler, he declared, not one had said, "We will take in Hitler's victims."[33]

Not until 1944 did the United States government finally make real gestures at relief. Secretary of the Treasury Henry Morgenthau, Jr., confronted Roosevelt and Cordell Hull with proof that State Department officials were hindering every effort at relief, and that men like Breckinridge Long were overtly anti-Semitic. Morgenthau presented a memorandum drafted by Randolph Paul, general counsel of the Treasury, carrying the unequivocal title "Report to the Secretary on the Acquiescence of this Government in the Murder of the Jews," which documented consular policies preventing refugees from gaining asylum, as well as the activities of senior officials in frustrating relief work. Roosevelt finally divested Long of responsibility for refugee policy and established the War Refugee Board, much to the satisfaction of Jewish leaders who had been pleading for such action.[34]

The War Refugee Board did establish some temporary havens, in-

cluding one in the United States, and oversaw the humane handling of
Jews liberated from Nazi hands as the Allies moved forward against the
Reich. But it should also be noted that by 1944, the horror of German
atrocities had moved public sentiment sufficiently to support such
"bold" measures.[35] By then, however, it was too late for the millions already dead, too late for those in Nazi death camps who would not live
to see VE Day, and too late for those who had waited helplessly and
hopelessly for a visa to safety. The Board, staffed by men genuinely
desirous of saving lives, showed what could have been done had there
been presidential leadership in the early years of the war to awaken
public understanding and compassion. Again, could a united Jewry
have done this? Not without the active support of a President willing
to override senior officials in the State Department as well as of
congressmen working to change public opinion rather than being held
captive by it. Such conditions did not exist, and even a united American Jewish community could not have called them into existence. And
while Breckinridge Long played upon anti-alien sentiment and manipulated red tape, his colleagues on the Middle Eastern desk were working
equally hard to make Palestine another dead issue.

*   *   *

"I really am inclined to believe . . . that there is a cabal in the State
Department deliberately and, I am afraid, effectively working against
those Palestinian interests which are precious to some of us."[36] So wrote
Stephen Wise in the fall of 1942, and by the end of the war, nearly
every Zionist leader shared this feeling. While one might dismiss the
sentiment as a product of frustration and/or depression, the evidence
indicates that Wise did not suffer from paranoia; an important group of
State Department officials assigned to deal with the Middle East most
certainly shared the anti-Zionist, pro-Arab biases of their colleagues in
the Foreign Office. Hiding behind the legalism that Palestine constituted a British rather than an American interest, they worked diligently
to deter any policy or statement that might have advanced the cause of
a Jewish homeland.

Once more, middle-level bureaucrats had their way because of a
lack of effective leadership and supervision. The Secretary of State on
several occasions pronounced himself in favor of a Jewish homeland as
originally proclaimed in the Balfour Declaration.[37] But Cordell Hull
faced conflicting pressures: On the one hand, Jewish groups wanted

him to support Zionist claims to Palestine and to force the British to repeal the White Paper; on the other side, both his own advisers on the Middle East as well as the British warned that Zionist propaganda could easily stir up Arab resentment and create unrest in that part of the world. The Secretary wavered with indecision, and finally allowed the anti-Zionists to direct policy. A good example of this can be found in a supposedly "definitive" answer given by Hull in response to a Senate enquiry on departmental policy. "Toward this matter," he wrote Senator Burnett Rhett Maybank, "I may say that Palestine is a British responsibility. Nevertheless, the Department maintains a close interest in the Palestine problem and follows closely all developments having a bearing upon the tragic plight of the Jewish people in Europe."[38] This was exactly the attitude fostered by the middle-level bureaucrats, although they had been far from reticent in the previous two decades in interfering in Palestine when American shipping and commercial interests were involved, or when American businessmen trading in Middle Eastern products felt discriminated against by British regulations.

Departmental officials followed a number of tacks to sidetrack Zionist pressure. Prior to the American Jewish Conference in 1943, Zionist delegations had to fend off charges that they spoke for only a small minority of American Jewry. Wallace Murray, head of the Middle Eastern Division, complained to Zionist leaders that they could not really expect the Department to support them when they did not have unified backing from their community. Chaim Weizmann retorted by asking why in all democratic countries a majority decision is deemed adequate, but Jews are expected to be unanimous.[39] Murray had no answer, but at subsequent meetings repeated that Zionists lacked a broad-based support. A similar complaint came from Assistant Secretary Adolph Berle, Jr., whose father, the Reverend A. A. Berle, had been a strong supporter of Zionism after the First World War. The younger Berle declared that he and his colleagues who dealt with Jewish matters were in a very difficult position. Because of the widespread disagreement within the Jewish community, a State Department official could not express any viewpoint without incurring the wrath of several factions who disagreed.[40] Of course, the last thing the bureaucrats wanted was such a unanimity, and they did their best to head it off. They tried pressuring the American Jewish Conference into postponing its meeting, and failing that, urged Judge Proskauer and other non-Zionists to defer any resolution dealing with Palestine. They attempted to get a joint Anglo-American statement calling for postponement of public debate on the Palestine question until after the war, but Zionist leaders nonetheless refused to keep quiet. The State Department pushed for such a statement until 1944, when the British advised that they no longer believed such a document would be of value.[41]

When all else failed to move the Zionists, one could always count on some undersecretary or assistant secretary to appeal to reason and humanity, with the supposedly unanswerable argument that the *Yishuv* would be slaughtered if left to its own devices, that Jewish settlers would be overrun by the Arabs. One of the most fantastic conversations between government and Zionist representatives followed just this line. A. A. Berle, in a conversation with Emanuel Neumann, suddenly began painting a horrific scenario of events in Palestine should the Germans conquer the area. Neumann asked what Berle thought the Zionists should do, and the assistant secretary promptly responded that they ought to make a deal with Ibn Sa'ud, renounce political claims in Palestine, and move a large part of the *Yishuv* to Kenya for the duration of the war. In return, they would receive a Vatican City in Palestine after the hostilities, as well as real territory, worthy of a nation, some place in Africa, such as Abyssinia.

"But Abyssinia is in the hands of the Axis—Italy," protested Neumann.

"Of course," countered Berle, "but it will be in Allied hands if we win the war."

"Quite true," Neumann answered, "but in that case so will Palestine, too, be in Allied hands—and if, God forbid, we lose the war, there will be neither Palestine nor Abyssinia."[42]

In the face of such responses, the Zionists found negotiations with the State Department extremely difficult. The Jewish delegations had a specific agenda and wanted the State Department to commit itself, at the very least, to the idea of a Jewish commonwealth in Palestine, if not to a specific plan for achieving it.[43] But the Department found one excuse after another to evade the issue. Even after Rabbi Silver gave Cordell Hull overwhelming proof that repeal of the White Paper and a homeland in Palestine enjoyed overwhelming support within the Jewish community,[44] lower-level officials continued to maintain that fringe groups like the American Council for Judaism, or the practically disowned American Jewish Committee, actually represented majority opinion. Less than one out of every ten Jews in America belonged to the Zionist movement.

Only one man in the State Department seemed to understand and sympathize with the Zionists, Under Secretary Sumner Welles, who eventually became a stanch advocate of a Jewish state. In early 1943, as prospects for victory in Africa brightened thus removing the military threat to the *Yishuv,* the State Department realized that it would at least have to listen carefully to what the Zionists said about Palestine. Welles met with Chaim Weizmann several times, but then had to turn the talks over to Wallace Murray who, as head of the division, had direct responsibility in the Middle East. But as the lower-level officials managed to evade the real issues, Welles continued his own talks with Weizmann and other Zionists leaders. The memoranda of those conversations indicate that they were the only serious discussions on Zionist aims and methods to take place in the State Department, and for a brief moment Jewish hopes rose that the bureaucratic roadblock might be broken. But Welles left the State Department in October, and, as Weizmann sadly wrote, his departure "is a great pity from every point of view."[45]

Failing to get anywhere with the State Department, the Emergency Council decided on an end run: It took its case to Congress, hoping that a resolution there might force the Administration to act on Zionist proposals. "Without political agitation," Abba Hillel Silver had declared, "forthright and direct, recovering our authentic voice and our authentic demands . . . without political action, we will not be able to solve the pressing refugee problem after the war."[46] Utilizing their contacts in Washington, especially the members of the American Christian Palestine Committee, the Zionists introduced resolutions calling for the repeal of the 1939 White Paper, so as to allow refugees into Palestine immediately, and for the establishment of a Jewish commonwealth in Palestine after the war.

State Department officials would have opposed the resolutions, but Cordell Hull, aware of the political risks of directly antagonizing American Jewry, hesitated. Before Hull could decide, the War Department came to his rescue. Secretary of War Henry L. Stimson wrote to the chairman of the Senate Foreign Relations Committee urging him to table the resolutions. Stimson had been advised by both army and foreign service officers that the resolutions might stir Arab resentment and possibly lead to a civil war in Palestine, a situation which would surely be exploited by the Axis. Roosevelt urged Stimson to make his letter public, thus placating the Zionists, but Stimson refused, since he did not want the War Department involved in a political controversy. Senator Thomas L. Connally, unwilling to take the blame for killing the resolutions, scheduled hearings instead. The Zionists, unaware of Stimson's opposition, continued their lobbying, and passage of the measures seemed assured.[47]

Under pressure from the British, the Administration could not allow Congress to act, and on February 23, 1943, Army Chief of Staff George C. Marshall testified before a secret session of the Foreign Relations Committee. According to Arthur Vandenberg, Marshall made an "utterly frank and blunt confidential statement" to the effect that the resolutions might incite an Arab uprising. At the same time, Roosevelt pressured several Zionist leaders to appear before the committee. Without having consulted Silver, they testified that delay in passage would not harm the Zionist program. The committee immediately tabled the resolution; when the House wanted to act on it, the Administration made Stimson's letter public on March 17.[48]

Silver, who had never been a Roosevelt enthusiast, was furious; he felt betrayed by the President's avowals of sympathy on the one hand and his manipulation of Zionist leaders on the other, especially since the Emergency Council had not been advised of the alleged military problems until Marshall's sudden and dramatic appearance. Shortly afterward, Silver publicly attacked the Administration for its duplicity. "Within the last few months, as if by concerted action, there has set in a very definite and noticeable withdrawal on the part of the official family from anything which might even remotely suggest a recognition or endorsement of the Jewish homeland." At the same time that government officials flooded Jews with messages of sympathy and outrage over Hitler's atrocities, "when pressed to do something about it, to help save a race from annihilation, they regretfully remind us how difficult it is to do anything for these poor unfortunate people under present war conditions. . . . The suggestion is even made that anything which may be done for these unfortunate Jews now might, in some way, postpone the day of ultimate liberation."[49]

Stymied temporarily in the Congress, the Emergency Council increased its campaign to generate local and state support, confident that at some time the Zionists would be going back to the capital. During

1943 and early 1944, seventeen state legislatures, representing nearly 60 per cent on the American people, endorsed Zionist-sponsored resolutions supporting a Jewish homeland in Palestine.[50] Within Congress, moreover, a growing number of senators and representatives continued to introduce resolutions which, although destined to be tabled in committee, nevertheless kept the issue alive in Washington. Sol Bloom believed that a majority of the Congress favored the plan, but could not even vote on it so long as the Administration justified its opposition on the grounds that the possibility of antagonizing the Arabs might adversely affect Allied efforts to win the war.[51]

The Emergency Council, under Silver's prodding, decided to push for passage of a strong measure at the beginning of 1944, and identical resolutions were introduced in each house of Congress, resolving "that the United States shall use its good offices to the end that the doors of Palestine shall be opened for free entry of Jews to that country, and that there shall be full opportunity for colonization so that the Jewish people may ultimately reconstitute Palestine as a free and democratic Jewish commonwealth."[52] Again, Hull and his associates felt that passage "although not binding on the Executive, might precipitate conflict in Palestine and other parts of the Arab world, endangering American troops and requiring the diversion of forces from Europe and other combat areas. It might prejudice or shatter pending negotiations with Ibn Sa'ud for the construction of a pipeline across Saudi Arabia." In his memoirs, Hull did not mention whether Jewish suffering in Europe was even discussed. But once again the War Department and Secretary Stimson intervened with another warning that "further action on [these resolutions] at this time would be prejudicial to the successful prosecution of the war."[53]

Frustration filled Emergency Council headquarters. The Administration's concerns about antagonizing the Arabs struck Zionist leaders as an empty worry, or worse yet, as appeasement, yet they could not set themselves up as military experts contradicting the War Department. After months of lobbying, the Zionists had secured statements of support from 77 senators and 318 congressmen, and felt certain that they could carry a strong resolution through the Congress. About the only positive note that Silver could strike was that the subject of Palestine, "which in the last year had become tabu in Washington, is now on the agenda again. . . . Our authorities now know how the American people and Congress feel about it."[54] The situation, however, became even more confused and more frustrating a few days later when Roosevelt met with Abba Silver and Stephen Wise. Although the President had worked behind the scenes to kill the resolutions, he now authorized the two rabbis to say that the American government "has never given its approval to the White Paper." The Zionists were immediately besieged by senators and representatives asking whether they should now reintroduce the measures, but in the light of continuing War Department opposition, it seemed best to let the matter rest for the moment.[55]

In the meantime, the Zionists decided to try still one more approach to move the Administration. Aware that Roosevelt enjoyed enormous electoral popularity among the Jews, Silver suggested that some cozying up to the Republicans might be in order. "Our movement," he announced, "is not wedded to any one political party. We have strong and warm friends in both."[56] Utilizing his close contacts with Republican Senator Robert A. Taft of Ohio, Silver secured approval by the Republicans at their 1944 convention of a strong plank endorsing a Jewish homeland in Palestine. Moreover, the Republicans articulated the thoughts of many Jews when they condemned Roosevelt for his failure "to insist that the mandatory of Palestine carry out the provisions of the Balfour Declaration and of the mandate while he pretends to support them."[57]

Some Zionist leaders did not like the idea of their movement being used in such a partisan fashion; others saw a need to protect Roosevelt. Stephen Wise, who viewed himself as the Democratic Party's emissary to American Jewry, took it upon himself to ensure that the Democrats came out just as strongly, if not more so, in favor of a Jewish commonwealth. Wise lobbied through his friends in the Senate and within the party, and several Jewish congressmen, realizing the potential impact of the Republican plank, joined in the campaign. Emanuel Celler reportedly told the Democratic Resolutions Committee that "it would be highly dangerous for my party not to include a Palestine plank. It would be particularly dangerous so far as my own bailiwick is concerned. You can't carry New York without Brooklyn, and you might not carry Brooklyn without such a plank."[58] Responding to such arguments, the Democrats declared that they favored "the opening of Palestine to unrestricted Jewish immigration and colonization, and such a policy as to result in the establishment there of a free and democratic Jewish commonwealth."[59] Roosevelt pronounced himself happy to support the platform, but many people wondered whether sincerity or political expediency had finally moved the President to endorse Zionist demands.

*   *   *

The more one studies the war years, the more one is puzzled by Franklin Roosevelt's behavior. Recognizing that the President was the compleat political animal, conceding that few men of his generation had his grasp of world affairs, even admitting that by nature he always worked both sides of the street, there remain elements of irrationality and duplicity in his actions. How does one reconcile the man who promised Stephen Wise that he would personally rescue Palestine for the Jews with the man who deliberately avoided every opportunity to come to grips with the issue? No one had more power to help the Jews during the war, yet Roosevelt failed to use it in any meaningful way.

On several occasions, Roosevelt cast himself in the role of a friend to the Jews. He met frequently with the presidents of major Jewish groups, and throughout the war condemned Nazi bestiality, pledging that a day of reckoning would come. To men like Stephen Wise and Emanuel Celler, he promised that the Jews would have a homeland in Palestine after the war.[60] Through advisers like Samuel I. Rosenman, he consistently assured Jewish spokesmen of his sympathy and friendly attitude. Even Jewish leaders from abroad, such as Chaim Weizmann, found it relatively easy to secure interviews with the President and to get a considerate hearing of their plans.[61]

At the same time, Roosevelt cleverly played off one group against another. In this he was abetted by Rosenman, who was less than enthusiastic over the Zionist program. After the American Jewish Conference, for example, both Zionist leaders and the American Jewish Committee sought interviews with Roosevelt. Rosenman blocked the appointments on the grounds that it would be highly impolitic to confuse the President with contradictory views on Palestine. Whenever it appeared that Zionist pressure might heat up, the White House would sidetrack the Zionists, forcing them to waste valuable time and energy trying to convince middle-level bureaucrats that they truly had community support behind them. Even when the Zionists secured an affirmative statement from Roosevelt, Rosenman saw that non-Zionists were reassured that little hope existed of creating a Jewish state in the foreseeable future.

Roosevelt moved cautiously—indeed, deviously—on Jewish issues for several reasons. Despite Biltmore and the American Jewish Conference, the influence of the American Jewish Committee and the noise of the American Council for Judaism seemed evidence that the community was far from united on major issues; it would be better to buy time until a clear consensus developed at a politically opportune time. On the refugee issue, he correctly gauged that if he came out strongly behind demands for greater refugee quotas, he could easily antagonize groups whose support he needed for other major programs. "First things come first," he told his wife, who had taken a keen interest in refugee problems, "and I can't alienate certain votes I need for measures that are more important at the moment by pushing any measure that would entail a fight."[62] American Jewry might have seen the refugee issue as *the* burning issue of the day, but the President did not.

Abroad, Roosevelt wanted to avoid the enmity of Arab leaders, especially the Arabian monarch, Ibn Sa'ud. While one can debate whether or not Roosevelt correctly assessed the depth of Arab hostility or their ability and willingness to oppose Western pressures, one must concede that the President had legitimate worries about how a pro-Zionist stance on the part of the American government would affect the progress of the war. A major American supply line to the Soviet Union ran through Arab lands around the Persian Gulf, and the goodwill, or at least the neutrality, of the people along this Lend-Lease conduit had to be maintained. Planning groups in both the State and War departments predicted a growing American presence in the region; Air Force and Navy officials wanted to acquire bases there, while American oil executives as well as government agencies could hardly wait to tap the immense oil reserves recently discovered in Arabia. The Near Eastern Division of the State Department constantly reminded the President of the potentially explosive consequences of an American endorsement of Zionist aims, including the possibility of having to divert troops from the Italian front to put down an uprising in Palestine.[63]

Roosevelt tried several approaches to dealing with the Arabs. Just as he quietly reassured the American Jewish Committee at home, so he would balance any pro-Zionist statement with a secret message to Arab leaders that no decision would be made regarding Palestine without consulting them.[64] In October 1942, the President dispatched Colonel Harold B. Hoskins to the Middle East to talk with both Jewish and Arab leaders regarding the possibility of a peaceful settlement in Palestine. Hoskins, whom many Zionists suspected of being pro-Arab, reported in early January 1943 that he saw no hope for resolving the problem, for tensions in the area were increasing. As a gesture of goodwill, the Administration invited Ibn Sa'ud to visit America. When the Emir Faisal agreed to come as his representative, the government sought assurances from Jewish leaders that no criticism would be directed against the President's guest.[65]

Throughout all of his dealings, both devious and direct, on the question of Palestine Franklin Roosevelt naïvely clung to the illusion that he could impose a peaceful settlement—one that would satisfy both Jew and Arab. Early in the war he toyed with the idea of a trusteeship. "What I think I will do," he told Henry Morgenthau, "is this. First, I would call Palestine a religious country. Then I would leave Jerusalem the way it is and have it run by the Orthodox Greek Church, the Protestants, and the Jews—have a joint committee run it. . . . I actually would put a barbed wire around Palestine, and I would begin to move the Arabs out of Palestine. . . . Each time we move an Arab out we would bring in another Jewish family."[66] Together with Winston Churchill, he played with the notion of calling in Arab and Jewish leaders, making them sit in the same room, and forcing them either to negotiate a settlement or accept one imposed upon them. Roosevelt gloried in what he saw as the effectiveness of his personal diplomacy and believed that he alone, as President of the United States, could bring about not only a solution to the Palestine question, but also a reconciliation between Arab and Jew. Herbert Feis, who listened to the President discourse on his plans one afternoon, left the White House muttering: "I've read of men who thought they might be King of the Jews, and other men who thought they might be King of the Arabs, but this is the first time I've listened to a man who dreamt of being King of both the Jews and Arabs."[67]

Because Roosevelt believed he could influence the Arabs, he made plans to see Ibn Sa'ud on the way back from the Yalta conference in 1945. At Yalta, Palestine did not appear on the formal agenda, although the Big Three discussed it informally. According to one observer, Roosevelt took a strong pro-Zionist stand and got Joseph Stalin to agree to a Jewish state in Palestine. When the Soviet leader pointed out the difficulties involved, especially Arab hostility, Roosevelt smilingly replied that he and Ibn Sa'ud would work that out.[68] Even while these discussions went on at the Crimean resort, an American destroyer had been dispatched to Jidda to bring the Arabian monarch eight hundred miles to Cairo. According to a White House release, "the destroyer's decks were covered with rich oriental rugs, while gilded chairs gave added touches of unusual splendor, as, also, did the flowing robes and accessories that make the Arabian dress so strikingly picturesque." In a lengthy luncheon meeting, the religious head of the Wahhabi sect hardly gave the President of the United States any chance to practice personal diplomacy. Ibn Sa'ud launched into a nonstop diatribe against Zionism, interspersing his comments with quotes from the Koran. When Roosevelt tried to point out the benefits the Jews had brought to Palestine through their modern farming methods, the King dismissed the whole issue with a curt "My people don't like irrigation." Harry Hopkins later wrote that the King had "overly impressed" Roosevelt.[69]

How much the ailing President had been impressed was demonstrated in Roosevelt's report to a joint session of Congress on March 1, 1945, when he declared: "I learned more about the whole problem, the Moslem problem, the Jewish problem, by talking with Ibn Sa'ud for five minutes than I could have learned in an exchange of two or three dozen letters."[70] This statement fell like a bombshell among Zionists and non-Zionists alike. The American Jewish Congress angrily attacked Roosevelt for reneging on his pre-election endorsement of the Democratic platform on Palestine. Emanuel Celler bitterly complained that of all the great issues discussed at Yalta, no one had seen fit to even mention the catastrophe overtaking the Jews. And on the way home, Celler added, Roosevelt did not have time to meet with any Jewish leaders from Palestine, but spent four hours with Ibn Sa'ud. Senator Edwin Johnson of Colorado, a member of the American Christian Palestine Committee, declared that "the choice of the desert king as expert on the Jewish question is nothing short of amazing. . . . I imagine that even Fala [Roosevelt's pet dog] would be more of an expert." Even Samuel Rosenman, a member of the White House staff, found the remark "almost bordering on the ridiculous." Bernard Baruch, although not a Zionist, told Ben Hecht that "despite my having been a lifelong Democrat, I would rather trust my American Jewishness in Mr. Dewey's hands than in Mr. Roosevelt's."[71]

Yet two weeks after his speech to Congress, Roosevelt met with Stephen Wise and assured him that he had not retreated from his earlier pledge. "I have had a failure," Roosevelt said. "The one failure of my mission was Ibn Sa'ud. Everything went well, but not that, and I arranged the whole meeting with him for the sake of your cause. . . . I have never so completely failed to make an impact upon a man's mind as in his case."[72] Less than a month later, Franklin Roosevelt died.

*   *   *

Few men in our nation's history are so controversial as Franklin Roosevelt. Few were so well-loved or so reviled as he, and the storms he stirred in his lifetime have not abated even now. This is especially true of the debate over Roosevelt's relationship with the Jews, a debate that began within days after his death. Meyer Weisgal believed that Roosevelt had truly "wanted to do the right thing for us," but was thwarted by the "puny advisers" who surrounded him. At a memorial service in the Free Synagogue, Stephen Wise lauded the late President as Israel's great and true friend, downplaying the Ibn Sa'ud episode with the explanation that the President had been misled by "some supersubtle counselors in the State Department." Sumner Welles also objected to the attacks leveled against Roosevelt, arguing that despite the "malicious misrepresentations," Roosevelt "in his conference with King Ibn Sa'ud did not modify in one iota the basic principles that he had constantly supported," namely, "a negotiated settlement of the Palestine question . . . that would provide the Jews with their promised national homeland."[73]

Yet even before his death, some Jews had begun to question just how reliable a friend Roosevelt was, whether in fact he held to any "basic principles" on Jewish issues.[74] In the time of European Jewry's great trial, the President had been morally indignant, but his wariness and not his indignation set the tone and pattern of administration policy. The State Department must certainly bear its share of the blame for placing obstacles in the path of rescue, but even Roosevelt admirer and biographer James Burns has conceded that the President "seemed unable to face the main problem—the millions of Jewish men, women, and children trapped in the Nazi heartland and headed for the gas chambers."[75] While the Near Eastern desk did all it could to retard Zionist plans, they never had to fight the commander in chief to have their way. Shortly after the war, Frank Manuel attacked the tendency to blame the State Department for American policy in the Middle East: "The decisions were his, and the Middle East was a world area of whose significance President Roosevelt was profoundly aware. He may not be held responsible for every stupid dispatch contrived by a desk man in the Near Eastern Affairs Division, but he was fully conscious of the main lines of policy toward both the Arabs and the Zionists."[76]

Numerous theories defend Roosevelt, and they have some merit— he could not lead a nation where it did not want to go, he had to preserve American influence in the Arab world, he had to safeguard American troops fighting in the Mediterranean, he had hundreds of pressure groups beseeching him to solve their individual crises, and above all, there was the sheer magnitude of the problem—not hundreds but millions of victims—and the determination of the Nazi regime to liquidate European Jewry. But where is the moral response of the man who showed such great compassion for the ill-housed, ill-fed, and ill-clothed? Where is the action regarding the refugees, the swift decision-making that marked the New Deal's energetic response to the Depression? Franklin Roosevelt personified twentieth-century liberalism; the New Deal was *the* liberal political-economic event of our century. Did Jews expect too much from it? Did they believe that if any democratic society could live up to its most humanitarian aspirations, then the America of Franklin Roosevelt would? But moral and humanitarian responses, claims Henry Feingold, are rare in history and particularly rare in wartime. For Feingold, "the villain of the piece, in the last analysis, may not be the State Department or even certain officials but the nature of the nation-state itself."[77] For all the pious statements, the Western democracies bore out Hitler's prediction that they would not lift a finger to save the Jews.

Centuries ago, Hillel asked, *"Im ain ani li mi li?"* (If I am not for myself, then who is for me?) During the war, American Jewry learned that they could not count upon the kind words or sorrowful bromides of their government. If Jews were to be saved, if Zion were to be redeemed, Jews would have to do so by themselves. But before they could do that, they had to put their own house in order.

Chapter 3

A HOUSE DIVIDED

The war years present an interesting paradox in American Jewish affairs. While a great majority of Jews and many non-Jews endorsed Jewish statehood by 1945, the community was actually on the verge of disintegration. Unity of sentiment could not be transformed into purposeful action. The American Jewish Conference failed to realize its initial promise,[1] and without a powerful guiding force, American Jewry became torn by conflicting demands. On the one side a bitter anti-Zionism *redivivus* arose, demanding an end to Zionist programs, while on the cther a Revisionist-inspired group called for a "Hebrew" army to fight both the Nazis and the British. The Zionists, who might have been expected to grasp the lead of a Jewry suddenly converted to a Palestinian program, found themselves beset by internecine strife. If the State Department middle managers misunderstood the temper of American Jewry, it saw quite accurately that a community so busy fighting itself had little time to fight them.

*　　　*　　　*

For decades, the strongholds of anti-Zionism in the United States were the temples and institutions of Reform Judaism. The Pittsburgh platform of 1885 explicitly renounced any hope of return to Zion: Judaism had a universal mission to spread the message of ethical monotheism, which precluded an outmoded and particularistic nationalism. Reform leaders in this country also feared that Zionism implied a dual allegiance; if one were to be a good American, one could not harbor any equal loyalty to Zion. Throughout the latter part of the nineteenth century, and well into the twentieth, Reform fought Zionism tooth and nail, with many Reform rabbis appalled at the implications of the Balfour Declaration.[2]

While there had always been some Zionists within Reform, their influence and numbers began to increase in the 1920s. The growing persecution of Jews in Europe and the influx of the children of eastern European parents into the Reform rabbinate led to a weakening of the anti-Zionist tradition. In 1932, Rabbi Barnett Brickner argued that Reform Judaism and Zionism must make their peace: "Jewish nationalism needs the dynamic of religion for its motivation and power, and Reform needs the whole household of Israel for its congregation." Reform's attempt to discard nationalism and include "Jews by religion only" led merely to assimilation and the loss of identity. By 1937, Zionists within the CCAR were able to insert a strong nationalistic tone in the "Guiding Principles of Reform Judaism," adopted to replace the five-decade-old Pittsburgh platform. Instead of a denial of Zion, the Columbus platform declared: "In the rehabilitation of Palestine, the land hallowed by memories and hopes, we behold the promise of renewed life for many of our brethren. We affirm the obligation of all Jewry to aid in its upbuilding as a Jewish homeland by endeavoring to make it not only a haven of refuge for the oppressed but also a center of Jewish culture and spiritual life." Despite strong resistance from some of its members, the CCAR incorporated these ideas into its ritual and practice.[3]

Reform anti-Zionism, however, remained strong, and it was only a matter of time until the anti-Zionists found an issue around which they could rally. That opportunity arose at the 1942 CCAR convention when the Zionists, on a roll-call vote, endorsed the creation of a Jewish army in Palestine.

Within a remarkably short time denunciations of the CCAR resolution appeared in the Anglo-Jewish press. A small group of Reform rabbis, led by Louis Wolsey of Philadelphia, met to discuss ways of restoring Judaism's "prophetic and universal" ideas. Unless the defenders of the faith acted, he argued, Reform would be lost to the incursion of "Jewish national chauvinism." Although reluctant to precipitate a schism within the movement, the anti-Zionists finally called a national rabbinical meeting in Atlantic City in early June 1942.[4]

It appears that the original intention of Wolsey was to downplay anti-Zionism and to emphasize the broad range of concern about recent developments within Reform. The agenda for the Atlantic City meeting covered numerous areas of concern, including development of Hebrew Union College and postwar problems. But opposition to Zionism had been the common bond which brought the rabbis to the resort city, and they received a heavy dose of anti-Zionism in the opening speeches. Ninety rabbis attended the conference, and eventually another six signed the "Statement of the Non-Zionist Rabbis" issued at the close of the meeting. It was the third principle of this statement that acknowledged "how dear Palestine is to the Jewish soul," yet denounced the "political emphasis now paramount in the Zionist program. We cannot but believe that Jewish nationalism tends to confuse our fellow men about our place and function in society."[5] Although the Wolsey group explicitly called themselves "non-Zionists," elements within the Jewish community immediately labeled their statement "the anti-Zionist manifesto."

In reply, seventeen leading Zionist rabbis, including the presidents of the Synagogue Council of America, the CCAR, and the Rabbinical Assembly, as well as a member of the presidium of the Union of Orthodox Rabbis, prepared a counterdeclaration entitled "Zionism: An Affirmation of Judaism." They proclaimed that the overwhelming majority of American rabbis "regard Zionism not only as fully consistent with Judaism but as a logical expression and implementation of it," and they went on to castigate the Wolsey group for misrepresenting and distorting "historic Jewish religious teaching." Circulated primarily under the direction of Stephen Wise, Abba Silver, James Heller, and Philip Bernstein, 733 rabbis originally signed it, and 85 more added their signatures within the next two months; the total included 215 Reform rabbis. Moreover, the student bodies of the five leading seminaries approved the statement, including Reform's Hebrew Union College, where it was endorsed by a vote of 42 to 9.[6]

Thus far, the battle had been primarily theological rather than political. Both Wolsey and James Heller, president of the CCAR, saw it as an internal feud, one with potentially serious consequences, but still one which could be contained within rabbinic circles. The manifesto, however, proved to be a rallying point for anti-Zionist laymen, who demanded that an organization be created to accommodate them. The rabbis, confronted by such overwhelming opposition from their colleagues, welcomed the new members and their financial support. By the end of 1942 the original rabbinical protest against the dilution of classical Reform theology had begun to shift to a lay-dominated war against Jewish nationalism.[7] With the creation of the American Council for Judaism, the rabbis were effectively shunted aside; although Rabbi Elmer Berger of Flint, Michigan, was chosen as executive director, he stood clearly with the laymen in their uncompromising hatred of Zionism.

Throughout 1943, as the American Jewish Conference worked to create a pro-Zionist consensus, the anti-Zionists girded for battle. Berger traveled throughout the land soliciting support. Local rabbis, such as Edward Nathan Calisch of Richmond, used their prestige to establish Council chapters. Thanks to major contributions from Lessing Rosenwald, former chairman of Sears, Roebuck who later became the Council's president, and a handful of other wealthy Jews, the Council generated its own flood of pamphlets responding to Zionist claims. Naturally, the State Department rejoiced in this "proof" of its contention that all American Jews did not really support Zionism, while a number of Christian anti-Zionist groups applauded openly. After all, Jewish anti-Zionist opinion proved attractive to a world wary of anti-Semitism.[8]

Perhaps the most stunning "victory" of the Council came in Houston, Texas, at Congregation Beth-Israel, one of the oldest and wealthiest Reform temples in the South. When the senior rabbi retired, a bitter fight ensued over the choice of a successor; eventually the nominating committee, dominated by anti-Zionists, chose Hyman Judah Shaftel, and the congregation ratified his selection on August 4, 1943, by a vote of 346 to 91. Because of this lopsided victory, the board, which included several Council members, decided to push through a set of "Basic Principles" that would "safeguard at least a segment of the Jewish people of this nation against indictment before the Lord for worshipping a false god, ZIONISM." The board changed the bylaws of the temple to allow for two classes of membership. Those whose advocated Zionism, observed the rules of *kashruth* (dietary laws), or desired the extensive use of Hebrew in the services could only have a second-class, nonvoting status. Full voting membership was reserved for those who unequivocally endorsed a resolution which stated: "We are Jews by virtue of our acceptance of Judaism. We consider ourselves no longer a nation. We are a religious community, and neither pray for nor anticipate a return to Palestine nor a restoration of any of the laws concerning the Jewish state. We stand unequivocally for the separation of the Church and the State. Our religion is Judaism. Our nation is the United States of America. Our nationality is American. Our flag is the 'Stars and Stripes.' Our race is Caucasian. With regard to the Jewish settlement in Palestine we consider it our sacred privilege to promote the spiritual, cultural, and social welfare of our coreligionists there." The resolution passed 632 to 168, whereupon 142 members and the assistant rabbi resigned in protest and founded a new, rival temple.[9]

The Council rejoiced in its Houston victory, and while some rabbis even proposed emulating the Beth-Israel program,[10] it quickly became apparent that the council had completely underestimated the temper of American Jewry. The Beth-Israel "Basic Principles" evoked near-universal condemnation. David deSola Pool, the distinguished Orthodox rabbi of New York's Shearith Israel, wondered why the statement did not begin "No Jews Need Apply!" Within Reform circles, aside from the Wolsey group, reaction was just as strong. When Shaftel visited Hebrew Union College, the students subjected him to endless recriminations and arguments; in the dining room they chanted the grace after meals with emphasis on the words *"boneh b'rachamav y'rushalayim"* (may God in His Mercy rebuild Jerusalem) especially for his benefit.[11]

The American Council for Judaism episode reveals a profound insecurity among its adherents, not only about their Jewishness but about their Americanism as well. Elmer Berger, who has never deviated from a strong anti-Zionist position, expressed this sentiment quite clearly a quarter century after the founding of the Council. The group coalesced, he declared, "because a number of American Jews considered Zionism a sufficiently serious threat to their identity as Americans of the Jewish faith. . . . The threat, to some, was to their Judiasm; to others it was the character of their nationality status that was threatened. To some it was also a combination of both. In most cases, the racial peoplehood character of Zionism was, on an ethical and moral basis, something to be particularly repudiated."[12]

In essence, those who joined the Council were afraid—afraid of too much attention being called to the Jews, afraid of *Ma yomru hagoyim?* (What will the gentiles say?), afraid that someone might question their American patriotism not because they were *Zionists* but because they were *Jews*. Council members, who preached about loyalty to America, did not understand that true Americanism went far beyond flags and symbols. They never really trusted the United States to accept them.

Ironically, this insecurity manifested itself in a group which had consciously tried to drop all appearances of being different. Upper-class, Reform, and assimilationist, they did everything they could to relegate their religion to a minor facet of their lives; they tried to hide their Judaism. Three generations of life in America had not, for them at least, wiped out the old ghetto mentality that if a Jew calls attention to himself, trouble will inevitably follow. Arthur Hays Sulzberger, publisher of the New York *Times*, worried that his non-Jewish friends would say to him, "What are you doing in America? Why don't you go where you belong? To a Jewish Palestine."[13]

For the Zionists, the Council proved a mixed blessing. At first, all they could see was a well-financed drive to split American Jewry, a group of renegades playing right into the hands of the State Department and the anti-Semites. In the beginning the Emergency Council moved cautiously vis-à-vis the Council, afraid that if anti-Zionism became too public it might well create the disunity within the community that the Zionists so assiduously tried to avoid.[14] But as the Council for Judaism stepped up its campaign of anti-Zionism, flooding the country with pamphlets and books critical of Zionist work, the Zionists began to respond in kind. In late 1943 and throughout 1944, through a committee headed by Rabbi Arthur J. Lelyveld, the Emergency Council waged an all-out war against the anti-Zionists. It established over 130 local Committees on Unity for Palestine to combat the American Council for Judaism, and distributed hundreds of thousands of pieces of literature. In the pages of *The New Palestine* and other Jewish journals, Zionist writers attacked the American Council for Judaism as traitors to their faith and to their country; the anti-Zionists, ran the argument, were the ones who had really renounced American ideals and principles.[15]

Eventually the Zionists discovered that in many ways the American Council for Judaism could be an asset. Nahum Goldmann had predicted fairly early that in having to fight the Council the Zionists would have to bury some of their internal differences in order to concentrate their forces.[16] But beyond that, by forcing the issue into such stark terms as Zionism vs. anti-Zionism, the Council compelled American Jewry to take a stand. Berger, Rosenwald, Rabbi Morris Lazaron of the Baltimore Hebrew Congregation, and others believed that most American Jews, when given a choice between "Zionism and dual loyalties" and "anti-Zionism and true Americanism" would choose the latter.

But American Jewry refused to allow the Council to define the problem in those terms. Most Jews, including the Reform segment, believed in Jewish peoplehood and were unafraid that their identification as Jews, or even as Zionists, impaired their status as Americans.

The Holocaust, moreover, proved that Jews needed a haven. The Zionists proposed Palestine as an answer, while all the Council could offer were platitudes about suffering humanity. The American Council for Judaism seemingly never confronted the one issue which more than any other gripped the minds and hearts of American Jewry; in the face of mass murder, all its talk about Jewish universalism, dual loyalties, and militant nationalism was irrelevant.[17] But the Zionists did see that, and by acting upon that recognition managed to turn the Council from a potential threat into a convenient whipping boy.

From its beginnings, the Council suffered one setback, defection, and castigation after another. The CCAR overwhelmingly condemned the Council, and in its strongest statement to that time approved a resolution denying any incompatibility between Zionism and Reform Judaism. When Hebrew Union College president Julian Morgenstern echoed Council doctrine, large numbers of alumni as well as virtually the entire Jewish press excoriated him. The Council tried to have the Union of American Hebrew Congregations repeal a pro-Palestine resolution, only to find that Abba Hillel Silver easily persuaded the executive committee to back down.[18] The strengthening and extension of the American Christian Palestine Committee especially upset the Council, since Christian endorsement of Jewish nationalism would endow Zionism with what, to the Council, would be unimpeachable legitimacy. The many Christian friends of Zionism must have thought it strange that influential Jews were trying to thwart their humanitarian response. Although Lazaron garnered the support of a number of Christian ministers and leaders, most followed the example of George W. Maxey, chief justice of the Pennsylvania Supreme Court and head of the Pennsylvania chapter of the ACPC, who told Berger that he considered it his duty to do all he could "in keeping open Palestine and the roads to Palestine for the tens of thousands of Jews who are struggling to escape the cruel fate which Hitler has already imposed on over three million Jews."[19]

As one Jewish group after another publicly condemned the Council, many of the ninety rabbis who had met in the Atlantic City conference withdrew. Over half had left by September 1943, only one month

after the legal incorporation of the Council; by 1946 less than a dozen
rabbis remained on the Council's roster. Many of these had been
worried from the start that the laymen's anti-Zionism would drown out
the larger theological issues involved. The most famous defection came
in 1946, when Louis Wolsey, the guiding spirit of the Atlantic City
conclave, resigned as vice president when the Council tried to block
Jewish immigration into Palestine. In a speech explaining his withdrawal, Wolsey, in sorrow and in anger, pointed out how the Berger-
Rosenwald leadership had betrayed his own and his colleagues' original
intentions. They had seen themselves not so much as opposing Zionism
but as promoting religion. The lay leaders who had taken over the organization ignored the rabbis, and concentrated only on fighting Jewish
nationalism.[20]

Perhaps the most telling indictment of the Council came from
within. Assessing its failure to rally American Jewry behind anti-
Zionism, the Council's *Information Bulletin* of June 30, 1944, noted:
"Always, the Zionists-nationalists could say to the dissenters, 'Whom
but yourself do you represent?' "[21] The answer, it seemed obvious to all
but the most radical anti-Zionists, was no one but themselves. Although
the American Council for Judaism created a stir, their extreme anti-
Zionism placed them, as Barry Silverberg has noted, "beyond the consensus" of Jewish thought in America. Until 1967 the Council could always
be counted upon to oppose Zionist policy and even Israeli existence.
But it always proved to be little more than sound and fury, with no
substance; it beclouded the Jewish scene temporarily in a storm of
protest, but having no real alternatives to offer a beleaguered community, it lacked staying power.

*   *   *

The American Council for Judaism has been described as a haven for
those ashamed of their Jewishness, composed of men who overempha-
sized the universalistic and ethical aspects of religion only to deny the
particularist, the ethnic sense of peoplehood. For the Council, like the
assimilationist leaders of the Reform movement in Germany a century
before, anything within Jewish life that might set Jews apart should be
denied, or if that proved impossible, at least downgraded or muted. Zionism scared the Council because it called attention to Jews and their
problems, it made them too "visible."[22]

At the other end of the religious spectrum stood another Jewish group equally opposed to Zionism, but for totally different reasons. The Agudas Yisrael, an ultra-orthodox movement dedicated to preservation of *halachic* life (life lived according to the strict precepts of the Torah), opposed Jewish nationalism because in its eyes Zionism contravened God's promise to redeem the Jewish people through messianic deliverance. The Zionists, according to the Agudas, were working to thwart God's will; man could not redeem himself, and any effort to do so would only postpone the final coming of the Messiah. Adding to their consternation was the fact that many of the Zionist leaders were secularists and not Torah-observant; how, they asked, could God's chosen people be led to redemption by men who were not even good Jews?

In many of the Orthodox communities of New York, the Agudas waged a bitter struggle against Zionism, with pietist rabbis imposing *herem* (excommunication) on their Zionist foes. For the Orthodox Jew, the battle with Agudas was just as disruptive and aggravating as that with the Council for the Reform Jew. Only the fact that the Orthodox community was relatively small, and the Agudas Yisrael minute, kept this battle from assuming the proportions it had with the Council.

If the Zionist movement in the United States during the early 1940s upset some Jews because of its secular nature, and appalled others because of its "militant nationalism," yet another Jewish group believed that American Zionism, in its response to Hitler and the White Paper, had been far too timid. Inspired by the Revisionists, this group openly and belligerently proclaimed their Jewishness, and denounced all Jews who would not join them in fighting fire with fire.[23]

The Revisionist movement has often been identified with one man, Vladimir (Zeev) Jabotinsky, who had almost single-handedly organized and promoted the Jewish Legion during the First World War. In the early 1920s, Jabotinsky played an important role in the World Zionist Organization, and seemed the heir apparent to Chaim Weizmann, who alone among major Zionist leaders had actively supported the Legion project. On the surface the two men had much in common—born in Russia, well-educated, brilliant, masters of several languages, at home both in Jewish and non-Jewish circles, and totally committed to rebuilding a Jewish homeland in Palestine. But during the decade following the war, Jabotinsky and Weizmann drifted apart on the question of how that homeland should be built. Weizmann saw growth as a necessarily slow process, or as he once put it, the *Yishuv* would grow dunam by dunam, house by house, goat by goat. Moreover, co-operation with the British must be fostered, for only under the Crown's benevolence could the Balfour promise ultimately be fulfilled. Although England had begun to renege on its commitment almost at once, Weizmann continued to urge accommodation and understanding.

Jabotinsky, on the other hand, did not view Palestine as a privilege granted by His Majesty's Government, but as a rightful possession of the Jewish people. The British had the moral and legal obligation to do all they could to foster, not impede, Jewish settlement; the Zionist task, as he saw it, involved rapid development of the *Yishuv*, with massive immigration so as to create a Jewish majority in Palestine in the shortest possible time. Any British moves to thwart this growth had to be resisted, and in protest against what he considered Weizmann's "minimalist" policy, Jabotinsky resigned from the Executive in early 1923.

Over the next several years Jabotinsky devoted himself to building a new Zionist movement, dedicated to creating a Jewish majority on both banks of the Jordan. As for the Arabs and the British, they must be made to understand that Palestine historically belonged to the Jews, who had now come to reclaim their heritage. Mollycoddling of the British, appeasement of the Arabs, would only cut the ground out from beneath the Zionists. The ultimate aim of Zionism—a Jewish state—must not be hidden; let the world know that the Jews would no longer be subservient to everybody else's interests, that they now had an agenda of their own.

By 1934 Revisionists had given up completely on any rapprochement with the British, and openly called for nonco-operation with the mandatory authorities. The following year the tension in the movement could no longer be contained, and the New Zionist Organization, with Jabotinsky as president, split from the world body. Over the next few years the Revisionists, almost alone of all Zionist groups, called for massive emigration of European Jews to escape fascism, and for armed resistance in Palestine.

In the *Yishuv*, the Haganah, the Jewish settlement's defense arm, had always followed a policy of *havlagah* (restraint), acting only in self-defense and reacting only to specific acts of Arab terrorism or aggression. Some Haganah members, however, desired a more active role in which they could move to head off Arab attacks by striking first. In 1937 the *Irgun Zvai Le'umi* (National Military Organization) came into being, ideologically linked with the Revisionist movement and accepting the authority of Jabotinsky as its leader. With the publication of the 1939 White Paper, the Irgun increased its activities, especially in smuggling refugees into Palestine and in fighting British authority altogether. The most famous member of the Irgun, Menachem Begin, later Prime Minister of Israel, assumed command of the organization in December 1943, and for the next three years the Irgun fought not only against the British, but also against the Haganah and the regular Zionist groups who were willing to co-operate with the British in the war against Hitler.[24]

In the United States, the Revisionist New Zionist Organization did not carry much influence, but through the Irgun, a number of committees organized by a brilliant young Palestinian, Peter Bergson, generated immense publicity, grabbed headlines, and made it appear at times as if they alone were fighting Hitler and the British. For the regular Zionists, the Bergson committees proved more dangerous than the American Council for Judaism, for they appealed to the same raw emotions as the Zionists, but seemingly could provide an outlet for the frustrations plaguing American Jewry.

Bergson arrived in the United States in 1940 with a handful of Irgun members. Shortly after Pearl Harbor, they issued a call for the formation of an "American Committee for a Jewish Army," and set about rounding up sponsors to endow the group with legitimacy. By May 1942, the Army Committee was circulating a letter claiming the endorsement of Eleanor Roosevelt, Secretary of War Henry L. Stimson, General Louis B. Hershey, William Green of the American Federation of Labor, and some three hundred other luminaries in American life.[25]

Despite the fact that Christians and Jews previously unaffiliated with Zionist work, like the journalist Pierre Van Paassen, nominally headed the Committee, the regular Zionists quickly perceived that the dominant figures were all Revisionists. David Ben-Gurion declared that the Army Committee was nothing more than an American branch of the Irgun terrorists, and wanted the Emergency Committee to have nothing to do with it.[26] But the American leaders, with the exception of Hadassah, felt that in the name of unity some effort ought to be made to reach an accommodation with the army group. None of the American Zionist leaders had major objections to a Jewish armed force fighting on the side of the Allies, and if agreement could be reached, then unnecessary and enervating factional strife might be avoided.

During the first six months of 1942, over Ben-Gurion's constant objections, Emanuel Neumann and Meyer Weisgal negotiated with the

Jewish Army Committee. Privately Weisgal conceded that the Emergency Committee had failed to take the initiative, and perforce had to co-operate with the Revisionists, trying to reach a satisfactory agreement, or publicly oppose them, which would create ill will within the Jewish community and misunderstanding on the part of non-Jews. The Army Committee was more than happy to reach some sort of *modus vivendi* with the Zionists, since, despite the presence of the big names on its letterhead, it as yet had little money and few people for day-to-day operation. Just when it seemed that some understanding was reached, Ben-Gurion, with the aid of Hadassah, managed to convince a majority of the Emergency Committee that it would be a grave error to work with the Irgun in any way, and scuttled the negotiations. The result, as Weisgal bitterly complained, was that instead of creating a common front against a common enemy, the Zionists now spent too much time and effort fighting each other.[27]

Bergson quietly watched as the negotiations between the Army Committee and the Zionists foundered. He then stepped forward, and in a series of brilliant maneuvers breathed new life into the Army Committee. He followed up with the Emergency Committee to Rescue the Jewish People of Europe (1943), the Hebrew Committee of National Liberation, and the American League for a Free Palestine (both 1944). Together these committees ran dramatic, if distorted, advertisements in major newspapers to call attention to the Jewish plight.

For example, in February 1943, word leaked out that the Romanian government was willing to allow seventy thousand Jews to leave the country in return for a "ransom" of approximately fifty dollars per person. Days later the New York *Times* carried a full-page advertisement calling upon the American public to save Jews by sending the necessary money to the Jewish Army Committee. The fact that the offer had to be approved by many governmental groups, both on the Allied and Axis sides, as well as by neutral intermediary agents, so as to make it virtually unworkable, was not mentioned in the ad, which brought in a considerable sum of cash—none of which was returned when the ransom scheme fell through. A few months later, during the Bermuda conference, the Bergson groups ran large ads calling State Department officials murderers; the wording of the text was so extreme that thirty-three senators rose on the floor of the Senate to disassociate themselves from the statement. Their names had appeared because they had originally signed up as sponsors of the Jewish Army Committee.[28]

Yet Bergson's success can be credited in part to his winning Ben Hecht over to his cause. Hecht was a successful playwright (he coauthored *Front Page* with Charles MacArthur), screenwriter, columnist, and novelist, but also, prior to the war, a classic case of the self-hating Jew. Hecht's literary portraits of Jewish figures were savage caricatures. In *A Jew in Love* (1931), he described his central protagonist, Abe Nussbaum, as a dark-skinned little Jew with a vulturous face and a reedy body; other Jews in the novel radiated ennui, obscenity, and a tired sophistication. All had sausage faces or other disfigurements and were stamped by a distorted Jewishness which could have been produced in Josef Goebbels' hate factory.[29]

The phenomenon of Hitler forced Ben Hecht to re-examine his Jewishness, and when he met Bergson and his fellow Palestinians, his former self-hatred boomeranged into militant assertiveness as well as admiration—indeed, a near idolatry—of this new breed of Jew—strong, self-reliant, and unafraid. In a defiant article entitled "My Tribe Is Called Israel," Hecht demanded that American Jews like himself, who had never considered themselves Jews, stand up to fight for Jewish rights and values then under attack. He called for "the sound of moral outrage over the extinction of the Jews [which] would restore human stature to the name Jew. In the silence this stature was vanishing. We Jews in America were fast becoming the relatives of a garbage pile of Jewish dead. There would be no respect for the living Jew when there was no regret for a dead one."[30]

Bergson and Hecht combined to produce some masterful propaganda events, whose quality and impact far surpassed the more mundane work of the Emergency Committee. Hecht wrote a pageant, *We Will Never Die,* which Billy Rose produced on March 9, 1943, in New York's Madison Square Garden. Directed by Moss Hart with a score by Kurt Weill, it blended traditional Jewish tunes with a theme of courage and hope. Dozens of stars, including Edward G. Robinson, Sylvia Sidney, and Paul Muni, acted their parts beneath two forty-foot-high tablets of the Law. The pageant toured the country, playing to sellout crowds and winning rave reviews everywhere.[31]

The hatred Hecht at one time had shown against all Jews, however, was now focused, with Bergson's help, on the so-called Jewish establishment. There is an almost paranoid quality in Hecht's autobiography as he discussed how the "leading Jews" tried to get him, tried to stop his work. There is also a great deal of naïveté in his reports of how

Bergson told him stories about this establishment, which Hecht thereafter accepted as truth.

The regular Zionist leadership, Chaim Weizmann and David Ben-Gurion, Stephen Wise and Abba Hillel Silver, opposed the Irgun and Bergson's activities, which they denounced as a shameful fraud.[32] Part of the trouble arose from a lack of co-ordination between the Bergson groups and the Emergency Council. The Zionists, aware of various political pressures and sensitivities, were trying to mount a sophisticated nationwide campaign to break through the apathy confronting them. Bergson and Hecht, under no discipline, could issue the most outrageous statements, well aware that they would face no reprisals. While the Zionists discounted so-called Arab might, they at least tried to avoid unnecessarily offending Arab opinion; Bergson damned everyone, scornful of the consequences, seemingly oblivious to the fact that potential friends, from Congress to the Cabinet to the White House staff, were being alienated. Wherever the Zionists went, they—not the Bergson group—reaped the reproaches for the latter's inflammatory newspaper advertisements and distorted news releases.[33]

The Zionist quandary could not easily be resolved, since the Bergson groups had touched an open nerve in American Jewry. The Zionists had worked to ease immigration laws, to cancel the White Paper, to open Palestine, all to no avail. They more than anyone knew of the tragedy in Europe and how the Western democracies had failed to act. The Bergson groups did not save a single Jew because of their activities; they did not alter British or American policy one iota. But they articulated the hidden anger of many American Jews; when frustration reaches a high enough level, screaming becomes therapeutic, and the semblance of action can be accepted in place of the substance.

When Bergson and Hecht began attacking specific individuals, however, they alienated many of their own supporters who knew the character and accomplishments of men like Stephen Wise, Abba Hillel Silver, Israel Goldstein, Louis Lipsky, and others. As a group they might be culpable, but individually they had earned the respect of the Jewish community. Judd Teller wrote: "However disappointed in Wise, once the roaring lion of Jewish protest, they still revered him for a lifetime of Jewish service. Ben Hecht was hardly fit to sit in judgment on him." Perhaps the most ludicrous incident occurred when Bergson brought charges against Wise in a rabbinical court, accusing him of obstructing passage of a congressional resolution in favor of a

Palestinian homeland.[34] American Jewry recognized the attack for what it was—a cheap publicity stunt—and it backfired badly against Bergson; nearly every Jewish paper in the country rose to defend Wise and condemn Bergson.

As the war dragged on, many American Jews began to perceive Bergson's policy as counterproductive and separatist. Supporters of a Jewish army could endorse the recruitment of Palestinian Jews and stateless refugees, but assumed that, as in the First World War, the fighting force would be under British command. But as the Army Committee raised its goal from ten thousand to two hundred thousand men, it called for an independent command under general Allied control.[35] The figure of ten thousand might have been realistic, but setting a goal—a *minimum* goal—of two hundred thousand struck many people as a publicity trick.

It gradually dawned upon sponsors and members of the committees that nothing had been accomplished. Protestant clergyman and journalist Pierre Van Paassen resigned from the Army Committee, and in a published letter, branded the Committee to Save the Jewish People of Europe a hoax, "a very cruel hoax perpetrated on the American public, Jewish and non-Jewish alike. That committee and its directors have but one aim in view: to increase the prestige of the outlaw group in Palestine known as the Irgun and the glorification of the Irgun's self-styled 'dynamic' missionaries in this country."[36] As Bergson and his cohorts played politics, more and more members deserted the committees, complaining that the purpose for which they had joined, the army or refugee rescue, had been abandoned.[37]

By 1944, Bergson attacked the Zionists as illegitimate spokesmen for the Jewish people, and demanded that the Zionist organizations, as well as the Jewish Agency, turn authority over to the Hebrew Committee for National Liberation, a self-styled "government in exile" which Bergson established on May 18, 1944, and which immediately raised the Star of David flag over its headquarters in Washington.

The Zionists, who for the sake of unity tried to avoid open fighting, now went on the attack. Nahum Goldmann, on behalf of the Jewish Agency, reaffirmed that the Agency was the only international body recognized in law as representing the Jewish people, and warned that "American public opinion should not allow itself to be fooled by the acts of a few men whom a normally organized people would deal with as traitors to the common cause and exclude from the community."[38]

The Zionist Emergency Council charged that the new committee "is made up of half a dozen adventurers from Palestine with no standing, no credentials, no mandate from anyone." *The New Palestine* called upon Jews everywhere to take action against the Bergson committees, and Hadassah shortly thereafter passed a resolution of condemnation at its annual convention.[39] Jewish congressmen, who had been most susceptible to the overt publicity pressures of the Bergson group, flocked to Zionist headquarters demanding that something be done. As long as the different committees had restricted their operations to the rescue field, there had been no problem; now they were issuing manifestos and meddling in military and political matters, and Samuel Dickstein, Emanuel Celler, and others were receiving irate phone calls from the White House, the military, and the State Department. Rabbi Leon Feuer bluntly told the congressmen that they should restrict their co-operation and support to the legitimate Zionist groups, and got them to agree to warn their non-Jewish colleagues in the House and Senate against Bergson's activities.[40]

The Zionists also activated a speakers' bureau composed of Zionist professionals and Palestinians, who toured the country as "truth squads," alerting local communities to the real conditions in Palestine and the terrorist nature of the Irgun. Leading Jewish figures in the *Yishuv*, including the chief Ashkenazic rabbi, whose alleged endorsements had appeared in Hecht's advertisements, issued strong denunciations dissociating themselves from the Revisionists and charging that they had never authorized the use of their names.[41] In October 1944, the Washington *Post* published an exposé entitled "Bergson Admits $1,000,000 Fund Raised, Vague on Its Use," and labeled Bergson a "self-styled nuisance diplomat."[42] The exposé questioned the financing of the various committees, and also deflated their claims to have smuggled forty thousand illegal immigrants into Palestine.*

The tragedy of Irgun operations in the United States during the war is that they wasted talent, energy, and money in a frantic and self-serving search for attention. Peter Bergson and Ben Hecht tapped a

---

* Several thousand Jews were indeed smuggled into Palestine during the war, but not by the Bergson groups. The real heroes of "Aliyah Bet" could not publicize their feats nor claim credit until after the establishment of the Jewish state in 1948. It was Haganah, and not Irgun, which ran the clandestine operation. The full story is reported in Ehud Avriel, *Open the Gates!* (New York, 1975).

vein of eagerness in American Jewry, an eagerness to do something to alleviate the tragedy of the Holocaust. There is no doubt that they called attention to the problems, but their methods confused both Jewish and non-Jewish supporters of Zionist goals and did much to weaken the unity necessary for the American Jewish community to exert any leverage on the government or public attitudes. In the end, in terms of real results—a Jewish army, rescued refugees, altered immigration quotas, changes in British policy in Palestine—they accomplished little.

*   *   *

The activities of both the American Council for Judaism and the Bergson groups detracted from the pro-Zionist consensus developing in the United States, but internal organizational disputes also sapped the movement of a great deal of strength. One of the saddest chapters in Zionist history was occasioned by the bitter infighting that took place during the Second World War, a fight not only over methods, but also over leadership.

Although the Biltmore conference had marked a shift in goals and tactics, it would be years before the changeover would be complete, a process prolonged by the egotism of the principal characters. The decision at Biltmore to seek actively the creation of a Jewish state after the war marked Chaim Weizmann's decline in influence over the world movement, and Stephen Wise's diminishment on the American scene, against the rise of David Ben-Gurion and Abba Hillel Silver. Unfortunately, unlike a political election, the winners could not be quickly determined, with a concurrent and orderly transition of power. In the years following Biltmore, it seemed at times that Zionist leaders fought themselves as much as outside opponents. It is a complicated tale, yet its outcome materially affected the postwar struggle for a Jewish state; it also prefigured the later transformation of American Zionism after the creation of Israel.

Weizmann had moved to establish an American base for himself in 1941, directing Meyer Weisgal to open an office of the Jewish Agency in New York; the following April Weizmann had also created an "office of the president of the WZO . . . to act as a liaison with the various agencies, Zionist, non-Zionist, governmental, scientific, and otherwise."[43] Weizmann's motives went beyond a desire to improve Zionist efficiency. The Jewish Agency Executive in Jerusalem had emerged as a rival center of power within the Zionist movement, and

David Ben-Gurion used his position as chairman of the Agency Executive to challenge Weizmann's authority. According to Ben-Gurion, Weizmann ran the World Zionist Organization as a personal fiefdom, in which all division heads reported only to the president and were not accountable otherwise. The fiery Palestinian thus sought "procedural" safeguards, purportedly designed to prevent Weizmann from engaging in his unique brand of personal diplomacy without consulting other Zionist officials. As Yehuda Bauer notes, "the debate was not in the least procedural." What Ben-Gurion sought was nothing less than undivided leadership in Zionism, a leadership based in the *Yishuv* and not in the world Zionist apparatus. The two men also differed in their view of the relative importance of the United States. Ben-Gurion believed that after the war, the United States would be the decisive influence in securing a Jewish state, while Weizmann clung to his faith in Great Britain. They also drifted apart on the meaning they attached to specific goals, such as a timetable for creating a state and the transfer of some two million Jews from Europe to Palestine. For Weizmann, such slogans might be useful in political games, but he had grown too old and weary to believe that they could be anything more than that in a cynical world. Ben-Gurion, on the other hand, seized upon them as banners around which to rally Jews. He realized that American Jews would labor endlessly for a specific task, even a visionary one, while they had little patience with theory, and even less with those who did not believe in their own dreams.[44]

Both Ben-Gurion and Weizmann came to the United States in early 1942, and the differences in their approach manifested themselves in the negotiations preliminary to the Biltmore conference. After Ben-Gurion had his way at the conference, a weary Weizmann went to Grossinger's Catskill resort to rest, and while there, invited his old friend Judge Louis Levinthal, president of the ZOA, to visit him. As the two men sat in a secluded bungalow, they discussed the implications of Ben-Gurion's threatened warfare against Weizmann's beloved England. Still grieving over the death of his son Michael, an RAF pilot, Weizmann said: "B.G. wants to be Bar Kochba.† I don't want to

---

† Simon Bar Kochba led the revolt against Rome from 132–35 C.E. For two years he managed to keep Roman legions out of Palestine and to restore an independent state, but in the end he was crushed by the might of Rome, and Palestine was laid waste.

be Bar Kochba. Maybe he's right, but I don't want to be a Bar Kochba. We've waited so long, fighting for our position, we'll wait a little longer. We don't want bloodshed."[45]

Anyone aware of the inner anguish Ben-Gurion later endured as head of the Jewish armed forces in the Israeli war of independence could testify that the last thing he wanted was to spill blood. But part of Ben-Gurion's genius lay in his sense of timing, his instinct for the right move at the right time. He sensed, he knew, that by 1942 the time of accommodation had passed; he did not seek the struggle so much as accept its inevitability. But he moved to consolidate his position in a blunt, even brutal, manner. Weizmann's moment in the sun had passed, and he should be pushed aside as quickly as possible. On June 11, 1942, Ben-Gurion wrote to Weizmann demanding he resign his Zionist leadership. Ben-Gurion accused the aging leader of having completely failed to harness the potential strength of American Jewry and of fostering disunity in Zionist ranks. The movement could not continue to be governed this way; either Weizmann must step down, or Ben-Gurion would refuse to work with him any longer.[46]

Ben-Gurion may have been right in his analysis of the situation, but he misjudged the emotional support Weizmann commanded within Zionist ranks, the result of decades of devoted service. Even in America, where he had antagonized the old Brandeis group for more than two decades, Weizmann had become a familiar figure on his annual pilgrimages to this country in search of funds for Palestine. In mid-1942, Ben-Gurion was still a relatively unknown quantity.

Stephen Wise tried to make peace between the elder statesman and the young lion, an attempt which within a few months he would recall with more than a trace of irony. Ben-Gurion and Weizmann agreed to meet in Wise's study, along with a handful of key American leaders— Louis Levinthal, Robert Szold, Louis Lipsky, and Meyer Weisgal, as well as Nahum Goldmann. There, in a painfully embarrassing scene, Ben-Gurion, in a two-hour tirade, accused Weizmann of playing a lone hand, of making serious political mistakes, even of preventing the creation of a Jewish army. Hayim Greenberg, the veteran Labor Zionist leader, walked out of the room practically in tears, and murmured to Weisgal: "I never believed I would live to see the day when such an outrageous discourse would be delivered by a leader of the Palestinian labor movement." Weizmann's reply, while much briefer, hardly tempered the tone of the meeting: He declared that Ben-Gurion suffered from hallucinations and that the whole affair added up to nothing less than political assassination.[47]

For once Ben-Gurion's sense of timing failed him. Four years later, with American Zionist backing, he repeated the charges against Weizmann at the Zionist Congress in Basel and forced his ouster as head of the WZO. But in 1942, even the Brandeisists in the group reaffirmed their personal confidence in Weizmann; this, however, led Weizmann to misgauge completely the tenor of American Zionists. He misread a vote of personal confidence as a mandate, and over the next few years made a series of errors in attempting to direct the movement in America. And just as Ben-Gurion had come to challenge his leadership, so another young Turk arose to overthrow the Wise regime in American Zionism.

Stephen Samuel Wise had been a major force in American Zionism for four decades.[48] During the Brandeis administration, Wise counted as one of the jurist's chief lieutenants and spokesmen. When Hitler came to power in the early 1930s, Wise was among the very few to recognize that the Nazis meant what they said, that the Hitler regime posed a real threat to European Jewry, and he had organized numerous protests and rallies to pressure the Germans into leaving Jews alone. But Wise's importance far transcended Zionist affairs, for he was an important secular reformer as well as a mover and shaker in Jewish communal life. Wise had been the first child labor commissioner in Oregon, and later he became a leading advocate of union rights and labor reforms. From the time he settled in New York in 1907 he had been involved in good-government campaigns on both the city and state levels. In an age which still admired oratory, Wise had perhaps the finest speaking voice of his time, a voice that could always be found in support of the rights of minorities, of the downtrodden, of those whom an industrial society had dealt a poor hand.

Yet Wise never neglected his Jewish responsibilities, and he had a major impact on American Jewish institutions and life. Perhaps Wise's most important work came in the democratization of Jewish life in America. More than any other man, he led the fight against the elitist mentality of the American Jewish Committee during the First World War, and organized and led the American Jewish Congress from its founding in 1916 until his death more than thirty years later. During the 1930s he established the first truly representative international

Jewish body, the World Jewish Congress, which not only fought Hitler's power but also took the lead after the war in securing billions of dollars of reparations for Nazi crimes against European Jewry.

Despite all this work for democracy in Jewish life, for new modes of congregational life and rabbinic training, for social justice and reform in civic affairs, Wise never lost his touch for the individual person. Nahum Goldmann once wrote: "Not only did he love the Jewish people, he loved every individual Jew. He would turn his hand to finding help for a poor refugee, arranging for the adoption of an orphan, or providing for a destitute widow as willingly as solving a great social problem. . . . Other Jewish leaders may have been more revered, feared, or admired than he, but none was so beloved."[49] This love enabled Wise to survive the vitriol thrown by a Peter Bergson or a Ben Hecht, but it could not withstand an assault from within the Zionist movement led by Abba Hillel Silver.

Silver had once been the *wunderkind* of American Jewish life, and his promise as a young man developed into extraordinary accomplishments as he grew older.[50] A brilliant orator as well as a respected scholar, he had at an early age become rabbi of the immensely prestigious and wealthy Temple Tifereth Israel in Cleveland, Ohio. From all reports, Silver was as devoted to his congregation as Wise was to his; the two men also shared great involvement in their respective civic lives and in Jewish affairs, although where Wise had been a pioneer, the younger Silver would frequently rejuvenate an ailing, lackadaisical organization. Both men were among the few committed Zionists within the Reform rabbinate; both were devoted to the growth and well-being of the *Yishuv*; they were outstanding orators.

But there the similarities ended. Where Wise was warm and open, Silver was cool and remote except to his closest associates. Where Wise's opponents respected him, even some of Silver's allies could not stand him personally. Wise acted on the grand stage, taking on giants, but was often a casual administrator, leaving many details to his loyal associates. Silver was an administrative and organizational genius, but he also knew how to delegate responsibility and authority. He gave his subordinates free hands in their areas of responsibilities, but if they failed to perform their tasks satisfactorily, he could be mercilessly harsh with them, as he was with Weizmann when, like Ben-Gurion, Silver thought the time for a change in leadership had arrived; like the Palestinian, he was blunt, even brutal, in effecting that change. Nahum

Goldmann, though often an enemy of Silver, summed up his strengths and weaknesses accurately: "Above all he had unyielding strength of will. He was a typical autocrat, possessing the authority and self-confidence to command but not the flexibility to understand his opponent. He was an Old Testament Jew who never forgave or forgot and who possessed no trace of the talent for keeping personal and political affairs separate. Once he had adopted a movement or an idea, he served it with utmost devotion, and he was a loyal friend to all those who followed his orders absolutely. Anyone who fought him politically became his personal enemy. He could be extremely ruthless in a fight, and there was something of the terrorist in his manner and bearing."[51]

For Silver, Wise's greatest sin lay in his willingness—indeed, his commitment—to work within established routes. Wise's fame and prestige, built upon a lifetime of service, gained him easy access to the inner offices of mayors, governors, congressmen, senators, and even the President of the United States. While he had no compunction about utilizing these contacts to help Jewish and Zionist causes, he did shy away from forcing confrontation with men he considered his friends and allies. Saddest of all, Wise trusted them, especially his "great and good friend," Franklin D. Roosevelt, and he could not believe that the President was playing a double game. Silver deeply distrusted Roosevelt, and in speech after speech warned American Zionists "to put not their trust in princes." Silver sought an aggressive campaign to force politicians out into the open, to put them on record for the casual promises so "sincerely" made in private. But Silver's battle also extended to Chaim Weizmann, whom he felt was interfering, unwisely and ineptly, in political activities in this country.

Silver was originally reluctant to take a leading part in day-to-day Zionist affairs, partly because he realized that his innate militancy would be out of tune with the established leadership. But his speech at the Biltmore conference impressed many people, and ironically, Chaim Weizmann made the first move to draw Silver into the inner circle. "Silver seems the most suitable," wrote Weizmann, and "would be prepared to take the part assigned to him, if it can be done with dignity and without friction, which is, I confess, not altogether easy to achieve."[52] Weizmann's concern grew out of the resignations of three key members of the Emergency Committee, David Petegorsky, Meyer Weisgal, and Emanuel Neumann, all of whom objected to the Committee's disorganization and its lack of leadership and initiative. Moreover,

Weizmann and other European leaders felt that American Zionists in general, and the ZOA leadership in particular, did not appreciate the gravity of the situation in Europe and were incapable of dealing with it. Weizmann's focus on Silver was an attempt to amend Weizmann's early efforts to interpose a WZO presence in the United States, efforts which had fed Ben-Gurion's charges that Weizmann had been playing a lone hand. Thus at Stephen Wise's urging, both for tactical reasons as well as to placate Ben-Gurion, the WZO expanded its American office to include all of its executive members from the United States, as well as a number of new American Zionist figures, including Silver.[53]

While Ben-Gurion refused to be pacified, he soon discovered in Silver an ally in impatience with the WZO, one who stood ready to agitate and fight for a Jewish state. For Ben-Gurion the hope of the Zionist movement lay in winning the support of the American public and government, and Weizmann's counsel of moderation and caution could delay, if not actually defeat, the realization of an independent Jewish state.

Silver came to partial power with the reorganization in August 1943 of the Emergency Committee into the American Emergency Council. Weizmann and other WZO leaders had been frustrated since the beginning of the war with the Emergency Committee's inability to unite the various Zionist groups in the United States. As late as mid-1943 the Committee had not established a Washington bureau, nor did it have a resident representative in the nation's capital. Moreover, the lack of leadership had allowed Ben-Gurion's advocates, in Weizmann's opinion, to take far too militant a stand in interpreting the Biltmore platform. Stephen Wise, then sixty-nine years old and the nominal head of the Emergency Committee, confessed to Weizmann that the burdens of the office exceeded his physical capacities, and he would welcome a younger man, like Silver, taking over.[54]

After protracted negotiations, Silver agreed to become cochairman with Wise of a reorganized Emergency Council, which would be recognized by the WZO as *the* representative agency of American Zionism. The Council consisted of twenty-six people, representing all of the major American Zionist groups. Even the fringe groups, such as Hashomer Hatzair, Achdut Avodah, and the Revisionists, were invited to send observers, so that the Council could claim that no one had been excluded. From that time on, however, Silver found himself fighting simultaneous battles within the Zionist camp. He not only opposed what

he saw as the unwarranted and dangerous interference of the world organization in American affairs, he also had to overcome his colleagues'
cautious approach to political activity.

Prior to the reorganization of the Council, the Jewish Agency
Executive established a political office of its own in Washington in
May 1943, with Nahum Goldmann and Louis Lipsky in charge.
Created not only to fill a void in the Zionist campaign, the office also
was intended to restrain what Weizmann saw as a heretical tendency of
American Zionists to ignore the world movement, a habit that had had
disastrous consequences after the First World War.[55] Weizmann promised the Council that this office would "closely co-operate" with it, but
in fact Goldmann hardly ever consulted with Silver, and seemed determined to establish himself as the "Jewish ambassador" to the American
government. By October 1943, Silver felt that either Goldmann had to
abide by the authority of the Council, or that the office should be
abolished. At a stormy meeting at the Dorchester House in Washington
on October 12, a reluctant Goldmann agreed, neither for the first nor
the last time, to clear with the Council office all his appointments with
government officials. Within a month, however, the two groups were
again at cross-purposes, one office arranging meetings without informing the other, bombarding confused congressmen and bureaucrats with
contradictory viewpoints, and trading accusations regarding who had
broken the agreement.[56]

The fight involved more than a mere "clash of temperaments."
Goldmann insisted that only the Jewish Agency had the prerogative to
deal with foreign governments in matters relating to Palestine, and the
proper function of any "local or national" Zionist group should be
propagandizing Zionism's goals, particularly among non-Jews. Emanuel
Neumann, speaking for Silver, sharply contested this view, arguing
that only American Zionists as American citizens could legitimately
deal with the American government; the proper role of the Goldmann
office would be contacts with foreign embassies. By January 1944
Neumann believed a showdown inevitable, and urged Silver to consolidate his forces within the ZOA in anticipation of a fight.[57]

The Zionist Organization of America was, in fact, the key to power
at that time within American Zionism, despite Hadassah's larger membership. The women's group had partisans of all factions on its board,
and for the most part tried to keep the Wise-Silver and Ben-Gurion-
Weizmann feuding out of its ranks. Whichever group could provide

real and effective leadership would find Hadassah ready to help.[58] The ZOA, on the other hand, thrived on politics, and Silver recognized that unless he established a power base within that organization, he would have no leverage on the Emergency Council. Although Silver made a bid for full control of both the Emergency Council and the ZOA, he failed to secure it. The compromise gave him more effective power than Wise within the Council, due to his second role as chairman of its executive committee; but Israel Goldstein, then an ally of Wise, became president of the ZOA in September 1943.[59] Silver's perception of the situation proved accurate when matters came to a head in late 1944.

The battle began over efforts to secure a congressional resolution calling for the rescission of the White Paper, with a number of Council members urging caution, while Silver called for "an active and vigorous attack." When the War Department killed the proposal in committee, a number of Zionist leaders asked Silver to soft-pedal the campaign, especially in an election year. Silver reacted angrily, declaring that "quiet diplomacy" would not bring any results; the alleged goodwill of government leaders could not be counted upon to produce concrete results.[60]

Throughout the spring and summer of 1944, relations between Silver, a Republican, and the ardently pro-Roosevelt Wise grew more tense, and Silver time and again suggested, not very tactfully, that the elderly Wise retire and stop interfering with his efforts to discipline the Council into an effective organization. The strain between Silver and Goldmann, who was allied with Wise through the World Jewish Congress, also increased, as Goldmann, with Weizmann's encouragement, continued to play a lone hand in Washington. Silver wanted the Goldmann operation closed, as he found his own work "becoming increasingly hampered and embarrassed." Silver complained that on all occasions he had kept the London office informed of developments in America, not only out of courtesy, but also so an overall Zionist policy could be created. But Goldmann acted as if he were the Jewish Agency incarnate. "Nobody has authorized him to speak on those basic Zionist policies," Silver declared, "and his actions and opinions are subject to no quick review by the parent body."[61] When Goldmann in late August saw Secretary of State Edward Stettinius without first consulting Silver, the Cleveland rabbi exploded. Goldmann had created a situation in which it was impossible for the Emergency Council to function effectively, Silver announced, and then submitted his resignation from the Council.

The members of the Council—indeed, the entire Zionist organization—reacted wildly to this unanticipated turn of events. The Council failed to convince Silver to withdraw his resignation, even after passing a resolution that all contact with officials of the American government could be made only after clearance with the Council's executive committee. Cables shot across the Atlantic urging the London office to take action, and Goldmann agreed, once again, not to act without consulting Silver.[62] Ben-Gurion personally urged Silver to stay on, saying that at such a critical point in Jewish history Silver could not withdraw. Finally, after Goldmann formally repeated his pledge of co-operation, and the peacemakers within the ZOA had soothed everyone's ego, Silver consented to resume his post.[63]

At first glance, the August resignation might appear as an overblown fuss, with a strong-willed, self-important Silver petulantly walking out because of the conduct of an equally temperamental Goldmann. But larger issues were involved. Weizmann at any time could have broken the impasse by ordering Goldmann, whom he had personally selected to head the Washington office, to obey the Council's directives. But Weizmann, seeing his base of power in Europe and Palestine eroding, hoped to preserve control of American Zionism despite the rise of a younger, more aggressive leadership; Silver and his friends were unwilling to be guided, or manipulated, by a man whom they no longer trusted. He and Ben-Gurion would not be able to oust Chaim Weizmann from the WZO presidency until the Zionist Congress in 1946, but they were not about to co-operate in his minimalist policy, which they believed totally unsuited for the times. Similarly, Stephen Wise, despite his age and growing physical impairment, did not want to yield power either. During the resignation episode he remained notably reticent in urging Silver to return, and Emanuel Neumann thought he detected a fair amount of manipulation by Wise's supporters, Robert Szold and Israel Goldstein, in turning the situation against Silver.[64]

The "reconciliation" hardly deserved the title. Goldmann "consulted" for a few weeks, but then kept only his own counsel. Wise actively worked for Roosevelt's re-election, to the chagrin of Silver, who felt that the Zionists should lobby both parties, and had gotten the Council to adopt a resolution of neutrality in the 1944 elections. At an Emergency Council meeting, Silver argued that "it was not proper for a

Zionist spokesman appearing on Zionist business to give the impression that the whole Zionist movement was tied to the Democratic Party."[65] To add insult to injury, Wise had not informed Silver on his much-publicized meeting with Roosevelt until afterward. Then, when Silver wanted to test Roosevelt's sincerity after the election by reviving the congressional resolution against the White Paper, he found Wise working to block him. An anguished Sol Bloom complained to Israel Goldstein that he did not know what to do. One moment Rabbi Silver tells him to go ahead with the hearings, and the next Rabbi Wise tells him to delay.[66] Within the Council, friction built to an intolerable level as advocates of the two men traded charges of "dictatorship" and "cowardice." Silver grew more and more secretive, refusing to discuss matters with any but his most trusted associates, and on several occasions acted as single-handedly as he had accused Goldmann of doing. Even Hadassah felt that the situation had gotten completely out of hand, and had to be resolved one way or another.[67]

Stephen Wise made the first move on December 12, 1944, resigning as chairman of the Council in protest against Silver's alleged dictatorialness and insulting manner. After Wise had defended his conduct in a private meeting with the president, the Council voted to refuse his resignation, a clear-cut vote of confidence in him, as well as a slap at Silver. On December 28, after a lengthy meeting, the resignations of both Silver and Wise were accepted. Pausing just long enough to tender appreciation to Silver for his devoted service to the cause, the Council then elected Wise as sole chairman, Rose Halprin of Hadassah as treasurer, and reorganized the structure to give Wise complete control of the Council and its activities.

Silver retired to Cleveland, sorry that against his better judgment he had ever agreed to join the Council. Left to himself, he probably would not have tried to regain control of the American Zionist apparatus. But the uproar in the Jewish press and the activities of his friends soon convinced him that while he had been outvoted on the Council, he had the support of the lay leadership. The editorials in the Jewish press for the most part eschewed attacking Wise so much as endorsing the Silver position. The *Jewish Morning Journal* (December 22, 1944), for example, declared: "At this moment we cannot afford to indicate lack of confidence in an outspoken Zionist policy—even when such a policy encounters difficulty," while *Der Tag* (December 23, 1944) insisted: "Only an aggressive, dynamic policy can lead to success, and Rabbi Silver is clearly the man to be entrusted with such a policy." Philip Slomovitz, in the Detroit *Jewish News* (January 26, 1945), wrote that Silver "is a consistent and vigorous fighter for justice for Jewry and Palestine, and the Zionist constituency will surely reject any plan to eliminate him from leadership."[68]

Silver's friends, heartened by this response, made their first move when two of the Council's leading members, Harry L. Shapiro and Harold P. Manson, resigned, and together with Abraham Tuvin and Emanuel Neumann, created the American Zionist Policy Committee to lobby among the rank and file for Silver's return to leadership. Their statements not only defended Silver, but also directly attacked Wise, and they portrayed the struggle as one between militancy and nonmilitancy, between democracy and *shtadlanuth*. At the Policy Committee's urging, local Zionist sympathizers organized debates on the issues and flooded the Emergency Council with telegrams and petitions demanding Silver's recall. At a ZOA administrative council meeting on January 7, 1945, Israel Goldstein, Judge Morris Rothenberg, James Heller, and Louis Levinthal defended Wise, while Emanuel Neumann and Jacob Fishman presented the Silver case. Wise interrupted Neumann's presentation to charge Silver's lieutenant with carrying on a "sewerage campaign." Neumann slowly turned, offered the opinion that Wise was taking advantage of his years, and then left the platform amid much applause. But when the vote came calling for Silver's return, it lost, 30 to 66.[69]

The Wise group, aware that the situation had deteriorated beyond saving, began searching for alternatives. While Wise was ready to resign, neither he nor his colleagues wanted Silver or one of his designees in power. Strangely enough, they thought they could promote Meyer Weisgal, Weizmann's closest friend in America but a person totally unacceptable to the Silver coalition. Weisgal was willing, but the mere mention of the plan raised such protest that it died immediately. As the controversy dragged on through the early months of 1945, the political activities of the Council came to a standstill; only the pro-Palestine propaganda work, by now routinized and handled by staff members, continued to give the organization semblance of life. Members of the WZO tried to find some solution, only to realize that there was no longer room for compromise.[70]

The Policy Committee worked feverishly generating support for Silver through a stream of newspaper articles, speeches, and testimonial dinners. Ostensibly, the Committee aimed at winning over the ZOA, the key to power in the American movement; in fact, it had set itself up as a rival to the Emergency Council and had the active backing of the Mizrachi and the Labor Zionists.[71] When Weizmann arrived on the scene in April, he found American Zionism completely split, and his efforts at peacemaking yielded only a growing criticism of his own policies. In urging American Zionists to unite so they could act, he found himself under attack for lacking any positive program. When Hayim Greenberg, the head of Poale Zion, resigned from the Emergency Council on June 15, the Wise group recognized that their coalition could not survive. Accepting the inevitable, they appointed a three-man committee to arrange a peace agreement with Silver.

In effect, it was a total capitulation. Although the final plan re-established Wise and Silver as cochairmen, Silver now had the effective power. He controlled appointments to the executive committee, which he chaired, and a majority of the other officers, as well as the key staff people, came from the Silver bloc. At a meeting on July 12, Abba Hillel Silver listened quietly as the Emergency Council adopted the peace plan, and then he gave what was, for him, a conciliatory speech: "I hope we will all turn our backs on what took place in the last few months, and that we shall begin to think of ourselves not in terms of friends or foes, or as members of this group or that group, but in terms of comrades working in a common cause."

*   *   *

And there was work aplenty. Even as Silver assumed leadership, the American public was trying to adjust to the great events of the previous months. On April 12, Franklin D. Roosevelt had died; a month later, the Germans surrendered. Even before the war in the Pacific had ended, Harry S. Truman, once a little-known senator from Missouri and now President of the United States, had convened the United Nations conference at San Francisco. Finally, in the pages of *Life* and other pictorial magazines, Americans could see the brutal evidence of the efficacy of Hitler's "Final Solution." Now, in a world where one change crowded another, the Zionists might find the opportunity to create their homeland in Palestine. Unity had not come a moment too soon.

Chapter 4

"OPEN THE GATES!"

If during the war, the apparent unity of American Jewry could not conceal the failure to secure a pro-Palestine policy from the Roosevelt administration or a relaxation of the immigration laws, in the three years following VE Day, surface illusion and reality reversed themselves. Now the appearance of failure masked the reality of achievement.

In these years American Jewry, stung by the full awareness of the Holocaust, moved from a passive endorsement of a Jewish homeland to a near-unanimous commitment to active work for its realization. Thanks to an amazing but secret supply network in the United States, the *Yishuv* managed to secure the essential material goods it needed in its fight for independence. Despite the opposition of both the Foreign Office and the State Department, the Zionists managed to win United Nations approval of a partition plan which called for a Jewish state in Palestine. And in the face of vested interests opposed to the Zionist dream, American Jewry mounted one of the most intense and successful lobbying efforts in American politics, one that led to *de facto* recognition of the Jewish state eleven minutes after its birth. Indeed, although the story has been told many times, the establishment of the State of Israel in the face of seemingly insurmountable obstacles remains a modern miracle, still capable of moving one to awe and wonderment. And it is a story in which American Jewry played a major role.

*　　　*　　　*

The long night of German barbarism that hung over Europe for nearly a dozen years began to lift in early 1945. After their desperate effort to contain the advancing Allied forces in Belgium, the German armies could do little more than fight rear-guard skirmishes, hoping to delay the inevitable. Despite Hitler's orders to stand and fight, to die rather than surrender, German lines buckled for lack of supplies, and new, half-trained recruits saw little reason to give up their lives for a Reich which itself teetered on the brink of collapse. By March Eisenhower's armies had crossed the Rhine, while Patton's tanks raced toward Frankfurt. The Ruhr, Germany's industrial heartland, fell into complete Allied control by mid-April, and a few days later Russian troops, under Marshal Georgi Zhukov, penetrated the outskirts of Berlin. At 4:40 in the afternoon of April 25, patrols of the American 69th Infantry Division and of the Russian 58th Guards Division met at Torgau on the Elbe. Five days later, in a bizarre imitation of Wotan's death in Valhalla, Adolf Hitler committed suicide in a Berlin bunker; the Third Reich outlived him by a week. On May 7, 1945, General Walter Bedell Smith, acting for Dwight D. Eisenhower, accepted the German surrender in a little red schoolhouse at Reims.

It would be years before the full horror of the Nazi reign—the millions killed, the havoc wrought on Western civilization, the economics shattered, the hopes for a moral life lost—could be assessed with any degree of objectivity. Now an exhausted world could only breathe a sigh of relief and silently pray that peace would accompany the victory. But many never lived to see that victory. In the last months of the war, as Allied armies liberated the death camps, the full extent of Hitler's "Final Solution" became known. Until then, there had been doubts that a whole people could be exterminated, there had been a lingering belief—a hope—that stories of genocide had been exaggerated. Now there would be no more doubts. As a shocked world stared at pictures of piled-up corpses, of mounded shoes torn from dead feet, of cattle cars with limbs grotesquely sticking out through the slats, they learned the statistics of death. Of the more than three million Jews who had lived in Poland prior to the war, less than 100,000 survived; of Germany's own 500,000 Jews, the most assimilated community in continental Europe, only 12,000 lived. The figures for other countries conquered by the Nazis were equally devastating: Czechoslovakia,

40,000 survivors out of 300,000; Holland, 20,000 out of 130,000; Belgium, 25,000 out of 90,000; Greece, 10,000 out of 75,000. Although losses in Romania and Hungary were lighter, the 320,000 surviving Romanian Jews and 200,000 Hungarians represented less than half of the previous communities. In the Soviet Union, one out of every two Jews was killed by the Nazis. All told, out of every 7 Jews living in Europe, 6 had been killed during the war, including one million children. All the major centers of Jewish population, of culture, of learning and piety, the legacy of a Jewish presence in Europe dating back more than a thousand years, had been wiped out.[1]

And what would become of those who had survived the hells of Auschwitz and Treblinka and Bergen-Belsen? What would happen to those starving, dead-eyed, stumbling ghosts who had somehow cheated the angel of death? Where would they go? Even if they wanted to return to their homes, there were no longer any homes for them; all of Europe lay devastated by 5½ years of war. For most of the Jewish survivors, soon to be classified as "displaced persons" and again herded into camps, there could only be one answer: *Eretz Ysrael!* But before they could go to their promised land, the peacemakers would have to meet.

Still another did not live to see the final victory, one of its chief architects, Franklin Delano Roosevelt. On April 12, 1945, while he sat for a portrait, the President died suddenly, the victim of a massive cerebral hemorrhage. As the nation mourned, few groups wept more than American Jews, who for the most part still believed that in Roosevelt they had had a great and true friend, one who would look after their interests after the war as he had watched over them during the Depression. Now Harry Truman sat in the White House, a man unknown to Jewish leaders,[2] and it would be he who convened the preliminary United Nations conference in San Francisco in May.

About a month before his death, Roosevelt had told Stephen Wise that he wanted the Jewish Agency officially invited to the meeting. Shortly after Truman took office, Wise visited him and, among other things, informed him of Roosevelt's promise.[3] But Truman was too new in the office, too in awe of its power, and too dependent upon the advice of his Cabinet and assistants to undertake an independent policy on Palestine. The last thing that either the Foreign Office or the State Department wanted was an official Jewish presence at San Francisco, since such a delegation would surely try to put the Palestine issue on the agenda. Since many other special-interest groups also clamored for a role in the conference, the State Department created a "consultant" category and invited representatives from forty-two different organizations to the United Nations meeting. Of these, two were distinctly Jewish—the American Jewish Conference and the American Jewish Committee—although another half-dozen or more Jewish groups sent unofficial observers.

The Zionists from the beginning realized that the deck had been stacked against them. Nahum Goldmann predicted a month earlier that Palestine would not be allowed on the agenda, and Secretary of State Edward R. Stettinius, Jr., confirmed this to Stephen Wise just before the latter's departure for the meeting.[4] The best that the Zionists could hope for, then, would be that their existing rights, as spelled out in the League of Nations mandate, would not be whittled away; at the same time, there might be an opportunity to elicit sympathy among the non-Arab nations present, not only to offset Arab propaganda, but also to plan for the day when the Palestine issue could no longer be swept under the rug. The American Jewish Conference and the Zionist Emergency Council began this campaign by sponsoring eighty-eight mass rallies around the nation to demonstrate the extent of public support for a Jewish commonwealth in Palestine. The largest of these drew sixty thousand people in New York on April 29.

In San Francisco, the Conference delegation of eleven persons found itself harassed by the actions of uninvited Jewish organizations and crippled by the rules of procedure. Israel Goldstein bitterly complained of "a vicious circle. They [the Jewish people] had no status there; therefore they could get no status." David Ben-Gurion portrayed the Jewish dilemma in classical Zionist terms: "We are a people without a state, and therefore a people without credentials, without recognition, without representation, and without the privileges of a nation, without the means of self-defense, and without any say in our fate."[5] The Conference delegation organized a coalition of the major Jewish organizations in the country, similar to the one which had been so effective at Versailles in 1919, but grew frustrated by the efforts of the more extremist groups. The American Council for Judaism, for example, called a press conference to deny that Jews constituted anything more than a religious fellowship, and Elmer Berger attacked the whole concept of Jewish "peoplehood" and the idea of a Palestinian state. As for the militants, Eliahu Epstein (later Elath), a member of the Con-

ference staff on loan from the Jewish Agency, disgustedly described
their activities: "The Bergson group made some noise like skilled circus
people, but no one took them seriously. The Revisionists came late and
their main occupation was to publicize their arrival to San Francisco so
that their members in other countries would know that 'we too were
present.' Professor Yehuda, their expert on Arab affairs, visits our office
often to ask what news there is in the Arab world. His main occupation
is to prove that there would be no Arab problem had Weizmann listened to him twenty-five years ago." The Conference delegates, in their
attempts to win support, were embarrassed to learn that these other
groups, who held no official status, had descended upon the conference
participants. When requesting an interview, a member of the official
Jewish group would often be told: "But I have already seen this and
this number of Jews. What more do you want from me?"[6]

Yet underneath the confusion, the Jewish delegation managed to accomplish a great deal, not the least of which was repairing some of the
damage done by earlier fraternal battles. At least one ultra-orthodox
group, Agudas Hahabonim, dropped its opposition to a secular state and
endorsed the American Jewish Conference Palestine program.[7] More
importantly, the breach between the American Jewish Committee, represented at San Francisco by Joseph Proskauer and Jacob Blaustein,
and the Zionist groups began to heal; both factions agreed to co-
operate not only on the issue of Jewish rights but also even to some extent on Palestine. The Committee began postwar planning with a
major emphasis on protecting the civil rights of Jews, both as individuals and as groups, assuming that many of the issues would be similar
in nature to those which had come before the peacemakers of 1919.
What many people had lost sight of in the struggle over the American
Jewish Conference was the Committee's support of Jewish immigration into Palestine and the protection of Jewish rights there. At San
Francisco, Henry Monsky and Maurice Bisgyer, executive secretary
of B'nai B'rith, met Judge Proskauer in the lobby of their hotel. The
three men, despite philosophical differences, remained on cordial terms,
and informal conversations soon turned to more serious business. At a
series of private meetings, Monsky and Proskauer agreed that past battles should be forgotten in the light of the current emergency. While
Proskauer was not yet ready to support fully a Jewish state, the impact
of the Holocaust made him realize that Palestine alone offered hope of
solution to the growing refugee problem. The Committee, while not

formally joining in the Conference-sponsored union of Jewish groups, endorsed the Conference's position papers. Proskauer, using his contacts with the Secretary of State, urged him to do everything possible in support of Jewish immigration into Palestine. The Conference, in turn, backed Proskauer in his successful fight to secure the United Nations Commission on Human Rights.[8]

The Jewish delegates at San Francisco also achieved much more than they had expected in lobbying the member nations. A nine-man Emergency Council team headed by I. L. Kenen distributed more than forty separate releases in three languages to assembled delegates and to the press, easily countering the poorly planned, if better financed, Arab propaganda campaign. Hardly any of the member delegations remained immune from the Jewish lobby, and Israel Goldstein recalled the extent to which the Jewish representatives went to win support. The Zionists had been having difficulty securing access to the Chinese minister, General Woo, said Goldstein, when "I remembered that in Canada I had recently met a Mr. Morris Cohen, who had a fantastic career. He was born in Whitechapel, London, a burly man—he was called 'Two-gun Cohen'—came to Canada, developed some friendships with the Chinese, and they recommended him to Sun Yat-sen as a bodyguard. He accepted the job. He rose in the esteem of Sun, not only because of his physical prowess, but also because of his mental agility. He became a financial adviser, and he returned to Canada to negotiate a loan for building a railroad, and then returned to China. When Sun died, Morris Cohen was inherited by Chiang Kai-shek, who also discovered in him important qualities. So during the war Chiang bestowed upon him a title of general, and Cohen took for his name as general the initials of his Hebrew name, Moishe Avraham, and called himself 'General Ma,' the same General Ma who won such a great reputation. After the Japanese invasion, Cohen became a prisoner of war, then escaped and returned to Canada.

"When I was in San Francisco worrying with my colleagues how we could get to the head of the Chinese delegation, General Woo, I thought of my friend Moishe Avraham Cohen in Canada. So I sent him a telegram to come out to help us meet General Woo. He was glad to do it. He had a conference with us at which he said, 'Gentlemen, I will get in touch with General Woo, try to make the appointment for you, but please bear in mind that he recently became converted to Catholicism. He's a very religious Christian. And bear that in mind, so as not to say anything that would offend him.' We bore it in mind. So the following Monday morning at the Fairmont Hotel an appointment was made for us to see General Woo. We appeared at 8:30 in the morning —Monsky, Lipsky, and Goldstein calling on General Woo. The general came out, greeted us warmly, and said: 'Gentlemen, you can't imagine how much your visit means to me. You know I became a Christian recently. I say my prayers every morning to Mother Mary, and this morning I said, "Mother Mary, your relatives are coming to see me today." ' Needless to say, he was on our side from then on."[9]

The wooing of General Woo involved more than public relations or even sympathy. The Arabs, as expected, introduced a resolution amending the safeguard clause in the proposed charter of the United Nations Trusteeship Council, the clause which preserved all of the rights and privileges granted by the League of Nations in its mandates. Had this clause been eliminated, the entire legal claim of the Zionists to Palestine would have been jeopardized. The Jewish delegates worked around the clock to counter this move, and when the final vote came on May 26, the endless hours of lobbying paid off: All but the five Arab members voted to retain the safeguard clause intact.[10]

Yet despite these solid achievements, most of the leaders in American Jewry evaluated the San Francisco conference in gloomy terms. Nahum Goldmann, Eliahu Epstein, Israel Goldstein, Gershon Agronsky, and others spoke of this first postwar meeting in extremely pessimistic tones,[11] and their reason is not hard to discern. At the end of the First World War, the great powers had seen the Jews as potentially useful allies in their political maneuverings in the Middle East. As a result, they had been cultivated at the peace conference and had secured a formal endorsement of their claim to Palestine. Now European Jewry had all but been eradicated, and the great powers sought the favor, not of the Jews, but of the Arabs, who were seen as the key to the power struggle in the Levant. It seemed as if concerted effort existed to keep a Jewish voice out of the council of nations. But now the witnesses to the evil of man would not allow the Western nations to table the matter as had happened at Evian and Bermuda.

*   *   *

Once the victorious Allies had opened the gates of the concentration camps, they came to realize that most of the survivors had no place to go. Many of those who came from France, Italy, and the Low Countries elected to return to their previous homes, but this group comprised only a fraction of the Jewish survivors. Few of those from Poland, Russia, eastern Europe, and above all from Germany itself would even consider going back to live among neighbors who had actively or passively condoned the murder of six million of their brethren. The Americans worked feverishly to meet the essential needs of the camp inmates—food, clothing, shelter, and medical assistance—and within a few weeks after the German surrender, representatives of the Joint Distribution Committee arrived to determine how they could help.[12] The problems seemed enormous, yet in the 18 months following the war, they grew even worse. The 100,000 Jews in the western camps swelled to 250,000 as refugees from the eastern zones fled from a new and vicious outbreak of anti-Semitism in Poland. Over 2,000 men and women, including hundreds of doctors and nurses and teachers, worked to make life worth living for those who had escaped the death chambers and crematoria. In Germany alone, the Joint maintained 67 schools, 47 kindergartens, and 75 Talmud Torahs (religious schools); it printed newspapers, magazines, and books, and launched an extensive employment and vocational training program.[13]

The Joint saved their bodies and worked to salvage their minds, but the Zionists gave them the will to live. In the fall of 1945, at a mass meeting of survivors in Landsberg, David Ben-Gurion told them what they longed to hear: "Do not be afraid," he said, "if you hear of new laws promulgated against us tomorrow or the day after. A Jewish power has arisen which will fight together with you for a proud, independent Palestine. I promise you that not only your children but also we, the white-haired ones, will live to see the Jewish homeland."[14]

Critics later charged that the DPs had been won over to Palestine by Zionist agents who infiltrated the camps as social workers, but contemporary accounts indicate that from the start, the survivors thought of only one thing: to leave Europe and go to Palestine. In the camps, the elders spontaneously set up schools to teach Hebrew to the young, and the bare, ugly walls of the barracks were festooned with imaginative pictures labeled artzenu (our land). When Richard Crossman visited the camps in 1946, he reported that the Jews would have opted for Palestine even if not a single foreign emissary or trace of Zionist propaganda had ever reached them. The United Nations Relief Agency took a poll of 18,311 DPs in one section of Germany; 13 said they wanted to remain in Europe. Of the 18,298 who wanted to leave, 17,712 chose to go to Palestine.[15]

While living in the camps, they refused to make even the slightest accommodation to domestic comfort, for that would have been an act of submission to the intolerable thought that they might live there permanently. Crossman drew a biblical parallel in describing the attitude of the DPs. They "assert that each day in Germany must be lived as though it were the last day, when food is eaten hurriedly, when bags are packed ready for the journey out of the Land of Egypt and into the Promised Land." Eleanor Roosevelt, who for a variety of reasons had not believed that the refugees were so single-mindedly determined, went to inspect the camps personally. In the mud of the Zilsheim camp an old Jewish woman knelt and threw her arms around Mrs. Roosevelt's knees, murmuring over and over, "Yisrael, Yisrael." For the first time the former First Lady realized what Palestine meant to the survivors.[16]

Where else could they go? Certainly not back to Germany or Poland or Hungary, for they neither had homes nor were wanted there. Some wanted to come to America, but the United States, even now, would not relax its discriminatory quotas. In a poll taken in January 1946, only 5 per cent of the respondents favored more immigration from Europe, while 51 per cent wanted either fewer newcomers or none at all. American Jews recognized this situation and offered Palestine as the solution to the refugee crisis: Palestine would absorb the DPs, thus easing the American conscience without bringing an unwanted population to these shores.[17] In the months following the German surrender, no American Jewish spokesman called for a lowering of immigration barriers to the United States. At hearings in early 1947 on the Stratton bill, which would have allowed more DPs to enter the United States, only two Jewish witnesses appeared: Herbert Lehman, representing the Joint Distribution Committee, and Rabbi Philip Bernstein, civilian adviser on Jewish affairs to General Lucius Clay, the Allied commander in Europe. Both supported the bill in terms of broad humanitarian needs, but neither they nor any Jewish organization made a special plea for the Jewish refugees. Most of the backing for the bill came from church groups.[18]

The Zionist strategy, cynical as it may seem, accurately assessed the mood of the American public. A major effort to get the Jewish survivors into the United States could not have succeeded; it might have defeated the modest goals of the Stratton bill and would certainly have diverted attention from Palestine. Public-opinion polls in early 1944 showed increasing support for opening Palestine to Jewish survivors of the war. But for the Zionists, the issue went far beyond the immediate relief of the DPs. "Are we again," asked Rabbi Silver, "going to confuse Zionism with refugeeism, which is likely to defeat Zionism? Zionism is not a refugee movement."[19] A Jewish state would, of course, take in refugees, but the goal of the movement extended far beyond that; it aimed at solving the Jewish problem so that there never need be Jewish refugees in the future. Zionism aimed at giving the Jewish people new pride and self-reliance. Jews never again would have to rely on the mercy of an indifferent world.

The Holocaust brutally drove home that point for thousands— indeed, hundreds of thousands—of Jews. In Europe many of the survivors wondered that they had failed to see this before. Isaac Breuer, a leader of the ultra-orthodox Agudas Yisrael, had been an outspoken opponent of Zionism; he now admitted that the leaders of the Agudas did not understand the times. "They saw the trees, not the forest; they lacked historical perspective." Dr. Zalman Grinberg spoke for many of the survivors when he told of how, during the long nights in the ghettos and concentration camps, he had beat his breast, asking: "Why didn't I go to the land of Israel? I could have avoided all this." In a heart-rending letter to her son in Haifa, Esther Sacks told how she alone of the family in Europe remained alive. After the first wave of roundups, her husband had said: "I am not afraid of Hitler. Me they cannot destroy, for I have a son in *Eretz Yisrael.*"[20]

American Jews, possibly worried about their own future, recognized that but for the grace of God and the courage of their parents, they too would have been on the death lists at Dachau. An American military officer wrote to John Slawson, executive vice president of the American Jewish Committee, in the summer of 1945: "I have before me your letterhead and a memorial roll from a concentration camp, and the names of your Committee can be duplicated on the memorial roll. Waldman, Lehman, Kaplan, Lazarus, Stern—are all names of persons in this concentration camp. It could have been they if their parents or grandparents hadn't moved to the United States."[21]

Many of those who had opposed Zionism before the war now came to support it. Julian Morgenstern, president of Hebrew Union College, confessed that the war years "have made Zionists in a certain sense of

all of us who are worthy of the name Jew." Nahum Goldmann put the
argument most succinctly: "Now we don't have to make a case for Zionism any more. Hitler has proved that a Jewish homeland is necessary
and the Jews in Palestine have proved that it is possible."[22]

Did the Holocaust make possible the State of Israel, as many writers
have suggested,[23] or would the *Yishuv* in any case have ultimately
demanded and fought for its independence? It is a difficult, an impossible question to answer. But the Holocaust certainly made Zionism not
only acceptable but also imperative in the eyes of American Jewry. The
sherit hapleita (surviving remnant) had to be protected, rehabilitated,
and transferred to the promised land, where it would serve as the core
of a reawakened Jewish consciousness. Tragically, these walking ghosts,
who had undergone the trauma of the death camps, would not yet be
allowed to rest in the one haven they sought. Britain, which had so
bravely withstood Hitler's assault, now added one more blot to its record in Palestine.

*   *   *

During the 1930s, one of the most eloquent voices in the House of
Commons attacking British policy in Palestine belonged to Winston
Churchill. When he took charge of the government in 1940, Churchill
informed Zionist leaders that he favored a change in the White Paper,
but that he could do nothing until Germany had been defeated; the
hard-pressed Empire could not divert any of its meager resources to
quelling a potential Arab revolt. Just as Stephen Wise had placed his
hopes for redemption in the hands of Franklin Roosevelt, so Chaim
Weizmann had pinned his faith to Churchill's promises of a postwar
change. With the German surrender in May 1945, Weizmann called
upon the Prime Minister to make good his wartime pledges; on
June 9, 1945, Churchill replied in a coldly formal note that the
Palestine question could not be "effectively considered until the victorious Allies are definitely seated at the Peace Table."[24]

"Put not your trust in princes," the Bible warned, and now Weizmann recognized its bitter truth. Yet despair turned to hope within
weeks, when the British electorate turned Churchill out of office and
voted in a Labour government. Here would be the Zionists' great opportunity and Weizmann's chance to prove that his faith in England
had not been in vain. The Labour Party specifically opposed the White
Paper, and in party conference had called for its repeal and the

fulfillment of the Balfour promise. "Put not your trust in princes" may as well have referred to would-be princes and their promises, for the new government headed by Clement Attlee and Ernest Bevin refused at the first opportunity to allow refugees into Palestine, destroying the Zionists' last shreds of trust in Great Britain.

Despite the rescue work of the American military forces, the Joint Distribution Committee, and the UN Relief Agency, conditions of Jewish DPs in the months following VE Day remained wretched and abominable. With no place to go, they remained behind the barbed wires of the concentration camps amid filth and disease that could not be quickly eradicated even with the best of goodwill. In May and June of 1945, eighteen thousand Jews died of starvation and disease in Bergen-Belsen, while at Dachau the death rate ran between sixty and a hundred people a day. At Landsberg, an unheated room twelve feet by twenty-five feet contained twenty-five people, who slept on wooden tiers. Protests against these conditions eventually reached President Truman, who dispatched Earl G. Harrison, former immigration commissioner and dean of the University of Pennsylvania Law School, as his special emissary to inspect the camps in the summer of 1945.[25]

The spectacle of DPs in striped pajama uniforms, existing on a bare subsistence diet, condemned to long hours of boredom and frustration, festering in unsanitary quarters, outraged Harrison, and in his report to the President on August 21, he did not mince words: "We appear to be treating the Jews as the Nazis treated them," he wrote angrily, "except that we do not exterminate them. Beyond knowing that they are no longer in danger of gas chambers, tortures, and other forms of violent death, they see—and there is—little change." But the most telling part of Harrison's report was his acknowledgment that Palestine promised the only viable solution for the Jewish DPs. For those who could no longer go home, or had no homes to return to, "there is no acceptable or even decent solution for their future other than Palestine. This is said on a purely humanitarian basis, with no reference to ideological or political considerations so far as Palestine is concerned." Harrison appealed for quick action and endorsed the Jewish Agency's request for a hundred thousand additional certificates of entry into Palestine. "The world owes it to the handful of survivors to provide them with a home where they can again settle down and begin to live as human beings."[26]

Truman responded immediately out of a sense of decency and outrage. However the pressures of domestic politics or international relations influenced his policies from 1945 to 1948, Truman at all times clung to an intense humanitarian desire to aid the victims of the European war. The President, without consulting the State Department, called for the admission of more Jews into Palestine, and then directed General Eisenhower to put an end to the practice of billeting Jewish refugees in the former concentration camps; if necessary, Truman said, Eisenhower should requisition German homes for the DPs. The general complied immediately, and during his administration of the camps proved receptive to requests from Zionist leaders for specific favors.[27]

The British responded cautiously, but did offer a maximum of fifteen hundred Jewish immigrants a month to enter Palestine. The proposal evoked an outcry from the American Zionist leadership; not only was the figure grossly inadequate to the refugee need, but also it represented no concession at all, since the number of visas would be deducted from the unused quota of the 1939 White Paper. On September 27, an open letter to Attlee, signed by Stephen Wise and Abba Hillel Silver, appeared in fifty newspapers throughout the United States. It warned that the Zionists had reached the limits of their patience; no solution other than unrestricted immigration and the establishment of a Jewish state in Palestine would be acceptable.[28] Then, in the middle of October, Truman startled the British and delighted the Zionists when he specifically requested that Britain allow one hundred thousand Jews to enter Palestine.

The British, still reeling under the physical and economic devastation wrought by the war, did not want the Palestine issue raised at all. Once in office the Labour government was given a rapid and thorough education in the politics of the Middle East by the permanent staff of the Foreign Office; Attlee and Bevin now accepted the view that the Arabs had to be placated at the expense of Jewish aspirations in Palestine. But the United States, alone of the great powers to emerge economically unscathed by the war, held the key to material aid and recovery. If its President refused to follow the advice of his State Department, then some way would be found to make the United States share the burden. Maneuvering to buy time, the British proposed a joint inquiry into the refugee problem, and even tried to have Palestine kept out of the scope of its investigation. This time, however, the Americans proved unwilling to participate in another Bermuda fraud. Prodded by the White House, the State Department insisted on the inclusion of Palestine in the committee's charge. Truman also informed the British that he did not agree with their approach and had not abandoned his appeal for one hundred thousand certificates.[29]

Even before the public announcement of the Anglo-American Committee, Truman received warnings that the Zionists would oppose the idea. On October 30, Stephen Wise and Abba Silver sent the President a lengthy wire begging him "not to countenance further commissions and inquiries at a continued cost in human life and human misery, which can only ascertain facts already well known." The rabbis urged Truman to demand immediate admission of the one hundred thousand, repeal of the White Paper, and reaffirmation of the Balfour Declaration. The British were only playing games and the Zionist leaders pleaded with the President not to become ensnared in the trap.[30] But Truman actually had little flexibility in his decision. He had originally called for the one hundred thousand admissions on a purely humanitarian basis, totally innocent of the promises, counterpromises, and subterfuges involved in the Middle East situation. He realized that the British were stalling, but believed that unless he agreed to go along with the investigation, he would have no leverage to enact his refugee plan. If, as he expected, the committee endorsed his proposal, he fully anticipated that the Attlee government would have no choice but to agree. Although Truman recognized that the Palestine issue would be likely to intrude in domestic political matters, he hoped to keep the discussions in their proper sphere of foreign affairs. The President's pragmatic, and simplistic, approach to the problem did not include a Jewish state; in fact, it precluded unilateral American action; instead he expected that the transfer of one hundred thousand refugees would relieve the pressures.[31] The delay of the committee seemed a fair price to achieve these goals. Harry Truman's education was about to begin.

The Anglo-American Committee found itself subject to subtle and not so subtle pressures from the Foreign Office and the State Department. Interestingly, this committee was composed of twelve men,* most

---

* The six Americans on the committee were Judge Joseph Hutcheson, of the Fifth Circuit Court, who had single-handedly broken the Ku Klux Klan in Houston; Frank W. Buxton, editor of the Boston *Herald*; James G. McDonald, former League of Nations High Commissioner for Refugees; Frank Aydelotte, director of the Institute for Advanced Studies; William Phillips, a career foreign service officer and former ambassador to Italy; and Bartley C. Crum, a San Francisco attorney. The British members were Sir John Singleton, judge of the King's Bench in London; Lord Robert Mor-

of whom had previously been ignorant of or opposed to Zionism, and who by personal observation and objective investigation came to understand the plight of Jewish refugees in Europe, as well as to agree that only Palestine could solve their problem. From the start, the committee realized that the entire refugee problem labored under the enormous emotions and guilt generated by the Holocaust. "Had a logical solution been possible," William Phillips observed, "our committee would not have been in existence."[32]

The committee split into four groups to visit the various refugee camps in Poland, Czechoslovakia, Germany, and Austria. There the members witnessed the intensity of feeling about Palestine among the survivors. In nearly every camp, they found banners reading, "Open the Gates of Palestine!" Judge Hutcheson reported to his colleagues that at the big Honne camp he found "a feeling not of hope, but of Palestine." At a refugee camp in Austria, Richard Crossman had a nerve-wracking interview with a sixteen-year-old boy whose mother reached the United States. "I have cut her off, root and branch," he said. "She has betrayed the destiny of my nation. She has sold out." Sir Frederick Leggett was disturbed by this fervid nationalism, and after he saw a group of young children singing *Hatikvah*, he complained that it smacked of indoctrination, "after the Nazi fashion." Bart Crum replied: "Would you feel the same way if you saw a group of British youngsters singing 'God Save the King'?"[33]

The sights and smells of the camps profoundly moved the twelve men. Crossman, who earlier had this shattering experience in a visit to Dachau, wrote to his colleagues: "They had smelt the unique and unforgettable smell of huddled, homeless humanity. They had seen and heard for themselves what it means to be the isolated survivor of a family deported to a German concentration camp or slave labour. The abstract arguments about Zionism and the Jewish state seemed curiously remote after this experience of human degradation. A door had been slammed shut behind us. . . . Now a nightmare, dimly apprehended in reports and interviews and newspapers, had become the everyday life, and everything else was a dream."[34]

---

rison, a Labour peer; Richard H. S. Crossman, a Labour member of Parliament; Major Reginald Manningham-Buller, a Tory member of Commons; Wilfrid Crick, adviser to the Midland Bank; and Sir Frederick Leggett, a labor mediator. Hutcheson and Singleton served as cochairmen.

If devastated Europe provided the darker side of the Jewish case, Palestine offered the committee its brighter, idealistic aspects. The contrast between the rundown Arab sections and the Jewish settlements amazed the members. In Tel Aviv, Crum stood on a corner and thought, "Here before your eyes is proof that Palestinian Jewry is bringing civilization to the Middle East." When Frank Buxton returned from a visit to a kibbutz, his eyes filled with tears. "I felt like getting down on my knees before these people," he said. "I've always been proud of my own ancestors, who made farms out of the virgin forest. But these people are raising crops out of rock![35]

Buxton eventually took a very pro-Zionist stand within the committee, and even the terrorist activities of the Irgun and Stern group failed to dim his enthusiasm for the *Yishuv*. In a remarkable letter to his British colleague, the anti-Zionist Manningham-Buller, Buxton described a fantasy he had: "I found myself thinking about the Boston Tea Party. My imagination must have run away with me, for I saw in my mind that my compatriots of the day were not satisfied with throwing the tea into the sea. They began shooting at the British soldiery, killing some of them. Then these American terrorists ran for their lives with your soldiers in hot pursuit. One of my terrorist-compatriots knocked at my door and asked me to hide him. At this point of my fantasy, I came back to reality. The dilemma, however, still stayed with me, and I was pondering it for some time. What would I have done? Would I have hidden an American 'terrorist' pursued by British soldiers, or shut the door in his face? Well, my friend, I would have hidden him."[36]

The Zionists, of course, had no way of knowing what the committee would decide. Although the members were chosen for their supposed neutrality on the Palestine issue, the Jews had seen too many royal inquiries in the 1920s and 1930s turn into attacks on Zionism, with a subsequent whittling away of the Balfour pledge. At first, Zionist leaders seriously considered boycotting the hearings in protest against further delay, but calmer heads prevailed. If Jewish leaders failed to appear, they would leave the field open to Arab spokesmen, Christian missionaries, and others who violently opposed further immigration and a Jewish state in Palestine. As a result, a parade of Jewish leaders and non-Jewish Zionist sympathizers appeared before the committee in Washington and Jerusalem. The concern of men like Albert Einstein and Reinhold Niebuhr, and the eloquence of Stephen Wise certainly impressed the panel members. Few of those testifying, how-

ever, took a moderate stance, and in the end the extremist statements of
Zionists and anti-Zionists, of Jews and Arabs and Christians, probably
canceled each other out. Chaim Weizmann may have made the greatest
impression upon the committee when he, alone of all the speakers, declared that the issue was not between right and wrong, but between a
greater and a lesser injustice, and he believed that denying Palestine to
the Jews would be the greatest of injustices.[37]

The Zionists proved more successful in countering what they saw as
State Department pressures on the American members to accept British
proposals. When Judge Hutcheson reportedly said that so far as "election platforms, congressional resolutions, and all that kind of stuff are
concerned, he felt himself a free agent," the Emergency Council immediately contacted the White House to retract the statement. As the
committee gathered in Lausanne, Switzerland, to prepare a final report, the Zionists worked feverishly through David Niles, a White
House aide, to have the President indicate that he expected, at the
least, approval of the one hundred thousand certificates for Palestine.
On April 16 Truman agreed; he wired Hutcheson of his hope that the
American delegation would "stand firm for a program that is in accord
with the highest American traditions of generosity and justice."[38]

Pressures from the White House held the Americans firm, but the
evidence of misery and suffering which the twelve men had seen in the
refugee camps played an equally important role. On Good Friday 1946,
the committee completed its work, and the twelve members initialed a
unanimous report of ten recommendations. They found no country
other than Palestine willing to admit large numbers of refugees; and
while Palestine alone could not meet the needs of the survivors, one
hundred thousand certificates must be awarded. The committee also
called for repeal of the 1939 White Paper, but were decided against a
Jewish *or* an Arab state. Some sort of British trusteeship should continue until a satisfactory form of government for the country could be
determined; in the meantime, the Jewish Agency should resume co-
operation with the mandatory and help put an end to terrorism in
Palestine.[39]

Zionist leaders learned of these recommendations upon the delegates' return to the United States. Bartley Crum met with Emanuel
Neumann and Rabbi Silver in New York shortly after his arrival, before delivering the report to the President. Crum realized that the Jews
would not be happy with all the provisions, but he was eager that

Zionist leaders not criticize the report on the basis of incomplete information; he also wanted to alert Truman to the Jewish response. Silver and Neumann expressed delight with the recommendations on the refugees and the White Paper, but were aghast at the suggestion that Palestine remain under British control and that there be no Jewish state; the Zionists of America, they told Crum, would never approve that.

All three men pondered the dilemma; If the President approved it, as Crum expected, how could the Zionists attack the report without seeming to oppose Truman? Neumann saw the obvious solution: Let the President accept and praise the constructive parts of the report, especially the admission of one hundred thousand refugees, and withhold his opinion on the other sections pending further study. Neumann immediately wrote out a draft statement for the President, which Crum took with him to the White House. Truman, aware of the political dangers involved in the report, followed Neumann's strategy in his public statement. The Zionists, keeping their part of the bargain, praised the President for his humane and constructive approach to the refugee problem.[40]

As it turned out, the recommendation for one hundred thousand refugees was the only part of the committee's report to gain widespread acceptance among American Jewish groups. The Zionists, while lauding Truman, attacked the report as "totally unacceptable. It offers charity, not justice; it goes again and again to the brink of understanding and then draws back in fright." The American Jewish Committee urged that all long-range plans be subordinated to the immediate relief of the refugees. The American Jewish Conference and the Emergency Council, however, condemned the idea that the Jews give up their "legitimate and natural aspiration to become a self-determining people." The most extreme reactions came from the fringe groups. In rejecting the report, Peter Bergson's Hebrew Committee of National Liberation insisted that the British allow Holocaust survivors to enter the promised land immediately; the American Council for Judaism, alone among American Jewish organizations, wholly accepted the report. Among the American people an overwhelming 78 per cent favored admitting one hundred thousand Jews into Palestine; interestingly enough, so did 74 per cent of the British public.[41]

The British leadership, however, was appalled. Ernest Bevin had led the members of the committee as well as Harry Truman to believe that if he received a unanimous report he would accept the recommendations. The twelve men had repeatedly sought compromise positions for the sake of unanimity, and both the American and British members considered the final proposals consonant with the vital interests of each country.[42] But the Foreign Minister had assumed that the British delegates would secure a report more in line with the Arabist views of the Foreign Office, and he certainly did not expect to see recommendations for the admission of one hundred thousand refugees or the repeal of the White Paper. A furious Bevin refused to accept the report, and in so doing profoundly affected Jewish history. By reneging on his word, he alienated an American President, wiped out the last traces of moderation within the Zionist leadership, and created a set of circumstances that made the establishment of Israel possible.

The first British response came from Prime Minister Clement Attlee on May 26, in a cable recommending consideration of forty-five points before either government took any action. The list included expenses of transportation, housing and maintenance of the immigrants, the elimination of terror and "private armies," and the role the United States would play in the process. Realizing that the British could not bear the financial burden alone, Truman, while insisting on quick action on the refugees, agreed that American and British experts should meet to iron out any problems; Secretary of State Byrnes even proposed asking Congress for up to $300 million in grants and loans to help implement the committee's recommendations.[43]

But the British had no intention of implementing the plan, as Ernest Bevin made clear at a Labour Party conference on June 12, 1946. There would be no surrender and no appeasement. To admit the one hundred thousand displaced persons would cost Great Britain £200 million and require another army division, a burden Britain could not and would not bear. And why were the Americans pushing this plan? he asked; because they did not want any more Jews in New York. It was a wild, free-swinging comment, typical of Bevin, to whom tact was frequently a stranger, and it caused an uproar in the United States. Truman, who had been working to amend the immigration laws, was furious, and the American public was also personally offended. When Bevin came to this country a few months later for a United Nations meeting, New York dock workers refused to handle his baggage, and at a football game the demonstrations against him grew so violent that police trundled him out of Yankee Stadium for his own safety.[44]

On a more diplomatic level, the career officials of the two countries, summoned to work out details for implementing the committee report, devised a new scheme in July 1946, the Morrison-Grady plan, which in effect endorsed the Foreign Office view of a proper solution to the Palestine muddle. Palestine would be divided into four areas—Jewish and Arab provinces, Jerusalem, and a district of the Negev—with a central British authority having exclusive control of defense, foreign affairs, and, among other things, immigration. As one British official summed it up: "It is a beautiful scheme. It treats the Arabs and the Jews on a footing of complete equality in that it gives nothing to either party while it leaves us a free run over the whole of Palestine."[45]

As details of the Morrison-Grady plan leaked out, the Zionists unleashed another barrage of pressure on the White House. The new proposals were a complete sellout to the British, and were not worth the price of the one hundred thousand, assuming that Bevin would still allow them entry. Jewish leaders descended on Washington to indicate directly to government officials their anger at the proposal; indirectly, they alerted Democratic Party leaders that if Truman sold out to the British, there would be hell to pay at the November elections. Paul Fitzpatrick, chairman of the New York State Democratic Committee, wired Truman that if the plan went into effect, "it would be useless for the Democrats to nominate a state ticket for the election this fall. I say this without reservation and am certain that my statement can be substantiated."[46]

The Zionists also arranged for the six American members of the joint inquiry to present their views to both the State Department and the White House. Dean Acheson, who admittedly did not favor either the one hundred thousand proposal in particular or Zionism in general, unwillingly presided over the initial meeting ("The Archangel Gabriel would have declined the assignment, but he had more latitude than under secretaries of state"). All six men condemned the Morrison-Grady plan as a complete negation of their own work. It would only create a new ghetto; it was "very pretty, even grandiose, but a sellout nevertheless." Even William Phillips, one of State's own, rejected it as "entirely unacceptable," and archly asked when the United States had become "the tail to the British kite."[47]

The six men repeated their views to Truman, and one of them, James McDonald, in a private interview arranged at the Zionist request, had an explosive confrontation with the President. McDonald told Truman that the Jews would rather not have the hundred thousand than have the plan, that if Truman gave in to the British, he would go down in history as anathema.[48] McDonald's blunt talk, as well as the more tactful prodding of David Niles, convinced the President to kill the plan.

The Morrison-Grady fiasco had far-reaching results. Truman finally recognized that despite his primarily humanitarian concern for the refugees, that problem could not be considered separately from the final disposition of Palestine. Truman still did not understand Zionism, but he was beginning to appreciate the deep emotions that the refugee/Palestine problem stirred up among American Jews and that this could have important political repercussions. The demise of the plan also marked the end of Truman's patience with the British; he would continue to press them to admit the hundred thousand, but he would no longer trust them nor join with them on any proposal regarding Palestine. Instead of involving the United States in a Palestine solution, as Attlee and Bevin had originally hoped, they had ensured that an angry President would stand by as they sank into the morass.

But Bevin's error in judgment had still greater implications. From Truman's initial proposal until the demise of Morrison-Grady in August 1946, the central issue had been the admission of one hundred thousand Jewish displaced persons into Palestine, a proposal that had widespread public support both in the United States and Great Britain. Had the British government admitted the hundred thousand, the Zionist cause might have been lost. The removal of the hundred thousand would have made the refugee problem in Europe less acute; thus American public opinion would have been assuaged, Anglo-American relations over Palestine would have improved, and Truman might not have been so amenable to Zionist pressures. After all, the great majority of American Jews were then mainly concerned with saving the refugees; by refusing haven to the DPs, Great Britain forced American Jewry into the arms of the Zionists. Now the Zionist argument for a Jewish state in Palestine assumed a burning urgency, because not only was there no place else to go, but also no one else to trust. Abba Eban went so far as to suggest that had the British allowed in the DPs, "the problem would have lost its unendurable tension, and it is doubtful if the State of Israel would have arisen."[49]

The Zionists and the British, of course, recognized the relation between the refugee issue and Palestine. Britain opposed both the short-term solution for the refugees and the long-term Zionist plans; the Zionists had to fight for both, but were aware that in the public mind the two could be separated. And indeed, by the summer of 1946 the simple idea had taken hold that all the Jews wanted was admission of one hundred thousand survivors of the Holocaust into Palestine, and that the British were refusing this one humanitarian and necessary request. According to Christopher Sykes, the key planks of the Biltmore program—a Jewish state and Jewish control over immigration—had been submerged by the hundred thousand issue. Bevin's obstinacy and crude anti-Semitism saved the Zionists by proving their essential premise correct: Only a Jewish homeland could be relied upon to save the Jews. And by betraying the Zionist movement once again, England cut the ground out from under the moderates. It was now clear to all that a Jewish state would never come to pass under British sponsorship or protection. Thanks largely to Ernest Bevin, the militants won complete control of the organization at the twenty-second Zionist Congress in Basel in December 1946.

*   *   *

In surveying the wreckage which would be postwar Europe, Chaim Weizmann in early 1944 had presciently described what the internal situation of the Zionist movement would be like after the war. There would remain only two major centers of Jewish life, one in America and the other in Palestine, both militant, and with no European Jewish community to provide balance and moderation.[50]

Weizmann's fears of a union between militant Americans and the *Yishuv* overcoming his own cautious approach were borne out once the war ended. In the summer of 1945 he convened a Zionist conference in London to resume the program of the world movement and to map future strategy. The gathering, he wrote, consisted of "seventy-odd delegates and pervading ghosts of our five million or more dead." From the start, the coalition Weizmann feared began an attack on his policies. David Ben-Gurion and Moshe Sneh, the young and brilliant leader of the Haganah, talked openly of armed resistance against the British. The mandatory would be given a choice, declared Sneh, "either to destroy the *Yishuv,* or to abolish the White Paper and to establish a Jewish state in Palestine." Silver, now paramount in American Zionism, attacked Weizmann, arguing that trust in England would yield the Zionists neither immigration nor a state. And much to Weizmann's surprise, the representatives of European Jewry, the delegates from the decimated communities of Poland and Hungary and Czechoslovakia, spoke for those whose lives behind the barbed-wire fences now had only one urgency: "We cannot wait. Our choice is either *Eretz Yisrael* or death!"[51]

But if a new mood of militancy, a desire for "actions, not debate," dominated the conference, there also lingered the old-time distrust of American Jewry, a heritage from the prewar struggles. Silver declared that the time had come for Americans to share in the Zionist leadership. "We are mature not only for solicitation for funds. We are politically mature. I suggest that you take us into your confidence." But this the Europeans were not yet ready to do, and by skillful exploitation of this latent antagonism, Weizmann stacked an enlarged Zionist executive with his own supporters, and even kept Hadassah from it. This mistake on Weizmann's part would cost him dearly, for the women's group, the largest single Zionist organization in the world, by its nature tended to support the moderate policies that he advocated. Now, instead of an ally, he had another potential antagonist in the midst of the militants.[52] For there could be no mistake that American Zionists were growing more and more militant. Silver, now the head of the Emergency Council, also became president of the ZOA, and the pages of *The New Palestine* and the records of the Council clearly show that Americans would no longer passively follow a policy of restraint. Even moderates such as Judge Bernard Rosenblatt talked of organizing a "government in exile" to fight the British.[53]

Weizmann, Stephen Wise, and Nahum Goldmann became increasingly estranged and isolated by this new tone. Meyer Weisgal, Weizmann's alter ego in the United States and a bitter enemy of Silver, had urged Weizmann to abolish the Emergency Council before it destroyed the movement. Wise and Goldmann consistently used the bogey of Silver and the militants to bolster their own standing with the American government, and even depicted their opponents as unworthy Americans and unrepresentative Jews, a policy which made it even more difficult for Silver to gain access to either the White House or Cabinet members.[54] Only a threat from the outside, such as the Morrison-Grady plan, could dampen this internal feuding long enough to produce a pressure campaign or a letter drive, and then the two sides were at it again.

Because of the organizational fractures within the movement, the dissidents could always find some shelter for their case. In America, the Emergency Council supposedly co-ordinated all American Zionist activities, yet each of the constituent organizations retained sufficient freedom to dissent openly and loudly. The world movement had two centers of power, the Weizmann-dominated Zionist executive in London, and the Jewish Agency executive in Jerusalem under Ben-Gurion; both either ignored or wooed the Americans as the occasion demanded. And the World Jewish Congress had its own power base, so that Wise and Goldmann could identify with that body, which remained aloof from and therefore free of Zionist control. It is little wonder that the Silver group felt frustrated and hampered in its work.[55]

The situation could not last indefinitely, as all factions realized as time drew near for the Zionist Congress in Basel, the first to meet since before the war. Here Weizmann's prophecy would be realized, a congress dominated by Americans and Palestinians. In the early spring, the political maneuverings began, the militants and the moderates each assembling as many delegates as possible. The two largest delegations from the United States were those of the ZOA and Hadassah, and the men pressured the women to join them in a common slate. Only through such a course would American Jewry exert its influence at the congress, ran the ZOA argument, yet Hadassah would have full parity in membership, committee assignments, and all other matters. Although the National Board agreed with most of the proposal, it finally came to naught over the ZOA's insistence on a joint caucus rule, under which all of the delegates would be forced to vote by majority determination within the caucus. The moderates within Hadassah recognized that nearly all of the ZOA representatives would be Silver supporters; together with the half-dozen Silverites on the Hadassah side, they could force their will on every issue.[56]

But the militants, despite Hadassah's reluctance and a strong opposition led by Wise and Goldmann, came to dominate most of the American delegations. Weizmann, who for so many years had been the great master of Zionist politics, could not believe that the movement would be so foolish as to entrust its future to Silver and Ben-Gurion. With a sense of power and sureness, though, the latter two began their own maneuverings, each wary of the other, but willing to co-operate on the militant policy they espoused. Ben-Gurion, Moshe Sneh, Peretz Bernstein, and Jacques Torczyner, representing Silver, met several weeks before the congress and worked out an agreement for the ouster of Weizmann from the Zionist leadership.[57]

Weizmann later claimed that he had intended to resign anyway, and fought at the congress not for personal glory but to vindicate his policies. And this he attempted to do in one of the most masterful addresses of his life. Speaking in Yiddish, he attacked those who advocated armed struggle and a political orientation away from Great Britain, and quoted Ahad Ha'am's famous maxim: "This is not the road." But Weizmann reserved his greatest scorn for the American militants, who said they would give full political and moral support to the *Yishuv*. "Moral and political support is very little when you send other people to the barricades to face tanks and guns," he cried. "The eleven new settlements in the Negev have, in my deepest conviction, a far greater weight than a hundred speeches about resistance, especially when the speeches are made in New York while the proposed resistance is to be made in Tel Aviv and Jerusalem."

Emanuel Neumann, angered by this tirade, called out "Demagogy!" Weizmann incorrectly heard it as "Demagogue!" His eyesight nearly gone, the old man could not see who had hurled the challenge at him, but in a burst of passion he summed up all that the Zionist movement meant to him.

"I—a demagogue! I who have borne all the ills and travails of this movement. The person who flung this word in my face should know that in every house and every stable in Nahalal, in every workshop in Tel Aviv or Haifa, there is a drop of my blood. You know I am telling you the truth. Some people don't like to hear it—but you will hear me. I warn you against bogus palliatives, against shortcuts, against false prophets, against facile generalizations, against distortions of historic facts. . . . If you think of bringing the redemption nearer by un-Jewish methods, if you lose faith in hard work and better days, then you commit idolatry and endanger what we have built. Would I had a tongue of flame, the strength of prophets, to warn you against the paths of Babylon and Egypt. 'Zion shall be redeemed in Judgment'—and not by any other means."[58]

The delegates interrupted him with cheers several times, tokens of the love and esteem they felt for this man who had given more than a half-century's service to the cause, but for Palestine's future they cast their ballots for Ben-Gurion and Silver. The issue that became the test of power between the militants and the moderates was Great Britain's invitation to attend still another conference on Palestine scheduled in London toward the end of January 1947. Weizmann wanted the Zionists to attend, arguing that even if England had not lived up to its obligations, a Jewish homeland would still have to develop under the framework of British authority. Abba Hillel Silver, in a speech as powerful as Weizmann's, urged the delegates to boycott the conference, to "serve notice on Great Britain that we have finally reached the limits of any possible concession which can be forced from us, that it cannot have its way with us all the time.

"A hundred thousand certificates? No! The Anglo-American Committee report? No! A moderate increase in the number of refugees permitted into Palestine? No! And on the final grand gesture of sacrifice which we made to surrender half of Palestine in order to be master in our own house in the other half? Again, no! And now we are expected to go to another Conference, convoked by the same Government, so callous and so willful for what purpose? Again to be told, No. How long can we follow this line of retreat or abnegation without tearing the heart out of our movement?"[59]

When the vote came, the congress rejected a motion to attend the London talks, 171–154,† which amounted to a vote of no confidence in Chaim Weizmann. He stepped down as president of the WZO, a post he had held almost continuously for twenty-five years, and the congress chose not to elect anyone as his successor.

Some saw the decision as a mark of respect and affection for Weizmann; having rejected his program, the delegates did not wish to hurt him personally. It would be equally true to say that the two contenders for the presidency, Abba Hillel Silver and David Ben-Gurion, canceled each other out. Hadassah, which distrusted Silver after the joint-slate fiasco, voted against him on several issues, thus denying him the large power bloc needed to win the presidency. Moreover, Silver's shabby treatment of Stephen Wise, blocking his appointment to anything but a meaningless ceremonial post, angered many of the moderates.[60] Ben-Gurion found his chances subverted not only by the greater strength of

---

† The final wording of the resolution left to executive discretion the choice of attending the conference, and fourteen of the eighteen members favored doing so. The vote was a measure of confidence in Weizmann, and it failed. Eventually the Zionists indirectly participated, but the conference was doomed to failure even before it began.

the Americans, but also by the internal party factionalization of the Palestinians. All of these groups, both American and Palestinian, agreed on lines of general policy but could not reach accord on a leader. The two men, therefore, divided the work between them. Silver now headed the newly created American Section of the Jewish Agency, and spoke not only for the American Zionists, but also was the ranking official of the world movement in America. The moderates, both in Europe and the United States, conceded to the militants.

What did the Congress achieve? According to Ludwig Lewisohn, a Silver partisan, "the political power now vested in the able and effective political leadership of American Zionism embodies the historic recognition of the devotion, the members, the wealth, the natural generosity of American Jewry."[61] Hardly that, but the Zionist Congress did mark the emergence of a new, postwar Zionist movement. The union Weizmann feared had come to pass, and a Zionist program built upon trust in and co-operation with Great Britain came to a formal close. The Congress did not so much signify a revolutionary change in orientation as a final acceptance of the truth. That realization led the delegates to accept the militant leadership of Silver and Ben-Gurion, and, in hindsight, we can say not a moment too soon. For in the next eleven months the dream of a Jewish homeland would be assaulted on all sides, by London and Washington, in Palestine and in the United Nations.

Chapter 5

HAMA'AVAK

In 1947 it became clear to Zionists, displaced persons, the British and American governments, and American Jewry that the situation in Palestine could not continue unchanged. No one, with the exception of the Irgun, wanted armed conflict between the *Yishuv* and British forces, but with the status of the Holy Land changed, with entry to it still closed to the surviving remnant of European Jewry, even the more moderate Zionist elements began talking of *hama'avak* (the struggle).

The center of the controversy, Palestine, had been a bone of contention among competing empires for over three thousand years. In early times, it had been fought over because of its geographic position, straddling the major trade routes among three continents. In more recent centuries, the geopolitical significance had been enhanced by its holiness to three great faiths, Christianity, Islam, and Judaism. In 1947, Great Britain controlled Palestine under a mandate awarded by the League of Nations in 1922, but the original promise of the Balfour Declaration had given way to stringent immigration and land-purchase restrictions on the Jews in a futile effort to placate the Arabs.

But the *Yishuv*, in spite of the British, had prospered, and by 1947 counted 630,000 people. Basic industries and thriving agricultural settlements provided a sound economic base for future development, while water-distribution plans promised to open new land to increased immigration. Despite British attempts to seize arms, the Haganah had built small arsenals throughout the country, and most of the men had had

some military training, either as British troops during the war, or as ci-
vilians in the Palmach (Youth Corps) and Haganah. All told, the
Yishuv represented, literally and figuratively, the front line of the
Zionist struggle.

But the *Yishuv* shared Palestine with an Arab population that in
1947 was estimated at somewhere between 850,000 and 1,100,000.
Most Arabs lived in small villages, eking out a subsistence living,
scratching and picking at the earth with the same tools and the same
methods as their ancestors used for centuries. Some, like the Bedouin,
still pursued a nomadic existence, while others settled as unskilled laborers or small merchants in Jaffa, Haifa, and Jerusalem. Many had
come to Palestine fairly recently, drawn from neighboring Arab countries by the prosperity and opportunities generated by Jewish settlement
and industry. Indeed, in absolute numbers, more Arabs settled in Palestine between 1917 and 1948 than Jews.

Relations between Arab and Jew in Palestine was, from the start,
ambivalent. Theodor Herzl and most Zionist leaders had assumed that
the two Semitic nations could live side by side in peace, with the Jews
benefiting from Arab knowledge of the land, and the Arabs enjoying
the increased wealth and higher health standards which would accompany Jewish settlement. While there have been thousands of cases of
good relations, even friendships, among individual Jews and Arabs,
there has also been constant friction between them as groups. The
Arabs did not see the Jews as Semitic cousins, but as European
colonizers. Zionist leaders like Shmuel Hugo Bergmann, Judah
Magnes, and Henrietta Szold tried desperately to find common ground
for peaceful coexistence, but their efforts were doomed from the start.
Even if there had been no fanatic Arab leaders wanting to use the Jews
as pawns against the British, traditional Muslim teachings made it impossible for the Arab ever to accept the Jew as an equal.

Presiding over this mare's nest was a dying British Empire. Both
the Foreign Office and the State Department feared that if Great
Britain either left or was forced out of the Middle East, Russia, which
traditionally had sought an opening in the Mediterranean, would rush
into the resulting power vacuum. The Americans had no desire to enter
the area themselves, and much preferred that Britain, with as little
United States assistance as possible, continue to police the region. To
the State Department, a Jewish state would be an open invitation first

to chaos and then to Communist domination of the oil-rich, strategically important Levant.

As career professionals, the middle managers of the State Department felt themselves above politics, insulated from public opinion; their only responsibility was to conduct the foreign affairs of the nation oblivious to partisan demands. The fact that the American public supported increased immigration into Palestine or the creation of a Jewish state there had little relevance to the Near Eastern Affairs desk, other than a grudging recognition that the President would be under pressure to accommodate foreign policy to domestic politics.

Although the polls proved overwhelming support for the Jewish cause,[1] a small but influential minority of Americans opposed the Zionist program. The center of this group could be found in those Protestant churches with large missionary commitments in the Middle East. The increase in Jews in Palestine per se did not worry them, but they feared the effect of American endorsement of Zionism on their own educational and conversion programs. When Congress passed a pro-Zionist resolution in December 1945, the Reverend Lewis G. Leary, an elderly Presbyterian minister who had taught at Beirut's American University since 1900, cried out that "everyone zealous for Christian missions must feel a veritable heartbreak for the way in which the hasty and ill-advised endorsement of the Zionist program by Congress has nullified the sacrificial labors of generations of missionaries and educators." A study by a joint commission of the Federal Council of Churches, the Foreign Mission Conference, and the Home Mission Council, entitled "The Palestine Question: A Christian Approach," was blatantly anti-Zionist, terming Jewish nationalism "a philosophy of defeatism."[2]

Small as they were, the missionary groups nevertheless had close ties to the State Department careerists and believed that they "knew" the Arabs better than anyone else. After all, they had lived with them, worked with them, and taught them for more than a century. When the Anglo-American Committee of Inquiry held its hearings, a number of missionaries lectured the committee members on how the Arabs actually felt and what would be in the best interests of the Arabs, the United States, and Great Britain. Not surprisingly, the missionaries favored maintaining the status quo, and, insofar as an increased Jewish population in Palestine might upset it, further Jewish immigration should be opposed. Virginia Gildersleeve, former dean of Barnard College and an ardent anti-Zionist, declared: "Almost all Americans with diplomatic, educational, missionary, or business experience in the Middle East fervently believed that the Zionist plan was directly contrary to our national interests, military, strategic, and commercial, as well as to common justice."[3]

American Catholics, too, had their problems with the Jewish program. Hitler had also persecuted their church, and Catholics constituted a large number of the refugees in the DP camps. Catholic leaders resented the popular impression that the refugee problem was primarily one of Jewish suffering, and as such could be solved by opening Palestine. More than any other group, American Catholics favored allowing European refugees to enter the United States, and they struggled to relax the immigration quotas. They saw the Zionists undermining their plan by linking humanitarian issues to a political program. As one commentator noted, "if the Jews would press for opening America's doors instead of Palestine's, the Catholics could ride on the crest of sympathy evolved for Jewish refugees and resettle their own D.P.s."[4]

Theological considerations accounted for much of Christian anti-Zionism. Millar Burrows spoke for many of the missionary-Orientalists when he wrote in *Christian Century*: "The central issue between Judaism and Christianity lies in their answer to the question: What do you think of Christ? . . . The present resurgence of Jewish nationalism is a repetition of the same fatal error that caused Israel's rejection of Jesus. It is the focal point at which Christian opinion, in all brotherly love, should make clear and emphatic its disagreement with the dominant trend in contemporary Judaism. For the authentic, dominating, just now apparently all-conquering devotees of political Zionism we would feel the sorrow that Jesus felt when he wept over Jerusalem. We must not relinquish or forget our conviction that the Messiah is Jesus, and that the fulfillment of the promises of the Old Testament is to be found in the universal Kingdom of God which He came to establish. The Christians' final attitude may be that of Paul: 'Brethren, my heart's desire for Israel is that they may be saved.' "[5]

Fortunately for the Zionist cause, nearly all of the Christian opposition to Jewish nationalism could be nullified by the stronger pro-Zionist sentiment found in the Christian communities. Luminaries like Reinhold Niebuhr, Paul Tillich, John Haynes Holmes, and Daniel Poling spoke out through the American Christian Palestine Committee. Among the large fundamentalist Christian groups, strong support for the Zionists abounded, as T. D. Raynor wrote in the *Moody Monthly*:

"The title deeds from the Original Owner of the earth naming the Jews as legal owners of Palestine are still extant in millions of Bibles the world around."[6] Thus, while the Zionists had some Christian opposition, especially from those groups with vested interests in the Levant, for the most part Christian America either looked on favorably or was indifferent to the Zionist struggle.

In addition to a prepared and confident *Yishuv*, the other key to Zionist success lay in a militant American Jewry, ready with material wealth and political strength to fight for a Jewish state in Palestine and to bring relief to the refugees in Europe. In the postwar years 1945 through 1948, the community taxed itself over $400 million to sustain and rehabilitate survivors of the Holocaust and then pay for their transportation to and resettlement in Israel. It was undoubtedly the most significant philanthropic effort a Jewish community had ever undertaken, and more than fulfilled the biblical command of *tz'dakah* (righteous charity). The United Jewish Appeal campaigns, which included the local federations as well as Zionist funds, collected $35 million in 1945, $101 million the following year, $117 million in 1947, and $148 million in the year of Israel's birth, and of this approximately 75 per cent went to overseas projects and relief. To those who remembered that the UJA had raised only $14 million in 1941, the thought of raising $100 million the year after the war seemed preposterous. The magnitude of the achievement is even more impressive when one notes that the United Jewish Appeal, soliciting a community of 5 million people, including children, brought in *four times as much* as the total national receipts of the American Red Cross.[7] In addition, an estimated $100 million more went to Palestine in those four years through nonaffiliated Zionist funds and through secret channels to help arm the Haganah.

A second feature of American Jewry during this period was its incomplete acculturation, a sense of belonging but not full acceptance. While the majority of American Jews could accept their Jewishness, a small minority found it uncomfortable, and like the German immigrants of a century earlier eagerly sought assimilation. In a study of Jewish students at Yale in 1946, only half said that they would continue to identify as Jews, and only one third opposed intermarriage.[8]

In part, this desire not to be different arose from fear of latent antiSemitism. Hitler had shaken American Jewry to its core, to the point that few Jews could say as confidently as they did a decade earlier: "It can't happen here!" While overt anti-Semitism became unfashionable, covert forms could still be found. A *Fortune* poll found that one third of the sample believed Jews wielded too much economic power, while one out of five felt Jews had too much political influence as well. An Anti-Defamation League study in 1947 found increases in discrimination in employment, housing, education, and exclusion from resorts, as well as a greater toleration among the public of anti-Semitic remarks from public officials. The following year, Arnold and Caroline Rose wrote in *America Divided* that "among Jews, the feeling has become widespread that the outside world is bent on their destruction. Individual fears are being compounded into a group panic. The attitude is growing that desperate measures must be taken for group defense."[9]

How much this fear reflected actual conditions and how much the emotional reaction to the Holocaust are impossible to determine. The Roses noted that non-Jewish Americans saw little reason for Jewish panic, but there is no doubt that fear existed. In many ways, this fear led to the third significant feature of postwar American Jewry, its commitment to the Zionist demand for an autonomous Jewish homeland in Palestine. An independent Palestine became a psychological necessity, according to Kurt Lewin, in order to resolve the ambiguous position that Jews found themselves in at the end of the war. Zionism became the unambiguous test of Jewish affirmation. Rabbi Jacob Weinstein asserted that a Jewish homeland would give American Jews respect in the eyes of their gentile neighbors, while saving themselves from "the demoralization and self-hatred that are the inevitable by-products of anti-Semitism."[10]

More than at any time in its history, American Jewry stood united behind the Zionists. On the eve of Jewish statehood, 955,000 men and women formally belonged to one of dozens of Zionist organizations. In addition, millions of other American Jews endorsed the Zionist position through their membership in groups affiliated with the American Jewish Conference or through any of the more than fifty national agencies engaged in practical work in Palestine or political support of Zionism in the United States.[11]

Here again the Holocaust played an important role, driving home the fact that bigots made no distinctions. "Zionist or not, Reform or Orthodox, shoemaker or lawyer," declared a Jewish leader in Atlanta, "there was no difference to Hitler. After the war all Jews were alike, and deep down we all knew it." While the fanatical anti-Zionists on the American Council for Judaism remained beyond this consensus, their numbers and their strength dropped sharply in the postwar years. Most of the founding rabbinic members left, as did some of the prominent laymen. Judge Jerome N. Frank, once a member of the executive committee, admitted that the tragedy of the war changed his mind, and in October 1947 worked as a consultant with the Jewish Agency in the negotiations at the United Nations over partition of Palestine and the creation of a Jewish state there.[12]

In Hebrew, the word *am* means people, but it connotes much more: the sense of peoplehood—*Am Yisroel* (the people of Israel). In early 1947, this sense of belonging and identification permeated the American Jewish community, imbuing it with a spirit of power and purpose and unity previously unknown. Robert Szold, who had played an important role in Zionist affairs in the interwar years, spoke of "a new generation, untrammeled by successive reverses in dealing with the Mandatory Power, uninhibited by fears of internal weaknesses, unaccustomed to Old World anti-Semitism, fortified by the deeds and character of the emerging *sabras*, unafraid to proclaim the maximal position."[13] Only a people filled with that spirit of unity could have succeeded in the ensuing struggle.

*   *   *

Great Britain, like most of the shattered nations of Europe, looked to America for financial assistance in rebuilding her economy. Before the United States rationalized its aid program through the Marshall Plan, it treated each country's application on an individual basis. When Great Britain applied for a loan of $3.75 billion, some of the Zionist leaders saw a chance to pressure the English into agreeing, at the least, to admit one hundred thousand refugees into Palestine. While the Zionists did not oppose the loan, several other groups, particularly Anglophobes, Irish Americans, and isolationists, wanted to kill the loan outright, and for several months stalled the enabling bill in Congress. The Zionists by themselves would not have been able to defeat the loan,[14] but their opposition, joined with that of the other factions, could possibly do the trick. In essence, the Zionists hoped to force Britain to open Palestine or lose the loan. In a speech to a mass rally in New York on June 12, 1946, Abba Hillel Silver linked Britain's Zionist opposition to Albion's perfidy: "In view of the shocking record of broken pledges . . . American citizens have the right to turn to their representatives . . . and inquire whether the Government of the United States can afford to make a loan to a government whose pledged word seems to be worthless. They should also inquire whether American money, including that of the Jewish citizens of the United States . . . should be used to back up a government whose Foreign Secretary has repeatedly given evidence of a virulent anti-Jewish bias." The Zionists were not alone in this sentiment. New York mayor Fiorello LaGuardia bluntly told the British ambassador that "if Britain wants credit, the best way to get it is the indication that the borrower knows how to keep his word." The Emergency Council, because of opposition by the moderates, never came out publicly against the loan, but agreed to work through congressional contacts to delay the bill until the English admitted the refugees.[15]

The plan fell through, however, because a number of leading Jews refused to tie the British performance in Palestine to their application for a loan. As early as April 1946, Stephen Wise, in an editorial in *Opinion*, declared support of the loan, but at the same time damned Britain for its record in the Holy Land. To deny the loan, he argued, would be wrong, and "a great wrong will not condone another wrong. Wrong is wrong, and if the general denial of the loan to Britain is wrong to the British people and to our own Country, we as loyal American Jews have no right to insist upon that." On July 9, Wise published a message he had sent in favor of the loan to Sol Bloom, which at the White House's request was read into the Congressional Record.[16] Two days later, twenty-six prominent Jewish leaders, including Proskauer and Blaustein of the American Jewish Committee, labor leader David Dubinsky, and former Cabinet member Henry Morgenthau, Jr., took an advertisement in the New York *Times* supporting the loan. Shortly afterwards, under intense prodding by the Administration, Congress approved.

From the beginning moderate Jews had felt uncomfortable over the effort to use the loan as a club with which to beat the British. Like Wise, they questioned whether the loan would be in the best interests of the United States, and if the answer was yes, they did not want to interpose Jewish interests against the common good. Moreover, most American Jews drew a sharp distinction between the British *government* and the British *people*. The government would be opposed at every step, but the people should not be hurt. Golda Meir, in writing of the Israeli attitude, spoke for American Jews as well when she

recalled that: "Despite the long, stormy, and often terrible conflict between us and the British . . . we Israelis still hold the British people in
great and truly affectionate esteem, and are more hurt by being let
down by the British than by any other nation. . . . Jews have never
forgotten the lonely British stand against the Nazis."[17]

Unlike their response to the British loan, American Jews were less
hesitant, though somewhat ambivalent, to use the Palestine issue in the
1946 elections. The Democratic Party in 1944 had pledged itself to support a Jewish homeland; President Truman had called for the admission of one hundred thousand DPs in 1945; a joint Anglo-American
commission in 1946 had recommended opening Palestine. The right
words were said; now American Jewry began pressing for action to bear
out the words. In the fall of 1946 Harry Truman found himself
besieged by numerous Jewish groups calling for implementation of the
Democratic Platform and the admission of refugees into Palestine, even
if this required the use of American troops.[18]

Emanuel Neumann, speaking to Hadassah, argued that the Zionist
movement had reached a crossroads with the Truman administration:
Either the President would make good on his promises, or Jews would
have to take their votes elsewhere. The idea of bloc voting, of casting
their ballots strictly on the basis of *Jewish* issues, offended many American Jews. One member of the Hadassah board declared that although
Zionism was one of the most important things in her life, she would
not vote under orders from the Emergency Council. The old argument
that American Jews owed their allegiance solely to the United States
would be totally discredited if they now voted purely on the basis of
Zionist demands. "How could we possibly dare say that there is no dual
allegiance if we make the Zionist issue the one criterion? It would be a
field day for the American Council for Judaism." When the matter was
raised for discussion in the Emergency Council, opposition by Stephen
Wise and Hadassah prevented the more militant members from establishing a political-action group, although the Council decided to continue its policy of keeping political leaders aware of Jewish interests.[19]

But if Hadassah and the moderate elements within the Council opposed bloc action, Silver and Neumann favored it, and the Democrats
feared it. Bureaucrats within the government had long complained
about the "Jewish vote," although there is no evidence that there ever
was any bloc voting by American Jewry. As one student of the period
has noted: "Whether a Jewish vote existed is, of course, difficult to de-

tect, but the important fact here is that leaders of all parties acted under the assumption that such a vote did exist." One seasoned party worker argued that voting blocs had become more important than the old party machinery, and that of these blocs, American Jewry was the most important.[20]

The militants hoped to cash in on this alleged political potency, and in this they were encouraged by a man who had been an ardent anti-Zionist and now quietly advised Silver behind the scenes, Bernard M. Baruch. The elderly financier once said: "You let me have the Jewish vote of New York and I will bring you the head of Ibn Saud on a platter! The Administration will sell all seven Arab states if it is a question of retaining the support . . . of the Jews of New York alone; never mind the rest of the country." To Silver he argued that "the only thing which will matter in Washington . . . is if the people in the Bronx and Brownsville and Borough Park begin to mutter in their beards that they'll be damned if they continue to cast their votes for a party that breaks its pledges to them."[21] Silver, of course, needed little encouragement on this score, but Baruch's advice counted heavily because it came not from the Republicans, but from within, from the elder statesman of the Democratic Party.

In early September, Bernard Rosenblatt, a vice president of the ZOA, announced a series of Zionist meetings to condemn the Democratic administration for its failure to implement the pledges on Palestine. The sponsor of the rallies would not be the Emergency Council, but a new and allegedly independent creation, the Zionist Political Action Committee. To reinforce its message, the new committee bought full-page newspaper advertisements in cities with large Jewish populations. "WE DO NOT SEEK NEW PROMISES OR NEW PLANKS," ran a typical ad. "THE OLD ONES ARE GOOD ENOUGH. WHAT WE ASK IS THAT OUR ADMINISTRATION FULFILL OLD PROMISES NOW!" Technically, the committee was nonpartisan, working to stimulate public interest rather than endorsing candidates; practically, it could only benefit the Republicans, a fact which antagonized both Lessing Rosenwald of the American Council for Judaism and confirmed Democrats like Stephen Wise. Within the Emergency Council, Wise and Silver clashed continually over the wisdom of such a course, while privately the New York rabbi fulminated over the idiocies of Silver, Neumann, Rosenblatt, et al.[22]

Harry Truman, whose interest in the refugees and Palestine was primarily humanitarian, resented the intrusion of the issue into domestic politics, and for as long as he could, avoided making any further announcements on Palestine. Then word reached the White House that Governor Dewey, the nominal head of the GOP and its likely standard-bearer in the 1948 elections, would make a strong pro-Palestine statement before the United Palestine Appeal on October 6. David Niles, the Zionists' friend on the White House staff,[23] as well as officials of the Democratic Party, beseeched the President to beat Dewey to the punch. At the suggestion of Abraham Feinberg, Truman issued his own statement on October 4, the eve of Yom Kippur, reiterating his previous demand for admission of one hundred thousand refugees into the Holy Land. Truman recognized that the statement would have political repercussions, but he wanted to indicate that he had lost patience with Great Britain.[24]

Silver, however, saw the President's Yom Kippur statement as merely a "political move . . . to counteract the great political pressure" of the Zionists. Wise, while admitting that Council pressure had helped, nonetheless saw the announcement in a more positive light. The political-action campaign had little effect on the elections, in which the Republicans recaptured control of the Congress for the first time in sixteen years. While the Zionists may have affected some local elections (such as the defeat of Herbert Lehman in New York), the GOP won nationally on domestic economic and political issues that had little to do with Palestine. Truman's Yom Kippur message may have helped the Democrats raise some funds, but it otherwise had little impact. What is most important is that the Zionists now believed they had political influence, and under the direction of Silver and Neumann would be less hesitant to exercise it in the future. As Truman noted a week after the election, it seemed impossible to keep Palestine out of politics.[25]

*   *   *

While American Zionists flexed their political muscles, the situation in Palestine deteriorated rapidly. Even before the end of the war the Jewish Agency Executive, headed by David Ben-Gurion, increased its active opposition to British rule. General Sir Henry Maitland Wilson recalled that the Agency "was in some respects arrogating to itself the powers and status of an independent Jewish government. . . . It was, in fact, defying the [colonial] government, and to that extent rebellion could be said to exist." In June 1945, Ben-Gurion had told the Hadassah national board that the strain in Palestine had become "unbearable," and a year later reported to that group that although he hoped never to have to fight the British, the *Yishuv* stood ready and able to do so if that proved their only option.[26] Within Palestine, clashes between individual British soldiers and Jews occurred frequently. The British disliked the Jews since they did not act as a typical "native" population should. Richard Crossman noted that the mandatory administrators resented the fact that Jews were a logical people who studied the facts and were not afraid to catch a British official in talking nonsense. The Jews were also a proud people. When a young English officer in a cafe in Tel Aviv ordered the waiter to "Hurry up, you dirty Jew," the waiter, a member of the Haganah, picked the customer up by the scruff of the neck and threw him out.[27]

By mid-1946, British forces in the Holy Land felt themselves besieged on all sides. The Agency disregarded the colonial government whenever possible; Irgun and Stern groups carried out attacks with seeming impunity; and even the Haganah ceased its efforts to hold the terrorists in line. Ben-Gurion and Moshe Shertok bluntly informed the British High Commissioner that they would not ask Jews to keep the peace when the government itself consistently violated the law by barring immigrants and conducting illegal searches. At a funeral for a Haganah member killed in a clash with the British, Golda Meyerson declared "*Ein Breira*" (There is no alternative).[28]

British forces proved inadequate to stop the large-scale smuggling of illegal immigrants, and the Attlee government ordered an entire airborne division from Malta to clamp down on the Jews by invading their settlements and seizing all guns and armaments. The *Yishuv* responded on the night of June 17, 1946. For the first time, Irgun and Stern forces co-operated with the Haganah in blowing up nearly all the major bridges and rail junctures in the country, practically crippling the British army's internal communications.[29] On June 29, "Black Sabbath," the mandatory power retaliated in a nationwide raid, arresting more than three thousand people and wreaking havoc among the kibbutzim where they searched for arms. Nearly all Jewish Agency members in Palestine at the time were arrested and sent to a detention camp near Athlit.

Thanks to advance warnings, the Haganah saved most of its arms caches, but the British raid had been carried out efficiently and ruthlessly. Despite the round of protests against the British action, those Zionist leaders not in captivity realized that, for the moment, Great Britain had the upper hand. Ben-Gurion, who had been out of Palestine on Black Sabbath, and Moshe Sneh, who had escaped in disguise, called the remaining members of the Executive to an emergency meeting in Paris toward the end of July. Weizmann, ill in London, did not attend, nor did Silver. In a gloomy mood, the Zionist leaders wondered if perhaps they had made a mistake a decade earlier in not accepting the Peel Commission report, which had recommended partition of Palestine. Nahum Goldmann seized the opportunity and persuaded the others to adopt a proposal that clearly marked a retreat from the Biltmore program. For the first time, the Zionists declared themselves willing to settle for autonomy over a portion of the Holy Land, provided the British would immediately allow a hundred thousand immigrants into the country and transfer administrative and economic autonomy to Jewish authorities over a "viable" area to be designated as a Jewish state.[30] None of the Zionist leaders sought partition, but accepted it as the only way to a Jewish state.

Goldmann quickly returned to Washington, where he hoped to convince the American authorities that the new plan offered a solution to the Palestine dilemma. As usual, Goldmann overplayed his hand. He met with Silver and Neumann and promised to confer with them before acting. Nearly all of the American Zionist leaders opposed the partition proposal, even Goldmann's mentor, Stephen Wise, who lamented the Paris decision and quoted Brandeis' dictum that "what you renounce, you can never regain. What is taken from you, you may regain."[31] But Wise had toured the refugee camps and believed that a haven had to be found for the DPs, even if in a truncated Palestine. Goldmann had been instructed in Paris to indicate to the American government that the Jews would discuss partition if it were offered by the mandatory. Instead, he presented partition as the Agency's main proposal, thus destroying any flexibility for bargaining in later negotiations.

Goldmann did accomplish, coincidentally, one important piece of business: He reconciled Judge Joseph Proskauer to the necessity of a Jewish state, the final step in the transition of the American Jewish Committee from an opponent of Zionism into an ally. When Goldmann arrived in Washington, he discovered that Proskauer was also there. Fearing that the Committee head had come to oppose his plan, he secured an interview with Proskauer on August 7. In the meeting, which lasted several hours, he convinced the judge of the necessity and justice of the plan. "Above all," Goldmann said, "I reminded him of the conflict of conscience that would afflict American Jewry if a prolongation of the Palestinian Jews' struggle against Britain would force it to choose between Jewish solidarity (and hence, having to attack America's first ally) and stabbing the Palestinian Jews and the concentration camp refugees in the back out of loyalty to American policy." The next day, Proskauer and Goldmann saw Secretary of War Robert Patterson and together urged upon him the need of a Jewish state.[32]

While Patterson and other officials in the Truman administration agreed with the Goldmann plan, and a number of Zionist leaders expressed interest in further negotiations with the British, the London conference of early 1947 found the British and the Arabs unwilling to concede even minimal Zionist demands. Finally Ernest Bevin, condemning the "unreasonableness" of both Jew and Arab, announced on February 14, 1947, that His Majesty's Government had been unable to formulate a workable solution to the Palestine muddle and would refer the entire matter to the United Nations. In a callous reference to the refugees languishing in the DP camps, Bevin remarked that "after two thousand years of conflict, another twelve months will not be considered a long delay."[33]

Bevin's anger could not be contained. He had once declared that he could and would solve the Palestine problem, and would stake his reputation as Foreign Secretary on it. In a speech before the Commons on February 25, he attacked not only Harry Truman and Earl Harrison, a troublemaker whose report on the horrible conditions of the refugee camps led Truman to call for one hundred thousand entry certificates, but also the New York Jews, whom he claimed dominated the Jewish Agency and prevented other Jews, "those who have been trained in England and grew up under English customs and practice," from cooperating with the Crown's efforts. The petulant Labour chief could simply not admit that the British Empire's moment in the sun had passed, that England's reneging on the Balfour promise and the mandate terms—and not the New York Jews—had led to the impasse in the Middle East. Now let the United Nations try its hand, he declared, and it was understood, though never articulated, that if the world body failed, then England would impose its own solution, one that would have meant the end to any hope for a Jewish homeland.[34]

*   *   *

The United Nations had not even reached its second birthday when the British dumped the Palestinian hot potato in its lap. Administrative machinery had been established, but only in skeletal form, and there were few precedents to which the world body could refer for guidance in this case. Within the State Department, a general malaise prevailed. For those committed to continued British hegemony in the Middle East, a "wrong" UN decision could easily create a power vacuum from which the Soviet Union could emerge as the dominant force in the region. Dean Acheson and others believed that the United States would have to assume some leadership, if for no other reason than to secure a "sensible" proposal that the American government and people could accept, since in all likelihood the United States would be asked to finance it. The State Department, which privately favored a partition plan, publicly adopted a neutral position, despite repeated requests from Zionist leaders and pro-Zionist congressmen for a clarification of policy. Secretary of State George C. Marshall and chief delegate Warren R. Austin refused to make any statement which, in their opinion, might limit the usefulness of the United Nations.[35]

The special session of the UN called to deal with Palestine met on April 27, 1947, and plunged into debate on the agenda. The Arab states demanded an immediate "termination of the Mandate over Palestine and the Declaration of its Independence," a proposal that received no support from the other nations. A touchier issue involved Jewish representation. The five Arab members would make a full presentation of the Arab case, but who would speak for the Jews? Asaf Ali, the Indian representative and a Muslim, argued that discussing Palestine in the absence of the Jews would be like "playing Hamlet without the Prince of Denmark." The Jewish Agency had already submitted a formal request to speak for the Jewish people, and after lengthy parliamentary maneuvering, the Agency was recognized as the sole organization to represent the Jewish case before any UN body deliberating the Palestine matter.

On May 8, 1947, Abba Hillel Silver, Moshe Shertok, and David Ben-Gurion took their seats between the Cuban and Czechoslovakian delegations to make the first presentation to the international assembly of the Jewish claim to homeland. Each delegation had a small signboard in front of it, denoting the country represented, and now, for the first time in nearly two thousand years, the Jewish people again stood in the family of nations. David Horowitz, who served on the Agency's UN staff, recalled the thrill that ran through the delegation: "It was, of course, still only a substitute, a state in the making, and not actual independence; nevertheless, it bore the hallmark of international recognition of Jewry. . . . After hundreds of years of discussion on the nature and national-territorial characteristics of Judaism, the discussion had seemingly been finalized by this modest shingle."[36]

Unable to reach agreement in the committee of the whole, the UN appointed an eleven-member Special Committee on Palestine (UNSCOP), consisting of smaller, neutral countries, with the Arab states and the great powers deliberately excluded. The Committee held hearings in Palestine from June 16 to July 24, and then went to Geneva to prepare its report. During its deliberations, the British managed to create an incident which focused both the Committee's and the entire world's attention on the plight of Jewish refugees.

A battered Chesapeake Bay ferry, purchased by the underground group, steamed to France, where it was refitted to hold some forty-five hundred DPs, and renamed *Exodus-1947*. As soon as it left French territorial waters, six British destroyers and one cruiser "escorted" the overladen vessel across the Mediterranean. Twelve miles outside of Palestine, the British ships closed for boarding. After several hours of hand-to-hand combat, the British resorted to machine guns and gas bombs, and in the ensuing battle killed three Jews and wounded more than a hundred. All the while, a detailed account of the fighting went out on the *Exodus-1947* radio to Palestine, where the Jewish Agency rebroadcast it on a clandestine network for the world to hear. The ship finally surrendered only after the British began ramming it, and stove in one side.

They towed the badly listing ferry into Haifa, where illegal immigrants normally would be transferred to detention camps in Cyprus. But as the two facilities on that island were already overcrowded, Ernest Bevin decided to make an example of the refugees by sending them back to Europe. British prison ships carried the DPs to Marseilles, but there, except for a small number of the aged, ill, or pregnant, the refugees refused to leave the boats. The French government offered hospitality, the British officers pleaded with them, all to no avail. The Jewish Agency managed to sneak a correspondent on board, and his description of the inferno beneath the decks did little to enhance British prestige: "Squeezed between a green toilet shed and some steel plates were hundreds and hundreds of half-naked people who looked as though they had been thrown together into a dog pound. For a moment I had the hideous feeling that they were barking. Trapped and lost, they were shouting at us in all languages, shattering each other's words. . . . The hot sun filtered through the grillwork, throwing sharp lines of light and darkness across the refugees' faces and their hot, sweaty, half-naked bodies. Women were nursing their babies. Old women and men sat weeping unashamed, realizing what lay ahead."

After three weeks the French, fearful of epidemics, ordered the ships to depart, and the British Cabinet, meeting in emergency session, decided to take the Jews to Germany. When the ships docked at Hamburg, the refugees again refused to leave, and British troops wielding clubs and rubber hoses literally drove the DPs off the boats and into railroad cars that took them to internment camps. For a month the British tried to register them, but no matter what questions were asked, the refugees had only one answer: "Palestine." A subcommittee of the UNSCOP visited the *Exodus-1947* camps, and in the words of the Yugoslavian member, "it is the best possible evidence we can have." Indeed, the experience of the UNSCOP teams duplicated those of the Anglo-American Committee a year earlier. Although the Arab states wanted the refugee problem dissociated from the Palestine question, the Committee's final report concluded that "if only because of the extraordinary intensity of the feeling displayed in this direction, such a situation must be regarded as at least a component in the problem of Palestine."[37]

Unable to reach unanimous agreement, UNSCOP submitted both a majority and a minority report. The minority proposal, signed by three members, called for the creation of a federal state, composed of two subordinate states, one Jewish and the other Arab, with two legislative bodies, one elected on the basis of population and the other giving both Jews and Arabs an equal vote. The majority called for the partition of Palestine into two states, joined through an economic union, with the city of Jerusalem placed under a special United Nations trusteeship.

The General Council of the World Zionist Organization received the report in Zurich and instantly rejected the minority plan as "wholly unacceptable." The majority proposal received a qualified endorsement: The Zionists welcomed the creation of an independent Jewish state, but the proposed boundaries limited it to only "a minor part of the territory originally promised to the Jewish people on the basis of its historic rights"; furthermore, it excluded "areas of the utmost importance." Yet Silver and Neumann, who had opposed the Agency's partition plan a year earlier, now seemed willing to take half a loaf, though on returning to New York, Silver reiterated his earlier plea that the Jews "demand all of Palestine and wait for such an offer on the part of the United Nations Assembly as will prove acceptable." Aware that American Jews overwhelmingly endorsed the partition plan, the Emergency Council urged caution on the part of local Zionist leaders and groups. "If the impression is created that the Jewish people regard the majority report as being in their favor," the Council warned, "the efforts of our enemies within the UN further to whittle down pro-Jewish recommendations will be greatly facilitated."[38] The final lines had not yet been drawn; should the Zionists appear too pleased with the UNSCOP report, it would be difficult if not impossible to secure better boundary lines in the UN debate.

But despite its shortcomings, the UNSCOP report gave the Zionists their first glimmer that a Jewish state might soon be established. Leaders of the movement began planning how to maintain this momentum, how to counter the anticipated British and Arab opposition. The United States would play an important role in the struggle, and the key to American support would be the attitudes and efforts of American Jewry. "It will not be worthwhile for the United States to incur Anglo-Arab wrath, or even to offer to co-operate with the British or the UN in implementing the committee's proposals, if they are not backed resolutely by the broad mass of the American Jewish community." The Zionists were therefore delighted when Judge Proskauer, in a public telegram to Secretary of State Marshall, on behalf of the American Jewish Committee, urged the United States government to endorse the UNSCOP majority report "vigorously and speedily."[39]

But while American Jewry welcomed the UNSCOP plan, reactions within the State Department ranged from incredulity to outright hostility. Anglophiles and Arabists rejected the plan as undermining the balance of power and British hegemony in the Middle East. The Joint Chiefs of Staff warned that implementation of the plan would require use of American troops, which would surely prejudice American influence and prestige in the Middle East. They urged Truman to take no action which would turn the peoples of the region against the Western powers. Intense opposition came from both military and foreign service officers concerned about access to the area's oil reserves. A special committee, headed by Herbert Feis, had been created in 1943 to study the problem of future oil reserves, and at that time had warned that "unless our ability to derive required supplies from abroad at all times . . . is safeguarded, the United States will be in hazard (a) of having to pay an economic or political toll to secure the oil; or (b) actually fail to secure it." Now led by Secretary of Defense James Forrestal, the "oil" groups in State and Defense mounted a vigorous opposition to the UNSCOP plan, fearing that it would so antagonize the Arab nations that American oil supplies would be endangered. As an alternative, they argued that since Great Britain could no longer maintain her position in the Middle East by cultivating the Arabs, the United States would do well to take over and follow the same formula; otherwise the Arabs would be driven into the arms of the Soviets. As Loy Henderson put it, "Arab friendship is essential if we are to have their co-operation in the carrying out of some of our vital economic programs," such as the Marshall Plan.[40]

The argument has been made that beneath the veneer of national interest, the true cause of opposition to the creation of a Jewish state was anti-Semitism. Government service, especially in the State Department, had long been an exclusive club, and few Jews held positions of influence there. Undoubtedly during the war years, Breckinridge Long's deep animus against Jews led him to thwart efforts to save a doomed people. After the war, James Forrestal, while not a bigot, came from a business and social milieu where Jews were excluded, and he tended to be indifferent, rather than hostile, to Jewish distress.[41] But the principal villain of the drama is usually identified as Loy W. Henderson. David Niles, Bartley Crum, and Eleanor Roosevelt were contemporary critics, charging Henderson with being the leading Arab advocate in the State Department, a man who consistently misrepresented the Jewish case and worked to thwart presidential directives. Joseph Schechtman, an ardent Zionist, disagreed. He argued convincingly that Henderson was neither anti-Zionist nor anti-Jewish; rather, he interpreted America's best interests as requiring close ties with the Arab world, and the creation of a Jewish state, insofar as it would drive a wedge between the United States and the Arabs, had to be opposed. "He undoubtedly misjudged the importance of the 'Arab factor' in the global United States policy, but his was a sincere and honest error," wrote Schechtman. "He frankly believed that his stand was in the best interests of America, and he acted accordingly, using his exceptionally wide knowledge of the Middle East and his official position to press unrelentingly for the implementation of the policies he deemed right."[42]

Henderson was a master at bureaucratic infighting, at interpreting directives so they were more in tune with his careerist thinking, but in the fall of 1947 he found the scales tilted too far for him to affect. Secretary of State George Marshall, despite whatever qualms he may have had about the wisdom of partition, believed that the United States had to support the UNSCOP plan as a matter of principle. The President, moreover, saw the UN proposal as the only way to extricate himself from the morass of competing Zionist and British demands. Within the UN delegation, Henderson found Eleanor Roosevelt a strong supporter of partition, while another friend of the Zionists, General John Hilldring (who had been appointed at the suggestion of David Niles), managed to offset the influence of Henderson and his chief aide, George Wadsworth.

The Zionists too were applying pressure; a mail campaign initiated by the Emergency Council inundated Washington with letters and telegrams supporting partition. In case Truman had not yet received the message contained in the more than sixty-five thousand pieces of mail, Clark Clifford reminded him that the Jewish vote would be very important in 1948.[43] At the beginning of October, Truman advised the State Department to announce the government's approval of partition, and on October 11, Herschel V. Johnson informed the General Assembly that the United States would approve the UNSCOP majority report, although it would suggest geographical revisions. Two days later, to everyone's great surprise, Soviet delegate Semyon K. Tsarapkin declared that the Soviet Union would also vote for partition. "Those damned Jews!" one delegate gasped. "They even bring America and Russia together when they want something."

The Soviet decision resulted in part from months of careful work by the Jewish Agency delegation, especially by Emanuel Neumann, who had made the first contact with the Russians as far back as 1941. When Chaim Weizmann visited the United States that year, Neumann arranged for an interview between the Zionist leader and Soviet Ambassador Maxim Litvinoff. The Russian surprised both Weizmann and Neumann when he declared that the Soviet Union did not oppose Zionism. "When Zionism first appeared on the scene it appeared as protégé of Great Britain, and Britain was our enemy, so naturally we were opposed to Zionism too," Litvinoff, a Jew, explained. "But now we're allies. And we have no Arabs. Britain has Arabs to think about. Why should we be opposed to it? As far as we're concerned it's a matter of indifference."[44] The Russians, of course, also wanted to see the lessening of British influence in the Middle East.

After the war, Neumann again led the way in contacting the Russians, and the Zionist delegation admitted that it sought aid wherever it might be. As David Horowitz noted: "We told the Americans that we were meeting with the Russians, and the Russians of our conferences with the Americans, without holding back anything. . . . We told both the Americans and the Russians that our sole criterion was the Jewish interest."[45] At one point, the United States and Great Britain wanted to have the Big Four meet with both Jews and Arabs in a final effort to reach agreement. The Russians, suspicious of the maneuver, refused to attend, and Silver insisted that if they did not participate, the Jewish Agency would also boycott the meeting. In response to the anti-Communist arguments of some of the labor Zionists, Silver lost his temper and declared that hatred for communism could not be allowed to interfere with the creation of a Jewish state.

Finally Neumann and Moshe Shertok (who Hilldring had said could sell ice to the Eskimos) went to the Russian embassy to see if the impasse could be broken. Shertok used all of his skill, but Andrei Gromyko insisted that the Russians had made their decision; they would not participate. Suddenly Neumann spoke up. After explaining again the difficulties facing the Zionists, who did not want to forfeit the friendship and goodwill of either the Americans or the Russians, he offered a suggestion: "You are unwilling to participate in such a discussion. Very well. But couldn't you—by way of protest—attend the meeting without 'participating'?" Gromyko's face broke into a broad grin as he repeated the idea; finally he promised he would let them know early the next day. As the Emergency Council met the following morning, they received a message from the Russian embassy that Gromyko would be at the gathering. Though nothing resulted from the meeting, as the

Jews had expected, the fine line of communication between the Agency and the superpowers was preserved.[46]

Despite optimism over the backing of both the United States and the Soviet Union, Zionist leaders recognized that many obstacles had yet to be hurdled before the UNSCOP report could be approved. The State Department careerists remained unhappy with details of the partition plan, and sought excuses to disparage the *Yishuv* and the Jewish Agency. Intermittent fighting in Palestine, as well as increased illegal immigration, the Aliyah Bet, led the Department to warn Zionist officials that unless the violence in the Holy Land were brought under control, the United States would be forced to speak out against the Agency. While Assistant Secretary Dean Rusk delivered this message to Lionel Gelber, the Secretary of State called Judge Proskauer to inform him that if there were any more *Exodus* incidents, the American effort on behalf of partition might be damaged.[47]

Of greater danger confronting Jewish interests was the Department's efforts to appease the Arabs by allotting them more territory under the proposed partition plan. The UN Special Committee on Palestine had recommended that Jaffa be included in the Jewish section for the sake of rationalized borders, despite the fact that its population was almost exclusively Arab. In negotiations at the United Nations, Jaffa became part of the Arab state, a more logical arrangement demographically, but one which reduced the already truncated Jewish area. When the State Department then proposed detaching much of the Negev (the arid southern section) from the Jews, the Zionists dug in their heels and prepared to fight. The small amount of land allotted to them was for the most part land they had already developed; to accommodate the immigrants, the new state would need open land. Moreover, if the Negev fell under Arab control, the Jews would have no water access to Asia. Through Aqaba, the Jews could reach the Persian Gulf and establish trade relations with the Far East; without it, they would either be restricted to dealing with Europe and America, or be dependent on the questionable goodwill of the Arabs for use of the Suez Canal.

American diplomats, however, were less interested in future trade routes for the Jews than in appeasing the British and the Arabs. They thought the Arabs might be placated by getting more land, and they pressed the Jewish Agency representatives to yield the Negev. When the State Department dropped hints that without this concession by the

Jews, the United States would have to reconsider its support of partition, the Emergency Council wired all its local chapters urging them to
see that huge numbers of telegrams were sent immediately to the State
Department and the White House "by all groups in their respective
communities, both Jewish and non-Jewish." And in this moment of crisis, the Zionists turned for help to one man who might possibly
influence the President. Chaim Weizmann, ill in a New York hotel
suite, was still the master diplomat of the movement, the one person acknowledged even by his opponents as the most persuasive apostle of Zionism to the non-Jewish world.

Truman, who had met Weizmann once before, greeted him warmly
on the morning of November 19. After only a few minutes of small
talk, the aged Zionist leader plunged into the purpose of his visit.
Guided by a memorandum and a map prepared by Eliahu Epstein, he
proceeded to give the President of the United States a lesson in political geography, and kept Truman's mind riveted to this one single issue.
A fascinated Truman, grasping the force of Weizmann's argument,
gave his assent and promised to inform the American UN delegation
that the Negev should remain under Jewish control.

The Jewish Agency representatives were scheduled to meet with
the Americans at three o'clock that afternoon to give their response to
the Negev question. Weizmann called New York immediately after his
interview with Truman to inform Moshe Shertok of the results. Unfortunately Truman, perhaps unaware of the scheduled conference, failed
to contact the American contingent with equal speed. At the United
Nations, General Hilldring told a confused David Horowitz that, as far
as he knew, the Americans were still under instructions to push for ces-
sion of the Negev to the Arabs. Horowitz intercepted Shertok outside
the building with news of the mixup, but, unable to evade the Americans, they sat down with Herschel Johnson shortly after three. Johnson,
after the usual polite phrases, asked them if they had any news about
the Negev decision.

Shertok, in a quandary, could not tell Johnson that Truman had already made a decision in their favor, nor could he accede to the State
Department's demands. Just then a messenger entered to inform Johnson of a telephone call for him; not wishing to interrupt his conversation, Johnson asked Hilldring to take the call. A minute later the general returned and whispered in Johnson's ear that the President was
holding at the other end of the line. The chief delegate, in Abba

Eban's phrase, "leaped to the telephone booth like a startled and portly reindeer." Twenty minutes later he returned and stammered: "What I really want to say to you, Mr. Shertok, was that we have no changes to suggest." The collective sigh that arose from Horowitz and Shertok could be heard across the lounge.[48]

The Negev had been saved, but the partition plan was still to be approved, and many of the smaller nations wavered. The British ambassador, Sir Alexander Cadogan, had announced that His Majesty's Government would do nothing to help carry out partition, and since it could not be put into effect peaceably, his government would not be a party to implementing it by force. Moreover, the British unilaterally set their own terms for withdrawal in such a manner as to guarantee bloodshed: no gradual transition, no interim councils, and no relaxation of the White Paper. If open warfare were to devastate the Holy Land, some delegates suggested, perhaps continued British rule might still be the most preferable option.

In the light of this argument, an enlarged Jewish Agency contingent, directed by Shertok and Silver, labored feverishly in the temporary UN headquarters at Lake Success, buttonholing delegates and drawing up numerous legal documents in support of their case. Leading American Jews, many of whom were non-Zionists, offered to use their contacts with foreign delegations, and Judge Proskauer, Bernard Baruch, Herbert Bayard Swope, George Backer, Edward M. Warburg, and Henry Morgenthau, Jr., some of whom had bitterly opposed a Jewish state a short time earlier, now did their best to bring it into being. Tens of thousands of telegrams descended upon the White House and the State Department demanding that the United States not only vote for partition, but also use its influence to persuade—indeed, to pressure —other nations to do so as well.

Until the last moment, the State Department resisted this pressure. Acting Secretary of State Robert A. Lovett told Loy Henderson that he could notify the Arab ambassadors that the United States planned to vote for partition but would not bring pressure on other UN members to follow its lead; Henderson gladly informed Herschel Johnson at the United Nations of this policy. The White House also tried to resist the demands of American Jewry. Truman later recalled: "I do not think I ever had as much pressure and propaganda aimed at the White House as I had in this instance. The persistence of a few of the extreme Zionist leaders—actuated by political motives and engaging in political threats—disturbed and annoyed me."[49] On the day of the scheduled vote—November 27, 1947—Shertok's calculations showed the partition resolution still three or four votes shy of the necessary two thirds. He decided to filibuster, thus postponing the vote, and thanks to the Thanksgiving recess, gaining another day in which to round up the crucial ballots.

Now the dam broke. Truman, inundated by the mail campaign and besieged by Democratic congressmen and party officials, gave David Niles the go-ahead. Niles phoned Johnson, and on the President's instructions, directed him to lobby actively for partition. Orders went to the State Department: American officials in wavering or opposed countries outside the Moslem world were to exert pressure for support.[50] The Emergency Council's long cultivation of non-Jewish friends now paid off as well; the tactics they adopted were far from subtle, but too much was at stake. Two justices of the United States Supreme Court wired Philippine President Carlos Rojas, "The Philippines will isolate millions and millions of American friends and supporters if they continue in their effort to vote against partition." At the same time that the Philippine ambassador to the United States received a "briefing" at the White House, twenty-six senators cabled Rojas urging him to change his country's vote from a no to a yes. Harvey Firestone, under threat of a Jewish boycott of his company's products, informed William Tubman, the President of Liberia, that if that country did not change its vote Firestone would have to reconsider plans to expand rubber holdings there. The Liberians too were prodded by South Africa's Jan Smuts, one of the fathers of the Balfour Declaration, who acted at Chaim Weizmann's request. Adolph A. Berle, who had once tried to convince Emanuel Neumann to accept Ethiopia in lieu of Palestine, now used his contacts in Latin America to induce Haiti to vote in the affirmative. And Bernard Baruch shocked Alexander Parodi, the French representative to the UN, with a blunt threat to cut off American aid if France went against partition.[51]

Long before the delegates arrived at the converted building which temporarily housed the world organization, the streets of Lake Success were thronged with Jews and their friends waving signs and placards. Around the nation and in Palestine people dropped their normal routines to tune in the radio, and with pencil and pad waited for the debate to end and the tally to begin. Emanuel Neumann, whose observance of traditional Jewish law would have normally prevented him from traveling on Sabbath eve, received a dispensation from a rabbi so that he could attend the crucial session. Shortly after 5 P.M. on November 29, 1947, Oswaldo Aranha of Brazil, the General Assembly president, gaveled the debate to a close and reached into a basket to pull out the name of the nation which would lead off the vote.

"Guatemala," he called.

As the Latin American delegate rose amid the dead silence that gripped the hall, a cry rang out from the spectators' gallery:

"*Ana adonai hoshiya!*" (O Lord, save us!)

In Jerusalem, Yitzhak Sadeh, father of the Haganah, and thirty of his followers, among the most wanted men in Palestine, listened intently. "If the vote is positive," he declared, "the Arabs will make war on us. This war will cost us five thousand lives. And if the vote is negative, then it is we who will make war on the Arabs."

Abba Hillel Silver, Emanuel Neumann, and Moshe Shertok all sat expectantly in the hall; near the Dead Sea potash works, halfway around the world, David Ben-Gurion slept.

One by one, the fifty-six member states rose to announce their votes: thirty-three for partition, thirteen against, ten abstentions. In New York and London and Tel Aviv and Jerusalem, wild celebrations broke out. "This was the day the Lord hath made," exulted one rabbi. "Let us rejoice in it and be glad." In Cincinnati, where the Young Zionists convention was in process, hundreds of delegates marched to Fountain Square to see Bernard Marks, captain of the *Exodus-1947*, burn a copy of the Mandate. In the refugee camps the day of deliverance seemed finally at hand, and more than one observant Jew noted that the United Nations vote nearly coincided with Channukah, the feast of lights, which marked the victory of the ancient Maccabees.[52] The next issue of *The New Palestine* carried on its cover the traditional Hebrew prayer of Thanksgiving, the *Sheheyanu*— "Blessed art Thou, O Lord our God, King of the Universe, who has given us life, sustained, and enabled us to reach this season."

*   *   *

Since that historic vote, the argument has been made by both friends and foes of the Jewish state that had it not been for the political pressure exerted by the American Jewish community, both on the American government and on the wavering nations, the necessary two-thirds vote would never have been gathered. David Horowitz wrote enthusiastically that the "one potent factor, which excelled all others operating on our behalf, was the strong action and pressure exerted by American Jewry. This great community, from the Zionists to the American Jewish Committee led by Judge Joseph Proskauer of New York, rallied massively to help in the political struggle. . . . American Jewry flung itself into the thick of the fray with an enthusiasm and dedication which had no parallel or standard of comparison in all past experience. The whole of the community, from coast to coast, was aflame with the zeal and ardor of the battle."[53]

Foes of the Jewish state were equally convinced that American Jewry played the decisive role. Edwin M. Wright has charged that "the Zionist propaganda machine was efficient and thorough, blanketing the American political processes in systematic campaigns targeted at the general population, city halls, state houses, and on up the ladder to Washington." A study of American periodical coverage of the Palestine debate confirmed that the Zionist viewpoint dominated the medium, with an emphasis on the humanitarian and religious aspects of the movement. Recent studies of Harry Truman's role in the propartition decision agree that Zionist-generated political pressure proved the major factor in the White House overruling State Department advice, a conclusion James Forrestal bitterly reached thirty years ago.[54]

While it is undoubtedly true that many considerations went into the creation of American policy, the fact remains that a sudden and dramatic shift took place in the fall of 1947, with Truman consistently overriding the State Department, and that the American public overwhelmingly supported partition. Moreover, the capacity to generate the propaganda, to organize mass rallies and telegram campaigns, to secure the help of important personages, both Jew and non-Jew, to touch the various nerve points in the political system—all this did not happen overnight. The success of the Zionist effort in 1947 represented nearly five years of work, organization, publicity, education, and the careful cultivation of key people in different fields. While the politicians may have reacted to the alleged existence of Jewish bloc-voting in major cities and states, the real power of the American Zionists resulted from their ceaseless and ultimately successful efforts first to win over the Jewish community and then the American public to its side, thus securing the help of influential men and women in the press, the church, the arts, and above all, the government. In the process, the plight of the displaced persons of Europe played an ever-present role.

But even though the United Nations had voted, there remained much to do. Rabbi Abba Hillel Silver, the architect of the American victory, declared: "November 29 was only the evening and the morning of the first day—the day when light broke through the darkness of our world. Our great community, providentially spared for this hour, must now shoulder the vast economic burdens involved in the setting up of the Jewish State. . . . Our people are fully aware of their new responsibilities and are resolved to meet them. Whatever aid may come from other sources, the primary responsibility is ours."[55] Silver could not yet know that American Zionists would have to wage one more battle with the State Department to save the partition decision. But he was well aware that while he had led the public drive to secure a Jewish state, another section of American Jewry had been secretly at work for nearly two years helping to arm the *Yishuv* in preparation for its fight for survival.

Chapter 6

THE RETURN TO ZION

"Zion shall be redeemed in justice!" thunders the prophet, and despite the military exploits of the ancient Hebrews, the Jewish tradition has always emphasized ethics and morality. The Jewish model has been the scholar, not the soldier, and it is one of the tragic ironies of history that after centuries of prayer and decades of back-breaking labor in reclaiming the land, Israel was reborn amid blood and fire. In the years between the Holocaust and the end of the Israeli War for Independence, American Jewry came to understand that, while in a messianic age the lion and the lamb may lie down together in peace, in a far less than perfect world the lamb will normally be slaughtered.

The leading exponent of "redemption through justice," Chaim Weizmann, opposed not only the militant political tactics of Silver and Ben-Gurion, but also, in the name of Jewish morality, could not accept either the terrorist struggle waged by the Irgun or the decision of the Haganah to move from purely defensive activity to more aggressive resistance to British policy in Palestine. "Our only force is moral force," he asserted. "A policy of destruction can rebound only on ourselves, and it is we who will be destroyed." The *Yishuv*, he lamented, has "chosen the revolver and the bomb as the salvation in the present calamitous situation and I confess I doubt the Messiah will arrive at the sound of high explosives."[1] Nearly all the major Jewish and Zionist leaders condemned the terrorism of the Stern group and Irgun, arguing that such activities only jeopardized chances of establishing a Jewish homeland. "Our bitterness," explained one editorial about the terrorists, "is, as Ben-Gurion said on a comparable occasion, as the very bitterness of death. What have these insanely misguided people done? They have given our brutal and stupid enemy a weapon of incomparable power and effectiveness against us. That is all—all they have accomplished."[2]

Yet in the face of British oppression in Palestine, what could the Yishuv do but resist? Some even justified, if they could not applaud, the terrorism. For years the mandatory authorities had applied a double standard: Arabs caught with illegal weapons had them confiscated; Jews received jail sentences. Even on the rare occasion when the courts imprisoned an Arab, the penalties proved relatively light. What justice could be found in meting out a seven-year sentence to a Jew caught with two rounds of ammunition, while an Arab with a rifle and eighty-six rounds got off with six months?[3] That the Jew should practice non-violence in a Christian world full of violence, Stephen Wise averred, is asking too much of a people who had suffered the Holocaust. Meyer Weisgal confessed himself beset by doubts. The Jews had nothing to apologize for to the Christians, since "nothing that we can do will ever expiate their sins. But it has no relation to our acts. . . . What does it do to us? It eggs on evil as an end in itself. But there is no compromise with evil. . . . It has succeeded in dragging us down to its own level. We were told, and a number of us believed, that this is the only language the goyim understand. It may be so, but not when the one who speaks it is a Jew."[4]

While the majority of American Jews continued to oppose terrorism, many gradually came to condone the Haganah's resistance to British rule. When the Haganah sank two British ships in Haifa harbor which were scheduled to deport illegal immigrants to Cyprus, Abba Hillel Silver hailed the incident in Boston and suggested that "the descendants of the Boston Tea Party will applaud them too, as well as all Americans who cherish the tradition of strong resistance to lawlessness and tyranny." A former Vice President of the United States, Henry A. Wallace, agreed that it had become "necessary for the Jews to conduct what amounts to a resistance movement of their own to arouse the conscience of the world."[5]

Some American Jews went even farther and publicly endorsed the underground war against the British. The Bergson group founded still another front, the American League for a Free Palestine, and once again Ben Hecht sounded the clarion. On September 5, 1946, *A Flag Is Born* opened at the Alvin Theater in New York. Starring Paul Muni, it portrayed the Irgun-British battle in terms of the children of light against the hosts of darkness. At the finale of each performance, when the Hebrew warriors called for young Jews to come "and fight for Palestine," the audience rose in enthusiastic applause, and a call for funds brought in thousands of dollars. As Eliahu Epstein exclaimed in frustration, the public "leaves the theater excited and impatient with everything that is not based on Irish methods of national struggle."[6]

The League pursued basically the same tactics it had during the war years—theatrical gestures, pageants, newspaper advertisements—all calling for Americans to help the Palestinian freedom fighters defeat the British. But during the war years the advertisements, however adversely they might have affected the Zionist public-relations campaigns, did not do any real damage; now, by openly endorsing terrorism, the League ran the risk of antagonizing powerful officials in Congress and the government. Despite appeals from regular Zionist organizations, the League would not desist. When Haganah moved to quash the Irgun and the Stern group, the League attacked the moderates as traitors. After the bombing of the King David Hotel in 1946, with the loss of ninety-one lives, the League openly applauded, and managed to portray General Sir Evelyn Barker's retaliatory policy in Hitleresque terms.[7]

Ben Hecht, in an open letter to the "Terrorists of Palestine" on May 15, 1947, wrote:

"My Brave Friends . . .

"The Jews of America are for you. You are their champions. You are the grin they wear. You are the feather in their hats.

"In the past fifteen hundred years every nation of Europe has taken a crack at the Jews. This time the British are at bat. You are the first answer that makes sense—to the New World.

"Every time you blow up a British arsenal, or wreck a British jail, or send a British train sky high, or rob a British bank or let go with your guns and bombs at the British betrayers and invaders of your homeland, the Jews of America make a little holiday in their hearts. . . ."[8]

Did the League accomplish anything? Other than generating spectacular publicity, the Bergson group had little to show for its labors in the two major projects it sponsored. In March 1948 it began a campaign to form a "George Washington Legion," and a few days after its initial call announced that more than three hundred men had volunteered. Early in May, the nominal head of the legion, Major Weiser, publicly registered with the government as a recruiting agent, and implied that the legion's services would be offered to the United Nations. However, no evidence exists of any "George Washington Legion" fighting in the Israeli War of Independence. One American, Harold Krausher, who did come to Israel, said that about twenty men on his ship from France had been recruited by the legion, and had their way paid, but of these, half actually came from Betar, the Revisionist Zionist youth movement. All twenty, the only known results of this flamboyant effort, served not in the Irgun, but in the regular army.[9]

The League's other project involved Aliyah Bet, the smuggling of illegal immigrants into Palestine. The League's "Repatriation Board" bought the S.S. *Abril* and renamed it the *Ben Hecht,* then sent it to France, where it picked up refugees to Palestine. On March 8, 1947, the British Navy intercepted the *Ben Hecht* near Haifa and transshipped 599 "illegals" to the detention camps in Cyprus. The League had a field day. Its first statement claimed that the *Ben Hecht* had left Europe "with over 900 Hebrew repatriates aboard. . . . News reports say that the ship was picked up with 600 passengers. Those 300 Hebrews unaccounted for did not disappear into thin air or into the Mediterranean. Let the British try to find them." No evidence has ever been produced to confirm the hint that 300 refugees had been landed before the boat's capture.[10]

But there was no doubt whatsoever that the eighteen American crewmen, all volunteers, subsequently languished in a British prison in Haifa. The League launched a major campaign to free the prisoners, and managed to arouse a good deal of anti-British sentiment. On March 21, 1947, Representative Andrew L. Somers of New York, who worked closely with the Bergson group, took the floor of the House to demand that Great Britain release the volunteers. "I want to emphasize," he said, "that the seamen in the crew of the *Ben Hecht* are not now in prison as a result of their irresponsibility or willful violation of any recognized agreement. Those men are in prison because they carried out what we—again and again—told them we wanted carried out. In perfect good faith, every one of those seamen had reason to believe, and I am sure they were right, that they were serving this country's interest in embarking upon such a merciful venture." The British, who had just received a large loan from the United States and hoped for more aid in the future, decided to free the men. They arrived back in New York on

April 16, and two days later received the city's welcome on the steps of City Hall, where Acting Mayor Vincent R. Impellitteri said they symbolized "American determination to save the Hebrews of Europe and to help transport them to Palestine."[11]

The *Ben Hecht* and the *Exodus-1947* were only two of the more publicized incidents in the long campaign to smuggle survivors of the Holocaust into Palestine. For the most part directed and carried out by a branch of the Haganah, it had an important American element. As early as 1944, the Joint Distribution Committee, which had always been exceedingly scrupulous in abiding by both the spirit and the letter of international law, had been stung by Zionist accusations that such an attitude could only result in the deaths of more Jews. The directors were forced to agree, and began actively defying the existing Palestinian laws on immigration; the JDC, undoubtedly with the knowledge of the American Jewish Committee leaders, channeled large sums of money to Mossad, the Haganah's agency for "parallel immigration," for its smuggling work. Indeed, nearly all of the money for Aliyah Bet, the illegal immigration, came from the United States, for the most part from the Joint and the Jewish Agency, and the British on several occasions complained of this to the State Department. Moreover, many Americans helped man this ragtag armada; ten ships with entirely American crews brought 40 per cent of the *ma'apilim* (illegal immigrants) to their new homeland.[12]

The Joint also stepped in to help care for the refugees on Cyprus after the British banned the Jewish Agency from those camps. Many of the JDC teams consisted of Haganah members who helped prepare the survivors for their eventual life in a Jewish state. The bulk of the welfare work, however, devolved upon Hadassah, which also operated under the aegis of the Joint. In charge was American-born Rose Viteles, a member of the Hadassah Council in Palestine, and, as it became known much later, one of the organizers of the Haganah in Jerusalem. Hadassah soon provided doctors and nurses, and Tamar deSola Pool arranged for an entire educational system, including teachers and books, to be moved from the Ruttenberg Foundation in Haifa to the Cyprus camps. The last Hadassah team left Cyprus with the last detainees, on February 16, 1949.[13]

*   *   *

Smuggling immigrants was undoubtedly the most appealing and most humane aspect of Jewish resistance, and the easiest to rationalize in terms of "breaking the law," since the Zionists had built up the case that the British White Paper itself broke the law of the Mandate. But while the *Yishuv* needed and wanted immigrants, it would never be able to win the anticipated battle for survival with bodies alone. An army needs guns and munitions and supplies with which to fight, and the British were doing their best to deprive the *Yishuv* of these materials. Yet for all the customs inspections and raids on kibbutzim, somehow the Haganah accumulated what it needed, not in great amounts, but just enough. Not until years later would details of how they did this become known.

The story began with David Ben-Gurion's visit to the United States in June 1945, following the London Zionist conference. He talked to Jewish leaders in all walks of life, and found them willing to help care for the refugees and to do political work, but they shied away from his suggestion that the *Yishuv* would have to fight not only to establish a Jewish state, but also probably for its very survival. Finally he called Meyer Weisgal to his hotel room in New York, and for three hours explained the situation as he saw it, and the problems he had encountered in America. Could Weisgal get thirty or so men who would follow him blindly, who would do what he wanted without asking questions? Weisgal promised him an answer within twenty-four hours.

"I suppose you want to discuss it with your boss," said Ben-Gurion; "Exactly," came the reply.

Weisgal immediately went to Weizmann, then also in New York, and repeated the story. Weizmann, torn between his own moderate views and the realization that Ben-Gurion's analysis could be right ("Perhaps they do need a Bar Kochba"), finally said, *"Nu, loz sich arumdreyn an eydem in shtub."** Weisgal returned to Ben-Gurion and said he would help. Together with Henry Montor, he drew up a list and invitations were sent out.[14]

At 9:30 in the morning of July 1, 1945, nineteen American Jews and three Palestinians—Ben-Gurion, Eliezer Kaplan, and Reuven Zaslani—met in the Manhattan penthouse of millionaire Rudolph G. Sonneborn. There Ben-Gurion asked a simple question: "Would

---

* Literally, "O.K., let's have a young son-in-law hanging about the house." The meaning of this folk idiom refers to a Jew who is looking for a son-in-law when he hasn't a daughter. A friend asks him, "What do you want with a son-in-law when you haven't a daughter?" The answer: "Who knows? Something good may come of it."

America take in the refugees?" He did not wait for a response, since all those present knew the answer. He launched into his reading of the situation: Only Palestine wanted the refugees; the British would not admit them; eventually the British would be forced to give up the Mandate; at that time the *Yishuv* would have to fight for its life; in order for it to carry on that struggle, it would have to prepare; to do that, the *Yishuv* needed help, now, from American Jews. Several years later, Sonneborn wrote: "On that memorable day, we were asked to form ourselves into an . . . American arm of the Haganah. We were given no clue as to what we might be called upon to accomplish, when the call might come, or who would call us. We were simply asked to be prepared and to mobilize like-minded Americans. We were asked to keep the meeting confidential."[15]

Over the next several months, Sonneborn and his associates gradually created the apparatus that did, in fact, become the American arm of the Haganah. The so-called "Sonneborn Institute" began meeting at luncheon sessions every Thursday in a private dining room at the Hotel McAlpin. Slowly the group around the horseshoe-shaped table grew, as new members, all sworn to secrecy, joined them. For a long time the Institute's main work consisted of identifying men in key industries, who in turn set up small committees to do the actual work. In mid-1946, Sonneborn began raising funds for purposes which could not be fully disclosed, much less publicized—purchase of boats and planes, of surplus arms and jeeps, as well as warehousing and shipping operations that moved all these goods to Europe where they could be stored until the termination of the Mandate.

On the grounds that the fewer people who knew about the operations, the less chance of their being discovered, even the gentlemen at the McAlpin were told next to nothing outside their own areas of responsibility. Yet not knowing made their work seem more mysterious, more dangerous, and in some ways this American branch could vicariously share in the danger and romance of the fighters in Palestine. "Haganah is the biggest romance," said one member from Philadelphia, "it is the greatest thing certain Jews have had happen to them in this country. I have known Jews all my life who were waiting for this day that they could point to another Jew that carried a gun and say, 'He represents me,' meaning not a gangster but a hero." Another man agreed, declaring that people totally unaffiliated with Zionism, some who did not even give to the UJA, had offered contributions. By the end of the year, the Institute, working through private parlor meetings, was raising a hundred thousand dollars a week for the Haganah.[16]

As the Jewish army-in-the-making began to form, the Institute members, together with Palestinians detailed to the United States, organized a fantastic network to gather the materials needed for the men and women in the field. Fortunately for the Haganah, the American army and navy were selling huge quantities of surplus materials at a fraction of their original cost. The sharp-eyed buyers of the Institute eagerly snapped up hundreds of radio sets, field tents, mobile kitchens, and the other paraphernalia needed by a modern army. Nor were Jews alone involved in this work; many non-Jews, aware that they were helping the Palestinians in their fight for independence, pitched in as well. A New Jersey amusement park owner covertly gathered thousands of rifles, while Connecticut state police officers overtly did the same. Guns and ammunition were packed in the bottom two thirds of huge oil drums, covered with tarpaper and a layer of plaster of paris, and the remaining six inches filled with real oil. Lead ballast would be added to make sure the drum of "oil" weighed what it should. Used machinery, capable of making guns and mortars, could also be secured through U. S. Army surplus. The "Institute" bought enough machines to stock a decent-sized factory, then disassembled them. The key elements, as well as the plans, could be smuggled into Palestine secretly, while the bulk of the equipment could be openly sent as "textile machinery."

No matter how carefully the network operated, there were bound to be leaks, and the police and the FBI were especially watchful for anything having to do with arms. But here also the "Institute's" members could help, for many of them had contacts with highly placed government officials. When buyers found and purchased two airplanes, for example, authorities refused them the necessary exit permits. Meyer Weisgal, purely on chance, approached Herbert Bayard Swope and explained the situation to him: These were the first planes they had been able to get, and would be the nucleus of the Jewish air force. Swope picked up the telephone and dialed Washington. When he reached the man he wanted, he said: "You remember when I was editor of the *World* and the Irish were fighting for their freedom, and you asked me to do something for you and I did? Now I'm going to ask you to do something for my people. I want you to give orders for those two planes to leave this afternoon. That's the only payment I want from you for my services to the Irish Republic." Two hours later the planes left.[17]

Another time a young Palestinian, bringing from Canada a small machine part in the trunk of his car, panicked when stopped at the border. He took off and drove through the night, with the police hunting him. At 4 A.M., he called Abraham Feinberg, chairman of the board of Kayser-Roth and a member of the "Institute," and told him the story. First thing in the morning, Feinberg, through Robert Nathan, arranged an interview with FBI Director J. Edgar Hoover. Nathan explained to Hoover that a number of men were engaged in a secret operation. "It is not damaging to the United States, but it is not straight and above-board. Some prominent people and some important organizations could be hurt."

Hoover asked whether any of the weapons were to be used *in* the United States.

"No."

"Are they to be used *against* the United States?"

"Absolutely not."

Hoover made no promises, but the young man agreed to plead guilty to a minor charge, the "Institute" paid the fine, and a ship full of "textile machinery" sailed a few days later for Palestine.[18]

Not all the help from non-Jews was so clandestine. A New York police raid on a deserted warehouse found a large cache of guns, grenades, and ammunition, some of them stuffed into large bales of used clothing. The police immediately cordoned off the warehouse, thus preventing the shipment of the arms. Feinberg went directly to New York Mayor William O'Dwyer and said: "Bill, I'm going to put everything on the table." After hearing the story the mayor asked what Feinberg wanted him to do. "I want the detectives guarding the warehouse to be sick for twenty-four hours. I promise you everything will be out by then." O'Dwyer agreed, and the American Haganah had the warehouse emptied in time.

On the premises at the time of the raid were two young men, Joseph Untermeyer, son of the poet, and his friend, Isaiah Warshaw. When they came up for trial, Paul O'Dwyer defended them, and told the court that the Sullivan Law had been enacted "to prevent gangsterism," while "these guns were to be sent to Palestine to protect people in their houses." The young men said they knew nothing of hidden weapons, and the presiding magistrate dismissed the case. A few months later O'Dwyer defended five other couriers, this time caught red-handed loading crates of rifles aboard a truck. Using the same argument as before, O'Dwyer went on to say, "If there is any conspiracy at all, that conspiracy exists with the State Department and—" Before he could finish the sentence, the judge had broken in and declared the case dismissed. In New Jersey, five rabbinical students from Brooklyn were arrested for firing rifles in a field. They claimed that they had purchased the guns as war souvenirs and were shooting them off in celebration of a Jewish holiday, *Lag B'Omer*. When asked if they were not, in fact, testing the weapons for the Haganah, the students replied that indeed they hoped to contribute the guns to the Jewish cause. The justice took all of this at face value, fined them twenty-five dollars each, and suspended the sentence.[19]

By the end of 1947, the "American arm of Haganah" had developed an elaborate and secret network of procurement, warehousing, and shipping, and established a covert radio station linking the Haganah to its friends in the United States. On January 3, 1948, however, it looked as though the whole supply apparatus would be exposed and destroyed. Longshoremen on Jersey City's Pier F were loading seventy-seven large packing cases marked "Used Industrial Machinery" aboard the S.S. *Executor*, bound for Palestine. As the huge winch swung the twelfth case upward, it cracked open, revealing a row of tins clearly marked "TNT." Within minutes police swarmed over the pier, followed shortly by agents from the Federal Bureau of Investigation. A brief examination indicated that several of the crates held explosives, "enough to blow up all of Jersey City," and the "Used Industrial Machinery" could make arms—all contraband under federal law. By tracing the truck manifests back to the warehouses, the FBI could easily expose the entire operation, and only Feinberg's earlier contacts with J. Edgar Hoover prevented that. But the cover was blown.

Nahum Bernstein, an ex-OSS man who directed much of the "Institute's" field work, had insisted that each of the underground's activities be run under a separate cover company. In the wake of the TNT affair, he followed another OSS maxim: If one cover blows, create new ones. Fortunately, the United Nations resolution now allowed Sonneborn and his colleagues to operate much more openly, and by the end of the month a host of new "companies" had sprung up in New York. At 250 West 57th Street, the previously unnamed tenant in suite 1905 put a sign up on the door indicating that the office now housed "Materials for Palestine, Inc.," while on the fifth floor, Service Airways, Inc., moved into rooms 515 and 516. At 245 Fifth Avenue, the elevator operator accepted mail for the Radio Communications Engineering Company, and in a loft on lower Broadway, Inland Machinery and Metals opened for business. A little while afterward, the Thursday luncheon group received a list from the Haganah's Teddy Kollek indicating what the Jewish army would need:

The list included: 2 million sandbags; 1,000 tons of barbed wire; 100,000 square feet of corrugated iron; 10,000 each of coats, pairs of boots, raincoats, cots, and canteens; 40,000 blankets; 30,000 pairs of socks; 1,000 pairs of binoculars; 1,000 telephones; 50 miles of telephone cable; 50 switchboards; 1,000 Jeeps; 200 motorcycles; 50 water trucks; 1,000 bicycles; 1,000 2½-ton trucks; 1,000 ¾-ton trucks; 300 searchlights; 30 drafting tables; 200 Hebrew typewriters; 10 English typewriters; a print shop; 200 megaphone systems . . .[20]

The list continued for three pages. Nothing in it was actually contraband. Solicitations could now be made openly, and all purchases and shipping could be legitimately handled through Materials for Palestine, Inc.

The time of testing would not be long delayed, and while the Jews of Palestine prayed that the end of the Mandate would pass peacefully, they prepared for the worst. The *Yishuv* now numbered about 650,000, of whom 54,000 belonged to the Haganah. But of these over 41,000 were either untrained adolescents or middle-aged men unfit for combat. The actual fighting strength consisted of the 3,000-member elite Palmach commandos, 9,500 regular troops, and perhaps 1,000 men of the Irgun. Their arsenal, comprised of homemade mortars, stolen British arms, antiquated surplus items (many dating from the First World War or even earlier), and smuggled goods, amounted to 10,500 rifles, 3,500 submachine guns, 900 heavier-caliber machine guns, 672 one-inch mortars, and for heavy artillery, 84 three-inch cannons.[21] Materials for Palestine, Inc., would get the auxiliary equipment needed by an army, while the secret purchase of weapons was shifted to Europe, where Haganah agents, using American money, found Czechoslovakia eager to sell arms with no questions asked and no restrictions on where they could be shipped.

But all this took money, and although the UJA now listed Haganah as one of its beneficiaries, the amounts raised through that channel would at most put a small dent in Teddy Kollek's list. At the Jewish Agency Executive meeting, Ben-Gurion warned that only if the Jews were armed would they be able successfully to establish the Jewish

state; a weak *Yishuv* might well lead the United Nations to back away
from the partition plan. American Jewry, Ben-Gurion told Silver, had
two supreme tasks: to maintain political pressure on the American government in support of partition, and to raise the funds needed to equip
the *Yishuv*.[22]

But Ben-Gurion worried whether enough cash could be raised.
Eliezer Kaplan, the treasurer of the Jewish Agency, had returned to
Palestine from the United States in early 1948 to report on "the growing sense of Jewish solidarity and of the widespread readiness to take
part in the struggle for our national future." But, he added, at best he
thought 10 million to 25 million dollars might be raised, less than half
of what the *Yishuv* would need.[23] Ben-Gurion wanted to leave for the
United States immediately to see if he could do better than that, but
Golda Meyerson told him that he could not leave Palestine. "No one
can take your place here," she said, "while I may be able to do what
you can do in the United States." When Ben-Gurion argued this, she
suggested that it be put to a vote. A few hours later, unable to return to
her flat in Jerusalem, she boarded a plane to America wearing the same
dress she had worn to the meeting, with a light winter coat over it, and
no luggage. She landed in a New York blanketed by its worst snow-
storm in sixty years, and sought out Henry Montor, who managed to
squeeze her onto the program of the Council of Jewish Federations and
Welfare Funds, then meeting in Chicago.

Golda—"our Golda," as American Jews would call her—had been
raised in Milwaukee, and after her *aliyah* in the 1920s had returned to
the States on several occasions to work for Pioneer Women. But while
some of the Zionists knew her well, the non-Zionists of the federations
had little idea of whom this woman was, in plain, unfashionable dress,
but with a commanding air about her. Yet a few minutes after she
started to speak, not a person in the hall had a mind for anything but
the message she brought from Palestine. The *Yishuv* would fight to the
end, she said. "If we have arms to fight with, we will fight with them.
If not, we will fight with stones in our hands.

"I want you to believe me when I say that I came on this special
mission to the United States today not to save seven hundred thousand
Jews. During the last few years the Jewish people lost six million Jews,
and it would be audacity on our part to worry Jews throughout the
world because a few hundred thousand more Jews are in danger.

"That is not the issue. The issue is that if these seven hundred thousand Jews in Palestine can remain alive, then the Jewish people as such is alive and Jewish independence assured. If these seven hundred thousand people are killed off, then for centuries we are through with the dream of a Jewish people and a Jewish homeland.

"My friends, we are at war. There is no Jew in Palestine who does not believe that finally we will be victorious. That is the spirit of the country. . . . But this valiant spirit alone cannot face rifles and machine guns. Rifles and machine guns without spirit are not worth very much, but spirit without arms can, in time, be broken together with the body.

"Our problem is time. The question is what we can get immediately. And when I say immediately, I do not mean next month. I do not mean two months from now. I mean now. . . .

"We are not a better breed; we are not the best Jews of the Jewish people. It so happened that we are there and you are here. I am certain that if you were in Palestine and we were in the United States, you would be doing what we are doing there, and you would ask us here to do what you will have to do. . . .

"You cannot decide whether we shall fight or not. We will. . . . That decision is taken. Nobody can change it. You can only decide one thing: whether we shall be victorious in this fight or whether the Arabs will be victorious. That decision American Jews can make. It has to be made quickly, within hours, within days.

"And I beg of you: Don't be too late. Don't be bitterly sorry three months from now for what you failed to do today. The time is now."

They listened, they wept, and they gave. Kaplan had said that all of American Jewry might raise fifteen million dollars, yet in that one afternoon the federation leaders, men who for the most part had been indifferent to the idea of a Jewish state only a few short years before, emptied their pockets for this small, intense, and magnificent woman. They wrote checks for themselves, and then they made pledges for their communities, committing their own personal assets, homes, and businesses as collateral against bank loans so that cash could be gotten immediately. In that one afternoon, American Jewry raised *twenty-five million dollars* for the *Yishuv*, and a buoyant Golda wired Tel Aviv that they had "twenty-five stephens," their code word reflecting their esteem of the venerable American Zionist leader who accompanied her on much of her tour. Astounded at her Chicago triumph, American Zionist leaders quickly arranged for her to speak in other cities, and from every stop went out a cable indicating the number of "stephens" that Ehud Avriel and his Mossad colleagues in Europe would have with which to purchase arms.[24]

She faltered only once. At Palm Beach, Florida, she was stunned at the elegance of the dinner crowd, their jewels and furs, and she mentally contrasted this scene of wealthy men and women vacationing in their posh resorts and that of Haganah soldiers freezing in the Judean hills. "These people don't want to hear about fighting and death in Palestine," she thought, but she was wrong, and before the evening had ended, they had pledged her $1.5 million, enough to buy a winter coat for every soldier in the Haganah.[25]

When she returned to Palestine, Ben-Gurion himself came to meet her at Lydda airport, and told her: "Someday when history will be written, it will be said that there was a Jewish woman who got the money which made the state possible." Golda demurred, and in her memoirs wrote: "I always knew that these dollars were not given to me, but to Israel."

*   *   *

While Golda Meyerson toured America raising "stephens," Abba Hillel Silver toured Palestine, seeing for himself the problems facing the *Yishuv*. Before leaving at the end of January, he issued a statement in response to fears he had encountered within the *Yishuv* that the United States would retreat from its endorsement of partition before the scheduled termination of the British Mandate in May 1948. "For America now to withhold positive support," he declared, "at the very moment when Arab violence is directed toward frustrating [the partition plan], would be a betrayal of the United Nations and the Jewish people. Knowing the spirit of the American people, I venture the prediction that this will not happen." Silver correctly assessed the pro-Jewish sentiment of the people; poll after poll that winter showed a vast majority of Americans in favor of the creation of a Jewish state.[26] But the *Yishuv*'s anxieties about shifts in governmental policy would be justified all too soon, and the Zionists would have to mount one more campaign before a Jewish state came into being.

The United Nations partition plan pleased Jewish leaders primarily for its recommendation that a Jewish state be created, but few of them were satisfied with the specific details. Weizmann labeled the UN decision "a great moral success," but worried whether the plan would work. Abba Hillel Silver bluntly pointed out that partition had never been a

Zionist objective, but the plan "represented all that a committee representing the nations of the world was prepared to give us," and now the Jews would have to do the best they could. But if the Jews accepted partition as a necessary price for a Jewish state, the State Department saw it as a disaster. Despite the American vote in favor of the plan, by mid-December Secretary of State Marshall was privately telling his staff that the government might have made a mistake supporting partition.[27]

Strategists within the bureaucracy began warning that only Russia would benefit from partition, supposedly because it would replace Britain as the dominant power in the Middle East. Kermit Roosevelt, who frequently publicized the private views of the careerists, argued that the Soviet Union's propartition vote represented only the most recent move in its traditional plan to penetrate the Mediterranean region. Moreover, the recovery of Europe might well depend upon an adequate supply of oil both to the United States and the Marshall Plan nations; the United States, in order to protect Western democracy, could not antagonize the Arab world. Before the House Armed Services Committee, both Secretary of Defense James Forrestal and Vice Admiral Robert B. Carney, the deputy chief of naval operations, sounded dire predictions that Muslim response would endanger the flow of oil. Vice President James T. Duce of the Arabian-American Oil Company, and other oil executives, prophesied terrible consequences unless the government won back Arab goodwill.[28]

The antipartitionists in the State and Defense departments recognized that they faced strong popular opposition, since the American people overwhelmingly supported the creation of a Jewish state. But they found and exploited the weak spot in the Zionist armor, the strong reluctance of the public to commit American troops to enforce the United Nations resolution. In mid-1946, when the British first raised the question of using American troops to keep order in Palestine, 74 per cent of the populace opposed the idea. On the eve of the partition vote, only 3 per cent of the sample were willing to have American soldiers keep the peace, although 65 per cent said they would favor a UN army. In February 1948, with shooting rampant in the Holy Land, only 43 per cent now approved of a UN force that would include Americans.[29]

General Alfred M. Gruenther, in charge of planning for the Joint Chiefs of Staff, informed the White House in mid-February that from

80,000 to 160,000 troops were required to impose the partition plan, and that if this were to be a UN force, then Soviet detachments would undoubtedly have to be included. Both Secretary of State Marshall and the chief UN delegate, Warren Austin, opposed the use of troops, even UN troops. The Security Council, Warren informed its members, "is dedicated to keeping the peace, and not to enforcing partition." The Alsop brothers also joined in the alarum, warning that use of American soldiers in Palestine could well result in anti-Semitism at home. Even a "serious proposal to send troops," they wrote, "let alone the actual sending of them, would fan the flames of racial hatred in a dangerous and terrible manner." Senators Arthur Vandenberg and Owen Brewster, both counted as friends by the Zionists, declared they would not like to see a single American soldier fighting in the Holy Land.[30]

Events in Palestine in the early part of the year only reinforced the misgivings of State and Defense. The Arabs from neighboring states had infiltrated hundreds of irregulars into the country, where they harassed the *Yishuv* in ceaseless guerrilla warfare. Later analysis would show that the Arabs had disrupted communications, besieged Jewish cities, and inflicted casualties, but they had not taken a single settlement away from the Jews. Military analysts, however, began issuing jeremiads about the imminent destruction of the *Yishuv*. The Jews labored under a double handicap: The British would not allow them to import arms for defense, and the United States arms embargo prevented them from purchasing weapons here. The embargo, forbidding arms shipments to troubled areas, was originally proclaimed as a gesture of neutrality; in effect it penalized only the Jews, since the Arabs secured the weapons they wanted from the British. Despite appeals from all sections of American Jewry, including the American Jewish Committee, Truman and the State Department refused to lift the embargo until after the War of Independence.

The Zionists, aware of the growing strength of antipartition sentiment in the United States government, reverted to their previously successful tactics of massive mail and telegram campaigns as well as personal contacts with Administration officials. The White House alone received more than three hundred thousand post cards on the Palestine question during this period, nearly all of them from Jewish groups and individuals urging action by the President to sustain the United Nations decision. But the enormous pressure caused an unexpected and dangerous reaction: Harry Truman got his dander up, and absolutely refused to see any Jewish leaders, while George Marshall gratefully followed suit. Chaim Weizmann, who had made an uncomfortable midwinter crossing to America at the Agency Executive's request in order to meet with American leaders, found all doors barred to him. A personal note to the President, pleading for "a few minutes of your precious time" in the interest of preventing a "catastrophe" in Palestine, brought only a brusque official reply that an appointment would be "out of the question." Even the efforts of Democratic political chieftains like Ed Flynn of the Bronx could not budge Truman, who, at the slightest provocation, would rail against the "extreme Zionists" who would not leave him alone.[31]

But the Zionists were not to be put off. Frank Goldman, now president of B'nai B'rith, telephoned Eddie Jacobson, a member of Kansas City Lodge 184, but more importantly, an old friend of Truman who had served under him in the First World War and had been his partner in an ill-fated haberdashery store. Goldman explained the situation, and the following day, February 21, 1948, Jacobson wired a personal appeal to Truman: "I have asked you for very little in the way of favors during all our years of friendship, but am begging you to see Dr. Weizmann." When Truman still refused, Jacobson went to Washington and arranged to see the President on March 13. As he waited to go into the Oval Office, Matt Connelly, Truman's secretary, pleaded with him not to even mention Palestine.

Although Truman was always glad to see old friends, as soon as Jacobson started talking about Palestine, the President tensed and said that he would rather not discuss the subject, letting the whole problem run its course in the United Nations. But Jacobson, by now very self-conscious, would not stop, even when Truman started complaining about "how disrespectful and how mean" some of the Jewish spokesmen had been. Jacobson urged him not to count Weizmann among his enemies; Truman agreed, but said that if he saw Weizmann, it would only result in more wrong impressions. "I suddenly found myself thinking," Jacobson later recalled, "that my dear friend, the President of the United States, was at that moment as close to being an anti-Semite as a man could possibly be." Suddenly the Kansas City retailer noticed a small statue of Andrew Jackson in the office.

"He's been your hero all your life, hasn't he?" Jacobson asked. "You have probably read every book there is on Andrew Jackson. I remember when we had the store that you were always reading books and pamphlets, and a lot of them were about Jackson. You put his statue in front of the Jackson County Courthouse in Independence when you built it."

Now he had the President's full attention.

"Well, Harry, I too have a hero. I have never met him, but I have studied his past as you have studied Jackson's. He is the greatest Jew alive, perhaps the greatest Jew who ever lived. I am talking about Dr. Chaim Weizmann. He is an old man and a very sick man. He has traveled thousands of miles to see you, and now you are putting him off because you were insulted by some of our American Jewish leaders. It does not sound like you, Harry, because I thought you could take this stuff they have been handing to you."

Truman, in the big swivel chair, spun away from Jacobson and for a moment or two stared out into the Rose Garden; then he spun back.

"You win, you bald-headed son-of-a-bitch. I will see him."

Truman quickly arranged an appointment for Weizmann, but insisted that it be private, with no public announcement and no press coverage. On March 18, an unmarked staff car drove in through the East Gate of the White House, and the ailing Weizmann had his long-deferred interview with the President, in which he pleaded for continued American support of the partition plan. Truman listened sympathetically, and assured Weizmann that the United States would press forward.[32]

Within twenty-four hours, however, Warren Austin proposed that the partition plan be abandoned and that a special session of the General Assembly convene in order to establish a trusteeship over Palestine. This *volte-face* by the United States set off a storm of protest and confusion. "It took the British 25 years to sell out," wailed one Zionist leader, "the Americans have done it in two and a half months." Bernard Baruch demanded that Austin explain "our weather-vaning attitude" on Palestine, in which the United States first asked the world to follow its lead, and then abruptly changed its mind. Clark Clifford reported that every Jew in America considered Truman a "no-good" who placed greater value on oil than on human lives. The Synagogue Council of America, an organization which crossed every line of division in American Jewry, called for a day of prayer "to give expression to the shocked conscience of America at the inexplicable action of our Administration in reversing its Palestine policy and to demand the fulfillment of the plighted word of this country and of the nations of the world, and to pray for God's help."[33]

Nor were Jews the only ones outraged by the shift in policy. *Time* magazine declared that "Harry Truman's comic opera performance had done little credit to the greatest power in the world." Eleanor Roosevelt offered her resignation from the American United Nations delegation, while Helen Gahagan Douglas, Leon Henderson, I. F. Stone, and other liberals condemned the President, with the Republicans, led by Thomas Dewey, in hot pursuit as well. At the White House, mail ran twenty-two to one opposing the reversal in policy.[34]

Many observers suggested that the shift represented a loss of control by the President over foreign policy, and a resurgence of State Department influence. In large part they were right, but they did not know at the time that the careerists, seizing upon Truman's earlier approval of a contingency plan, had decided to implement that strategy, despite the fact that the necessary preconditions for its adoption did not exist. Truman had agreed that if the situation in Palestine deteriorated, the United States might seek some form of trusteeship to hold things in order until a peaceful solution could be worked out. The Middle East desk decided that the guerrilla fighting warranted such a move, and instructed Austin to propose abandonment of partition. Truman, livid with rage, ordered Samuel Rosenman to New York to explain the situation to Weizmann, and more importantly, directed his special assistant, Clark Clifford to find out how the mixup had occurred in the first place. From this point onward, American policy toward Palestine took on a new tone.

Much of the historiographical debate over Truman's recognition of Israel—indeed, his entire Palestine policy—has concerned the extent to which domestic political considerations intruded in the realm of foreign policy. Certainly the Zionists used every weapon in their arsenal to bring pressure on the President. Truman had shown through his demand for entry of the one hundred thousand refugees that he had been deeply moved by their plight. Yet time and again he insisted that domestic politics could not and should not be allowed to dictate the nation's foreign policy. From the fall of 1947 through the spring of 1948, Truman did his best to resist the demands of Democratic Party chieftains for a more pro-Zionist Palestine program. Within the Administration, Secretary of State Marshall and Secretary of Defense Forrestal urged Truman not to yield to political expediency.[35] In large measure, the shifts in American policy reflected Truman's ambivalence; with the emergence of Clifford as a key adviser on domestic affairs, political and humanitarian considerations achieved dominance over the oil-centered *realpolitik* of State and Defense strategists.

Clifford made no bones about the fact that Truman, in running for election in 1948, would need Jewish votes, and that he could not get those votes unless he actively supported the creation of a Jewish state. The Democrats had been losing Jewish support even before the March debacle; at a special election in the Bronx, normally under the control of Democratic boss Ed Flynn, a minor-party candidate, running primarily against Truman's Palestine policy, easily defeated three opponents. On April 4, an estimated 50,000 Jewish war veterans paraded down New York's Fifth Avenue in protest against the partition reversal, and another 250,000 people held a mass rally at which speaker after speaker denounced the Administration. Moreover, as Clifford pointed out, not only the Jews but also many segments of the American people wanted to see a Jewish state established, and were confused and angry about American reversals in policy. As for the oil argument, the Arabs could really do very little other than cut off production completely, a step not likely to be taken since the Arab governments had no other source of revenue. Public support of a humanitarian policy which would reap great political benefit—all this Truman could have, but only if he decided upon a firm policy and stopped vacillating.

Was Truman's Palestine policy, therefore, nothing more than political expediency? Politics certainly played a part, but to look at it only in that light is to miss the complex interaction of foreign affairs and domestic politics in a democratic society. For a foreign policy to be successful, it must have popular support; moreover, the demands of particular segments of society, providing they do not antagonize other groups, must be taken into account. The State Department experts, for all their supposed sophistication about international relations, proved themselves remarkably naïve in this area. Richard Crossman, in a speech in Commons defending Truman against one of Bevin's tirades, proved more perceptive about the workings of the American system than most of the members of the Middle East desk. "It is easy to make jibes about the votes in New York and to insult the President of a great republic," he said. "But if we had a million Jews in this country, our Cabinet might have been slightly more careful to keep their election pledges. Do not let us attack American politicians for what we ourselves would have done. . . . Anyone who thinks that it was just the Jewish vote in New York that made Mr. Truman a sincere and ardent Zionist must be very badly informed; and anyone reckless enough to take the word of a State Department official who thought that he would wangle the White House into letting down the Jews cannot have much experience and should not believe it. America could have nothing but a Zionist policy in Palestine. Politicians have to face the facts, and we ought to have faced the fact that America could not be persuaded to condone the destruction of Israel, or its overrunning by the Arabs, or anything of that sort."[36]

On April 23, 1948, the eve of Passover, the holiday of freedom celebrating the Hebrew exodus from Egypt, Truman sent word that he had decided on a policy. As Chaim Weizmann prepared to leave his hotel suite to attend a Seder service, he received an urgent request to come to the Essex House, where Samuel Rosenman lay incapacitated by an injured leg. Rosenman, whom many of the Zionists suspected of being unfriendly to their cause, told Weizmann that the President had spoken to him earlier that day, and had begun the conversation by saying that he had "Dr. Weizmann on my conscience." Truman wanted Rosenman to reassure Weizmann that the United States would not desert the Zionists. A few days earlier, the President had directed that conduct of the Palestine policy be transferred from Loy Henderson to General Hilldring; the new trusteeship proposal would not be pushed in the General Assembly; and most importantly, if the Jewish state were declared, the United States would recognize it immediately. But Truman would deal only with Weizmann, not with the militant Silver, and the substance of the conversation could not be made public.[37]

Much anxiety within Zionist ranks could have been avoided had Weizmann been able to tell his colleagues what he now knew. A meeting of the WZO Actions Committee in Palestine that same day had wrestled with the decision of whether or not the Yishuv should declare independence on May 15, and finally, agonizingly agreed that no other course was possible.[38] Moreover, American Zionist leaders would have greeted the final State Department campaign with less resentment had they known that the careerists had been outflanked. But they did not know this, and in the final weeks before the Mandate was scheduled to expire, they had to resist an enormous amount of pressure from George Marshall on down to delay, if not give up on the idea of a Jewish state.

Military analysts in the government believed that the Yishuv, with little more than 650,000 people, could not withstand a concentrated military assault from an Arab world numbering over 50 million, and in the early months of 1948 the Haganah seemingly fared poorly at the hands of Arab irregulars. Weizmann, Silver, Neumann, and other Jewish leaders were implored to give up statehood, at least temporarily, in order to avoid the bloodbath which seemed sure to follow British withdrawal. When Jewish leaders resisted this argument, subtle and not so subtle threats crept into the conversations—governmental edicts prohibiting raising money in the United States for foreign arms purchases; the publication of documents detailing American support of Palestinian terrorism; pressures on American Jewry to support their government and not the Zionist leadership; and resort to the Security Council to have it proclaim Palestine a danger to world peace.

At the end of April, Dean Rusk, then an assistant secretary in charge of UN affairs, approached Moshe Shertok and Nahum Goldmann with a new plan, calling for delay of statehood while an emergency conference of Arab states, the Jewish Agency, and the UN committee on Palestine convened at which an amicable solution could be found. The President's own plane, the *Sacred Cow*, would be available to take the delegates to the meeting. The Zionist leaders were incredulous: Why did Rusk—or anyone else, for that matter—think that what had been impossible for thirty years of discussion would now be accomplished in ten days? At a midnight meeting of the American executive of the Agency on May 3, Silver, Neumann, Rose Halprin, and Rabbi Wolf Gold voted against the proposed delay, while Shertok and Goldmann voted for it. The following morning, with members of the political committee brought in, the American Section was still split, but with a firm majority opposed to any deferment. Shertok wired Rusk that acceptance of the new American procedure, which ignored the United Nations decision, "would involve us in a moral responsibility in respect of those proposals which we cannot possibly accept."[39]

A few days later, Secretary of State Marshall personally invited Shertok to meet with him in Washington. On May 8, one week before the scheduled end of the Mandate, Shertok, Marshall, and Under Secretary Robert A. Lovett met for an hour and a half. Marshall led Shertok to a map of Palestine. "Here you are surrounded by Arabs," he said, pointing to the Negev, "and here, in the Galilee, you are surrounded by other Arabs. You have Arab states all around you and your backs are to the sea. How do you expect to withstand this assault?"

"Believe me," Marshall continued, "I am talking about things which I know. You are sitting there in the coastal plains of Palestine while the Arabs hold the mountain ridges. I know you have some arms and your Haganah, but the Arabs have regular armies. They are well trained and they have heavy arms. How can you hope to hold out?"

When Marshall finished, Lovett suggested that if the Jewish Agency refrained from proclaiming a state, and the Arabs did attack, then the United States would have some grounds for intervention; it would be helping individuals rather than taking sides in a war between nations. But if the Agency persisted and war followed, the Jews would not be able to look to the United States for aid; they would have to fend for themselves.[40]

Shertok, obviously shaken, tried to remain as noncommittal as possible, but promised to deliver the Secretary's message to his colleagues in Palestine, as he planned to leave for the Holy Land within a few days. But he did push for some clearer understanding of American intent. Did the government actually want a Jewish state, and was trying to remove the difficulties in its way, or did it prefer to abort statehood? He appreciated Marshall's concern about the military problems, but the Secretary had to realize that the Jewish people stood on the threshold of fulfilling a two-thousand-year-old dream. For the Jewish Agency to consent to postponement, without the absolute assurance that statehood would inevitably follow the delay, meant that he and other Jewish leaders would be answerable to Jewish history for that decision, and this they could not do.

Before leaving for Palestine, Shertok returned to New York, where he reported to the American Section's political committee and unburdened himself of his fears. Silver and Neumann, aware that an adverse report by Shertok could sway the *Yishuv*'s leaders, called Rose Halprin aside and suggested that she go with Shertok. The Hadassah president knew full well how worried Shertok was about the risks involved, but refused, as she said, "to put myself in the *chutzpadik* position of accompanying Shertok." Instead, she wrote a letter to Ben-Gurion and asked Shertok, who was aware of its contents, to take it. In it she told Ben-Gurion of some of the pressures the American government had exerted to prevent statehood, but declared: "Don't worry about us. The American Jewish community is not to be worried about, and doesn't have to be worried about. You have to make up your mind. Your boys are going to die or not. You know whether you can fight the war, but for goodness sake don't let anybody talk about the pressure that we are under because we're not going to yield to that."[41]

When Shertok arrived in Palestine, Ben-Gurion had him brought to his office immediately, and they went over the situation fully. A few hours later, both men went into a meeting of the national council of the *Yishuv*, the elected body which would ultimately make the decision for or against proclaiming the state. Shertok described the fears in Washington, but nonetheless came out in favor of immediate statehood; he also brought word from Chaim Weizmann urging immediate action. Ben-Gurion, for the first time, revealed what the millions raised by Golda Meyerson in the United States had wrought: The Haganah had adequate arms, enough to offset the numerical advantage of the larger Arab armies. When Ben-Gurion called for a show of hands, the men and women around the table slowly, gravely, but unanimously agreed that the time had come for a Jewish state to be born.[42]

*   *   *

As the clock drew nearer to the end of the Mandate, tensions rose not only in Palestine, but also in London, Washington, New York, and in every Jewish community in the world. Only three weeks before, millions of Jewish families had concluded the Seder service of Passover, the festival of freedom, with the traditional chant *"l'shanah haba'ah b'yerushalayim!"* (Next year in Jerusalem!) Now that dream stood on the edge of realization. Although the Foreign Office still hoped that the United Nations would call on Great Britain to continue governing Palestine, Sir Alan Cunningham put in motion the final plans to have all of His Majesty's troops out of the Holy Land by midnight, May 15, 1948.

In Tel Aviv, a drafting committee appointed by David Ben-Gurion several weeks before now put its last revisions on the Declaration of Independence.

In New York, Chaim Weizmann wrote a letter to the President of the United States urging immediate recognition of the new state, and Weizmann's private secretary, Josef Cohn, took the night train to Washington to deliver the letter personally at the White House on Friday morning, May 14.[43]

In Washington, Harry Truman summoned his advisers once again to discuss what they should do. At a meeting a few days earlier,

Marshall and Lovett had strongly opposed recognition. When Clark Clifford pointed out that the President had already gone on record favoring an independent Jewish state, Marshall's face flushed. "Mr. President," he said, "this is not a matter to be determined on the basis of politics. Unless politics were involved, Mr. Clifford would not even be at this conference. This is a serious matter of foreign policy determination, and the question of politics and political opinion does not enter into it."[44] For the time being, Truman agreed; no decision would be taken.

But if ever any foreign policy issue was intertwined with domestic politics, Palestine was that issue. Much as the State Department had tried to keep the matter on a "professional" plane, American Jews and their friends had managed to make it the most emotion-laden question of the day. Jacob Arvey, Herbert Lehman, and other leaders of the Democratic Party besieged Truman to recognize the new state immediately. The few pro-Arab voices, like John Badeau, president of the American University at Cairo, were drowned out in an avalanche of letters and telegrams calling for recognition, while the media almost unanimously demanded the same policy.[45] Finally, even Marshall realized that the tide could not be stopped; moreover, the Haganah, in a series of quick victories beginning in late April, convinced the former chief of staff that the Jews might very well be able to handle the Arabs. So on May 14, he and Lovett informed the President that they no longer objected to recognition; but they urged caution rather than any precipitate move.

Clifford and David K. Niles, however, pushed Truman for immediate action. If the new state were to be recognized, let it be done at once. Such a move would not only bolster the position of the new nation, it would also win political support at home. Since it appeared that the Soviet Union too would extend recognition, the United States could also steal a march on its cold war opponent. Truman, determined that his pledge to Chaim Weizmann would not be undercut again by the State Department, agreed, and Clifford called up the Jewish Agency's Washington representative, Eliahu Epstein, and told him: "You'd better write a letter asking us for recognition."[46]

At almost the same moment that Epstein prepared to draft his letter, David Ben-Gurion rose and called to order a meeting in Tel Aviv's municipal museum. There, in front of a portrait of Theodor Herzl, he picked up a parchment scroll and slowly began to read:

"Eretz-Israel was the birthplace of the Jewish people. Here their spiritual, religious, and political identity was shaped. Here they first attained to statehood, created cultural values of national and universal significance, and gave to the world the eternal Book of Books.

"After being forcibly exiled from their land, the people kept faith with it throughout their Dispersion and never ceased to pray and hope for their return to it and for the restoration in it of their political freedom. . . .

"We, members of the People's Council, representatives of the Jewish community of Eretz-Israel and of the Zionist movement, are here assembled on the day of the termination of the British Mandate over Eretz-Israel and, by virtue of our natural and historic right and on the strength of the resolution of the United Nations General Assembly, hereby declare the establishment of a Jewish State in Eretz-Israel, to be known as the State of Israel. . . .

"Placing our trust in the Rock of Israel, we affix our signatures to this proclamation at this session of the Provisional Council of State, on the soil of the Homeland, in the city of Tel-Aviv, on this Sabbath eve, the fifth day of Iyar 5708 [May 14, 1948]."

At midnight in Jerusalem—6 P.M. in Washington—the British Mandate of more than a quarter century came to an end. The British flag now flew over no buildings in the Holy Land; in its place, in all areas under Jewish control, the blue-and-white ensign carrying the Star of David rose for the first time over sovereign soil. Eleven minutes later, President Harry Truman announced that the United States, the world's oldest democracy, had extended *de facto* recognition to the world's newest, the State of Israel. He then telephoned his special assistant, David Niles who had pleaded the Jewish case so effectively, and said: "Dave, I want you to know that I just announced recognition. You're the first person I called because I knew how much this will mean to you."[47]

At the United Nations a few minutes later, I. L. "Sy" Kenen slipped into the Assembly chamber and handed a slip of yellow paper, torn from the teletype machine with the news of Truman's announcement, to Abba Hillel Silver. The Cleveland rabbi read it, incredulously at first, and then showed it to his colleagues, Rose Halprin, Emanuel Neumann, and Nahum Goldmann, who rose and broke into cheers. The news spread like wildfire, and soon Philip Jessup found himself surrounded by angry and confused delegates demanding to know if it were true.

Jessup charged out of the hall to a telephone, and a few minutes later, white-faced and shaken, returned and made his way to the rostrum, where he read Truman's two-sentence statement. In the corridor, Garcia Granados of Guatemala, who had labored behind the scenes to aid the Zionists, encountered an aide to the American delegation and asked about the news. "That is White House language," came the curt reply, "not State Department." Years later, in his memoirs, Truman allowed himself more than a touch of self-satisfaction when he wrote: "I was told that to some of the career men of the State Department the announcement came as a surprise. It should not have been if these men had faithfully supported my policy."[48]

In Tel Aviv, a little after midnight, the phone rang in Golda Meyerson's apartment. Expecting the worst, she picked it up to hear a jubilant voice tell her of Truman's announcement. "It was like a miracle," she recalled, "coming at the time of our greatest vulnerability, on the eve of the invasion. I was filled with joy and relief. All Israel rejoiced and gave thanks." Over the furious pleas of Paula Ben-Gurion, Ya'acov Yanai, the Haganah communications chief, pushed his way into the old man's bedroom to ask him to make a radio broadcast to the United States. The sleepy leader pulled a coat over his pajamas and had barely begun his statement when the crash of falling bombs rocked the studio. "Listen," Ben-Gurion told his audience, "those are the sounds of bombs falling on Tel Aviv." Near the Catholic Terra Sancta College in Jerusalem, Farnsworth Fowler, a CBS correspondent, picked up the news of American recognition on the BBC, and ran to tell Jewish policemen guiding military vehicles. For a few minutes they were all too busy dodging stray bullets, and all the Israelis could say was "Fine—that means we can get arms." When Walter Eytan of the Jewish Agency heard the news, he was skeptical, and in his diary wrote: "How one wished it were true, but surely the man was a babbler."[49]

In the United States people danced the *hora* in the street, waving small blue-and-white flags, and shouting *mazel tov* over and over again. At 2210 Massachusetts Avenue in Washington, where the Jewish Agency had its office, a group of congressmen, including Emanuel Celler, Jacob Javits, and Sol Bloom gathered with Eliahu Epstein. After a rabbi intoned a prayer, two children raised the Star of David, the old

Zionist flag and now the proud emblem of a new nation. When the flag reached the top of the pole, the crowd of hundreds spontaneously burst into *Hatikvah*—"So long as still within the inmost heart a Jewish spirit sings, so long as the eye looks eastward, gazing toward Zion, our hope is not lost—that hope of two thousand years, to be a free people in our own land, the land of Zion and Jerusalem."

1   Backdrop for a mass meeting in New York's Madison Square Garden in March 1945, protesting Britain's continued enforcement of the 1939 White Paper, which kept Jewish refugees from fascism out of Palestine. (Alexander Archer)

2 Jewish War Veterans march on Washington in July 1946 urging the
American government to force Great Britain into opening the gates of
Palestine to survivors of the Holocaust. (Alexander Archer)

3 Jewish Agency delegation at the United Nations waiting for the debate on the Partition resolution to begin. Left to right: Hayim Greenberg, Emanuel Neumann, David Ben-Gurion, Moshe Shertok (later Sharett), Nahum Goldmann, and Rose Halprin. (Alexander Archer)

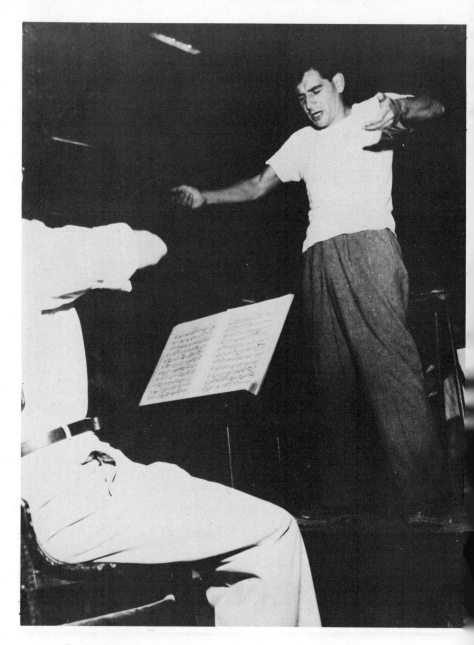

4 Leonard Bernstein conducting the Israel Philharmonic Orchestra at a special concert given for Israeli soldiers in November 1948. (Zionist Archives and Library)

5 Chaim Weizmann, first President of the State of Israel, presents Harry
S. Truman with a Torah scroll shortly after American recognition of the
Jewish State in 1948. (Zionist Archives and Library)

6   A delegation of Jewish leaders asking President Truman to extend economic aid to the Jewish State.

7   A similar delegation waiting to see Secretary of State John Foster Dulles during the Eisenhower administration about American foreign policy in the Middle East. (Zionist Archives and Library)

8   A *ma'abarah* at Holon, one of dozens of refugee camps hastily erected in Israel to accommodate the hundreds of thousands of refugees who poured into the Jewish State from Europe and Arab lands between 1948 and 1951. (Zionist Archives and Library)

Part Two

Zion and *Galut*

When the Lord brought back those that returned to Zion,
We were like unto them that dream.
Then was our mouth filled with laughter,
And our tongue with singing;
Then said they among the nations:
"The Lord hath done great things with these."
The Lord hath done great things with us;
We are rejoiced.

Psalms 126:1–3

Chapter 7

THE THIRD JEWISH COMMONWEALTH

Although Jews throughout the world had hoped that the new State of Israel could be born in peace, and that the states bordering Palestine would accept the United Nations resolution, the grim reality of Arab hostility soon dashed that dream. Even before the Mandate expired on May 14, 1948, Arab irregulars from Jordan, Syria, Lebanon, and Egypt began guerrilla attacks upon Jewish settlements and towns. Efforts by the *Yishuv* to reach King Abdullah of Jordan, the most moderate of the Arab leaders, merely brought news that the monarch privately welcomed the Jewish state and could live with it, but that if his brethren declared war he would have no choice but to join with them.[1]

Within hours after the Israelis declared their independence, Arab armies poured into the new state from Lebanon, Syria, Iraq, Jordan, and Egypt, all fully equipped with artillery, tanks, armored cars, and personnel carriers, and with more than adequate supplies of ammunition, oil, and gasoline. Egypt, Iraq, and Syria had air forces, and as sovereign states had little difficulty in purchasing additional military supplies on the world market. On May 15, the Haganah had very few weapons on hand, but with the proclamation of statehood, Israel could bring in the weapons it had purchased and stored in Europe. While still outsupplied, outmanned, and outgunned, the Haganah could now operate free of British harassment. There was no real battle plan. The Israelis had only one objective: to survive. Each settlement, each town, each outpost had somehow to make do with whatever it had, to hold off the invading forces until scarce supplies could be brought in to bolster the Jewish cause.

Despite a clear quantitative superiority in men and material, the Arab armies were unable to win the quick and easy victory predicted by Arab leaders, and both sides eagerly accepted the first UN truce, which went into effect on June 11, 1948. On July 9, after both armies had regrouped and resupplied, a new series of battles began, but this time the Israeli forces clearly dominated the action. The Arab siege of Jerusalem was broken, although the Old City remained in Jordanian hands, and the borders of the new state were extended to include all of the Negev, the Galilee, and the Jezreel Valley. Eventually, under UN mediation, the belligerents signed a number of armistices on the island of Rhodes in early 1949. The new Jewish state had been established, but at a cost of twenty months of fighting and six thousand lives, almost one per cent of the Jewish population at the time. The *Yishuv* had borne out David Ben-Gurion's prophecy on the night of May 15, 1948. Touring Tel Aviv after the first Egyptian bombings, he had scanned the faces of his countrymen. He saw worry and concern, but no fear or panic. Returning home, he wrote in his diary: *"Eilah ya'amdu."* (These will stand.)[2]

And as they endured, American Jewry, figuratively and literally, stood with them. American aid during the War for Independence manifested itself primarily through political and financial channels— raising huge sums of money, pressure on the American government, public relations, and, on a limited scale, the fighting of American Jews alongside Israelis.

As early as May 1945, Palestinian Jewish leaders, preparing for the possibility that they would have to fight for independence, had looked to the United States as a possible reservoir of soldiers. "In the near future," wrote Reuven Zaslani, "hundreds of thousands of young Jews serving in the American army overseas will be returning home. The experience of these men in the army and their contact with conditions in Europe has made them potentially good and devoted and keen Zionists." Zaslani's analysis seemed to bear fruit a year later, when four thousand members of the Jewish War Veterans marched on Washington in support of Truman's proposal to admit one hundred thousand refugees into Palestine. If the United States needed troops to help in implementing that demand, they said, they were ready to raise two divisions of Jewish ex-servicemen for that cause.[3]

Haganah began serious recruitment of these veterans in the fall of 1947 through such cover agencies as Land and Labor for Palestine, the Palestine Vocational Service, and Service Airways. Under the guise of informing prospective settlers about Palestine, these front groups, all connected and financed through the Sonneborn Institute, spread the news that a variety of interesting jobs were about to open in the Holy Land. The Intercollegiate Zionist Federation, B'nai B'rith Hillel, and rabbis steered volunteers to various Zionist youth groups, especially Habonim, while workers at the National Jewish Welfare Board combed through their servicemen's files for the names of pilots, bombardiers, and navigators.[4]

All told, between one thousand and fifteen hundred Americans eventually served in Mahal, the Israeli acronym for *mitnadvey huts la'-aretz* (volunteers from outside the country), the five-thousand-member international volunteer brigade. In order to protect the citizenship of the Americans, Israeli officials administered a limited oath of allegiance, so that it could be said they served "with" rather than "in" the Israeli armed forces. As Joseph Heckelman, who has done the most complete study of American volunteers, has written: "Under the then current [American] law, taking an abstract oath of allegiance to a foreign government (or voting in a foreign election) was clearly a cardinal offense, whereas actually risking one's life in the service of a foreign government could be presumed to be less reprehensible."[5]

Nearly all of the volunteers fought without pay, and the reasoning of one former merchant marine officer, born in America to a Polish immigrant laborer, is typical of hundreds of others. "There was nothing Zionist in my life," he later said, "no Zionist youth movement, nothing. When I got out in 1946, I began to read about the situation. When I heard about the call for the illegal immigration ships, I decided to find out about it. I asked only one question: Was it for pay or for no pay? They said it was for no pay, and I said, O.K., I'll go. If people were going to be paid, they could find better qualified people than me, and I wasn't interested. But if it's a volunteer deal, I said, O.K. I'd go. That was the beginning of my Zionism. Why? How do we know? There was what happened in Europe and what didn't happen. It's what the Nazis did and what the democratic countries didn't do. I'm a Jew, maybe I ought to put that first in explaining why. I really don't know where that fits. Then there's the fact that I was brought up in the American tradition, whatever that is. To me it means you're for the underdog, and these Jews were really the underdog."[6]

While Americans in Mahal served in all branches of the Israeli services, they were concentrated in, and made their greatest contribution to, the fledgling air force. During the war, the operational personnel—pilots, flight engineers, and navigators—were nearly all Americans; Israelis did not take over the bulk of the flying until 1949. American terms and procedures set the tone for the air force, and for the minuscule navy as well.[7]

Undoubtedly the most famous of all Mahal volunteers was Colonel David "Mickey" Marcus, a West Point graduate who had served on Esienhower's SHAEF headquarters staff during the war. Under the name "Mickey Stone," he brought a sense of administrative order and discipline to the Haganah, reorganized it, wrote the first training and procedures manual, and taught the officers the latest military tactics. The presence of such a high-ranking American officer did much to boost Israeli morale, and he had immediate access to Ben-Gurion and all the army leaders at all times. Tragically, he was the last Israeli casualty before the June 11 truce, killed by a nervous sentry in Jerusalem days after his brilliantly conceived strategy had lifted that city's siege. The Israelis flew his body home to America, accompanied by two young officers, Yosef Hamburger, a member of the *Exodus-*1947 crew, and a tough one-eyed *sabra*, Moshe Dayan. The governor of New York, the mayor of the city, and a former Secretary of the Treasury attended his funeral at a Brooklyn temple. Of the more than three thousand men buried at the United States Military Academy at West Point, Mickey Marcus is the only one to have been killed while fighting under a foreign flag.[8]

Marcus was not the only American to die for Israel; thirty-seven other Mahal volunteers also gave their lives in the fight for independence, together with a number of Hadassah medical personnel killed during the war. Yet for a number of years, the Israeli government ignored Mahal. During the early years of the state one could ascribe this official silence to the desire, both of Israel and the American volunteers, to avoid legal complications which might arise if the extent of the latter's involvement became widely known. However, there is no justification for the omission from official Israeli literature of any mention of the memorial forest planted halfway between Jerusalem and Tel-Aviv in memory of the fallen American and Canadian members of

Mahal. Nor can one find a reason for the government's tabling of a 1965 proposal to celebrate Israel Independence Day in the United States with Mahal as the theme.

Heckelman suggests that the explanation lies in part in the insecurity of the young nation, born in fire and not yet mature enough to concede that outsiders helped achieve the victory. But he also notes the resentment that many Israelis felt toward American volunteers.[9] On a ratio of volunteers to size of the overall Jewish community, American Jewry sent a minuscule contingent, proportionally only one fiftieth that of the much smaller South African community. Moreover, very few of the Americans involved in either the Aliyah Bet rescue work or Mahal remained in Israel as settlers. One air force officer described the volunteers as "Americans first of all, and they remained that way throughout everything." When the war ended, they went home, inviting bitter denunciations by Israelis that their land was good enough to die for, but evidently not good enough for Americans to live in. Only in the afterglow of the 1967 victory did the Israeli government finally begin acknowledging the Mahal role in the struggle for statehood.

The Israelis proved more willing to acknowledge the financial and political support extended by American Jewry during the war. Golda Meyerson, who earlier in the year had secured $50 million with which to arm the state-in-the-making, returned to this country in May 1948 with another blunt message: The war would not be won by speeches or declarations or even tears of happiness. Americans had their role to play, and they could do their share in the establishment of the Jewish state by paying the bills. "We cannot go on without your help," she told dozens of audiences. Once again they responded to this plainspoken woman who personified the heroism and determination of the new state.[10] In 1948, American Jews gave $150 million to the United Jewish Appeal, and the following year, even though the immediate crisis had passed, $103 million, most of which found its way to Israel. And while Golda raised the money, Ben-Gurion turned to another American woman to spend it.

Almost immediately after declaring its independence the Israeli government had applied to the United States for a $100 million development and reconstruction loan, but the Truman administration could not approve it while the fate of the new nation still hung in the balance. In the meantime, the Israeli economy suffered from the dislocations of war, with arms purchases devouring most of the available cash.

Selig Horwitz and Pinhas Sapir, on Ben-Gurion's instructions, approached Hadassah's president, Rose Halprin, and asked her to head
a finance committee in the United States composed of leaders of all the
Zionist fund-raising agencies as well as the consul general of Israel, with
the specific task of spending money for nonmilitary purchases, especially
food.

The committee met nearly every day, and every day it realized that
no matter how they cut corners, the demands—the basic needs—of the
Yishuv cost more than they had in hand. "So we went to Hadassah, we
went to the Palestine Endowment Fund, we went everyplace," she later
recalled, "and we said to them, 'Listen, we ain't got anything in the
treasury.' We would make out checks that did not hit the bank until
after three o'clock, so we could gain twenty-four hours to cover them.
We did this, we did that, and the grant still wasn't there.

"Finally we were down to $5 million, and the question was, 'what
do we do? Do we buy grain and the necessities, and then, if necessary,
go bankrupt, or do we hoard it?' And I decided that we'll buy, and trust
to God.

"Now every man I knew, including my good friends Meyer Weisgal and Abe Tulin, thought I was wrong. They all said to me, 'You
idiot. You know nothing about finances. What are you doing?'

"And I said to them, 'My dear friends, why do you think I was
asked to take this job? Because any businessman would have fallen flat
on his back long before this. Any businessman knows that one and one
make two. But we can't do that. We are adding one and one, and it has
got to make five.' And somehow we did it. Somehow we got through."[11]

*   *   *

"Somehow we got through" might have been the *leitmotiv* of the entire
effort to found the Jewish state. Somehow the *Yishuv* survived the
mandatory power. Somehow it got partition through the United Nations. Somehow it managed to raise the money and buy the arms to
fight the war and win it. And somehow it even survived the Department of State's various efforts to undo the "damage" of partition and
Truman's recognition.

In the months following Truman's *de facto* recognition of the Jewish state, its supporters pursued three main goals: *de jure* recognition
and the establishment of full diplomatic relations, a lifting of the arms
embargo so that Israel could buy weapons in the United States, and the

granting of a large reconstruction and development loan. The achievement of these goals, however, depended upon the successful prosecution and conclusion of the War of Independence, and the election of a duly constituted government. Had the State Department been willing to await the natural settling of events in the Middle East, Israel's friends would not have worried. But the State Department actively involved itself in United Nations efforts to mediate the struggle, and the UN chief negotiator's plan would have severely truncated the territory of the Jewish state.

The diplomatic maneuvering began almost immediately following Truman's decision to recognize Israel. Fortunately, Chaim Weizmann, elected President of the provisional government, remained in the United States until the end of the month, and he used his influence with the White House to press for more active assistance from the United States. Specifically, he wanted the government to lift the arms embargo, and hoped that the President would issue a direct warning to the Arab states to "stop their destructive and murderous attacks and withdraw their irregular troops and regular forces."[12] At Truman's invitation, Weizmann journeyed to Washington for a meeting at the White House. But this time, instead of sneaking in a side door as a supplicant, the Zionist leader arrived as the proud President of Israel, stayed at Blair House, and received all the honors and panoply due a foreign head of state, including a parade down Pennsylvania Avenue. At the White House, Weizmann presented Truman with a Torah scroll, the sacred five books of Moses. With the ceremonial amenities over, the two men turned to a discussion of practical matters, including sale of arms, long-term loans, and full diplomatic relations.[13]

While the President promised Weizmann to do all he could to help, subsidiary executive agencies proved less amenable. Egypt and Syria proclaimed a blockade of the Palestine coast, which the State Department had *pro forma* protested as invalid. Yet the United States Navy on May 28 began warning ships of the existence of the blockade, and on June 4 the Maritime Commission ordered Haifa omitted as a port of call for American ships in the Mediterranean. The Zionist Emergency Council immediately telegraphed Secretary of State Marshall that by doing so, the American government had legitimized an illegal act and penalized Israel. Instead of appeasing aggressor states, the United States should insist on the freedom to carry on lawful commerce. Subsequently Haifa was returned to the approved list, but on June 11, just before the S.S. *Marine Carp* sailed from New York, ten American citizens bound for Israel were forcibly detained and prevented from sailing. The federal agent responsible for this action informed the other passengers that "this is the means the United States Government has used to insure the strict observance of neutrality on the Palestine question." In Washington, a department spokesman explained that under the new truce, no fighting personnel were to be introduced into the area, and the ten detainees were potential soldiers for Israel.[14]

The State Department's strict and legalistic interpretation of neutrality had the practical effect of supporting the Arab position, whether in regard to the arms embargo or blockade resolutions. The State Department continued covertly to support British policy in the Middle East, which had become even more pro-Arab now that the Jewish state had defied Ernest Bevin by coming into existence. His Majesty's Government had imposed an oil embargo on Israel, and through its financial and contractual arrangements managed to get most of the big oil companies to accede to it—with the knowledge and approval of the State Department.[15] The State Department also wanted to move slowly, very slowly, in establishing diplomatic relations with Israel; after all, one never knew if the new country would survive. And if it did, then it would be essential to have a man with the "right" views assigned as envoy there. But in this area, at least, Harry Truman outmaneuvered the "striped-pants boys."

On June 21, at Chaim Weizmann's behest, Eddie Jacobson called on his former haberdashery partner, the President, to renew the request for diplomatic relations, and also conveyed some of the Zionist fears about State Department intrigues. Events, with obvious White House prodding, suddenly began to move much faster. The very next day, Truman convened a small group of his advisers and informed them that diplomatic relations with Israel were to be established immediately, and he wanted their advice on whom to appoint as minister to the new nation. The State Department representatives strongly urged that a trained foreign service career officer be nominated, but the President, after politely listening to their nominees (nearly all of whom came from the Middle East desk), chose James G. McDonald—an outsider to the careerist club, a pro-Zionist member of the Anglo-American Committee, and former League of Nations High Commissioner for Refugees. Clark Clifford, at Truman's direction, called McDonald to see if he would accept; when McDonald hesitated, Clifford told him not to worry about "details." Before McDonald knew what had happened, he was informed that a press announcement would be made shortly.[16]

At 4:20 P.M., with McDonald's acceptance in hand, Clifford called Under Secretary of State Robert Lovett and told him that Truman wanted the State Department to announce McDonald's appointment that evening. Lovett protested that it would be impossible; an envoy could not be appointed until he had been declared *persona grata* by the country to which he had been assigned, and this would involve an exchange of cables. Moreover, Lovett questioned whether McDonald's known sympathy for the Zionist cause ought not to disqualify him. Clifford quickly set the Under Secretary straight: This was the President's decision, and he did not want a discussion of the matter, just action. He suggested that Lovett call Eliahu Epstein, the Israeli representative in Washington. Epstein immediately assured Lovett that he had full authority from his government to act, and that McDonald would be most welcome in Israel. A special messenger would leave within minutes carrying the required note of approval.[17] The seven-o'clock evening news carried the story of McDonald's appointment, less than three hours after Clifford's first telephone call.

For the Zionists, McDonald's nomination capped a week of achievement. That same day, the Republican Party convention, at Rabbi Silver's prodding, had adopted a strong plank on Israel, and the Democrats could be expected to follow suit.[18] Eddie Jacobson relayed Truman's decision to stand by his commitments to Israel. At their meeting on the twenty-first, the President had told Jacobson that the State Department and their allies in Whitehall had "pulled the rug from under me before. They will not do it again." Truman had also asked Jacobson to relay to Chaim Weizmann the message that the United States would not support Anglo-Arab attempts to reduce Israel's territory; that full *de jure* recognition would be extended as soon as a permanent truce was signed; and that Israel would receive a long-term development loan to help resettle the displaced persons.[19] Even the bloody *Altalena* affair* redounded to Israel's credit, showing the new

---

* Although the Irgun had agreed to stop all independent arms purchases and unite its forces with the Haganah, the Israeli government learned at the beginning of June that a ship called the *Altalena* (Jabotinsky's pen name) was on its way from France carrying 900 immigrants,

government capable of maintaining domestic order. As Abba Eban put it, "the single act was worth more than a thousand *memoranda.*"[20]

McDonald's appointment not only reassured Israeli and American Jewish leaders of Truman's sincerity and good wishes, but McDonald's presence over the next 2½ years also did much to establish and preserve good relations between the two countries. His personal access to Truman allowed him to bypass potential stumbling blocks in the State Department, while Israeli perceptions of him as a friend, together with his close ties to Ben-Gurion, Weizmann, and other top officials, allowed him to deliver even tough American communications in an atmosphere of trust rather than suspicion.

Hopes for a "real peace" at this time centered on the activities of Count Folke Bernadotte of Sweden, who headed the UN mediation team. During the period of the first truce (June 11–July 8), he had presented a plan calling for an economic and political union of a Jewish state and an Arab state (including Transjordan), with Jerusalem and a large part of the Negev under Arab control. In early September, Bernadotte abandoned the idea of union in the face of Arab hostility. But while he called for Arab acceptance of Israel, he still proposed Arab control of the Negev, internationalization of Jerusalem, and severe restrictions on immigration into the new Jewish state. In many ways, the Bernadotte plan merely resurrected the Morrison-Grady scheme, and both the State Department and the Foreign Office saw another chance to settle the Palestine question in a "proper" manner. When Jewish terrorists assassinated Bernadotte in Jerusalem on Sep-

---

250 light machine guns, 5,000 rifles, and a large quantity of ammunition. Also on board was the Irgun leader, Menachem Begin. The government, headed by Ben-Gurion, demanded that the ship and its cargo be handed over to it, but the Irgun refused. On June 20, when the *Altalena* approached shore near Kefar Vitkin, government forces were sent to prevent unloading, and a battle erupted between Haganah and Irgun troops. The Irgun detachment surrendered, but the ship escaped and reached Tel Aviv. There another battle broke out between the Irgun and a Palmach brigade. Ben-Gurion, who believed that the Irgun was about to attempt a coup, ordered the ship fired upon, and the immigrants on board barely escaped before the ammunition-laden vessel exploded. In the battle, 83 people were killed or wounded, and the affair left much bitterness in Israel. But it also made it clear that no separate armed forces would be allowed to exist outside the framework of the Israel Defense Forces.

tember 17, his plan assumed the aura of a memorial to his martyrdom. Four days after the count's death, Secretary of State Marshall, addressing the General Assembly in Paris, endorsed the plan as "a generally fair basis for settlement" and "the best possible basis for bringing peace to a distracted land," a view seconded by the British.[21]

But it was directly counter to both party platforms, which had approved the boundaries laid down in the United Nations resolution, and which held that no territorial changes should be made which were not fully acceptable to Israel. Chaim Weizmann, alarmed by the apparent reversal of American policy, cabled Jacobson on September 27 that Truman should be reminded "of his own encouragement to me, on which we all very implicitly rely." Truman already recognized the danger, and had been bombarded by Zionist demands for a clarification of American policy. He ordered his staff to prepare a statement reaffirming the party platform, but then a sudden agenda change in Paris postponed debate on the Bernadotte plan. Truman decided to let the matter cool down, and kept silent.[22]

Matters came to a head, however, in the two weeks before the 1948 presidential election. On October 14, an Egyptian attack on an Israeli supply convoy triggered what the Israelis termed "Operation Ten Plagues," which in eight days completely routed Arab forces in the Negev and left the entire area, with the exception of the Gaza Strip, in Jewish hands. The General Assembly, aware of the impending American election, voted to postpone debate on Palestine until after the balloting. American Zionists, elated by both moves, stepped up their pressure for a clearer commitment by the President. In a full-page advertisement in the New York *Times*, the Zionist Emergency Council pointed out how the Bernadotte plan, backed by Secretary Marshall, differed from the UN partition agreement endorsed by the Democratic Party. "Mr. Truman: Where Do YOU Stand on This Issue?" Party leaders agonized over Truman's silence, and New York congressional candidates, who feared the effects of the Henry Wallace third-party campaign, repeatedly tried to see the President, who steadfastly refused to meet with them.

Within the White House staff, some advisers feared that anything Truman said would be interpreted as blatant politics and lose him votes; others, including David Niles, wanted Truman to reaffirm the party's pledge to "Americans of Jewish faith who have lived through the liquidation of six million of their fellow Jews." Truman stubbornly kept silent, except for a telegram to Marshall on October 17 directing "that no statement be made or no action be taken on the subject of Palestine by any member of our delegation in Paris without obtaining specific authority from me." Then on October 22, just ten days before the election, Thomas Dewey announced that he had always believed that the Jewish people were entitled "to a homeland in Palestine which would be politically and economically stable," and that he fully endorsed the Republican platform with its support of the partition plan. Although the Republican candidate had not specifically mentioned boundaries, Truman jumped at the opening. Dewey's injection of foreign policy into the campaign now made it "necessary" for him to restate his position, namely, that he stood unequivocally by the Democratic platform. At a mass rally in Madison Square Garden, the President developed fully his record of support for Jewish refugees after the war and of Zionist dreams for a Jewish homeland.[23]

Truman, despite the pollsters, defeated Dewey that year, but the President received little overt support from the official Zionist organization. Abba Hillel Silver, who was a friend of Senator Robert A. Taft, favored the Republicans, and thought the Zionists would fare better with an administration in which Taft would have a major voice.[24] Even so, the President did well in predominantly Jewish precincts; the timely contributions of some wealthy Jews in the closing weeks of the campaign helped Truman buy valuable radio time as well as finance his last-minute train swing; and the Labor Zionists in Ohio turned out *en masse* to work for him—all evidence that his efforts on behalf of refugees and the Jewish state had borne fruit. A few weeks after the election, Truman wrote to Chaim Weizmann: "I have interpreted my reelection as a mandate from the American people to carry out the Democratic platform, including, of course, the plank on Israel. I intend to do so."[25]

In the year following his election, Truman fulfilled several of his promises to Weizmann, yet without losing his own sense of perspective in the Middle East. He strongly supported Israel's existence, but he would not condone continued Israeli military action which violated UN truce agreements. Throughout 1949, the two sides gradually disengaged their forces, but a series of border incidents, which evoked strong Israeli countermeasures, had James McDonald delivering one note after another to Ben-Gurion expressing Truman's displeasure. Yet when Israel shot down some British planes on reconnaissance flights over the

Negev, President Truman wasted no time in informing London that he considered the Israeli action completely justified.[26]

Within the State Department, hostility to Israel gradually lessened as the careerists realized that Israel would survive, and that far from being a Russian outpost in the Middle East, the new Jewish state, despite its stated position of nonalignment, ideologically stood with the Western democracies. Although Achdut Ha'avodah, Israel's leftist labor group, pushed for closer ties with the Soviet Union, the Ben-Gurion administration gradually drifted into the American camp, a path eased by McDonald's skillful work. On his trips back to the United States, the American envoy took especial pains to convince State Department officials that Israel was America's real friend in the Middle East.[27]

As Israel solidified its territorial holdings, its government took steps to change from a provisional, besieged, *ad hoc* hodgepodge of formal, semiformal, and informal groupings into a permanent institution with sound legal bases. The first national elections took place on January 25, 1949, and three weeks later the first Knesset met to adopt the basic laws of the country. The United States had held up *de jure* recognition, which, the State Department pointed out, would follow only after a permanent government was elected by constitutional means as the UN partition resolution demanded. Six days after that election, the United States extended *de jure* recognition both to Israel and to the Hashemite Kingdom of Jordan. A short time later, Israel received its long-awaited development loan.[28] A series of armistices was signed on Rhodes, and in early March, Israel took its seat in the United Nations. Now a new personality emerged on the American Jewish scene: young, stoutish, loose-jointed Abba Eban. During his first speech to the United Nations, a correspondent raced down the corridor in search of the Zionist press officer to find out the name of "that Johnson's Baby Powder kid" addressing the General Assembly. As Judd Teller wrote: "Speaking Churchillian rhetoric, Abba Eban, then just turning thirty-three, captured the affection of American Jews. Immigrants and the sons of immigrants, they could envision nothing more appropriate for an Israeli diplomat than a British accent."[29]

*   *   *

While most American Jews eagerly welcomed the Third Jewish Commonwealth and wholeheartedly joined in fund-raising and other pro-Israel activities, a faint residue of anti-Zionism lingered. Within the

Union of American Hebrew Congregations, for example, Dr. Maurice N. Eisendrath, president of the Reform group and a warm supporter of the new state, expressed his dismay and frustration at the caution with which his colleagues had greeted the birth of Israel. At the annual meeting in November 1948, he chastised the members for their faint-heartedness. During the weeks and months of agony and tension and rejoicing, "your Union stood silently on the sidelines, while our sister religious organizations issued calls to prayers of thanksgiving, and secular institutions of every kind—even those composed of memberships of Zionists and non-Zionists such as our own—rejoiced in this momentous event. . . . Your Union, I do believe, was just about the only organization which calls itself Jewish—with but one conspicuous exception—which was compelled by the demands of our neutrality resolution to seal its lips and to stay its hand and heart from participation in the drama which the past year of Jewish history presented." Eisendrath had repeatedly polled the executive committee to see if there was any way to break this silence, only to find half of the members either firmly opposed to Israel or indifferent.[30]

That "conspicuous exception" was, of course, the American Council for Judaism, which had consistently opposed the creation of a Jewish state. At its annual meeting in February 1948, the Council had reacted angrily to Golda Meyerson's fund-raising tour to buy arms for the Haganah, and had adopted a resolution entitled "Relief Funds vs. Political Funds," condemning the drive. Moreover, the Council warned, if the United Jewish Appeal and the Joint Distribution Committee continued to allow relief funds to be diverted to other purposes, the Council would establish its own charitable apparatus for American Jews who did not want to support Jewish nationalism.

When the nightmare of a Jewish state became real, the Council issued a lengthy statement objecting to phrases in the Israeli Declaration of Independence regarding "the self-evident right of the Jewish people to be a nation." In tones pregnant with fear, the Council announced: "We therefore emphatically declare that the state of Israel is not the state or homeland of 'the Jewish people.' To Americans of Jewish faith it is a foreign state. Our single and exclusive national identity is to the United States. Our exclusive spokesman in all international affairs is the government of the United States through its authorized representatives."[31]

Equally concerned about the political claims that Israel might make upon American Jews, the American Jewish Committee chose to define its position in terms of reason rather than fear. Judge Joseph Proskauer, for example, had declared in 1943 that "there can be no political identification of Jews outside of Palestine with whatever government may there be instituted." In January 1948 he repeated these words, but this time in direct response to the Council's shrill cry that a Jewish state would impose intolerable political stress on American Jewry. "There is no such problem," Proskauer said. "The Jews of America suffer from no political schizophrenia. Politically we are not split personalities, and in faith and in conduct we shall continue to demonstrate what the death rolls of our army on many a battlefield have attested: that we are bone of the bone and flesh of the flesh of America." But American Jews would not hold themselves at arm's length from their brethren; there were mutual obligations, and American Jews had the responsibility to see that the United Nations partition resolution was carried out, that a democratic state was not overrun. In so doing, Proskauer saw no contradiction between his duties as a Jew and as an American. "This is not a pro-Jewish position," he concluded, "it is a pro-American and a pro-United Nations position." Shortly after the establishment of the State of Israel, Proskauer put his words into action when he requested that the State Department use its influence to force the British to release thousands of Jewish detainees, the "illegal" immigrants, held on Cyprus, since Israel wanted to accept them.[32]

Proskauer's calm resulted in part from earlier assurances he had received from the Jewish Agency that a Jewish state would not claim any loyalty from American Jews or interfere in American Jewish affairs; Israeli officials, shortly after the creation of the state, repeated these promises. In early 1949, a Committee delegation, headed by the then president, Jacob Blaustein, visited Israel at Ben-Gurion's invitation, and the Prime Minister personally reiterated the substance of the earlier pledge. Thus Committee officers were shocked when a few months later Ben-Gurion allegedly called for large-scale *aliyah* of American youth to Israel, and they protested vehemently to Israeli Ambassador Eliahu Elath (formerly Epstein) and Abba Eban, head of the United Nations delegation. Although Proskauer wanted to issue an ultimatum threatening dissociation from the state, Blaustein and the others prevailed in their desire to work things out, in true AJC fashion, quietly.

In the summer of 1950, Blaustein again journeyed to Israel as a guest of the government, and after a series of long and hard bargaining sessions, Ben-Gurion indirectly admitted that American Jews did not live in exile, and therefore the ingathering of the exiles did not apply to them. "The Jews of the United States," he declared, "as a community and as individuals, have only one political attachment, and that is to the United States of America. They owe no political allegiance to Israel. . . . The State of Israel represents and speaks only on behalf of its own citizens and in no way presumes to represent or speak in the name of the Jews who are citizens of any other country. We, the people of Israel, have no desire and no intention to interfere in any way with the internal affairs of Jewish communities abroad." Israel would welcome an American *aliyah* and the technical knowledge that would accompany it; however, such immigration would have to be voluntary. But Israel, he asserted, was "anxious that nothing should be said or done which could in the slightest degree undermine the sense of security and stability of American Jewry."

Blaustein, in his response, stressed that "to American Jews, America is home. There, exist their thriving roots; there, is the country which they have helped to build; and there, they share its fruits and its destiny." As to the safety of American Jews, he warned that "in a world in which it would be possible for Jews to be driven by persecution from America would not be a world safe for Israel either; indeed, it is hard to conceive how it would be a world safe for any human being."[33]

Of course, it would not be possible for Israel to completely abstain from "interfering" in American Jewish affairs. Some Israeli actions, especially in religious matters, by their very nature affected American Jews, and very often American Jewish communities would appeal to Israeli officials to take part in issues of strictly local concern. In the years following the Blaustein-Ben-Gurion agreement, the Israelis would periodically violate the protocol by "interfering"—at least in the Committee's opinion—in American Jewish affairs, and then both sides would reaffirm the 1950 understanding.

As time went on and the ties between Israel and the American Jewish community strengthened, the issue of interference died down. But in 1949 and 1950, American Jewry had not yet grown accustomed to the existence of a Jewish state, nor worked out what relations to it should be. In some ways, the Blaustein-Ben-Gurion agreement marked the final playing out of the Committee's old fears of Jewish nationalism, its worries over dual allegiance. The Committee stood prepared to accept and support Israel. Committee leaders recognized that the new state—indeed, much of Zionist ideology—rested upon European philosophical assumptions which did not apply to the United States. If Israel, at that time, had persisted in describing America as *galut* (exile), in demanding that American Jews make *aliyah* in advance of another Holocaust, in interfering with local Jewish matters, the new state would have confirmed the worst fears of the American Council for Judaism. By avoiding such blatant steps, Israel allowed American Jewry to isolate the Council,† and allayed the concerns of those not yet comfortable with the presence of a Jewish state. In the future, all of these issues would be raised, time and again, but by then American Jewry would be able to respond in a more secure manner.

*   *   *

For most American Jews, however, the main concern in the years following the establishment of Israel focused on providing the material resources needed by the new nation. During this period, the state's economy seemed to hover on the edge of total collapse, as the country struggled not only to build a viable economy, but also to absorb hundreds of thousands of immigrants at the same time. Between May 1948 and the end of 1951, Israel's Jewish population more than doubled, from 650,000 to 1,324,000. They came from all over: 25,000 from the camps on Cyprus, 75,000 Displaced Persons from Germany and Austria, 33,000 from Turkey, and 14,000 Europeans who had escaped the Holocaust by making their way to China. Entire Jewish communities were transplanted from Arab countries, with much of the costs underwritten by the American-financed Joint Distribution Committee. Operation Magic Carpet flew in 49,000 Jews who had escaped from Yemen and found refuge in the Crown protectorate of Aden, where they awaited redemption in Israel. These Jews, from one of the most backward countries in the world, had never before seen an airplane, but knew that the strange-looking machines had been sent to carry out the biblical prophecy of Isaiah: "They shall mount with wings as

---

† American Zionist leaders were unhappy with the agreement for a number of reasons (see below, Chapter 11), but did not criticize the Committee for fear of driving it into the arms of the Council. In October 1949, the Committee had, in fact, publicly criticized the Council's methods and its anti-Israel propaganda, even though Lessing Rosenwald sat on the AJC executive committee.

eagles." On planes designed to hold 56 passengers, the Joint crowded 125 to 145 people in on a flight. As Oscar Handlin noted, this "caused no great difficulty; life in Aden had reduced the weight of the average adult male to 80 pounds." Shortly afterward, Operation Ezra and Nehemiah airlifted 114,000 Jews from Iraq to their new home, nearly three times the number who had returned from Babylonia with the two prophets 2,500 years earlier.[34]

The Jewish state had been founded to accept them; indeed, a prime rationale of Zionism had been that only a Jewish homeland could be relied upon to provide refuge for persecuted Jews. But these newcomers had to be housed and fed and clothed and trained to become economically independent members of society, and that task required expenditures far in excess of the young state's meager resources. Yet Israelis did not suggest that immigration be halted, or even limited. They tightened their belts, and austerity (*tzena*) became the watchword of the country. Stringent price controls and the rationing of food and other necessities ensured minimum standards for everyone. Israeli exports barely rose from $43 million in 1949 to $45.8 million in 1950, but imports jumped from $263 million to $327.6 million. The gross national product in 1950 was only $1.282 billion, a per capita output of only $3,752.[35] Still, immigrants crowded in wherever they could; many Israeli families opened their doors and took in refugees on a "temporary" basis. But most of the newcomers were to be found in *ma'abarot* (transit camps), where they lived in tents and shacks awaiting permanent housing; not until mid-1954 would the last *ma'abara* be closed or converted into a new agricultural village.

Part of the effort to rehabilitate or retrain the refugees fell to the Joint Distribution Committee. Among the immigrants pouring into the country were thousands of aged and handicapped people, many of them permanently crippled, physically and emotionally, by their experience in Hitler's death camps. The JDC had been supporting them in Europe, and no country other than Israel would take them in, though Israel had no resources with which to care for them; every available dollar had to be diverted into programs of reconstruction and development, for which these people could not qualify. The Joint and the government, therefore, signed an agreement in 1949 to create a new agency, *Malben*, to take care of these men and women, by establishing a network of homes for the aged, hospitals, clinics, sheltered workshops, and other institutions. The government would simultaneously develop, as much as its resources allowed, public facilities and housing near the *Malben* installations so that the aged and the ill would not be isolated from the society. The JDC made an initial allocation of $15 million in 1949, but within a year managed all of the financing and administration of the *Malben*.[36]

Decent housing stood near the top of Israel's priorities. Men and women who worked would have a sense of pride and responsibility, a psychological necessity after years of persecution; in addition, they would be contributing to the growth of the country. As long as they lived in *ma'abarot*, however, the majority of them were condemned to boredom, with their lives little better, materially, than in the DP camps. Yet no matter how much the government wanted to build houses, it had only limited resources; no matter how fast it built even the most primitive housing, immigrants came faster than they could be accommodated. In April 1949, when Golda Meyerson, now Golda Meir, became Minister of Labor in charge of housing she went to the Knesset, the Israeli parliament, and secured approval of a plan to build thirty thousand additional units; the only problem was that the Knesset could not appropriate any money for their construction.

So once again Golda returned to the United States to ask for funds, this time "not to win a war but to maintain life." It is worth quoting from her speeches to American Jewry on this trip, because more than anything else, they give one an idea not only of the deprivations facing new immigrants in Israel, but also of the type of appeal that touched so responsive a chord among American Jews. It is doubtful if any Israeli leader has ever been so attuned to the American Jewish community as this Milwaukee-raised woman.

"I went to our parliament," she told them, "and presented a project for thirty thousand housing units by the end of this year. Parliament approved it, and there was great joy in the country. But actually I did a strange thing; I presented a project for which I didn't have the money.

"What we want to do is give each family a luxurious apartment of one room; one room which we have built out of concrete blocks. We won't even plaster the walls. We will make roofs, but no ceilings. What we hope is that since these people will be learning a trade as they build their houses, they will finish them, and eventually, one day, add on another room. In the meantime, we will be happy, and they will be happy, even though it means putting a family of two, three, four, or five into one room. But this is better than putting two or three families into a single tent. . . .

"It is an awful thing to do—to forge a signature to a check—but I have done it. I have promised the people at home and the people in the camps that the government is going to put up these thirty thousand units, and we have already started to do so with the little money we have. But there isn't enough for these thirty thousand units. It is up to you either to keep these people in camps and send them food packages or to put them to work and restore their dignity and self-respect."[37]

She got the funds, and despite many difficulties, the new housing units went up.

But there were still other areas in which American Jewry responded to Israeli needs. Just as the Joint Distribution Committee, through the *Malben*, undertook to care for the aged and infirm, so Hadassah assumed much of the responsibility for refugee children through the Youth Aliyah program. The women's Zionist organization had begun to rescue boys and girls from fascism during the 1930s, and had continued the task, as best it could, during the war. Many of the children who survived the Holocaust had been orphaned, and Hadassah, through Youth Aliyah, brought some twenty thousand of them to Israel, settled them in *kibbutzim* and youth villages, educated and trained them, and tended to their psychological and physical needs. It was a task which, despite the enormous costs, Hadassah gladly assumed. "There was a tremendous sense of commitment," Charlotte Jacobson, former president of Hadassah and later chairperson of the Jewish Agency, American Section, recalled; "the children who survived were a very special obligation."[38]

But Hadassah's major work in Palestine had always been health care. Under the direction of Henrietta Szold, a network of hospitals, clinics, and social services had been developed in the *Yishuv*, capped by the Hadassah Hospital on Mount Scopus in Jerusalem, the finest teaching and research medical-care facility in the Middle East. After the Holocaust, when the major centers of European medicine had been wiped out, a visiting committee of American physicians described the hospital on Scopus as potentially the finest medical center east of London. It had been designed as a showcase, where the latest in American medical and nursing techniques would be taught, where the best medical care would be available to Jew and Arab alike. But Scopus had been cut off during the war, and although still technically in Israeli hands, it was surrounded by Arab East Jerusalem, and inaccessible.

Ben-Gurion asked Rose Halprin, then president of Hadassah, if the women would start again. She recalled her shock at the thought that Scopus would be gone for good. Not for good, Ben-Gurion said, but it will be years before we have it again. On her way back to the United States, she was fearful of the reception this news might receive from the national board. What would the members say? After all, they had just finished the Scopus facility in 1939. Perhaps they would say no, enough, we can't do it.[39] She need not have worried. It would take time, but the membership never even considered the possibility that there would be no Hadassah hospital in Israel. When the new Hadassah Medical Center-Hebrew University Medical School opened at Ein HaKerem in 1961, Israel had the finest hospital in the Middle East, and in 1967, when Jerusalem was reunified, Hadassah reopened and expanded the old hospital on Mount Scopus.

Good medical care, however, required good nutrition, and while Israel was capable of growing enough food for its people, it could not do so in the postwar turmoil. Hadassah, as a member of the President's Advisory Committee on Voluntary Foreign Aid, had the right to receive surplus foods for free distribution. In Washington, Hadassah representative Denise Tourover haunted bureau offices and read hundreds of government information releases to find out what foods might be available. One time she discovered that tons of potatoes were stored at Presque Isle, Maine. The Israeli government said they would take them, provided they were fumigated first. So Hadassah found itself in the business of fumigating and shipping tons of potatoes every month. As late as 1953, Hadassah still worked to get additional foodstuffs to Israel, and in Operation Reindeer, secured $12 million of kosher meat, dried fruits, and staples. Packed in bags with both the American and Hadassah insignia, they were sent as a Christmas present by the U.S. government for free distribution to both Israeli Arabs and Jews. As Marlin Levin noted, "the project was something to ponder: an American Christmas gift handed out by a Zionist organization to Palestinian Arabs."[40]

Many of the projects—emergency housing, *Malben*, Operation Reindeer, even the rebuilding of the Hadassah hospital—despite their magnitude, were essentially of limited duration and expense. But it became clear very early that if Israel were to develop a viable economy, if immigrants from different cultural and economic backgrounds were to be absorbed, if a democratic society were to be sustained, then long-term plans had to be adopted. In the early years of the state, however, the immediate problems, with their terrible urgency, crowded long-range planning off the agenda. People had to be fed and housed and clothed at once, not in five or ten years, and that meant raising funds for current use.

Daniel Frisch, in his acceptance speech as president of the ZOA in 1949, clearly established the priorities: "In the very foreground of our attention, of course, is the United Jewish Appeal. The Appeal must command the priority of all American Jews, no matter what their special interests in Israel may be. A failure, God forbid, of the Appeal to achieve the total goal, would have nearly the same effect as if Bevinism would have succeeded. Heroic, willing, and self-sacrificing as the *Yishuv* is, it will not be in a position to continue the open-door policy unless we provide the means. Thereafter we must look to the setting up of projects, through private investments and otherwise."[41]

This type of appeal, that help had to be found now, was a common theme not only at Zionist meetings, but especially at UJA rallies. Philip Klutznik, president of the B'nai B'rith, reported that at one such meeting, after listening to the speaker run down the litany of needs, a volunteer said he had a small question. "Friend," he began, "what you said here is all too true—the desperate need to save . . . a new life for them in Israel . . . jobs and homes . . . security . . . rescue dollars . . . run to the banks to borrow millions, run a campaign to collect the millions . . . repeat it all next year—I understand all that.

"But just one question. These constant crises . . . one-hundred-million-dollar campaigns—when will it all end? Give us an inkling, something to look forward to, can you?"

The UJA official thought for a moment. "Sure," he said.

"Well—when?"

"In the year of the Messiah," the UJA man said, "plus one."

The volunteer sadly nodded his head in understanding, except—"Why the extra year?"

The UJA man explained. "One final campaign, to pay off the banks."[42]

The short-term funding came primarily from the UJA and from a series of grants-in-aid and loans from the American government, a program that, unlike some foreign-aid allocations, received widespread public support. Columnists as diverse in their viewpoint as Eleanor Roosevelt and George Sokolsky agreed that the United States should aid Israel generously. The Hearst chain, "opposed to the general concept of thoughtless giveaway schemes to squander the substance of the American people," believed it fully in the American tradition to assist the young republic, not only for humanitarian reasons, but also because "Israel is another potential island of defense against aggressive Communist penetration." The proposal for a $150 million supplemental grant in 1951 received bipartisan support, as did one for $73 million the following year, although it took some Zionist lobbying to get that full amount.[43]

But this hand-to-mouth method of financing allowed Israel no economic breathing space, no margin upon which to build for the future. As early as February 1949, fund-raisers and government officials began talking of "gift dollars vs. investment dollars." A publication of the United Jewish Appeal, in advising its volunteer workers, warned that they "should avoid building up the myth that Israel is an almost permanent relief recipient." At the same time, in seeking private investors, it would have to be admitted that "Israel's economy is a profit economy only to the extent to which the security and daily needs of a growing population allow individual profits." Golda Meir, who in these early days was one of Israel's chief fund-raisers in the United States, also worried that a "continued dependence on philanthropy violated the most elementary concepts of Zionism, of self-reliance, and self-labor, to say nothing of national independence."[44]

Preliminary discussions among Golda Meir, Ben-Gurion, Eliezer Kaplan (Israel's first Minister of Finance), Henry Montor, and other Americans began early in 1950, and culminated in a three-day conference of fifty American Jewish leaders in Jerusalem in early September 1950. There Ben-Gurion proposed that, in addition to the UJA, American Jewry could help Israel by purchasing development bonds which would give the state capital for long-term economic growth. Few of the communal representatives pretended any great enthusiasm. What if the bond drive undercut the United Jewish Appeal? Who wanted to make money off of Israel? Who wanted to lose money? A UJA gift could be deducted from one's taxes, but not a bond purchase. What if the American government opposed their sale? Reluctantly, the conference approved the bond idea, but only after linking it to a four-point program which incorporated increased UJA support, private investment, and government aid.

Fortunately, one member of the group responded positively, Henry Morgenthau, Jr., former Treasury Secretary and now head of the UJA. On his return to the United States, he went to the White House to learn whether the government objected to the proposal. Truman understood the need for long-term financing for economic growth as opposed to short-term aid, and gave his blessing to it. Late in October, the National Planning Conference for Israel and Jewish Rehabilitation met in Washington, and once again Ben-Gurion tapped Golda Meir to sell the bond program. She presented to the 1,100 delegates a three-year plan for economic growth costing $1.5 billion. The Israeli people, despite their staggering problems, would be responsible for one third of that amount; but the Diaspora, and especially the Jews of America, would have to raise the balance in various ways, including the purchase of bonds. An important financial and psychological impetus to the bond proposal was the commitment made by Benjamin Browdy, president of the Zionist Organization of America, that ZOA members would purchase $100 million worth of bonds. When Morgenthau reported White House approval and support, the assembly decided they would proceed, and set up plans for launching the Israel bonds program in May 1951.

For that auspicious event, Prime Minister David Ben-Gurion himself came to the United States, the only visit he made outside of Israel during his first term as Prime Minister. His visit provided an occasion for enormous public demonstrations of sympathy and support for Israel, all of which gave added impetus to launching the American Financial and Development Corporation for Israel (later the Israel Bonds Organization), which in its first year sold $52.5 million. From its inception to the eve of the 1967 war, the bond program raised more than $850 million in the United States alone, and an additional $150 million in Canada, Western Europe, and other free world countries.

Although many of the organizers' fears proved groundless, for a number of years American Jewry suffered some confusion over the exact nature of the bond program. For one thing, the term used to describe the sales drive—"campaign"—invariably conjured up the image of a charity, such as the UJA "campaign." Since banks and other large financial institutions were unwilling to underwrite the bond issues, the Israel Bonds Organization decided to sell them directly to the public using volunteers, another reflection of the UJA style. The fact that the bonds constituted a loan, a real interest-paying obligation, did not easily penetrate the minds of American Jews, who considered them a kind of gimmick, a new fund-raising device, to increase the flow of cash to Israel under the pretext of investment.

The early years also saw misunderstanding between the bond supporters and UJA officials, and a co-ordinating committee of representatives from Israel Bonds, the United Jewish Appeal, the Jewish Agency, and the Israeli embassy had its hands full trying to keep things on an even keel. Gradually, however, both UJA and bond drives settled into a pattern, with contributions to the UJA, which solicited for domestic needs and the Joint Distribution Committee as well as for Israel, getting a significantly larger share of the monies American Jewry gave each year to the Jewish state (see Table 1). In 1963, Israel redeemed the first $170 million worth of bonds coming due, thus putting the imprimatur of fiscal responsibility on the securities, and removing the last doubt that the bonds were indeed an investment and not a charity.[45]

TABLE I

UJA Pledges and Israel Bond Sales, 1951–61

Year	UJA Pledges ($ thousands)	Bond Sales ($ thousands)
1951	80,100	52,506
1952	69,800	46,516
1953	65,000	31,551
1954	60,000	34,361
1955	60,000	36,681
1956	75,000	45,699
1957	82,000	40,696
1958	68,000	37,763
1959	73,000	42,628
1960	61,000	41,390
1961	60,000	45,287

SOURCE: *American Jewish Year Book*, Vols. 52–62.

Beyond the pride in the new state, beyond the happiness that the refugees from Hitler's infernos would now have a home, beyond the sense of responsibility which American Jewry had for their brethren, there was—and has been—a fear for Israel's survival, a dread that somehow this tiny nation could not survive surrounded by hostile Arab states. And although they paid little attention to it at the time, American Jews were aware that in the birth pains of the Third Jewish Commonwealth, a new group of refugees had been created, the Palestinian Arabs. Their presence and their gross manipulation by Arab politicians would poison every peace effort for the next three decades.

In the thirty years between the Balfour Declaration and the United Nations resolution, many more Arabs entered Palestine than did Jews since, ironically, the development of the *Yishuv* generated economic opportunities for laborers and small businessmen, which attracted Arabs seeking better living conditions. Yet the centuries-long antagonism between Muslim and Jew prevented harmony from ever developing, despite numerous examples of good relations between individual Jews and Arabs, as well as between Arab villages and nearby Jewish settlements. Many writers, and nearly all of the various royal investigatory commissions who blamed Arab resentment on the intrusion of Jews into the Holy Land missed the historic bases which generated this hostility, and even today many Arab apologists talk about the "good relations," the "golden age" of Arab-Jewish amicability which predated the "Zionist invasion."

However, traditional Muslim teachings, based upon the Koran, have always held Jews to be an inferior people, whose downfall is inevitable "because they misbelieve the revelation of Allah and slew the prophets wrongly." Anwar Sadat, talking of Jerusalem in 1972, declared: "We shall take it out of the hands of those whom the Koran said, 'It is written that they shall be demeaned and made wretched.' . . . We shall celebrate the defeat of Israeli arrogance so that they shall return and be as the Koran said of them, a people 'condemned to humiliation and misery.' "[46]

The Old Testament, of course, does not treat the children of Ishmael gently: "His hand shall be against every man, and every man's hand against him; and he shall dwell in the face of all his brethren" [Gen. 16:12]. The ancient Hebrews were, moreover, directed to deal harshly with the Canaanites, the Midianites, the Moabites, and other local tribes who resisted them. The difference, however, is that by the time of the First Commonwealth under Solomon, these practices had been discarded and had become part of history. Talmudic and modern Judaism, while striving to keep the Jewish people intact and free from outside influences, does not downgrade other groups, but ignores them. And for nineteen centuries, Jews did not rule over subject peoples.

Throughout the centuries following the rise of Islam, the Muslims sought to keep Jews in an inferior position. As a *dhimmi,* or non-Muslim, a Jew lived in a *mellah* (ghetto), could not own a horse, built his house smaller than that of neighboring Arabs, paid heavier taxes, and wore special clothing, which frequently included some form of yellow badge. In different lands and at different times, the conditions of Jews might temporarily improve, and individual Jews might even rise to posts of importance in business, universities, or the government. But for the most part, the life of Jewish communities under Arab rule was one of harsh and unrelenting persecution.[47]

Yet some modern analysts have suggested that, even then the Jews had a love-hate attitude toward the Arab. "On the one hand," writes Hillel Halkin, "he was unwashed, ignorant, untrustworthy, treacherous, emotional, violent, temperamental; he stole Jewish crops and animals, waylaid Jewish travelers, harassed Jewish settlements when he could. On the other, he was bold, brave, graceful, spontaneous, and lived close to nature and to the earth; he was the embodiment of that physicality, that closeness to the natural passions, that the Jew had lost in his exilic life; he was, in however fallen and degraded a state, a precious missing link with the Jews' own past, a living gloss on the imagery of the Bible."[48]

Despite the hostility of the Arabs, the dominant policy of the *Yishuv* took the form of *havlagah* (restraint), in which the Haganah never initiated attacks, but only responded to Arab assaults. *Havlagah* influenced security measures well into the 1950s, when Israel felt compelled to adopt a policy of stern reprisals. Throughout these early years, moreover, a variety of Jewish groups, such as B'rith Shalom and Ichud, as well as numerous individuals, tried to initiate a dialogue of peace with their Arab neighbors. One Zionist leader after another attempted to reassure the Arabs that they meant them no harm, that the Jews were, in fact, the Arabs' true friends. Emanuel Neumann, for example, explained that a Jewish commonwealth did not mean driving the Arabs out of Palestine, but that within the state every Arab right would be protected, and they would share fully in the modernization and prosperity of the country. Gradually it became clear, however, that the Arabs cared not at all for modern amenities if they came from Jewish hands. When Shmuel Hugo Bergmann and Moshe Shertok tried to discuss these benefits with an Arab leader, Mussa Alami interrupted them to say that Palestine had been a desert wasteland for a thousand years, and could remain so for another thousand, until the Arabs themselves improved it.[49] Jews, caught up in their own dream of national restoration, failed to recognize emerging Arab nationalism.

When the war came, Israeli leaders did their best to convince their Arab neighbors not to run away. But as early as January 1948, Arabs began leaving Palestine to avoid the inevitable war. Some saw this as plain fear of the Jews, but as Christopher Sykes notes: "To flee the wrath to come is an Arab way. . . . There is a certain feudal dependence in Arab life, and more than in any Western society men tend to follow the example of the mayor and the notable and the local clergy."[50] By May 1948, nearly 175,000 Arabs had fled, and the momentum picked up once full-scale fighting broke out. There has been an ongoing debate whether the Arabs left out of fear or on orders from the Arab High Command. The London *Economist* on October 2, 1948, carried the report of a British eyewitness that such an order had been given, that the local Arabs should remove themselves to safety while the Arab armies "drove the Jews into the sea." The Greek Orthodox archbishop of Galilee, himself an Arab, confirmed that "the refugees had been confident that their absence from Palestine would not last long, that they would return within a few days—within a week or two. Their leaders had promised them that the Arab armies would crush the 'Zionist gangs' very quickly."[51] Some historians have dismissed this argument by pointing instead to the total collapse of Palestinian Arab leadership and political institutions.[52] Nor should the element of terror in wartime be ignored. While there were only one or two outright attacks on Arab civilian populations, like that at Deir Yassin,[53] war inevitably breeds fear, and fear will drive thousands of innocent people away from their homes. By the end of the fighting, some 700,000 Arabs had left Palestine.

While the treatment of these refugees in camps and their political exploitation by Arab leaders is well known, what is frequently ignored is the fact that an equal number of Jews living in Arab lands also became refugees, driven out by the waves of frenzied frustration generated in Arab countries by the Israeli victory. Out of nearly 900,000

Jews who lived in Arab lands, 700,000 went to Israel in the three years following the War of Independence, and another 130,000 Jews from Tunis and Algeria migrated to France; in 1976, the once-sizable Jewish communities in the Arab countries numbered little more than 35,000. But where Israel took in and absorbed the *edot hamizrachi* (the people of the East), the Arab nations, despite their vast undeveloped areas, despite their talk of Arab solidarity and unity and brotherhood, refused, with the exception of Jordan, to make room for the Palestinians, and instead shut them for years in squalid camps, where hatred and a lust for vengeance festered and grew.[54]

The great tragedy in all of this, as Chaim Weizmann had noted before the Anglo-American Committee, was that the issue could not be resolved as one of right vs. wrong. There were two rights here—the right of the Jews to return to their ancestral homeland, and the right of Arabs to develop their own nationalistic vision and to continue to live in a land they had occupied for centuries. For the most part, Zionist leaders had either been blind to or had ignored the Arab nationalism which arose after the First World War. They continued to cling to the idealistic vision that Arabs ought to welcome Jews into Palestine so that they could both benefit from a modern development of the ancient land. In retrospect, it appears that such dreams were doomed to failure, that just as the Jews would not allow Arab nationalism to prevent their return to Zion, so the Arabs would hardly consider Zionism, which they saw as an alien ideology, to grow within their own national awakening.

American Jews, at least in the 1930s and 1940s, remained oblivious to this dilemma. For them, the issue was simple—redeeming Palestine as a refuge for the survivors of the Holocaust. Even in the months following the establishment of the State of Israel, the plight of the Palestinian Arab refugees caused little concern in the American Jewish community. What did matter was saving Jewish refugees, whether the displaced persons of Europe or the Jews fleeing the *mellahs* of Islam. American Jews opened their hearts and their purses for their brethren, and had little time or thought to spend on a situation in which it appeared that the Arab states would not do as much for their kin as American Jewry was doing for Israel.

American Jews were proud of the role they had played in bringing into existence the new State of Israel, the Third Jewish Commonwealth, to govern in *Eretz Yisrael,* and they had many achievements of which to be proud. In that moment of triumph it is understandable that they paid so little attention to those refugees who had fled from Palestine, and that they failed to see how this problem would prevent the arrival of the peace which American and Israeli Jews so fervently desired.

Chapter 8

HOMO JUDAICUS
AMERICANUS

The establishment of the State of Israel in 1948 marked far more than the successful culmination of fifty years of organized Zionist labors. In the aftermath of the Holocaust, the new state appeared as a sign of redemption, an indication that the God of Jacob had not forgotten His ancient promises. Beyond that, the victory of the beleaguered *Yishuv* did much to mend the psychological trauma and guilt feelings of the war years. The old stereotype of the weak and helpless Jew was challenged by a new image of the strong, healthy, and courageous Israeli. The Third Jewish Commonwealth meant many things, but the question of timing must be taken into consideration when looking at the nature of American Jewry during these years. The creation of a Jewish state provided a crucial background as well as a point of focus in the midst of enormous changes that were then transforming the American Jewish community.

*   *   *

On the eve of the tercentenary celebration of the Jewish arrival in Nieue Amsterdam in 1654, an observer would have been hard put to find any immigrant group which had prospered in the United States as swiftly as had American Jews. Numbering slightly more than five million, they could be found in all the states of the Union, in small towns and hamlets, and even a few on farms; for the most part, however, they clustered in the urban northeast. Although comprising only 3.5 per cent of the population, their income and status distribution skewed wildly from national norms. One out of every five Jewish families made over $10,000 yearly, as compared to one out of twenty gentile families; Jews were proportionately underrepresented in that part of the population near or below the poverty line. William Attwood found that American Jews earned about 10 per cent of the nation's total personal income, and constituted one fifth of the country's 9,000 millionaires.[1]

A number of surveys also indicated that American Jewry was becoming remarkably homogeneous, but in a way which also defied the statistical norms. In the 1930s, most Jews had been employed as laborers or in low-level white-collar jobs, such as clerks and office help, but by the early 1950s over 55 per cent worked in professional or technical fields, or as managers, officials, and proprietors, compared to only 23 per cent of the populace as a whole. Correspondingly, the number of Jews employed in manual labor dropped precipitately, confined for the most part to pockets of first- and second-generation immigrants such as those still involved in the New York garment trades. While there would remain large groups of poor Jews (whose existence would be practically a family secret until the early 1970s), there is no doubt that the children and grandchildren of the great eastern European immigration had raised themselves to middle- and upper-middle-class status, as had the older German Jewish community two generations earlier.[2]

Like other upwardly mobile groups in the postwar years, Jews left the cities in search of more pleasant surroundings in the suburban belts. In doing so, they did more than exchange a tenement apartment for a small house with a postage-stamp lawn; the inner-city communities had provided a particular Jewish ambiance, a cohesiveness that made it easier for one to retain a sense of Jewish identity. Schools, synagogues, stores, butcher shops, bakeries, and restaurants in close proximity reinforced one's Jewishness; most importantly, to live in one of these ethnic enclaves meant to be surrounded by other Jews. By moving out of this protected environment, would these pioneers on the suburban frontier lose their identity? Would they assimilate and cease being Jews? Certainly Albert Gordon, in his study of Jews in suburbia, found that a number of those who left the city wanted to escape their past. They played down their Jewishness, which they saw as something separate and different from normal—that is, gentile—American practices.[3]

But surprisingly, the majority of these newly middle-class suburban Jews did not forsake their heritage. To the contrary, finding themselves cut off from the familiar props of the urban ghetto, they set to work creating new communal structures. They found that even in suburbia, certain areas tended to have higher concentrations of Jews. Some saw this as a sign of group cohesiveness, while others complained that gentiles moved out of neighborhoods that became "too Jewish."[4] Whatever the cause, the new suburbs soon saw the construction of elaborate synagogue-communal centers, all-purpose buildings which catered to the educational, religious, social, and cultural needs of the community. Mordecai Kaplan's prediction of the emergence of the "synagogue/ center" as the new focus of Jewish life in America seemed to be borne out with striking rapidity in the early fifties. The Conservative movement, which had claimed 250 synagogues and 75,000 member families in 1937, reported an affiliation of over 500 congregations and 200,000 member families in 1956. Reform, with 290 temples and 50,000 families in 1937, now claimed 255,000 families belonging to 520 congregations. Overall, the total number of synagogues in the country only rose from 3,700 to 3,900 in this period. Hundreds of small Orthodox congregations in the inner cities closed their doors as their members— and their children—moved outward.[5] The growth of Reform and Conservative Judaism, often at the expense of Orthodoxy, reflected much more than demographic changes, however; the 1950s witnessed the development of a more secularly oriented Judaism, one which, in Kaplan's old terms, tended to resemble a "civilization" rather than a traditional "religion."[6] Much to the dismay of many religious leaders, the social needs of the individual and the communal needs of local Jewries became the prime foci of American Judaism.

Much of the ritual observance of traditional Orthodoxy disappeared —the *mikvah* (ritual bath), segregation of the sexes at worship, strict rules regarding the celebration of Sabbath and holidays, and *kashrut* (dietary laws)—yet even while this new generation seemingly abandoned traditional *Judaism,* they clung to *Jewishness,* to their sense of group identity. They joined the local temples and synagogues, not so much to pray there as to send their children to the religious schools so that they might learn about their heritage, or to join the sisterhoods and brotherhoods for Jewish companionship. In the so-called religious revival of the fifties, a tolerant America did not care to which religion one belonged, but did expect that every family would belong somewhere. The Yiddish-speaking culture of the cities did not survive the move to the suburbs, and a new milieu had to be created. All too often this new life-style reflected the garishness and pretentiousness of the *nouveaux riche*—the emphasis on objects rather than ritual, on form rather than substance, on the lavish weddings and *bnai mitzvot*, the gastronomical "bagels and lox" Jewishness so devastatingly parodied by Philip Roth in *Good-bye, Columbus.*[7]

It would be easy to denigrate this life-style, to emphasize its shallowness and excesses. But to do so is to miss the psychological and emotional search which lay behind the façade of lavish and ornate temples. This generation of American Jews, unlike other ethnic groups, confirmed Marcus Hansen's prediction of the behavior of the third immigrant generation. According to Hansen, the first generation, those who actually made the long journey to these shores, arrived with a set of cultural baggage they could never jettison; while they might adapt to America, English would always be their second language, and their standards, ideals, and even behavior would reflect their Old World origins. Their children, the second generation, seeking to affirm their Americanism, would deliberately reject the cultural heritage of their parents; they would speak only English, discontinue old customs and traditions, and in many cases "Americanize" their names. The third generation, the grandchildren of the original immigrants, secure in their Americanness, would be willing to "remember" what their parents had striven so hard to "forget."[8]

This postwar generation of American Jews, the third generation, did just that: They sought to "remember," to discover who and what they were. And if we think this was easy, if we lose sight of the fact that this generation had little in the way of a Jewish upbringing to fall back upon, then we miss the meaning and depth of their plight. In the words of one young college woman in the late 1940s: "I am on the fence. I haven't quite made up my mind as to what I think or why I think it. And in that, I am typical of the Jewish people. Look at me. I'm neither here nor there. As a Jewess, I don't amount to much. . . . I've been told that mine is a precious heritage, but I've not the slightest idea what it is. . . . Occasionally I discover something in me that is characteristically Jewish, and I am surprised, almost estranged from myself. I know I'm Jewish because I've been told so, because I have Jewish friends. Aside from that, it doesn't mean very much to me. So, you see, as a Jewess I don't amount to much. But I'm not much better as an American either. . . . So what am I?"[9]

Unfortunately, this young woman's complaint reflected more than her own sense of confusion; it also mirrored the sad state of much Jewish education, with the exception of the Orthodox. Traditional religious schools emphasized Jewish subjects rather than secular matter, a pattern which may have given their children sound Jewish knowledge, but which varied considerably from the desires of the vast majority of American Jewry, which wanted to acculturate. Throughout the 1950s there would be one lament after another about the failures of Jewish education, and fears about whether or not this new generation would remain Jewish.[10]

Lacking the European experience of a shared, religiously oriented life, deprived of a sound Jewish education, this third generation began to grope, uncertainly at first, then more surely, to recapture their heritage. They would not be able to resurrect Yiddish, but they avidly read the works of Mendele Mocher Sforim, Sholom Aleichem, I. L. Peretz, and other Yiddish writers in translation. They would never be able to restore the group solidarity of the *shtetl,* so they endowed it with near-mythic qualities and sentiment, which would later erupt in the fantastic success enjoyed by *Fiddler on the Roof.* Unfamiliar with many of the rituals and traditions, they surrounded themselves with objects and symbols such as *mezuzot,* candelabra, paintings, and prints with "Jewish" motifs, as well as countless books on "the meaning of Judaism." They no longer felt at home in the old Orthodox *shul,* with its lengthy, Hebrew service, its segregation of the sexes, and its seeming lack of order, so they joined an American Conservative or Reform congregation, which attempted to bridge the gap between ancient beliefs and contemporary needs. "Religious association," wrote Will Herberg, "now became the primary context of self-identification and social location for the third generation."[11]

To the more observant Jews, those who maintained the traditional customs across the generations, much of the new religious fervor of American Jewry seemed extremely shallow, devoid as it was of so many of the old rituals. Immanuel Jakobovitz feared that "for the first time in our history . . . the sheer survival of Jews and Judaism is now at stake," while Jacob Neusner wondered if there had ever been a Jewish community "less religiously concerned than our own."[12] Yet, as Marshall Sklare and Marc Vlosk discovered, the selection of what to keep and what to discard had been far from haphazard. "The rituals which had special appeal," they reported, "were those which were joyous, which marked the transition from one stage of life to another, which did not require a high degree of isolation from non-Jews, which did not demand rigorous devotion and daily attention, which were capable of acceptance to the larger community, and which this larger community had itself reserved for the sacred order."[13] What American Jews now sought was a religion which would meet not only their spiritual needs, but also the social, cultural, and communal demands which conformed to American expectations.

This interplay between religion and secularism, which alarmed the traditionalists, fit perfectly into the scheme of the third generation, who saw no conflict between Jewish and Americans values and obligations. In large measure, the secularization of the churches proved to be a widespread American phenomenon during the 1950s. A committee of Presbyterian leaders, chaired by Henry P. Van Dusen, the president of Union Theological Seminary, found that the American people were simultaneously becoming more religious and more secular. In "Elmtown," according to August B. Hollingshead, the church had become "a community facility like the school, the drug store, the city government, and the bowling alley." The synagogue, commented C. Bezalel Sherman, "has gone even farther along the road to secularization than its Christian counterparts."[14]

Horace Meyer Kallen, whose writings on "cultural pluralism" had done much to foster the legitimacy of continued ethnic diversity, agreed that the Americanization of American Jewry had led to a partial abandonment of the traditional Judaic nucleus of creed, code, and conduct. But he noted that even in doing so, American Jews had not departed from their faith. "However radical the mutation," he noted, "however extreme the social and psychological distance from the starting point, Judaism, Jewish, and Jew remain the distinguishing terms."[15] American Jews were not *assimilating*—that is, they were not losing their particular identity in being swallowed up by the larger society—but were *acculturating*, bringing their life-style into conformity with the larger community while at the same time retaining their sense of Jewishness and identification as Jews. Certainly, by all reports, the most frequently accepted indicator of assimilation, intermarriage with non-Jews, remained remarkably low during this period, with most estimates running at 10 per cent or less.[16]

The only group for whom these general trends did not seem to hold true was the Jewish intellectuals. Various surveys indicated that the rate of intermarriage, for example, among the intellectuals ran two or three times higher than for the community as a whole. One study found that young Jewish intellectuals, writers, artists, and academics in their midthirties, while valuing the universalist ethical principles of Judaism and taking pride in the State of Israel, had little interest in ensuring that their children received a solid Jewish education, or even caring about whether their offspring remained Jewish. Elia Kazan accepted the fact that he was Jewish, but did not consider himself at all involved in any meaningful Jewish life or culture. Irving Howe declared in 1952 that the Jewish intellectual "has largely lost his sense of Jewishness, of belonging to a people with a meaningful tradition." Nearly a quarter century later, looking back at these times, Howe, who had done more than anyone to popularize Yiddish writers, recalled: "Even though most of the New York intellectuals were Jewish, statements beginning 'I am a Jew and . . .' were hard for them to make. They resisted identifications or assertions of Jewishness, just as the East Side Yiddish-speaking socialist of half a century earlier had quailed before the heresy of 'Jewish nationalism.' To speak openly out of Jewish sentiments or interests seemed too 'parochial' for writers who, often enough, had emerged a few years earlier from immigrant neighborhoods in Brooklyn and the Bronx and now liked to think of themselves as radical internationalists, spokesmen for cultural modernism, men of letters transcending 'mere' ethnic loyalties."[17]

In many instances, the *cri de coeur* of intellectual Jews seemed to be that they had not rejected Judaism, so much as it had excluded them. In a widely read article, Leslie Fiedler stated: "What does the [Jewish] Intellectual, fumbling his way 'back' toward a Jewish faith, discover in our Jewish institutions? In the orthodox *shuls*, the *hassidic* fire, the old unity of devotion are moribund beneath an emphasis on *kashrut*, and the endless *pilpul*, long since turned into a substitute for any moving faith. In the Reform Temples, the glib young Rabbi, with his tags from Freud, his sociological jargon, speaks his conviction that God is a 'cosmological blur.' Like the more debased Protestant Churches, the Temples have tended to substitute 'social service' for religion, felt to belong to the unenlightened past. These conditions do not prevail universally, of course, but in general, American Judaism has made everything its center but God in amateur psychoanalysis, collecting money for the Jewish Appeal, hating all Germans, worshipping force, bowing down before a revived nineteenth-century nationalism." When anybody else asks me, Fiedler confessed, "I am a Jew; when I question myself, I am not so sure." Fiedler was far from alone in feeling uncomfortable both with the traditionalism of Old World Orthodoxy and the secularism of the new Judaism; the fact that this latter phenomenon was endemic in all American religious institutions in the fifties did not make the plight of the intellectuals, their sense of loneliness, any less acute.[18]

*   *   *

Rabbi Israel Goldstein, a noted Zionist leader and longtime spiritual leader of New York's Conservative Congregation B'nai Jeshurun, while agreeing that Jewish life in America remained centripetal, wondered how much of Jewish self-identification rested on a desire to preserve a heritage and how much resulted from social anti-Semitism. "I believe that anti-Semitism is not far beneath the surface," he wrote, "and I believe that most American Jews feel it and fear it in the secret chambers of their hearts."[19]

A number of studies during the 1950s indicated that Jews for the most part did tend to associate primarily with each other. A survey in Detroit found 77 per cent of the Jewish sample reporting "all" or "nearly all" of their close friends were Jewish, a finding duplicated in other cities.[20] A study of suburban life seemed to confirm that Jews remained socially segregated even after leaving the cities. "Our husbands do business with [gentiles]," explained one typical suburban matron. "We see them in the town's shopping area. It's always a very pleasant 'Hello, how are you?' kind of superficial conversation. We may even meet at a meeting some afternoon or even perhaps at a PTA school affair, but it is seldom more than that. It is a kind of 'nine to five' arrangement. The ghetto gates, real or imagined, close at 5 P.M. 'Five-o'clock shadow' sets in at sundown. Jews and Christians do not meet socially even in suburbia. If we do, you bet that it is to help promote some cause or organization where they think we Jews may be helpful. But after five o'clock there is no social contact, no parties, no home visits, no golf clubs—no nothing!"[21]

Moreover, Goldstein also correctly assessed that Jews, after witnessing what had happened to their "accepted" brethren in Germany only a few short years earlier, felt anxious, even fearful, no matter how much they seemed to be at home in America. As late as 1970, Jews almost leaped off the charts in terms of their intrinsic distrust of others. A study done for the National Institute of Mental Health attempted to assess various white ethnic groups' comparable levels of distrust. The scale went from +4 (most trusting) to —4 (least trusting):[22]

Group	Score
Irish Catholic	2.506
Scandinavian Protestant	1.583
Slavic Catholic	1.481
German Protestant	0.767
German Catholic	0.757
Italian Catholic	0.502
White Anglo-Saxon Protestant	0.242
Jewish	—3.106

In terms of group consciousness, it would be very strange indeed if Jews could wipe away the memories of centuries of persecution and pogroms, of the Holocaust, even in a land of religious freedom and tolerance. Yet even if we concede that Jews tended to stick together and remained fearful, this would hardly confirm the existence of anti-Semitism in the United States in the postwar years. In fact, explicit studies seeking anti-Jewish activities found a consistently decreasing level in the 1950s.

The first major study of prejudice after the war, *America Divided* (1948) by Arnold and Caroline Rose, found practically no legal restrictions against Jews but a fairly widespread set of informal barriers. Resort hotels, private schools, clubs, fraternities, and country clubs tended to exclude Jews, as did certain businesses, such as banking and insurance. Medical and law schools, while accepting Jewish students, had unwritten quotas to limit their numbers, while many stores would hire only one or two Jewish salespersons, mainly to cater to their Jewish clientele. The Roses found that in almost every metropolitan area with a significant Jewish poulation, restrictive covenants denied Jews the opportunity to buy or rent homes in the more desirable areas. Confirming the suburban housewives' reports, they concluded: "It is in interpersonal relations that segregation of Jews is most extensive. Not only are they kept out of social clubs, but they are not invited to informal gatherings or parties in many circles. They are talked about behind their backs and kept at a distance in neighborly relations. . . . Scorn, disgust, and studied indifference are frequent attitudes manifested by non-Jews in their personal relations with Jews."[23]

In the years following publication of *America Divided*, the evidence gathered in successive studies by the American Jewish Committee registered an increasingly favorable attitude toward Jews. In 1950, for example, 69 per cent of the sample declared it would make no difference to them if a Jewish family moved in next door; in 1954, the figure rose to 88 per cent. One analyst, looking at all the data available for this period, concluded that "anti-Semitism in all its forms massively declined in the United States between the prewar or war years and the early 1960s. . . . Thus, as of 1962, significantly fewer people than formerly believed that Jews as a group had distinctive undesirable traits or considered them a 'race.' Fewer thought Jews were clannish, dishonest, unscrupulous, or excessively powerful in business and finance. Fewer believed colleges should limit the number of Jewish students. Fewer still objected to Jewish neighbors or employees."[24]

Anti-Semitism, of course, had not disappeared. An employment survey in the middle of the decade showed large areas where Jews faced substantial discrimination. The civil rights movement, which broke down many barriers confronting Jews, tended to drive more conscious or organized anti-Semitism underground, where it simmered until it exploded in the two-month-long "swastika epidemic" that began in the last week of 1959.[25] Yet a number of events which might have triggered any large-scale latent anti-Semitism had no perceptible effects. The creation of Israel did not raise any cries that American Jews would no longer be loyal to the United States; neither did the 1956 Israeli invasion of Egypt, which directly challenged the policies of the American government.* Despite the long-standing canards that Jews were all radicals, during the spy trials of 1950–51 and the subsequent McCarthy Red scare, no evidence could be found that the nation associated Jews with communism, espionage, or loyalty to the Soviet Union. Even Arnold Forster and Benjamin Epstein, who argue that a new and potent anti-Semitism developed in the United States in the late 1960s, concede that in the twenty years after World War Two, "American Jews achieved a greater degree of economic and political security and social acceptance than has ever been achieved by any Jewish community since the Dispersion."[26]

* See below, Chapter 12.

As John Higham has argued, anti-Jewish feeling in this country has never been based on ideological arguments, such as had been the case in Hitler's Germany or in Europe under the medieval church.[27] Social discrimination resulted primarily from what Israel Goldstein called the "dislike of the unlike." As American Jewry became more Americanized, it perceived itself as more accepted, as moving into the mainstream of American life.

Perhaps the classic document marking this feeling of acceptance was Will Herberg's *Protestant-Catholic-Jew*, first published in 1955, at the crest of the move to suburbia. In it, Herberg argued that although American Jews numbered little more than 3 per cent of the population, their cultural and social values affected the general society in an extremely profound manner. Taking his cue from Kallen's thesis of cultural pluralism, Herberg posited a triad of Protestantism, Catholicism, and Judaism sharing dominant values in American religious life. While Herberg noted the lengths to which the Jewish community went to assert its legitimacy and to protest real or alleged slights, he also placed the pattern in the broader sociological framework of American religion in general. To these Jews departing from the strict orthodoxy of their parents, or worried about the superficiality of their Jewishness, Herberg brought the reassuring message that such developments were natural in the pattern of American society, and were shared by the other major religions. He ignored much of the peoplehood concept of Judaism, the *gestalt* that had blended religious and secular activities into a harmonious whole, and described Judaism mainly in terms of religion—more specifically, as religion was practiced in midcentury America. Herberg became a popular speaker on the synagogue lecture circuit, preaching the comforting message not only of acceptance but also of parity.[28]

Not everyone accepted the Herberg thesis, although it enjoyed a lengthy vogue. Some critics challenged what they saw as his rationalization of Judaism's degradation; they did not like these new forms of Americanized Judaism, and saw no reason to praise them. The fact that the stereotyped Jew had disappeared, only to be replaced by the stereotyped American, gave them little cause for celebration. Others contested the thesis that Jews had been admitted into the American establishment; things might have indeed gotten much better in recent years, but Jews, in their minds, would always remain tolerated outsiders rather than accepted equals. Abraham Duker, without mentioning Herberg, attacked those who sought "to divest Jewishness of its elements of peoplehood," who represented American Jewry "as predominantly if not exclusively religious," and who deliberately tried "to present Judaism as a purely religious development."[29]

The question about the nature of Judaism, however, remained. Was it strictly a religion, like Methodism or Congregationalism, or was it an all-encompassing way of life, a civilization? Were Jews defined only by their modes of worship, or did they see themselves as part of a people or as both? Herberg took the first view, yet in the end American Jewry itself rejected the idea that it could be defined only within religious parameters. Support for Israel could in no way be explained as a strictly religious matter, or even as purely humanitarian. These considerations were, to some extent, put aside in the early 1950s, as American Jews pursued a style of life acceptable both in Jewish and American terms, but they were not forgotten. In a time of testing and adjustment, American Jews worked out the psychological mechanisms necessary for living in two cultures. One culture, as C. B. Sherman explained, "identifies him with the totality of the American community, and induces a separateness from the Jews of the rest of the world; the other draws him to the latter, creating needs and interests apart from his fellow citizens. He is thus within and outside the mainstream of American life at the same time."[30] This learning to live simultaneously in two cultures underlies much of American Jewish development in that decade. The Americanization of Jewish practices facilitated one part of this process; the growth of communal and national organizations marked the other.

*   *   *

Although the phrases "American Jewry" and "the American Jewish community" are widespread in use, there is a certain irony inherent in them. They seem to imply that the Jews of the United States form an organized, coherent, and unified corporate body, when this is in fact far from the truth. On a few issues, such as support for Israel and opposition to anti-Semitism, America's 55 million Jews do share a high degree of consensus approaching unanimity. In times of crisis, such as the campaign to create the Jewish state or the 1967 and 1973 Israeli-Arab wars, they come together and even act in a more or less co-ordinated way. Some politicians claim that a Jewish bloc vote exists, and many if not most Israelis, especially since 1967, share the belief that American Jews can swing into action at a moment's notice.[31] American Jewish leaders, on the other hand, while publicly asserting the unity and power of the community, privately smile at such naïveté, and say "*halevai!*" (were it only so!). The recurrent crises in Israel have, in fact, strengthened the organizational structures of American Jewry, and enabled them to raise large sums of money as well as to lobby in Washington on behalf of Israel and other causes, such as the emigration of Soviet Jews. But even today, American Jewry is far from monolithically organized, and in the postwar decade confusion rather than coherence marked its structural arrangements.

Recently noted Judaic scholar Joseph L. Blau contended that there never has been, nor can there be, a normative American Judaism, one that could be organized within the confines of a centralized control. He ascribes this condition to four influences derived from the general American religious culture: Protestantism (in the sense of denominationalism), pluralism, moralism, and "voluntaryism." All of these factors work against the development of any overall control and foster diversity, rather than unity, within the community. The very Americanism of American Jews in their cultural, political, and social views makes it impossible for them ever to re-create, even locally, the unitary socioreligious organization of the *shtetl*. Only crises can override these constraints, and then only temporarily and with far from a total control.[32]

The crisis of the Second World War had brought about the American Jewish Conference, whose early history paralleled that of the American Jewish Congress a quarter century earlier.[33] But where the Congress had managed to create for itself a permanent role, albeit a diminished one, in Jewish communal life, the Conference, with its emphasis on Palestine, never accomplished even that. The Conference died an obscure and unlamented death, and in the years following the establishment of Israel, old patterns of diversity reasserted themselves. One seeking to discern the structure of the American Jewish community would have to look at several groupings, all of them overlapping, without any common denominator other than identification as Jewish.

In the directory of Jewish organizations for 1954, the *American Jewish Year Book* listed over three hundred national Jewish organizations, divided into the following rough categories:

Civil defense, political	16
Cultural	32
Overseas aid	19
Religious, educational	89
Social, mutual benefit	54
Social welfare	29
Zionist and pro-Israel	62

Mordecai Kaplan, in reviewing this situation, lamented what he termed "Jewish self-segregation" and condemned the fact that "each institution, organization, and financial drive is viewed as an end in itself, unrelated to any overall pattern of Jewish life which should normally animate all of them."[34] Yet, if one accepts Joseph Blau's suggestion, the very diversity and voluntaristic aspect of American life in general precluded any other pattern in Jewish affairs.

Within the specifically religious area of Jewish life, attempts at central organization proved somewhat successful. The Reform movement, thanks to the early leadership of Isaac Mayer Wise, began its organizational efforts in the latter part of the nineteenth century and developed three major institutions. In 1873 Wise founded the Union of American Hebrew Congregations, which became the lay arm of Reform Judaism in the United States. Although the UAHC developed a number of programs in such fields as religious education, brotherhood and sisterhood, youth work, synagogue administration, and social action, prior to the Second World War the UAHC remained the weakest of the three Reform agencies. In 1941 a radical change began with the appointment of Rabbi Edward Israel as executive secretary. Under Israel, and especially under his successor, Rabbi Maurice N. Eisendrath, the UAHC became the national spokesman for Reform, representing the movement in its dealings with comparable Catholic and Protestant agencies. In 1951 the Union moved its offices from Cincinnati to New York, a step which not only marked the end of the old midwestern domination, but also symbolized the UAHC's intention to play a major role in Jewish affairs above and beyond the needs of local congregations. By the late 1950s, the Union had clearly emerged as the dominant force within American Reform.

The second stage of Wise's plan had been the creation of an American seminary to train rabbis, and in 1876, under the sponsorship of the UAHC, the Hebrew Union College opened its doors in Cincinnati. Over the following decades, HUC became the chief source of rabbis for American Reform congregations. The college also took the lead in developing Reform practices and theology, and in adopting traditional Jewish beliefs and laws to suit contemporary conditions. In 1948 it merged with the Jewish Institute of Religion, which Stephen S. Wise had founded in New York in 1922 as a more theologically flexible and socially conscious alternative to what he saw as the parochialism endemic in Cincinnati.[35]

The graduates of HUC formed the third arm of Reform, the Central Conference of American Rabbis, founded by Isaac Wise in 1889, and which he led as president until his death in 1900. At first most of the HUC graduates and CCAR members followed the classic proto-German Reform position, with its stark opposition to Zionism and its insistence on modernity. Gradually, however, as more and more sons of the eastern European migration entered the movement, the rabbinate became not only sympathetic to Zionism but also much more traditional in outlook, blurring some of the ritualistic differences between Reform and historic Jewish practices. The CCAR pioneered in such areas as social action, church and state problems, interfaith relations, military chaplaincy, and college youth work, and its *Union Prayer Book* became a common link among Reform congregations throughout the country. Thanks to strong rabbis like Wise and David Philipson, the CCAR dominated Reform until after the Second World War, when the UAHC, representing the congregations, assumed control.[36]

A different pattern developed within the Conservative movement. There the premier organization from the start has been the Jewish Theological Seminary of America, founded in 1887 and reorganized in 1902 with the installation of Solomon Schechter as president. Under Schechter and his successors, Cyrus Adler and Louis Finkelstein, the seminary became the leading center of Jewish scholarship in the country as well as the arbiter of Conservative practices and beliefs, a system that retained much of traditional Judaism with some concessions to contemporary conditions. Like Isaac M. Wise, Schechter founded a congregational organization, the United Synagogue of America, in 1913, which sought to provide its affiliates with help in meeting religious and educational needs. The United Synagogue's Commission on Jewish Education conducted numerous studies on the operation of congregational religious schools, which eventually led to the formulation of standardized curricula and texts.[37]

Conservative Judaism's rabbinical arm, the Rabbinical Assembly, predated Schechter's arrival in the United States by only a year. Even more than the CCAR, the Rabbinical Assembly has devoted itself to religious problems, especially the furtherance of Jewish ritual. It published a large number of *responsa* dealing with how the modern Conservative Jew can fulfill such varied obligations as *kashrut*, Sabbath observance, and life rituals. Unlike Reform, however, the Conservative rabbinate has retained its control over the movement. A much closer tie exists between the Assembly and the Seminary than between the CCAR and Hebrew Union College, which is financed primarily by the UAHC. The word of the Seminary has been considered authoritative in theological matters, and the lay leadership has, for the most part, been deferential to rabbinical authority not only in religious matters, but in secular policy as well.

Undoubtedly the least organized, in fact one might say the most disorganized, group has been the Orthodox, where there has been no centralization at all. Despite the eminence of the Isaac Elkanan Yeshiva and the founding of Yeshiva University, the old European pattern of local *yeshivot*, where one group of rabbis trained the next generation in Talmud and Jewish law, was replicated in America with each *yeshiva* jealously guarding its independence. From time to time there were attempts to create a national organization, but instead of a single agency, there have been at least four rabbinic groups, and the Union of Orthodox Jewish Congregations has only a minority of Orthodox synagogues affiliated with it. As much as anything, the absence of strong nationally known leaders such as Isaac Wise and Solomon Schechter within Orthodox circles has prevented national consolidation.[38]

In the 1950s, both Reform and Conservative Judaism experienced enormous growth, a situation which central organization and administration not only facilitated, but which in turn strengthened the national agencies. New congregations, receiving financial and administrative assistance from either the UAHC or the United Synagogue, saw the value of some form of affiliation not only for religious uniformity but also for the ancillary services that local congregations by themselves could not provide. Orthodoxy, on the other hand, underwent a decline in these years, and such a condition did not prove amenable to calls for new national organizations.[39]

To many observers of the religious revival in this country during the 1950s, the most striking aspect seemed to be the vitality and growth of the synagogues. Only in retrospect can we see that this effort to define, or redefine, Jewishness entirely in synagogal or religious terms had to fail. A century earlier, the German Jewish immigrants had also discovered that in order to maintain Jewish life they had to create a number of institutions outside the synagogue—welfare agencies, benevolent associations, and fraternal groups. As Daniel Elazar has observed, "We Jews need a communal infrastructure and not simply houses of worship precisely because we are a 'polity' and not simply a 'religion.'

. . . [In the 1950s] we tried to define ourselves ideologically in 'religious' terms and, in functions from the community as a whole to the synagogues, it did not work."[40]

Here is one of the distinguishing marks of American Jewry, the fact that its interests and needs far exceed the relatively limited confines of the strictly religious idiom. No other religious group in the nation requires the extensive combination of welfare funds, educational agencies, cultural programs, benevolent associations, or defense arms that American Jews do, because no other religious grouping also sees itself as an ethnic bloc, as a people. The majority of "Jewish" agencies in this country have little to do with directly fostering or protecting Jewish religiosity, but concern themselves with the support of the Jewish people. Various attempts to unify American Jewry, to bring it under a single centralized organization, have failed because not one of those efforts could encompass a definition of Jewish needs broad enough to cover all those aspects of life which can, in various ways, be related to "Jewish" living. In large measure, the central religious organs of Conservative and Reform Judaism had the easiest task, since by definition they focused on a fairly narrow level of Jewish life.

It would be impossible to describe in even superficial detail the more than three hundred national organizations supported by, and supporting, American Jews in the 1950s. The range and activities of dozens of educational, cultural, and social associations proved as diversified as American Jewry itself. But two specific types—the welfare campaigns and the defense agencies—deserve some examination.†

*   *   *

William Zuckerman, then editor of the *Jewish Newsletter,* dubbed postwar American Judaism as "Campaign Judaism," and in a scathing attack declared that the community "has almost consciously emptied itself of all higher aspirations and spiritual needs and has willingly limited itself to the role of a financial milk cow for others. . . . How can a community such as this, whose highest ideal is mechanical fund-raising, be the source of nobility and greatness? Can the interminable big-and-even-bigger Bond and UJA drives, the Hadassah teas, the gaudy banquets, the garish publicity and appalling bad taste, be the soil from

† A more detailed analysis of Zionist organizations will be made in Chapter 11.

which greatness will spring? Can salesmanship, even when clothed with the mantle of philanthropy, be anything but shallow and sterile?"[41]

Like similar attacks on the superficiality and *gaucherie* of Jewish life in these years, Zuckerman's plaint had many elements of truth, but it also missed the deeper significance of the elaborate welfare system developed by American Jews. Undoubtedly for too many people and for too long, the measure of one's "Jewishness" could be found in the amount written on a check to the United Jewish Appeal; rather than honoring the scholar, as had been the custom for centuries of Jewish life, the community seemed hell-bent on making a hero of the big giver, no matter how lacking in knowledge or how unobservant in ritual he might be.

The yearly fund drive in local Jewish communities actually encompassed two different campaigns: one to meet local needs—hospitals, schools, family services, and the like; the other, the United Jewish Appeal, which in turn consisted of two previously separate funds, the Joint Distribution Committee and the United Palestine (later Israel) Appeal, which had merged, after long and acrimonious debate, in 1939.

In the early years, the division of monies raised through the UJA was negotiated annually by the major beneficiaries, with the amounts varying according to common perceptions of need. In the immediate postwar years, the JDC, with its responsibilities in the European refugee camps, took a high priority; in addition, certain amounts were also then appropriated to the National Refugee Service and its successor, the United Services for New Americans, and to the United HIAS Service. After 1948, by common agreement, the lion's share of overseas aid went to Israel.

Perhaps the most important change in the campaign occurred in 1949 following a 20 per cent drop in UJA contributions, a falling off attributed to the relaxation of the crisis mentality after the successful establishment of the State of Israel. From 1945 through 1948 fund-raising had been of an "emergency" nature, with every possible dollar channeled to the UJA. The more than two hundred local Jewish federations and community councils had postponed numerous programs, diverting funds first to the refugees and then to Israel; now, just as revenues fell, they clamored for the UJA to reduce its goals, arguing that they could no longer ignore local needs. At the UJA conference in Atlantic City in late 1949, angry delegates demanded precampaign agreements on the local share of the 1950 total as their price for continued co-operation. When the UJA general chairman, Henry Morgenthau, Jr., warned that hospitals, schools—in fact, every Jewish need in America—would have to wait upon more pressing problems overseas, Justice Meir Steinbrink and others rejected his pleas. "Neglected problems at home," declared Steinbrink, "have now to be met and solved if Jewish life in this country is to continue strong and healthy."[42]

The UJA leaders recognized that since Israel was in desperate need of long-term assistance, the haphazard "emergency" mentality would have to give way to systematic planning. In 1954, the JDC and the United Israel Appeal signed their first five-year agreement, stabilizing apportionment of UJA funds; since then the pact has been renewed periodically, with only minor modifications. In recent years, the distribution has settled at 67 per cent for the UIA and 33 per cent for the JDC of the first $55 million after campaign expenses, and 87.5 per cent and 12.5 per cent, respectively, of all sums beyond that.

In the seventeen postwar years of 1946 through 1962, American Jews raised $2.29 *billion* for their various communal charities, of which more than half went to the UJA. Fund-raising became a major activity and reached into every nook and cranny of American Jewish life. Every town, every industry, every profession, every association of Jews developed its own campaign committee with its own tactics designed to get the most money. In New York, for example, leading manufacturers of ladies' undergarments would gather for luncheon at a midtown hotel for their annual fund-raising event. Although the surface mood appeared pleasant, these men, locked in bitter competition in the Seventh Avenue clothing jungle, carried that competitiveness into the campaign. No one dared not to give, with the eyes of the whole industry upon him. An increased pledge meant business had been good (let the other fellows choke on that!), while any suggestion of a decrease might be regarded as a sign of slipping sales. As one commentator wryly noted, "Might as well tell Wall Street as inform the UJA that things were not going too well at Adorable Undies!"[43]

In different cities and for different groups the approaches would vary, sometimes assuming an air of casual relaxation. At a private dining room in downtown Miami, for example, fifty lawyers finished lunch and lit their cigars as Dore Schary, motion-picture producer and playwright, talked to them about the work of various Jewish groups. He concluded with a story about a chicken who struck up a conversation with a salmon swimming upstream. After two hours of talk, the chicken suggested to the salmon that they pause at a nearby restaurant for lunch.

"Nothing doing," the salmon replied. "When we get in there, all they will want from you is a token contribution. From me they will demand total commitment."

The audience chuckled, and reached for their pens to fill out their pledge cards.[44]

While certain groups gave readily, others proved harder to reach, and the UJA adopted various approaches to meet specific situations. Some communities published an annual list of donors with the amount given by each one, a process designed to shame people into giving more.[45] Others used peer pressure, and high-powered fund-raisers were known to fling pledge cards back in donors' faces, telling them that they had not given enough. During the campaign season there would be an endless marathon of parlor meetings, conferences, fashion shows, and cocktail parties, all with one aim: raising money. In New York City, the Federation of Jewish Philanthropies estimated that more than five thousand such gatherings took place in the city alone during the drive. Buttonholing probably reached its peak when Rabbi Irving Koslowe, the Jewish chaplain at Sing Sing, asked his parishioners to contribute to the UJA. The prisoners, who earned five cents a day, averaged donations of $2.50—fifty days' pay—with 100 per cent of the Jewish inmates contributing. When Koslowe pointed a suspicious finger at his Collections Committee, they put on their most sincere expressions and declared, "Honestly, Rabbi, we didn't use any strong-arm tactics," and compared to some of their counterparts over the wall, they were probably telling the truth.[46]

Such stories abound endlessly, some funny, some appealing, and some appalling. Yet the fact remains that through the drives, countless Jews were drawn into communal life, even if only in a temporary and peripheral manner. Moreover, despite the prominence of the big givers, several studies indicated that the percentage of Jews contributing to the annual campaigns was extremely high. One study of general American charities in the early sixties determined that 975,000 private-service and cultural agencies received contributions from 40 million donors. But the base of overall giving did not seem to be very broad. Citing a college that had raised $655,000 in one drive, the author discovered that this sum included one gift of $400,000, a few others that totaled $245,000, and the remaining $10,000 in small amounts.[47]

Jewish philanthropies, on the other hand, seemed extremely broad-based, with, at that time, three out of every four contributors giving between $10 and $100. In one drive in Detroit, out of a total of 23,778 pledges, 16,863 were for $50 or less, and another 4,500 for between $50 and $100. At the end of the 1950s, conservative estimates suggested that more than one million people contributed annually to federated campaigns out of a total population of 5.5 million men, women, and children; in the smaller communities, there was close to total coverage.[48]

Instead of reacting to the cruder mechanisms of fund-raising, or even its pervasiveness, critics might better have complained that Jewish leadership in this country failed to use the nexus to develop stronger ties between the individual and the community. At a time when observers like Jacob Neusner, Albert Gordon, and others feared for the breakdown of group consciousness and cohesion, the UJA had fashioned an instrument which, properly used, could have been the point of contact between the purveyors of Jewish education and culture and those who needed—and wanted—it. The real tragedy of "Campaign Judaism" in the 1950s is that its leaders were men of such small vision.

*   *   *

In Europe, Jews had been helpless before the onslaught of pogroms or the less bloody but equally debasing legal restrictions on their activities and rights. In the United States, they discovered that they had little to fear from physical violence, and had legal means to redress a number of wrongs. Only in the area of social discrimination did they recognize a sense of helplessness, and since this type of bias did not interfere with their political, religious, or economic liberties, they ignored it as best they could. But it is a mark of the sense of brotherhhood and responsibility that they felt obligated to protect not only American Jews but also Jews threatened anywhere in the world; the American Jewish Committee, the oldest of the defense agencies, came into being not in response to domestic anti-Semitism, but to a pogrom halfway around the world.

By the 1950s the Committee, while still an elitist organization, had

taken several steps toward reorganization after the American Jewish
Conference debacle. Beginning in 1944 it instituted a chapter system,
and within five years had established 38 branches and raised its membership from 400 to 18,000. But it still aimed for like-mindedness rather
than mass support, for articulating Committee opinion rather than
broadening its leadership base. As described by Naomi Cohen, the average member of the Committee's executive in the mid-1950s was a man
in his early sixties, affluent, established, and respected in his business or
profession, American-born (though of old German stock), Reform, and
non-Zionist. Well-educated, he was moderate to conservative on political issues and had joined the Committee primarily out of a sense of *no-
blesse oblige*. The Committee deliberately sought out members of eastern European background, but only those who had "arrived" in terms
of social status and wealth. It would not be until well into the 1960s
that the organization would open its doors to all classes in the community and work *with* rather than only *for* Jews.[49] In the late forties, the
Committee also joined the civil rights struggle, and through a well-
financed drive attempted to educate Americans to the fact that discrimination against any minority group threatened the liberties and
well-being of all. It set up offices in several foreign countries to aid their
Jewish communities in developing civic programs, but, no matter what
ends it sought, the Committee continued to eschew public controversy,
preferring to spread its message through low-key contacts with influential officials.

The American Jewish Congress, on the other hand, always retained
its founder's belief in the political benefits of public indignation. As
David Petegorsky explained, "discrimination and prejudice cannot be
eliminated by propaganda or pious preachment but only by vigorous
and affirmative action in the legislatures, the courts, and the public forums of the land to transform public policy and practice."[50] In 1945 it
adopted a program based on proposals by Alexander H. Pekelis, who
argued that the welfare of Jews depended on a liberal political and social climate. The Congress thereafter became increasingly involved in
crusades on behalf of blacks and other minorities, as well as in the
struggle to maintain a firm separation of church and state. Overseas activities were conducted in co-operation with its sister agency, the World
Jewish Congress, also founded by Stephen Wise, and directed by
Nahum Goldmann.

The only lynching of a Jew in America occurred in Georgia in 1913 and led directly to the founding of the Anti-Defamation League of B'nai B'rith. Of all the defense agencies, the ADL has most consistently served as a watchdog, ever alert to the slightest signs of anti-Semitism in any form. The League periodically conducted surveys measuring public attitudes on issues of importance to the Jewish community, kept a close watch on anti-Semitic organizations, and funded a series of studies on prejudice. With the emergence of the civil rights movement, the ADL added interracial and interreligious understanding to its agenda.

The Jewish Labor Committee evolved from an informal gathering of New York trade union leaders in 1933. In its early years it concentrated on helping victims of fascism, and with the assistance of the American Federation of Labor, it succeeded in rescuing hundreds of European labor leaders, both Jewish and non-Jewish, from Hitler. After the war it shifted its energies to the clearly delineated tasks of representing Jewish interests within the American labor movement, and labor interests in the Jewish community. It frequently acted as organized labor's representative in a number of actions involving racial and religious issues.[51]

In 1944 these groups, together with the Jewish War Veterans, the Union of American Hebrew Congregations, and about two dozen local agencies, established the National Community Relations Advisory Council in an attempt to eliminate duplication of effort and act as a forum for the exchange of information and ideas. While the Council succeeded somewhat in co-ordinating its constituencies, it failed in eliminating much of the overlapping activities and jurisdictional conflicts. In fact, the problems grew so acute that in 1950, at the insistence of several of the larger welfare funds, the Council commissioned a study of Jewish community-relations work under the direction of Columbia University professor emeritus Robert M. MacIver.

The MacIver Report consisted of three sections: a theoretical analysis of the nature of the American Jewish community; a review of the activities of community-relations agencies on both the national and local levels; and the key section, a series of recommendations on the future organization and functions of the defense groups. MacIver suggested that the agencies were overreacting to a fairly limited and low-level amount of anti-Jewish prejudice in the United States. Moreover, neither together nor separately had they ever examined in a scientific manner the nature or extent of anti-Semitism in America nor the effect, if any, on it of their various programs. He scored their parochialism and accused them of catering more to their own constituencies and perpetuating themselves than to developing a comprehensive and effective program of combating discrimination.

To remedy the situation, MacIver suggested that the powers of the Council be greatly expanded, and that it have the means and authority to assign specialized tasks and then enforce these decisions. In the areas of greatest overlap, he proposed that the Anti-Defamation League and the American Jewish Committee divide responsibilities for activities in youth work and intercultural education, and that their respective fact-finding apparatus, which consistently duplicated each other's work, be combined into a single agency. Finally, MacIver recommended that the greatest authority and activity be transferred from national bodies to local community-relations councils, where he believed the most effective work could be done.[52]

The reaction of the Council and its constituent organizations was predictable. Those like the Jewish Labor Committee, the Jewish War Veterans, the UAHC, and the local agencies, which had been assigned specific tasks and enlarged responsibilities, endorsed the report fully. The American Jewish Congress also approved the recommendations but differed sharply with MacIver in his analysis of the extent of anti-Semitism and the nature of the Jewish community.[53] The Congress especially liked the idea of a continuous assessment of progress and the establishment of an overall policy-planning group.

The two groups which had the most to lose, the American Jewish Committee and the Anti-Defamation League, severely criticized the report both in its theoretical aspects and its practical suggestions, and took special exception to what they considered MacIver's misreading of the nature and extent of anti-Semitism in the United States. When the Council adopted the majority of MacIver's proposals at a plenary session in September 1952, the Committee and the ADL withdrew from the organization. Since neither agency depended on welfare fund financing for its programs they could afford to go their separate ways, thus effectively nullifying any efforts by the Council to establish a coordinated policy.[54] The ADL did not return to the umbrella organization until 1965, and the Committee remained out until the following year; but both returned on terms which emphasized the independence of the member organizations. Thus still another attempt to foster unity and co-operation foundered on the particularism so characteristic of American Jewry.

*   *   *

While certainly not so large as the nation's Bicentennial would be in 1976, American Jewry's celebration of its three hundred years on these shores in 1954 held a meaning of equal importance to the more than 5.5 million Jewish U.S. citizens. In no other place since the Dispersion had Jews prospered or enjoyed such a wide range of political and economic freedoms or had lived in such harmony with their neighbors. To be sure, the Tercentenary was not unabashedly self-congratulatory; nearly everyone recognized that American Jewry had far to go before becoming, in Simon Dubnow's terms, a Jewish center, with its own well-defined set of social, religious, and educational institutions, and with a positive sense of its own worth and of its relations to the whole of the Jewish people. The first condition seemed well on its way to achievement, but few people suggested that American Jews had taken more than a few steps in the direction of defining themselves as a community. Since the great majority of American Jews had arrived in the United States after 1880, the community was really less than a hundred years old, "a mere infant if looked at from the perspective of Jewish history."[55]

Yet, as Eugene Borowitz has pointed out, a review of American Jewish life in the 1950s does not indicate indecision or even hesitation, but a clear determination to do what had to be done. Economic mobility led tens of thousands of Jewish families out of the cities and into the suburbs; there they found no established institutions, no patterns of communal life, so they did what had to be done—build schools and synagogues and community centers and organizations. They saw their brethren across the seas in Europe and Africa and Asia in distress, and raised undreamed-of sums of money to help them start anew in life. They took pride in the new Jewish state of Israel, and gave generously of their time and money and prayers to help it succeed. And this attitude, according to Borowitz, came not from the top, not from professional Jewish leaders or national organizations, but from the people themselves, from an American Jewry imbued "with what can legitimately be called an irreplaceable faith in man's capacity to know the righteous act and accomplish it successfully."[56]

The excesses—lavish synagogues, tactless fund-raising, tasteless wed-

dings and *bnai mitzvot*—were certainly no greater and no worse
than those of American society in general in the 1950s, an era marked
by Dwight Eisenhower in the White House, Elvis Presley on television, and enormous tail fins on cars. There were also failures, in the
area of education, in the informal opportunities lost through "Campaign Judaism," and in the breakdown of efforts to unify and co-ordinate the organizational structure. But on the whole, for a group
caught up in the swirls of rapid social and economic change, American
Jewry had no need to feel ashamed.

And during these transition years, the fact of Israel's existence became an ever more important consideration in American Jewish life.
Abba Eban, at the formal ceremonies of the Tercentenary, considered
his presence there symbolic of the growing ties between the new Jewish
state and the world's largest and most powerful Jewish community, and
he predicted a long and fruitful union between the two.[57] Yet even as
Israel loomed larger in the hearts and minds of American Jews, it also
raised a number of troubling questions about that special relationship.

Chapter 9

THE MEANING OF ISRAEL

To look at Israel strictly in terms of a foreign state—albeit a Jewish one —or even to regard it in the foreshortened historical perspective of modern Zionism's half century of labor is to miss the deeper meaning of Israel in the collective consciousness of the Jewish people. Zionism has been the only modern national movement based on the idea of return. Other peoples—Czechs, Poles, Indians, and various African groups— had never been physically separated from their land; they sought political autonomy, but even as subjects of foreign imperialist powers, they lived in their homeland. Jews, before becoming politically independent, would have to reclaim the land they considered their birthright. "We are the sons of the Homeland," wrote David Ben-Gurion, "disciples of the Bible, and bearers of the vision of the great redemption of the Jewish people and of humanity—and the expression of that idea in the original, in the ancient original which has been renewed and rejuvenated in our time, is to be found in the prophets of Israel."[1]

The relation of the Jewish people to the land of Israel goes back nearly four thousand years. Judaism's sacred writings are replete with references to the ties that bind the people of Israel to the land of Israel, beginning with God's promise to Abraham: "Lift up thine eyes, and look from the place where thou art, northward and southward and eastward and westward; for all the land which thou seest, to thee will I give it, and to thy seed forever." In times of stress and danger, the prophets reminded the ancient Hebrews that the Lord would not forget his pledge. "I will plant them upon their land, and they shall no more be plucked up out of their land which I have given them."[2]

In the early centuries of the Dispersion, the rabbis of Babylonia, in devising the Talmud, that great compendium of law and lore, reminded the people of the importance of the Holy Land even for Jews who did not live there. The land of Israel, *Eretz Yisrael*, was seen as the potential ideal of earthly dwelling places, lacking in nothing (Ber. 36b). Even the soil of Palestine is endowed with holiness and will help man earn a portion of *olam habah* (the world to come) (J. Kil. 9), a belief which led to the practice of putting a small bag of Palestinian soil into the coffins of observant Jews. Because so many of the commandments in the Torah relate to the land, a Jew could lead a more religiously observant life within the borders of *Eretz Yisrael* than outside. Yet at the same time a number of Talmudic sages emphasized that it was more important to lead a Jewish life, within a thriving Jewish community, than merely to reside in Palestine. *Eretz Yisrael* was valuable only insofar as it was a Jewish land, one which reflected and supported the ideals and customs of Judaism. If it were not, if Palestine were in the hands of non-Jewish conquerors or of nonobservant Jews, a person should stay wherever he might be surrounded by Jewish learning and practices. During the time of the Babylonian exile, the rabbis declared, "If one goes from Bavel to *Eretz Yisrael*, one transgresses a positive commandment" (Ber. 24b). Babylonia, and not Israel, then constituted a greater center of Jewishness, and there the Jew should stay.[3]

Now Jews were once again in their own land, but in a way unforeseen by most of the ancient writers. The Hebrew prophets had assumed that all of the Jewish people would live together; dispersion or exile, whatever phrase one chose, had been seen as a temporary condition, an abnormal state of affairs that would in one way or another be set right at the time of return. Theodor Herzl had argued that with the creation of an autonomous Jewish state the Jewish problem would be solved. Jews who wanted to remain Jews would move to Palestine; the others would then be free to assimilate and within a generation or two, having intermarried and converted, would cease to be Jews. Even before 1948, however, it became obvious that not all of the world's twelve million Jews could or even wanted to settle in Israel, and the great debate began over the meaning of Israel for modern Jewry—a debate which continues to this day.

*   *   *

For the two extremes of American Jewry, there were no questions. The ultra-orthodox rejected the Jewish state as an abomination, a sinful attempt by man to precipitate the coming of the Messiah; only God, not frail men, could redeem the Jewish people.* Epitomized in Israel by the Neture Karta and in the United States by the Satmar Hassidic sect, these ultrareligious Jews, as much as they could, denounced Israel, and have never taken any significant role in the general discussion of its meaning. Small in number, they have little to do either with the world, or even with other Jews, most of whom they consider apostates at worst or religious malingerers at best.[4]

At the other end of the spectrum stood the ultra-assimilationists of the American Council for Judaism, with their profound fear that a Jewish state would somehow impugn the status of American Jews. The leader of a Council chapter in the South later recalled how disturbing an event Israel's creation had been. "I was afraid that Judaism would become a political issue here because Israel would change us from a religion into a race; that Jews would be persecuted more because people would think that they were more loyal to a country across the sea." Perhaps the classic statement of assimilationist fears is contained in Alfred M. Lilienthal's polemical *What Price Israel?* published in 1953. Unconsciously reiterating Herzl, he argued that those Jews who believed in a Jewish state should move to Israel, after which the rest of American Jews who "remain just that—Americans of the Jewish faith—will

---

* Prior to 1948, this view was held by a number of the ultra-orthodox groups, although there had been for nearly fifty years a religious Zionist group, the Mizrachi, that believed man could seek to establish a Jewish state, and that this did not contradict traditional beliefs regarding the messianic age. Following the establishment of Israel in 1948, many of the ultra-orthodox changed their views. It was no longer a question of whether or not to create Israel, but how to deal with the *fact* of a state already in existence. Undoubtedly, the Holocaust, which wiped out so many of the European centers of piety, affected their thinking, and this seems to be true in the case of one of the most famous of American hassidic leaders, the head of the Lubavitch, Rabbi Menachem Mendel Schneersohn. Israel now existed, and hundreds of thousands of Jews lived there; therefore they had to be supported and protected, and toward that end—the sustaining of the Jewish people—he could accept the existence of Israel.

then be able to normalize their lives . . . to free themselves of the spell
of 'unity' . . . [to] live at inner ease with their countrymen." In
Lilienthal's eyes, Israel was prostituting the Jewish faith, violating the
commandment against idolatry. "In contemporary Judaism," he lamented, "the worship of the State of Israel is crowding out the worship
of God."[5]

Both the Council and the Satmar were unrepresentative, minuscule
sects; they constituted the extremes of American Jewry who stood outside the overwhelming consensus of support for the new Jewish state.
Most American Jews believed that Israel would affect them positively,
although few had any specific or articulate notions of the shape such
influence might take. Nathan Glazer, writing in 1957, tended to dismiss much of the talk about the meaning of Israel as "largely an expression of ebullient feelings." Aside from replacing Poland as a source of
Talmudic scholars for Orthodox *yeshivot*, he concluded, the idea that
Israel "could in any serious way affect Judaism in America, or Judaism
in general, is recognized as largely illusory."[6] Yet whatever effects Israel
may have had on the religious aspects of Jewish life, it had an enormous
impact on Jews. Elliot Cohen, editor of *Commentary*, pointed out that
this meant far more than accepting Israeli artifacts in one's home or
dancing the *hora* at weddings. Everywhere he went, he heard serious
Jews discussing how Israel would affect the ideals and goals of American
Jewry even as the Jewish state developed its own distinctive culture.[7]
In the decade following the creation of the state, it became clear that
Israel had made a profound impression upon American Jewry, although
the depth of that relationship would not be fully understood or appreciated until June 1967.

To begin with, Israel affected American Jewry—indeed, all of
world Jewry—as a partial recompense for the Holocaust. This is not to
say that the existence of Israel could ever redeem that evil, but rather as
Abba Lessing wrote, "without Israel the Holocaust is totally unbearable. . . . We *felt* Israel as a relief, genuine hope. With Israel, our cry-
ing signified new energy, strength, power. Without Israel our tears
would have been only anguish and resignation." In a similar vein,
Abraham Joshua Heschel declared: "The State of Israel is not an
atonement. It would be a blasphemy to regard it as a compensation.
However, the existence of Israel reborn makes life less unendurable."
We have had enough, he said, of extermination camps, of expulsions,
of pogroms. Should he go to Poland or Germany, "every stone, every

tree there would remind me of contempt, hatred, murder, of children killed, of mothers burned alive, of human beings asphyxiated. When I go to Israel every stone, every tree is a reminder of hard labor and glory, of prophets and psalmists, of loyalty and holiness. Jews go to Israel . . . for renewal, for the experience of resurrection."[8]

For Jews, the Holocaust means far more than the extermination of six million of their brethren; it is the darkest side of man's nature and raises frightening questions about a God who permitted evil of such magnitude to exist. Elie Wiesel, in stating the grim meaning of the death camps, declared that "at Auschwitz not only man died but the idea of man. It wasn't worth much to live in a world where there was nothing else, where the hangman acted as God and judge. For it was its own heart the world burned at Auschwitz."[9] The Holocaust became the burning memory of the modern Jew, never far below the surface, a subject that both drew and repelled. Yehuda Amichai used the telling analogy of Lot's wife: we are afraid to face it, yet we cannot resist turning back to look. For twenty years after the war, the Holocaust lay in the Jewish subconscious, growing like a cancer, yet writers and intellectuals and theologians seemed somehow unable to deal with it. Perhaps, as Richard Rubenstein suggested, the wound was still too painful, or, in Irving Howe's phrase, "we were still stunned into unresponsiveness."[10] Whether or not religious man can ever understand the Holocaust is doubtful, but there is no question of its dreadful results: Fifteen million dead, six million of them Jews, one out of every three Jews in the world; the great Jewish centers of learning and piety in Europe gone; the promises of the Enlightenment turned into bitter ashes. "To realize you are a survivor is a shock," Saul Bellow's Herzog says. "At the realization of such election, you feel like bursting into tears." Not until Hannah Arendt's *Eichmann in Jerusalem* (1964) did the pressure burst and erupt into a cascade of books and short stories and historical studies.[11]

During all these years Israel provided some counterweight to the oppressiveness, to the memory of disaster. As a partial redemption of the Holocaust, Israel assumed a symbolic as well as a real role in the continuity of the Jewish people. If anything happened to Israel not only would the Jewish state be lost, but also the one saving grace of a world gone mad would also be destroyed, and Hitler would have won his victory. Perhaps no other theologian has caught this meaning so perfectly as Rabbi Emil L. Fackenheim, who has taught that the "commanding voice of Auschwitz" has given modern Jewry a 614th commandment in addition to the traditional 613 rules of the Torah: "The authentic Jew of today is forbidden to hand Hitler yet another, posthumous victory." Israel was the mark that Hitler had not won, that the Jewish people, despite the Holocaust, still lived and still retained its faith.[12]

A second way in which Israel significantly affected American Jews also derived, in part, from the Holocaust. Part of the controversy surrounding Hannah Arendt's *Eichmann in Jerusalem* resulted from her charges that the Jews in Europe had been excessively passive—indeed, even "collaborationist"—in their response to the Nazi extermination program. Later documentation has shown a large involvement of Jews in the anti-fascist underground movements. But in the 1950s many believed the Germans met with practically no resistance in implementing their "Final Solution," that with the exception of the Warsaw ghetto uprising in 1943, European Jews marched passively to the gas chambers.[13]

This painful judgment accounted in part for the postwar literary silence concerning the Holocaust. Not only did the wounds hurt, they were also too shameful. How could six million people quietly allow themselves to be degraded and tortured and killed without fighting back? Because so many Jews agreed with this verdict, Jay Gonen suggests, they reacted with the passionate cry of "Never Again!" Not never again Jewish casualties, but never again Jewish victims who would not resist their oppressors. In Israel, where for a variety of reasons the psychological impact of the Holocaust was greatest, the same emotions were expressed in the phrase *Asur shehasho'ah tachazor* (It is forbidden for the Holocaust to return).[14]

The new Israeli provided a solution to this problem of shame and guilt. The new Jew, the Israeli, born and raised in freedom, farmer and warrior, he or she would be the hero to whom American Jews could proudly point. And Israel, their spiritual land, had been victorious; it had not gone quietly and helplessly to the slaughter, but had fought and won. The triumph of Israel restored dignity to the Jewish name; no longer would "Jew" summon up the caricature of a yellow-badged, stooped, servile creature. The poet Karl Shapiro, who had long been estranged from much of Jewish life in America, first expressed this changing attitude in a poem published shortly after the establishment of the state:[15]

When I think of the liberation of Palestine,
When my eye conceives the great black English line
Spanning the world news of two thousand years,
My heart leaps forward like a hungry dog,
My heart is thrown back on its tangled chain,
My soul is hangdog in a Western chair.

When I think of the battle for Zion I hear
The drop of chains, the starting forth of feet,
And I remain chained in a Western chair.
My blood beats like a bird against a wall,
I feel the weight of prisons in my skull
Falling away; my forebears stare through stone.

When I see the name of Israel high in print
The fences crumble in my flesh; I sink
Deep in a Western chair and rest my soul.
I look the stranger clear to the blue depths
Of his unclouded eye. I say my name
Aloud for the first time unconsciously.

Speak of the tillage of a million heads
No more. Speak of the evil myth no more
Of one who harried Jesus on his way
Saying, *Go faster*. Speak no more
Of the yellow badge, *secta nefaria*
Speak the name only of the living land.

Israel had quite simply added a dimension of dignity and pride to
Jews the world over, especially those in America, who never faced the
insecurities and degradations of the European ghetto or the Arab
mellah. David Ben-Gurion claimed, with a large measure of truth, that
Israel "straightened the back of the Jew everywhere. . . . It showed
that the Jews are capable of undertaking all forms of creative labor. It
revived Jewish heroism."[16] Study after study indicated that American
Jews shared this view,[17] that just as the creation of the state compen-
sated, in a small way, for the destruction and death of the Holocaust, it
also redeemed, in a large way, the sense of shame felt over the seeming
passivity of six million martyrs. In literature this new and positive attitude could be seen in a number of works, especially two fine novels by
Michael Blankfort, *The Juggler* (1952) and *Behold the Fire* (1965).
Israel now seemed to offer the modern Jew a free choice of how to live

his life. For Arthur Koestler and others who, by their own account, had remained Jews only out of a sense of honor and obligation, the creation of Israel gave them the freedom to assimilate. They would no longer feel guilty of deserting a besieged people, but could now leave, if they chose to, confident that Israel and Judaism would survive. For Meyer Levin, on the other hand, this new freedom would allow American Jews to build their lives on a new foundation, one of pride and affirmation.[18]

Perhaps the most striking example of this new pride in Israel was the reception accorded Leon Uris' runaway best seller *Exodus* (1958), a novel on the birth of Israel. Despite the fact that critics considered the book little better than a "TV soap-opera novel," four million people bought copies, the movie version (starring Paul Newman and Sal Mineo as Jewish freedom fighters) enjoyed immense popularity, and the theme song (sung by Pat Boone) climbed to the top of the record charts. According to Sol Liptzin, Uris "performed a great deed of immeasurable propaganda value for Israel and American Jewry." Philip Roth conceded that although "the image of the Jew as patriot, warrior, and hero is rather satisfying to a large segment of the American public," he questioned if, in the light of the European disaster, there was not some "higher moral purpose for the Jewish writer, and the Jewish people, than the improvement of public relations."[19]

Roth, I would suggest, missed the importance of Uris' work, and certainly his own caricatures of Jewish life hardly fulfilled the mandate for a "higher moral purpose." What American Jews sought was not propaganda (although no one objected to the adoption of a more positive view of the Jewish character), but reassurance that at long last a Jew need not be ashamed of his alleged cowardice. Perhaps one needed the pot-boiling emotionalism of an *Exodus* to allow other writers to treat Jews more realistically, to concentrate on the moral and intellectual values which had played so important a role in Jewish life and history. But there is little doubt that psychologically a certain *machismo* in Jewish literary characters at that time confirmed American Jews in their ideas of their own self-worth. Noah Ackerman, the hero of Irwin Shaw's *The Young Lions* (1948), has the moral sensibilities and intellectual strength prized by Roth, but Ackerman is neither a weakling nor a coward; he establishes his intellectual interests by proving his physical courage, resorting to Esau's fist to justify Jacob's voice.[20] Perhaps, as Roth implied, this balance is not to be admired, that the Jew loses too much in becoming *ke'hol hagoyim* (like all the other nations).

But in the post-Holocaust era, this new image, generated by Israel, gave American Jews the emotional counterweight they needed to move beyond the painful doubts of the Holocaust.

* * *

To see Israel only in this light, however, is to ignore many other and more positive aspects of its meaning to American Jews. Perhaps the most important single effect Israel had was to reinforce the concept of the continuity and vitality of the Jewish people. For ages Judaism has been a religion which emphasized group consciousness and cohesiveness. While Judaism had great respect for the individual, and especially for individual life, it manifested itself primarily in a sense of peoplehood. In prayer, for example, the Jew, except when it is impossible, always worships in a group of at least ten men, a *minyan*. In response to God's commandments, the people, not the individual Jew, responded, *Na'aseh v'nishma* (*We* will do and *we* will listen).[21] Moreover, it is not a question of the *we* of the moment, but a *we* of all times, cutting across temporal and spatial boundaries. Each year at the Passover Seder, the story of the exodus from Egypt is retold, because each Jew, in his own time, is as if he himself had followed Moses out of bondage. For nearly two millennia, the Jewish people had maintained their ties to their promised land, and now the Third Jewish Commonwealth would reinforce and renew these communal ties.

Palestine, Ludwig Lewisohn wrote in 1925, "does not exist for itself alone . . . it exists for the Jewish people, everywhere in the world." A half century later, Golda Meir echoed this sentiment. "We in Israel are only one part of the Jewish nation," she wrote, and noted that Israelis fully understood and accepted their responsibilities in this manner. The first director general of the Israeli Foreign Ministry, Walter Eytan, recalled that from the start everyone assumed that foreign representatives of Israel would have a dual role: minister plenipotentiary to the accredited country, and envoy extraordinary to its Jews.[22] For Israel, both among the people and the political elites, Jewishness permeates all aspects of the country's life, and all believe that it is through this Jewishness that the real links between Israel and the Diaspora are forged. Israel has not been made for the Diaspora, nor does the Diaspora exist to support Israel; both exist as part of a larger *Klal Yisrael* (a Jewish people).

Ironically, few of the early Zionist philosophers developed any comprehensive proposals for future relations between Jews in the Diaspora and the Jewish state; nearly all of them concentrated instead either on the mechanics of securing their goal or on the internal structure of the new nation. A significant exception was Asher Ginzberg, who under the pen name Ahad Ha'am (One of the People), suggested a general theory of cultural relationships between Israel and the Diaspora. According to Ahad Ha'am, the essential task of the Jewish nation was to serve as a "spiritual center" for world Jewry. By "spiritual" (*ruchani*), however, he did not mean theology, but rather a cultural and ethical center reflecting the finest Jewish values. In contrast to the political Zionism of his time, Ahad Ha'am emphasized what he called *kultura* as the primary purpose of the movement. Schools, academies, and artistic workshops were more important than settlements, and would serve as the foci of a new Jewish life which could then be emulated by Jews in other countries. Underlying much of Ahad Ha'am's writings was the fear that Jewish unity stood on the verge of disintegration and that only a strong cultural center could provide the cement to hold the Jewish people together. Naturally, this center would be Palestine, while various Diaspora communities would reflect the distinct traits of their local cultures. The Jewish state would serve as a "refining crucible and unifying bond" for a common national consciousness.[23]

During the first decade after the creation of Israel, American Jews looked eagerly to the Jewish state for some evidence that this prescription would be filled, and clutched pathetically at any trace of Israeli influence. Abraham Duker, for example, found evidence in "the little synagogue shops, in the Israeli seder plates and pictures in homes committed to Judaism, in the substitution of the *hora* for the [eastern European] *sher* at weddings and other *simhot*."[24] It soon became clear, however, that while American Jews welcomed the surface artifacts of Israel, they had little desire to base American Jewish life on Israeli standards. Ahad Ha'am wrote out of his own experience in eastern Europe, where Jewish communities were isolated from the gentile culture, where life in the *shtetl* reflected, above all else, Jewish norms. He assumed that Jewish existence in Europe would perpetuate this pattern, that the common and pervasive bonds of Jewishness could be shared, that essentially the Jewish state and the Diaspora communities would have many more similarities than differences. In the United States, on the other hand, as in western Europe, the Jewish communities tended to acculturate, and once the second-generation immigrants left the cities, whatever had been left of an all-encompassing Jewish ambiance dissipated.

Despite the hopes that many Jewish leaders had for an ever-increasing Israeli influence, the one area which might have seen the development of a fruitful cultural connection, the Hebrew language, proved to be a less than popular challenge for American Jews. As one critic put it, American Jews spoke with pride *about* Hebrew, but not *in* it. Hebrew courses sprang up all over the country, but few students completed the first year, while intermediate and advanced classes had at best a handful of devotees. Even those who managed to survive the basic course could do little more than order meals in an Israeli restaurant or perhaps ask instructions on a Tel Aviv street. As indigenous Israeli literature developed in the 1960s, it would be available to the vast majority of American Jews only in translation, recognizable as Israeli only from the story line or setting. At best, Hebrew would be a second language for only a small minority of the community.[25]

With the establishment of the state, however, a number of Jewish leaders began to pay serious attention to just what Israel would mean for Jewish survival in the United States, and to the kind of relationship which would develop. With the exception of the fringe groups, most Jews could echo Stephen Wise's prayer for "the potency of inspiration in every direction that is to come to all the people Israel from the new and blessed State."[26] One man in the United States who had given deep, consistent, and systematic thought to the problem of Israel and its ties to American Jewry was Mordecai M. Kaplan. Whether they have agreed with him or not, all writers and critics at some point have had to deal with Kaplan's proposals for the reconstruction of modern Jewish life.

Kaplan, who for many years taught at the Jewish Theological Seminary, built his philosophy around the basic proposition that Judaism constituted a total civilization for the Jewish people, a construct which included organic relationships of people to land, language, mores, laws, and social structures. The problem with earlier attempts to "reform" Judaism was that they paid attention only to strictly religious aspects and tried to reduce Jewishness to a narrow and specialized area; in doing so, they emasculated Jewish life, made it sterile by divorcing it from its history and culture. The denial of Zionism made sense in Reform Judaism, since, as it aspired to be only a religion, it had no need for a geopolitical anchor. The people of a civilization, on the other hand, must be rooted, it must have a physical center, a home of its own, where it can develop its own culture and language and folkways. This center would then have an impact on Jews elsewhere.[27]

So far Kaplan had apparently followed the basic lines of Ahad Ha'am's cultural Zionism, but Kaplan's genius, and the importance of his philosophy, lay in extending the argument and adapting it to modern conditions. Where Ahad Ha'am saw a Jewish homeland primarily in terms of its influence on the Diaspora, Kaplan posited a dual relationship in which the Israeli center and the Diaspora would affect each other and intersect in all areas of Jewish concern. In *A New Zionism*, Kaplan demanded that, in order to see Jewish life steadily and whole, one "should relate the Jewish people, the Jewish religion and the Jewish way of life, to *Eretz Yisrael* as the alpha and omega of Jewish existence." But such a development could not be limited to the Holy Land alone. "Should Jewish civilization fail to be at home in *Eretz Yisrael* it would disappear everywhere else. Should it disappear everywhere else, it is bound to give way to some new Levantine civilization in *Eretz Yisrael*."[28]

Kaplan emphatically rejected the contention of Arthur Koestler, and before him of Heinrich Heine, that being a Jew in the Diaspora made no sense. The creation of Israel did not make the Diaspora or Jewish life in it superfluous. Rather it rounded out and fulfilled the basic requirements of peoplehood, and for Kaplan confirmed the covenant between God and Israel. With all the necessary components once more united—God, people, and land—it would now be possible to revive Judaism in all its manifold dimensions. By emphasizing the interrelationship, Kaplan restated the definition of Judaism as a totality and argued that a Judaism which knows only God but not His people is not authentic in the Jewish tradition. A Jew could thus be seen as a person who not only affirmed his faith in God, but also acknowledged that a special relationship existed between each Jew and the Jewish people as a whole. The Jewish state now provided the anchor for this reconstruction and rejuvenation of Jewish life. "Jewish peoplehood," he suggested, "is no longer possible without a Jewish community in *Eretz Yisrael*," one which would build a civilization there and "provide the setting in which the Jewish people could become a fit instrument of this-worldly salvation for every Jew, wherever he resides." But it could not be done by Israeli Jews alone; the building of the new Jewish civilization was a partnership among Jews everywhere, a commitment of the people, and its results would not belong only to the Israelis, but also to all of Jewry.[29]

Kaplan's concept of peoplehood and the centrality of Israel in Jewish life eventually became the dominant model in describing relations between Israel and Diaspora Jewry. He claimed that the centrality of *Eretz Yisrael* could be traced back to the original election by God of Israel for His people, and was at the heart of the covenantal relation. Despite the unyielding opposition of classical Reform Jews, the acceptance of peoplehood was affirmed by the majority of American Jews within a relatively short time. Simon Rawidowicz had earlier argued that "we must see, and teach others to see, a one and indivisible Jewish people, imbued with a Jewish spirit, so that the State of Israel and the various Diaspora communities are only different manifestations, or aspects, of the same organic entity." More recently, Rabbi David Polish, president of the Central Conference of American Rabbis, indicated that Reform Judaism had also come to accept the doctrine of unity; should Israel and the various Diaspora communities try to go their own separate ways, it would surely mean the end of the Jewish people.[30]

The doctrine that Israel occupied the central position in Jewish life has also been accepted, but not with the ease that most Jews could affirm their sense of peoplehood, nor has this concept itself been as understandable. For centuries Jews recognized themselves as an *am* (a people) and also accepted an ultimate return to Zion as a focus and unifying factor in their existence. In modern times, as the possibility of a real Zion grew, philosophers like Martin Buber began exploring how the presence of a Jewish state in Palestine would affect world Jewry. For Buber, the Jewish state would serve as a paragon, an ideal, of what an authentic Jewish life could be. A Jewish society in Palestine would be the core around which other Jewish groups could build their own sense of community.[31] While few people assumed that Israel could overnight become a messianic society, there has been a continuing expectation that Israel, its people, and its leaders would strive to reach the goals of full economic and social justice. "The Jews in the Diaspora," wrote Ben-Gurion, "ardently wish to see in Israel an unblemished, perfect state, one that exemplifies in its conduct and regiment the very best of Jewish and universal ideals and aspirations." The fact that Diaspora Jews wanted Israeli Jews to lead a more moral and idealistic life than they did not upset Ben-Gurion at all. Difficult as it might be, Israel had the obligation to conduct itself so that it might once more be "a beacon to the nations." When Israel failed to live up to this ideal, as in the so-called Kibya massacre in October 1953, the aggrieved reaction of Henry Hurwitz, for example, mirrored the disappointment and anguish many Jews felt about a retaliatory raid which took the lives of a number of Arab civilians, that it "should be perpetrated by men of a people that has prided itself for centuries on being *rachmanim bnai rachmanim* (merciful sons of the merciful)."[32]

For some Jews, in the United States and in Israel, this idea of Israel's "centrality" implied that in time it would become the only legitimate context for Jewish life, the bright center of Jewish existence, with Diaspora communities merely pale reflections of Israeli glory. The chancellor of the Jewish Theological Seminary, who had been a non-Zionist before 1948, readily agreed to such a formulation, and described American Jews as contentedly standing "on the periphery of Jewish inspiration. . . . Always we turn to Zion not only in prayer but also in the hope of instruction. We gladly assume the role of amanuensis to our brethren who have been given the superior privilege of serving God and studying Torah in the land . . . [that role] in itself will be a privilege."[33] This attitude evidently was fostered in Jewish day schools, with one study indicating that students praised Israel at the expense of Diaspora Jewry. One critic asked how a meaningful Jewish life could be fostered in America if young people were taught to be ashamed of being in the Diaspora. In Israel, similar attitudes could be found in the small but noisome Canaanite movement, which distinguished between the "Israeli" and the "Jew." Only the "Israeli" really mattered, and the sooner the "Jew" in the Diaspora faded away, the better, and more authentic, Israeli religionationalism could triumph.[34]

During the 1950s the idea of centrality grew very slowly, and, in fact, did not fully emerge as a major tenet of Jewish thought in the United States until after the 1967 war. In part this can be attributed to the overwhelming preoccupation of American Jews with creating their own niche in American society. Also, the enormous needs of Israel, especially in terms of financial support, obscured the two-way relationship developing between Israel and the American Jewish community; most people could see only the constant giving by Americans and the constant taking by Israel. A sympathetic observer like Carey McWilliams could describe Israel as "the lamp of Jewish life and culture in the world today," a lamp fueled and protected by American Jewry, but few Americans were sure just what sort of light had been lit. For a number of younger intellectuals the Israeli beacon was not a moral light unto the world but just another nationalistic brushfire, an ethnocentric anachronism which flew in the face of a much-needed universalistic outlook.[35]

Yet among many American Jews there could be little doubt that in one way or another Israel had become important in their lives. The old canard of dual loyalty died hard, mainly because of periodic transfusions of passion into the moribund concept by the American Council for Judaism, but it did die. By the mid-1950s few people paid any serious attention to charges that American Jews were more loyal, or might become more loyal, to Israel than to the United States. An extensive study of Jewish attitudes in 1958 found that American Jews clearly drew a distinction between their roles and loyalties as American citizens and their obligations to help other Jews. Moreover, most believed that the basic interests of both the United States and Israel were compatible; helping Israel, therefore, became a means of furthering American ideals of freedom and justice. Israeli diplomats went out of their way to emphasize these common bonds, while at the same time scrupulously denying any political claim on non-Israeli nationals.[36] American Jews found themselves perfectly comfortable with this relationship, but there was one area which from the beginning proved a source of friction and which could not be harmonized with the ideals American Jews as Americans had for the Jewish state.

*   *   *

Many of the early Zionist leaders, such as Herzl, Nordau, Brandeis, and even Weizmann, were relatively indifferent to the role that religion would play in the Jewish state. All Zionists agreed that there would be no laws preventing observant Jews from carrying out traditional rituals and practices; the state would be Jewish, though, primarily because its citizens were to be Jews rather than because it imposed Jewish laws. Orthodox Jews, however, saw no value in having an autonomous homeland in Palestine unless it were to be governed by the Torah, with all Jews, if not required to lead observant lives, at least prevented from publicly violating some of the more important commandments, such as Sabbath observance. Since religious Jews from the beginning constituted only a minority of the *Yishuv*, the Mizrachi, the Orthodox wing of the Zionist movement, could not impose its wishes on the country as a whole.

With the establishment of the state, however, the Mapai, the leading labor party, found that it could not put together a majority coalition
in the Knesset, the Israeli parliament, without the co-operation of the
various religious blocs. The Mizrachi cared little about economic policy,
and was willing to let Mapai run the secular affairs of the country as it
wished, provided the Orthodox rabbinate had a free hand in religious
matters. Since Mapai included a large number of nonobservant, even
secularist, Jews, a period of hard bargaining ensued before an agreement was reached between Ben-Gurion and the religious leaders. The
Orthodox secured control over marriage and divorce proceedings, enforcement of Shabbat closings of business and public transportation,
control of *kashrut*, a religious educational track, and other concessions.
While the religious leaders claimed that they did not want to institute a
theocracy, they did not long remain content with the original agreement. They pushed the Ben-Gurion government to adopt more Orthodox practices, including a ban on the importation of nonkosher meat.
Leading Orthodox rabbis declared that they would not be satisfied until
Israel became a Torah-true state. The Orthodox also saw religion as a
means to unify the new Jewish state, by appealing not to the lowest
common denominator but to the highest, and as Abraham Barth put it,
"there is no thing apart from Jewish religion and tradition that satisfies
this condition."[37]

The religious bloc found surprisingly little opposition to their program within the Israeli public as a whole. There were many religious
Jews in the regular parties who endorsed Mizrachi demands. A majority of the European refugees, as well as those from the Arab lands, had
long tried to lead lives which conformed to Orthodox practices, and saw
no reason why, in a Jewish state, all Jews should not do so. A study
conducted by Aaron Antonovsky of the Israeli Institute for Applied Social Research found that 23 per cent of the respondents believed that
the government should "definitely" enforce religious traditions in community life, while another 20 per cent felt that such regulation would
"probably" be wise. Over one out of every three Israeli children attended either the state-supported religious schools or the independent
schools run by Agudat Israel.[38]

Even nonreligious Jews did not oppose the Orthodox drive. For one
reason, it seemed peculiarly fitting that Israel, as a Jewish state, should
follow traditional practices. On a day-to-day level, few of the demands
of the religious bloc really affected them. Stores closed on Shabbat, but

no one said that individual Jews had to observe the day in any special way; bus companies also closed, but no rules prevented people with private cars from using them. The state supported Orthodox rabbis, but did not require attendance at services. On a more positive level, the traditional Jewish holidays, which had originally been based on an agricultural calendar, now made sense once again; there was a definite beauty and satisfaction, for example, in celebrating Shavuot, the feast of the spring harvest, and to see schoolchildren bedecked in garlands of flowers. And, as one nonobservant Jewish educator admitted: "We owe them something. All those years when Jews suffered pogroms and were killed and tortured and exiled, those Orthodox Jews kept the faith alive. They made it possible for me to be a Jew today. For all they suffered during the centuries for me, I can afford to be slightly inconvenienced for them."[39]

In the Diaspora, Orthodox Jews of course welcomed efforts to introduce a Torah-directed life into *Eretz Yisrael*. The more progressive elements hoped that a new and enlightened rabbinate would develop with the authority to make rulings to bring certain archaic practices into congruence with modern conditions, thus facilitating the maintenance of traditional Jewish life outside Israel. And, of course, there were those Jews who, while totally nonobservant in their own lives, expected the Jews of Israel to be strictly Orthodox, the type portrayed in the character of Paul J. Zodman in James Michener's *The Source* (1965).

Had the Orthodox rabbinate been more modern in its outlook, and had its leaders possessed the prestige and courage to make new rulings, it is possible that efforts to make Israel into a more religiously observant state might have met with more success.[40] But instead of re-examining Jewish law, the rabbinate declared that not one jot or tittle would be changed, an attitude totally at variance with the whole Talmudic tradition. In the past, Judaism had thrived by retaining its essential moral and religious principles while adapting outward practices to meet local conditions. The Talmud itself is replete with discussions on how particular rituals should be changed to fulfill the substantive commandment rather than its form. But the rabbinate insisted that practices dating back hundreds of years, originating from conditions in other places and other milieus, must be enforced.† And beyond that, they totally denied

† One example of this rabbinical rigidity dealt with the question of levirate marriage. In ancient times, when a woman became widowed

the validity of marriages, divorces, and other functions performed by non-Orthodox rabbis, even when done in strict conformity to *halachah*.

This last attitude raised the hackles of Reform and Conservative rabbis in the United States. After all, the bulk of American Jewry adhered not to Orthodoxy, but belonged to either the Conservative or Reform movements. They, and not the Orthodox, had been the leaders of the Zionist movement that had laid the groundwork for American support in the mid-1940s. Now they were being asked—indeed, told— to raise more and more funds for a state which denied their legitimacy as rabbis and cast doubts on their congregants as well. Conversions, for example, performed by Reform or Conservative rabbis were not recognized as valid in Israel. Reform Jews rarely bothered to seek a religious divorce when dissolving a marriage; their divorces and subsequent remarriages normally took place through civil decrees. In the eyes of the Orthodox these people were living in adultery, and their children were illegitimate and forbidden to marry Jews. That Jews, who for so many centuries had been victimized in other lands because of their religious beliefs, should now in a land dominated by Jews discriminate against other Jews, was to Horace Meyer Kallen and others "a blasphemy beyond pardon." For Mordecai Kaplan as well, an imposed Judaism was useless; somehow the state would have to institute voluntaristic religion, involving free choice. Any other path would destroy Judaism.[41]

The Conservative movement, because it shared many of the basic assumptions of Orthodoxy, would not attempt to establish itself in Israel until the 1960s. But Reform, which considered Orthodox dogma antiquated, thought that the "secular" Israelis would welcome a modernized and more flexible Judaism in Israel. The Reform movement in the United States, moreover, had progressively abandoned its earlier anti-Zionist stand, and with the establishment of Israel sought a positive and constructive relationship with the new state. This was of ne-

---

it was incumbent upon the dead man's brother to take her for a wife. The object of this law was clearly humane, to protect and provide for a widow and her children in a society where they otherwise would have had nothing. In modern Israel, if a woman is widowed and a brother-in-law is alive, he must renounce his rights before she is free to remarry. If he cannot be reached, or, considering the process absurd, refuses to participate, the woman is not free to remarry. In recent years, under strong public pressure, the rabbinical courts have relaxed such rulings, quietly and on a case-by-case basis, but publicly they still uphold the ancient *halachah*.

cessity a slow task because of opposition not only from the Israeli rabbinate but also from classical Reform leaders in the United States. In 1953, on the fifth anniversary of the state, the Union of American Hebrew Congregations sponsored a pilgrimage to Israel, and Maurice Eisendrath reported that those who participated, whatever their earlier attitudes, had come away firmly committed to the new Jewish state. If Reform Judaism acknowledged its love of and support for Israel, declared Theodore Lewis, it "will not only become authentically Jewish but be better prepared to fashion the minds and mold the hearts of its followers. No Jewish movement, religious or otherwise, is entitled to Jewish loyalty unless it embodies in its teachings devotion to the Holy Land."[42]

The movement decided to establish congregations in Israel, and under the leadership of Nelson Glueck, president of Hebrew Union College and a world-famed archaeologist, moved to open a biblical and archaeological school in Jerusalem. The Israeli rabbinic reaction to this latter proposal verged on hysteria. The chief rabbi of Tel Aviv vowed: "We shall fight against it. . . . It is not a question of a place of worship but of making a niche for a new interpretation which misrepresents Judaism. . . . There is no place for it here." Both chief rabbis, Nissim of the Sephardic community and Herzog of the Ashkenazic, objected to the inclusion of a Reform synagogue in the school as a cause of religious divisiveness in Israel. The Minister of Religion, Zerah Warhaftig, personally attacked Glueck before the Supreme Rabbinical Council, which latter issued a declaration condemning the Reform movement and asserting that it "must not be allowed to strike root in this country and to defile the Holy City." The religious party vice mayor of Jerusalem, Moshe Porush, warned on Israeli radio that the presence of Reform in Israel would be nothing less than a "disaster to Jewry and would bring about the destruction of the state." Thanks to the support of Mayor Gershon Agron of Jerusalem and Prime Minister Ben-Gurion, both of whom recognized that turning down the proposed building could generate severe repercussions in the United States, Glueck managed to get the necessary permits.[43]

But hopes for the growth of Reform in Israel proved barren. By 1965 there were only six Reform congregations in the entire country, and their first national convention passed practically unnoticed. For the most part they served American and British immigrants, and one poll indicated that a full third of the country did not even know they existed. The average Israeli, while probably not sharing the bitter hostility of the rabbinate to Reform, did share its contempt. For the Israelis, even the anticlerical and secular Israelis who did not subscribe to Orthodoxy, an authentic Jew conformed closely to the Orthodox model. They did not understand, and had no respect for, rabbis who were not learned in Talmud nor observant in the traditional mode. "Scratch an Israeli," Yehudah Avner claims, "and you'll find an Orthodox Jew." Indeed, Emil Fackenheim observed wonderingly that despite the fact that so many Israelis claim not to be religious, the visitor from abroad is astonished by the religious quality of the "secularist" Israeli Jew.[44]

*   *   *

The meaning of Israel, at least in the first decade or so after its creation, might better be described as a process rather than a finished product. Elements of assuaged guilt, of vicarious pride, of ethnic unity, of religious devotion, and of centrality were all there, some more easily perceived than others, some already well defined, and some still embryonic. It would be years, however, before American Jews were able to express what Israel meant to them in more than vague generalizations. Part of their inability to define Israel resulted from a preoccupation with finding their own niche in American society. But soon after the establishment of Israel another and very important consideration arose from the bitter debate about the nature—not of the Jewish state—but of the Jewish community in the Diaspora. If Israel was in the process of becoming the center of Jewish life, what then was the status of the Jews in the United States?

Chapter 10

ZION AND *GALUT*

During a visit to the United States in the early 1950s, a veteran Zionist leader who had escaped Nazi Germany remarked wonderingly: "It is not *shver tsu' zein a Yid* (hard to be a Jew) in America today."[1] Benno Weiser's comment, marveling at the comfortable position enjoyed by American Jews, underscored one of the bitterest conflicts to erupt between American and Israeli Jews, a dispute which was not only ideological, but also involved practical matters as well.

For centuries, religious Jews considered themselves living in *galut* (exile), as punishment for having abandoned the ways of God. For decades it had been accepted Zionist doctrine that only in a Jewish state, where Jews could lead a normal life, would this psychological burden be lifted. The Holocaust only intensified the Zionist belief that a Jew could never be at home anywhere in *galut*, and would be safe only in a Jewish state. Why, then, did American Jews persist in living in the United States, in exile? Israel had been created not only for the Jews of Europe and Africa, but of America as well. Moreover, Israel desperately needed people with technological and industrial skills, men and women familiar with Western bureaucratic and political practices. American Jews were needed in Israel, but they insisted on staying in the *goldenah golus* (the golden exile).

* * *

The idea of exile dates back more than twenty-five centuries in Jewish history, to the destruction of the First Temple in 586 B.C.E. and the carrying off of thousands of captives to Babylonia by Nebuchadnezzar. This exile, however, proved to be of relatively short duration, for in 537 B.C.E., Cyrus, King of the Medes and Persians, defeated Babylon and issued an edict permitting all of the children of Judah to return to Palestine to build a new temple to the Lord. As it turned out, however, during those fifty years of captivity a number of Jews had grown accustomed to life in Babylon and chose to stay, so that throughout much of the Second Temple period, as many if not more Jews lived outside of Palestine as in it.[2]

Were these Jews, who voluntarily remained outside *Eretz Yisrael*, in exile? Did they "weep by the waters of Babylon"? They did not, and they used the word "dispersion," which omitted the painful meanings of exile associated with forced expulsion from one's home. "Diaspora" bore no psychological freight; it implied no more than a geographical description, the area of residence of non-Palestinian Jews.[3] Yet even then, some sought the reunification of all Jews in Palestine, and a number of prayers at that time call for the "ingathering of exiles." Ecclesiasticus contains the prayer: "Give thanks unto Him that gathereth the outcasts of Israel," while another book of the Apocrypha, the Psalms of Solomon, pleads for God to "gather together the dispersed of Israel." But, as Jakob Petuchowski observes, since the Temple still existed and the "outcasts" had left of their own free will, the imagery expressed more of a hope for the spiritual unity of Israel than an end to the Diaspora.

The destruction of the Second Temple, the devastation of Palestine, and the forced exile of nearly the entire Jewish population there led to the creation of an extensive literature on the idea of exile. Until the end of the fifth century, the general sentiment was that the Jewish people, out of its homeland, was deprived and suffered from a sense of displacement. A few rabbis, however, saw redeeming elements in the expulsion. R. Johanan and R. Eleazar, for example, agreed that "the Lord did not exile Israel among the nations except in order that there should be added converts" (Pes. 87b). Other writers, such as Saadia Gaon, saw the exile "partly as a punishment and partly as a test." The trial would have a purifying value, "to refine our dross . . . and to terminate our impurities. . . . He has exiled us and scattered us among the nations, so that we have to swim in the roaring waves of the kingdoms, and, as the smelting of silver in the furnace, in their fires, we have been purified." Nowhere, however, in the *halachic* vocabulary of the Talmud is the word *Gola* (exile) to be found.[4]

During the Middle Ages, with rising persecution and expulsions, the modern meaning of *galut* (or in Yiddish, *golus*) came into use. It signifies not only that Jews were displaced physically, but had been rejected socially and psychologically as well. Through sinfulness the "chosen people" had broken their covenant with God, and exile was the price they had to pay. There is bitterness in the writings of sages like Menachem ben Solomon Meiri over the suffering of the Jew while the gentile waxed powerful and wealthy. Yet even here, a variety of interpretations on *galut* is possible. Moses ben Nachman, the famed Ramban, visualized the exile as a crisis not only for the Jewish people but for their God as well, for *galut* disconnected the people from their land and God from his subjects. Few writers were as explicit as Nachmanides about Judaism and its God being capable of full realization only in *Eretz Yisrael*. Century after century since, Jews have prayed for redemption, for a return to the land where they would be religiously fulfilled and politically free.

With Emancipation in the early nineteenth century, a split occurred between those Jews eager to be accepted as part of the general society, and those who believed that full freedom would not be achieved until Jews were restored to their ancient homeland. In many respects the new arguments reflected the diverse opinions that had characterized the debate throughout the centuries: Some saw exile as punishment, others viewed dispersion as a challenge. Reform leaders in particular interpreted the dispersion as a task to bring Judaism's universal message to all the nations. Reflecting the general optimism of the age, Reform foresaw an era of greater acceptance and full equality of Jews in Western society, and totally rejected both the idea of exile and the hope for return to the land.[5]

Zionism, however, never accepted the notion that Jews would be totally free anyplace but in their own homeland. Anti-Semitism did not result from ignorance, but flowed as an inevitable result of *galut*. So long as Jews had no home of their own, they would remain an unassimilable minority, forever aliens and unwelcome. The Holocaust, erupting out of the very land where Reform leaders had proclaimed their vision of Jewish equality, vindicated the Zionist viewpoint; the shabby, callous treatment of refugees during and after the war added still more weight to the argument that Jews were in *galut*—religiously, geographically, and psychologically. The State of Israel, in classic Zionist terms, would supposedly end the abnormality of Jewish existence in the Diaspora. "In Israel everything is Jewish," Ben-Gurion told the B'nai B'rith in 1959, "just as everybody around him is Jewish. The roads are paved by Jews, the trees are planted by Jews, the harbors are built by Jews, the mines are worked by Jews—even the crimes are committed by Jews!"[6]

Ben-Gurion delivered these words before an American audience, in a country where the majority of Jews had rejected the notion that it was in exile. America was different: Here there had never been an Emancipation of Jews, since there had never been enslavement of Jews; here anti-Semitism had never been more than an occasional flare-up of extremists, and had never been an institutionalized phenomenon of the political structure; here Jews had never been forced to choose between Judaism and assimilation, for opportunities had always been available to them as Jews to participate in society. Not all American Jews subscribed to the "America is different" hypothesis, but the dissenters were more often than not Zionists.[7]

Prior to the establishment of the State of Israel, the question of America as *galut* had been soft-pedaled, partly to avoid antagonizing non-Zionists committed to developing the *Yishuv* and, more importantly, because the political fights against the mandatory and Hitler, and then the struggle to establish Israel, diverted attention from such seemingly theoretical matters. During the first few years of independence, critical issues such as housing and absorption of immigrants precluded serious discussion, but by the early 1950s Israeli leaders, and especially David Ben-Gurion, would no longer allow the matter to rest. America was *galut*, they declared, and the only way to save American Jews from the fate of European Jewry was to initiate massive emigration from the United States to Israel.

No matter how well off financially or how much freedom he enjoys, the Jew in the Diaspora, even in the United States, Ben-Gurion argued, still has a "split personality," since he must try to live as a Jew in a non-Jewish environment. He named four characteristics of all Jews in *galut*: They are a minority, always dependent upon the sufferance of the majority; they are economically different, usually professionals and businessmen, while the majority are farmers and industrial workers; they are constantly torn between their desire to lead Jewish lives and the pressure of the society on them to assimilate; and they can never, in such a setting, lead fully Jewish lives. "Whoever lives outside *Eretz Yisrael*," he declared, quoting the Talmud, "may be regarded as one who has no God" (Ket. 110b).[8]

At the twenty-third Zionist Congress in July 1951, the first to be held in Jerusalem, Ben-Gurion led the campaign for *kibbutz galuyoth* (the ingathering of exiles). Despite their numerous internal differences, all of the Israeli delegates, no matter what their political party, stood united behind the idea that Jews living outside Israel were in *galut* (exile), not dispersion, and that Zionism must gather the Jews of the world to live in the State of Israel now that it had been established. The Israeli position, clearly and simply, divided the Jewish world into *Moledet* and *Galut* (Homeland and Exile), and whoever was not in the first was in the second. All Jews, and especially Zionists, had to shake off the dust of exile and make *aliyah* as quickly as possible.

The protests of Western delegates, and especially of the Americans, went unheeded, and only the threat of total disintegration of the movement led to a partial compromise. The resulting Jerusalem declaration set forth the "tasks" of Zionism, rather than its "aims," thus avoiding for a while the thorny issue; but those tasks were "to strengthen the State of Israel, to gather the exiles in the Land of Israel, and to guarantee the unity of the Jewish people."[9]

The Congress touched off the major Zionist ideological debate of the decade. The Israelis, almost without exception, insisted that Jews outside the state lived in *galut*, and the only remedy for that situation was massive *aliyah*. In 1957, at the special Jerusalem Ideological Conference, one Israeli after another rose to offer changes on this theme; Halper Leivick: "A Jew who for one reason or another is not in Israel —the land from which his people was driven and to which it was bound to return—is in exile. Even America is, in my opinion, complete *Galut*." Yitzhak Tabenkin: "There is such a thing as *Galut*, and the Jews of America are also in one. . . . For this reason we say to the Jews: 'Leave the Diaspora and don't take generations to do it; do it within a period of one generation!'" Shmuel Yavnieli: "*Mene, mene, tekel upharsin!* This should be written on the walls of every Jewish home." Golda Meir: "We have nothing against Jews in the *Galut*. It is against *Galut* itself that we protest."[10]

For most Jews in the United States, the debate over exile or dispersion had little personal impact, but in the context of relations between the new Jewish state and the American Jewish community, it held enormous significance. If American Jewish leaders accepted the Israeli viewpoint that all Jews living outside the Jewish state were in *galut*, then that automatically placed American Jewry in a permanently inferior and subsidiary role vis-à-vis Israel. If one denied *galut*, and insisted on the legitimacy of the Diaspora for Jewish life, then one could argue for a partnership between Israeli and Diaspora Jewries. Among articulate Jewish leaders in the United States, spokesmen represented all points of view.

Even before the 1951 Congress resolution, one could find support for the view of America as *galut* in this country. In 1946, for example, Israel Knox attacked the emphasis in Jewish education on the denigration of Jewish life in the United States. In 1950 Jewish journalist Mordecai Danzis conceded that in America Jews indeed enjoyed the fruits of freedom, "but there is more than one kind of *galut*. . . . There is the *galut* of physical suffering, of pogroms and concentration camps and gas chambers. But there is also the *galut* of spiritual suffering, of not being able to live a full Jewish life and of constant pressure from the environment. This latter *galut* leads to assimilation either consciously or unconsciously. It means that our children are turned away from their people, swallowed up by an alien culture. . . . This may not be physical suffering, but it is *galut*."[11]

This theme of spiritual *galut* permeates much of the writings of those who sided with the Israelis. Milton Konvitz described the Jew as essentially a "double being," a person simultaneously at home and homeless. David Polish and Eliezer Berkovits, Reform and Orthodox respectively, agreed that outside *Eretz Yisrael*, Jewish life could not be described other than in terms of exile. Even Mordecai Kaplan, who denied the bulk of the Israeli argument, conceded that there was an element of exile in all Diaspora communities, but if one symbolically conceived of *galut* as night, then there were some exiles of pitch-black night, and others, like the United States, of bright moonlight.[12]

This moonlight, this freedom which seemed to run counter to the darker meanings of exile, actually reinforced its consequences, according to supporters of the *galut* theory. The problem of exile, above everything else, was the survival of the Jewish people. In some countries, oppression had been physical, with death or forced conversion the result. In America, no one killed Jews, but the threat to survival was just as real. "Never was such a great Jewish community in danger of gentler extinction as American Jewry," warned Ben-Gurion. American Jews would, God willing, not face the tragedy of a Holocaust, but he recalled the *mitat n'shika*, the legend of Moses being called to his end not by the Angel of Death, but by a kiss from God Himself. This could very well be the end of American Jewry, by *mitat n'shika*, he feared, for it would succumb to the sweetness and freedom of America.[13] Liberty would prove a greater peril to the Jewish people than persecution. Moshe Davis, Immanuel Jakobovitz, Shmuel Margoshes, and others complained that gently, but surely, American Jewish life was being sapped of vitality by the freedom of America, by the lack of any challenge to Jewish values. Only by turning away, by rejecting the siren song of liberty, could Jews survive.[14]

Perhaps the most consistent and thoughtful analysis of the America-as-*galut* argument appeared in 1956 in a slim book by Ben Halpern entitled *The American Jew: A Zionist Analysis*. For Halpern, long a leading ideologue of Labor Zionism in America, there could be no question of the existence of *galut*. "We in America are not in exile, we say, because nobody keeps us here nor does anyone keep us out of Israel. The argument is sound—but it is not an argument. The debate is not about exile, it is about Exile—*Golus, Galut*. . . . Exile means a disordered condition of the Universe as a whole, which is epitomized in the fact and symbol that the Jewish people live outside their own proper place, the land of Israel." Zionism rejects *galut*; it does not deny its existence, but rejects the consequences, and the vitality of the movement arose from its opposition to *galut*, its demand that Jewish life be normalized. But normality for the Jew is impossible unless he can lead a Jewish life, in all the rich connotations of religion and culture and civilization, unhindered by the environment, be it hostile or friendly.

But Halpern proved to be as perceptive an observer of American Jewish life as he was an ardent advocate of Zionist ideology. Zionism's greatest creation, the State of Israel, did not have to sunder the world into Homeland and Exile, good and evil. The act of creating the state forged a new vitality into Jewish life in the Diaspora and gave many Jews new strength and insight into how to cope with the Jewish problem. By establishing Israel, Zionists made it easier for non-Zionists, those who did not accept the idea of *galut*, to survive. Israel gave Jews all over the world a new pride, a new reason for continuing to be Jews. But it now imposed a new burden on those who claimed to be Zionists. Prior to 1948, they could maintain that they were in exile without any options; now if they remained in exile, it was their own choice. They could say that America was different, and indeed it was; they could argue that they had a mission to help preserve a viable Jewish life in the Diaspora, and indeed such a task, while possibly hopeless, could not be denigrated. But however one looked at the problem, the inescapable fact was that America was *galut,* and even a comfortable, self-imposed exile remained an exile.[15]

*   *   *

Theorists of America as *galut* did not go unchallenged, nor were the advocates of "America is different" necessarily defensive. They made positive arguments in behalf of Diaspora communities, as well as negative statements about Israel as the ideal center of Jewish life or the redemption of exile. The spectrum of argument ranged from the bellicosity of a Jacob Agus, who charged that those who had no "faith in America obviously cannot be trusted with the tasks of building the future of Jewry in America," to the "yes, but" attitude of Trude Weiss-Rosmarin, who considered herself in exile, but, since Israel could not possibly absorb all of the world's Jews, she would have to stay in America and "make the most of the *Galut.*"[16]

Nearly all of the defenders of American Jewry agreed that the negative aspects of *galut* were not present, that one thing Jews in America did not feel was a sense of homelessness.[17] There were many things wrong with the American Jewish community—lack of a definable center, no censensus on its identity, a deplorable absence of organizational unity, distressing internal friction among the various secular and religious groupings, to name but a few—but one could certainly not caricature the American Jew as a *golus yid,* "a pitiful creature, weak, ill-mannered, without pride and lacking in manly dignity, one who was willing to humiliate himself before those stronger than he, ever fearful and self-deprecating before the *Goy.*" The physical, and even psychological, burdens of *galut* as expressed in classical terms did not fit American history or society. Whether the Israelis accepted the fact or not, *America was different,* and the American Jew could not and would not be confused with the persecuted, long-suffering, inhibited Jew of the exile.[18]

Moreover, American Jewry did not care to accept a position of inferiority, either implied or explicit, vis-à-vis Israel. While the Jewish state would occupy a central place in Jewish thinking in all matters relating to the survival and welfare of the Jewish people, American Jews during the 1950s grew increasingly restive with Israeli attitudes. Arthur Hertzberg, visiting Israel in 1949, detected a deep-seated resentment toward its American benefactors. "One hates to be a poor relation," he reported. "Israel's reaction to American Jewish aid seems startlingly similar to the mood of England toward America and the Marshall Plan. Like England, Israel wants more and more aid, and yet wants to be on her own."[19] At the 1951 Zionist Congress, the popular slogan was "Hebraizing the *Galut*," with its implication that Israel had a mission to "civilize" the ghetto Jews, especially those of America. Boaz Evron confirmed that Israeli Jews felt superior to those of the Diaspora, because, by Zionist logic, only they could lead fully Jewish lives.[20] Israelis were not shy, either, about flaunting their alleged superiority. A young Israeli rabbi insultingly told an American audience: "I was born in Palestine, and the Jews of Palestine have status and dignity; the Jews of the *Galut* have no status or dignity." At the end of the Jerusalem Ideological Conference in 1957, called to bring Israeli and American Jews closer together, a weary and dispirited Oscar Handlin found that the only unity evident at the affair had been the nearly unanimous Israeli resentment and derogation of American Jewry.[21]

American Jews might have been willing to accept Israeli assumptions of superiority had there been any indications that the Zionist ideal of a just and humane state had been created, that once again "out of Zion shall go forth the law, and the word of God from Jerusalem." But the new nation faced enormous social and economic problems, and while Israel may have had a more "Jewish" society and population than any place else, there was little evidence that it had become a utopian state. A survey of American rabbis found that ninety-three out of a hundred believed religious life in Israel was unsatisfactory. Spiritually, one observer sadly noted, "the Jews in the State of Israel are not more favored than their brethren in America. Nor, for that matter, is Zion's potential greater than that of the United States." To the contrary, the larger financial resources of the American community could conceivably build the institutions necessary for a flourishing Jewish life in this country.[22]

Nor were Israeli attitudes toward the Jewish people and its history any more encouraging. The older Israelis, veteran Zionist leaders from

Europe and the *Yishuv* who had built the state, clung tenaciously to a siege mentality, ever expectant of another Munich or Holocaust, while younger Israelis, even if they did not embrace the Canaanite view, seemed to have little interest in or concern for Jewish history between Masada and the modern resettlement of the land. Maurice Samuel, in a chapter entitled "If Thou Forget Me, O Jerusalem," accused Israel of trying to break the continuity of Jewish history that linked one generation to another for four thousand years, of denying the great cultural and philosophic achievements of the Diaspora. "American Jewry," he urged, "must counteract Israeli Jewry's growing illusion that it stands before the world as an immediate self-resurrection of the bimillennial past."[23]

If one wanted to talk about *galut* of the soul, about spiritual exile, one could talk about Israelis being in *galut* as well. In a brilliant and sensitive article, Milton Konvitz recalled that traditionally the idea of exile applied not only to the Jewish people, but to the *Schechina* (Holy Spirit) as well, and that as long as the Spirit of the Lord had no sanctuary—that is, until the messianic age—Israeli Jews would be as vexed as Americans over the nature and meaning of Jewish life. Neither the Israeli nor the American was superior. "After he abstracts from himself his Americanness or his character as an Israeli, he sees himself as a Jew, and he begins to feel the pain and the glory of his exile, the pain and the glory of the dream that would bring an end to his homelessness." This dream, at least before messianic times, could not be limited to *Eretz Yisrael* alone, and Konvitz quoted the prophet Jeremiah: "Build homes and live . . . and seek the welfare of the city where I have sent you into exile."[24]

Robert Gordis too emphasized that the type of redemption needed to end the exile had always been conceived of in messianic terms, and since all things were possible to God, the belief in *kibbutz galuyoth* (ingathering Jews to Zion) could proceed without thought of petty details such as housing and logistics for those redeemed. Zionism, by interjecting the idea of auto-emancipation, radically changed the entire nature of the problems of *galut* and redemption, and now such realities as population, economic and political factors, and geographic limitations could no longer be ignored. The Zionists, and especially the Israelis, erred when they changed the agent of redemption from God to man without rethinking the whole problem. *Galut* and redemption either remained a matter of divine will, in which case all Jews were still in exile, or it became a matter of free human choice, in which none were.[25]

Unlike the "negators of the *galut*," Gordis, Konvitz, and others did not want to set up a dichotomy between Israel and the Diaspora communities, a tension between the alleged choices of homeland or exile. On the eve of statehood, Gordis had warned against establishing two opposing factions; not "Palestine or the Diaspora, which can survive?" he urged, but rather "Palestine and the Diaspora." For Simon Rawidowicz, both Israel and Diaspora were but components of an organically unified *am Yisrael*, and both had to complement and supplement one another, a process which Mordecai Kaplan defined as one of the major tasks of the New Zionism. But in the at times raucous argument, these voices of reason went, for the most part, unheard.[26] Nor should one assume that this was a sterile debate, a matter of nitpicking. Depending on how one philosophically viewed Jewish life, as exile or as dispersion, might well determine how one answered the very specific and practical demand of Israel for an increased American *aliyah*.

*   *   *

Aliyah, or emigration to *Eretz Yisrael*, had been a touchy issue among American Jews since the first Zionist Congress. The European assumption was that given a choice between a homeland of their own in Palestine and anti-Semitism in *galut*, Jews would naturally emigrate. This idea, of course, met with intense hostility from Americans who saw the United States as their Zion and certainly did not feel oppressed in exile. The Brandeisian synthesis, which saw the large majority of American Jews staying in this country while helping those who wanted to make *aliyah* and develop the land, solved the question for most American Jews, and writers like Ludwig Lewisohn and Maurice Samuel spread the idea that by doing this work, American Jews would be redeemed from the morass of assimilation and cured of "the sloth in their hearts."[27] In the thirties and forties, the pressing need was to rescue European and Middle Eastern Jews, not those living in freedom and security. But even before Israel had won its independence, Ben-Gurion began his campaign to promote an American *aliyah*. During an Egyptian air raid in July 1948, Rabbi Morton Berman, representing the UJA, asked the Israeli leader what the new state required of American

Jewry. Without a moment's hesitation, Ben-Gurion replied, "What we need is Jews."[28]

The Israeli demand for an American *aliyah* rested on four arguments, two of which flowed directly from the conceptual dimensions of the debate on America as *galut*. The Jews of the United States stood endangered; the history of other Diaspora communities, especially the supposedly "safe" ones in Spain and Germany, proved that at some time, even if not in the immediate future, American Jewry would face a pogrom. "Is the America of McCarthy," challenged Yitzhak Tabenkin, "superior to the Germany of Weimar? Did Germany not have liberals, Social Democrats, Communists, Humanists, Thomas Mann—and nevertheless six million Jews were burned by German Nazis?" Shmuel Yavnieli warned that it would not even take a Hitler, only a major social disturbance. American Jews would then run to the Constitution to take out its guarantees, but who, he asked, "will be the police, who will be the judge in time of need? Have there not been instances of this kind before?"[29] Time and again American Jewish leaders and writers reported that in meetings with their Israeli counterparts they were bombarded with versions of "You American Jews are an alien body in the organism of the American people; you are cherishing vain illusions; you forget that other Jews had the same illusions in other countries, and you know what happened to them." Israelis *knew* that what had happened in Germany would happen in the United States; Zionist ideology demanded that they believe this.[30]

The spiritual danger confronting American Jews—indifference, assimilation, and estrangement from Hebrew culture and the Judaic heritage—was Israel's second argument. Ben-Gurion reminded his contemporaries of the sage's belief that "Whoever dwells outside the land of Israel is considered to have no God."* As long as Jews lived outside of

---

* Ben-Gurion, while quoting the Talmud accurately, did not interpret it correctly. Talmudic discussions consist of two parts: *halachah*, which is legally binding upon Jews, and *aggadah*, homilies which reflect the individual viewpoints of various rabbis but which have no legal force. The passage in question (Ket. 110b) is clearly an *aggadah*, and includes several explanations, including one that God does not reveal Himself to His prophets outside the Holy Land. Maimonides read the "dwell" as "leave," and interpreted it to mean that the rabbis were upset not at those outside the land, but at those who would leave it. According to J. K. Mikliszanski, "Jewish law does not assert, nor does it even imply, that the Land of Israel is the

Israel, they lived in exile, "a wretched, poor, backward, and inadequate form of life," and their Jewishness had "few and feeble foundations." Other voices besides the Prime Minister's warned that America could not provide a meaningful Jewish life, and Golda Meir admitted that she felt pity for American Jews because "a true, free Jewish life" just was not possible in the United States, and the only way to remedy that deficiency was through *aliyah*.[31]

The third round in the Israeli salvo reflected a practical, almost desperate, need for Western-trained men and women familiar with modern technological and industrial skills. In the years following independence, Israel absorbed several hundred thousand refugees from Arab countries, many of them illiterate, most unskilled, and nearly all bewildered by modern society. They would ultimately learn, and become useful citizens of the new state, but they would never have the familiarity and comfort that comes naturally to those raised in sophisticated, industrialized societies. "I would give you ten Arab Jews for one American Jew," a high-ranking Israeli government official said, and while others did not voice this opinion too loudly, it was implicit in their often-frenzied demand for American *aliyah*. Had American Jews only come, Eliezer Livneh lamented, "the entire course of Israel's development in these fateful years would have been changed. Its population would have been more vigorous, more enterprising, more civilized, more progressive."[32] Levi Eshkol, Yigal Allon, and Ben-Gurion never missed an opportunity to chide Americans that, no matter what else they did, they were failing Israel if they or their children did not settle in the land. At the dedication of the new Hadassah hospital at Ein Kerem, Ben-Gurion paid lavish tribute to Hadassah's founder, Henrietta Szold, because she came and lived in *Eretz Yisrael*, and he pointedly urged those who revered her memory to follow her example. In a series of lengthy discussions with Israeli writers and leaders, Maurice Samuel was thunderstruck to realize that the only thing that

---

only place for worshiping God in the Jewish manner." Nor is there a religious obligation for Jews to make *aliyah*. "Going up" to the land is treated as a good deed, but failure to do so is not considered a sin. The religious status of Jews, at least in the Talmud, is not affected at all by the fact of living in the land or *l'chutz ha'aretz* (outside the land); the words *gola* and *galut* are unknown in the *halachic* vocabulary. See Mikliszanski, "The Question of Aliyah in Jewish Law," *Judaism* 12 (Spring 1963): 131–41.

mattered to these men was the development of Israel; they saw American Jewry merely in terms of providing a source of skilled immigrants.[33]

The final component of the Israeli demand proved, to American Zionists, the most difficult to deal with, the charge that the Zionist mission required individual *aliyah*. In December 1953, Ben-Gurion, then out of office, wrote to the Zionist General Committee convening in Jerusalem, asking whether "a Zionist movement particularly after the establishment of the State [is] feasible without the duty of personal immigration." Zionist ideology required not only a Jewish homeland, but also that a majority of Jews live there. We will not compromise, Golda Meir vowed, with only one seventh of the Jewish people living in Israel and the rest in *galut*. The true Zionist could fulfill his or her obligation only through their own or their children's *aliyah*, and Israel launched a missionary program to convince young American Jews to make *aliyah*.[34]

There were very few Jews in the United States who agreed with any or all of the Israeli argument.[35] Those who rejected the idea of America as *galut* could only wonder at Israeli warnings of doom. And if America should go fascist, Hayim Greenberg asked, "if we should ever see a bestialized America, how long could the State of Israel exist in a world capable of producing such a monster, even if Israel's population be increased by several million Jews?" American Zionists, who did support the idea of an increased *aliyah*, vainly tried to explain to Israeli leaders that such scare tactics could have no effect on American Jewry, that they could not, in Maurice Samuel's words, "move a community to great action by playing its funeral march."[36]

The only appeal that would generate a significant *aliyah* would be one that did not denigrate America, but instead emphasized the challenge of pioneering in a Jewish homeland. When he thought of Jews migrating to Israel, Greenberg explained, he did not envision a flight from catastrophe, but rather "Jews departing from America with a blessing on their lips, with love and gratitude in their hearts, and even with homesickness for America at the very moment when they wish it farewell. For we must not assume that all situations call for a choice between love and hatred. Sometimes it is a choice between two loves, one of which transcends the other." Nor did Jews see America as a place where they lived without God. Rabbi Simon Greenberg, vice chancellor of the Jewish Theological Seminary, saw nothing in American life that required him to reject Torah or to violate its precepts, while the Orthodox communities of Williamsburg and Borough Park hardly understood how nonobservant Israelis could tell them they were not good Jews.[37]

In some areas of the community, the Israeli demand for *aliyah* evoked outright hostility. The American Jewish Committee saw the call for emigration as an unwarranted infringement by Israel in domestic American Jewish affairs, and consistently—and fruitlessly—petitioned the Israeli Government, and Ben-Gurion in particular, to desist from its campaign.[38] A number of welfare fund and UJA leaders also protested, and demanded to know if monies raised in local campaigns had been used to foster American *aliyah*. Edward Warburg, UJA head in the early 1950s, threatened to resign if UJA funds were used to encourage emigration of American youth to Israel. While the Israelis denied this, it is probable that "bookkeeping devices" were employed to mask the expenditure of some receipts for *aliyah* propaganda.[39]

On a more personal level, many Jewish families felt bewildered and resentful of this demand for their children. This sentiment was deliciously satirized by Meyer Levin in "After All I Did for Israel," a short story about Jews who belong to various Zionist organizations and devote enormous time and energy to raising money for the Jewish state, but who are totally upset and confused when their own children indicate that they would, perhaps, like to try living there.[40] In a more serious vein, Edwin Samuel suggested that for American Jews with adolescent children, their generous contributions to Israel often included an element of *pidyon haben* (the redemption of the first-born). Perhaps the organizational response of the Committee and the gut response of individuals also reflected a lingering sense of insecurity.[41]

For some people, however, the personal response proved to be emotionally difficult, as they stood torn between a love of Zion and a love of America. "More than once," Maurice Samuel wrote, "I felt the inclination to settle in Palestine, perhaps to throw in my lot with the pioneers on the land. Reflection showed that it was not for me." This hesitation, this feeling of being torn between two poles, involved far more than the simple explanation that Americans were just too attached to the "fleshpot," too comfortable and sloth-ridden, to move.[42] As one young Zionist intellectual confessed, he faced an impasse: "I know that I am something other than the Israeli, by upbringing, by my allegiance to America, and by my decision to be part of the cultural tradition of the Western world. And yet Zion has been part of the underpinning of my life, that part which gave it the greatest zest and vitality. It is not easy to let it go."[43] And as he sat down to recite the Passover Seder, with its eternal prayer for a return to Jerusalem, Milton Konvitz realized that he, and other American Jews, now had their chance, yet deliberately chose not to return. Now and in the future, he would have to tell not only how he had gone out of Egypt, but also out of Jerusalem, a decision "enacted each day of his life by every American Jew, that agitates our hearts, that gives us no rest." Yet without denying the eternal Zion, American Jews had chosen to build their personal Zion in the United States, and that placed certain responsibilities on them and on their children. "For my son is an American," Konvitz concluded. "As an American, he must feel at home here; and I as an American and as his father must do all I can to make his home here secure, peaceful, wholesome, prosperous, and a happy one—*so that he would not want to leave it.*"[44]

*   *   *

Not everyone rejected *aliyah*. Most American Zionist leaders eventually came to support the idea of an increased American presence in Israel, of a greater spirit of *chalutziut* (pioneering), which would benefit not only Israel but American Jewry as well. Mordecai Kaplan, David Polish, Ludwig Lewisohn, and Daniel Frisch all endorsed the principle of *aliyah*, but objected to the methods and reasoning employed by Israelis to promote that goal.[45] But even as they praised an idealistic emigration, they themselves did not go, and it would not be until 1960, when Rabbi Israel Goldstein moved to Israel, that the first American Jew from the community's leadership made *aliyah*. Nor did the average Jew feel differently. In Marshall Sklare's Riverton study, 94 per cent of all adults and 87 per cent of the children felt positively about Israel, but only 4 per cent wanted to live there. Other studies, including several on American rabbis, reflected the same attitude—very high support for Israel and practically no interest in living there.[46]

Yet despite this, there had been a small, at times minuscule, stream of American *olim* (immigrants) to the Holy Land for well over a century. Although precise figures are not available, between 1860, when the first known American *chalutz* (pioneer) arrived, to 1948, between 7,000 and 9,000 Americans settled in Palestine, out of a total of more than 500,000 immigrants, or less than 2 per cent. During the mandatory period the flow had varied, but never rose to more than 3 per cent, and between 1936 and 1945 was less than 500 people, the smallest percentage of any Jewish community, including the Russian, in the world. During the first twelve years of statehood, estimates vary from 5,500 to 7,600 net *olim*.[47]

The inexactitude results in part from insufficient records, from deliberate omissions, and from the various types of Americans who entered Israel. Many became *de facto* immigrants, permanent settlers who did not want to lose their American citizenship, thus never declaring themselves as *olim*. A large portion of the American group were tourists who decided to stay in the country, also not filing permanent papers. A number of elderly Americans, both for economic and religious reasons, decided to spend their last years in the Holy Land, either in retirement homes built by fraternal groups like the B'nai B'rith or independently, and again no one was quite sure how to classify them. Perhaps the most significant factor is that no one knows how many Americans who came on *aliyah* left; nearly all estimates indicate that upward of 80 per cent of all Americans settling in Israel returned home. In 1959, a former president of the Association of Americans and Canadians in Israel (AACI) estimated that 6,000 North Americans, 10 per cent of whom were Canadians, remained of the 35,000 who had come.[48]

Although there have been several studies on American *olim*, there does not seem to be any clear pattern of why they came, but there is general agreement that few moved to Israel out of fear or great dissatisfaction with life in the United States. "I live here by choice," wrote Moshe Kerem, formerly Murray Weingarten, "not from compulsion. Since I am a native American, Israel does not represent an escape from an 'intolerable' way of life. I have faith in American political and social development, and I have no fears about my ability to take my place in American society." Very often the *olim* came from a strong Zionist background. One Ivy League Ph.D. recalled that he had joined a Zionist youth group in New York at age eleven. "I grew up with the intention of coming to Palestine, to go on a kibbutz, to become an ideological farmer, and in 1949 I came." When a middle-aged university professor, who came from "an old Zionist family always oriented on Israel" met and married his wife in 1944, they never set up a real home, "for we expected to be going to Palestine." This Zionist background predominated in those Americans who emigrated in the first few years after the establishment of the state, especially if they had not been born in America; it diminished among *olim* arriving in the middle and later fifties. Interviewers found a variety of reasons behind the decision to make *aliyah*: idealism, job opportunities, religious motivation, marriage prospects; or coming on a visit, some liked what they saw, and decided to stay. Calvin Goldschneider, who has done the most scientific sampling of American *olim*, found that they had been exposed to a much more intensive Jewish education than normal for American youth. Fully 85 per cent had some Jewish education, and 63 per cent had attended six or more years. One third of all American *olim* had attended either a Hebrew day school or a *yeshiva*, and of these, 70 per cent did so for ten or more years. Over one third of the respondents identified themselves as Orthodox, and 46 per cent said they were either "religious" or "very religious"; only 14 per cent came from homes described as "not at all religious."[49] If there is any ideological factor involved in post-1948 American *aliyah*, it would appear to be less "Zionist" and more "religious" in its broadest sense.

Another aspect of the immigrant profile which could not fail to please—and frustrate—Israeli officials is that the *olim* had the educational and occupational background necessary in a developing society. Over 60 per cent of the men and 67 per cent of the women were classified as professionals on their arrival in the country, and they quickly found employment; of those who went into the labor field, four out of five men and nearly all the women had white-collar occupations, a percentage which surpassed even the distorted occupational pattern of American Jewry as a whole.[50] American *olim* in the 1950s, therefore, represented an educational and occupational elite in Israel. Not the quality, but the quantity of this immigration, which rarely rose over 200 or 300 a year, angered and puzzled the Israelis.

Despite this elitist portrait, American *olim* did not have an easy time settling into Israeli society and culture; in fact, the very attributes that made an American *aliyah* so desirable to Israeli officials often proved a handicap in winning acceptance. The novelty of living in an entirely Jewish surrounding, of no longer feeling unique because of one's Jewishness, soon wore off, only to be replaced by a sense of being different because one was an American. Jacob Neusner, after spending a sabbatical year in Israel, observed that to Israelis, "one is mostly an American, or less appropriately, an 'Anglo-Saxon,'" a situation which he felt certain exclusive hotels and clubs back home would find interesting. Even though he wanted to feel part of a Jewish society, he found himself constantly treated as a foreigner; in the end, he affirmed his own deepest loyalties to the United States.[51] Neusner, of course, was not technically an *oleh*, but the regular American immigrants reported the same problem. They had come to Israel expecting to be accepted, but instead frequently faced hostility from the native population. It often took years before American *olim* felt themselves fully at home in their new land.

Part of the *sabra* (native-born Israeli) resentment was only natural; the Americans enjoyed a high standard of living in the United States, and thanks either to professional salaries, savings, or help from home, frequently lived better than other Israelis. One American spoke of his difficulties in adjusting to life in Israel, and especially to the envy directed at Americans. One day, while visiting a couple in Jerusalem during the winter, he mentioned in passing how cold it was. The woman turned to him with a terrible look of contempt: "Well, of course not all of us were raised with central heating; we poor peasants had to grow up with the cold." He was stunned, since Israelis themselves spent a lot of time complaining about the cold. "But an American is not allowed to," he said. "Everybody there is so suspicious of Americans, so jealous. For the past two thousand years, the world has been suspicious and angry at the Jews because they were supposed to be rich. Now the Israelis feel the same way about the Americans." Even in the communal life of a kibbutz, Americans frequently found themselves thought of as "rich." In the eyes of those who had nearly nothing, those who have even a small something may appear to be wealthy. The term "American" carried connotations of wealth and ease in the frontier conditions of Israel in the 1950s, and made it difficult for even a poor American to be accepted.[52]

Another cause of resentment was the desire of most Americans not to give up their United States citizenship. Prior to 1967, Americans could not hold dual American-Israeli citizenship. Few American *olim* wanted to take the legal, and even greater psychological step, of renouncing their American ties. One American who became an important figure in the Israeli government recalled how difficult the decision to become an Israeli citizen had been. He had come to help build a new Jewish society, not to repudiate the United States. "But if I give up my American citizenship, then I *am* repudiating America, and this is not the way I feel. *Why should one have to choose?*" Israelis, so many of whom had been persecuted in Europe and elsewhere, could not fathom this depth of loyalty, and Neusner suggested that for many

Israelis, the American loyalty "was similar to the loyalty of 'Egyptian' Jews for the fleshpots of Pharaoh, and similarly reprehensible."[53] And, of course, that blue-green passport could always take one back home, to comfort, to security, to the fleshpots; it was a ticket to safety, if you will, unavailable to Israelis.†

Nor did they always find Israeli society and customs to be all they expected. Most of them, for whatever reason they came, shared some idealistic—and unrealistic—view of what a Jewish state should be, but were inevitably disillusioned. They found that it took at least ten thousand dollars to see a family through the initial period of adjustment, of finding a place to live, learning the language, and settling in; and at least fifty thousand dollars if one wanted to open a small business. Money, however, lasted only so long, and goods were terribly expensive. The deliberate and unadorned frankness, so highly prized by Israelis, scornful of Westernized and "assimilated" manners, struck Americans, accustomed to some courtesies in life, as downright rude. (As late as 1965, a study of bureaucratic behavior in one large Israeli enterprise disclosed that 60 per cent of officials in contact with the public did not believe in greeting a visitor, nor would they reply to his greeting; an even higher percentage would not offer him a chair, simply letting him stand during the interview.)[54]

Some adjusted, some did not, and the latter, by far the larger group, went home.[55] The reasons for their not making it in Israel varied as much as their reasons for coming—failure to learn the language, inability to adjust to Israeli mores, unhappiness in job or personal life, attachment to American life-styles. For some, the Zionist ideology had become passé. "We are middle-class American Jews who need to find a place where we can fit; we are not people who are going to find our satisfaction in physical labor," said one dissatisfied *oleh*. Another, a Conservative rabbi, thought the Orthodox religious monopoly repellent, and went home to the United States, which he believed "more conducive to

† The North Americans, in forming an association for mutual help, had, like other national *olim* groups, adopted the Hebrew title *Hitachdut Olei America Canada*, which properly translated would mean the Association of American and Canadian Immigrants. But the English title they adopted was the Association of Americans and Canadians in Israel. The omission of that word *olei* (immigrants), tiny as it is, highlights the ambivalence of the Americans; they wanted to be Israelis, but were unwilling to cease being Americans.

religious living than Israel." Ironically, American Jews, the children
and grandchildren of immigrants, suddenly came face to face with the
generational gap which had so troubled their own parents. "The American parents speak Hebrew," explained one returnee, "but not well and
not easily, and all of the children speak it as a matter of course. I
remember when I was a child how embarrassed I was—let's face it—by
the broken English my parents spoke. Do I want to raise my children to
think of me as a greenhorn?"[56] For any American, the idea of being inferior in an alien culture is difficult to tolerate under the best of conditions, and in the Israel of the 1950s this may have been of all the burdens of the *olim* the one they were least prepared to handle.

The low point of Western *aliyah* came in the mid-1950s; in 1956,
only 187 Americans immigrated. That same year, the World Zionist
Congress, either out of disgust or frustration, decided to forgo the usual
harangues on the failure of Americans to immigrate. As one reporter
noted: "On the whole, it seemed that the matter of *aliyah* from the
United States was treated as a subject one does not speak of in polite
company, like sex in Victorian England." But there were two groups of
Americans who were coming in increasing numbers each year—tourists
and students—and from these groups the Israelis hoped a new pool of
potential *olim* could be developed. In 1952, 33,000 tourists entered Israel, and by the end of the decade the figure topped 100,000 (of this
total, approximately one third were Americans); moreover, in every
year except 1956, fewer tourists left the country than had entered.[57]

American students had been attending the Technion and the Hebrew University in Jerusalem since before the founding of the state.
During the 1950s, the various Israeli universities established a number
of programs for visiting students, many in co-operation with the "home"
schools in the United States. In addition, it became an increasingly
popular practice for many Orthodox boys to attend a *yeshiva* in Israel
for at least one year. While precise figures in this area are also lacking,
some rough indicators point to a larger percentage of students staying
on in Israel as *olim* than of regular immigrants.[58] Yet the majority of
students, while their studies in Israel gave them an increased appreciation and understanding of the Jewish state, were beset by the same
ambivalences and suffered the same problems of adjustment as their
elders.

While still on shipboard, Simon Herman reported, the students
overwhelmingly expected, and desired, that their Israeli counterparts

see them as fellow Jews rather than as visiting Americans, yet within a short time of landing, 86 per cent recorded their disappointment that Israelis would see them only as Americans. As time went on, they found to their dismay that they were not succeeding in establishing close relations with the younger Israelis; the friendships they had anticipated did not materialize, and the Israelis kept them at arm's length. Many students, being consistently identified as Americans, began to reaffirm that identity, and in turn resented Israeli ignorance and deprecation of life in the United States. While the students continued to hold a high opinion of Israel, they differentiated sharply between Israel and Israelis, and their estimation of the latter dropped. By the time their semester or year of study had been completed, the majority of them went home.[59]

*   *   *

The debates over Zion, *galut* and *aliyah*, which had been dormant during the prestate era, inevitably surfaced as soon as Israel emerged from the day-to-day crises of the first few years of her existence. Classic Zionism had been predicated on the view of life outside *Eretz Yisrael* as life in exile, a misfortune which could only be remedied by the ingathering of the Jewish people in its own homeland. For Israel's leaders, all reared in that tradition, the problem seemed unequivocally clear: Jewish life in the Diaspora faced constant danger; Israel had been created to solve that problem; the development of Israel required emigration from Western, industrialized nations; survival and growth of Israel was the responsibility of the entire Jewish people. The only conclusion to be drawn from these "facts" was for Jews in the Diaspora, especially in America, to make *aliyah*. To continue to live in *galut*, in danger, in disgrace, made no sense. Why then did American Jews persist in doing so?

For their part, American Jews rejected, as they always had, the assumptions of European-Israeli Zionism: They did not live in exile, or in danger, and while willing to make enormous sacrifices to sustain the Jewish state, did not consider living there to be one of their obligations. They also resented the air of superiority that Israelis assumed. "You addressed us with unyielding authority," complained Elie Wiesel, "as though you had every right over every one of us. You knew all the answers—and even all the questions. The final word had to be yours—and the first one, too. Nothing pleased you more than to make us feel inferior. . . . In your eyes, we are second-class Jews. Worse: second-rate Jews."[60]

American Jews objected to a rationale of *aliyah* based on what they considered a false, distorted image of life in the United States. Time and again American Jewish leaders called for an *aliyah* based on the idealism of *chalutziut*, or, as an alternative, shorter periods of service along the model later popularized in the Peace Corps.[61] They were willing to base an argument for *aliyah* on the *pull* of Israel, on its challenges, its idealism, its opportunities, its religiosity, or any of the positive virtues which one had always sought in a Jewish state. But Israelis seemingly could not understand that American Jews had no intention of fleeing the United States, and efforts to implant an element of fear in the community aroused only resentment. Unless a revolution, horrible even to contemplate, took place in the United States, a large-scale *aliyah* from America was then, and remains today, in the realm of fantasy.

Not until late in the 1970s did some Israelis begin to understand the difference between an emigration caused by "push" and one caused by "pull." In a study of American and Russian *olim*, Ephraim Tabory of Bar-Ilan University discovered that the Russians had left the Soviet Union because they did not want to live there any more, and while choosing Israel, would have left for any place which gave them freedom. The Americans, on the other hand, came to Israel because of what they saw as opportunity in Israel; they would not have left the United States to go anywhere else.[62]

Regrettably, Israeli leaders never understood the pride, love, and sense of acceptance that Jews felt in America, and the debate over Zion and *galut* deteriorated into a dialogue of the deaf. One might use this same analogy when examining the other major Israeli-American controversy in the 1950s, the effort to redefine Zionism, especially American Zionism, in the poststate era.

Chapter 11

ZIONISM:
THE VISION DISRUPTED

Two weeks before the 1947 United Nations vote to partition Palestine, the lead editorial in *The New Palestine* attack "foolish speculation" that the creation of a Jewish state would "absolve the organized Zionists of the world, particularly in America, from further responsibilities. On the contrary, the real task for the ZOA and for Zionists throughout the Diaspora will only be starting."[1] In the light of historic Zionist philosophy, one could not argue with that statement. Zionism had never seen the establishment of a political state as its only goal; rather, the state together with the movement would become the chief instrumentalities for the rejuvenation of the Jewish people. Israel would be a haven for the persecuted and a refuge from anti-Semitism, but that would only be the first step in the process of creating a modern, thriving, and creative Jewish life for those settling in the homeland as well as for those who chose to remain in the Diaspora.

American Zionists, however, had been so wrapped up in the fight to build the *Yishuv* and establish the state that they had given scant thought to just what an American Zionist movement would be once such monumental tasks had been accomplished. They realized that certain functions, especially those of a political nature, would be taken over by the new nation; after all, Israelis, not American Jews, should speak for Israel in the United Nations and to the governments of the world. American Zionists fully expected, however, that a number of responsibilities would devolve upon them and that they and the Israelis would remain partners in the greater work of the movement, even if the terms of the partnership perforce had to be altered. They could scarcely have anticipated a full-scale attack on them, nor a denigration of their role as Jews and as Zionists, nor a dismantling of the apparatus they had labored so diligently to build. Yet in the decade following the Israeli War of Independence, that is exactly what happened. By the late 1950s, American Zionism as a movement had been rendered nearly impotent, a pale shadow of its once powerful self, with few members, little status, and no purpose.

*   *   *

In 1948, the membership of the leading Zionist organizations in the United States stood at about 711,000, with another 244,000 belonging to various smaller groups (such as the Revisionists) and affiliates:[2]

Religious Zionists		125,000
Mizrachi	75,000	
Mizrachi women	50,000	
Labor Zionists		93,000
Poale Zion	65,000	
Pioneer women	28,000	
General Zionists		493,000
ZOA	250,000	
Hadassah	243,000	
Affiliates and other organizations		244,000

Thus, out of a total Jewish population of 5 million, nearly one fifth belonged to organized Zionism; of all Jewish movements and organizations in the United States at that time, there can be little doubt that Zionism was the strongest and had most effectively permeated the community. And within Zionism, the Zionist Organization of America stood as the pre-eminent leader and as the largest single Zionist organization in the world.

Yet to the leaders of the new Israeli government, nearly all of whom held positions of importance in the World Zionist Organization.

the very strength of the ZOA seemed menacing. It had been one thing to have the power of American Jewry on their side in the fight against the British, and to have the wealth of the world's richest Jewish community thrown into the balance during the War of Independence and later to help bring in the refugees; it would be quite another to have such a potent group looking over one's shoulder and possibly even interfering in the affairs of a sovereign state. Moreover, with the disappearance of eastern European Jewry in the Holocaust, the Israeli Labor Zionists had lost the base of their Diaspora power in the WZO; opposition parties within Israel, especially the centrists, could conceivably utilize their ties to the large American Zionist bloc to thwart the will of the ruling Mapai coalition.

Everyone, of course, recognized that some reorganization of the Zionist movement would be necessary to accommodate the fact of Israeli sovereignty. Emanuel Neumann, president of the ZOA, put forward the first plan, namely, that Israel should be responsible for all those activities directly related to its internal security and needs and for relations with other sovereign states, while the World Zionist Organization/Jewish Agency would control Diaspora activities, including cultural affairs and the transfer of Jews to the new state. On the face of it, Neumann's proposal made a great deal of sense: It divided responsibilities along familiar lines, since the WZO had been primarily a Diaspora agency since the early thirties, while the *Yishuv* had controlled its own affairs in Palestine. Naturally, there would be some overlapping where co-operation would be necessary; in the resettling of immigrants, for example, the WZO would bear much of the cost, although once the refugees set foot in Israel they would be under Israeli control. Another reason for establishing separate WZO functions, as Neumann pointed out to the 1948 ZOA convention, was that the world organization in the course of years "has created many institutions. It has legal title to many valuable assets, which it holds in trust for the Jewish people; there are funds, banks, movable and immovable properties. Shall they be turned over at once to the Republic of Israel—that is, to its Jewish and Arab citizens?" These were the assets of the Jewish people as a whole, for the benefit of those in the Diaspora as well as those in Israel, and could not be summarily disposed.[3]

Neumann wanted one more thing: the complete separation of the Israeli government and the Zionist Executive. From the American standpoint, it would hardly do to have the head of a foreign government directing the affairs of American Zionists via his role as chairman of the Executive. The possible embarrassments resulting from this arrangement would only play into the hands of non-Zionists and anti-Zionists, ready at a moment's notice to revive charges of dual loyalty. And, while they did not say so, the Americans wanted not only a free hand to run their own affairs, but also saw an opportunity to take over the world organization. Restrict Ben-Gurion, Sharett, Meir, Ben-Zvi, and others to Israel, and the resulting power vacuum in the WZO could conceivably lead to an American assumption of leadership and responsibility.

The Silver-Neumann faction strengthened its hold over the ZOA at the July 1948 convention and prepared to present its plan at the WZO Actions Committee meeting in Israel the following month. Yet even before they left, a growing opposition group, headed by Stephen Wise's old ally Henry Montor, flew to Israel to learn how far Ben-Gurion was prepared to co-operate with a Silver-dominated American Zionism. They saw the ingrained friction between Ben-Gurion and Silver as their opening to depose the Cleveland rabbi and his allies. If they could not gain control of the ZOA, they proposed establishing new organizations of "friends of Israel" to circumvent the ZOA, a project already quietly blessed by Golda Meir. When the Executive met in August, one could detect a distinct coolness between Israeli and American Zionist leaders.[4]

The question of *hafrada* (separation) dominated the Actions Committee meeting, with none of the Israelis willing to yield his position on the Zionist Executive. The Americans could not understand the Israeli attitude, since, in effect, by becoming cabinet members they had assumed responsibilities and power far greater than they had exercised within the Zionist movement. During the debate, Zalman Shazar, later to become President of Israel, invited Emanuel Neumann to lunch, and proposed that they settle the question in a "quiet, Jewish way," implying that a private agreement, so familiar in Zionist politics, would resolve the dispute. Neumann declined the bait, but agreed that there would be no need for a ruckus. "Let each one express his views and then have an orderly vote taken, and whatever comes out will be the decision." Neumann went on to suggest that, if the Israelis feared American domination, then those seats on the Executive vacated by cabinet members be filled by representatives from the same parties, so as not to change the political makeup of the leadership. The issue was not resolved until Selig Brodetsky, chairman of the Board of Deputies of British Jews, finally went to Ben-Gurion's home and pointed out how impossible the situation would be for the Diaspora leaders if the Prime Minister of Israel remained chairman of the Zionist Executive. Ben-Gurion then relented, and the Israeli leaders resigned from the Executive.[5]

The plan for separation of responsibilities and authority, designed in the light of past experiences, proved inadequate to meet the needs of the current situation. The idea of channeling money from the Diaspora to Israel through the Jewish Agency, as had been the case before 1948, did not take into account the fact that certain large sources of capital, such as the Import-Export Bank, the International Bank for Reconstruction and Development, and the United States government, would not deal with the quasiprivate Jewish Agency, but only with an established government. Moreover, the rate of immigration into Israel exceeded the highest estimates of both government and Zionist officials, and the money for settling them proved more than the Zionists could raise, thus requiring the Israeli government to take a hand. Here one came face to face with how much the very fact of independence had changed the situation. Prior to 1948, the Jewish Agency had had to bear all the costs of resettlement because the mandatory refused to help in any way; now the Israeli government was not only willing to help, it also demanded a voice in such affairs. All of the established Zionist institutions, such as the Jewish National Fund, had to surrender some of their independence. The whole mental frame of the leaders had to be readjusted; they were no longer working against a hostile British regime, fighting to eke out every small victory. The government was no longer an enemy of the Jewish people, but a friend; it was still a government, however, and therefore jealous of its prerogatives as a sovereign state.

The new situation did not seem any more comfortable for the Israeli leaders. For decades they had been in opposition; now they were in power, with a responsibility to develop a government and a nation. They could no longer issue orders to Diaspora groups, and on some points, such as *hafrada*, found themselves opposing colleagues who had been lifelong allies in the battle to build a Jewish state. They also had to deal with men like Nahum Goldmann, the president of the WZO, who presumed to take a very active role in affairs of state, and who wanted to attend and participate in Israeli cabinet meetings.[6] On one thing both Israeli and Zionist leaders agreed: A special arrangement had to be worked out between the World Zionist Organization/Jewish Agency and the State of Israel, an arrangement which preserved Israeli sovereignty while granting the WZO rights and duties to justify its continued existence. At the same time, in deference to non-Zionist Jews, this agreement clearly had to differentiate between the roles and responsibilities of Jews in the Diaspora and citizens of Israel.

The first bill granting the WZO/JA a special status passed the Israeli parliament in 1951, but was too vague in a number of areas to satisfy many Jewish groups. The second bill, resulting from more than eighteen months of drafting and negotiation,[7] passed the Knesset on November 24, 1952. In the debate, Ben-Gurion acknowledged that while the State of Israel had the advantages of sovereignty, this could at times be a source of restriction. Four out of five Jews in the world lived outside the state, beyond its jurisdiction, and Israel "cannot intervene in the internal life of the Jewish communities abroad, cannot direct them or make demands upon them." But the Zionist movement, a voluntary worldwide association, could "achieve what it is beyond the power and competence of the State, and that is the advantage of the Zionist Organization over the State." In the Status Law, the Israeli government authorized the WZO/JA to continue operations within Israel in areas of development and settlement, absorption of new immigrants, and co-ordination of Diaspora-based institutions operating in these fields. In order to preserve Zionist agencies, such as the Jewish National Fund, the law also conferred legal corporate status on the Executive, giving it the power to hold and acquire property, and exempting these holdings from Israeli taxes. The specifics for implementing the Status Law were then worked out by special committees representing the government and the Executive, and in a formal convenant signed in Jerusalem on July 26, 1954.[8]

Theoretically, the Status Law resolved the problems of relations between the Zionist Organization and the State of Israel, and in legal and financial matters it has been the guiding document for settling a number of questions. In fact, however, the issue has never been settled, because the underlying assumption, that the Zionist Organization would continue to be the predominant Jewish organization in the world concerned with Israeli development, was even then being radically altered. Ben-Gurion had already set out on a deliberate policy of emasculating the ZOA, and then called into question the entire ideological underpinning of Zionism as a movement.

In October 1948, less than two months after the ZOA leaders won their argument over *hafrada*, eighty Jewish community leaders, representing over thirty major welfare funds, called for an overhaul of the United Palestine Appeal. The UPA, which received that portion of funds raised for Palestine through the United Jewish Appeal, had since its inception been under the control of the ZOA, and had been the Zionists' chief instrumentality for raising money in the United States. The dissidents constituted themselves the "Committee of Contributors and Workers of the United Palestine Appeal," and called for the reorganization of the UPA as an independent, self-governing body with full power over disbursements and operations in the United States; the Jewish Agency in Jerusalem would control expenditures in Israel. They also demanded a 50 per cent representation in the new UPA for the local welfare funds and federations. Within a very short time it became clear that the Israeli leadership endorsed this "palace revolution," led by such anti-Silver stalwarts as Henry Montor, Abraham Feinberg, Rudolph Sonneborn, and Harold Goldenberg, and that some of the other American Zionist groups, such as Hadassah and Mizrachi, did not necessarily object to the revolt. Robert Szold, who had led the Brandeis faction in the 1930s, opposed the threat of a separate campaign, but endorsed the purpose "of limiting the dictatorial and arbitrary power of Silver and Neumann."[9]

The charges of dictatorship and arbitrary abuse of power against Rabbi Silver and his lieutenants dated back a number of years, and on several occasions had nearly split the movement. During the critical period between the end of the Second World War and the establishment of the state, there is no doubt that only the single-minded and powerful leadership of Silver welded American Zionists into the effective instrument which had played so important a role in the creation of Israel. But with the establishment of the state, the underlying resentments and jealousies that had festered so long finally erupted. At a meeting of the American Section of the Jewish Agency in late December, after Emanuel Neumann had defended the integrity of his administration in handling UPA matters, Rose Halprin, president of Hadassah, rose to declare that the question was not at all one of financial probity; no one questioned Neumann's honesty. In the blunt language for which she had long been famous, Mrs. Halprin told Neumann that other Zionist leaders were tired of being treated as lackeys; they had had enough of being informed after the fact whenever Silver or Neumann decided something in the name of American Zionism; they resented not being consulted over matters in which they had vital interests; and above all, they refused to see the fight in terms of loyalty to Silver. American Zionism had to be loyal, not to any one leader or faction, but to the movement itself, and that meant to the Agency in Israel.[10]

The crisis culminated swiftly in early 1949, after several leading UPA staff members resigned to join the Committee of Contributors. Berl Locker, chairman of the Agency Executive, and Eliezer Kaplan, now Israeli Minister of Finance, came to the United States, and on their own initiative called a special meeting of the UPA directors. Despite the opposition of the Silverites, the dissidents—backed by the Israelis—managed to secure control of the board of the UPA and to reconstitute it as a separate body to co-ordinate Zionist fund-raising in the United States.[11] Although the ZOA would continue to have representation on the board, power had shifted away from the ZOA leadership to the communal leaders, who would look more to Jerusalem than to New York for guidance in managing the operation. Moreover, since Mizrachi, Poale Zion, and Hadassah agreed to co-ordinate their drives with that of the UPA, soon to be renamed the United Israel Appeal, they demanded and received a larger voice in its direction.

The effect of this agreement on American Zionism in general, and on the Zionist Organization of America in particular, was immense. Prior to 1948, American Zionism, led by the ZOA, had had three main areas of responsibility: political affairs, education, and fund-raising. The establishment of Israel effectively removed political matters from Zionist hands; a sovereign state had to speak and act for itself. The reconstitution of the UPA shifted the burden of fund-raising from the Zionists to the non-Zionist communal leaders. From an Israeli point of view, this made essentially good sense, since the wealthier Jews, while friendly to the new state, were rarely Zionists, and could be reached more easily, and more efficaciously, through the local welfare funds. The educational activities of American Zionism had never been particularly effective, and the diffuse organizational pattern of American Jewish life prevented any single body from taking the lead in a major educational campaign. Moreover, there is little doubt that Labor Zionists, who dominated and led the Israeli government, were glad to see the more conservative ZOA reduced in influence.

Within American Zionism, those bodies with specific goals retained their strength. Hadassah and its medical program, Pioneer Women's social service facilities, and Mizrachis' religious programs grew over the years, but only because their members directed all efforts into specific projects encouraged by the Israeli government out of need, and because they posed no threat to the political leadership of the Jewish state. The Poale Zion basked in the reflected glory of a labor government in Israel,[12] but had nothing to offer American Jews, who were less and less interested in socialism. The ZOA foundered, losing members, groping for something to do, watching helplessly while new institutions and agencies, non-Zionist for the most part, assumed the work of public relations, lobbying, and fund-raising on behalf of Israel, tasks which the ZOA had always assumed would be its responsibilities after the creation of the state.

The ZOA also suffered from a lack of strong leadership. Silver, embittered by the battle, retired to his pulpit in Cleveland. While frequently consulted by Abba Eban, he never again played a major role in Zionist affairs, and appeared content to devote himself to his congregation and to his studies. Neumann shifted his activities to the American Section of the Jewish Agency and founded specific organs to further Zionist education, such as the Tarbuth Foundation, the Herzl Institute, and *Midstream* magazine. Although he would serve another term as ZOA president in the mid-1950s, by then the trend had became irreversibly fixed, and the ZOA, from being the strongest of American Zionist organizations, soon lost much of its power and influence.

There have been charges that David Ben-Gurion deliberately sabotaged the ZOA to prevent Silver from challenging his leadership. There is no doubt that the reorganization of the UPA and the establishment of separate non-Zionist bodies to aid Israel, all bypassing the ZOA, had Ben-Gurion's approval, while his negotiations with the American Jewish Committee, without even consulting American Zionists, contributed to the declining prestige of the ZOA. Despite his many admirable characteristics, the founder of modern Israel inevitably turned against those whom he suspected might challenge his leadership, such as Chaim Weizmann and Moshe Sharett, who were treated shabbily and often cruelly. It is doubtful if Silver even desired the responsibility of directing world Zionism, and a number of Silver's close friends have denied the charge that he wanted to oust Ben-Gurion.[13] The Cleveland rabbi wanted no more—but no less—than that American Zionism should play its role as a partner in Israel's development. Ironically, and sadly, the egocentrism which had helped split the Zionist movement in the Brandeis-Weizmann dispute in 1921 now seemed to recur, but this time with a more ominous note for the cause. Ben-Gurion not only seemed intent on destroying the ZOA, but also on dismantling the Zionist movement itself.

*   *   *

The dispirited condition of American Zionism in these early years impressed itself on a number of observers. Judd Teller, a frequent commentator on the American Jewish scene, returned from a speaking tour for the UJA, to write that "the sorriest lot in some communities are the Zionists," who object to the domination of the welfare funds yet really do not know what to do with themselves. One Zionist after another called upon the movement to reassert itself, to redefine its mission. Shlomo Katz argued that the Zionists, if they had the will, could provide the leadership necessary for developing a creative Jewish consciousness in the United States. At a symposium on "redefining Zionist Education," nearly all of the speakers agreed that with the establishment of the Jewish state, the Zionist movement as a whole, but especially the American branch, would have to create new tasks.[14] Yet by the time of the twenty-third Zionist Congress in 1951, American Zionism seemed at a loss over what it should do. Hadassah and Pioneer Women had their projects, but the very success of those endeavors merely underscored the philosophical emptiness of the movement. The state had been created; now what did one do? Ben-Gurion's affirmation that Zionism's "responsibility and mission have become incalculably greater" seemed insincere, especially in the light of his constant denigration of Zionists outside Israel.

The World Zionist Congress, the first to be held in Jerusalem and in a Jewish state, should have been an occasion of great joy, but it was not. The ghosts of European Jewry haunted the convention hall, and the tension between the two largest delegations, the Israeli and American, was manifest.[15] The Israelis demanded a renewed spirit of *chalutziut* (pioneering) and called for American Jews to emigrate *en masse* to Israel. No matter what the Americans proposed, the Israelis found fault, and deliberately ignored American Zionist leaders. When ZOA spokesmen suggested that Americans be assigned the major responsibility for organizing Diaspora Jewry, the Israelis reacted vigorously, and in effect said to forget the *galut* and make *aliyah*. Only the threat of an American walkout kept the Congress from adopting an ideological statement based entirely on *aliyah* and *chalutziut*.[16]

The attack of the Israelis, led by their fiery Prime Minister, did more than just disparage the Diaspora and demand Western *aliyah*; it also called into question some of the basic assumptions of Zionism. Although Ben-Gurion, when supporting the Status Bill, had declared that a positive and essential role still existed for the Zionist Organization, at other times he seemed to go out of his way to describe the movement as an anachronism. "It is doubtful whether there is any remedy for the old generation of Zionists in the Diaspora," he said, and younger men and women "will neither be discovered nor activated by the 'Zionist' Organization, which has lost its meaning." While willing to concede that the movement, especially in America, had been of great help in bringing Israel into existence, he would not allow present Zionists to live on past credits. The Zionists of the Diaspora, he argued, were not "partners" in the upbuilding of the state, "but only helpers." At one point he described the Zionist movement as a mere "scaffolding," useful in the preliminary stages of construction, but now with Israel established, the superfluous scaffolding could be dismantled.[17]

Ben-Gurion reserved his sharpest attacks for those who presumed to call themselves Zionist leaders but did not fulfill the basic requirement of *aliyah*. At the 1951 Zionist Congress he belittled the entire American Zionist movement for its failure to produce *olim*. "If only ten American Zionist leaders had come," he said, they would have supplied an inspiring example to other American Jews; instead, the movement in the United States teetered on philosophical bankruptcy. "Jewish history won't forgive them," he told Moshe Gurary, but it was not too late. "There is enough for them to do here. Let them come. . . . What are they waiting for, God forbid, another catastrophe like in Europe?" He would certainly never reject any form of assistance to Israel, but he denied the Zionists any special claims in their roles *vis-à-vis* the Jewish state. So long as American Zionists "do not personally accept the ideological and practical content of Zionism," he saw no reason to place them in any category separate from all Jews who wished Israel well.[18]

Perhaps Ben-Gurion's strangest bolt came when he suggested that Zionism no longer really existed. Those Jews who did not make *aliyah* were not entitled to call themselves Zionists, while those who had come to *Eretz Yisrael*, having fulfilled the Zionist mission, could now discard that label. "I am not a Zionist," he proclaimed, "yet I live in *Eretz Yisrael*. Was Joshua a Zionist? Was Ezra a Zionist? Both lived in *Eretz Yisrael*, and never in their lives did they know there existed such a thing as Zionism."[19] The rise of the Third Jewish Commonwealth had put an end to the dysfunctional character of the Jewish people; the movement had succeeded; now all that was left was the ingathering of the exiles, and once in Israel, the term "Zionism" had no further meaning.

The theme that Zionism had become outmoded ran like a *leitmotiv* through Zionist debates and articles in the 1950s. Joachim Prinz, president of the American Jewish Congress, concluded at the end of the decade that "Zionism is—for all practical purposes—dead." Within Israel the very term was demeaned; *al tekashkesh Tzionut*, a common colloquialism, meant "don't give me that claptrap."[20] One could no longer "talk Zionism," at least in the Diaspora; one had to fulfill Zionism, and in so doing, liberate oneself from the need for Zionism. That single act of *aliyah* became, according to Eliezer Livneh, "the heart of Zionism and its acid test."[21]

But what of those who could not, or would not, make *aliyah*? For Rabbi James Heller, a veteran Labor Zionist leader who had long fought for Zionism within the often hostile ranks of Reform Judaism, it was too late, his life was too far along, for such a radical change of direction. "Does this make me no better than a 'friend of Israel'? Am I to be relegated to this place of coldness and remoteness? What of all the years I have thrown into the battle for the ideas of Zionism, and the aid in its task of winning the American Jewish community?" There would never be more than a small emigration from the United States; the bulk of American Jewry would not leave. "For the rest, must Zionism be written off?"[22]

American Zionists were not willing to be written off. They knew, better than anyone else, the magnitude of the problems facing them. They too could run down a lengthy litany of organizational and philosophical problems confronting the movement in the United States. Indeed, some of the most trenchant criticism of American Zionism came not from the Israelis, but from Americans themselves. But where the Israelis denigrated Zionism in the Diaspora as an outmoded anachronism, American Jews bemoaned the failure to build a movement capable of meeting not only the physical needs of the new state, but also the spiritual and cultural needs of Israeli and Diaspora Jews.

Perhaps the chief failure of American Zionism had been that it had assumed primarily a philanthropic function. The Brandeisian synthesis had assigned American Jewry the practical task of raising funds to be used for the rebuilding of Palestine. Through Zionist education, personal involvement in various programs, and other devices, American Zionists would acquire the knowledge and commitment necessary to prevent their work from deteriorating to the level of a common charity. For a variety of reasons, however, the Brandeisian program was only partially implemented; the personal involvement, the educational programs, the development plans fell by the wayside, leaving only fund-raising and political action.

Few Israelis were as candid as Zehava Epstein in admitting that the European and Palestinian leaders of Zionism had welcomed the financial contributions of American Jews but had never really wanted them to get politically involved in the movement. For all their talk about education, the Zionists had done nothing to teach American Jews either about the *Yishuv* (other than that it constantly needed money) or about Zionism itself.[23] In many ways, Zionism had merely supplanted the old *chalukah* system. Instead of Orthodox Jews supporting pietistic scholars in Palestinian enclaves, the Zionists had managed to get the majority of Jews to support the *Yishuv* in its efforts to build a Jewish society. *Chalukah* had been a charity, but much more than just alms-giving, since both donors and recipients saw themselves as participating in the same task—the worship of God through the study of Torah. The donor never felt superior, nor the recipient inferior; each had his own task. Ideally, Zionist fund-raising should have operated in a similar fashion, but it failed to be so because Americans and Palestinians did not share the same value system. The Palestinians saw themselves as building a new Jewish society, ending the suffering of *galut*; the Americans saw themselves as helping suffering Jews escape *European* persecution, while they continued to build their lives in a new Zion. For one brief period, from 1945 to 1948, the emotional, political, and financial needs coalesced so that Americans and Palestinians could see themselves as fighting the same battles, with the immediacy of the crises blotting out the ideological differences. Support of Zionism—that is, support of the Jewish-state-in-the-making—for a while became one's way of identifying as a Jew, but once the crisis passed, the old divisions reasserted themselves. The Israelis now demanded a personal involvement unessential to American Jewish ideals, and when the Americans rejected this approach, the Israelis wrote off the movement in the United States as a failure.[24]

The philanthropy would continue. Israel needed help, and the Jewish tradition of *tzedakah* would ensure a steady flow of cash to the new state. Henry Morgenthau, chairman of the UJA, declared that "the most important Jewish issue before the Jews of America is the success of the State of Israel," and nothing would be allowed to interfere with that policy. Mordecai Kaplan described Israel as the front line in the battle for Jewish survival, and assigned American Jews the role of the home front, providing the material and emotional support Israel needed.[25] This need for funds led Israeli officials to court such non-Zionist groups as the American Jewish Committee and the welfare-fund leaders; that, after all, was where the money would be found. They went out of their way to distinguish publicly between the obligations they expected of American Jews, primarily financial in nature, and those of Zionists, so that the bulk of American Jewry remained largely unaware of the bitter disputes within Zionist ranks. They continued to give, and to give generously, and saw themselves as "friends of Israel." That was all they wanted to be, but American Zionists wanted much more.

*   *   *

In many ways, American Zionists in the poststate decade reverted to the more classical ideas of the movement, especially those of Ahad Ha'am. They had exerted all of their efforts to create a Jewish state, and now found themselves, as one observer noted, in the position of a mother who has given her last child in marriage. All along, however, there had been voices calling for an orientation in American Zionism which went beyond the creation of a state. Now those ideas received a fresh airing, as American Zionists, unwilling to be just "friends" of Israel, and unalterably opposed to a definition of Zionism limited to *aliyah*, sought new directions for their labors.

First of all, they argued, one had to recognize that the State of Israel had been created not only by the heroic endeavors of the *Yishuv*, but also by the entire Jewish people acting primarily through the Zionist movement. Had there been no Zionist Organization created at the end of the nineteenth century, no instrumentalities such as the Jewish National Fund and Keren Hayesod, the greatest exertions of the early immigrants would have come to naught. It had been funds from the Diaspora that had enabled the purchase of land in Palestine, funds from the Diaspora that had supported the early settlements and industries, and political support from the Diaspora, especially in Great Britain and later in the United States, that had made possible the Balfour Declaration, the United Nations partition, and the creation of Israel. Maurice Samuel, in commenting on the Israeli equation of Zionism and claptrap, said he could forgive them if they had referred only to windy speeches, pretentious idealism, or political bluster. But he objected strenuously to the attack on Jewish unity and the ties between the Jewish state and the Jewish people. "It is an intolerant assertion," he wrote, "that the Jewish State is a thing in itself, self-justified, self-explanatory; it is a demand not to be burdened with Jewish history and tradition and larger significance."[26]

Yet Zionism had been integral to Jewish life and religion since the time of the first exile. Those concerned primarily about religion did not necessarily welcome this phenomenon, since they saw it as a pushing aside of the God-centeredness of Judaism; the primacy of Israel in Jewish life merely appeared as the modern equivalent of idol worship.[27] But to a majority of Zionist thinkers, the state and the movement could provide the cohesiveness which would hold the Jewish people together.[28]

This, then, would be the continuing mission of Zionism, the perpetuation of a Jewish people united not only by ethical ideals and religious observance, but by nationalism as well. "What makes us Zionists," Ben Halpern declared, "is the doctrine that the Jews throughout the world are One People." Moshe Sharett and Abba Eban, two Israelis who dissented from Ben-Gurion's negation of Zionism, agreed with Americans that the aim and purpose of the movement could be nothing less than the survival of the Jewish people, and for this task, the State of Israel, important as it was, constituted a means and not an end in itself. In the United States, Hayim Greenberg, Maurice Samuels, Mordecai Kaplan, and others agreed that the creation of the state had been but the first stage of Zionism; the second phase now had to be just as revolutionary, "to reconstitute the Jewish people, to reunify it, and to redefine its status vis-à-vis the rest of the world."[29]

At the first Zionist Assembly in 1953, Nahum Goldmann, president of the WZO, argued that "Zionism will hereafter be judged by its efforts for Jewish survival outside Israel more than by its efforts on behalf of Israel," yet the dangers which Goldmann and others warned about—indifference, assimilation, as well as physical attack—were not restricted to the Diaspora alone. Indeed, as far as physical danger went, Jews in Israel suffered a far greater threat to their lives than did nearly any of the Diaspora communities. Moreover, the establishment of the state, despite Israeli claims, had not fulfilled some of the basic Zionist goals. Jewish life had not been normalized nor anti-Semitism erased. Few would agree that life in Israel represented a normal existence, while anti-Semitism in the Diaspora had decreased (having been discredited by the Holocaust) but had certainly not disappeared. In a trend that would reach epidemic proportions in the late 1960s and early 1970s, anti-Zionist and anti-Israel sentiments became the new form of Jew-hatred. For Meir Ben-Horin, the bitter truth had to be faced: "The coalition of Zionicides is, in fact, a coalition of Judaeocides. For Zionism and Judaism are one, and the effort to destroy the one is the effort to destroy the other."[30]

Americans also refused to accept another aspect of the Israeli version of Zionist history, the failure to distinguish between a *Jewish* state and a *Zionist* state. Israel had indeed become a Jewish state insofar as a majority of its citizens and nearly all of its leaders were Jews, as it allowed Jews full civic and religious freedom, and as its patterns of daily life permitted observant Jews to lead a religious life without either direct or indirect interference from the government or the society. But the Zionist dream had been to create an ideal state, one marked by social and economic justice, fulfilling the ancient prophecy that "out of Zion shall go forth the law, and the word of God from Jerusalem." Martin Buber recalled that the early Zionists and the Lovers of Zion had not wanted merely a country of Jews in Israel; they had dreamed of creating a Zion in Palestine, and it had been this idealism which brought the early settlers to *Eretz Yisrael*. Eliezer Livneh, despite his basic agreement with Ben-Gurion over the superfluousness of Zionism, conceded that Israel had not come near being a Zionist state.[31]

Some of these arguments were admittedly retaliatory and self-serving in nature, but they all pointed up the American belief that Zionism, far from having outlived its usefulness, still had much work to do. It was hardly a dialogue, and no one on either side changed his or her views.[32] It would take the trauma of the June 1967 war to shake both sides into a greater realization of how deeply committed the Diaspora and Israel were to each other. American Zionists might have achieved greater understanding and respect from the Israelis if instead of merely

defending American society and rejecting Israeli arguments, they could
have put forward a positive and specific program of their own. But that,
above all else, constituted the essential weakness of American Zionism
in the 1950s: It did not have any clearly defined philosophical basis.

*   *   *

American Zionists, with their immediate goal of a Jewish state realized,
found that their own vision had soured. Horace Kallen spoke tellingly
of the abyss that separated the ideal Israel from the earthly Israel: "Students of philosophy know, of course, even more than students of history, that ideals enacted are ideals corrupted, conceptions implemented
are conceptions maculated, visions realized are visions disrupted. To
keep your conceptions immaculate, don't employ them; to hold your vision intact, don't realize it; to retain your ideals, don't live up to them.
Reality and its actualizations transform. They bring unforeseeable distortions and shocking shapes and colors. . . . Whatever renders the
ideal potent and fruitful deflowers it."[33]

The ideal Israel, at least for the moment, no longer existed; the
dream of a Jewish state, the vision of two millennia, had come to pass.
The ache of possessing proved as painful as the ache of longing, perhaps even more. Not to possess at least meant that one had something
to work toward. Now what did one do? American Zionists felt, they
knew, that somehow a choice must be available, a new synthesis of
ahavath Yisrael (love of Israel) and *ahavath America* (love of America); there must be a new merging of seemingly contradictory values,
much as Brandeis had developed a generation earlier.[34]

Everyone agreed that unless Zionism instituted a positive and energetic program, it could not survive. How far the deterioration had gone
by late 1954 could be seen in the founding convention of the Student
Zionist Organization, convened at Columbia University by the American Zionist Council. The whole affair lacked the vigor and élan of the
"old days," and one observer wondered aloud whether the Zionist revival might not die of boredom. Jacob Neusner questioned if some of
the delegates were Zionists at all. He asked one coed the burning question of the day, whether she considered herself living in *galut,* and she
wanted to know what the word meant; her entire exposure to "Zionism" had been through a novel she had read about Israel's War of Independence. At their socials in the evenings, they all danced the *hora* du-
tifully, but seemed relieved when the record player switched back to

fox trots. Neusner left the convention with a sense of unreality about the entire meeting. Perhaps Judah Shapiro, the secretary of the National Foundation for Jewish Culture, had been right in his opinion that since 1948, the Zionist movement had nothing to say to American Jews.[35]

Gradually, however, gropingly, hesitatingly, American Zionists began to shape in the rough outlines of what might hopefully emerge one day as a new synthesis, and the key figure in this area is undoubtedly Mordecai M. Kaplan. Nearly all of the themes that appeared throughout this period derived in large part from his work, or were transmuted by him from stray thoughts into integral parts of a uniquely American Zionist philosophy. In a variety of articles and speeches, but especially in *A New Zionism* (1955), he spelled out a program which both responded to Israeli challenges and provided American Zionists with constructive goals.[36]

Kaplan had one advantage over other Zionist ideologues: For many years prior to 1948 he had been thinking of how an autonomous Jewish state would fit into his overall view of Judaism as a civilization. Axiomatic to Kaplan's system was the belief that Israel and the Diaspora had interdependent, but unique, roles to play in Jewish life. The detractors of the Diaspora failed to take into account how much the Jewish state would rely upon Diaspora, especially American, Jews for material, political, and psychological help. Given the enormous internal burdens upon the state, as well as the hostility of the surrounding Arab states, it was doubtful whether Israel could survive without Diaspora aid; but the relationship should not be allowed to deteriorate to that of a rich relative supporting a poor cousin with charity.

The new Zionism, he suggested, should be concerned less with *Medinat Yisrael* than with *Am Yisrael* (less with the Jewish state *per se* than with the Jewish people as a whole). It would continue to battle for the survival of Israel, but primarily because Israel would be the touchstone for the survival of Judaism and the Jewish people. As Zionists, Kaplan declared, "we have to reconstitute our peoplehood, reclaim our ancient homeland, and revitalize our Jewish way of life." Each of these objectives would have to be pursued not only in the Diaspora but in Israel as well. The survival of the Jewish people universally, with Israel as its living center, would be the essence of the new Zionist movement, and all efforts had to be directed toward that goal.

What Kaplan proposed in his "new Zionism" was in many ways a restatement rather than a radical alteration of the "old Zionism." Herzl, Pinsker, Ahad Ha'am, and the other founders of the movement all saw no way for the Jewish people to survive without an autonomous homeland. For them, the world was anti-Semitic, and once a Jewish state came into existence, they saw little reason or hope for a continued Jewish life in *galut*. The danger in this line of reasoning is that the distinction between the Jewish people and the Jewish state eventually blurred, a process accelerated by the tragedies of the 1930s and 1940s, when the need for a state became the paramount consideration in every facet of Zionist work. Kaplan once again differentiated between people and state, and recognized that Diaspora Jews expected to continue living in the lands of freedom as Jews.

For Kaplan, the new danger would be a schism between the Jews of Israel and the Jews of the Diaspora, a split already evident in the Canaanite movement. In order to preserve the unity of the people, Zionism had to foster a sense of interdependence and interaction between Israeli and Diaspora Jewries, a process that went far beyond mere material aid, and at the same time to provide individual Jews with a sense of meaningful participation in that process. Only if individual Jews were part of the larger peoplehood would they and the Jewish people survive. Religion, nationalism, culture—all of the aspects that made up Judaic civilization had to be relevant to each individual Jew; otherwise the people would die, whether the Israeli state existed or not. Kaplan did not demean the efforts which had gone into securing that state, but demanded that Zionism should view the establishment of Israel "only as the first indispensable step in the salvaging of the Jewish people and the regeneration of its spirit. To attain these objectives, Zionism had to be viewed not merely as a cultural and political movement, but also as a religious movement for our day."

This required, of course, that Zionist leaders in Israel cease their attacks on the Diaspora, that they stop viewing world Jewry only as a source of money or of potential *olim*, and that they start treating Zionist movements in the United States, Great Britain, and elsewhere as partners in the great tasks facing the entire Jewish people. In the 1950s, the Israelis were not willing to do so. In the United States, few people objected to Kaplan's proposal that Zionism focus on the survival of the Jewish people, but the organizational strength and influence no longer existed. Membership in the movement had dropped precipitately, and had it not been for the vitality of the women's groups in pursuing their projects, the figures would have been even worse. Moreover, Israel was still the glamorous focus of Jewish attention, and thanks to the growing importance of the local welfare funds, Jews interested in Israel could get involved with the Jewish state and completely bypass the Zionist organizations.

The philosophy of the "new Zionism" was not so much antithetical to American Jewish interests as it was premature and irrelevant. In the 1950s all of American Jewry felt strong and confident, growing in wealth and status, with the young Jewish state as a symbol of its pride. American Zionism, which had done so much to bring that state into existence, now stood forlornly on the sidelines, shunned as inadequate by the Israelis and as outdated by American Jewish communal leaders. Not until the crisis of 1967 would the sense of a unified Jewish people again dominate American Jewish thinking; for the meantime, Horace Kallen's evaluation of the Zionist trauma would have to stand: Visions realized are visions disrupted.

Chapter 12

MARKING TIME

In any marriage, no matter how great the love of one partner for the other, there is an unavoidable period of adjustment, a settling in, a learning of the strengths and weaknesses, likes and dislikes by one or the other. The 1950s constituted that period of adjustment between Israel and the American Jewish community. The attempts to define such areas as exile and dispersion, Zionism, and the meaning of Israel in contemporary Jewish life may appear as a rather stormy beginning for a marriage, yet by exploring these subjects, even when agreement could not be reached, both Israeli and American Jews slowly established the basis for an enduring relationship. In the area of political action as well, the decade following the creation of the state saw both sides gradually work out an acceptable arrangement, the strength of which easily withstood what might have been the trauma of the Sinai campaign of 1956.

*   *   *

Organizationally, the Zionists had little flexibility, since each of the individual bodies would yield practically none of its sovereignty or initiative to a central committee. The crises preceding 1948 had forced the Zionist factions to join together in the Emergency Committee, which disintegrated soon after Israel's War of Independence. It was reorganized in 1949 as the American Zionist Council, headed by Louis Lipsky, and composed of the fourteen leading Zionist groups. From 1949 to

1954 the Council floundered, trying to find a niche for itself. It launched propaganda campaigns, lobbied in Washington on behalf of Israel, fought the American Council for Judaism, and made a fruitless stab at co-ordinating Zionist activities in the United States. The Council even tried, with limited success, to dovetail its work with that of some pro-Israel but non-Zionist groups, such as the Anti-Defamation League of B'nai B'rith.[1] But from the start the centrifugal forces at work on the Zionist scene undermined the idea of a powerful co-ordinating council. Israel had assumed responsibility for speaking to the American government; the crises in the Jewish state from 1949 to 1954 focused on absorption of hundreds of thousands of immigrants, a process that required large sums of money, and here the UJA's role became crucial. The absence of leadership following the Ben-Gurion-Silver controversy, as well as the residue of antagonism to the Silver regime, precluded the emergence of a strong figure. Lipsky, by now an elder statesman in Zionist ranks, exercised little real control over Zionist affairs.

At the end of 1953 it was evident that American Zionism, as a movement, had little importance or even a sense of where it was going. At the first Zionist Assembly in December of that year, the delegates did not even try to deal with the problems of how a Zionist movement might fit into the larger patterns of American Jewish life. Zionism is what Zionism *does,* they decided, and those gathered identified their three major tasks as assuring the unity of the Jewish people, promoting Hebraic education, and relating Diaspora communities to Israeli life. As to *how* these tasks could be achieved, and in a specifically Zionist context, the Assembly could not say. Although some editorialists professed to see the Assembly as a sign of new life and vigor in American Zionism,[2] in terms of practical results the gathering accomplished nothing.

The following months, however, saw a number of organizational changes designed not only to infuse vitality into the movement, but also to channel its work into those areas where Zionist activities could be most useful and effective. Rabbi Irving Miller replaced the aging Lipsky as head of the Council, and soon afterward the Council decided to discontinue all of its distinctly political activities. In March 1954 it established the American Zionist Committee for Public Affairs, an organization created specifically to lobby the federal government on matters affecting Israel. The Committee, which former newspaperman I. L. "Sy" Kenen directed from its inception until his retirement more than

two decades later, served two purposes: First, it removed the growing
pressure by the State Department on the ZOA and other Zionist groups
to register as agents for a foreign government, a move which would
have deprived them of their tax-free status; more importantly, it allowed, for the first time since 1948, all pro-Israel lobbying to be co-ordinated through a single office. There would continue to be some individual efforts from time to time by the different Zionist bodies to
advocate particular points, but thanks in part to Kenen's genius as a
lobbyist as well as the Israeli government's support of and co-operation
with the Committee for Public Affairs (later the American Israel Public Affairs Committee), the Committee eventually became, as was intended, the focal point and co-ordinator of pro-Israel lobbying in the
United States.[3]

The Committee for Public Affairs gave American Jews a central
office through which they could try to exercise their political influence
for Israel; in turn, the Israelis needed an equivalent agency through
which they could consult and advise American Jewry on matters of mutual concern. The American Zionist Council had been devised as that
agency, but the insistence of individual organizations on maintaining
their own contacts with the Jewish state negated that route. Moreover,
the Israelis also wanted to involve the powerful non-Zionist groups,
such as the American Jewish Committee and B'nai B'rith. Following
anti-Jewish incitement in the Soviet Union in early 1953, Abba Eban,
Israeli ambassador to the United States, sent invitations to the presidents of some of the leading Jewish organizations, both Zionist and
non-Zionist, to meet with him in Chicago on April 16.[4] Nahum Goldmann, Maurice Eisendrath, Phil Klutznik, Emanuel Neumann, and
others had been pushing for some sort of high-level group, and in 1955,
a conference in Washington on problems of peace in the Middle East
led to the creation of an informal "presidents' club," which over the
next decade met more and more frequently and gradually acquired its
own staff. By 1966 the initial wariness between Zionists and non-
Zionists had declined, and the presidents decided to form a representative body of their respective organizations, which would provide
the conduit that Israel needed to funnel information into the American
Jewish leadership as well as secure its views on a variety of issues.
Eventually the Conference of Presidents of Major American Jewish
Organizations grew to include twenty-four members, representing

Zionists and non-Zionists, fraternal groups, welfare boards, and all three religious branches.[5]

Another area of organizational development involved finances. The UJA provided annual subsidies for health and welfare work, especially the absorption and resettlement of new immigrants, while the Israel Bond Corporation raised money for long-term capital investments. In addition, several major investment-management companies funneled monies into Israel for private development. The PEC Israel Economic Corporation had originally been founded in 1926 by the Brandeis and Marshall groups as a supplement to the Keren Hayesod, the Zionists' principal fund-raising instrument, and supplied technical expertise as well as investment capital. The Brandeisians, despite charges by labor Zionists, never wanted to limit Palestine to a single economic mode; rather, they saw a mixed economy of private, co-operative, and government-sponsored ventures as providing an ideal balance for a small state. PEC invested in more than ninety enterprises through stock purchases, loans, or a combination of both, and in many instances helped establish such basic industries as chemicals, citrus products, paper, textiles, and plastics, as well as organizing the distribution of Carmel Mizrahi wines in the United States.

A second option for would-be American investors in Israel was AMPAL, the American Palestine Corporation, established in 1942 under the aegis of Labor Zionism. During its early years, AMPAL primarily guaranteed loans to finance projects in Palestine, since wartime restrictions forbade the sale of Palestinian securities in the United States. After the war AMPAL began financing construction in basic industries and utilities, as well as housing, and organized subsidiaries to deal with specialized problems. The Jewish Agency provided a third avenue for investment funds through RASSCO, the Rural and Suburban Settlement Company, founded in 1934 to be the central instrument for the settlement and housing of middle-class immigrants. Although originally interested primarily in housing, RASSCO later branched out into real estate, land development, prefabricated buildings, hotels, and other enterprises.[6]

It would be several years before all of these formalized channels would be able to do what was expected of them—provide means of communication between American and Israeli leaders on matters of mutual concern. During the early 1950s, before the creation of the presidents' club and the Political Affairs Committee, chaos frequently reigned as everyone tried to "speak" for Israel. Abba Eban, in recalling those years, once confided that his most trying day of the week was Monday when he, the Israeli ambassador, read in the newspapers what various Jewish leaders had declared to be Israel's policy at Sunday meetings in New York.[7]

The Israelis recognized, however, that American Jewry, properly mobilized, could be a great asset in the diplomatic arena, and they went to great lengths to cultivate that community. One assistant director of the Israeli Foreign Office told a visiting member of Congress that "the two pillars of Israel's security are the Israeli Defense Forces and American Jewry." Another official, in explaining the situation to a State Department dignitary, said: "The Almighty placed massive oil deposits under Arab soil, and the Arab states have exploited their good fortunes for political ends during the past half century. It is our good fortune that God placed five million Jews in America. And we have no less a right to benefit from their influence with the United States Government to help us survive and to prosper."[8] Developing this resource became a prime objective of all Israeli officials. Abba Eban, while ambassador to the United States, traveled indefatigably from one Jewish community to another, speaking at UJA dinners, Hadassah luncheons, and welfare board receptions, while at the same time "selling" the Jewish state to influential Jews who had not yet seen the light.[9] Whenever high-ranking members of the Israeli government or army came to the United States, they would inevitably end up "campaigning," meeting with Jewish leaders, addressing mass meetings, visiting Jewish schools and hospitals, and helping in financial drives. Moshe Sharett, Israel's first Foreign Minister, set this pattern, which Golda Meir and all of their successors have followed.[10] Michael Brecher, in his analysis of Israeli foreign policy, described world Jewry as the "most important component" in Israel's global perceptions, and, in Ben-Gurion's phrase, "Israel's only absolutely reliable ally."[11] And in world Jewry, the most powerful section could be found in the United States.

*   *   *

American Jews, after doing so much to help bring Israel into existence, had no inclination to abandon her, and in the early 1950s worked in a number of political areas to help the Jewish state. They took an active part throughout the long negotiations between Israel and the German Federal Republic in securing a reparations agreement, in which Chancellor Konrad Adenauer officially accepted Germany's responsibility toward the Jewish victims of the Nazis.[12] American Jews also swung into action in 1951 when Israel applied to the United States government for a $150 million grant-in-aid. Abba Hillel Silver and I. L. Kenen helped in drafting the bill, and secured Republican senators Edward Martin of Pennsylvania and Robert A. Taft of Ohio as cosponsors. The American Zionist Council alerted all of its committees to begin lobbying their local congressmen, while Abba Eban, at the United Nations, kept tabs on the entire effort, indicating to local leaders where extra doses of persuasion might be needed. The success of the drive was crucial, since the grant-in-aid provided Israel with desperately needed cash until German reparations began.[13]

American aid to Israel, as well as the influence American Jewish leaders began to exert on Israel, accounted in part for Israel's shift during these years from a policy of nonalignment to a definite pro-Western stance. Israel, it will be recalled, had the support of both the United States and the Soviet Union during the 1947–48 United Nations session, and both countries recognized the new Jewish state immediately following its Declaration of Independence. In Israel's early years, Ben-Gurion would instruct a diplomat going abroad to "do everything possible to please the Americans and nothing to displease the Russians."[14] Unfortunately, this tight-rope balance could not be maintained as relations between the two superpowers deteriorated during the Cold War.

The moment of decision came in June 1950, when communist troops from North Korea invaded South Korea, and the United Nations, led by the United States, decided to intervene. Although the communist countries of eastern Europe had not restricted Jewish emigration to Israel, and had allowed the local Jewish communities to join the World Jewish Congress, the Soviet Union's initial friendliness failed to develop into close ties, and Israeli requests for aid from the Soviet Union had been rebuffed. In light of the enormous assistance from both the American government and American Jewry, Israel felt great pressure to "stand up and be counted." Through David Niles, President Truman passed the word to Eliahu Elath that he wanted Israel's support; more than that, he expected it as an act of friendship in return for all that the United States had done for Israel. At the United Nations, American pressure was intense, and the Israeli delegation received the message that Washington assumed the Jewish state would be on its side. The Korean War thus marked the great divide in Israel's foreign policy.

On July 2, 1950, Ben-Gurion convened an extraordinary Cabinet session at Rehovot, so that the ailing President of Israel, Chaim Weizmann, could participate in the discussion. Moshe Sharett, Abba Eban, and others recommended that Israel contribute diplomatic and political support—thus endorsing American policy—but no more than that. Ben-Gurion alone favored sending a token force of troops, though in the end agreed to limit support to nonmilitary areas. The July 2 decision, which clearly marked Israel's move away from nonalignment, reflected the widely held belief in the Jewish state that its future was tied to that of the United States and that nothing should be done to endanger that tie. Ben-Gurion later responded unequivocally that the prime consideration had been "sympathy for America; it was merely for the sake of America. I knew that Truman wanted peace." Abba Eban conceded that American presssure "was not easy to ignore or resist" and that pressure came from private as well as governmental sources. All in all, Jews in both countries perceived closer ties between the United States and Israel as natural in the light of the democratic nature of both societies, the strong bonds between Israel and American Jewry, and the flow of millions in aid and investment dollars from the United States.[15]

While the Korean resolution strengthened ties between Israel and Harry Truman's Democratic administration, it was clear by early 1952 that the Republicans would probably capture the White House in the fall election. Here again Abba Hillel Silver, although holding no Zionist office, proved immensely valuable as the only major Jewish leader with ties to the Republican Party. In 1948, Silver had won Senator Robert Taft's gratitude by arranging a mass meeting in Cleveland, where he enthusiastically endorsed the senator as a friend of the Jewish state. On Election Day, Thomas Dewey, the Republican presidential candidate, lost Cuyahoga County by 112,000, the party's gubernatorial nominee ran 192,000 votes behind his opponent, but Taft lost by only 96,000, a margin he was able to overcome with his heavy downstate support. During the recount, the Republicans discovered that many Democratic voters who had supported Taft by splitting their tickets came from the heavily Jewish precincts.[16] In 1952, Silver supported Taft for the Republican presidential nomination, and together with I. L. Kenen managed to secure a strong pro-Israel plank in the Republican platform. At the same time, the American Zionist Council cultivated its Democratic contacts to produce an equally strong endorsement by the Democrats, a feat very much appreciated by Israeli leaders. Just prior to the election, Silver convinced Dwight D. Eisenhower, the Republican nominee, to give his personal endorsement to the bipartisan "tradition" of American friendship toward Israel.[17]

The first five years of the Eisenhower administration, however, marked the low point in relations between the Israeli and American governments. One analyst has suggested that Eisenhower, as the only President from Truman to Ford who did not serve in Congress, had never been exposed to Jewish political pressure. Eisenhower's military career had shielded him from this experience, and of all recent Presidents, he showed the least inclination to befriend the Jewish community.[18] In addition, for nearly twenty years American Jews had overwhelmingly backed the Democratic Party, and with the exception of a man like Silver, had few points of access to the GOP. American Jews were liberal, the Republicans conservative; Jews lived in the cities, while the GOP drew most of its strength from suburban and rural areas. Although individual Republicans like Taft and Jacob Javits of New York expressed sympathy for "Jewish causes," the inner circle of the Eisenhower regime did not. The American Jewish Committee, for example, had secured candidate Eisenhower's assertion that "the McCarran Immigration Law must be rewritten," and after the election discreetly urged the President to act on his campaign promises. In April 1953, Irving M. Engel, a liberal Democrat and president of the Committee, approached Taft on the matter. A few days later, Taft reported back to Engel that the Administration had discarded any plan for revision of the national-origins formula and that neither Eisenhower nor Vice President Richard M. Nixon recalled advocating such a revision during the campaign.[19]

It is more than likely that even if Adlai Stevenson had been elected President in 1952, relations between Israel and the United States would have deteriorated to some extent during these years. On a number of issues, the Israeli government adopted policies which ran counter to what almost any American President might have supported. In such areas as removal of the Israeli capital from Tel Aviv to Jerusalem, the effort to secure a Middle East equivalent of NATO, arms purchase, and water policy there was bound to be some friction between the two governments, regardless of which party occupied the White House. Under a Democratic administration, however, the efforts of American

Jewry might have eased tensions, whereas under Eisenhower there was little receptivity to such political activities.[20]

This does not mean that American Jews ceased lobbying for Israel, only that the amount of effort produced fairly meager results. For example, a number of Arab countries declared an economic boycott against firms doing business with Israel, and then put restrictions on Jewish entry into Arab states. Some Arab nations refused outright to grant visas to American Jews, and Jewish servicemen and civilian laborers employed by the American government were banned by Saudi Arabia from the United States' own air base in Dhahran. The American Jewish Committee and other defense agencies vigorously protested that American acquiescence in these practices violated traditional American policy. Yet despite occasional *pro forma* statements condemning such discrimination, the government meekly abided by Arab policies. The *Air Force Manual* for 1953 listed Arab travel restrictions in the instructions to servicemen. The Agriculture Department and the Commodity Credit Corporation agreed that American ships carrying goods to Arab countries, sold under the foreign-aid program and therefore paid for by American taxpayers, would not stop at Israeli ports. When the New York State Commission Against Discrimination investigated a complaint that the Arabian-American Oil Company was making illegal inquiries into the religion of job applicants, the State Department took the view that the situation was a domestic affair of the Arab states and could not be altered; any nation, after all, had the right to define and then exclude "undesirable aliens."[21]

Perhaps the greatest frustration resulted from attempts to have the United States supply arms to Israel. The process had begun early in 1950, when Israel requested that the American government sell it arms to balance British sales to Arab nations. (Israel had been secretly buying arms from France.) While the Truman administration was sympathetic, it feared the possibility of an arms race in the Middle East. On May 25, 1950, therefore, the United States, Great Britain, and France issued the Tripartite Declaration, which declared the three countries' desire to maintain peace in the area without creating an arms imbalance. While not granting Israel what it wanted, the declaration soothed the Jewish state because it implied a guarantee of the borders as well as a promise of future arms sales should it ever become necessary for national defense.[22]

Had the Middle Eastern nations been able to purchase military equipment only from the United States, Great Britain, or France, the Tripartite Declaration might have worked to stabilize the area. Despite occasional border skirmishes and raids, and diplomatic name-calling in the press and in the UN, the Arab-Israeli situation seemed fairly stable. Certainly the outbreak of a full-scale war did not seem imminent in the early 1950s. But then it began to look as if the Soviet Union would also become an arms supplier, and the Eisenhower administration, in an effort to curry Arab favor, proposed an increase in American military aid to Egypt and other Arab states without a corresponding expansion of aid to Israel.

American Jews were aghast. The editor of the Yiddish newspaper *Der Tag* sounded the clarion call: "American Jews cannot look on indifferently when economic help and military equipment is being delivered to countries at war with Israel who might use these armaments for a new war against Israel which might break out with the help of Communist incitement. In the present critical moment . . . it is the duty of America to stand with both feet and with its full weight on the side of democratic Israel and not to seek new friends who might rather be an obstacle than a help to a democratic front as long as the Arabs are opposed to peace with Israel." The Eisenhower administration, surprised at the vehemence it had aroused, tried to play the matter down and gave private assurances to the Israeli ambassador that the United States would not leave Israel undefended.[23]

By 1954 American Jewish leaders seriously doubted the Eisenhower administration's friendliness toward Israel. In the spring, Assistant Secretary of State Henry A. Byroade, drawing heavily on material supplied by the American Council for Judaism, weighed in with a series of speeches which questioned the whole rationale of Israel as a state created by the Jewish people. "To the Israelis I say that you should come to truly look upon yourselves as a Middle Eastern state and see your own future in that context rather than as a headquarters or nucleus, so to speak, of worldwide groupings of peoples of a particular religious faith who must have special rights within and obligations to the Israeli state." Byroade went on to characterize Israel as a conqueror, and deplored its policy of retaliation against Arab raids; in somewhat softer tones, he urged the Arab states to accept Israel "as an accomplished fact." In the face of protests both by American Jewish organizations and the Israeli ambassador, Byroade maintained that while he did not question Israel's sovereign right to regulate immigration, Israel's

Zionist ideology and its free admission of Jews were legitimate matters of concern to the Arabs and to the Western world. The only hope for Israel, he declared, would be "integration" into the Arab Middle East.[24]

The Administration, in a number of small and not so small ways, indicated that Israel no longer enjoyed the special status accorded it during the Truman years. The State Department refused to recognize Jerusalem as the capital of Israel, and kept the embassy in Tel Aviv (a policy which greatly inconvenienced the American ambassador, since it effectively isolated him from close touch with many of his colleagues), and forced Israel to abandon some civilian development in the demilitarized border regions. From time to time, State Department officials would issue strange statements suggesting possible reductions in Israeli territory or the inclusion of the Gaza Strip—and its thousands of Arab refugees—in Israel proper. When Secretary of State John Foster Dulles proposed a defensive alliance in the Middle East, he deliberately excluded Israel from participation, so as not to offend Arab nations such as Iraq, which he considered essential to the success of the pact.[25]

This last policy led to a sustained but unsuccessful drive by American Jewry to reverse the Dulles strategy of supplying arms to Arab nations, supposedly so they could defend themselves against communist aggression. The Committee for Public Affairs worked to secure statements from congressional candidates either opposing military aid to Arab states and/or supporting arms supply to Israel.[26] On October 25, 1954, the heads of sixteen national Jewish organizations met with the Secretary of State to explain to him how concerned they were over the government's apparent pro-Arab policy and its potential harm to Israel. The tone of the meeting was extremely conciliatory. Philip Klutznik, president of B'nai B'rith, explained that the represented groups all recognized Dulles' past support of Israel, and that, above all, they did not wish to make Israel a matter of partisan politics. But unilateral grants of arms to the Arabs and the exclusion of Israel from American defense plans in the Middle East appeared extremely inequitable. Dulles responded in the same tone: He had in mind, above everything else, the best interests of the American people, but he was also trying to promote peace and stability in the area. He then hinted darkly that it was a good thing he was sympathetic to Israel, because he had been under strong pressure to do a great many things concerning the Jewish state, things he could not discuss just before an election.[27]

Over the next two years, Jewish organizations tried to keep as much pressure on the government as possible. Rabbi Barnett Brickner, in his presidential message to the CCAR, declared that, as Americans, they had the responsibility to make plain to the government that support of Israel was the best American policy in the Middle East. At the founding meeting of the presidents' conference in March 1955, the major topic of discussion was how to prevent the United States from abandoning Israel. Abba Hillel Silver, the only Jewish leader with ready access to the White House, explained to presidential aide Sherman Adams the frustration of both Israeli and American Jews when they saw the American government denouncing Israeli retaliatory responses to Arab raids, being unable to dissuade the Arabs from such a course, and then sending the Arabs more and more arms.[28]

When Silver went to Israel in early 1956, he carried a private message from Eisenhower to Israeli President Itzhak Ben-Zvi, and evidently tried to reassure Israeli leaders that the United States remained friendly and sensitive to the Jewish state's problems. Silver met with Eisenhower and Dulles on April 26 to brief them on his trip, and the Secretary of State took the occasion to complain of the pressures to which he had been subjected. Silver lectured him gently on the subject: "In a democracy, my dear Mr. Dulles, such pressures are unavoidable—at times desirable as an index of public opinion. It is the accepted way that any group which feels keenly about a subject close to its heart has of giving expression to its views and of defending its interests. . . . One must, however, be on guard against *refraining* from an indicated action on the possibility that such action might be interpreted by some people as yielding to pressure. This is a negative and fatal form of pressure. Thus if the Israeli request for the sale of defense arms by the United States is justified . . . then that request should be granted regardless of the pressures at times unrestrained which would have been brought to bear upon you by those who feel very keenly that the thing *should* be done."[29]

Dulles remained silent, however, and despite the fact that 1956 was an election year, the Republicans did not feel it necessary to go out of their way to court the Jewish vote. While both parties pledged to prevent war in the Middle East and to preserve the integrity of Israel, the Democrats proposed arms sales to Israel, a subject on which the GOP maintained an obvious silence.[30] But the Israelis had in the meantime managed to secure the needed arms, and with the backing of France and Great Britain, launched a surprise attack into the Sinai that would have a significant impact on the Middle East and on the Western alliance.

*   *   *

The origin of the 1956 war can be found in a number of sources: the quasiwar, quasipeace stalemate between Israel and her Arab neighbors; the lingering antagonism between former colonial powers and newly independent nations; and the Cold War competition between the United States and the Soviet Union, to name only a few. For our purposes, one can date the start of the Sinai campaign from September 1955 and the consummation of the first Soviet-Egyptian arms deal. Until then, the 1950 Tripartite Declaration had worked fairly effectively in keeping all of the Middle Eastern nations in short supply of war materials. Suddenly Egypt began receiving artillery, fighter and bomber aircraft, tanks, and other weapons in such profusion as to upset totally the balance of arms. Although the Tripartite Declaration had acknowledged the need for maintaining parity, the United States and Great Britain refused to counter Soviet arms shipments to Egypt with sales to Israel.[31] The Soviet-Egyptian arrangement also had repercussions throughout the so-called Third World and in Western capitals. Gamal Abdel Nasser, the Egyptian leader, in turning against the former colonial powers in defying the West, won much applause from other emergent nations.

The Western powers reacted with alarm to the Soviet Union's first successful breakthrough into the Mediterranean, thus breaching the wall of "containment" thrown up around the communist bloc. Unable to nullify the arms agreement, the Western powers rushed in to woo the Arabs from their newfound Soviet friends, a situation made to order for Nasser, who now cleverly began to play off one side of the Cold War against the other for Egypt's benefit. Secretary of State Dulles began repeating with growing frequency his earlier assertion that the United States would steer a course of "friendly impartiality" between Israel and the Arab states. In practice, however, this "impartiality" turned into efforts to draw Arab states into defensive alliances with the United States, and an American offer to help finance the Aswan High Dam, the keystone in Nasser's plan to modernize the Egyptian economy.

For Israel, the developing American policy seemed fraught with danger. The refusal to sell arms to Israel, as well as the proposed alliances, pointed to a growing imbalance of arms, with the Jewish state not only outmanned but also outgunned by hostile neighbors. When the Israelis tried to point out these dangers to Dulles, the Secretary of State responded that he was actually promoting Israeli security; if the Arab states could be brought into the Western fold, they could be prevented from attacking Israel. In effect, Dulles was asking Israel to entrust its security to the United States, but without any formal treaty or guarantees. Given the history of Western pledges to Jews over the previous four decades, Israel not surprisingly placed little faith in the Secretary's assurances. Nor did it appear that the other Western powers would intervene to protect the Jewish state. Great Britain, trying to retain her hold on the Suez Canal, was actively courting Egypt, and shortly after the Soviet arms sale had publicly advised Israel to concede some territory in order to make peace with the Arabs. Even France, which had little love for Nasser because of his aid to the Algerian rebels, sent Foreign Minister Pineau to Cairo in an effort to prevent Egypt from sending its obsolete weapons to dissident groups in French North Africa.[32]

Only the fact that Nasser overplayed his hand finally stopped the spiraling threat to Israel. When Egypt indicated that it intended to accept American aid and still purchase Russian arms, the highly moralistic Dulles abruptly and clumsily withdrew the offer of American assistance at Aswan in July 1956. Nasser struck back by nationalizing the Suez Canal, thus earning the enmity of both France and Great Britain. The British now sought an opportunity to get back into the canal and to reassert themselves as an imperial power; the French, partners in the Suez Canal Company, also wanted to retaliate for Nasser's aid to the Algerians. For Israel, the time seemed propitious, not only to strike against Egypt before it became too powerful, but also to put an end to the *fedayeen* attacks on her border carried out under Egyptian sponsorship, and to break the Arab blockade of her water access to the Indian Ocean. Moreover, the work of the Public Affairs Committee in the United States had gradually built up resistance to the Dulles policy, both in Congress and with the public,[33] to the point where a bold Israeli thrust might be perceived as a natural move in its own self-defense. Over the summer, David Ben-Gurion flew secretly to Europe to meet with British and French leaders to co-ordinate their actions. When the Arab states established a unified military command under an

Egyptian general on October 24, 1956, Israel put these secret plans into action and mobilized its forces.

The Sinai operation, also known by its code name *Kadesh,* achieved its objectives within one hundred hours. On October 29, a parachute battalion landed near the Mitla Pass, about forty miles east of the Suez Canal and well behind the bulk of the Egyptian forces in the Sinai. Operating on three fronts, with effective air support, *Zahal* (the Israeli Defense Forces) overran the entire Sinai Peninsula in four days, inflicting casualties of 1,000 dead and capturing over 6,000 prisoners, at a cost of 180 Israeli casualties and only 4 captured. By prearrangement, the British and French, in order to "protect the canal," invaded Egypt and then "warned" the Israelis not to come any closer than ten miles to the waterway. It was an incredible victory, with possibly the most brilliant tank maneuvering of modern warfare, and the ease with which Israel vanquished the Egyptians stunned not only the Arab world, but the Soviet and American governments as well.[34]

Ben-Gurion had correctly perceived that the Soviet Union, tied up by the revolt in Hungary, would not intervene, but he also recognized that the United States could easily force the Israelis to withdraw. The day before the campaign began, he told his cabinet, "The United States wouldn't need to send troops; it would be enough for them to announce that diplomatic relations were being broken off, that collections for the Jewish funds were forbidden and loans to Israel blocked."[35] And Dwight Eisenhower was indeed furious. When he had first learned of the Israeli mobilization, he had tried to stop Ben-Gurion from initiating any military operations. As for the French and British, the President was doubly angry, since America's two closest allies had kept their plans secret from him and had launched their invasion of the canal zone without consulting the United States. Dulles shared Eisenhower's resentment, and according to Emmet John Hughes, Dulles "felt *personally* incensed for the inconsideration of others in frustrating his diplomacy in the Middle East," despite the fact that Dulles's own bungling, as Townsend Hoopes has shown, had done so much to force Britain and France to play a lone hand. The United States wasted no time in condemning the Sinai campaign, and calling on Israel, Great Britain, and France to withdraw completely from Egyptian territory. Possibly only a message from Russian Premier Nikolai Bulganin urging joint action by American and Soviet naval units in the Mediterranean against Anglo-French "aggression" prevented the United States from pursuing a more active policy.[36] But the Eisenhower administration did bring tremendous pressure to bear on Israel and tried to use American Jewry to force the Israelis to back down.

Even while hostilities raged, the United States began its campaign to force Israeli withdrawal. Eisenhower, through Sherman Adams, contacted Abba Hillel Silver in Cleveland; asking him to use his connections with the Israelis; Silver replied that the Jewish state had an embassy in Washington, which was the proper channel for such messages.[37] In the United Nations Security Council, U. S. Ambassador Henry Cabot Lodge introduced a resolution calling on all UN members to "refrain from giving any military, economic, or financial assistance to Israel" until it withdrew to the 1949 armistice lines. Britain and France, about to launch their own attack, vetoed the resolution. Three days later, on November 2, the General Assembly, by a vote of 64 to 5, adopted an American resolution urging an immediate cease-fire and withdrawal of all invading troops. Finally, on November 5, the United Nations voted to establish an emergency international force to police the proposed cease-fire. Israel, having achieved its military objectives, agreed to stop fighting, and even said it would "willingly" withdraw its forces, on conclusion of satisfactory arrangements with the UN in connection with the emergency force. The terms of a satisfactory arrangement became the stumbling block, and the next 4½ months, as Golda Meir recalled, were "heartbreaking" as Israel tried to convince the American government that a return to the *status quo ante* would only mean a war in the Middle East in the not too distant future.[38] Ironically, Dwight Eisenhower, the general who presided over the liberation of Europe in 1944–45, and John Foster Dulles, who prided himself on his realistic grasp of international affairs, both refused to look at the strategic implications of Israeli policy, and talked instead of the abstract morality and legalism of the situation.

For American Jews, the Sinai campaign produced both pride and worry; pride in the military accomplishments and in the postbattle offer of the Israelis to exchange 6,000 Egyptians for the four captured members of *Zahal*; worry over the fate of the Jewish state if it refused to accede to American and United Nations demands. In a statement issued on October 31, the presidents of sixteen major Jewish organizations urged the United States to undertake a "fresh appraisal" of the conflict "between the Free World and Nasserism backed by Moscow." Four days later, the American Jewish Committee wrote Secretary

Dulles that "to return to the *status quo* is to restore the very conditions which have caused bloodshed, misery, and turmoil."

The period from 1948 to 1956, while relatively quiet compared to the ensuing years was not marked by any efforts toward a lasting peace between Israel and its Arab neighbors. The borders situation had settled into an uneasy truce, marred by periodic raids. The development of the Jordan River, which could have provided much-needed water and power to Israel, Jordan, Syria, and Lebanon, was never begun because of Arab objections and suspicions of Israeli motives. The Jewish state, surrounded by hostile Arabs, had to devote nearly 60 per cent of its budget to defense, while the Arab states also ignored pressing domestic social and economic needs in order to maintain large armies.

Perhaps the Middle East situation, like a festering boil, needed lancing to allow healing, and American Jewish leaders suggested that the Sinai campaign might, with proper support from the United States, prove to be the fateful first step toward peace. Instead of condemning Israel, the United States should now take the lead in the United Nations in requiring Arab states and Israel to enter into real peace negotiations. Moreover, the United States should not condemn Israel for acting in a way so consistent with American policy and ideals. Emanuel Neumann, president of the ZOA, declared in a radio address that while the West followed appeasement, Israel alone stood up to the threats of Nasser and communism. In their propaganda campaign, the Zionists frequently compared Israel's response against *fedayeen* attacks to American acts in 1916 against border raids from Mexico.[39]

But surveys of American public opinion, while still favorable to Israel, overwhelmingly endorsed Eisenhower's policy of reliance on the United Nations, and only a minority felt Israel justified in its attack; where in April 1956 there had been five critics of Egypt for every two of Israel, in November the ratio had dropped to three to two. Fearful that public opinion would turn completely against the Jewish state, Nahum Goldmann wrote Ben-Gurion on November 7: "I must tell you that it will be impossible to mobilize an American-Jewish front to support this posture [of nonwithdrawal]. If there will be an open dispute between Israel and the United States Government on this point. . . . I foresee great difficulties. . . . What is needed is a step that will prevent an open split with Eisenhower."[40]

Although American Jews agonized over Israeli intransigence, they did not worry about the old charge of dual loyalty. Here was the classic case that the anti-Zionists of the American Council for Judaism had so fearfully predicted: a clash of policies between the United States and Israel, with American Jews caught in the middle. What would they do? They bombarded Congress and the White House with demands and protests that the Eisenhower administration pursue a more pro-Israel course. Some experts believed that American Jews would hesitate before contributing—even indirectly—to a nation at odds with their own. Yet just the opposite happened. UJA contributions jumped 20 per cent, from $58.8 million to $70.6 million; in one day during the crisis, over $2 million poured into UJA coffers in spontaneous contributions.[41] Moreover, among the non-Jewish population, there was an actual increase in the percentage who rejected any idea of linkage between American Jews and problems in the Middle East. Those who did blame American Jews came, for the most part, from that segment of the sample which were anti-Semitic in the first place, and believed in such fantasies as a worldwide Jewish conspiracy.[42]

While American Jews labored to help Israel, the Jewish state itself refused to buckle under to American demands for immediate withdrawal until the United Nations dealt with "the root of the tension . . . Egypt's continuing maintenance of a state of war" against Israel. In response, the Eisenhower administration increased its pressure. At American ports, officials examined shipping documents of materials headed for Israel with unprecedented bureaucratic zeal. In Washington, the Commerce Department, which had hitherto routinely handled export licenses for Israel, now had to clear matters interminably with the State Department. Private banks which in the past had been eager to make loans suddenly held back, despite Israel's excellent credit rating. On February 5, 1957, Dulles announced that the United States would give "serious consideration" to applying economic sanctions unless Israel complied with the UN withdrawal resolution.[43]

This proved too much for Israel's friends in the Congress, and the patient work of Sy Kenen and others began to pay off as one congressional leader after another stood up to oppose the President and his Secretary of State. Senate Majority Leader Lyndon B. Johnson personally informed Eisenhower that the Congress would never approve economic sanctions. The use of coercion against Israel struck many as involving a double standard, and Johnson pointedly reminded the moralistic Dulles that the Administration had done little more than wag its finger when Russian troops bloodily intervened to quash the uprising in Hungary.

The Administration response—that it expected more from Israel because it was "imbued with a religious faith and a sense of moral values"
—merely infuriated Johnson. "Israel has become a showcase of democracy," he argued, "and it is up to all believers in democracy everywhere to support Israel in every possible way." On this issue, the President could get very little support even from his own party. Senate
Republican leader William Knowland of California backed Johnson's
stand and threatened to resign his seat on the UN delegation if Dulles
pushed sanctions. Forty-one Republican congressmen called upon the
President to oppose Israeli withdrawal until Egypt began to negotiate
for peace in earnest.[44] The President also came under fire when Dulles
threatened to lift the tax-exempt status of the United Jewish Appeal.
Dulles seemed to labor under the illusion that American Jews could
somehow direct events in Israel. In a last-ditch effort to save his
policy, he called in eight non-Zionist leaders to meet with him so that
he could explain the Administration's point of view. According to a
State Department release, the Secretary hoped the Jewish leaders
would exercise a "helpful influence" upon the Israeli government. The
Jewish press, as well as a number of daily papers, castigated Dulles for
his blundering approach; the Philadelphia *Inquirer,* for example, described the meeting as "an arrogant intimidation of one group of American citizens . . . something that is unwholesome and a disservice to the
cause of peace in the Middle East."[45] The fears of the assimilationists
seemed to have been in vain.

Ultimately, of course, Israel had to back down, but in doing so she
still achieved some gains. Her stubbornness in standing up to Eisenhower and Dulles won her many friends in the United States, and in
the end the Eisenhower administration showed that it too had gained
some understanding of Israeli perceptions on self-defense and the Middle East situation. Whether or not Israel was correct in these assumptions, the United States would have to take them into account, because
those would be the axioms upon which Israel acted. On March 1, Foreign Minister Golda Meir announced that Israel was ready to withdraw, and cited "assurances" in an American *aide memoire* of February
11, 1957, regarding rights of passage in the Gulf of Aqaba. She also
took note of the Eisenhower Doctrine regarding the security and territorial integrity of nations in the Middle East. Following an exchange of
letters between Eisenhower and Ben-Gurion repeating these assurances,
the Israelis withdrew their forces from the Sinai.[46]

The Sinai episode highlighted the limited ability of American Jewry to affect governmental policy and to create public opinion. They had been totally unable to influence the Eisenhower administration directly, and only by working through congressmen and senators finally forced Dulles to back away from threats of economic sanctions and eliminating the UJA's tax-exempt status. Public opinion split over the correctness of the Israeli move and could not be mobilized to force the Administration to alter its policy until it had gone so far as to create an impression of unfairness. If any lesson was to be drawn, it was that continuous work would be required by pro-Israel lobbyists, not just in times of crisis, in order to build up an ongoing sentiment that would prevent a hostile administration from pursuing what Israel's supporters perceived as an anti-Israeli policy.

* * *

In retrospect, the 1950s appear to be a period of marking time, of a settling in between Israel and American Jewry. There were numerous points of friction, especially over the relationships between Israel and the Diaspora, and the role of the Zionist movement. At the same time, both Israel and the American community went separate ways in developing their own lives—a new, tough, semifrontier society in Israel, and a comfortable, upwardly mobile, acculturated subsociety in the United States. If one is looking for a pattern of partnership during these years, the best one can point to is a skeletal arrangement, with some of the institutional features coming into focus, but with no clear indication of which directions the relationship would take. One would find only the beginnings of that closeness which developed in later years, the cultural and educational interchange, the centrality of Israel in all Jewish affairs.

The 1956 Sinai campaign did not alter this general picture in any marked way. The secrecy surrounding the preliminary planning, and the swift execution of the operation itself precluded any major emotional upheavals such as had accompanied the War of Independence in 1948, or which would be seen in such intensity in 1967 and 1973. At best, the 1956 war, for a brief moment, led American Jewry to unite in political support of Israel against the perceived unfriendliness of the Eisenhower administration. For the rest of the decade, however, the United States government seemingly pursued a policy of courting the Arabs at the expense of Israel, even to the point of collaborating in the economic boycott against companies dealing with Israel, and in breaking a 1960 longshoreman's strike called to protest the boycott.[47] One unexpected development following the war, however, was a rise in American *aliyah*. Only 187 Americans had entered Israel on immigrant visas in 1956, the lowest number in the entire history of the Jewish state. The following year 271 Americans went, and in 1958, 378, a number still small in absolute terms but nearly twice as large as before; moreover, the figures rose each year until 1964, when for the first time more than 1,000 Americans made *aliyah*.[48] Whether they journeyed in response to Israel's need, or to escape the McCarthy Red scare or the doldrums of Eisenhower's America, is impossible to say.

There is, however, a coda to the 1950s. In late 1957, Walter Eytan, Director General of the Foreign Ministry, put through an urgent call to Isser Harel, the head of Israel's secret service, the *Mossad*, asking for an immediate meeting. A few hours later, in a corner of a cafe in Ramat Gan, Eytan told Harel that he had received evidence that Adolf Eichmann, the man who had carried out Hitler's "Final Solution," was living in Argentina. For the next two and a half years, the *Mossad* investigated the report, tracked down Eichmann, kidnaped him, and flew him out of Argentina to Israel. On May 23, 1960, David Ben-Gurion rose to inform the Knesset that Eichmann had been found and would stand trial in Israel for his crimes against the Jews.[49]

Ben-Gurion called it "historic justice" that Eichmann be tried by a Jewish state,[50] and few voices protested either the legal issues involved in the kidnaping or the *ex post facto* nature of the Israeli law; the enormity of the crime made such questions irrelevant, and the Nuremberg trials had confirmed the right of an outraged humanity to call to account those who had so debased civilization. All in all, Israel succeeded in winning the public to its view of the trial's legality as well as the bestiality of the crime. But at all times, the strictly legal aspects of the prosecution remained secondary to its greater educational goals. By 1960, memories of the Holocaust had begun to fade, both in Israel and in the Diaspora. The survivors, of course, could not forget. But for those not personally touched, it was necessary to remind them of what had happened, of why there *had* to be a Jewish state. And it was also necessary to remind the Christian world of what had been done. Israel had taken the first steps in this process of education in 1953, when the Knesset had conferred posthumous Israeli citizenship on the six million, and then established Yad Vashem as a memorial to the martyrs with a mandate to gather and publicize as much as could be learned about the *Shoah* (Holocaust). "May every person in Israel," declared the law, "every Jew wherever he may be, know that our People has its own reckoning, the reckoning of the generations of the Eternal People—a reckoning of an Eternal People whose entire history is proof and evidence of the prophetic promise: 'And I said unto you in your blood, "Live!" ' [Ezek. 16:6]."[51]

The United States shared this need for education. Christmas Eve 1959 witnessed a brief but widespread outbreak of swastika painting and synagogue vandalism, which vanished almost as quickly as it began. Yet in a symposium in *Commentary* magazine in 1961 on the state of Jewish belief, there were no questions asked about the Holocaust, no indication that the European tragedy had affected Jewish life in America.[52] Moreover, in the one scientific sampling of reaction to the trial, the educational process could be described as only partially successful. About a third of the Oakland public did not pay enough attention to the trial either to know that it was happening or even to have an opinion on Eichmann's guilt. More people knew about the Freedom Riders and the death of Gary Cooper than knew about the trial, while about the same percentage of the sampling had heard about the tractors-for-rebels exchange with Cuba, Marilyn Monroe's operation, and Ernest Hemingway's suicide.

Yet the Israelis managed to generate not only media coverage of the trial, including daily telecasts, but documentaries and analyses of the Holocaust as well. Editorial opinion across the nation ran overwhelmingly in support of Israel's decision to try the Nazi chieftain. The majority of Americans, and of American Jews, however, even when they knew of the trial, remained more or less apathetic.[53] Somehow it just did not sink into their consciousness; they were still floating along in that placid euphoria which had marked so much of life during the Eisenhower era. Yet even as Eichmann stood in the glass box in the Jerusalem courtroom, the entire fabric of American Jewish life and of the community's ties to Israel was on the verge of great and far-reaching changes.

Part Three

"We Are One!"

For Zion's sake will I not hold My peace,
And for Jerusalem's sake I will not rest,
Until her triumph shall go forth as brightness,
And her salvation as a torch that burneth.
And the nations shall see thy triumph,
And all the kings thy glory;
And thou shalt be called by a new name,
Which the mouth of the Lord will mark out. . . .
Thou shalt no more be termed Forsaken
Neither shall thy land any more be termed Desolate.

Isaiah 62:1–4

Chapter 13

A SENSE OF BELONGING

For those who would like to see history as a relatively straight line leading with inexorable progress from one point to another, the study of relations between Israel and American Jewry must surely seem confusing. There is no lineal development, but rather a complex matrix of ties among Jew and Jew, Israeli and American, Jew and gentile, all affected and shaped by events and trends beyond the control of the central protagonists. American politics, the civil rights struggle, the ongoing Zionist debate, and cultural and social changes all contribute to the rough portrait, and the fine lines emerge only when concentrating not on the whole, but on specific aspects. But one thread runs throughout the picture, the ages-old belief that all Jews, everywhere, constitute one people, an eternal people (*am olam*), transcending spatial and temporal limits. At times this thread has been obscured by the internecine bickerings within one community or the other, or by the open and bitter debate over such issues as Zion and *galut*, but that thread, if nothing else, has run straight and true, a *leitmotiv* to this history.

In the period between the Sinai campaign of 1956 and the Six-day War of June 1967, one might have had some difficulty discerning that unifying thread. The initial honeymoon came to an end as American Jews no longer saw Israeli rebirth as the all-consuming passion of their lives, while Israelis wondered if they had been deserted. In the United States, American Jews reached a level of acculturation and acceptance which their immigrant grandparents would have found unbelievable, and became even more involved than before in American politics, passing well beyond the *arriviste* stage. In many ways, this growing Jewish influence could be and was used to help Israel, but it exacerbated the still open sores of the Zion-*galut* debate. And American Jews found that they could not ignore domestic questions such as civil rights, which touched them both as Americans and as Jews.

*   *   *

Natan Rotenstreich, an eminent Israeli philosopher, once termed American Jewry as a "post-Emancipation community," by which he meant that American Jews bypassed the European struggle for civil rights, and also did not have the lingering sense of alienation which permeated European Jewish communities even after the removal of legal restrictions. As a result, American Jews moved into the mainstream of American life as did other major immigrant groups, although the memory of centuries of religious conflict as well as the more recent experiences of the Holocaust and the rebirth of Israel heightened Jewish ethnocentrism. Yet in the late 1950s and early 1960s there seemed little to set American Jews apart from their fellow citizens. Civic and religious leaders spoke in all seriousness of "the Judeo-Christian tradition," clubs and colleges dropped discriminatory quotas, and anti-Semitism seemed on a permanent decline. By 1962 only 1 per cent of respondents in an opinion poll named Jews as a threat to America, and only 3 per cent said they would dislike having a Jewish family live next door. By 1965 the issue of anti-Semitism had become so trivial that the *American Jewish Year Book,* for the first time in its more than sixty-year history, dropped that subject from its front articles, and replaced it with a section, "Civil Rights and Intergroup Tensions."[1]

Yet American Jews did not quite fit the generalized patterns. They were solidly middle-class; by 1965 nearly half of all Jewish families had annual incomes between $7,500 and $15,000, while only a quarter of all American families had reached that level. The percentage of Jews in white-collar jobs was nearly three times the national average, while only one Jew out of five worked in factories. Despite the long tradition of Jewish involvement in the labor movement, by the early sixties American Jews had moved upward, so that only one Jew in ten belonged to a union.[2] In a society which glorified success, American Jews were in the process of writing the greatest success story of all. How comfortable American Jews felt can be seen by the way they confronted several issues which only a generation earlier they would have desperately sought to avoid.

One area of potential conflict arose from the civil rights movement, the drive for black equality triggered by *Brown* v. *Board of Education* in 1954. Jews had long been involved in this struggle, with men like Stephen Wise and Louis Marshall calling for equal rights for Negroes long before that cause became fashionable. The American Jewish Congress, which Wise led for nearly three decades, had a long record of participation in civil rights, and Wise's son-in-law, Shad Polier, was for many years one of the nation's leading civil rights attorneys. This commitment, however, certainly did not stretch across the entire spectrum of American Jewry. Even within the American Jewish Congress, some voices questioned whether Jewish organizations ought not to concentrate on protecting Jewish rights and not divert scarce resources and energies into other areas.[3] In the South, while Jews may have been somewhat more liberal than their white gentile neighbors, for the most part they shared the same basic racial attitudes.

Attacks on any one minority group however, usually trigger assaults on others, and in the southern backlash, white extremists struck out against blacks and against Jews also. Bigots in many southern communities used the integration crisis to launch vicious acts of anti-Semitism. From November 1957 through October 1958, eight temples were bombed in southern communities where the tensions of integration ran high. The bombings took place not only where southern Jews had spoken out but also where they had remained silent as well. Interestingly, southern Jews reacted not by castigating the Ku Klux Klan or the White Citizens' Councils but by denouncing northern Jews for publicly advocating racial equality. The activities of the American Jewish Congress and the Anti-Defamation League had drawn attention to the Jews, the argument ran, and therefore caused trouble.[4]

This notion, that Jews should not in any way call attention to themselves but should try to be inconspicuous, as much like their Christian neighbors as possible, had of course been the guiding rationale of an entire generation of American Jewish leaders. Jacob Schiff, Louis Marshall, Cyrus Adler, and the other founders of the American Jewish Committee had not been ashamed of their Jewishness, nor had they tried to hide it; rather they believed that in the United States one's religion was a private matter and by calling attention to things Jewish one only caused trouble.

How far the Committee had come can be seen in its response to the bombings and to pleas from its southern members that it abandon its civil rights work. At a meeting in New Orleans in 1958, Judge Joseph Proskauer, now the Committee's elder statesman, reminded the audience that he had been born in the South and respected its traditions, but that the Committee's tradition of defending human freedom ranked higher. "I would not ask the Committee to recede from its fundamental thesis that no man is free unless all men are free." Another southerner by birth, President Irving Engel, forcefully argued that he did not share "the wistful belief held by some that if only Jews and Jewish organizations would say nothing and do nothing in this situation, the trouble would somehow magically depart. . . . Out of tragic experience our generation certainly has learned one lesson and learned it well: Jews cannot buy security or status for themselves in an atmosphere where injustice is tolerated, or even worse, is sanctioned." Not only would Jews continue to work for black equality, they also had an obligation to do so, both as Jews and as Americans.[5]

Ironically, despite their long and extensive involvement in the civil rights struggle, American Jews found that they had to face the wrath of both white and black bigots. A writer like Judd Teller might hopefully suggest that Jews and blacks, because of their common heritage of persecution and suffering, ought to have an understanding of each other,[6] but the sociology of the ghetto often pointed black rage at the Jewish landlords and shopkeepers who allegedly exploited and cheated the black poor. One ran into a fascinating paradox here. Because of the fact that Jews had also been the victims of prejudice, Negroes expected more support and tolerance from Jews than from non-Jewish liberals or from non-Jews in general. At a 1964 colloquium on black-Jewish relations, novelist and essayist James Baldwin remarked that "an understanding is expected of the Jew such as none but the most naïve and visionary Negro has ever expected of the American gentile." On the other side, because blacks frequently moved into neighborhoods previously tenanted by Jews and where stores and buildings were still Jewish-owned, Jews were the nearest and most familiar target for black resentment. According to Jeremiah X, a Black Muslim minister, Jews "infiltrate the Negro neighborhood with stores, and then exploit the Negro more than any other white group—housing, food, clothing—controlling the three basic things Negroes need. They claim to be friendly with Negroes but, when pushed to the wall, they are more injurious, more ruthless, than other whites."[7]

As the civil rights struggle heated up in the sixties, Jewish involvement increased, as did black extremism. Jewish students might ride freedom busses and be killed in Mississippi, Jewish writers might explore differences and suggest that the two groups had much in common, but more and more one would find such searing incidents as when Clifford A. Brown, an official of the Congress of Racial Equality, told a Jewish audience in Mount Vernon, New York, that "Hitler made one mistake when he didn't kill enough of you." The "tepid and ambiguous response" of many black leaders to this outrageous statement led Will Maslow, executive director of the American Jewish Congress and a longtime fighter for civil rights, to resign from CORE's national board. Many other Jews wondered why they should back a movement whose leaders seemed as intent on persecuting Jews as on winning freedom for their own followers.[8] These early anti-Jewish remarks by blacks were but a portent, however, of the hysterical anti-Israel and anti-Semitic campaign which would erupt from the black left after the 1967 war. For American Jews, however, the willingness to participate openly in the civil rights struggle, to expose the community in such a sensitive matter, bespoke a growing maturity and sense of belonging in American society.

Another incident that highlighted American Jewry's sense of confidence occurred in 1962. On June 25, the United States Supreme Court held that prayer in public schools violated the constitutional barriers between church and state.[9] Among the petitioners requesting the Court to rule against the legitimacy of school prayers were several Jewish organizations, including the American Jewish Congress, the Union of American Hebrew Congregations, and the Central Conference of American Rabbis. The following September, the influential Jesuit magazine *America* ran a lengthy lead editorial entitled "To Our Jewish Friends," in which it noted "disturbing hints of heightened anti-Semitic feelings" since the prayer decision. While not blaming American Jewry in general, the editorial criticized the petitioning groups, and singled out Leo Pfeffer, counsel to the American Jewish Congress.

"We wonder," said the editorial, "whether it is not time for provident leaders of American Judaism to ask their more militant colleagues whether what is gained through the courts by such victories is worth the breakdown of community relations which will inevitably follow them. What will have been accomplished if our Jewish friends win all the legal immunities they seek, but thereby paint themselves into a corner of social and cultural alienation?

"The time has come for these fellow citizens of ours to decide among themselves precisely what they conceive to be the final objective of the Jewish community in the United States—in a word, what bargain they are willing to strike as one of the minorities in a pluralistic society. When court victories produce only a harvest of fear and distrust, will it all have been worthwhile?"[10]

Jewish leaders responded to the editorial quickly and vigorously, pointing out that in a free society, minority groups did not have to abandon their basic principles and rights in return for supposed security. The American Jewish Committee, while not a party to the suit, defended the right of people—of any faith—who objected to public prayer to pursue constitutionally protected means of redress. As for creating prejudice, the Committee pointedly suggested that *America* might well have lectured its own Catholic readers, who in the past had vilified the King James version of the Bible and attacked the opponents of parochial education. Jews were heartened to find that some liberal Christian journals immediately joined in their protest. The Catholic *Commonweal* said that if there was a danger of anti-Semitism among Catholics, "then it is Catholics who ought to be warned. Indeed, 'warned' is too mild a word: They ought to be told as sharply as possible of the sin of any form of anti-Semitism." The *Christian Century* called *America*'s stand a "thinly veiled threat to the Jewish community of our country."

Yet as a mark of how secure American Jews felt, *Commentary* ran an article by Arthur Hertzberg which said that while Jews had been rightly offended by the tone of the *America* article, the question itself was a fair one. Jews ought to examine their role in a pluralistic society, but Christians too had to rethink their commitment to separation of church and state and what it implied. This surely marked a long step away from the earlier posture of silence and a low profile; American Jews no longer seemed obsessed by *ma yomru hogoyim?* (what will the gentiles say?)[11]

In fact, as the *America* incident demonstrated, when the gentiles did say something, American Jews felt no compulsion to be defensive—whether about their roles in the prayer suit, or in the civil rights movement, or on behalf of Israel. They lobbied incessantly for American aid to the Jewish state, and by the midsixties over $1 billion in loans, grants, and technical assistance had been secured. Under the Point 4 program, 340 American technicians served in Israel, providing invaluable expertise in such areas as agriculture, animal husbandry, mining, and construction, while 640 Israelis were brought to the United States for specialized training. Point 4 aid terminated in 1962 after eleven years, when Israel no longer met the qualifications of an underdeveloped country. Shortly after that termination took place, however, Charlotte Jacobson of Hadassah appeared before a congressional committee to request funds to assist Hadassah's medical education work in Israel. William Gaud, the head of the Agency for International Development (AID), testified against the grant, on the grounds that since Israel was no longer underdeveloped, it did not qualify.

"I have been to Israel," he declared, "and I don't think we should provide funds on a grant basis."

"Your personal views don't count here," responded Mrs. Jacobson. "The law says grants, not loans. So it's only a question of eligibility."

"Is this the last year you are making this request?" the committee chairman asked her.

"Oh no," she replied. "I intend to come back every year, as long as the law provides for American sponsorship of institutions of higher learning abroad."

After several more hearings before both houses of Congress, Hadassah secured $1 million to construct a doctors' residence at the Hadassah-Hebrew University Medical School and to expand the nurses' training program. Moreover, Senator Claiborne Pell of Rhode Island spoke in the Senate and on behalf of himself and fourteen other senators, praising the women's Zionist organization for its work in Israel, and calling on AID to co-operate with the women in "maintaining an institution which serves the highest objectives of our foreign-aid program."[12]

A less pleasant incident took place, also in the Senate, which a decade or two earlier might have frightened American Jews. In 1960 Paul Douglas of Illinois and Kenneth Keating of New York sponsored an amendment to the Mutual Security Bill, denying aid to any nation which blocked the use of international waterways to other countries. Aimed clearly at Egypt, which denied Israel use of the Suez Canal, the amendment called forth an angry protest by J. William Fulbright, the powerful chairman of the Senate Foreign Relations Committee. "I hope no one in the Senate is so naïve," he declared, "as to believe that the

amendment will accomplish its ostensible purpose, which is to open the
Suez Canal to Israeli shipping and to end the Arab boycott against Israel. What it will accomplish is to annoy the Arabs and fortify them in
their conviction that in any issue arising from the Arab-Israeli controversy the United States, because of domestic political pressures, will be
on the side of the Israelis." Then in words loudly applauded by the few
remaining members of the American Council for Judaism, Fulbright
charged that "in recent years we have seen the rise of organizations
dedicated apparently not to America but to foreign states and groups.
The conduct of a foreign policy for America has been seriously
compromised by this development."[13]

Fulbright may have been right in his assessment of Jewish pressures
affecting American foreign policy; certainly such analysts as Robert
Dahl, Franklin Burdette, and Roger Hilsman have noted the influence
of American Jewry upon the country's actions and attitudes toward
Israel.[14] As far as positive achievements are concerned, American Jews
have been more successful in their lobbying efforts than have other ethnic groups, such as the Poles, Irish, or Czechoslovakians. Yet the old
fears about dual loyalties, which at one time might have magnified
Fulbright's comments into crisis proportions, no longer existed. American Jewish activity on behalf of Israel had been legitimized, in part because most Americans saw no conflict or contradiction in their Jewish
neighbors working to help a small democratic state surrounded by hostile Arabs. If this pro-Israel influence was a burden upon American
foreign policy, as Fulbright charged, it was not perceived as such by the
great majority of Americans, Jew and non-Jew alike, who saw Israel in a
unique relation to the United States, a country occupying a special
place in the international scheme of things. Jewish organizations could,
and did, respond to the senator's accusations without fear that their loyalty to the United States would be impugned because of their support
for Israel.

*   *   *

The early 1960s also saw the end of the Eisenhower-Dulles era, with its
indifference (or even intimations of hostility) toward the Jewish state.
The election of John F. Kennedy to the presidency not only returned
the Democrats to the White House, but also marked the resurgence of
liberalism in national affairs. And if American Jews were anything politically, they were liberal. Of all the anomalies of American Jewish

life, this persistent attachment to liberal ideas and policies has most fascinated and puzzled political analysts. By class and status, American Jews should have become more conservative, more Republican, as they rose out of the ranks of factory workers into the more affluent business and professional classes, as they moved from city to suburb. Yet they did not. Income, education, and occupation, all of which are considered determinants in political behavior, seemingly did not affect Jews at all. They had good incomes, were highly educated, and chose prestigious occupations, comparing favorably to upper-class Protestants, who were overwhelmingly Republican. Yet four out of five Jews remained with the party of Wilson, Smith, Roosevelt, and Truman.[15]

Moreover, despite their high ethnic self-identification, Jews consistently chose liberal gentile candidates over conservative Jewish politicians, and even managed to transcend traditional ethnic prejudices if they perceived particular non-Jewish or nonwhite candidates as the more liberal choice. Lucy Dawidowicz and Leon Goldstein amassed a great deal of evidence to show that Jews will easily vote against a fellow Jew in favor of a liberal Catholic. In the 1961 New York City Democratic Party mayoral primaries, 63 per cent of the vote in a heavily Jewish neighborhood went to a Catholic, Robert Wagner. His opponent was Arthur Levitt, who had an outstanding record in Jewish civic and religious affairs but was perceived to be the machine candidate. In the fall mayoral elections, when Wagner faced Republican Louis Lefkowitz, Wagner again gained a majority of the Jewish voters. And in the 1960 presidential elections the Jewish vote went overwhelmingly for that most ethnically Catholic of candidates, John Fitzgerald Kennedy.[16]

The love affair between Kennedy and American Jewry had started slowly enough, with little indication that any strong and enduring ties would ever emerge. Kennedy's father, who had been ambassador to the Court of St. James's in the late thirties, had been widely suspected of being anti-Semitic and an admirer of Hitler.[17] Traditionally, Jews and Catholics stood on opposite sides of the political fence; Jews saw Catholics as illiberal, isolationist, pro-McCarthy, and anti-Semitic, and only the exceptional candidates, such as Senator Robert F. Wagner (a German Catholic) and his son, received much Jewish support. Kennedy recognized this problem as a fact of political life, and as soon as his ambitions expanded beyond his congressional district, he took positive steps to secure Jewish backing.

When Kennedy ran for re-election to the Senate in 1958, he discovered that a number of Jewish voters in Massachusetts blamed him for cuts in a particular AID grant to Israel. He went to John McCormack, who later succeeded Sam Rayburn as Speaker of the House and had excellent relations with Massachusetts Jewish leaders, for help. McCormack called a meeting of leading Jewish businessmen and philanthropists who carried influence in the community. "Look," he told them, "there were ten million dollars in the original proposal earmarked for Israel, and I found that the [Eisenhower] Administration wanted to cut it to five. I called Jack Kennedy in and said to him that we're going to lose five million dollars. I want you to make a motion to reduce the grant to seven million, to see if we can save as much as possible. The motion was made and carried, and Israel got the seven millions. So instead of blaming Jack Kennedy for losing three million dollars, you ought to praise him for saving two millions." While the Jewish leaders present may not yet have trusted Kennedy, they did respect McCormack and took his word for what had happened. As a result, much of the anti-Kennedy sentiment in the community lessened.[18]

In the 1960 election, Kennedy worked diligently to win over the Jewish vote, and he did this, according to Saul Brenner, by emphasizing his own liberal image in contrast to Richard Nixon's illiberalism, by putting distance between himself and the Catholic Church, and by portraying himself as a victim of discrimination. The manifesto issued by a group of well-known Protestant clergymen led by the Reverend Dr. Norman Vincent Peale shocked Jews by its open bigotry and its attempt to impose a religious test for office. The fact that the American Nazi Party proclaimed Kennedy to be the candidate of the Jews did not hurt him either. Placards declaring "Nazis for Nixon, Kikes for Kennedy" and "FDR and JFK mean JEW deal" led many Jews to take a closer and more sympathetic look at the Democratic nominee.[19]

What they saw was somewhat reassuring. While Kennedy's record on Israel did not match that of Hubert Humphrey, for example, it was still fairly solid. He had nearly always voted "right" on matters concerning the Jewish state, and in speeches to various national Jewish organizations had gone out of his way to emphasize that support of Israel transcended party lines and was far more than just a Jewish cause, just as the battle for Irish independence involved others than those of Irish descent. "Because wherever freedom exists," Kennedy told the ZOA's national convention, "there we are all committed—and wherever it is in danger, there we are all in danger." In the midst of the campaign Kennedy took time to give an interview to Jacob Rubin, a correspondent of the Israeli newspaper *HaBoker*, and Kennedy's remarks received wide coverage in Israel. In contrast, Nixon had to bear the burden of the Eisenhower-Dulles doctrines, and seemingly wrote off the Jewish vote; perhaps Nixon knew he would get little sympathy from Jewish voters and did not want to waste his time or money on them.[20]

Probably the key incident in the Kennedy wooing took place shortly after the Democratic convention. Meyer Feldman, an influential Washington lawyer and adviser to Kennedy, Senator Abraham Ribicoff of Connecticut, and philanthropist and businessman Abraham Feinberg gathered about thirty of the nation's top Jewish leaders at Feinberg's apartment in the Hotel Pierre in New York to meet the Democratic candidate. Kennedy had agreed ahead of time that there would be no limits on the type of questions asked, and after an initial fifteen-minute presentation the candidate fielded a wide range of questions which were, in Feinberg's words, "hard, even brutal," and dealt with his father's alleged anti-Semitism and Kennedy's own stand on key issues. After over an hour of this, the thirty skeptical men who had entered the apartment had changed their minds about the Massachusetts senator. Although there was to have been no fund-raising, after Kennedy left, the group spontaneously put together a loan fund of $500,000 to be made available to the Kennedy campaign.[21]

In the closely fought election Jewish votes played a significant role, perhaps *the* significant role in electing the nation's first Catholic President. In New York, which Kennedy carried by 384,000 votes, Jewish precincts gave him a plurality of more than 800,000. In Illinois, which went Democratic by a scant 9,000 ballots, Jewish votes gave Kennedy an edge of 55,000. While the Michigan Survey Research Center concluded that Kennedy's Catholicism cost him some 1.5 million votes nationally, he actually did much better among Jewish voters than had Adlai Stevenson, that epitome of liberalism, in 1956. The traditionally liberal Jewish vote was cast against Nixon as much as it was for Kennedy, but in 1961, when the now President Kennedy paid a courtesy call on David Ben-Gurion in New York, Kennedy said to him: "You know, I was elected by the Jews of New York, and I would like to do something for the Jewish people."[22]

If an American political leader in 1961 wanted to "do something for the Jewish people," he did not have to go far to discover what that

something should be: support for the State of Israel. Yet if one were
the President, competing demands and opposing views of American national interests also had to be taken into account. John Kennedy, as any
President, had to confront the Arabists in the State and Defense departments, men such as John S. Badeau, William Crawford, Phillips Tal-
bot, and Francis Plimpton, who decried Jewish political influence for
warping the judgment of foreign-policy makers.[23] One can say that
Kennedy did as much for Israel in the negative aspect as he did for the
Jewish state positively—that is, he managed to avoid pressuring Israel
into situations or policies which would have been inimical to Israel's interests and which would have placed the Israelis in opposition to stated
American policies. Meyer Feldman believes that Kennedy's exquisite
political sense, the intuitive knowledge of how far a leader can go and
still be politically safe, determined much of his policy toward Israel. He
recognized that in such areas as refugee repatriation, Arab-Israel negotiations, and plans to divert Jordan River waters for large-scale agricultural and power projects, all of which had become extremely sensitive
matters thanks to Eisenhower and Dulles, no government in Israel
could survive which conceded as much as some of the State and Defense departments analysts demanded. What Kennedy did, much of it
through Feldman, was to signal Israel on how to distinguish between
rhetoric and action.

Thus, although the American government publicly called on Israel
to settle the refugee problem and joined in the United Nations censure
of Israel after the 1962 retaliatory raids on Syria, the Administration
also increased foreign aid, quietly buried a number of potentially dangerous anti-Israel proposals, and entered for the first time into a long-
term military-assistance program. When the United States finally decided to sell Hawk missiles to Israel, the Department of Defense
wanted cash on the line, and each Hawk battery cost $25 million. The
Israeli government said it could not pay cash, that it never paid for
anything in cash, but always bought on credit. Feldman checked and
discovered that the United States had been selling weapons to Australia
on a ten-year loan program at 3.5 per cent interest. The President
called in Defense Secretary Robert S. McNamara, who conceded that
this was true; but McNamara then pointed out that Australia was the
only nation in the world to receive such terms—everybody else paid
cash or got three years to pay at 6 per cent. Kennedy smiled when
McNamara produced a memorandum prepared by the Middle East

desk "proving" that Israel could pay cash. He directed that Israel be given the same terms as the Australians. "After all, $25 million isn't much in a $100 billion budget." Once the precedent was established, the Israelis insisted upon and received similar loan arrangements in future purchases of tanks and airplanes.[24]

If Israeli leaders could distinguish between rhetoric and action, the American Jewish community often could not. In part, this resulted from the very public nature of the rhetoric in the United Nations and in the press, and the very quiet nature of some of the arms and aid agreements. So in 1962, shortly after Feldman returned from a secret mission to Israel to inform them of the Hawk decision, he set up two meetings for the President, one with senators and congressmen identified as strong friends of the Jewish state, and the other with about sixty Jewish communal leaders to explain the Hawk agreement. Philip Klutznik expressed the gratitude of the community, since many observers believed that without the Hawk batteries Israel would be defenseless against the supersonic planes supplied by the Soviet Union to the Arab states. Kennedy nodded his agreement, reaffirmed his support of Israel, but then went on to explain that the sale would also be in the best interests of the United States. However, he insisted that the knowledge he had just shared with the Jewish leaders and congressmen be kept, at least for a while, completely secret.

Kennedy knew, of course, that such "secrets" could not be kept long, but his strategy of maintaining open lines of communication to American Jewish leaders meant that they would be able to blunt some of the criticism inevitably arising from the supposedly anti-Israel rhetoric. Thus, before the United States joined in condemning Israel for its raids on Syria in March 1962, the White House contacted a number of leading Jewish figures to inform them that the United States had no choice in the matter, since it did not want to antagonize the Arab world. Sy Kenen, in his role as chief lobbyist on behalf of Israel, kept Feldman notified of what AIPAC would be doing, so as not to embarrass the Administration.[25]

The Kennedy administration, of course, could at times make its actions as well as its rhetoric public. For example, in response to an appeal from the American Jewish Committee, the White House ordered a reversal of the Eisenhower-Dulles policy of acquiescing in Arab restrictions on Jewish servicemen being posted to American bases in Arab lands.[26] The President, shortly before his death, also began looking into a new problem, the desire of Jews to emigrate from the Soviet Union in order to escape persecution there. Since the status of relations with the Russians was hardly conducive to any American attempt to intervene in this matter, all the President could do was convey to the community the feeling that he understood the problem and sympathized with their anxieties, and convinced them of the limits on his maneuverability.[27] In addition, the White House made clear that the American Council for Judaism, whose memoranda had been so eagerly received by the State Department during the Eisenhower years, no longer had the ear of the government.[28] Much of this was wholly symbolic, of course, but symbols are often as important as facts. Through these gestures, Kennedy reassured American Jewry that he was concerned, that he understood their worries, and that he considered them a legitimate matter within the purview of American interests.

It is little wonder that when John Kennedy fell so suddenly in Dallas that November day, the American Jewish community reacted with such grief and outrage. Here was a man who had indeed proved himself a friend to Israel, who had assured American Jews not only of his support but also had contended that more often than not American and Israeli interests coincided. It is ironic that of all American Presidents since World War II, the one who most seized and held the admiration and affection of Jews both in Israel and in the United States was a quintessential Irish Catholic politician, and that in a forest south of Jerusalem stands a shrine, erected by American Jewry, to the son of a man who reputedly admired Hitler.

*   *   *

The understanding that marked relations between the Kennedy administration and American Jews reinforced the sense of belonging that characterized Jewish life in the early 1960s. In fact, for the first time since World War II and the establishment of Israel, American Jews felt secure enough in their new status to engage in a serious and critical look at themselves, at Zionism and at the State of Israel. In some ways this would prove intensely painful, as old perceptions proved illusory. In other ways it would be helpful, since a group which cannot look at itself honestly and searchingly has little hope for growth or of survival. Unfortunately, this introspective examination would be cut short by the 1967 war, and it would be nearly a decade before American Jewry once again picked up the threads.

Regarding the future of Judaism in America, the prospects in the early sixties struck some commentators as much bleaker than they had been a decade before. The great migration to the suburbs and the creation of Jewish institutions there had failed to live up to their earlier promise. The so-called religious revival of the Eisenhower years had collapsed, with little to show in terms of long-run structural or theological results. America in general, and not just American Jews, seemed tied to a superficial religiosity, one that bore a surface resemblance to Jeffersonian deism but completely lacked its intellectual rigor. Even among those who still saw vigor in American Jewish life, a note of anxiety seemed ever present. Judah Shapiro stated categorically, "Jewish life is very active with a multiplicity of organizations carrying out myriad tasks." But, he continued, despite the overt sense of Jewish security, "the danger would seem to lie in the possibilities of inner dissolution rather than pressures from without." Jacob Neusner was even more pessimistic about the lack of inner substance in American Judaism. He wondered whether in all of Jewish history there had ever been any community "more ethnocentric, and less religiously concerned, than our own." Despite all the exterior trappings of living "Jewishly," despite all the activities and buildings, despite all the emphasis on Jewish ethnicism, the real sense of being Jewish, the "visceral ethnic consciousness," seemed to be rapidly diminishing.[29]

The outward dynamism of American Jewry all masked, in the eyes of some critics, serious dangers. There seemed little doubt that Jews had become acculturated in the United States. But were they also becoming assimilated, were they being swallowed up by the secular society, were they forgetting who they were? Nahum Goldmann warned that "the larger and the wealthier Jewish communities become, the more dynamic they are in their own community life, the more they develop tendencies to become independent of other parts of the Jewish people . . . and to forget the great truth of our history, that no isolated Jewish community, however strong and numerous it was, has ever survived, but disappeared once it had lost its consciousness of being part of the Jewish people."[30] The very success of American Jews in becoming American now posed a danger. In examining a 1961 *Commentary* symposium on Jewishness, Milton Himmelfarb noted that a number of the participants begrudged American Jewry its accomplishments, even while conceding that its very success had won the respect and admiration of the greater society.[31]

Had success become the great danger? Had acceptance become the threat to survival? In a major address to the National Jewish Welfare Board in 1966, former Supreme Court justice Arthur Goldberg publicly worried about "the danger of losing our identity as Jews, or seeing that identity so watered down that we forget who we are and whence we came." Christian and Jew must indeed meet as brothers, he declared, but not necessarily as identical twins. Fraternal relations, however, were not what a number of younger Jews had in mind. According to some studies, the rate of intermarriage between Jew and gentile had jumped alarmingly, and might be running as high as 25 or 30 per cent, far beyond the estimated rate of 10 per cent in the 1950s.[32] Among intellectuals as well there seemed a strong desire to become part of the larger society, to emphasize their Americanness rather than their Jewishness. This had gone so far that many Jewish social scientists actively avoided research on Jewish life, lest they become too closely identified with their subject.[33] Ironically, Jews had finally found a place where they could be free; they had prospered beyond the wildest imaginings of any previous Diaspora community. Now their being "at home in the secular world," as Emil Fackenheim warned, threatened to eradicate that Jewish particularism which had been so zealously guarded for centuries against the most perverse forms of persecution.[34]

What generated these fears? Were there real dangers in freedom, the *mitat n'shika* which Ben-Gurion and other Israelis had warned about in their earlier attacks on the Diaspora? Or, as Simon Rawidowicz once suggested, were Jews "an ever-dying people," always in fear that their generation would be the last, and therefore inveighing against the real or imagined hazards of their times in order to give Judaism the strength and courage to survive? Certainly American Jews of the 1960s, whom Eugene Borowitz termed "the first free generation of Diaspora Jews," had to seek their answers in an environment completely different from that of their ancestors. Even some of the questions were completely new; diverse forms of Judaism had expanded the scope and meaning of Jewish life and values, while the United States itself, with its commitment to cultural pluralism and openness, had made some of the older considerations irrelevant.

Zionism in its classic terms had never dealt with such a situation— an established Jewish state open to all Jews who wanted to go there *and* a large community openly supportive of that homeland, yet tied intimately to a society which had welcomed Jews. By the 1960s even some

Israelis were suggesting that Zionism still had to confront the basic question of Jewish survival.

Yet how could this be done? Wherever one turned in the United States, for example, Zionists seemed to run into other Jewish groups already at work. Zionism no longer seemed to offer an opportunity for Jewish leadership, Arthur Hertzberg maintained, primarily because it had cut off Reform and Conservative Judaism, to which the majority of American Jews were aligned. Zionism, according to Judah Shapiro, "exists but does not lead," and even in supposedly "Zionist" activities such as fund-raising and politicking for Israel, non-Zionists directed the work. When Max Bressler took over the leadership of the ZOA, he demanded that the gulf between Zionist affairs and Jewish communal activities had to be bridged, that Zionists had to assume their rightful places in American Jewish leadership.[35] Yet no one knew how to even begin this process; the dismantling of the movement in the previous decade had been too thorough.

Fortunately, the process of re-examination led some Zionist leaders to frame constructive questions rather than jeremiads; they might not have had the answers, but at last they had begun to ask the right questions. David Polish, for example, in *The Eternal Dissent* (1961), conceded that if American Jews chose not to make *aliyah*, then they had to create a positive role for the Diaspora which would complement that of the Jewish state. "What system of thought can we develop," he asked, "to justify this thesis that a Diaspora existence is not only possible but desirable?"

For Polish, one of America's leading Reform rabbis, the answer might be found in the universal message of the Jewish faith. In some ways, he took Koestler's argument, that the creation of Israel made assimilation not only possible but even desirable, and stood it on its head. The establishment of the Jewish state now gave Jews freedom to live fully Jewish lives wherever they chose, and in doing so could create a much more vital Judaism than one hemmed in by sociolegal restrictions and prejudices. As long as Jews remembered that they belonged to an eternal people, that wherever they lived and whatever they did could affect for better or for worse the future vitality of Judaism, both in Israel and in the Diaspora, Jews would face specific challenges; how they met them would determine the Jewish future. Zionism, as the only movement combining both secular and religious appeals, could thus

serve to bridge the gap and unite the efforts of both Israeli and
Diaspora Jewries.[36]

A somewhat different viewpoint can be found in the speeches and
writings of Israel Goldstein, who served as rabbi of Congregation B'nai
Jeshurun in New York from 1918 to 1960 and also held many important posts in the Zionist movement, including the presidencies of
Young Judea, the ZOA, the World Confederation of General Zionists,
the Keren Hayesod, and the American Jewish Congress. Yet even
though he personally made *aliyah* in 1961, in a series of speeches and
writings in these years he reaffirmed the importance of the Diaspora,
and did so in terms not only of Jewish survival but of Israeli as well. As
long as the Jewish state stood beleaguered and in need of aid to meet its
social obligations to new immigrants, a strong and healthy Diaspora
would be needed. Like the Reform Polish, the Conservative Goldstein
believed in the Zionist movement as an instrument of Jewish survival,
and he reaffirmed the thesis that Israel could provide the anchor of Jewish existence.

Yet while maintaining the need for a Diaspora, Goldstein insisted
that it be intensely Jewish. He dismissed the analogies between modern
Jewish life in America and that in ancient Babylonia, since the circumstances differed so greatly. Babylonian Jews, no matter how comfortable
they became, never forgot that they lived in *galut* and clung tenaciously to their Jewish rituals and beliefs. Unless American Jews could
create as Jewish an existence, they had little hope for survival. One
need not berate American Jewry for the comfort of its existence or the
freedom it enjoyed, but one could exhort them to recapture the attachment to Jewish tradition which had marked previous Diaspora communities. The failure of Jewish education, the lack of a complete commitment to the Jewish people and its survival, had to be remedied, and
this should be the task of Zionism. By emphasizing the centrality of Israel in Jewish life, by battling for Jewish survival everywhere, Zionism
could once again become a dynamic force in the community.[37]

Both Polish and Goldstein accepted the centrality of Israel as axiomatic, but for Jakob Petuchowski, even this assumption had to be questioned, In *Zion Reconsidered* (1966), he raised serious doubts about
the supposed benefits of diverting so much of the community's resources and energies toward the Jewish state. How could American
Jews see themselves as authentic if all they learned was to give money,
automatically and passively, a condition sure to breed a sense of inferi-

ority? How could Jewish creativity be fostered if so much of communal and welfare work took its marching orders, as it were, from Israel? Few American Jews, he maintained, realized the political implications of their supposedly philanthropic gifts, and he chastised both the UJA and Israel for not being completely honest with American Jewry.*

As for Zionism, Petuchowski did not see the movement as an instrument for Jewish survival; rather, its obsession with serving the need of the Jewish state was counterproductive. Too much of the money raised in the United States, ostensibly for charitable purposes, wound up serving the bureaucratic and political needs of the World Zionist Organization and of its cohort, the Israeli government. If American Jews really wanted to help the needy in Israel, they could do this best by setting up American-run offices in Israel and administering the money directly. Distinctions had to be drawn, he argued, between the State of Israel and the Jewish people; American Jews had to recognize that support of the one did not by any means guarantee the survival of the other. The Jewish religion and the Hebrew nation were not identical, and unless Zionism learned to make that distinction clear, it would only continue to harm the future of a Diaspora-based Jewish life.[39]

*   *   *

The debate over proper relations between Israel and the Diaspora also benefited from the growing assurance of American Jewry that it had a viability of its own and something to offer the Jewish state other than money. The earlier eagerness to glorify and imbibe everything Israeli passed, as American Jews came to see not only Israel's very real accom-

---

* A similar argument had been put forward by James P. Warburg in a highly controversial speech in 1960, attacking what he saw as the duplicity of the UJA/Israel nexus. Why should donations to the UJA be tax-deductible, he asked, "when so large a proportion of them flow directly or indirectly into the hands of a foreign government which openly engages in propaganda attempting to influence the policy of the government of the United States?" He attacked many Israeli policies, especially its attitude toward Arab refugees, in terms which would have done justice to Elmer Berger, but he was especially hostile to the alleged philosophy of the UJA/Israel clique "that those Jews who do not recognize their obligation to return to Israel thereby incur an obligation to support those who do." This thesis, he maintained, "is an invitation to worldwide anti-Semitism . . . [and] a piece of almost incredible arrogance."[38]

plishments but some flaws as well. Regrettably, there is little evidence
that Iraelis came to have a comparable understanding of Jewish life in
America. In part this resulted from the relatively little exposure Israelis
had to the United States. Other than Zionist and government officials,
and a few professors on leave at American universities, few Israelis traveled in the United States. Those who did often marveled at what they
found. Ya'acov Tsur, one of the leading proponents of an Israelcentric
Zionist ideology, expressed his amazement after a tour of the country. "I
didn't expect an institution of these dimensions in spirit could exist in
the United States," he wrote after visiting Abba Hillel Silver's congregation in Cleveland. "I must confess that many of my ideas about
American Jewry will probably have changed after this hasty visit to
different cities in the country." Mati Meged reluctantly accepted an invitation to speak to a study group of young adults in New York, and
was amazed "to discover that this [Jewish intellectual] tradition was
still very much alive in America . . . where, I admit, I had never really
expected to find it."[40]

Unfortunately, as Maurice Samuel reported, most Israelis refused to
admit that American Jews had anything to teach them, or that anything worthwhile could be found in the American Jewish community.
And Marc Lee Raphael, in a study of articles appearing in Ha'aretz,
one of Israel's leading newspapers, found a completely distorted view of
American Judaism. Most of the articles were summaries of pieces in the
American Jewish press, with a complete lack of firsthand reporting by
an Israeli staff. Nearly all emphasized negative aspects, and monoto-
nously repeated the idea that Jewish life in the United States was
doomed to extinction. In a typical piece, Shulamit Aloni declared:
"American Jews cannot live full lives as Jews in America. Attachment
to Israel means attachment to a tangible land, a geographic entity.
America is a land of strife and disunity. Israel is a breast at which to
suckle and a source of inspiration for the collective Jewish identity."[41]

This is not to say that Israelis had no exposure to American life.
The fledgling Israeli television network relied almost entirely on American programming, while American movies, books, and records dominated those areas. Hundreds of movie stars, actors, athletes, artists, scientists, scholars, journalists, and politicians, and tens of thousands of
American Jews came to see the Jewish state. Unfortunately, American
television of the late fifties and early sixties had little to say about Jewish life, and did not even accurately reflect American society. The Jew-

ish tourists, for the most part, came from the more prosperous classes, and were frequently active in Zionist or communal affairs. The image they projected, while not quite that of the "ugly American," also did not mirror either the breadth or depth of American Jewish life. The fact that there were poor Jews in the United States, or that there were local concerns that competed with Israeli fund-raising, did not penetrate the Israeli consciousness.

In the Zionist dialogue, however, one began to pick up traces of a theme of partnership, a recognition that both Israel and the Diaspora could benefit from and support one another. Joseph Serlin, a member of the Knesset, actually used the word "partnership" in his opening remarks to a ZOA-sponsored symposium in Tel Aviv in October 1960, and other Israelis, from time to time, began to concede that modern Jewish life might fruitfully extend beyond the borders of *Eretz Yisrael*.

Levi Eshkol, Moshe Sharett, and Golda Meir, for obvious political reasons, could not espouse a bicentrist philosophy, but they too began to speak in terms of a Jewish universe with both Israel and the Diaspora playing significant yet separate roles. Some Israelis recognized that the Jewish state undergirded life in the Diaspora, strengthening it at the same time that those communities supported Israel. The predictions of Herzl and Weizmann that a Jewish state would increase respect for Jews everywhere seemed to be coming true. Richard Crossman, for example, noted that thousands of Englishmen who regarded their country's participation in the Suez venture as a disaster could not suppress their admiration for Israel's Sinai campaign.[42] At the twenty-sixth Zionist Congress in 1965, the situation of Jews in the Diaspora communities received serious attention, and Israeli delegates were now willing to discuss the *galut* as a permanent fact. *Aliyah* remained the optimal Zionist goal, but preservation of Jewish life, even outside Israel, was preferable to Jewish extinction.[43]

Naturally, not everyone conceded this point. Ben-Gurion never wavered in his assertions that Jews living outside *Eretz Yisrael* violated Torah. Rabbi Mordecai Kirshblum of Mizrachi despaired of American Jews having any real future. "From the point of view of the spiritual future of Jewry," he warned, "it is doubtful whether one can even speak about the U.S.A. today as a land of freedom." Zvi Lurie protested against attempts to build up Jewish culture in the Diaspora as "an old philosophy that has gone bankrupt and which does not hold water." Why waste all this effort, he asked, when the only center of

Jewish life could and should be Israel? Only the Jewish state could halt the force of assimilation.[44]

It is doubtful that any of these issues could have been fully settled then; indeed, they continue high on today's Zionist and Jewish agendas.[45] But the early 1960s saw at least the beginning of a dialogue, even if only a few voices participated. Such a discussion had been impossible a decade earlier because neither Israeli nor American Jewries had yet reached a level of maturity capable of dealing with these matters as part of an ongoing Jewish historical process rather than as current political needs. Unfortunately, the press of contemporary events rudely cut short these beginnings and sidetracked debate of significant issues for nearly a decade. But the growing assuredness and self-confidence of American Jewry allowed it to deal with the traumatic events of spring 1967 and to prove to the Israelis that Jews everywhere did, in fact, see themselves as one people, and that there was a strength and a love of Zion in the Diaspora the depths of which had been unsuspected.

9   With Mount Scopus surrounded by Arab territory after 1948, Hadassah embarked upon building a new teaching and research hospital at Ein Kerem outside Jerusalem. Chief Rabbi Herzog delivered the invocation to two thousand people at the ground-breaking ceremony on June 5, 1952. (Zionist Archives and Library)

10 During his tenure as ambassador to the United States, Abba Eban spent a great deal of time winning friends for the new Jewish State. Here he is inducted as an honorary chief of the Oklahoma Otoe Indian tribe and received the name of Na-hi-ra-sa-ha (Young Leader). (Zionist Archives and Library)

11 Jewish groups often sponsor missions to Israel to educate American Jews about the state and its needs. A group of young men who have just been *bar-mitzvah* and their parents are about to board a mission in honor of Israel's *bar-mitzvah,* or thirteenth birthday, which in Jewish tradition marks the passage from youth to manhood. (Zionist Archives and Library)

12 Israeli officials have been frequent guests at the White House. Mrs. Golda Meir, then Foreign Minister, chats with President John F. Kennedy. (Zionist Archives and Library)

13   President and Mrs. Lyndon B. Johnson host a state dinner for Israeli Prime Minister and Mrs. Levi Eshkol in 1964. (Israeli Information Services)

14 Israeli paratroopers gaze at the Western Wall of Solomon's Temple after recapturing the Old City of Jerusalem in the Six-Day War. (Israel Office of Information)

15 American youth flocked to Israel every summer to work as volunteers on Kibbutzim. Here fruit trees on the Plain of Sharon are harvested by American volunteers. (Israel Government Tourist Office)

16 Celebrating Israel's twenty-fifth anniversary, Yom Ha'atzmaut (Independence Day) 1973, at a New York synagogue. Seated in the first row, left to right: Rose Halprin, Israeli Minister of Tourism Moshe Kol, New York Governor Nelson A. Rockefeller, Senator Abraham Ribicoff of Connecticut, Yitzhak Rabin, then Israeli ambassador to the United States, and Mayor John V. Lindsay of New York. (Alexander Archer)

Chapter 14

SIX DAYS IN JUNE

A few weeks before Israel launched its Sinai campaign in 1956, David Ben-Gurion met with some of the senior officers of *Zahal*, the Israel Defense Forces. "After every war," he told them, "and after every war from which we will emerge victors we will again face the same problem . . . the threat of a third round, fourth, fifth—and so on with no end. . . . We must remember that the vision of peace is a Jewish vision. However, even without the moral motive, this actual situation compels us always, together with increasing military preparedness, never to forget that our historical goal for the long run is peace. . . . War must never be viewed as a goal in itself."[1]

Unfortunately, Ben-Gurion's prophecy was fulfilled with disheartening accuracy. All efforts by the Israelis, the Americans, and United Nations officials to lead the Arabs to peace negotiations came to naught. The United Nations Emergency Force (UNEF) created in the wake of the Suez crisis took over at Sharm el Sheik, thus opening the Strait of Tiran to Israeli shipping. But the Egyptians, not UNEF, rushed into the Gaza Strip, thus giving the *fedayeen* a base from which they could once again launch guerrilla raids against Israel. Because Jordan and Syria had stayed out of the 1956 war, and because the French and British had intervened, the Egyptians and other Arab states came to believe that, without outside interference, they could overwhelm Israel if they fought together against an isolated Jewish state.[2] In the decade following the Sinai campaign, the Arab press was filled with denunciations of

Israel, rejections of any suggestions of peace until the "Zionist aggressor" was destroyed, and the revival of such blatantly anti-Semitic documents as the "Protocols of the Elders of Zion," which purported to show that the Jews had a master plan to take over the entire world. The Soviet Union encouraged the Arabs both by supplying Syria and Egypt with vast amounts of weapons and by condemning Israel as a tool of Western imperialism.

Nor were American Jews exempt from Arab propaganda attacks. Claiming that American Jewry had manipulated and tricked the United States into support of Israel, Arab spokesmen tried to "enlighten" Americans about the situation. In 1965 the United Arab Republic embassy in Washington distributed an anti-Israel pamphlet which consisted of stock anti-Semitic charges, such as that Jews killed Christians and ran the world. The Syrian ambassador declared that Jews were aliens, and "the American Jew is not an American emotionally or even ultimately." Both Hussein of Jordan and Faisal of Saudi Arabia denounced American Jewish support of Israel, and Arthur Goldberg, the American ambassador to the United Nations, came in for special censure. One Cairo newspaper called Goldberg's appointment a most logical choice, since "Zionists are the ones who direct American policy."[3]

In these years, the Israelis learned to see the United States as its best friend on the world scene. The Americans, beginning with the Kennedy administration, advanced Israel the bulk of her weaponry, and both Kennedy and Lyndon Johnson assured Israeli leaders that a "special relationship" existed between the two countries.[4] The United States tried to reassure the Israelis that it would honor its 1957 commitments regarding the right of access to international waters, and that in the crunch, the Jewish state could depend upon America for protection. Kennedy in particular did not believe that tiny Israel could hold off one hundred million Arabs. "You just have to rely upon the United States," he would say. "We'll always keep the Sixth Fleet there." Shimeon Peres, then a member of the Knesset and later Defense Minister, remained skeptical of these assurances, and told Meyer Feldman that "the United States would never come to the defense of Israel. We have to defend ourselves and we know it. We're not asking you to do that; we are just asking you to keep out of it and try to keep Russia out of it." In the light of subsequent events, Feldman admitted, Peres was right.[5]

Tensions began to rise perceptibly in early 1967. Egypt desperately needed food after a series of bad harvests, but the United States withheld a request for $150 million in surplus foods in disapproval of Nasser's intervention in the war in Yemen. The Johnson administration was also unhappy about a series of vitriolic anti-American speeches by Nasser, and because the Egyptian leader continued pouring millions into arms purchases while expecting the United States to donate food. In January the Soviet Union agreed to provide 250,000 tons of wheat in the following three months, and Nasser stepped up his anti-American diatribes. Moreover, he threatened to default on Egypt's debts, which amounted to $1 billion, of which short-term loans from Western banks accounted for a quarter of the total.[6]

During this time, the incidence of border violence and terrorist attacks increased, and Israeli Chief of Staff Yitzhak Rabin warned that Israel would retaliate against nations sponsoring the infiltrators. War almost broke out in early April after Syria shelled several Israeli villages in the Galilee, and Israeli jets flew in to silence the Syrian gun positions on the Golan Heights. In the ensuing aerial combat the Israelis shot down six Syrian MiG 21s, and pursued the rest as far as Damascus. In the following weeks Israel maintained heavy troop deployments near its northern borders, a situation which the Russians decided to exploit. On May 13 the Soviet ambassador to Egypt informed Nasser that Israel was concentrating its forces in order to launch an attack on Syria within a week.[7]

The Egyptian President needed little encouragement. The Arabs had taken proper measures, he announced; now it was up to Israel to capitulate or fight. "Should Israel provoke us or any other Arab country, such as Syria, we are all prepared to face it. If Israel chooses war, then, as I have said, it is welcome to it." As for Israeli aggression, Nasser left little doubt as to what he meant: "Israel's existence in itself is an aggression." A few days later, Radio Cairo declared that "the existence of Israel has continued too long. We welcome the Israeli aggression, we welcome the battle that we have long awaited. The great hour has come. The battle has come in which we shall destroy Israel."[8] That same day, May 16, Nasser demanded the complete withdrawal of the United Nations Emergency Force, and U Thant, the UN's Secretary General, gave in without consulting either the major powers or Israel. On May 19, the UNEF commander informed Israel that the force had ceased to function and was in the process of complete evacuation.

In the next two weeks, events tumbled one upon another, all of them boding ill for the Jewish state—the mobilization of Egyptian forces; the closing of the Strait of Tiran to Israeli shipping and to all vessels carrying goods to or from Israel; a stepup in Syrian sabotage and border raids; a pact between Jordan and Egypt providing for unified military forces under Egyptian command; the calling by Muslim religious leaders of a *jihad* (holy war) to drive the infidels out of Palestine; and the dispatch of troops from Iraq, Algeria, and Kuwait to Egypt and of Saudi Arabian and Iraqi forces to Jordan. Israel in turn mobilized its own forces on May 29 and created a "wall to wall" government of national unity, embracing all of the country's political factions. Prime Minister Levi Eshkol also sent Abba Eban to the United States to see just how firm the American commitments would be and just what the "special relationship" between the two countries really meant in times of crisis.

Lyndon Baines Johnson, now President of the United States, faced a serious problem. His commitment to Israel was of long standing; in 1957, as Senate majority leader, he had personally forced Eisenhower and Dulles to back down from their threat of sanctions against Israel. He had close ties with a number of Jewish leaders, and, according to Abraham Feinberg, who knew him long and well, this interest in the Jewish state was not politically motivated; he sincerely believed in the right of the Jewish state to survive. At John F. Kennedy's funeral, when, as the new President, he had received the visiting foreign dignitaries, he had stopped Golda Meir for a moment in the receiving line, put his arm around her, and said: "I know that you have lost a friend, but I hope you understand that I, too, am a friend."[9]

Johnson had, however, already become bogged down in the Vietnamese quagmire, and opposition to that war was mounting steadily both in the Congress and among the people at large. American Jews, including many prominent in the peace movement, would draw distinctions between American involvement in Indochina, in support of a corrupt and brutal regime, and the defense of Israel, a beleaguered democracy. But Johnson saw two small countries, Israel and Vietnam, threatened by outside attack, and America should be willing to aid both. Yet he also recognized that he would have little support in Congress for any unilateral effort to aid the Israelis. So he desperately sought some formula for international co-operation, one in which a number of the leading maritime powers would stand up for freedom of the seas, thus forcing Egypt to abandon its blockade of the Strait of Tiran.

In the meantime, he asked Israel to hold off on any retaliatory action until the United States could put such a plan into action. When Abba Eban met with Johnson on May 26, the President was full of friendly bluster—"I want to see that little ole blue and white Israeli flag sailing down those Straits"—but he could make no firm promises. Under American pressure, however, Eban and Prime Minister Levi Eshkol promised that Israel would wait as long as it could, to give the United States a chance to avert a major war. Eshkol later recalled that he was ready to fight in May, but gave in to warnings from Johnson and Secretary of State Dean Rusk that one-sided Israeli action would be disastrous. "I did not want to give [Johnson] a pretext to say later: "I told you so.' "[10]

But the United States had no plan. Negotiations for a flotilla representing the maritime powers dragged on, and the proposal for a "Red Sea regatta" came to naught. The United States had the Sixth Fleet in the Mediterranean with three aircraft carriers, and the British had about a half-dozen ships in the area but no carriers. In the Pentagon, military planners made no secret of their misgivings, and feared the proposal of a "second Vietnam" in the Middle East; no one in the Administration even suggested that the American public be alerted to such a possibility. At the White House and State Department, even those who supported the right of free passage through the Strait could not agree on how to back this principle in practice. Shimeon Peres had indeed been right.

In Israel a pervasive sense of isolation and gloom filled the air. "Nobody who lived those days in Israel will ever forget the air of heavy foreboding that hovered over our land," Eban declared. "For Israel there would be only one defeat. . . . There would be a ghastly sequel, leaving nothing to be discussed—an ending with no renewal and no consolation."[11]

*   *   *

The period of *hamtana*, of waiting, came to an end in the early morning hours of June 5, 1967. Even today the sequence of events crowded into six short miraculous days seems impossible to grasp. The Israeli Air Force in lightning raids wiped out the entire Egyptian and Syrian air forces on the ground, destroying over four hundred planes while losing only nineteen. The tank corps virtually repeated its 1956 performance, punching through the Sinai all the way to the Suez Canal in three days. Although the northern front was to have been of secondary importance, the Israeli Defense Forces, in bitter fighting, stormed the supposedly impregnable Golan Heights, from which the Syrians had shelled Israeli settlements for nearly twenty years. Only the cease-fire on June 10 halted Israeli columns in their drive toward Damascus.

But the greatest prize of all would be taken from Jordan. Although King Hussein had been warned publicly and privately to stay out of the fighting and had received firm assurances that Israel would not attack Jordan, the young monarch felt bound by his treaty with Nasser. Jordanian artillery opened fire on Jewish Jerusalem on the morning of June 5. Two days later the Israelis broke through St. Stephen's Gate and took the Old City in hand-to-hand combat. Here *Zahal* suffered its heaviest casualties, since in order to avoid damage to any of the holy places it refrained from using artillery or air support. The entire West Bank was overrun up to the Jordan River. But of all the emotional events of the war, none could compare to the recapture of the *Kotel ha'Ma'aravi* (Western Wall), the holiest site in Jewish tradition, the last remnant of Solomon's great temple. There on June 7, the chief chaplain of the army sounded the *shofar* (ram's horn) as Jews for the first time in nineteen years could once again pray at the Wall. Defense Minister Moshe Dayan stood before the Wall and declared: "We have reunited the torn city, the capital of Israel. We have returned to this most sacred shrine, never to part from it again." And on June 11, the S.S. *Dolphin*, flying the Israeli flag, passed through the Strait of Tiran and anchored at Eilat.

The rapidity and extent of Israeli victory could only be matched by the reaction of American Jewry during the tense weeks of crisis in May and the actual days of fighting, and by the emotional outburst which erupted following the victory. But the joy of the victory must be seen in contrast to the gloom and despair which characterized American Jewry during May 1967. Despite a number of public-opinion surveys showing overwhelming support for the Israelis (one Gallup poll taken in late May showed 55 per cent for the Israelis and 4 per cent for the Arabs), the imagery of the Holocaust dominated American Jewry—the fear that twice in their lifetime the Jewish people would be slaughtered and would be able to do nothing about it.

"Terror and dread fell upon Jews everywhere," wrote Abraham Joshua Heschel. "Will God permit our people to perish? Will there be another Auschwitz, another Dachau, another Treblinka?

"The darkness of Auschwitz is still upon us, its memory is a torment forever. In the midst of that thick darkness there is one gleam of light: the return of our people to Zion. Will He permit this gleam to be smothered?"[12]

The fear was not just for the Jews of Israel. Even in America, there was a widespread feeling that the lives of all Jews, that the fate of Judaism itself, hung in the balance. If Israel perished then Jews everywhere would perish, not so much by the sword but because their faith could not survive a second onslaught. Elie Wiesel commented on the ages-old convenant between God and Israel: when the Torah was threatened, the Jews fought; when the Jews were threatened, then God fought. But in Europe from 1939 to 1945, God had not kept His part of the bargain. If He were to fail again, how could the Jewish faith survive? Rabbi Irving Greenberg's terse answer to a congregant's question reflected the mood of most American Jews:

"What shall we do if Israel fights and we lose?"

"You will find a sign outside our synagogue that we are closed."[13]

Unlike previous years, American Jews in May and June 1967 *felt themselves to be in a crisis of survival!* The American Jew no longer savored the dual Zion of the *goldenah medina* while vicariously enjoying the homeland in Israel. All Jews, Elie Wiesel said, had become children of the Holocaust.[14]

Israel stood, symbolically, as a redemption of the Holocaust; Israel made it possible to endure the memory of Auschwitz. Were Israel to be destroyed, then Hitler would be alive again, the final victory would be his. It is little wonder that American Jews, like Israelis, thought in terms of *"ein breira!"* (There is no alternative!). Nor could they think in terms of a Yavneh, the academy established by Rabbi Yochanan ben Zakkai which kept Jewish piety and learning alive after the Roman destruction of ancient Palestine. Now the image would be that of Masada, where Jews had killed themselves rather than surrender to the Romans. "When Masada is an ever-present possibility," wrote Richard Rubenstein, "there can be no second Auschwitz. Eliezer ben Yair [the commander at Masada] would never have submitted to the Nazis. Like the defenders of the Warsaw ghetto, he had found a way to resist. Before submitting to the Germans, he would have killed himself and his family." American Jews now had to resist or die.[15]

But what could American Jews do? Some, who were in Israel, chose to stay there, to stand—and possibly die—with their fellow Jews. In late May the United States embassy advised American citizens to leave, and cables poured in from parents to students in Israel imploring them to come home. The American students at the Hebrew University called a meeting, and, while no formal resolution was taken, a group consensus clearly emerged: The waverers fell into line, and not a single student left.[16] Of one hundred young men and women in the country under the Sherut La'am volunteer program, only one left, a woman who received a cable that her mother was seriously ill. At the Jewish Agency's Institute for Youth Leaders from Abroad, out of two hundred boys and girls only two left, one of whom was a girl whose parents were in Israel on business and literally dragged her onto the plane with them. One group of sixty Americans at the Greenberg Institute completed their year of study and had plane reservations to return to the United States; all of them canceled their flights and asked to be assigned to volunteer work in hospitals, schools, and settlements.[17]

One American woman wrote to her parents explaining her decision to stay in Israel: "After learning all my life about Hitler and the destruction of the Jews and the rise of a Jewish state, I cannot just run out like this. There is so much to do here. We are working with schools, youth groups, kibbutzim, and hospitals to fill the jobs that the men who are sent out from the reserves left vacant. I want to stay and do whatever I can so that the country can continue to function while others may have to fight. I feel it is my duty to my religion, my people, and my country to stay here and do whatever I can."[18]

In the United States, thousands of Jewish college and high school students rushed to sign up for volunteer work in Israel. At Case Western Reserve University in Cleveland, five hundred students jammed the Hillel House to pick up volunteer applications, while at New York's City College one hundred students signed up in four hours for the Sherut La'am volunteer program. On the first day of the war, at least ten thousand Americans of all ages swamped Israeli consulates and Zionist offices, despite repeated pleas from Israel that a deluge of foreign volunteers would only complicate a difficult situation, and despite a State Department ban on Americans traveling in a war zone. In the end, only a handful managed to get to Israel before the fighting ended, although seventy-five hundred arrived over the course of that summer.[19] When Golda Meir came to the United States shortly after the war she could not believe the stories she heard of American youth—the very group which refused to make *aliyah*—fighting to get to Israel. She insisted on meeting some of them, and over a thousand of the would-be volunteers showed up at the hastily called gathering.

"Tell me," she asked, "why did you want to come? Was it because of the way you were brought up? Or because you thought it would be exciting? Or because you are a Zionist? What did you think about when you stood in line last month and asked to be allowed to go to Israel?"

There were many reasons given, but one young man seemed to sum up the feelings of all those present.

"I don't know how to explain it to you, Mrs. Meir, but I do know one thing. My life will never be the same again. The Six-day War—and the fact that Israel came so close to being destroyed—has changed everything for me: my feelings about myself, my family, even my neighbors. Nothing will ever be quite the same for me as it was before."[20]

One group which could and did swing into action found it had all the work it could manage on hand. Even before the war broke out, Hadassah began storing drugs, supplies, linens, and the other equipment its medical complex in Jerusalem would need to serve as Israel's major military hospital. At a special crisis center in the New York headquarters, staff and officers worked around the clock for two weeks handling thousands of calls from members, doctors, and nurses—all volunteering goods and services. Faye Schenk, then Hadassah's treasurer, later reported that she had not had to spend an additional cent from the operating budget; everything had been contributed. Moreover, Hadassah was able to send all of the drugs and medical supplies to Israel in time at no transportation cost. Despite the fact that airlines were cutting back flights to the Middle East in anticipation of the war, both KLM and TWA offered to transport the goods *gratis*. El Al, of course, also carried supplies, and informed Hadassah president Charlotte Jacobson that next to ammunition, Hadassah shipments had top priority for cargo space on El Al flights.

During the crisis Hadassah was inundated with gifts of cash and supplies. Over $1.2 million came in, practically all unsolicited, and the women's Zionist organization had already raised its annual budget of

$18 million for the hospital. What it now needed were the thousand and one items to treat the wounded. Johnson & Johnson, like many other pharmaceutical firms, donated supplies outright, and later told Hadassah that the twelve hundred cases of surgical dressings it had furnished would be matched in future years as an annual gift. An official from S. Klein, a New York department store, called and asked Gladys Zales, Hadassah's purchasing director, if she could use linens. Upon receiving an affirmative response, he told her they would be over in an hour. One hour later, a burly truck driver walked into Hadassah headquarters and said he had some linens.

"Fine," Gladys replied automatically. "Please put them over there in the corner."

"Lady, I don't want to bother you, but I think maybe you better come outside and have a look."

Annoyed at the interruption, she stepped outside to find a fifty-foot trailer filled to overflowing with seventy-five hundred sheets, forty-five hundred pillow cases, and twelve hundred blankets. She managed to find a warehouse and within a week had the linens on a ship to Israel.

At the end of the war, the medical staff in Jerusalem reported that despite the wide variety of wounds and the thousands of soldiers, Jew and Arab alike, treated during the war, not a single item had been lacking except a No. 7 cannula needed for a tracheotomy; the surgeon had made do with the next larger size. For one operation, an ophthalmologist needed a pair of human eyes. One morning Mrs. Zales received a call from the executive director of the International Eye Foundation in Washington; he had two fresh eyes, but they had to be transplanted within twenty-four hours. A member of Hadassah's national board met an Eastern Air Lines plane from Washington, picked up the seven-pound vacuum canister containing the eyes, and delivered it to the next El Al flight to Israel. The eyes arrived in time to restore one soldier's sight.

For Hadassah, the greatest reward for its work came with the return of Mount Scopus. On June 8, the flags of Hadassah and of the State of Israel rose once again over the hospital that for nineteen years had stood unused and rusting, protected from total vandalism only by the small contingent of *Zahal* allowed there under the truce terms. Despite the State Department's ban on travel to a war zone, Charlotte Jacobson managed to get clearance and arrived in Jerusalem just as the war ended. She immediately went to visit the wounded at the Ein Kerem

facility, and then with Dr. Kalman Mann and other staff members
went up to Scopus. There they wept as they saw the deteriorated buildings, the rusting hospital beds, the smashed windows, and Henrietta
Szold's precious garden overgrown with weeds. Then they saw a message scribbled on the wall by one of the Israeli guards who had maintained the lonely vigil for nearly two decades: "If the day comes and
this building is filled again with patients, let them remember those who
watched over this place in difficult years."

Less than two weeks after the fighting ended the army formally
turned Scopus back to Hadassah, and despite shortages, broken equipment, and a hundred other obstacles, the woman immediately ordered
the facility reopened. Not the entire hospital—that would take a few
years and several million dollars—but one or two clinics, as a symbol
and a gesture that Hadassah had returned. And, most amazing of all,
Arabs from East Jerusalem came to the Scopus clinics on the day they
reopened, many of them clutching their pre-1948 medical cards and
asking for doctors and nurses who had treated them before the city had
been split.[21]

* * *

Members of Hadassah and some of the other Jewish organizations had
specific work to do, but for the overwhelming majority of American
Jews only one way seemed open to them to help the Jewish state—the
giving of money. Whether it was the fact that Israel had been the recipient of American funds for so many years, or fear, or guilt, or the
tradition of *tsadakah* (charity), or a sense of frustration, or a combination of all these things, there is no doubt that the American Jewish
community gave as it had never given before. Many cities and towns
had just finished their annual UJA drives in the spring, before the war
scare, and had raised about $65 million.

Now came the crises in May and the war in June, and money—
above and beyond the regular pledges—flowed in such quantities and
from so many people that even the professional staff and leaders of organized Jewry could not believe it. Synagogues froze their building and
expansion funds; businessmen applied for personal loans and turned
the proceeds over to the UJA. Word spread that "even the doctors are
giving like mad," a seeming miracle, since in the professional fund-raising business physicians are known as extremely reluctant contributors.
Many communities launched emergency campaigns even before the na-

tional UJA acted, and the response was phenomenal. In New York, the participants at one luncheon raised $15 million in as many minutes; one man pledged $1,550,000, and four others gave $1 million each. In Boston fifty families opened the drive by contributing $2.5 million. The Jews of St. Louis raised $1.2 million overnight, those in Cleveland more than $3 million. In Chicago, the community council expected only a hundred or so people to show up at a hastily called meeting; more than a thousand came, and shattered all the previous records for giving.[22]

Nor did all the money come from just the wealthy Jewish givers. Everyone in his or her own way did as much as possible. Ruby's Dry Cleaners in Pittsburgh ran special advertisements announcing that the entire cleaning price of every incoming garment, including box storage, would go to the Israel Emergency Fund. A New York youngster went into the streets with a Manischewitz borscht bottle and collected $72.79 from passers-by in a few hours. All across the country, Jewish children armed with milk bottles, tin cans, plastic buckets—anything that would hold money—improvised fund-raising campaigns of their own. Four *yeshiva* students stood in Times Square holding the corners of a bedsheet, soliciting funds. "There is no food being produced in Israel," they explained. "All able-bodied men are at the front. Give for medical supplies, for food and shelter for children." And there were many non-Jewish givers as well. The president of Catholic Fordham University gave $5,000; former Army Secretary Robert T. Stevens, a textile manufacturer, donated $250,000; and a girl in Minnesota called a rabbi to find out how she could become Jewish so she could make a contribution.[23]

During the first three weeks of the emergency campaign, more than $100 million came in; by the end of the summer the figure had climbed to $180 million with an additional $100 million worth of Israel bonds purchased. Between the regular and emergency campaigns, American Jews raised $240 million for Israel in 1967, and bought $190 million in Israel bonds, a total of $430 million! Jews who had never identified with Israel, or even as Jews, seemed to come out of the woodwork, checkbook in hand. In Chicago, when they finally managed to sort out the money and the pledge cards, they discovered twelve thousand Jewish families which had never been listed on the rolls of any Jewish organization in the city. In the South, where Reform Jews had been almost rabidly anti-Israel, some of the oldest families were suddenly pledging substantial sums to the emergency campaign. Ben Cone, Jr., of Greensboro, North Carolina, converted from the Episcopalian Church back to Judaism, and headed up the Israel Bond campaign. Pro-Israel rallies took place in Reform temples where, as one rabbi reported, "it used to be that the mere mention of the word 'Palestine' on Yom Kippur was enough to ruin the sacredness of the occasion."[24]

In fact, in the wake of the war, anti-Zionism among Jews as it had been known for decades practically ceased to exist. The New York Times carried an article that some of the leaders of the American Council for Judaism looked upon the war as an act of Israeli "aggression," and considered the "massive Jewish support for Israel in America . . . as amounting to 'hysteria.'" This certainly was the attitude of executive director Elmer Berger, but some of the leading members of the Council, including Donald S. Klopfer, vice chairman of Random House, John Mosler of the Mosler Safe Company, Walter N. Rothschild, Jr., president of Abraham & Straus, Stanley Marcus, head of Nieman-Marcus in Dallas, and others immediately repudiated his position, taking care to note that they supported Israel and had made substantial contributions to the emergency campaign. Several of these men soon resigned from the Council.[25]

Those still left in the group now realized that they had been nursing a vain delusion all these years; there was no hidden core of large anti-Zionist sentiment among American Jewry; to the contrary, the community overwhelmingly supported Israel. Berger wanted the Council to play a prophetic role, preaching its message of anti-Israel, anti-Zionism in the American wilderness. But the directors had had enough; in the glow of solidarity and pride following the Six-day War, they no longer wanted to be outcasts from the community. One member of the Council resigned because, as he told Berger, "the Israelis have made me feel ten feet tall." In "Lakeville," another member wrote a blistering letter to Berger denouncing his criticism of Israel, and later told Marshall Sklare that "what Berger said was right, but it was bad timing. I hate negativism. If he couldn't say anything good about Israel why couldn't he have kept his big yap shut?"[26]

This man now described himself as "pro-Israel" and "anti-Zionist," a strange condition evidently shared by other members of the Council. Although the group decided to stay in existence, despite the large loss in membership, it announced that it would no longer consider matters of Israeli existence or policy but concentrate on opposing Jewish nationalism within the United States; Zionism, not Israel, was henceforth the enemy. Berger claimed that one could not "departmentalize Zionism" that way, and finally resigned from the Council in 1968. Together with some other diehards, he founded the American Jewish Alternatives to Zionism, hoping to keep the faith pure. Although both the Council and Berger's group still exist on paper, they are notoriously weak. Their main purpose, other than occasionally providing an outlet for anti-Israel propaganda, seems to be as whipping boys for a variety of Zionist and pro-Israel orators.

All American Jews, it seemed, now basked in the pride of victory. For some, the pride was of long standing; for others, it was a new experience. One Reform Jew in the South, long an opponent of Israel because he feared charges of dual loyalty, shed his worries when his neighbor, a retired admiral, called him on the telephone and said, "Ed, I'm glad you Jews kicked the shit out of 'em." The *Intermountain Jewish News* proclaimed to its readers that "the glorious fighters of Israel have made an automatic hero of every Jew in America, yea of the world." One no longer had to be ashamed of being a Jew. One woman admitted that, although neither an observant Jew nor a Zionist, "I felt a pride in being Jewish that I've never felt. It was a real change from seeing the Jews as the long-suffering victims."[27] Even among Jewish professors, long thought to be apathetic about Israel, surveys found a striking response, and many of the academics reported amazement at their newly discovered passion for the Jewish state. One history teacher took to calling his colleagues every morning to give them the latest news and the battle positions of *Zahal*. Polls found a level of identification and support for Israel among Jews in general approaching near unanimity; at the height of the war, ninety-nine out of every hundred Jews expressed their strong sympathy with Israel.[28]

*   *   *

How does one explain this sudden eruption of feeling? What happened to cause this outbreak of identification and solidarity? First of all, it must be remembered that emotions of such magnitude are not created in a matter of days or even weeks. The Six-day War did not *manufacture* this sentiment, but *awakened* it. American Jews had never been anti-Israel, but in the nineteen years of the state's existence had come to take it for granted, had assumed its continuation as a matter of course. Now, when it appeared to face destruction, the love and energy and time that had gone into establishing the *Yishuv,* in securing partition and recognition—even vicarious involvement and sentiment—came rushing to the fore. The memory of the Holocaust and the guilt Western Jews felt for not having done enough to save their brethren awoke a need for action, for identification, for unity. Israel, God willing, would not perish, but no matter what happened, no one must be allowed to say that American Jews had again stood by passively. Here, more than in any other situation, the cry of "Never Again!" rang loudest and truest. Nasser was Hitler incarnate, and the Arab threat of genocide had to be taken seriously. As Elie Wiesel so poignantly wrote, behind the army of Israel stood another army of six million ghosts.[29]

American Jews also perceived intuitively that their destiny and that of the Jewish state were inextricably bound together. One of the young volunteers wrote that the war had been a moment of truth: "Two weeks ago, Israel was they; now Israel is we. . . . I will not intellectualize it; I am Jewish; it is a Jewish we. Something happened. I will never again be able to talk about how Judaism is only a religion, and isn't it too bad that there has to be such a thing as a Jewish state. Roots count." For Arthur Waskow, long active in the peace movement and radical causes, the war provided an "existential" moment in which he and other American Jews "discovered a great attachment to Israel that was so deep that they surprised themselves. . . . They felt about Israel as they felt about America: Somehow they were responsible for its existence and/or for its injustices. Simply because they were Jewish."[30] In earlier years, the anti-Zionists would have pointed to statements such as these and charged "dual loyalties"; now American Jewry felt secure enough to dismiss the isolated protests of the one or two Elmer Bergers left.

This sense of belonging as Americans and as Jews, this rebirth of Jewish identity, was probably the greatest legacy of the Six-day War, and forged new bonds between Israeli and American Jews. In the three decades of Israel's existence, it is doubtful if there has been a period of less divisiveness and greater harmony between these two communities than during the war and its immediate aftermath. One could find the evidence everywhere—in the near obsession with Israeli news and personalities, in the spurt of Israel-related activities in Jewish communities, in the rise of *aliyah* over the next few years, in the new and friendly attitudes of Israelis toward American visitors. "I have discovered a new land," sang Rabbi Heschel. "Israel is not the same as before. There is great astonishment in the souls."[31] Indeed, there was astonishment at the magnitude of the military victory, exaltation at the reunification of Jerusalem, pride in the dignity and humility with which the victors carried their accomplishments,* and the joy of belonging to one people.

Even the always sensitive subject of *aliyah* suddenly became a common concern, rather than a barrier. Some, like David Polish, found new force behind his argument that America constituted a *galut*. Others re-examined their own commitment in the light of their new recognition of the importance of Israel and its survival in their lives as Jews. If the state meant that much, then perhaps the logical response would be resettlement. A new generation of young Jews, many of whom had grown disillusioned with America because of the Vietnamese war, could accept Eliezer Schweid's declaration that *aliyah* constituted "the supreme test of their loyalty to themselves," that their going up unto the land would strengthen not only Israel, but also the interconnectedness of the Jewish state and the Jewish people.[32]

Zionist officials, both in Israel and the United States, were quick to encourage this sentiment. Emanuel Neumann stated that every Jewish family should be represented by at least one member in Israel. At the seventieth convention of the Zionist Organization of America, held in Israel in the summer following the war, Prime Minister Levi Eshkol told the delegates that "Zionism and *aliyah* are one and the same thing," and the assembly rose to cheer him—a far cry from the reaction to Ben-Gurion's nearly identical words over a decade earlier.[33] In phrases recalling Cyrus's edict to the Jews of Babylonia over two millennia earlier, the Israeli government and the World Zionist Organization issued a call to the Jewish people:

---

* There is little to be found in history to compare with the behavior of the Israelis after the war, their humility, almost sadness, in victory. See above all the speech by Yitzhak Rabin, then chief of staff, in accepting an honorary degree from Hebrew University, which he claimed on behalf of *Zahal*, and the moving reminiscences of young Israelis in war, *The Seventh Day* (New York, 1970).

"Arise and come up to build the land." . . .

In the present hour of deliverance, though the time of danger is not past, new vistas have been opened and immense challenges present themselves. A holy duty to upbuild the country speedily and to ensure the future of the Jewish State now faces the Jewish people. The inescapable call of this hour is for *aliyah*—the *aliyah* of the whole people young and old, a return to Zion of the House of Israel. . . . Every family should as a sacred obligation contribute one of its sons in this fateful hour. Let us be worthy of this historic moment with all that it offers for the future of the individual and of the Jewish people.

"Who is there among you all of His people? His God be with him and let him go up."[34]

Rose Halprin, head of the American Section of the Jewish Agency, agreed that *aliyah* was the key item on the Zionist agenda, and pointed with pride to the thousands of volunteers who had rushed to Israel to help. But she cautioned that the millennium had not yet arrived. Calls for "two million immigrants in two years" totally misread the situation. Such a mass immigration could result only from a *pogrom;* what Israel could hope for, and what it was seeing, was an idealistic *aliyah,* the resettlement of those moved by the nobility of the challenge. Now it was up to Israel, and to the Zionist movement, to help absorb these young people successfully into Israeli society; if that could not be done, then the expected breakthrough in Western *aliyah* would not materialize.[35]

The American *aliyah,* upon closer examination, proved to be rather small. In the three years following the war, 2,700 Americans declared themselves as immigrants, while another 16,141 entered the country as "temporary residents." But in terms of percentages, one could see an impressive jump in American *olim.* The number of immigrants rose nearly 50 per cent, while temporary residency doubled; more important, the proportion of all immigrants entering Israel coming from the United States rose from 91 per 1,000 to 192 per 1,000.[36]

A United States Supreme Court decision (*Efroyin* v. *Rusk*) on the eve of the war facilitated American *aliyah.* The justices, reversing a number of precedents, held that Congress did not have the power to deprive Americans of their citizenship without their consent. Now Americans could hold dual citizenship, Israeli and American, and the

Israeli government quickly revised its immigration laws to enable Americans to "back into" Israeli citizenship without having to give up their American rights.

For the Israelis, however, even this small jump proved welcome, but they, as much as the Americans, could not fathom the depths of emotion exposed by the war. The Jews of the Diaspora, of *galut*, who had refused to make *aliyah*, who had seemed so indifferent, so unresponsive to Israel, had shown that they cared. "There was no doubt that Israel would have to go the way alone, politically," Teddy Kollek wrote to an American friend, but "the unbelievable support we have received the world over . . . is overwhelming." Pinhas Sapir termed the response of Disapora Jewry a revelation. "These people are not mere friends or even partners," he told Israeli leaders, "they are our brothers." American students in Israel, nearly all of whom had refused to leave the country during the crisis, now reported a new warmth and openness on the part of Israelis. The barriers they had complained about dropped away, and many of them, for the first time, felt "at home" in Israel.[37]

In a series of interviews held in 1975, Israeli academics, government and Zionist officials, and military men all said the same thing—1967 had been the turning point. "We thought that American Jews did not care," said Yehudah Avner, then aide to Prime Minister Rabin, "and then we knew that they did care, and that was tremendously important to us." "We always talk about Jews as one people," Golda Meir explained, "but in the years before 1967 many Israelis had ceased to believe it. The American response proved to younger Israelis especially that all of us, all Jews, are *mishpachah*, are all one family." The generation which had seen American Jewry in action from 1945 to 1948 knew this, of course, but now they remembered anew, while the younger *sabras*, those who had grown up after the establishment of the state, realized the American commitment as well.[38] And, as David Ben-Gurion and others had long argued, the only ally the Israelis could ever count upon was world Jewry. In 1967 many Israelis came to agree with that sentiment for the first time.[39]

*   *   *

It would be pleasant to report that the Six-day War generated nothing but good feelings among American Jewry, but there were problems as well. Some newly minted chauvinists were carried away by the magnitude of the Israeli victory, and for the next few years too many people walked around saying, "Look at what *we* did to the Arabs!" No Jewish event, and certainly not one which related to Israel, seemed complete without some Israeli colonel telling his enthralled audience, "Yes, Jews make gread soldiers." At numerous fund-raising events, otherwise sober businessmen, long experienced in problems of procurement and delivery, acted as if the money they raised that evening had been responsible for the military victory. Moshe Dayan, the one-eyed Defense Minister, became the new hero of American Jewry, a second Moses, and numerous wits, including several members of Congress, suggested that the United States sell, or better yet give away, all the Phantom jets Israel wanted if in return Dayan would take over operations in Vietnam. One might better have kept in mind the humility of Yitzhak Rabin, the chief of staff and real architect of the Israeli military achievement. Moreover, when some critics suggested that excessive pride in war was somehow unbecoming to a Jew, that the Midrash taught that the angels were forbidden to exalt in the drowning of the Egyptians in the Red Sea since all men are created by God, they encountered a deep and resentful hostility.[40]

In Wheeling, West Virginia, for example, an Israeli colonel told a victory rally how many Arabs *we* had killed, how many tanks *we* had captured, how many planes *we* had destroyed. Rabbi Martin Siegel, watching the audience, described his congregants as literally bouncing in their seats with delight: "I, the shoe salesman, killed an Arab; I, the heart specialist, captured the tank." When the colonel finished, Siegel was called upon to deliver a fitting benediction to celebrate *our* military conquest. "I only want to say one thing," he said, "I'm pleased that Israel has survived. However, I don't think that an Arab mother weeps for her dead son any differently than a Jewish mother does. I simply refuse to take any joy in the killing of Arab children, any more than I would take joy in the killing of Jewish children." The audience sat stunned, and the Israeli colonel turned on his heel and left.[41]

The reaction of many Christians also left American Jews disturbed. The June war did call forth an unprecedented number of non-Jewish contributors to the emergency fund; it did evoke Philadelphia mayor James H. J. Tate to pledge his best efforts to work for Israel; it did lead a number of Catholic, Protestant, and fundamentalist Christian personalities as well as a very few Christian journals of opinion to support publicly Israel's political integrity and navigation rights.[42] But for the most part, the silence, or the outright hostility of many Christians shocked American Jewry. After all those years of dialogue, how could they keep still when the very life of Israel was imperiled?

Samuel Sandmel, a professor at the Hebrew Union College and long active in the interfaith movement, expressed the dismay he and his fellow Jews felt: "We Jews and you Christians had co-operated on the national level in many enterprises, such as civil rights [and] many Jews assumed that the same outpouring of sympathy for the beleaguered Jews that animated next-door Christian neighbors would be reflected in the organized Christian bodies. Beyond this expectation, some Jews in the acuteness of their anxiety, solicited support from Christian organizations, and even pressed for it; perhaps unduly. To the consternation of these Jews, such support was not forthcoming. . . . In the dismay at the Christian neutrality, some Jews felt completely abandoned by precisely those Christians with whom they had had so much affirmative co-operation, and there were those who said bitter things. Indeed, some Christians, not at all neutral, wrote to newspapers letters as venomous about Israel as the words of the Russian delegate to the United Nations, and wrote those letters as 'Christians.' "[43]

While many Jews may not have expected an all-out endorsement of Israel by Christians, they stood baffled at the "neutrality" of national church groups, and bitter at comments from the likes of Henry P. Van Dusen, the former president of the Union Theological Seminary, who compared Israel's actions with those of Nazi Germany. The Israeli "onslaught [was] the most violent, ruthless (and successful) aggression since Hitler's blitzkrieg across Western Europe in the summer of 1940, aiming not at victory but at annihilation." Van Dusen's resentment at Israel's "success" highlighted one facet of the problem: Christians could not get used to the idea of a potent Jew, one who would not be content in the role of victim. Franklin H. Littell, chairman of the Department of Religion at Temple University, and a strong supporter of Israel, acutely summed up the difficulty: "The thing the nineteenth-century Liberal Protestant, the Christian humanitarian, cannot grasp is the Jew who is a winner, a citizen soldier of liberty and dignity, who does not have to beg protection of a patron or toleration of a so-called Christian nation, who can take the Golan Heights in six hours if necessary. This is precisely the reason why Israel is a stone of stumbling, and why also the generally covert anti-Semitism of liberal Protestantism can be just as dangerous as the overt anti-Semitism of the radical right."†[44]

Christians somehow or other could not grasp the meaning of Israel to contemporary Jewry, its symbolic importance. Some Jews blamed their own efforts for this gap of understanding. "We have failed to clarify its meaning, its value to our existence," wrote Rabbi Heschel. "We have failed to convey its significance to our Christian friends." Rabbi Marc Tannenbaum, who had played such a significant role in speaking for the Jewish people at Vatican II, also shared this explanation.[46] And, as Alan T. Davies conceded, the Christian community never understood that Israel "is a symbol in some sense analogous to the Christian symbol of resurrection; after death (Auschwitz), God miraculously raised his people to life (Israel) in the midst of the nations." Few Christians proved as perceptive as John Delury, secretary of the San Francisco Archdiocese Commission on Social Justice, who saw the survival of Israel not just as a Jewish concern; in the broadest theological terms, the survival of Israel was a prime Christian concern.[47]

Whether or not the Jewish-Christian dialogue would continue now seemed problematical. Balfour Brickner, head of the CCAR's Commission on Interfaith Activities, Pesach Z. Levovitz, president of the Rabbinical Council of America, and David Polish all considered the dialogue if not dead, at least silenced, and wanted to leave the initiative for resuming it with the Christians. Others, including Professor Malcolm L. Diamond of Princeton, Richard Rubenstein of the B'nai B'rith Hillel Foundation in Pittsburgh, and Jacob Neusner of Brown believed that the crisis might yet provide the opportunity for meaningful under-

---

† Michael Frayne brilliantly satirized this attitude in a letter to "My dear Israel" from "Your affectionate Great-aunt Britain": "I have felt obliged to condemn your *unseemly haste* in opening hostilities [and] your insistence on *winning* the war—particularly in such a brash and violent fashion. . . . To insist upon defeating your opponents is a discourtesy which they may find *very hard to forgive*. . . . What makes your behavior all the more perplexing is that when the war commenced you enjoyed the approval and sympathy of polite society as a whole. There you stood, surrounded on all sides by greatly superior hostile forces, whose proclaimed intention was to destroy you utterly. Everybody was *deeply touched!* We shouldn't have let you down! If things had gone badly, we had ships standing by which could have evacuated *several thousand* Israeli survivors—who would have had *the unreserved sympathy* of the entire world!"[45]

standing between Christian and Jew.[48] In any event, the blithe optimism that Vatican II had ushered in a golden age could be counted as one casualty of the war.

Still another area of reaction could be found in the growing friction between supporters of Israel and those active in the peace movement, a counterpoint to the earlier tensions between the Johnson administration and those who opposed his Vietnam policy. In the summer of 1966 Lyndon Johnson had hinted his displeasure at the dovish views of some prominent Jewish intellectuals and communal leaders, and suggested that one day they might find themselves in the awkward position of petitioning the United States to save Israel. Jewish organizations responded energetically that the Jewish community was as divided as the rest of the country on the Indochina war, but that Jews had every right, as did other citizens, to take individual or collective stands on any issue. The vigor of the reaction caught the Administration by surprise, and the President, UN ambassador Goldberg, and other officials spent several days placating and explaining the President's statement to leaders of a number of national Jewish organizations.

When the June war broke out, American Jews had in fact requested American support of Israel, not in terms of troops, but for material aid and political backing. A number of intellectuals, many in the peace movement, signed a public appeal, and the list included Robert Penn Warren, Marianne Moore, Lionel Trilling, Daniel Patrick Moynihan, and Robert Heilbroner. But Arthur M. Schlesinger, Jr., refused to do so, on the grounds that it would be inconsistent to oppose unilateral intervention in one part of the world and favor it in another, while poet Robert Lowell also declined, because he opposed all wars. The confusion and ambiguity which Israel caused within the peace movement amused some White House aides, who suggested that the signers call themselves "Doves for War." Conservative columnist William F. Buckley, Jr., who supported Israel, derived a wry satisfaction that the war in the Middle East had "most of the critics of our policy in Vietnam on the run." But Theodore Draper saw neither humor nor inconsistency in the situation; in Vietnam he opposed the abuse of American power, while in the Middle East he criticized its abdication.[49]

In fact, the June war was just the first breach between the majority of American Jews and those who stood on the far left of the political spectrum. In the next few years leftist opposition to Israel and to Zionism became a major problem for American Jewry, but in 1967 the ideological debate still centered on Vietnam. While one could draw distinctions, the more committed young Jews in the peace movement now found themselves torn between ethnic ties they had not believed existed, and ethical principles now called into question.

*   *   *

The real anguish of the postwar period would not surface for several months, and in the summer of 1967 American Jews basked in the glory of an Israel saved by its own skill, daring, and courage. A second Holocaust had been averted. American Jews had redeemed themselves; they had come to the aid of their brethren, and still retained their sense of belonging in America. A harmony had been re-established between Israel and American Jewry. It had been a time of trial and fear and hope, and the victory had unleashed depths of emotion undreamed of by most American Jews. If one had to take a single example of how the war affected American Jewry, perhaps one might choose Henry Roth, author of *Call It Sleep* (1934). Although the book is now considered a classic, its poor initial reception led Roth to stop writing and become a semirecluse. The 1967 war caused him to break his silence, to feel that he had to rejoin the world, and rejoin his people. He wrote of his experience and emotions at the time:

"And then came the 1967 War in the Middle East, and the gloom that settled on him, despite his so-called Marxist orientation; the Arab states, the progressives, were going to drive the Jews, the Zionist-imperialist-pawns, into the sea. Jesus Christ, another holocaust of Jews! Sympathy flared up in the face of doctrine. And lo! the forlorn hope: by skill, by daring, by valor, Israel prevailed. A miracle! The pall lifted that had so long encompassed him. What the hell was he waiting for? Here was a people reborn—*his* people—regenerated by their own will. Was he mad not to share in that regeneration? He had been seeking it these thirty, almost forty years, ever since he had first opened *Ash Wednesday*. (And how many times had he thought with pity of his great master, Joyce, who couldn't make it home, and ended in that blind alley corruscating with his genius.) Here was a regeneration, tenable, feasible, rational—not in the direction of grandfather's medieval orthodoxy, but in the direction of a renascent Judaism, a new state. . . . And it was Israel, a revitalized Judaism, that revitalized the writer, his partisanship, a new exploration into contemporaneity, a new summoning of the word—however inept in the service of a cause. Threescore and ten, he climbed the stairs to the screendoor. A good morning to you, Lord God Almighty."[50]

Chapter 15

"A PEOPLE
THAT DWELLS ALONE"

At the end of André Schwartz-Bart's powerful novel of the Holocaust, *The Last of the Just*, in a heart-rending scene, Ernie, together with his wife and some children, goes into the gas chamber. "Oh Lord," he cries, "we went forth like this thousands of years ago through the Red Sea of salt, bitter tears. Oh let us arrive soon." In an ecstatic article published shortly after the Six-day War, Harold Fisch, as if in answer to Ernie, exulted: "The sea has split. We have walked through the Red Sea from the Egypt of Auschwitz to the coast of the promised land with the power of God holding the waters back at the right and at the left."[1]

But just as the despair of American Jews in those weeks in May had given way overnight to the joy of defeating Amalek, so now the sweet taste of victory turned to ashes in their mouths. The Arabs, defeated for the third time in nineteen years, instead of choosing to make peace with Israel, stepped up their campaign of vilification; with Russian aid they soon replaced lost arms, and began preparing for the next round of conflict. In the United States, the Johnson administration left office under the cloud of Vietnam, and Richard Nixon, a man with practically no political obligations to American Jewry, entered the White House determined to impose a peace settlement on the Middle East. Moreover, his chief foreign-policy advisers, Henry Kissinger and William Rogers, both seemed willing, for different reasons, to sacrifice Israeli interests for the sake of détente with the Soviet Union.

Anti-Semitic attacks from a number of sources left the community horrified. The New Left, which included many young Jews, turned viciously against "imperialistic" Israel, while angry blacks rioted and yelled that Hitler had been right. Christian groups which had seemingly sought a rapprochement with American Jews now turned against Israel, and could not or would not understand that, as far as Jews all over the world were concerned, anti-Israel and anti-Semitic comments had become synonymous. In the years following those exhilarating six days in June, the old biblical prophecy bore a new meaning: "Lo, it is a people that shall dwell alone, and shall not be reckoned among the nations" (Num. 23:9).

*   *   *

The New Left arose in the United States in the midsixties from two main sources: the peace movement to end the war in Vietnam, and the civil rights crusade to bring equality to American blacks. Eventually the radical agenda grew to include a neo-Marxist critique of American society as a whole, and thousands of young men and women, disillusioned by the Indochina war, by economic and social inequities, by racial prejudice, and by other perceived defects in "Amerika" rallied to the cause. While Jews did not constitute an undue percentage of the leftist leadership, they did figure disproportionately in the rank-and-file. Tom Milstein characterized Jewish participation in the New Left as falling roughly into three categories. There were Jewish youth drawn to the movement because of the traditional Jewish commitment to progressive social change. A second category included the "red-diaper babies," the sons and daughters of Communist Party members and sympathizers, who found their parents' political views suddenly reborn in a new and exciting wave of protest. It was from this group, although small in number, that most of the Jewish leaders of the New Left came; their prior attitudes, their contempt for democracy, their ability to rationalize away seemingly unpleasant or contradictory facts, and their organizational skills found a ready outlet. The third group Milstein described as "the passing generation," those who found in the New Left a medium of assimilation into the dominant Christian culture, an area of activity where they could shed their Jewishness and the status anxieties associated in their minds with it.[2]

Prior to the Six-day War, the New Left paid relatively little attention to Israel. Occasionally there would be some expressions of sympathy for the Palestinian refugees, but since Israel was, in obvious comparison to the Arab states, a democratic state with a strong socialist labor tradition, and was also fighting for its existence, the radical movement more or less ignored the Middle East. Civil rights and Vietnam took priority, and besides, an attack on Israel might alienate some of the wealthier Jewish "fellow travelers," liberals and former radicals, who helped finance New Left activism.

The first signs that Israel had become one of the enemies came when the Communist Party in this country began echoing Soviet charges in the United Nations that Israel had been the aggressor in the 1967 war. The fact that both the Soviet Union and China opposed the Jewish state led to the denunciation of Israel as an outpost of Western imperialism. The Arabs, ran the new orthodoxy, constituted an authentic Third World people struggling for freedom and independence; that several of the Arab states were among the most reactionary regimes in the world was conveniently ignored. Israeli supporters spoke in vain of Arab military dictatorships, of feudal sheikdoms which still practiced slavery, of the complete absence of civil liberties, of the oppression of women, of the fact that the oil-producing Arab states worked hand-in-glove with the capitalist nations, and of the fact that the Arabs had sought for two decades to destroy Israel, not vice versa. Efforts to point out Israel's democratic nature, its strong labor organizations, and its egalitarian nature proved just as futile.[3]

As far as the leftists were concerned, Israel had become the villain. George Novack, a longtime leader of the radical Socialist Workers Party, compared Israeli attitudes and treatment of the Arabs with that of American Jews toward blacks. "The upper and middle ranges of American Jewry," he wrote, "comfortably ensconced in bourgeois America, some of them bankers, landlords, big and little businessmen, participate in the system of *oppressing and exploiting* the black masses, just as the Zionists have become oppressors of the Palestinian Arabs." I. F. Stone, who had once been an ardent defender of the Jewish state, after June 1967 attacked American Jewish support of Israel as a perversion of traditional Jewish liberalism, a sellout to American imperialism. Jews in the Diaspora should make their contributions as citizens to their own nations; if Israel were to survive, then it would have to accommodate itself to the Arab world, and join in "a renascent Arab civilization." Noam Chomsky, one of the intellectual gurus of the New Left, went so far as to compare Israeli treatment of the Arabs to German treatment of the Jews.[4]

The left found further support for its portrayal of Israel as imperialistic when several leading Jews backed the American war in Vietnam. For some Jews, and Israelis, the real issue in Indochina was American resolution and ability to keep its commitments. If it withdrew from Vietnam, then how could Israel believe that in the future the United States would not allow it to fall victim to a renewed Arab attack? When Jacques Torczyner, president of the Zionist Organization of America, publicly adopted a hawkish position on Vietnam, he did so, he announced, to guarantee the support of the Nixon administration for Israel.[5] In a television interview with William F. Buckley, Jr., Abba Eban said, "There are those who believe that if the United States allowed Israel to be eliminated, nobody would have any trust in American security commitments anywhere else."

"Like Vietnam?" Buckley interrupted.

"Yes," Eban replied, "and Asia, Europe, Latin America."

"Amen," declared Buckley.[6]

Within the New Left, a host of leftist-oriented peace groups were spawned between 1967 and 1973. A partial list would include the Jewish Radical Committee, Committee on New Alternatives in the Middle East, the Israeli League for Human and Civil Rights, the Jewish Peace Fellowship, Arab-Israeli Research and Relations Project, Committee on the Middle East, International Committee of the Left for Peace in the Middle East, Middle East Research and Information Project, Students Against Middle East Involvement, Co-ordinating Committee of Jewish Intellectuals and Organizations for Peace and Justice in the Middle East, and the Search for Justice and Equality in Palestine. Many of them made no secret of their opposition not only to Israeli policy but even to the very fact of Israel's existence.

For many of the Jewish leftists the movement not only provided an outlet for their anger and frustration as Americans at the inequities in American life, but it also confirmed their ethical Jewish impulse. There have always been two major strands in the Judaic tradition, the ritualistic and the ethical, the priestly and the prophetic. "Justice, justice shalt thou pursue," the Torah had commanded, and now young Jews could claim that in opposing racial bigotry and economic exploitation as

well as an unjust foreign war, they were in the highest sense living
their faith. Their parents, who may not have agreed with all of their
politics, often saw in this rebellion ethical roots which had been fostered at home; the parents in their day had also protested, and had not
done enough. How could they now say no to their children carrying on
such a Jewish tradition?

But when it came to Israel, a great schism appeared within the
ranks of Jewish radicals. On the one hand, there were those who, in
earlier years, would have been described as "self-hating Jews," young
men and women unhappy with their Jewishness, actively seeking to rid
themselves of it. What better way to deny one's identity as a Jew than
by attacking Israel, which had become so central in contemporary Jewish life. Indeed, one generation of self-denying Jews reached out to another; Elmer Berger reported joyously to his latest anti-Zionist organization on the cordial reception he received on college campuses. This
new generation was emancipated from all of the old hypocrisies, and he
quoted one supposedly typical Jewish student as saying: "We cannot
identify with Israel's efforts to anesthetize the world's conscience with
respect to the Arabs and we reject any intellectual or moral obligation
to a state which cannot find a way other than force to sustain itself."[7]

For some radicals, criticism of Israel did not mean the rejection of
their Jewishness. Rather, they rebelled against the community's seeming closed-mindedness about Israel. Not everything the Jewish state did
was praiseworthy, not all of its actions admirable; moreover, within Israel there were Jews who opposed their government's policies. Why,
therefore, could not radical Jews be critical of Israel and not be read
out of the community? Did their efforts to seek justice really depart
that much from the castigations of an Isaiah upon his people? Radical
Jews, wrote Arthur Waskow, "must tell the Palestinians that we in
some sense understand and share their anguish at what they have lost
and at what they suffer. Who, after all, should better understand the
pain of those who feel cut off from the Dome of the Rock on the Temple Mount than we, who were deprived of the Temple? And if some
Jews—most Jews—do not understand this pain, we are all the more obligated to do so."[8]

Yet for most Jews in the New Left, the attack on Israel by the leadership wounded them deeply. Too young to remember the Holocaust,
they had grown up with Israel as a central feature of their Jewish life.

Unless they were willing to renounce their Jewishness, they could not denounce Israel. They began to perceive that attacks on Zionism and on the Jewish state were in fact attacks on Judaism and on them. Aliza Samuel recalled how she suddenly grew very uncomfortable with the movement's slogans. "Fine lines began to appear between terms which had run together smoothly. American Imperialism was one thing, but what about when coupled with Zionism? My Comparative Religions teacher compared Israel's raids on Lebanese terrorist bases to American bombing in Cambodia. Both 'imperialist acts of aggression.' The distorted analogy struck a part of me which was more basic than my identification with the New Left."[9]

Even among the most committed radicals, the events of May and June 1967 awoke emotions which overrode other concerns. Waskow, who would later be accused of fomenting anti-Israel propaganda, declared that in 1967, the Jewish community in Israel suddenly proved to be "ours."[10] The Six-day War, which evoked memories of the Holocaust for the older generation, made clear to their children what the Holocaust had been all about—not only the murder of six million human beings, but also their annihilation because of the fact that they were Jews. For the first time they now feared the possibility that there might not be an Israel, and it frightened them. They rejected the idea of a radical humanistic movement which had no room in it for a Jewish state. For many, the insight that as Jews they were still excluded came as a searing revelation.

Martin Jay Rosenberg, a senior at the State University of New York at Albany and a founder of the Jewish "underground" press, lashed out at American leftists "who put down everything Jewish," and particularly at "those Jewish students who are prepared to die for the Vietnamese, the Biafrans, the Greeks, and the Czechs, yet who reject Israel—they are our shame. The Jew must accept his identity. . . . A man who cannot accept his identity is a hypocrite and a liar when he pretends to accept someone else's." From that moment on, Rosenberg vowed, "I shall join no movement that does not accept and support my people's struggle. If I must choose between the Jewish cause and a 'progressive' anti-Israel SDS, I shall choose the Jewish cause. If barricades are erected, I will fight as a Jew."[11]

In a similar vein, Menachim S. Arnoni, who for a decade had published the sprightly *Minority of One*, declared that he had spoken out for the Cubans, the Puerto Ricans, the Algerians, the Guianans, the Angolans—now who spoke out for the Jews? All of his former allies now stood exposed: "Overnight many of my friends became enemies, partisans of the other side of the barricade. A whole world of associations collapsed around me. My former comrades, had they been pulling triggers instead of hitting typewriter keys, would have been shooting at me. What fervor they displayed in their new role as crusaders denying a small nation the right to exist! What enthusiasm! How much hidden bloodthirstiness suddenly found an outlet, sanctified by the 'progressive' equivalent of psalm and prayer! And how much Gentile anti-Semitism and Jewish self-hatred freed themselves from frustration and self-denial."[12]

Just how anti-Semitic the New Left actually was is hard to determine. Some critics have denied that Jew hatred actually constituted a part of the radical creed, but concede that it would have been only a short step to take from opposing Israel and Zionism to condemning Jews. Maurice Samuel, at the Arden House conference on the New Left, took a far more caustic view. "The New Left, so called," he declared, "is an old left in disguise with certain little gimmicks, *ota hagveret b'shinui aderet* [the same old hag in a new rag]. . . . Fundamentally or predominantly, the left was opposed to the existence of the Jewish people as a people, because it stood in the way [of their international program]." The fact that the words had changed, or that there was no uniformity within the movement, made no difference; those who stood on the far left were against the Jews.[13]

Whether or not, as Samuel claimed, anti-Semitism was an endemic feature of the political left, there is no doubt that by the late 1960s more than one leftist ideologue could be found preaching a barely disguised Jew hatred, and some, like Harold Cruse, a social critic and writer, did not even bother to hide their vitriol under the cover of anti-Zionism.[14] In response, many Jewish students, committed both to progressive causes and to the survival of Israel and Judaism, gradually split away from the movement's more radical leadership. Before the Six-day War, the Jewish New Left could easily have been described as Jews in New Left organizations. By the early 1970s, however, one could discern within the leftist framework a specifically Jewish grouping, consisting of individuals and organizations committed not only to the survival of Israel, but also concerned with problems of democracy within the American Jewish community. Like earlier Jewish radicals, they rejected the notion implicit in much leftist ideology that solution of economic inequities would solve the Jewish problem, with its assumption that "one of the payments Jews would make to the Left for having liberated them would be to disappear."[15]

Now one began to hear, not apologies for Israel, but defiant assertions of the Jewish state's legitimacy and of its centrality and meaning in Jewish life. "No Jew need rationalize his support of Israel," wrote Sleeper and Mintz. "And if the existence of Israel is a thorn in the side of the 'Third World,' then so be it. If the fact of Jewish self-rule in the Middle East serves 'imperialist' interests, let it. If the survival of Israel complicates matters for Soviet and American cold war strategists, that is their problem. It is not ours. After Auschwitz it is not in our province to lighten the burden of the superpowers. . . . Every Jew must join Israel in the struggle. He must see that for the Jew nothing changes. As Marxists and international bankers, millions of Jews were murdered by Hitler and Fascists. As imperialists, reactionaries, and capitalists, Jews are being murdered by Soviet Russians and their Arab puppets. Yesterday we stood in the way of Hitler and had to be removed. Today we stand in the way of the Soviets. And tomorrow . . ."[16]

The attempt to equate Auschwitz and Vietnam could now be seen for what it was, an empty and irrelevant analogy; indeed, if one sought historic parallels, the hysterical rantings of Arab leaders bore a frightening resemblance to Nazi proposals three decades earlier. And for many younger Jews, an old lesson was now being painfully learned anew. "We learned," wrote Bill Novack, "more dramatically than in any history class, the tragic lesson which seems to be the paradigm of the Jewish people: When it comes down to the crisis, we have only ourselves. . . . Yes, the New Left would save the Jew, we discovered, like it saved Spain, Greece, Czechoslovakia, and the six million."[17]

One could now find challengers to the leftist orthodoxy on such questions as the Arab desire for real peace and democracy. Where, asked Sol Stern, was the Arab equivalent of *Siach* [an Israeli leftist group seeking an accommodation with the Palestinians]? Where was there any evidence within the Palestinian movement of a sincere desire to come to terms with Israel, rather than a fanatic mania to destroy it?[18] When Arthur Waskow and Paul Jacobs, through their Ad Hoc Committee on the Liberation of Palestine and Israel, sought support for a series of pro-Palestinian advertisements in the *New York Review of Books* and the *Village Voice*, they found a number of previous sympathizers reluctant to participate in this new venture. Joseph McCarty, of Students for Peace and Justice in the Middle East, refused to sign because he found too many inconsistencies in Waskow's position, too many efforts to rationalize Arab intransigence and hostility.* Rabbis Arthur Lelyveld and A. Joseph Heckelman, while accepting the need for some resolution of the refugee plight, believed that the advertisements would not help achieve that goal but only cause divisiveness in the community. Especially after the murder of eleven Israeli athletes at the 1972 Munich Olympics, it seemed rather specious to talk of Arab democracy and a desire for peace.[19]

Early in 1970, a Radical Zionist Alliance sprang into being, with affiliates on seventy-five campuses. While aligning themselves with *Siach* and other Israeli critics of the Meir government, the Alliance "rediscovered" the radical strand in Zionism, and its members reprinted, studied, and quoted with enthusiasm the ideologues of early Socialist Zionism, Ber Borochov and Nachman Syrkin. From this group one began to hear that Zionism was nothing less than the national liberation movement of the Jewish people, and the true Jewish radical should become a Zionist. "Be a Zionist in the revolution," they proclaimed, "and a revolutionary in Zion." Critical of much of American communal life as well as of the Israeli government's alleged hard-line stand, the RZA epitomized what the Jewish New Left had become, but the existence of RZA was short-lived. Among other things, many RZA

* In one of their advertisements, Waskow and Jacobs wrote: "We think the Palestinians are entitled to self-government. At present, this urge toward self-determination sometimes expresses itself in the demand to abolish Israel and in acts of killing Israeli civilians. We deplore such demands and condemn such acts. Yet we would not penalize the whole Palestinian people for the acts of some Palestinian groups. We even dare hope that if all Palestinians were free to choose their own leadership with the promise of self-determination they would choose leaders who would negotiate with Israel. Present U.S. policy does not effectively protect either the lives and rights of Israelis or the lives and rights of Palestinians. We ask you to change that policy. We ask you to announce publicly that the goal of the United States is to assist the achievement of security and self-determination of all the people of the Middle East. We ask you to support the rights of Palestinians on both sides of the Jordan and Gaza for self-determination."

leaders made *aliyah* to Israel; with their loss the alliance soon foundered.[20]

*   *   *

Tied in closely to, yet distinct from, the attacks by the left was the upsurge in black hostility toward American Jews following the June 1967 war. While many Jewish liberals recognized that anti-Semitism had always been present in the far left, they were unprepared for the waves of black anger, because Jews had been prominent in the civil rights movement since the founding of the National Association for the Advancement of Colored People. Jewish philanthropists had played crucial roles in supporting several national black organizations, while Jewish attorneys had long been involved in the court battles leading up to the *Brown* case and beyond. In the freedom rides of the 1950s and 1960s, in the lunch counter demonstrations, in voter registration drives, Jews, more than any other segment of the white community, had turned out to work for the rights of black Americans to enjoy equality. In the most vicious episode of the southern struggle, three youths, two Jews and a black, had been killed and their bodies dumped in a dam.

But a whole complex of factors contrived to undermine what seemed to be understanding and co-operation between blacks and Jews. As early as 1946, Kenneth Clark had described the conditions that bred anti-Jewish feelings in black ghettos, and predicted that in the future such emotions would intensify.[21] Blacks often moved into deteriorating neighborhoods which had only recently been vacated by Jews, to find that the small shops and stores serving the area continued to be owned and operated by Jews. Undoubtedly, some economic exploitation took place, but blacks also found that Jewish merchants often extended them credit and served them as no other white men did. Many of the whites working in civil rights organizations were patronizing, and ultimately an authentic black movement would have to be able to stand by itself, free from the help and guidance of even the best-intentioned whites.[22] No other white group empathized with the blacks as did the Jews, themselves victims of centuries of persecution and bigotry, and no other group experienced such resentment at the turnabout of black militancy in the late sixties.

The nexus where the civil rights crusade, the peace movement, and other liberal and leftist causes came together was in the New Left. At the National Conference of the New Politics in Chicago in September

1967 blacks and radical anti-Semites joined forces in response to pressures which had been long building. The Watts riots of that year saw many Jewish-owned stores pillaged, and the year earlier a similar sacking had taken place in Philadelphia. A leader of the Philadelphia NAACP at that time had denounced Jewish leaders in the civil rights movement as "a bunch of phonies," and he berated the "thieving merchants" as the worst of the Negroes' exploiters. The only black-owned store to be burned in that city's riots, he noted, had been owned by a man named Richberg, because the looters thought he was a Jew.[23]

At that time, most American Jewish leaders tended to downplay black anti-Semitism as an aberration. I. F. Stone, still an acceptable figure among American Jewish liberals and intellectuals, wrote that "it will not hurt us Jews to swallow a few insults from overwrought blacks." Dore Schary, chairman of the Anti-Defamation League, warned against exaggerating fears of black-Jewish antagonisms, such as when the *Jewish Daily Forward* had described the Watts riots as a pogrom. The chairman of the National Jewish Community Relations Advisory Council insisted that Jews had a major stake in resolving the urban crisis and ought not to be diverted "because some Negroes are violent or ungrateful or anti-Semitic."[24]

But the consistency with which militant black leaders attacked Israel after the 1967 war could not be dismissed as isolated incidents. The newsletter of the Student Nonviolent Co-ordinating Committee began carrying virulent attacks on Israel and Zionists, and Ralph Featherstone, SNCC's program director, admitted that much of the material had been supplied by Arab embassies. He denied, however, that SNCC had become anti-Semitic; its sole target was "Jewish oppressors," whether in Israel or "those Jews in the little Jew shops in the ghettos." Placards sprang up in Harlem and other black areas identifying American Jews with the Israeli "killers of Middle East black people," and demanding that "Jews get out of Palestine, it's not your home anyway. Moses was the first traitor, and Hitler was the Messiah!!!" Harold Cruse condemned Israel as part of the world conspiracy against black people, and denounced American Jews as involved in an international plot aimed at keeping blacks enslaved. When the New Politics convention met that fall, the Black Caucus demanded as the price for its participation and co-operation with the white radicals the adoption of thirteen resolutions, one of which condemned the "imperialist Zionist war."[25]

The crescendo of intolerance continued to build. Cecil Moore demanded that American blacks rid themselves of "those Jews who claim draft deferments, raising the quota of our boys to die in Vietnam, but yet can raise ten million dollars to send to Israel and give up their draft deferments to go to Israel." Articles in the Black Muslim *Muhammed Speaks* repeatedly used such loaded phrases as "Israeli persecutors" and "Israeli occupation of Palestine," or spoke of "Nazi-like tactics exercised by the Zionists against the defenseless civilian population in the occupied Arab lands." Audia Masoud, the black publisher of *News-Gram,* deplored the Zionist readiness "to ply every advantage of the premeditated mass murder of untold thousands of Muslim Arabs," and also warned of alleged Zionist schemes to undermine African independence through "Zionist labor unions." The militant *Liberator* ran material in nearly every issue denouncing "Israeli aggression" and pledging fealty to the fanatics of the Syrian Ba'ath Party, supposedly the blood brothers of American blacks.[26]

(One of the great mysteries of this whole affair is how American blacks came to see Arabs as their brethren and allies. Arabs were the most important slave traders in East Africa, selling blacks not only to Europeans and Americans in the sixteenth and seventeenth centuries, but also to Arabia and other Muslim lands well into this century. When Zanzibar, once the leading slave market of the world, became independent in 1963, its black majority almost immediately rebelled against the ruling Arab elite, exiled the sultan, and massacred or deported thousands of Arabs, whom the blacks openly denounced as oppressors. As one reader of *Ebony* wrote, "For any black man to think of himself as being a natural ally of the Arabs is comparable to the final thread of the screw being turned. The Arabs, in league with the Portuguese, were the chief instigators and the main profiteers of the slave trade, the ones who set tribe against tribe in bloody massacre and then sat back and collected the human debris; the ones who raped and razed defenseless villages, enslaving men, women, and children, after slaughtering the aged, infirm, and those considered unsalable. Indeed, it was the Arab who showed the white man what a fortune could be made in black flesh. I do not see how any black brother with even a passing acquaintance with our history can proclaim himself in spiritual league with the Arab."[27])

The tensions burst out into full-scale conflict in the 1968 New York teachers' strike. A complicated matter involving teacher security, community control, urban politics, intrablack power struggles, and at least two dozen other issues, it pitted the predominantly Jewish United Federation of Teachers against black leaders for control of policy in several schools in black ghetto areas. Ironically, the UFT had an almost unblemished record on civil rights; its president, Albert Shanker, had marched in Selma, and the union had publicly backed many civil rights programs. The UFT, in fact, had originally proposed Ocean Hill-Brownsville as one of the experimental districts to try out decentralized community control. In the strike which paralyzed the nation's largest school system, the union repeatedly accused black leaders of anti-Semitism, and militant blacks, many of whom had no connection with the school system, in turn seemed willing enough to validate the charge. They flooded the city with leaflets carrying messages such as: "It is impossible for the Middle Eastern murderers of colored people to possibly bring to this important task [educating black children] the insight, the concern, the exposing of the truth that is a must if years of brainwashing and self-hatred that has been taught to our black children by these blood-sucking exploiters and murderers is to be overcome."[28]

The teachers' strike, which lasted fifty-seven days, did more than anything to polarize blacks and Jews, but in many ways it represented only the culmination of tensions which had been building for much of the decade. Not all blacks hated Jews, nor did all Jews detest blacks; it is doubtful if, aside from the militant extremists, many black people cared one way or another about Israel.† But the attacks on the Jewish state led a number of groups and individuals to withdraw their support from civil rights organizations. The American Jewish Congress led the walkout from SNCC, and ZOA president Jacques Torczyner urged a reassessment of American Jewish involvement in black affairs. Men like Theodore Bikel and Harry Golden, long active in civil rights, dissociated themselves not from the call for black equality, but from any organization that would raise up one group at the expense of another. Will Maslow, executive director of the American Jewish Congress, de-

---

† Shortly before he was assassinated, the Reverend Dr. Martin Luther King, Jr., met with a group of black students at Harvard. One of the young men happened to make some remark against the Zionists. King snapped at him: "Don't talk like that! When people criticize Zionists, they mean Jews. You're talking anti-Semitism." Other pro-Israeli black leaders included Bayard Rustin and the late Whitney Young.

clared that "there is no room for racists in the fight against racism. As
partners in the common struggle for social justice . . . the Jewish community has a right to expect that those who claim to seek equality will
neither give voice to nor tolerate anti-Semitism, publicly proclaimed or
privately whispered." Whether or not the confrontation with blacks
proved an "acid test" for Jewish liberals is debatable, but certainly the
schism between the two groups left American Jewry feeling a bit more
isolated and exposed as the decade came to an end.[29]

*   *   *

A third area in which American Jews felt their security weaken somewhat also followed the 1967 war, as they saw the much-touted "dialogue" with Christians nearly collapse.

Here again, as in the confrontation with blacks, a number of Christian leaders unequivocally supported the Jewish state. Cardinal Cush-
ing of Boston, Cardinal Shehan of Baltimore, and Bishop Hallinan of
Atlanta spoke out forcefully in Israel's defense, while noted Catholic
philosopher Jacques Maritain declared in no uncertain terms that anti-
Israelism and anti-Semitism were one and the same thing. The executive editor of *Christianity Today*, L. Nelson Bell, rejoiced when
Jerusalem was reunited, and claimed the event gave "a student of the
Bible a thrill and a renewed faith in the accuracy and validity of the
Bible." A voluntary fellowship, "Christians Concerned for Israel," pub-
lished an occasional newsletter and tried to counter both Arab and
Christian attacks on the Jewish state. But these were the exceptions,
not the rule.[30]

For the most part, Christians remained indifferent to Israeli and
Jewish fears during the 1967 crisis. The official Catholic position was
one of neutrality, as set forth by Archbishop Dearden of Detroit, the
president of the National Council of Catholic Bishops, in a call to "all
who believe in God to join in a crusade of prayer for peace throughout
the world," a call which avoided any mention of Israel's fate. The Reverend James L. Kelso, a former moderator of the United Presbyterian
Church who had worked in the Middle East for many years, wrote of
his horror "that great numbers of Christians in the United States applaud Israel's crimes against Arab Christians and Arab Muslims. How
can a Christian applaud the murder of a brother Christian by Zionist
Jews?" Malcolm L. Diamond noted that while many Christian laymen

supported Israel, the clerical leadership for the most part remained prisoners of Christianity's ancient hatred of Jews.[31]

Perhaps the most interesting example of this prejudice came from a wholly unexpected quarter. Most Jews expected the missionary churches, with their Arab members and Middle Eastern institutions, to be anti-Israel. But when the Quakers, long noted for ethical sensitivity and their courage to oppose unjust rulers, came out with their report *Search for Peace in the Middle East* (1970), its conclusions astounded both Jews and many of their Christian friends. The report distorted Middle Eastern history and assumed that only Arab refugees had been created by the birth of Israel; no mention at all was made of nearly seven hundred thousand Jewish refugees who had escaped or been driven from Arab lands and had been taken in by Israel. The Quaker task force, relying primarily upon Arab information and contacts, built up a case harshly critical of Israel, and ignored the historical train of events that had led to the emergence of the Third Jewish Commonwealth. This happened, wrote Franklin H. Littell, "because Christians are subconsciously accustomed to accept as normal the misery of Jews. Men of the Free churches, like men of the legally established churches, are riddled with ancient anti-Jewish prejudices which they have not even acknowledged—let alone repented of."[32]

All of this—the attack from the left, the schism with blacks, the faltering of the Christian dialogue—led to a growing sense of unease among many American Jews. A four-year study by the Anti-Defamation League released in April 1969 reported a far higher level of lingering anti-Semitism than many analysts had expected. According to the study, 37 per cent of the American people still retained negative images of Jews based on "old canards that Jews control international banking, engage in shoddy business practices, are too powerful, clannish, or ambitious." Should there be a severe economic dislocation, the survey found, more than 50 per cent of the respondents would vote for an anti-Semitic candidate.[33] This prejudice for the most part remained below the surface, but it cropped up often enough so that the American Jewish community once again saw bigotry as a distinct threat to itself. Sometimes it was innocuous, as when Judge Louis Levinthal's friends told him how they resented Jews picketing Japan Air Lines (after the 1972 Lod Airport massacre) and telling them which lines they should patronize. Sometimes it was more virulent, as when Norman E. Isaacs of the Louisville *Courier-Journal*, the first Jewish president of the

American Society of Newspaper Editors, criticized Vice President Spiro
Agnew's attacks on the press. Although Isaacs did not mention the anti-
Semitic undercurrent of many of Agnew's statements, he was inundated with hate mail attacking him as a Jew. Similar filth flooded into
the offices of newspapers and columnists across the country, all responding to that raw nerve of hate Agnew touched. As Eugene Borowitz
wrote, the "glow of the apparent American-Jewish cultural synthesis"
was suddenly dimmed by a recrudescence of fear and prejudice. For
Alan Miller, the conclusion was inescapable: "To be a Jew in the twentieth century is to be marginal. . . . There is no hiding place for the
Jews."[34]

The communal leadership, in the main, while alert to danger, preferred to minimize it. There had been no overt acts, no laws passed, no
sudden appearance of quotas. To call undue attention to the lunatic
fringe would only increase its relatively feeble strength. But for Rabbi
Meir Kahane, such a policy could only prove suicidal, a ghastly replay
of the illusions of security cherished by German Jewry in the early thirties. What had happened then could happen again, and American Jews
were deluding themselves to think otherwise. "We see what we wish to
see," Kahane wrote. "We believe what we wish to believe. The myth of
a melting pot and of honorable and subtle Jewish assimilation to escape
into a Land of the Free and Home of the Brave has been shattered a
thousand times over in the past decade. Our leaders assured us and we
were misled; it is time for an age of maturity and honest soul-searching.
The reality that is the American Jewish present and the specter that is
the American Jewish future must be looked at, with the proper amount
of honesty."[35]

Kahane demanded that Jews fight back, that they resist the small
pressures before large ones could be brought to bear. In the transitional
neighborhoods of Brooklyn, where pious Jews were frequently assaulted, his Jewish Defense League organized street patrols to guard the
area and deter would-be hoodlums. When news of fresh persecution of
Jews in the Soviet Union reached these shores, the JDL picketed the
Soviet embassy and may have been responsible for several bomb blasts.
He attacked the Jewish establishment for being blind, for being too
comfortable and secure, for being too afraid to speak out. He and his
followers cultivated their image of paramilitary defenders of Jewish
rights, and in assuming a tough posture played upon the vicarious
identification of American Jews with the tough Israelis. If the Israelis

surrounded by enemies in 1967 had been able to take care of themselves, why then could not American Jews handle domestic bullies? When dealing with "a Neanderthal type and a vicious anti-Semite," one did not reason—one fought.

Kahane touched a raw nerve in the late sixties. Alarmed by racial unrest, harried by the Left, afraid of potential anti-Semitism, still guilty over their failure to rescue the victims of the Holocaust, American Jews responded to Kahane's cry of "Never Again!" His extremism, his constant efforts to gain publicity, his distorted views of contemporary affairs, as well as his repudiation by the Jewish establishment and the apparent ability of the regular defense agencies to deal with problems effectively and quietly, ultimately led to the decline of the Jewish Defense League, while Kahane himself became little more than a shrill voice on the fringes of the community. Yet as Gerald Strober notes, Kahane raised questions about the character and quality of Jewish life in America which could not be easily dismissed, and he forced some American Jews, at least, to question whether their political attitudes, still attuned to the Roosevelt era, made sense during a Nixon presidency.[36]

*   *   *

The Nixon years proved to be strange ones for American Jewry. Traditionally liberal (in 1968, 81 per cent of American Jewry voted for Hubert Humphrey), they distrusted Richard Nixon. He had been too closely identified with the McCarthy witchhunts, he had been Eisenhower's Vice President and Kennedy's opponent, and he had absolutely nothing in his record to justify any sort of confidence in him. Yet he proved puzzling, for while he continued to be conservative on domestic issues, his foreign policy, so far as it affected Israel, appeared much more attractive.

The emergence of Henry Kissinger as architect of Nixon's foreign policy, first as presidential adviser and later as America's first Jewish Secretary of State, did little to reassure American Jews. While it was true that the German-born Kissinger had been a refugee from Hitler, he himself offered contradictory evidence of how it had affected him. Sometimes he said he could recall little overt anti-Semitism in his youth, while at other times, especially when trying to soothe Jewish leaders, he would declare that he could never forget what had happened to him and to his family. When Nixon nominated Kissinger to be Secretary of State the right-wing New Hampshire *Sunday News*, published by archconservative William Loeb, headlined an editorial entitled "Kissinger the Kike?" But the Jewish press was not particularly enthusiastic about him either. Marvin Schick, in his weekly column, noted that "the circumstances of Henry Kissinger's swearing in as Secretary of State did little to allay Jewish fears that his appointment does not auger well for our people. The ceremony took place on a Shabbos morning, a somewhat gratuitous bit of insensitivity, since it could easily have been held on another day. Mr. Kissinger took the oath of office with his hand resting on the King James Bible. The offensiveness of this act is both patent and inexcusable."[37]

Kissinger proved to be as much of a puzzle, if not more so, than Richard Nixon. At the top of Kissinger's priorities stood the goal of détente with the Soviet Union, an easing of Cold War tensions and of hot war potentialities; both sides would make accommodations and learn to live in peace, if not in love, with one another. Yet Moscow had become allied with the Arabs in their crusade against Israel. The Soviet Union armed the Arabs and the Palestinian guerrillas, and at every confrontation in the United Nations used its influence to prevent any castigation of the terrorists. In the Middle East, communist Russia's policy did not vary from that of czarist Russia—an opening into the Mediterranean and the establishment of a power base there, a strategy that now required co-operation with the "progressive" Arab states against "imperialist tool" Israel. Some analysts have asked whether in fact Russia really did desire the destruction of Israel. Such an event would have left the Arab nations independent of Russia, without any need for the massive arms aid she supplied, without any obligations to her. Moreover, as long as Israel existed, the Soviets could exploit the ties binding Israel and the United States in an effort to undermine American influence in the Arab world, a policy followed with great success after the 1967 war.[38]

Nixon shared Kissinger's vision of détente, and he felt free to pursue any policy leading toward it. Because Nixon owed so little to Jewish voters or contributors, he had few constraints to hinder his efforts to break the deadlock in the Middle East. He had conceded that the United States "stands by its friends and Israel is one of its friends," and he recognized that he could not pressure Israel into making concessions which endangered its security. But Nixon and Kissinger were willing to go much farther than Lyndon Johnson in cultivating good relations with the Arabs. Special emissary William Scranton toured the Middle East shortly after the 1968 election and promised the Arab states that a Nixon administration would pursue a more "even-handed" policy in the region. The State Department developed what came to be called the Rogers Plan in 1969, urging Israeli withdrawal from nearly all of the territory conquered in 1967 in exchange for peace, coupled with a declaration of a "balanced" American policy.[39]

The Rogers Plan failed not only because Israel refused to accept it, but also because the Arabs rejected it. The Soviet Union encouraged Nasser in his "war of attrition" and stepped up its arms supply. Moreover, Kissinger and Nixon had been aware that such a peace move might fail, leaving the United States with only Israel as a firm ally in the region. As Wallace Barbour, an experienced Middle East diplomat, told Nixon, "You know Israel may be a small horse, but it's the only horse we are riding with four sound legs."[40] So while Secretary of State Rogers was pressuring the Israelis, Kissinger quietly assured them that they would not be "punished" if they refused to give in. In mid-1971, for example, Rogers pushed Israeli ambassador Yitzhak Rabin to make "unilateral concessions" so that Egypt could reopen the Suez Canal, and even threatened to hold up the delivery of jet planes if Israel refused. When the Rogers-Rabin dispute broke into the open, Kissinger, with Nixon's approval, assured the Israelis that deliveries would continue.

In fact, the Kissinger-Rabin relationship played a crucial role in Israeli-American negotiations during these years. Rabin had been a student of Kissinger's in one of the international seminars the former Harvard professor had run. The two men met frequently, usually privately, yet the closeness of their ties surfaced just a few weeks before the 1972 election. At a gala concert of the Israel Philharmonic in Kennedy Center, Kissinger occupied the presidential box as Nixon's representative, and the grand tier was filled with prominent congressmen, journalists, lawyers, and government officials. When the concert ended, and everyone began filing out, Rabin and Kissinger were to be seen still standing in the presidential box, engaged in an obviously serious and earnest conversation. No one in the hall could miss this rare public display of the closeness between the two, and what it implied for Israeli-American relations.[41] But Rabin, as it turned out, came very close to openly interfering in American domestic politics in the 1972 elections.

The Republicans that year believed that it would be possible to break the long-standing Democrat lock on the so-called Jewish vote. George McGovern, the Democratic candidate, was considered to be not a liberal but a radical, and Jews were still smarting from the attacks made upon them by the New Left only a few years before. Following the seeming Russian betrayal of détente in sabotaging American peace efforts in mid-1970, the Nixon administration had agreed to Israeli requests for more tanks and Phantom jets, and in a series of well-publicized statements began asserting the need to maintain the balance of power in the Middle East—that is, of supplying Israel with materials to counter Russian aid to the Arabs. Prime Minister Golda Meir was welcomed by Nixon in an elaborate White House ceremony, and when she left, announced that the President had been very helpful in filling her "shopping list." When some American Jews later protested to her about her effusive praise of Nixon, she asked them whom they supported. "We are liberals," came the answer, to which Mrs. Meir replied, "Have you any liberals who can supply us with Phantoms? My business as Prime Minister is to ensure that we have Phantoms and that we have the answers to missiles and that if we are going to lose lives in the next war we have a chance to win."[42]

Nixon, who had practically been anathema to American Jewry, now emerged as a champion of Israel. He might never be a hero to American Jews, wrote one staffer in the Committee to Re-elect the President, but "they like what he's doing on Israel." Max Fisher, Rita Hauser, and Laurence Goldberg, who had previously led rather lonely political lives because they backed Nixon, now found they had many friends and allies. Taft Schreiber, the executive vice president of the Music Corporation of America and a loyal Republican, said, "I used to have trouble finding any supporters when I walked into the Hillcrest Country Club [the swank Jewish club in Los Angeles]. Now it's like everyone had a revelation. People come rushing up to me and say, 'I just want to tell you how I'm going to vote.' "[43]

The Republican Jewish strategy was simplicity itself: "Stick with Nixon and do not risk a fundamental change in United States policy toward Israel." And the Israelis endorsed this view. At one gathering of American and Israeli academics in Jerusalem that summer, an American historian was trying to explain his opposition to Nixon in terms of domestic policies, poor nominations to the Supreme Court, Vietnam, and other considerations. "That's irrelevant," come the reply from one Israeli. "He sends us Phantoms and tanks, and that's all that counts."

This attitude was understandable among the Israeli population, but it raised the hackles of American Jews when Israeli government officials began to voice it in a number of ways. "Nixon is our friend," the not too subtle message ran, "and we want him to remain in office. Nothing matters more to us than military aid from the United States. We ask you, as supporters of Israel, to subordinate any other concern." Ambassador Rabin, the architect of the 1967 military victory, traveled Washington's cocktail circuit openly endorsing the President, and in a radio interview told a reporter that friends of Israel "should reward men who support it, in deeds rather than in words." While Republicans were delighted with Rabin's statements, many American Jews, and some Israelis, were appalled at this undiplomatic gesture. The Jerusalem *Post*, in a front-page editorial, urged Rabin's recall for remarks which "have been construed as unwarranted interference in American politics." Rabbi Eugene Borowitz, while conceding that Israelis had no important interest in the election results and the right to make their views known, concluded that "the heavy, unrelenting pressure the Israelis have put on American Jewry to vote for Richard Nixon is utterly inappropriate to the issues and thoroughly demeaning to American Jewry." The Central Conference of American Rabbis, at its annual convention, passed a resolution viewing "with distress the reported intervention of Israel's ambassador to the United States into the coming presidential election."[44]

The normally astute Israelis had embarrassed American Jewry, and had done so in the most sensitive area imaginable. The old battle cry of the anti-Zionists had been that a Jewish state would lay claim to American Jewish loyalties and tell them how to behave, and now it had done so. The pro-Nixon statements and pressure forced American Jewish spokesmen to issue disclaimers about Israeli interference. Professor Mark Krug declared that if a candidate's support for Israel was the only criterion of interest to the Jewish voter, then "we will be branded by the American public as parochial, narrow partisans of a foreign state who lack interest in the fate of this country, and who in turn do not deserve much public attention."

The Israelis could also be faulted on their incredible lack of understanding and appreciation of American Jewry's political sophistication and acuteness. American Jews did not need the Israelis to point out to them what Nixon had done, nor that McGovern's record and attitude toward Israel did not seem very promising. Partisans within the com-

munity, aided by the well-financed Nixon re-election committee, were
perfectly capable of doing that. Nor did it ever appear that Nixon
would not win; only the most idealistic and dreamy-eyed optimist in
McGovern's camp gave him even an outside chance of defeating the
President.

In the end, nearly three times as many Jews cast their ballot for
Nixon in 1972 as had in 1968. He ran best among middle- and lower-
middle-class Jews and in neighborhoods which had experienced racial
strife, groups which responded like many other Americans to Nixon's
law-and-order campaign. In the Hassidic sections of Brooklyn, for example, Nixon ran up an incredible majority of 75 per cent of the vote.
Despite the fact that 60 per cent of the overall Jewish vote went to
McGovern, the ice had been broken. As columnist Victor Lasky wrote,
"Jewish hands did not fall off when they pulled Republican levers in
the polling booth." Republican analysts rejoiced, and Democrats feared,
that the more than fifty-year alliance of Jews and the Democratic Party
had begun to crumble.[45]

Looking back now, we can see this prognosis as premature. Many
Jews voted Republican less out of love for Nixon than out of fear of
McGovern, whose candidacy was seen by many as a departure from the
left-of-center liberal tradition and pro-Israel policies of Truman, Stevenson, Kennedy, Johnson, and Humphrey. They had not deserted the
Democratic Party; it had abandoned them. For the first time since 1924,
the Democrats had fielded a candidate totally alien from and unfamiliar
with Jewish political needs. Had a Humphrey or Jackson been the
Democratic candidate in 1972, there is little doubt that he would have
pulled a much larger percentage of the Jewish vote.

One can question whether, in such circumstances, Israeli interference had been at all effective. Only four years later, when Jimmy
Carter ran against Gerald Ford, the Israelis, this time much more
subtly, let it be known that they favored Ford, a known quantity, who
had more or less continued the Nixon policy, to Carter, a born-again
Christian who appeared to the Israelis and indeed to most American
Jews as an unknown and possibly dangerous entity. But Carter ran on a
moderately liberal platform, he went to great pains to cultivate the Jewish vote, and he assured American Jews that he understood and shared
their concerns about Israel. American Jews, as a result, flooded back to
the Democrats and gave Carter almost as high a percentage of their

votes as they had given Humphrey eight years earlier; in fact, the Jewish plurality in key industrial states provided Carter with his narrow margin of victory.[46] In 1972, then, all the Israelis had done was fire a blunderbuss when not even a pinprick was needed, and had added a further burden to an already harassed community.

Chapter 16

MISHPACHAH

If one were asked to sum up the relationship between Israel and American Jewry in just one word, the answer would have to be *mishpachah* (a Hebrew word meaning "family"). But it means far more than just consanguineal ties; when one talks about *mishpachah*, one conjures up a whole host of emotions and obligations. Family members may fight with one another, may hate each other as well as love, may go at one another tooth and nail, yet join together should any outside party threaten, may even at times ignore the family without being driven out. In the years following the June 1967 war, Israeli and American Jews constituted and recognized themselves as *mishpachah*, and demonstrated all the traits one would expect to find in so varied, opinionated, and contentious a family. Yet despite the many differences, they also shared a belief that from then on their destinies were intertwined, and as they faced their respective and common problems they did so with an awareness that they indeed constituted one people.

*   *   *

American Jews, despite the problems confronting them in the late 1960s, nonetheless still thought of themselves primarily as Americans, and did not see themselves as alienated from or rejected by American life. "After four generations," wrote Jacob Neusner, "to be Jewish is a mode of being American, taken for granted by Jews among other Americans, and no longer problematical." Eugene Borowitz also commented on how Jewish life in this country had changed in three decades: "Self-hatred, or at least ambivalence, dominated in the thirties, the decade of furtive changing of names, the straightening of noses, the suppression of accents and gestures, the cultivation of non-Jewish manners and non-Jewish approval. Though some of these symptoms are still to be found, negative attributes no longer characterize today's Jews. They are, on the whole, self-accepting. They know that they are Jewish, and assume that others know and respect them for it. And they do not hesitate to do some things, at least, that identify them with the Jewish community. Their children, too, are growing up with the notion that it is natural to be a Jew." Other commentators also noted that some of the overt signs of trying to assimilate, such as having a Christmas tree, had declined considerably. Instead of trying to hide their Jewishness, American Jews were now proud, at times even defiant, about their identity.[1]

Yet here again one must be careful in talking about American Jewry as a homogeneous whole. Depending on where one looked, and who did the looking, one could also find evidence that some Jews were falling away from the faith, not just acculturating but assimilating, swallowed up by the larger society, no longer identifying as Jews, perhaps even converting to Christianity. A full spectrum of choices now existed for the Jew in American society, ranging from living in a self-imposed pietistic ghetto to total assimilation, with countless way stations in between. Some termed themselves "Orthodox" and paid rote attention to some of the rituals, yet their daily lives showed very little commitment or devotion to Judaism; at the same time, some of those labeled "Reform," despite the abandonment of many traditions, identified strongly as Jews and worked to help keep the Jewish people alive.

Perhaps the greatest problem in this area was intermarriage, which, contrary to earlier projections, seemed to be sharply on the rise.* Some

---

* The definition of "intermarriage" varies according to the user. For some, an intermarriage is any union in which one party is Jewish and the other non-Jewish; others consider a situation in which the non-Jew converts to Judaism as also an intermarriage. Traditional Judaism, however, declares that once a person converts to Judaism, he or she must be accepted as a full Jew, and, indeed, very often the converted partner is more devoted to sustaining Jewish life than the born Jew who wears his or her Judaism more casually. For my purpose, intermarriage involves a non-Jewish partner who does not convert, since it is in these families that the children most often fall away completely from Judaism, frequently gravitating to one of the liberal Christian groups such as Unitarianism.

people estimate that between 1967 and 1973, the rate of intermarriage ran as high as 40 per cent, and predicted that if this trend continued the Jews in America would marry themselves out of existence. Compounding this problem is the fact that American Jews, reflecting their socioeconomic status, have seen a steady drop in their birth rate, until in the early 1970s they were barely reproducing themselves. Milton Himmelfarb, the editor of the *American Jewish Year Book,* has been the most persistent critic of this trend in American Jewish life. Jewry lost one out of three of its people in the Holocaust, and they have not been replaced. Why, Himmelfarb wants to know, have American Jews decided to be so conscientious about zero population growth? Why are they not out there having larger families in order to ensure the survival of the Jewish people? Only the very Orthodox are obeying the biblical injunction to be fruitful and to multiply, and he predicts that within a generation or two only the Orthodox will be left of American Jewry. Everyone else will have intermarried, and one will have a community of pietists in which the *Habad* Hassidim will be the liberal left wing.[2]

Himmelfarb's jeremiads are reflected in the more sober and scholarly analysis of Daniel Elazar, who is acknowledged as the leading contemporary authority on the structure of the American Jewish community. According to Elazar, American Jewry can best be described as a series of concentric circles, uneven in size, with a central magnet of those totally committed to "Jewishness," the very Orthodox who have completely rejected any integration into American life lest their Judaism be endangered, as well as those who are committed Jews, but still live and function in an accepted American milieu. Going out from this core one finds those actively involved in "Jewish rhythm." Then there are those who are affiliated but less active, and beyond them, various circles of those who identify as Jews, but are not actively involved in Jewish communal or religious affairs. At the periphery are the very marginal Jews, those who do not know or care if they are Jewish, people who are intermarried with a nonconverted partner, and the children of such marriages who have no Jewish background at all. Like Himmelfarb, Elazar also predicts that within the next two generations, forces in American life will increase the centrifugal pressures, pushing more and more Jews away from the inner circles toward marginality, and from there on to assimilation.[3]

It is this confluence of trends that began to worry Jewish leaders most acutely in the late 1960s. With a low birth rate, a community can survive, even prosper, providing it retains all or nearly all of its offspring. But if it is going to lose many of its children and even more of its grandchildren through intermarriage, and still have a low birth rate, then its future is bleak indeed. Yet intermarriage, aside from its implications for Jewish survival, must also be seen as the ultimate mark of belonging. Sociologists measure the degree of acceptance of an ethnic or cultural minority within the host society by the level of intermarriage between the two. A low level means that the majority looks down upon the minority as outsiders, as inferior; when they allow their children to marry the newcomers' children, then equality and acceptance are much more complete.[4]

But acceptance also means assimilation, the absorption of one group by the other, and here we have one of the central dilemmas of American Jewish life. For centuries, Jews have been on the outside, scorned and rejected. Now a predominantly Christian society has said that religion is a private matter, that Jews can and will be accepted, that the choice will be theirs, and to prove the sincerity of that pledge, the children may intermarry. How alluring is this vision! Indeed, it was no longer a vision, but an all too evident reality, with its implicit and logical development leading to the end of American Jewry as a separate and distinct group.

American Jews could protest against this trend as *Jews*, but as *Americans* they could hardly object to the idea of total acceptance and equality. There are two sides of the intermarriage problem. One is the Jewish side, where Jews feel that somehow they, as Jews, have failed in communicating to their children, in teaching and making them understand that being Jewish is a very precious heritage, that it is worth suffering for, that millions died for it, that being apart, being separate is not too high a price to pay to be the bearer of such a noble tradition. But American Jews are also very much American, and their predominant value system is an amalgam of Jewish teachings and American democratic norms. They have not rejected America, but see themselves as part and parcel of this society. They are consciously American, and the very troubles besetting them as Jews are also a mark of their acceptance and acculturation within American society.

It is indeed a dilemma, one recognized by many, if not most, American Jews. On the one hand, they do what they can to prevent assimilation. Reform rabbis, who for many years were willing to officiate at such unions, voted not to do so anymore. When some zealous Christian

students at Yale formed a group to proselytize among the Jews, some of
the Jewish students took out an ad in the school newspaper declaring
they "would rather fight than switch." At the annual Easter egg-rolling
on the White House lawn, the small son of one government official
showed up with a jar of matzoh balls, declaring, "After all, it's Passover,
too." One rabbi was amazed that his daughter openly read her Hebrew
books on the bus to school each morning. "When I was a kid," he
recalled, "I kept my Hebrew books under my coat, even if the bus was
filled with Jews. You just didn't do things like that in America in those
days."[5] In the years following the Six-day War, more and more Jewish
parents, even those with minimal Jewish background and knowledge,
enrolled their children in Jewish day schools. For them, and for most
American Jews, it still seemed possible to preserve one's Jewish
identification as an active and open member of American society.

One no longer talked of America tolerating Jews, nor even of a
triadic division within the society. Jews not only had entered American
life, they had also become an active force in shaping and molding it.
Jewish words and phrases crept into the common vocabulary until, like
the words and phrases of earlier immigrant groups, they became
American words. When Walter Kerr reviewed a musical based on Leo
Rosten's *Education of H*Y*M*A*N K*A*P*L*A*N*, he marveled
at how these earlier immigrants and their ways had not so much disappeared as had entered and become a part of the mainstream; they
were no longer the outsiders, but flesh and bone of the nation. American literature seemed dominated by Jewish writers and critics such as
Saul Bellow, Norman Mailer, Herman Wouk, Philip Roth, Leon Uris,
Lionel Trilling, and Irving Howe, to mention only a few. Yet only in
rare instances could their works properly be described as Jewish; they
wrote about American situations and subjects, some of which were
Jewish.[6]

On campuses all over the country, new departments and programs
in Judaic Studies grew rapidly, and few questioned their legitimacy
within the framework of either private, nonsectarian (or at times even
Christian) schools or at state-supported universities. Indeed, if one
wanted to look for young American Jews, one automatically turned to
academe. No other group in the nation sent so many of its children to
college. While only one fourth of the general population in 1971
twenty-five years or older had some college training, 54 per cent of all
Jews in that range had some higher education; in fact, projections

showed that by 1985, one half of all American Jews under sixty-five would not only have gone to college, but would have graduated. While there, they would have been taught by a large number of Jewish professors. Prior to the Second World War, discrimination had kept most Jews out of jobs in higher education; yet a study by Lipset and Ladd found that while only 3 per cent of the national population, Jews composed one tenth of all faculty members, and one sixth of those at the major research-oriented institutions. In a survey to determine the nation's top seventy intellectuals, the quarterly *Public Interest* produced a list which was half Jewish.[7]

And yet, as one rabbi asked, "What becomes of our individuality, our unique Jewish identity? Are we really prepared to give that up because of some indefinite synthesis that may not even exist?" Can one resolve that dilemma, to be both intensely Jewish and intensely American? Could an American Jewry have a long-range future, could it survive without hostile forces bearing in on it, forcing it to seek strength and courage from its inner Jewish resources? Could they develop, in time, a new theology which spoke to their needs not only as Jews but also as Americans? Or would it happen, as Daniel Elazar feared, that those Jews who chose to be active and full members of American society would reach a point where they would have to limit their involvement as Jews, and following that, give up their Jewishness?[8]

Even the existence of Israel, which had become so central in American Jewish life, could not resolve this problem completely, but in many ways only exasperated it. Some critics saw the adulation accorded to the Jewish state as undermining a real religiosity. Daniel Elazar coined the phrase "Israelolotry," signifying that worship of Israel, and not Israel's God, had seemingly become the central facet of Jewish life in the Diaspora. Israel Knox denounced this obsession with Israel as a modern form of idolatry, a perversion of Judaism that exalted "a piece of space with magical powers." The chairman of the governing council of the World Jewish Congress, Rabbi Joachim Prinz, warned that spiritual Judaism in the United States was headed for extinction, and the two main causes were intermarriage and the preoccupation of American Jewry with Israel.[9]

One way in which this preoccupation could be seen was in the priorities determined by the national fund-raising groups. The National Jewish Community Relations Advisory Council prepared a master plan in early 1973, listing what it considered the main issues facing American Jewry. The extensive list included concern for Soviet Jewry, social justice at home, amnesty for war resisters, civil rights, anti-Semitism, Jewish security, church-state relations, and many others, including, of course, Israel. Moreover, this list also reflected the fact that the American Jewish community had discovered in the late sixties that there were indeed a large number of Jewish poor, many living in older, run-down neighborhoods in the inner cities. Yet in its budgetary request to the Large City Budgeting Conference of the Council of Jewish Federations and Welfare Funds, the advisory council indicated that in the previous year, 65 per cent of all its expenditures had gone to just two beneficiaries, Israel and Soviet Jewry, and that in future years it expected the percentage of Israel-related funds to increase.[10]

Perhaps in no other area, however, did Israel prove so negative an influence as in one which many had hoped would be a bridge between the two communities: religion. Most orthodox Jews could accept the religious Zionist view of the establishment of the Third Jewish Commonwealth as a "beginning of redemption." But even for them, Israel could be a holy land only if it were governed by the Torah. If Israel could not be made into a Torah-true state, then it would be a sacrilege at worst and an irrelevancy at best. The Torah-true Jew would continue to live his life, either in Israel or in America, as he had always done—observing the commandments, studying Talmud, and praying for God to redeem man.[11]

Reform and Conservative Judaism departed from this essentially timeless milieu, in the belief that man had to live in the present, had to deal with contemporary problems and situations. The ultimate test of this belief would be whether they could adapt traditional Jewish beliefs, as expressed primarily in the ethical teachings of the prophets, in a way which would be meaningful and fulfilling in a free and modern society. Conservative Judaism was not as willing as Reform to undergo radical departures from ritual, and in many eyes, has remained primarily the left wing of orthodoxy. The Orthodox, in turn, have condemned Conservatives for not being fully Jewish, but have considered them as Jews, whereas they have often condemned Reform Jews as apostates. The ultra-orthodox Agudas Yisrael have gone even farther, and see both Conservative and Reform Jews as totally fallen away from the true faith.

By the midsixties, Reform leaders in the United States had grown increasingly resentful of the Israeli rabbinate's refusal to concede the authenticity of Reform. In 1964, the CCAR executive board had adopted a strong resolution deploring "the fact that non-Orthodox religious leaders are denied legal status which would permit them to officiate at such religious rites as marriage. We also deplore the harassment by the representatives of Orthodox Jewry of those wishing to worship in other than Orthodox forms. This infringement on religious liberty is contrary to the true nature of historic Judaism." Citing the success of the American system of church and state separation, they urged the Israelis to adopt a similar policy, one which would enhance voluntary religious observance and guarantee individual freedom.[12]

The problem confronting non-Orthodox Jewry revolved around the status of Orthodox Judaism as a quasi-established state religion in Israel. The national and local governments supported synagogues and rabbis; the government decreed that in all personal matters, such as marriage and divorce, Halachic rules would be enforced; and the chief rabbinate and its subordinate councils, all staffed by Orthodox rabbis, would be the final arbiters in Halachic disputes. Only those rabbis recognized by the rabbinical councils could perform religious duties in Israel, and the Orthodox made sure that no Conservative or Reform rabbis were recognized.

As Zalman Abramov has made so poignantly clear, the dilemma of traditional Jewry is that its codex is derived primarily from the experience of centuries in exile, where the Jewish communities deliberately avoided any contact with the civil authorities. The Talmud, the *Shulhan Arukh,* the comments of Maimonides, deal mainly with man's relation to man or to God, and only incidentally if at all with man's relation to a state. Jewish legal codes, however, had not always been eternally fixed. Essentially, the Talmud is an effort to take the strictures of Torah and interpret them to apply to a different time and place; the famed rabbis of Babylon often came up with some interesting devices to mitigate unnecessary suffering created by strict adherence to the letter of the law. Tragically, the spiritual leaders of Israel were afraid to engage in similar innovation, to try to bring the ancient principles to bear on modern problems and conditions. The Orthodox, led by the pietist wings, declared that no changes would be made; if it came to a choice of preserving the law or preserving the state, all would preserve the law.[13]

The Israeli rabbinate found the adaptations made by Conservative

and Reform Jewry in the United States unacceptable. Jews had lived
and suffered and died for centuries in defense of the Law, and now that
they had returned to the land, why should they abandon that which
had preserved them for so many centuries? Moreover, they did not see
these innovations as strengthening Judaism in America, but weakening
it. Like all fundamentalist groups, they saw strength only in uniformity; there were no varieties of Judaism, but only one Judaism.
Since the ruling Labor Party always needed the Religious Party as a
partner in its coalition governments, the rabbinate easily secured its
minimal demands for a free hand in the administration of religion as its
price for supporting Labor's foreign and other domestic policies.[14]

The 1967 war increased the desire of American Reform Jews to become tied more closely to Israel. Rabbi Bertram Korn, visiting Israel
shortly after the war, wrote to his congregants of his feelings when he
had been called to the Torah at the HUC chapel. "The Haftorah portion from Isaiah made referene to Jerusalem—not a far-away place
but right here. I was simply and literally overwhelmed by the reality of
history and the presence of God during the service."[15] To demonstrate
its solidarity with Israel, the World Union of Progressive Judaism held
its 1968 international convention in Jerusalem, the first time that body
had met in Israel. The Reform group was widely welcomed by government leaders, but met only cold hostility from the official rabbinate.

The great gulf dividing Jew from Jew became painfully apparent
when the convention committee announced its intention of holding a
prayer service at the Western Wall, a service to be conducted in the
Reform manner, with men and women praying together. Rabbi Zerah
Warhaftig, the Minister of Religious Affairs, announced that he would
not permit such a service. Speaking for the Orthodox, he angrily announced, "It is an incontrovertible law that men and women must not
pray together at the Wall." Many secularist Jews in the country were
outraged that fellow Jews should be the victims of such blatant discrimination in, of all places, the Jewish state. The issue reached the floor of
the Knesset, the Israeli parliament, where it was referred to a special
committee. Despite efforts by government leaders to reach some sort of
compromise, the Orthodox held firm. During the debate, the Agudas Israel newspaper *HaModiyah* called Reform Jews "traitors to their people, their land, and their God," and suggested that they "build a wall
near one of their temples and go pray there with their wives and
mistresses." The ultra-orthodox groups threatened to block physically

Reform access to the Wall. On the morning of the scheduled prayer meeting, the Reform leaders, in order to avoid bloodshed and further embarrassment to the government, canceled the service at the Wall.[16]

Such encounters can only cause divisions between Jew and Jew both in Israel and in the United States. Orthodox Jews in America, despite their familiarity with the workings of a pluralistic society, agree in principle with the Israeli rabbinate's policy that there can be only one Judaism.[17] Moreover, even secular Jews in Israel see Orthodoxy as authentic Judaism, even if they themselves do not follow its precepts. Despite claims by Reform and Conservative leaders that Israelis would flock to non-Orthodox synagogues if only they had a chance, this contention lacks proof.[18] The handful of Conservative and Reform synagogues in Israel are attended primarily by American *olim* and have been notably unsuccessful in attracting native-born Israelis. The secular Jews display the same contempt as the rabbinate toward non-Orthodox varieties of Judaism; they protested the Wall incident not out of identification with Reform as Jews, but out of their secularist concern for individual freedom. Until a significant Conservative or Reform presence can develop in Israel, either through *aliyah* or through the attraction of native-born Israelis, there appears little chance that either movement will be able to challenge Orthodox domination of Israeli religious life.

* * *

The struggle between Orthodox and non-Orthodox Jews occurred in, as it were, a remote corner of American-Israeli relations. Aside from the leaders of the Reform and Conservative movements, few American Jews took part in the debate, because it really did not affect them. They saw themselves as Americans, and as such did not accept the Halachic rulings of the Israeli rabbinate as applicable to them. Secure in their status in this country, they could afford to ignore such tirades as those of Yitzhak Ben Aharon when he derided American Jews as still living in *galut*. "There are no Jews and there are no Jewish congregations," he charged, "under whatever conditions they live, if they have gold and silver and dreams and equality and all other good things, and destitution and sanctity and purity—it is all *Galut!* Whatever is not Israel, what is not *Eretz Israel* is *Galut!*"[19] The debate over Zion and *galut* had lost all immediacy and relevancy for the vast majority of American Jews.

There remained, of course, the question of *aliyah*, and it would continue as long as Israel needed men and women to build its society. But even here a more relaxed attitude could be seen. Some Zionist leaders began to talk about *aliyah* less in terms of individual obligations than as a primary organizational goal. Israel's Moshe Rivlin, in addressing a Brooklyn Hadassah group, said that he did not share Ben-Gurion's notion that any person who did not move to Israel could not be called a Zionist. "I subscribe to another thesis," he said, "that any Zionist organization whose chief concern is not *aliyah* is not a Zionist organization. I do not know whether we can impose *aliyah* as an individual duty. It is a fact that such an obligation was never imposed upon Zionists, even in the most glorious days of *chalutziyut* (pioneering). We must create a Zionist climate, an atmosphere that enourages *aliyah,* in which *aliyah* is not taboo." Such a climate did seem to be growing in this country, an attitude which Marshall Sklare found in such repeated statements as "While I would not consider *aliyah* for myself, there is no denying that life in Israel has much to recommend it," or "I've been to Israel and I can understand how someone could be very happy there."[20] Drugs, urban crime, the New Left, and other American conditions made life in Israel in the late sixties look more attractive than ever before. In the years between the 1967 and 1973 wars, more than thirty thousand Americans moved to Israel.

The new emphasis would be on youth, where idealism still existed and where one could yet instill love of Zion and more extensive Jewish learning. Hadassah decided that youth work at home would become a major activity of the organization, and began spending over a million dollars annually on Zionist camps and other programs aimed at young people. Impressed by the high percentage of Jews in the Peace Corps, the Zionist organization stepped up its Sherut La'am program to give young men and women an opportunity to serve Israel on a temporary basis. For a number of observers, the idealism of American youth recalled the spirit of sacrifice of the early settlers in Palestine; if only they could be induced to come, then perhaps a new spirit of *chalutziyut* could be rekindled in the Jewish state. In one study of young American *olim,* a group of Sherut La'am volunteers who decided to stay in Israel, idealism and a high sense of Jewish identification seemed to have been the paramount factors in their decision.[21]

The only fly in the ointment was the Israeli failure to develop better immigration procedures. A new Cabinet-level department, the Ministry of Immigration Absorption, was created in 1968 to facilitate the integration of *olim* into Israeli society and to eliminate the previously overlapping functions of government and Jewish Agency programs. Over the next several years, the new ministry proved to be a dismal failure, incompetently staffed, totally unfamiliar with the needs and attitudes of Western immigrants, and, at times, downright apathetic. The new American *olim* represented just that type of educated, technologically sophisticated Jew which Israeli society so desperately needed. They expected to be given accurate information on what life would be like in their new land, a realistic appraisal of the problems which would confront them, and some help in overcoming these early obstacles. Instead they were told, and believed, that they would receive a red-carpet treatment.

Their first experience with Israeli bureaucracy was, in the words of one *oleh*, "a seeming nightmare of inefficiency. Due to Shabbat we were kept standing in line for hours on end (with friends and relatives waiting on the piers) while innumerable officials applied rubber stamps to endless pieces of bureaucratic paper. By 11:00 P.M., we were finally disgorged amidst cries of hundreds of wailing children to spend the next few hours trying to find the pieces of hand baggage that had been strewn around at random. Finally the waiting busses and taxis took us to our destinations—our group arrived at the camp in Netanya at 3:00 A.M.! Lest you think that taking the plane will spare you all this—a South African family complained that when they arrived, well after midnight at Lod [airport], they were greeted by munching and tea-sipping officials, who casually and very deliberately attended to the *olim*'s affairs after finishing their repast. My friend was ready to take the next plane back to South Africa—except there wasn't any."

In fact, a large number of the Americans did return home, although no exact figures are available. Yet Jewish Agency officials, the most persistent in their demand for Western *aliyah*, casually dismiss the problem of immigrants who leave. "We don't know how many American *olim* are leaving every year and we don't worry about them," one investigator was told. "They'll be back again, they come and go." Even if this were true, which is doubtful, obviously many Americans who have come on *aliyah* do not integrate into Israeli society. In many cases the fault is the individual's; all immigrations, including the great nineteenth-century waves to the United States, had sizable numbers of people who chose to return to the old country. But given the Israeli need for *olim,* such a cavalier attitude can hardly help keep American Jews there.[22]

But criticism of Israel in these years did not surface very frequently, a situation which would have serious repercussions after the Yom Kippur War. There seemed to be an unwritten rule in the American Jewish community that one did not criticize, or even question, Israeli actions and policies. "If there is one sure way to turn off a Jewish congregation," noted one rabbi, "it is to attack Israel, even affectionately." Eugene Borowitz charged that one of the worst things ever done by Zionism and by Israel was "to give us another topic in America which cannot be debated. We now have a subject on which no arguments are allowed, no criticism. A new sacred cow is introduced. Open your mouth in a Jewish audience to raise a question critical of the State of Israel, critical of Zionism, and if you're talking with Israelis, that's all right; if you're in the State of Israel and getting into an argument, that's all right; but to an American Jewish audience you are not allowed to say anything bad about the State of Israel. It is assumed either that you are a paid agent of Mao Tse-tung or of the American Council for Judaism or that there is something the matter with you as a Jew."[23]

Yet things were not all that well in Zion, as was becoming increasingly obvious to many sincere Jews who loved Israel yet found it difficult to defend the Jewish state constantly. Jerome Grollman summed up the anguish of many when he finally gathered his courage and wrote of American Jewry's responsibility to reprove Israel: "Some years ago after my first visit to Israel, in a conversation with my father . . . I mentioned a few things about Israel that disturbed me. My father listened patiently and then responded, 'But you wouldn't say anything that would hurt Israel, would you?'

"The impact of my father's comment was overpowering. Subsequently, I assiduously refrained from discussing anything that might reflect adversely upon Israel. When that was totally unavoidable, I would invariably apologize and minimize the issue.

"This, of course, is the posture that most of us have adopted because we are deeply devoted to Israel and are dedicated to its survival and well-being. I submit, however, that for those of us who are *Hovevai Tzion* (lovers of Zion), rather than hurting her, we help Israel grow and fulfill its sacred destiny when we speak critically out of the honesty of our convictions. . . .

"There are those who are passionately dedicated to Israel who have on occasion lifted their voices and suggested that all is not as well in Jerusalem as it should be. They have spoken in sincerity, but have been branded as traitors to the Jewish people. Yet Jeremiah and Isaiah and Amos were critical of their fellow Israelites and the ruling circles, and we read their utterances regularly on *Shabbos* morning. The time has come when honest criticism should not be labeled betrayal."[24]

The silence was, of course, not universal. Some American Jews did speak out against the Israeli raid on the Beirut Airport, against the bombings of Palestinian camps, against the shooting down of an Arab airliner over the Negev, against the seeming Israeli intransigence in peace negotiations. But for the most part, an unhealthy attitude permeated American Jewry in the late sixties and early seventies. Perhaps because Israel was under attack from so many other sources, it seemed unfair to burden it still further with complaints from within the family. Perhaps American Jews were in such awe of the Israelis, those giants who had conquered their enemies so brilliantly, that they could not say anything against them. Perhaps as tens of thousands of American Jews visited Israel for the first time, the beauty and excitement and Jewishness of the land led them to ignore, deliberately, anything less than perfect. Perhaps, after centuries of persecution and despair, no one wanted to utter a single syllable which might destroy this magical moment of power and strength.

American Jews glorified Israel, adored its military heroes, studied its history and geography, and some even went on *aliyah*. But they did not speak openly with Israel, they did nothing to deflate the growing arrogance both in Israel and in the United States, an arrogance that would be toppled in October 1973. Nor was this the fault of American Jews alone; Israel did not want to hear bad news either. For six years Jews in Israel, in America, and elsewhere wanted only to enjoy the military prowess of the Israeli army, the country's booming economy, its new stature in the world, and deluded themselves that all was well and would continue to remain that way. Golda Meir, after she left office, conceded that while it had been nice to believe all that, the Israelis knew better, and should have engaged in debate and dialogue and criticism; it might have precluded that arrogant pride which affected so many Jews before Yom Kippur 1973.[25]

And there were things to discuss, for in the aftermath of the 1967

war the ties which bound Israel and American Jewry together had not
only become stronger, but also had taken on a new tone, and it was far
from clear just what this meant. Irving Horowitz, for example, questioned whether in fact the Israeli victory meant a greater or lesser unity
of the Jewish people. With the Jewish state able to stand on its own
feet, might its relations with Diaspora Jewry change to become more
like that of other nations and their dispersed minorities, such as Italy
and Italian communities in America and elsewhere; instead of American Jewry worrying about its *responsibilities for* Israel, perhaps it
should start looking more to the question of its *freedom from* Israel.
Ehud Ben Ezer also noted that in the eyes of the world, there seemed
to be less and less differentiation drawn between Israelis and Jews.
While this, of course, gave comfort to those who believed in the concept of all Jews constituting a single people, *am Yisrael*, it could prove
detrimental if Diaspora Jews were to be held responsible for the actions
and policies of Israel.[26]

Had Israel itself somehow changed? Had victory, a phenomenon
unknown in Jewish history since the days of the Maccabees, altered the
self-image of the Israelis in a negative manner? One could understand
the joy, even the headiness, which followed in the wake of the war, but
there was also a tone of despair, of defiance, a recognition that even in
victory, Israel remained besieged. Yael Dayan, a young Israeli novelist,
noted that the war had not brought peace, but did provide security, and
if one had to choose between the two, Israelis would opt for security.
But this implied that Israel could never become the "normal" state of
the Zionist dreams, nor the embodiment of Jewish hopes. For centuries
Yavneh, the symbol of learning, had sustained Judaism; now Masada,
where Jews had chosen self-destruction rather than slavery, stood as the
ensign of the Jewish state. But Masada, despite its message that Jews
should live free or die, represented a dramatic departure from the biblical commandment to choose life; it implied a fatalistic attitude that
there were no other options, no other avenues open to the Israelis, that
Jews everywhere would abandon life before they would return to the
ghettos of depression and despair. Two poems illustrate this defiant yet
fatalistic note that now intruded more and more into the Jewish consciousness. One, by Yehuda Amichai, acknowledged the continuity between past and present generations of Jews, yet accepted as a given
the idea that Jews would always have to fight, that they could never
live in peace and freedom.[27] Four years later, in 1972, Stanley

Cooperman declared that Jews were tired of dying, that they would fight, but somehow, he expected that in the end the result would be the same:[28]

> The function of a Jew
> is to die.
> That is his function;
> that
>   was
> his function. We have come home
> and if we die
> it will be without your permission,
> and without your love;
> we have tasted your love
> and it burned us . . .
> it flows through the world
> like a sewer of used blood.
>
> Listen: our hands are no longer empty
> and our dreams
> are of olive groves,
> oranges
> planted on the edge of despair;
>
> if we die
> it will be here,
> if we die
> it will be as the lion dies
> protecting his young.

Perhaps, as Israeli novelist Amos Oz observed, the Israelis, like Jews everywhere, could not shake off the memory of the Holocaust. "Every day we fight the Arabs and win," he told Joseph Kraft. "Every night we fight the Nazis and lose." As Irving Horowitz commented on this, the *Israelis* have the victories, but the *Jews* continue to suffer defeats. American and Israeli Jews might well ponder if under such circumstances it would ever be possible to build the idealized state of the Zionist dreams.[29]

No one even thought of abandoning Israel; one did not desert *mishpachah*. But one could have questioned whether or not Diaspora Jewry should have tied itself so emotionally to Israel. Was it a good thing for American Jews to feel, as Irving Howe confessed, that if Israel were to perish, then so would contemporary Judaism? Where would one then find the saving remnant? Could the pietistic communities of Crown Heights, still wrapped in a world of long ago, survive and sustain the driving intellectual and moral force of the Jewish people if there were no Jewish state? Rabbi David Polish affirmed that when Israel is in mortal danger it unquestionably dominates our concerns. "But when a community like American Jewry is struggling to preserve itself politically and to save itself spiritually—yes, [even] with Israel's help—to advise such a community that it must take its lead from Israel, is to contribute to and hasten the process of disintegration." Should the Diaspora, especially in the United States, go into decline, Israel itself would be bereft, "a center without a periphery." Polish did not want to cut the ties between Israel and American Jewry, but even though he believed, more than did most American Jewish leaders, in the concept of *galut*, he saw the continued existence of the Jewish people as dependent upon both a strong Diaspora as well as a strong Israel.[30]

All of the old assumptions—about the meaning of Judaism, the importance of a Jewish homeland, the unity of the Jewish people, the continuity of the Diaspora—all had to be re-examined, even if, in the end, we only confirmed our original beliefs. Sometimes one would merely be covering old ground, rediscovering old truths; Albert Memni, the brilliant Algerian Jewish writer, in effect did little more than reinvent Pinsker's "Auto-Emancipation," but he did so for a new generation which had forgotten Pinsker. Could any foreign state be a spiritual and cultural center for millions of people living outside of it, as Ahad Ha'am had projected? Absolutely not, said Eliezer Schweid; one could not feed passively, one could not imbibe nourishment *in absentia*. Yet Jews did just that for centuries, dreaming and yearning for a rebuilt Zion. Perhaps Horace Kallen was right—an ideal realized is an ideal corrupted.[31]

*   *   *

One place a debate did continue was within and about the Zionist movement. Indeed, how else would one know if Zionism were still alive without this constant squabbling? What were the duties of a Zionist? Why did not American Zionists make *aliyah*? What would the functions of the organization be in the future? These were all the old questions, not yet resolved not likely to be, as long as American Zionists and Israelis each looked at these problems through different sets of spectacles, as it were, representing the differing attitudes and values and experiences of each country.

In part, one thought that by the early seventies there would be a bridging of this gap. Israeli society, for one thing, had become increasingly Americanized. A public-opinion poll taken after the 1967 war indicated that two thirds of the country considered American culture the most important foreign influence on their lives. American programs dominated Israeli television, while American magazines, books, and technical and professional journals overflowed in Israeli bookstores. In the universities, the majority of Israelis who took advanced degrees abroad went to the United States, while a high percentage of visiting scholars, as well as the largest bloc of foreign students, came from the United States. English was widely accepted as the common medium of international communication, both in business and scholarship. Israeli intellectuals read American-produced scholarly works, even in the specialized realm of religious studies, and were familiar with leading Jewish "middle brow" journals such as *Midstream, Commentary, Judaism,* and others.

This was true not only of the higher culture, but of the popular culture as well. Israeli children flipped bubble-gum cards (substituting, of course, Israeli soccer stars for American football and baseball players), while teen-agers deliberately tried to dress American, talk American, and sing American. Across the land one could find billboards proclaiming *Yoter tov im Koka Kola* (Things go better with Coke), while rising middle-class women eagerly scanned American magazines to copy the latest fashions and hairdos from New York. Even the American style of weddings and *bnai mitzvot,* so maligned and lampooned in this country, became the latest trend for Israelis. In fact, except for the Hebrew billboards, a casual visitor walking down Dizengoff Boulevard in Tel Aviv would have been hard put to distinguish the store windows, well-dressed women, and teen-age styles from that of any comfortable suburban shopping area in America or Europe.[32]

And yet, despite all this, despite the large number of American Jews who visited Israel each year, there was an obvious lack of knowledge by Israelis about the American Jewish community, and this ignorance extended beyond the man or woman in the streets into the leadership as well. American Zionists who sat on international committees were stunned at the distorted views their Israeli colleagues had of American Jewish life. In the universities, Israeli students had an image of their American counterparts that ran somewhere between *Beach Blanket Bingo* and *Easy Rider*; the fact that some of the American students in Israel tried to live up to this model did nothing to help matters.[33] Israeli textbooks used in secondary schools were full of distortions about American Jewry and, according to one study, deliberately magnified minor aspects of American life to make it appear that American Jews, while all rich, lived in constant danger. Israeli leaders, including some who had spent time in the United States, confirmed that the vast majority of Israelis have totally unrealistic views of American Jewry, of its wealth, its political power, or its religiosity. Moshe Betan frankly conceded that "the ideas current in [Israel] about American Jews are the ideas of the 'Establishment,' which we are transmitting to the younger generation. They are the ideas of forty and fifty years ago. Even the ideological concepts are forty or fifty years old."[34]

In the flush of victory, however, all Zionists felt the need of somehow coming together, of somehow blurring or burying their differences. At the twenty-seventh Zionist Congress, in June 1968, the first to be held in reunited Jerusalem, the movement adopted a new ideological statement, the Jerusalem Program, which would be binding on all members. The aims of Zionism, it declared, are

> —the unity of the Jewish people and the centrality of Israel in Jewish life;
> —the ingathering of the Jewish people in its historic homeland, Eretz Yisrael, through *aliyah* from all countries;
> —the strengthening of the State of Israel, which is based on the prophetic vision of justice and peace;
> —the preservation of the identity of the Jewish people through the fostering of Jewish and Hebrew education and of Jewish spiritual and cultural values;
> —the protection of Jewish rights everywhere.

Like many umbrella statements, the Jerusalem Program could be accepted by the different Zionist factions, but it did not necessarily satisfy all of them, and a number of Israelis, aware of the acute manpower shortage in their state, did not hesitate to point out that if one truly and sincerely accepted the Jerusalem Program, one logically had to make *aliyah*. Three and a half years later, at the twenty-eighth Congress in January 1972, the Israelis pushed through an implementing statement,

"Duties of the Zionist as an Individual," which spelled out just what the Jerusalem Program should mean to each Zionist:

—the implementation of *aliyah* to Israel;

—active membership in the local Zionist organization;

—continual effort for the realization of the program of the Zionist movement;

—the study of Hebrew, the provision of Jewish education for one's children and their education toward *aliyah* and the realization of Zionism in their lives;

—contributions to the national funds, work on their behalf, and active participation in the economic consolidation of Israel;

—active participation in the community's life and institutions, and efforts to ensure their democratic character, the extension of Zionist influence in them, and the improvement of Jewish education;

—activity in defense of the rights of the Jews in the Diaspora.

Here the Americans balked, and while all enrolled members in any American Zionist organization carry a copy of the 1968 Jerusalem Program on the back of their membership cards, they do not carry the 1972 statement of individual responsibilities. In fact, when a group of Israeli "young Turks" tried to force the actual implementation of the 1972 statement, it threw the Congress into an uproar and led to the walkout of Hadassah.

The American Women's Zionist Organization, together with other American leaders, were apprehensive from the start over the manner in which the Congress and its programs had been organized, with an almost total lack of opportunity for Israeli and Diaspora representatives to engage in any meaningful dialogue. Moreover, it appeared that a number of Israeli leaders were willing to let the Americans be embarrassed, and wanted to show up their lack of real Zionist devotion after the passage of the statement on individual duties. Their chance came when members of the Israeli youth delegation decided to introduce a resolution which would require the leadership of all Zionist organizations to make *aliyah* within two years, or resign their offices. The Israeli-dominated presidium of the Congress well understood that such a motion could divide the movement, since it would be obviously unacceptable to the Americans. But the Israelis allowed it to come to the floor, confident that after prodding and annoying the American delegates it would be voted down.

Instead of the debate on this resolution beginning in the daytime, however, when the full membership of the Congress was present, it started at a night session, and the vote did not occur until 3 A.M., when it was doubtful if even a legal quorum still remained in the hall. With the exception of Faye Schenk and Charlotte Jacobson, the entire delegation of Hadassah rose and walked out when the resolution passed. (The two women stayed, not to signify approval of the motion, but to demonstrate that Hadassah was not walking out of the movement, but only from the meeting. They encouraged the other Hadassah delegates to leave, but resisted Rose Halprin's plea that they come too, lest their gesture be misinterpreted.) But the leaders of the Congress, as well as the youth representatives, were aghast; they had never expected the resolution to pass, nor that the Americans would do anything other than sit in embarrassed silence. Now they went running up to the Hadassah leaders, begging them to reconsider, apologizing for what had been a dreadful mistake, but the women stuck to their position until the presidium found a parliamentary loophole which enabled it to nullify the resolution.[35] The Americans won their point, but the issue of *aliyah*, and its meaning for Zionists, remains unresolved.[36]

*   *   *

The *aliyah* problem primarily involved those within the Zionist movement, but in the surge of emotion which united all Jews after the 1967 war, a new problem confronted Israeli and Zionist leaders; how to utilize and direct the vast pro-Israel sentiment which now existed among all American Jews, the vast majority of whom did not belong to any Zionist organization. In every community across the country, support of Israel had become the *sine qua non* for leadership in local organizations. One might be nonobservant, or even intermarried, but one could not be neutral about Israel and still be considered a Jewish leader. For the everyday Jew Zionism meant something far different from the organizational definition. It had become a web of feeling and response and identification with Israel, a true *ahavat Tsiyon* (love of Zion). It had become, as Moshe Rivlin and other Israelis recognized, a Zionism of deeds and action, even if these were not yet the classical Zionist duties.[37]

Nearly forty years earlier, Chaim Weizmann had tried to tap this nascent sentiment when he and Louis Marshall founded the enlarged Jewish Agency. But a variety of factors, including Marshall's untimely death, the Depression, and the lack of a mass organizational basis, had precluded the Agency from ever developing into the type of partnership envisioned by its founders. By 1941, the Agency had, for all practical purposes, become another operating arm of the World Zionist Organization. Now in the late sixties, conditions seemed ripe for a new attempt to establish a partnership.

First of all, involvement and concern for Israel among American Jews extended far beyond the limited interests of an earlier generation of non-Zionists. Marshall's peers had feared what the effects of a Jewish state would be upon their status as American citizens; their descendants felt secure enough as Americans to extend themselves to a full-hearted identification with Israel. In the 1920s, there had been a great gulf between the Zionists and the non-Zionists; in the 1960s, in practical terms, little separated the two groups within the community. Most important of all, the growth of local federations and welfare funds, capped by national co-ordinating bodies, gave the non-Zionists the widespread organizational and financial base to carry their share of the responsibilities.

In fact, the non-Zionists had been forced to take a more active role since 1960, when the Internal Revenue Service ruled that funds raised in the United States for expenditure abroad had to be spent under the supervision of a nongovernmental agency controlled by American citizens. To meet this requirement, the United Israel Appeal, Inc., came into being as the recipient and disburser of UJA funds for Israel. Theoretically, from that time on, the non-Zionists had a larger voice in the activities of the World Zionist Organization-Jewish Agency, but American Zionists also sat on the UIA, and the new group did not initiate programs; it merely designated programs, such as education, it would support. What the UIA did do, however, was to accustom American fund-raising leaders to a greater sense of participation in Zionist programs in Israel, and make them more informed about Israeli problems. The age of merely transferring funds, the "era of the blank check," came slowly to an end. But the new arrangement did not satisfy the fund-raisers either. The only real decisions they could make were basically negative in character; they could withhold monies from cer-

tain projects, but they could not initiate new ones, or even supervise or
alter the ones they supported.

The impetus for a total reorganization seems to have come from
Louis Pincus, a former South African lawyer and director of El Al Israel Airlines, who had become first treasurer and then chairman of the
Jewish Agency Executive. Together with Detroit industrialist Max
Fisher, he convened the Conference on Human Needs in Jerusalem in
June 1969. Fisher, as president of the Council of Jewish Federations
and Welfare Funds, chairman of the UIA, and chairman of the executive committee of the American Jewish Committee, probably enjoyed
more individual prestige and power than any other Jew in America at
that time, and his willingness to co-operate with Pincus in establishing
a new mode of operation was crucial to the success of the enterprise. At
the 1969 conference, Louis Fox, a federation official, indicated the spirit
which had motivated the non-Zionists, or as most of them preferred to
be called, "non-WZO members." "We have come here," he said, "to
offer a more personal contribution to Israel in terms of thinking, planning, and doing. We call it 'involvement.' Israel's leaders agree that the
days have passed for us just to be silent partners. And we agree. Meaningful participation in the progress of Israel will enrich not only Israel
—it will enrich our own lives and will enrich the depth and scope of
our own communities."

From that conference, a planning committee was appointed to work
out a new organizational format, and it met to complete its work in
Jerusalem in August 1970. At that meeting, Pincus pointed out that the
differences between the Zionists and the non-Zionists had indeed
diminished, and he said that he had "warned Max Fisher that the day
will come when I shall call him a Zionist too, when that gap is closed
completely, and we will be unable to differentiate in the approach to
the problems of Israel between those who come from here or there."
But Pincus also made it clear that the Zionists would not be taking a
back seat in the new arrangement; it would be a fifty-fifty arrangement.
The World Zionist Organization did not view this separation as anything more than a necessary evil; it would have preferred to have
blurred the differences even more. But Israel was still a Zionist state,
and the movement would not be shut out.

The planning committee proposed a three-tier arrangement for the
reconstituted Jewish Agency. At the base is a 296-member Assembly,
half of whom are designated by the WZO, 30 per cent by the UIA,

and the remaining 20 per cent by national fund-raising groups outside Israel and the United States. The Assembly meets once a year to provide general guidelines, approve a budget, and elect a board of governors. Representation on the board is distributed in the same proportion as the Assembly; the board meets three times a year to oversee the Agency's activities and to elect the Executive which is the actual operating unit of the Agency. The Executive includes the heads of the operating departments, but also tends to follow the general division of membership as the Assembly. Not surprisingly, the day-to-day operation of the Jewish Agency is influenced most heavily by the Israelis representing the WZO, but Diaspora Jewry makes its voice heard through the policy-making board, of whom half the members are Americans, either Zionists or non-WZO members.

According to Zelig Chinitz, head of the UIA's Jerusalem office, and the man directly responsible for disbursing millions of American dollars annually in Israel, most of the prestate ideological questions are now passé, but the Zionists are still worried that, with their lack of access to large reservoirs of cash, they will eventually be forced into a secondary role in the Agency despite the constitutional parity mandated for the Assembly and the board. Yet the most important effect has been to give Diaspora fund-raisers, especially American businessmen, an opportunity to influence the spending of the sums they raise and bring their expertise to bear upon familiar problems in Israel. For example, Jack Weiler, long a leader in Jewish philanthropic circles, has been able to apply his knowledge of the American building industry to housing problems in Israel.

Charles Liebmann, who has done an extensive analysis of the reconstituted Agency, sought to determine whether the Americans only wanted to help Israel, or if they actually wanted to influence Israeli policy. He could find no instance in which the Agency attempted to have the government follow specific programs. Even in such areas as higher education, where the Agency provided 61 per cent of the funding for Israeli universities, the Agency deliberately avoided discussions of internal university policy. The Americans wanted the money spent well, but they preferred not to have a say in determining any of the broader issues confronting Israeli education. The reasons for this, he suggested, are that the non-WZO members are not ideologues, and want to avoid the political morass that surrounds so many issues in Israel; second, they do not seek personal power, they do not want to get too immersed in the responsibility for carrying out Agency plans; third, they do not represent group interests, but are involved only in fund-raising in the local communities; and finally, because they do not live in Israel, they are willing to defer to Israeli officials in interpreting what "the larger picture" involves. Liebmann points out that at no time in the sessions of the Jewish Agency Assembly does one ever hear the type of criticism of Israel that is so common at the Zionist congresses. The non-WZO fund-raisers wanted to get involved, but they also wanted to avoid politics and controversy. In order to do that, they basically abdicated responsibility to the Israelis and to the Zionist members who are tied to the governmental establishment and to Israeli parties.[38]

* * *

The years between the 1967 and 1973 wars saw major changes within the American Jewish community and in its relations to the State of Israel. The anti-Semitism of blacks and of the New Left, as well as the coolness of the Nixon administration, left American Jews a little less assertive about their secure status in American life, although it did not essentially alter their overall view of themselves as Americans nor shake their resolution that their proper place was in this country. Within the Zionist movement, Israelis and Americans continued to quarrel, but they did so as *mishpachah* (family), and even as they fought over such things as *aliyah* and religious tolerance, they worked together to perfect a new institution for channeling aid to Israel and providing a greater sense of participation in the building of the Jewish homeland. Despite all the problems, these were heady years for both American Jewry and Israel, years which came crashing abruptly to an end on Yom Kippur 1973.

Chapter 17

YOM KIPPUR: LESSONS LEARNED

The Jewish "family," despite its internal quarrelings, never even entertained the idea that its disagreements should spell disintegration or abandonment of the ages-old concept of *am Yisrael* (a unitary Jewish people.) And on Yom Kippur morning of 1973, the most solemn of all Jewish holy days, the day tradition maintains that God seals his judgment on mankind for the coming year, Jews reaffirmed that unity. As American Jews rose to spend the Day of Atonement in fast and prayer, they learned that the armies of Egypt and Syria had attacked Israel, precipitating the fourth Arab-Israeli war in a quarter century. Unlike 1967, no publicized buildup of tensions, no ringing Arab declarations of *jihad* preceded the attack. And for the first time, the Israeli defense forces did not win a quick or overwhelming victory. Perhaps most disturbing from the viewpoint of American Jewry, the imposition of an oil embargo by the Arab states set American and Israeli interests on a course of inevitable conflict. Many lessons were to be learned from the Yom Kippur War, some of which have still to be absorbed. Whether or not it marked a turning point in Middle East history is another question, which has yet to be answered.

*   *   *

Even before the war, the superpowers, the United States and the Soviet Union, had become inextricably involved in the region, their policies inevitably affecting Israel and her Arab neighbors. Following the 1967 war, a number of Arab nations broke diplomatic relations with the United States, on the pretext that American "intervention" had enabled the Israelis to achieve their stunning victory. The Soviet Union moved quickly to exploit this situation; the Kremlin rapidly resupplied the Arab armies, replacing all of the lost, captured or destroyed equipment with modern weaponry. Thousands of Soviet technicians arrived to train the Arabs in the use of extremely sophisticated military hardware, especially a radar-controlled surface-to-air missile network designed to prevent the Israeli Air Force from repeating pre-emptive strikes. During the war of attrition in 1970, the Soviet Union made no move to stop either Egypt or Syria from using these weapons to harass Israeli forward positions in the Sinai or on the Golan Heights. In the United Nations Security Council, the Arab states and the Palestinian terrorists could always count on a Soviet veto to prevent the international body from reprimanding them, while the Russians led the chorus of denunciation against Israel.

The problem, however, went far beyond the idea of the two superpowers having client states in the Middle East; that would have been a relatively simple proposition, with the United States backing Israel against the Soviet-sponsored Arabs. But while Russia may have had no advantage to gain in promoting closer relations with Israel, the United States, both in political and economic terms, had much to lose unless it could mitigate some of the Arab hostility. The United States had, more or less by default, taken over the British role in the Middle East, and did not wish to see the Soviet Union extend its influence in that region. Moreover, each year the United States imported an increasing percentage of its oil from the Arab states; should that source be cut off, America would face a severe energy shortage.[1]

These were but some of the considerations involved in the Nixon-Kissinger plan to promote détente with the Soviet Union. As long as tensions remained high in the Middle East between their respective client states, relations between the superpowers themselves would be strained; on the other hand, if an understanding could be reached between the Soviet Union and the United States, it might lead to the imposition of some peace plan on the region. Beyond that, the Russians' willingness to restrain their Arab allies would be one sign that they took détente seriously, that they were in fact searching for some peaceful mode of coexistence and co-operation with the West.

Neither Kissinger nor Nixon anticipated the possibility that American Jewry would object to their efforts to ease Soviet-American tensions. Obviously, any proposals which might be interpreted as weakening Israeli security or imposing unilateral concessions on the Jewish state would meet with stiff resistance, as the reaction to the Rogers Plan in 1971 had clearly demonstrated. But the monkey wrench thrown into the gears of détente did not result from opposition to any Middle Eastern peace plan, but from a new and totally unexpected area: American Jews suddenly wanted their government to pressure the Soviets into allowing Russian Jews to emigrate.

For many years, one hardly heard anything about the once-thriving Russian Jewish community. Communist efforts to abolish religion had supposedly weakened Jewish feeling in the younger generation, while the Second World War had taken the lives of hundreds of thousands of Soviet Jews. Common knowledge had it that only the very elderly still clung to Jewish practices, that the younger generations had for the most part assimilated. The leadership within Zionist circles and communal organizations wrote off Soviet Jewry, believing it would never again play an important role in world Jewish affairs. Gradually, however, a new picture began to seep out to the West.

Russian Jewry still lived! Despite official rules and regulations, the older Jews had managed to transmit some Jewish culture and learning to their children. Despite government censorship, news of Israel found its way to the Russian Jewish communities. Despite state proclamations against prejudice, Jews still found themselves the targets of discrimination. Despite all the communist efforts, Judaism still survived. Golda Meir discovered this when she was named Israeli minister to the Soviet Union in 1949, and thousands, tens of thousands, of Jews turned out to greet her when she came to worship on the High Holidays at Moscow's Great Synagogue.[2] Elie Wiesel told the world about the depths of Jewish feeling still alive in the Soviet Union in his moving *The Jews of Silence* (1966). In the late sixties and early seventies Russian Jews themselves defied their government and sought exit permits to go to Israel. Jewish unity ran so deeply among American Jews that they immediately made the cause of Soviet Jewry their own cause as well.

Demonstrations outside Soviet embassies and consulates, and pickets confronting Soviet artists and musicians demanded "Let My People Go!" As news of Russian anti-Jewish crackdowns and harassment reached the West, the tempo of the protest campaign increased. National and local Jewish agencies saw the Russian emigration problem as second in importance only to Israel. By the end of 1972, the majority of members in the National Jewish Community Relations Advisory Council and the Council of Jewish Federations and Welfare Funds had formed special committees on Soviet Jewry, while such organizations as B'nai B'rith, the American Jewish Congress, the American Jewish Committee, and the Anti-Defamation League were turning out reams of articles and statements, sponsoring conferences and meetings, and organizing mass letter-writing campaigns to Soviet Premier Aleksei N. Kosygin. The National Conference on Soviet Jewry came into being to help co-ordinate all of these efforts, and synagogues and homes across the country recited special prayers, including a "Matzoh of Hope" section in the Passover Seder.[3]

Throughout 1972, American Jews turned more and more to their government leaders to intercede on behalf of Jews who wanted to leave Russia and emigrate to Israel. A group of visiting congressmen met with Jewish activists and dissidents on their tour of the Soviet Union; eight governors who visited Russia in the spring insisted on making public visits to synagogues in Moscow and Tiflis, and repeatedly questioned Soviet officials on their policies toward Jews. Before Richard Nixon left for a summit meeting with the Russians in May, American Jewish leaders pressed him to raise the subject of Jewish emigration, and both Nixon and Kissinger later announced that the topic had been "mentioned" in the course of the talks.

Such measures, while focusing attention on the problem, did not produce results on the scale desired. The Russians had, in fact, allowed some 13,000 Jews to leave for Israel in 1971, and over 32,000 in 1972 (compared to 5,675 from 1966 through 1970). But any Jew seeking an exit permit found himself subject to mistreatment, loss of job, expulsion from school, and similar harassments. Then on August 3, 1972, Russian authorities imposed a new exit fee scaled to the educational attainments of the applicant, which could range as high as $35,000, thus setting off a new storm of protests in this country against the "ransom tax." At a meeting of the National Conference on Soviet Jewry on September 26, American Jewish leaders decided that what had been primarily a public-relations campaign should be transformed into a political effort to bring stronger pressures to bear on the Soviet Union.

Senator Jacob K. Javits, in a speech at a New York rally on August 30, first broached the idea of linking trade benefits to emigration rights, and soon afterward aides to Senators Javits, Hubert Humphrey, Abraham Ribicoff, and Henry Jackson began planning their strategy. Jackson himself presented the proposal to the September 26 conference and secured overwhelming approval from the 120 Jewish leaders present there. In essence, the extension of trade and credit benefits by the United States would be tied to Russian removal of hindrances upon emigration. By the time Jackson formally introduced the plan in October, as an amendment to the East-West Trade Bill, it had 76 cosponsors in the Senate.[4]

The introduction of the Jackson amendment seems to have stung the Russians, who were eagerly seeking expanded trade with the United States, into an awareness of how sensitive Americans could be to harassment of would-be emigrants; in late October, a large number of well-known Jewish activists were allowed to leave the Soviet Union without paying the educational tax. The Soviets, at the same time, told the Nixon administration that outside interference would not determine their internal policies. Nixon and Kissinger both saw the Jackson amendment as a deterrent to the development of détente, and in early January 1973, contacted several senators (but not Jackson and Ribicoff) in an effort to prevent reintroduction of the measure in the new Congress. The President assumed that limited pressure from the White House, as well as the Soviet concessions, would convince the sponsors that the prod was no longer necessary. The Jewish community and its congressional allies, however, far from seeing the battle as won, believed they now had the key to achieving greater success. Not only did Jackson reintroduce his proposal, but Congressman Charles Vanik of Cleveland sponsored a similar bill in the House. Following a massive letter-writing campaign by the Jewish community, 238 representatives, including the then powerful chairman of the House Committee on Ways and Means, Wilbur Mills, decided to become cosponsors.

Pressure to pass the amendment increased throughout the early months of 1973, much to the discomfiture of the Nixon administration and Soviet authorities, who hoped that continued issuance of exit permits, up to 2,500 a month, would lead Congress to drop the matter. Finally, at Nixon's invitation, 15 prominent Jewish leaders met with the President for over an hour on April 19, a meeting they had long sought but which the White House had hitherto avoided. At the session, the President emphasized his commitment to human rights and his sensitivity and sympathy for their problem, but he also wanted them to understand how difficult it would be for him to secure a relaxation in East-West tensions if the Jackson-Vanik proposal passed. He asked Henry Kissinger, who had just recently become Secretary of State, to share private "communications" from the Kremlin assuring the President that Soviet Jews would be able to emigrate without interference. Following the meeting, three of the conferees—Jacob Stein of the Presidents' Conference, Charlotte Jacobson of the Conference on Soviet Jewry, and Max Fisher—issued a statement reaffirming their commitment to Soviet Jewry as well as their gratitude to Nixon for his assistance, but they remained vague as to whether or not American Jewry would still press for the trade legislation.

The three had hoped to avoid an open decision, but the deliberate vagueness of the statement backfired. Congressional cosponsors demanded to know whether they should press ahead, while the grass-roots Jewish organizations wanted a clarification of just where they stood. Then on April 23, a group of one hundred dissident Soviet Jews sent an open letter to American Jewish leaders pleading with them not to abandon the fight, that free emigration did not exist, and that the Kremlin's word could not be trusted. "Remember," their statement concluded, "the history of our people has known many terrible mistakes. Do not give in to soothing deceit. Remember—your smallest hesitation may cause irreparable tragic results. Remember—your firmness and steadfastness are our only hope. Now, as never before, our fate depends on you. Can you retreat at such a moment?"[5]

The message solved the dilemma of the leadership. While aware of the Administration's problems, they decided to stand firmly behind the Jackson-Vanik bill, and congressional sponsors, despite strong Administration pressure, moved ahead. The Yom Kippur War temporarily halted the legislative maneuverings, but Soviet policy during and after that conflict only confirmed the impression that the Soviet Union could not be trusted. On December 11, 1973, by an overwhelming majority, the House passed the Trade Reform Act with Title IV, the Jackson-Vanik amendment, intact. The vote, according to Vanik, was "a clear mandate on the part of Congress in support both for human rights and decency." Although a full year passed before the Senate approved the measure—a year in which the Soviet Union, the Nixon and then Ford administrations, and big-business interests fought the measure—its final approval gave marked evidence that American Jewry and Congress were unwilling to buy détente at the price of human liberties.

Throughout the debate, Israel deliberately maintained a low profile, despite the fact that the major objective of the struggle was to allow large numbers of Soviet Jews, many with needed educational and technical skills, to make *aliyah*. It was not that the Israelis were not concerned; on the contrary, the possibility of saving tens of thousands of Jews, of again confirming the Zionist dream, was a matter of extreme importance. But the Israelis recognized the multiple dangers inherent in their involvement. If they tried to influence the American Congress, they would be charged with interfering in the internal affairs and policies of another state. If they called openly upon the Russians to let the Jews go, they could be sure that the Soviet Union would slam the door closed completely. The Arab nations were already complaining to the Kremlin that every Russian Jew coming to Israel added strength to the Jewish state. The imposition of the ransom tax had been described to the Arabs as a device to make sure not too many skilled Jews could leave. Israel's position, in any event, was obvious, and for many years Israeli representatives at the United Nations had led vigorous attacks on the Soviet Union for violating human rights in its policy of forced assimilation.[6] And on this issue, there was not one iota of difference between Israel and American Jewish leaders.* Israel saw no need to intervene, since American Jews by themselves, efficiently and effectively, did what had to be done.

Nor did the Soviet Union do very much to win over American pub-

---

* Later differences would appear when a growing percentage of Russian Jews, who had secured exit permits to go to Israel, decided to emigrate to the United States or other Western countries instead. The Israelis argued that these people endangered the entire program, since it would give Russian authorities an excuse to cancel all exit permits, and they called upon the international Jewish assistance agencies, such as the Joint Distribution Committee and HIAS, not to extend help to these "dropouts." The Americans, while recognizing the Israeli desire to secure more immigrants as well as to keep the Russian doors open, were divided on this matter. While some groups agreed, others responded that the battle had not been fought on the narrow issue of allowing Russian Jews to go to Israel, but on the broader concept of human rights. The principle was for the right of any Soviet Jew to leave freely, or return, there; to coerce the immigrants to going to Israel, if they did not want to do so, was as much a violation of human rights as forcing them to stay in the Soviet Union.

lic opinion. Aside from Kissinger, Nixon, Ford, some of their colleagues, and businessmen and farmers who stood to profit from increased trade, there was little trust in the country of either the Russians
or détente; the American people did not believe in the good faith of the
Kremlin. Détente implied close communication and consultation, yet
the Russians deliberately attempted to hide or camouflage Arab war
preparations, and did not inform the American government that they
knew how close the Middle East was to war. Détente demanded that
the superpowers cool down potentially dangerous situations, yet the
Russians did all they could to encourage the Arabs, providing them
with extremely sophisticated weaponry and upsetting the balance of
arms in the region. Détente required co-operation, yet the Soviet Union
did nothing but hinder American efforts to stop the war until Israel
suddenly turned the tables and had the Soviet client states on the run.[7]

In the end, however, it would be the Soviet Union and the United
States who imposed a cease-fire on the combatants. The United States
pressured Israel, while the Soviet Union, under American insistence,
brought its influence to bear on the Arabs. Despite Kissinger's shuttle
diplomacy[8] and the supposed increase in American prestige in the Middle East at Russia's expense, one lesson of the war which all parties recognized was that no settlement could be reached, and no war fought,
without the involvement of the superpowers. The history of relations
between the governments of the United States and Israel since October
1973 has reflected this fact. Israel has faced great pressure from the
United States to make concessions, to take risks on the chance that
peace might result, and it has had to call upon all of the political resources available to American Jewry to mitigate this pressure so that it
could retain flexibility and avoid steps which, in its opinion, would
jeopardize the security of the Jewish state.

*   *   *

A second lesson of the war, but one which has still to be learned in
many parts of the West, is that the Arabs have remained constant and
consistent in their rejection of a Jewish state in their midst. It took the
Israelis a long time to learn this, but it is a lesson that they are not
likely to forget.

Taught by the Koran that they are destined to lead the world, the
Arabs have seen Israel as a mocking of their insufficiency, of their inability to carry out their heaven-ordained mission. In Arab schoolbooks,

YOM KIPPUR: LESSONS LEARNED

the Zionists stand condemned because they constantly remind the Arab world of its failures and loss of glory. The Iraqi Minister of Justice, 'Ali Mahmud al-Shaykh'Ali, wrote in 1941 that Judaism constituted a threat to all mankind, and for more than three decades this Judeophobia has been evident in numerous Arab statements. An Egyptian teachers' manual asserted that Jews are "the monsters of mankind, a nation of beasts lacking the good qualities which are characteristic of humanity." At a conference in 1968 the mufti of Lebanon depicted Zionism as "the enemy of man, of truth, of justice, and the enemy of Allah," while the mufti of Tarsus in Syria declared that Jews "have always been a curse that spread among the nations and . . . sought to . . . extinguish all manifestations of civilization."[9]

The Arabs have been quite candid; they want the Jews killed and Israel destroyed. Nayef Hawatmeh, leader of the Marxist Popular Democratic Front for the Liberation of Palestine, a supposed moderate (and the self-acknowledged organizer of the massacre of children at Ma'alot), declared that even if a Palestinian state were established alongside Israel, his organization would remain unwavering in its determination to wipe out Israel. Yasir Arafat, the leader of the Palestine Liberation Organization whom many Westerners have touted as a realist and a moderate, put it even more bluntly in an interview with Oriana Fallaci: "We don't want peace, we want victory. Peace for us means Israel's destruction and nothing else. What you call peace is peace for Israel and for the imperialists. For us it is shame and injustice. We shall fight on to victory. Even for decades, for generations if necessary." Nor should it be supposed that only the leaders hold these views; as Moshe Ma'oz has shown, the Arab masses share the same prejudices. For two generations, bitter anti-Jewish, anti-Israel sentiment has saturated Arab textbooks, newspapers, magazines, radio, and most recently television, cultivated and inflamed by political and religious appeals to nationalism.[10]

The Israelis have been equally determined that they would inhabit and rebuild and keep the land they believe was promised to them. One does not have to be a right-wing adherent or a religious zealot in Israel to quote Scripture and believe in the biblical promises to Abraham and to his seed. Even before the State of Israel, among groups such as Hashomer Hatzair which wanted to develop friendly relations and ties with the Arabs, a determination existed that no matter what attitude the Arabs ultimately took, there could be no compromise on the right of the Jews to their homeland in *Eretz Yisrael*.[11]

Ironically, Arab intransigence itself has been a major cause of the growth and expansion of Israel. At the St. James conference in 1939, the Arabs refused to accept a partition plan which would have limited the *Yishuv* to a relatively small area of Palestine. In 1947 the Arabs refused to accept the United Nations proposal, and as a result of the 1948 war the State of Israel came into existence covering a significantly larger area than had originally been allotted to it. During the negotiations to end that war, the Arabs rejected the Bernadotte Plan, which would have given them part of the Negev, and thereby lost all of the Negev. Following the 1967 war, Israel immediately offered to exchange nearly all of the territory it had conquered in return for peace and normalization of relations, but once again the Arabs refused, and as of this writing, Israel still holds the West Bank, the Golan Heights, and most of the Sinai. Arthur Nutting summed up this trend, which has characterized Arab-Jewish relations for so many years, when he wrote: "Foolish and daring to the end, the Arabs had thrown away those few but nevertheless real opportunities to settle for half a loaf. If they were left with a dry and bitter crust, some of the blame must be attached to the false prophets who misled them and whose blind extremism demanded the rejection of any compromise."[12]

Of course, as in any war, those who suffer most are not the leaders but the people, the men and women and children who see their fathers and husbands and brothers go off to war, some never to return, who are forced out of their homes, never to see them again, who wonder whether there will ever be a time of peace or a return to normal life. Saul Bellow, in a poignant passage in *To Jerusalem and Back*, wrote of sitting "at dinner with charming people in a dining room like any other. Yet you know that your hostess has lost a son; that her sister lost children in the 1973 war; that in this Jerusalem street, coolly sweet with night flowers and dark green under the lamps, many other families have lost children. . . . you do know that there is one fact of Jewish life unchanged by the creation of a Jewish state: You cannot take your right to live for granted."[13]

On the other side have also been tragedies, especially the several hundred thousand Arabs who fled Palestine in 1948 and for the most part have lived a dreary and hopeless life in refugee camps ever since. What is most tragic, however, is how the Arab states have used these people as political pawns, isolating them from their own societies and deliberately cultivating a festering hatred of Israel. There have been nearly a dozen refugee migrations since the Second World War larger than that of the Palestinian Arabs. Israel itself absorbed two of these waves, Jews fleeing from Europe and from the Arab lands. But in every other case, every non-Arab land which has faced a similar problem has attempted to integrate the refugees into their societies. India, Pakistan, West Germany, Biafra, South Vietnam, and Hong Kong all launched successful programs of absorption. But the unprecedented callousness of Arab leaders was openly political. If the Arab refugees had found new jobs and homes in Syria or Egypt or Lebanon, they might have settled down and lost any sense of identity as Palestinians.

And there has been room for them. Nearly all of the Arab lands are grossly underpopulated, and have desperately needed additional manpower, even if unskilled labor, in their efforts to modernize industry and agriculture and raise their standards of living. The Palestinian refugees could have provided this pool, but no Arab leader would even consider such a solution. In 1956, for example, a British newspaperman was discussing Iraq's development plans with an Iraqi Cabinet member, who lamented his country's lack of manpower. "Why don't you bring over the Arab refugees from Palestine?" the correspondent asked. "Oh we couldn't do that," the official replied. "That would solve the refugee problem." When David Ben-Gurion in July 1957 suggested that Israel would be willing to help seek a solution to the refugee dilemma if the Arab states would join in meaningful moves toward peace, Radio Cairo, speaking for the government, made the Arab attitude quite clear: "The fact that Israel is trying to solve the refugee problem proves that she has an interest in its solution. This alone is enough to damn any such attempt in Arab eyes."[14]

However inhumane Arab policy toward their "brethren" has been, there is no doubt that it has been a brilliant political success. The whole world knows about the sufferings of the Palestinian Arabs, but it seems to have forgotten Israel's herculean and largely successful efforts to integrate an even larger number of Jewish refugees driven from the Arab nations, together with the survivors of the Holocaust—all of this in a tiny state with barely adequate resources and burdened by many other problems.[15]

Israelis have not been unaware of Arab suffering, although they have been unable to alleviate it. The most obvious reason is security. Israel just could not allow all of the refugees back; nor, it should be noted, has any other country from which large numbers of refugees have fled been subjected to such international pressure to do so. But one can at times find a note of shattering historical continuity, an awareness of the agony of the situation.

In a short story by S. Yizhar entitled "Hirbet Hiz'ah" (the name of an Arab village), an Israeli soldier, considering the banishment of the residents from their homes, is suddenly traumatized at the realization of what he is witnessing: "*Galut.* Why, this is *galut.* That's the way *galut* looks." *Galut* (exile), the bitter burden of centuries of Jewish life, unknown to this *sabra,* is suddenly borne home to him with paralyzing acuity by seeing it manifest again, this time for another people. As Robert Alter notes, the soldier's sympathy is not just humanitarian, "it is made possible, and is emotionally colored, by the collective past experience of the Jewish people."

It is doubtful that those who fled Palestine three decades ago will ever return. Indeed, by now most of the inhabitants of the refugee camps are not those who took part in the 1948 exodus, but their children and grandchildren, who have never known life elsewhere. Even in the unlikely event of the establishment of an independent Palestinian state—a development which, despite all of their propaganda, the Syrians and Jordanians oppose as much as does Israel—they could not return to their original homes in Yaffo or Haifa or the Galilee or other towns and villages in Israel proper. Of what was originally Palestine, Israel today occupies but a small fraction, and its people are determined to hold onto that.[16]

*   *   *

One lesson, learned so painfully over the preceding years and reaffirmed during the war, was that the lone ally that Israel could count upon remained American Jewry. From the time the first word of the concerted Syrian and Egyptian attack reached the United States until after the cease-fire, the American Jewish community rallied around Israel, raised massive sums, lobbied the White House and the Congress, and, in as many ways as it could, gave moral support and encouragement to the Israelis. Yet the circumstances surrounding the Yom Kippur War and American Jewish reaction to it differed significantly from those of the war in June six years before.

In 1967, there had been an agonizingly slow buildup of tensions and fears that Israel would be destroyed; in 1973, the war came with a numbing rapidity, with few discernible events before the surprise attack to indicate that conflict was even in the offing.

In 1967, American Jews had little awareness of the power and efficiency of the Israeli army, and before they quite knew what had happened, the war was over, with Israel barely bloodied and the Arab states in disarray. In 1973, American Jews and Israelis, as well as the American government, shared an exaggerated view both of the Israeli Defense Forces' strength and of the supposed Arab weakness.

In 1967, gloom gave way to an incredible joy; in 1973, an initial confidence soon dissipated into an unrelieved despondency which even the military turnabout at the end, when *Zahal*, in a brilliant maneuver, crossed the Suez Canal and cut off the Egyptian army from behind, could not alleviate.

Moreover, before 1967 relations between Israel and American Jewry had settled into a rather tranquil, possibly even indifferent, state of affairs, one which had led some Israelis to believe that American Jews, while continuing to donate financial support, really did not care too much about what happened in or to Israel. In 1973 an intensive and extensive set of relationships existed between the two communities, yet one possibly on the verge of change. The original "idolatry" surrounding Israel and Israelis had begun to pass over into a more serious mood of questioning certain assumptions about respective roles. Leonard Fein, writing on the eve of the war, noted that "a growing number of Jews in America are becoming somewhat restive, are beginning to search for a new and more mature understanding of Israel. And the time for such a reassessment, painful though it must be, may be said to have arrived." Despite the hoopla surrounding the celebration of Israel's twenty-fifth anniversary in the spring of the year, with its countless parades and festivals and television specials, there was also a growing awareness that certain Zionist expectations had not come to pass.[17]

Whatever reservations American Jewry may have had about trends in Israel, the outbreak of the war on October 6, 1973, soon plunged national and communal organizations into a flurry of frenzied activity, whose pace increased during the following week, when it became apparent that Israel would not win a quick or easy victory. Over one hundred of the UJA's fund-raising and organizational leaders flew to New York for an emergency meeting less than twenty-four hours after the start of hostilities, and announced a goal of $100 million to be raised within a week; seven days later, at a second national gathering, they called upon American Jewry to raise $750 million for Israel in the coming year. Unlike 1967, when the enormous sums raised did not reach Israel until after the fighting had ended, the Jewish state in 1973 needed cash for its immediate expenses. Israel purchased most of its goods overseas on credit, and found its normal sources of financing suddenly shut off. It was not a question of buying arms—those Israel eventually got from the American government—but of securing foodstuffs, medicines, and other goods needed to maintain its economy and provide the backup for its military effort. Local fund-raisers did not ask for pledges; they wanted the old pledges paid immediately and the new donations in cash, either through outright gifts to the UJA or through the purchase of Israel bonds. Elaborate mechanisms were devised to transfer the daily collections in towns and cities across the country into New York within twenty-four hours.[18]

Despite the fact that the UJA call came at the worst possible moment for many national Jewish organizations, then in the initial stages of their own fund-raising campaigns, they pushed everything else aside to work for Israel. To use such words as "hysteria" and "panic" in describing the community at this time would not be inappropriate. They gave, and gave again, and gave still more. One man in Chicago, after hearing Pinhas Sapir, the Israeli Finance Minister, speak at a noon rally, went to his bank and borrowed $50,000; four hours later he attended another meeting where Sapir spoke, and pledged another $50,000. The board of the Isaac M. Wise Temple in Cincinnati voted unanimously to postpone construction of a new building and to invest the proceeds from the sale of the old facility in Israel bonds. Other synagogues around the country also called emergency meetings of their congregations to authorize the investment of trust funds in Israel bonds, or to contribute some of their assets to the UJA. The Orthodox Young Israel movement set up bicycle brigades on Saturdays to collect money; the principle of *Pikuach Nefesh* (the saving of lives) took precedence over normal Shabbat restrictions. In New York, where mass fund-raising meetings are impracticable, WPIX-TV became the vehicle for an Israel emergency fund telethon, which featured many celebrities and raised several million dollars. Men borrowed money on their business or personal credit, women sold jewels, and families mortgaged homes.

One man in his forties donated over a third of all his assets, although he was far from well-to-do. When asked to explain why he was making such a sacrifice, he replied that once he had asked his father what he had done to help fellow Jews during the Holocaust, and his father had no answer. The man went on to say that he wanted his conscience to be clear, that if his children ever asked him what he had done to help the Jewish people, he would be able to answer: "I did everything I could."[19]

The campaign worked; $107 million was raised in the first seven days. But the war did not end, and the campaign went on. Practically all other communal activities came to a halt, and operating funds were diverted to Israeli needs. Sound trucks drove through Jewish neighborhoods in big cities asking for contributions, and many of the phenomena of 1967 repeated themselves. Merchants held special sales or promotions, with the proceeds going to Israel. Tens of thousands of people spontaneously mailed in checks to their local Federations, so that a month after the fighting stopped, volunteers were still opening envelopes. And the educational programs run by the Federations and the Zionists and the national agencies following the 1967 war, to teach American Jews more about Israel, paid off. Postwar surveys indicated that the young men who took out additional mortgages on their homes to secure more funds for Israel had almost invariably been through one of the UJA or Federation "young leadership" programs, or had been on an in-depth study mission to Israel, or had attended one or more Israel-oriented conferences. Faculty members, who normally are not large contributors, gave more freely when they had been involved in one of these programs. Student response also improved, thanks to the various efforts made from within their own ranks to organize between 1967 and 1973.[20]

The other major effort of American Jewry fell under the rubric of "community relations" and was aimed at securing the most favorable public sentiment possible for Israel. This drive had three major goals: first, continued American military and economic aid to Israel; second, preclusion of American pressure to force Israel into an unsatisfactory settlement; and third, the separation in the public mind of the oil embargo from the issue of Israeli survival.[21] This last issue was undoubtedly the most sensitive, because the Arab embargo on oil confronted American Jewry for the first time with a situation in which American and Israeli interests had collided, with adverse effects upon the American public. As long lines queued up at gas stations and oil prices skyrocketed, many Jewish leaders recalled that economic dislocations had often triggered outbursts of anti-Semitism. Predictably enough, some commentators raised the old accusations of dual loyalty, as conservative commentator Jeffrey St. John did on CBS radio. Many of the old anti-Semitic organizations, quiescent since 1967, suddenly came alive, and one analyst argued "the plain fact is that expressed anti-Semitic sentiment, spontaneous and unorganized, has increased a hundredfold since the outbreak of fighting in the Middle East."

Yet despite domestic hardships and dislocations and massive propaganda efforts by pro-Arab groups and the New Left, a more detailed analysis of the last quarter of 1973 did not find any massive upsurge of resentment against American Jews. Most people blamed higher prices on oil company gouging; Americans saw the embargo, not as a result of Israeli action, but as an attempt by the Arab producers to blackmail the United States, and resented it. And while few Americans wanted this country to get involved militarily in the Middle East, public-opinion polls continued to show supporters of Israel outnumbering Arab symphathizers by seven to one.[22]

Much of this pro-Israel sentiment resulted from twenty-five years of lobbying and propagandizing and education, but one could not rely on old emotions alone. The Vietnamese experience caused a majority of Americans to suspect foreign involvements. As Earl Raab noted at the time, "Americans sympathize with Israel, but not so intensely that they are ready to sacrifice a great deal to save her." The defense agencies—the American Jewish Committee, the American Jewish Congress, the Anti-Defamation League—all mounted extensive campaigns to explain the Israeli case and convince Americans that Israel did not want to involve U.S. soldiers in the conflict, and that support of a beleaguered ally would not harm American interests.

Here they had to contend with a wide array of charges that the United States would be "sucked in" to the conflict, that the politically potent American Jewish community was calling the tune in Washington. Senator J. William Fulbright, chairman of the Senate Foreign Relations Committee, appearing on "Face the Nation" the day after the war started, declared that as "a fact of life" the Israelis and their Jewish sympathizers in the United States "control the policy in the Congress and in the Senate." Jeffrey St. John echoed this assertion, charging that American policy in the Middle East "has been, and continues to be, shaped in large measure by the financial and political power of American Jewry." The same day, October 15, a WCBS-TV station editorial in New York, while moderate in tone, came down firmly against any American resupply of Israel, despite its acknowledgment of Russian shipments to the Arabs.[23]

On another front, the community-relations campaign had to counter the massive oil lobby and Arab propaganda. The oil companies took out full-page advertisements in newspapers calling for more "even-handedness" in the Middle East in order to end the embargo. The chief executive officers of Texaco, Exxon, Mobil, and Standard Oil of California delivered a memorandum to the White House urging that no American aid be extended to Israel, lest there be Arab retaliations against their oil holdings. The *Christian Science Monitor,* a longtime Arab sympathizer, editorialized that the Soviet Union had acted reasonably in giving the Egyptians and Syrians "the means to defend themselves and to try to regain their lost lands," and that it was not aggression on the part of these countries to try to recapture their own territory.[24]

While Christian support for Israel in general was stronger in 1973 than in 1967, due in part to the educational campaign of the defense agencies to make Christians realize the importance of Israel for all free people, some Christian leaders remained ready to abandon Israel. Professor Robert E. Cushman of the Duke University Divinity School declared that American support of Israel contravened the Jeffersonian dictum of "decent respect to the opinion of mankind." The price of Israel's existence, he wrote, was too high, it was not worth all this trouble. The governing board of the National Council of Churches, with its large number of missionary members, held its regular semiannual meeting during the war, and its sessions were marked by outspoken, viciously anti-Semitic speeches. In the end, the board passed a resolution designed to be "even-handed and balanced." The American Jewish Committee, however, immediately assailed the statement for its "total inability" to condemn Egypt and Syria morally for their violations of the cease-fire.[25]

Probably the most bizarre attack on Israel came from the then hero of the New Left, Father Daniel Berrigan, in a speech on October 19 to the Association of Arab University Graduates in Washington. In his talk, Berrigan equated Israel with South Africa, and declared that "the wandering Jew has become the settler Jew; the settler ethos had become the imperial adventurer . . . the slave master had created slaves . . . the coinage of Israel is stamped with the imperialist forces whose favor she has courted." While asserting Israel's right to exist, he charged that the Jewish state "has not abolished poverty and misery; rather she manufactures human waste, the by-product of her entrepreneurs, her military and industrial complex." Nor did American Jews escape his wrath, for he claimed that "the fate of the Vietnamese was as unimportant to the Zionists in our midst as was the state of the Palestinians." Ironically, though, Berrigan summed up by describing himself as a marginal man, as "a Jew" in his resistance to Israel.[26]

The speech evoked cries of outrage from both Jews and Christians, but perhaps the most effective rejoinder came from one of Berrigan's coworkers in the peace movement, a man ideologically close to the renegade Jesuit. Arthur Waskow, who in the next few years would become a major critic of Israeli policy, attacked Berrigan's position both privately and in public. To Berrigan, he wrote: "You after all are *not* a Jew. You do not stand in the particular ambivalence Jews stand in when they deal with God, the Torah, and *Eretz Yisrael*. You may stand in other ambivalences but not those. Would you have thought to say you are a Black standing perhaps before some Asians who had been chased out of Uganda and using your asserted Black identity to justify your criticism of Uganda? . . . *I* can say that the covenant obligates us to a certain course of action because I am bound to suffer the joys or disasters, to share in the results, that flow from my choice. But one of the deepest sufferings of Jewish history has been to have to cope with others' insistence that *they* could define our inwardness, our covenant for us. At its loftiest, at its most serious, at its least brutal, this is what Christian theological anti-Semitism has meant." And in the *Village Voice*, Waskow reminded its readers that "Dan Berrigan is no anti-Semite, but what Jews remember was that from roots like these in the past have flowered the most serious, the least brutal, the loftiest anti-Semitism, and the deepest."[27]

Other voices from the liberal and academic communities also rose in defense of Israel, voices which had not normally been quick to identify with the Jewish state previously. Irving Howe spoke for those who, despite their earlier silences, were now deeply troubled. "We live with the thought that the men who hold power in the world are preparing a political course that will end with the destruction of Israel. Some do so out of malevolence, others out of no visible hostility—indeed, for the highest of motives—but all aim toward the same result. It would be good if we brought this fear into the open, good for us personally and as a way of stirring ourselves into action." Irving Kristol, a widely respected intellectual and writer, spoke for many of his Jewish colleagues when he described in the *Wall Street Journal* how he found himself "getting up at dawn to listen anxiously to the radio reports." He went on to ask himself: "Why am I so deeply affected? I am not an Orthodox Jew, and only a barely observant one. I am not a Zionist and I did not find my two visits to Israel to have been particularly exhilarating." Yet he cared desperately about what was happening to the Jewish state, because he sensed "deep down, that what happens to Israel will be decisive for Jewish history, and for the kinds of lives my grandchildren and great-grandchildren will be leading."[28]

There is no doubt that American Jews were vitally concerned about the fate of Israel in October 1973, yet a number of commentators detected significant differences from the crisis of six years earlier. Elie Wiesel believed that the community had become polarized: "The dedicated ones were better, the aloof ones drifted away, and the huge mass in the middle went about business as usual." He suggested that the framework of 1967 had been the Holocaust, while that of 1973 had been a victorious Israel. Arnulf Pins saw the cause in the divided emotions of American Jews; as *Americans,* they worried about the impact of the war upon the United States, and this reduced their commitment as *Jews* to Israel. Albert Arent perceived a sort of schizophrenia within a community suddenly and simultaneously confronted by two almost inconceivable horrors: a grave danger to Israeli survival and a grave danger to American democracy. American Jews found themselves partially paralyzed at the thought of having to support the Nixon administration, then entering the worst throes of the Watergate scandal, in order to sustain Israel.[29]

Yet the college students turned out in even stronger force than in 1967; the communal and national organizations and their leaders performed even more heroic labors; because of an increased American *aliyah,* many more members of the community felt very personal links with Israeli trauma; more Jews took to the streets to demonstrate their solidarity with the Jewish state than had ever done before; some Israelis even went so far as to proclaim all of world Jewry Zionized. And yet, beneath all of the work and prayers and contributions, one could find a lingering malaise. This could be sensed not only among intellectuals disillusioned by Israeli secular policies and among the religiously observant mourning Israel's failure to become a Torah-true state. This strange alliance of the intellectual left and the religious right, as Norman Lamm described it, resulted from the excessive pride they associated with the Jewish state. "Not by might, but by My spirit, saith the Lord," and this biblical exhortation, declared Lamm, which is fundamental to the entire Judaic *Weltanschauung*, is what made the oft-repeated assertion that "we can rely on our own strength" sound so abrasive, even sacrilegious, to many Jews. Not that Judaism is pacifist, but it rejects the type of power which relies on armed might alone.[30]

Yet at no time did Israel, or American Jewry, reject the spirit entirely. Sometimes a picture can sum up the essence of a situation far better than words, and of the many words and pictures that came out of these two wards, two in particular caught and held the imagination of American Jewry. In 1967, a news photo showed young Israeli paratroopers, helmets on their heads and machine guns on their shoulders, eyes wide with innocence and wonder, standing and praying at the Western Wall of the Temple which they had captured only hours before; this epitomized what Israel had been fighting for, the right to live as Jews, to be free in their historic land, to return to worship the God of their fathers. In 1973, photographers with the Egyptian forces crossing the Suez Canal on Yom Kippur sent back a picture of an equally young Israeli soldier leaving the bunker at the Bar Lev line, wrapped in a *talith* (prayer shawl), carrying a Torah as he was led away into captivity. Force had for the moment prevailed, but the spirit, which many thought had been forgotten, had not surrendered.

*   *   *

Perhaps the hardest lesson of all, both to Israel and American Jewry, was that the interests of the two countries would not always be in harmony, but might at times clash, and in the reality of a world dominated by superpowers, small states like Israel would find their autonomy and maneuverability severely limited. Despite Israel's historic and special relationship with the United States, American leaders would have no scruples about manipulating Israel to achieve the aims of their foreign policy. Even before the Yom Kippur War, Joseph Sisco, the Assistant Secretary of State for Near Eastern Affairs, in an interview on Israeli television, had warned that American and Israeli interests ran parallel in many instances, but not in all, and he cited oil as an example. Sisco implied, and the Israelis understood him to mean, that in cases where the interests of the two countries clashed, the United States could not be expected to work against its own national needs.[31]

Prior to the war, the United States under both Johnson and Nixon had held steadfastly to three basic principles: Israeli withdrawal, in accordance with UN Security Council resolution No. 242, from territory taken in 1967, with some boundary changes; direct Arab-Israeli negotiations; and a binding peace treaty. American policy had excluded the imposition of a settlement either by the big powers or by the United Nations, and outside guarantees, according to Sisco, could add "as a minimum, an important psychological and political support for the agreement between the two parties," but no more.[32] Throughout these years, the Middle East rarely intruded on American policy-makers, whose prime concerns focused on Southeast Asia.

So long as the Arabs gave no signs of being willing to enter serious negotiations leading toward peace, this situation suited both Israel and her American friends. Ezer Weizman, the father of the Israeli Air Force, declared in early 1973 that "the present situation is ideal and we should not be in a rush to negotiate, certainly not through jarring, the United Nations, or the U. S. State Department. Right now we have no official specific boundaries. All right, that's not terrible. We control our *de facto* frontiers. There is no war, no fighting, no shelling, and we are strong. . . . And we don't need advice from Russians who send their armies into Hungary and Czechoslovakia, or America, which sends its men and planes to Vietnam. They are not fighting for national survival but for power reasons. We are fighting for survival. It is life or death for us. Who are they to give us lessons?" Weizman's attitude seemed to be widely held by the Israelis as a whole. Even among those who criticized the Labor government as being too inflexible regarding the Arabs, few were willing to pull out of the administered territories without some specific assurances that Israeli gestures would be reciprocated by the Arabs.[33]

And so the picture remained fairly static—Israel and the Arabs in a deadlock, the Soviet Union and the United States each providing arms to their client states, and an occasional meaningless prod to move toward peace talks—until the late summer of 1973, when the pace of the Arab military buildup increased sharply. Yet both the Israeli and American intelligence agencies failed to interpret the signals correctly. Just twelve days before the attack, Kissinger, recently installed as Secretary of State, told the United Nations that "many of the crises that haunted past General Assemblies have been put behind us. Agreement has been reached on Berlin; there is a cease-fire in the Middle East." He then listed eleven specifics of American foreign policy, not one of which mentioned the Arab-Israeli conflict. Even as Yom Kippur approached, Kissinger and the State Department continued to believe that, despite their extensive military maneuvers, the Arabs would not be so foolish as to start a war. They were too disunited, their political leadership too undistinguished, their military men too incompetent to co-ordinate an effective assault against Israel. Many State Department bureaucrats were still calling Sadat a "clown" and Faisal a "religious fanatic."[34]

When Israel became concerned about the size of the buildup and *Zahal* analysts began predicting an imminent Arab attack, Kissinger remained dubious. He had but one message for the Israelis, a message he repeated over and over to Ambassador Simcha Dinitz: "Don't ever start the war. Don't ever pre-empt! If you fire the first shot, you won't have a dog catcher in this country supporting you. You won't have presidential support. You'll be alone, all alone. We wouldn't be able to help you. Don't pre-empt it." Israel, dependent upon the United States for arms, could not afford to ignore such advice, and Mrs. Meir and her Cabinet reluctantly agreed that Israel would have to let the Arabs make any first move. Kissinger was also relying upon the Russians, either to head off any Arab assault or to inform the United States of its immediacy. This, as much as anything, would be a sign of Russian sincerity in creating détente. Yet on September 28, a week before the war, Soviet Foreign Minister Andrei Gromyko visited Nixon and Kissinger in the White House and told them nothing about the war, although the Russians by that time had certain knowledge of Arab war plans. When fighting broke out Kissinger was angry and disappointed. Years before he had written, "the test of statesmanship is the adequacy of its evaluation *before* the event." By that standard his own judgment of the situation and of Soviet intentions had been proved terribly inadequate.[35]

Hampered by the American caveat, Israel had to absorb the first blow. She then discovered not only how well equipped her opponents were, but also that the myth of Arab military incompetence generated by three earlier wars no longer held true. The Egyptians managed to launch sophisticated and complicated crosscanal landings, and executed them successfully. No one doubted any more that Arab soldiers, properly armed and led (conditions lacking in earlier wars) could fight well. The worst blow came when Israel realized that Egypt and Syria, supplied with the latest Soviet surface-to-air missiles, could effectively neutralize Israeli air superiority. Standing Israeli plans to strike deep behind enemy lines to disrupt troop and supply movements could not be put into operation.[36]

For the first time since 1948, Israel had to fight an essentially defensive war, and against well-trained and well-equipped soldiers. While she could field the world's third largest tank corps and sixth largest air force, she found that the Arab plans had effectively nullified Israeli strengths; before long, Israeli reserve supplies fell dangerously low, and troops in the field began running short of ammunition, fuel, and replacement parts. Now was the time for the United States to fulfill its often made promise that in the final analysis Israel would be able to rely upon America for its security and survival. Now the Jewish state needed help, not in the form of American soldiers, but in desperately needed supplies. She received promises and assurances and excuses, but not the goods. Various writers have said that Kissinger expected a quick Israeli victory, that he did not want to antagonize the Russians, that the Administration was under heavy pressure from the oil companies to allow the Arabs to recover at least part of the territory lost in 1967. If he could only delay committing himself, then perhaps the issue would resolve itself in Israel's favor. Ambassador Dinitz, by then practically living at the State Department, could get no positive response to his endless queries. Day after day the Israelis waited for the expected airlift, and Golda Meir called Dinitz constantly to find out when the planes would be on their way. One time she called at 3 A.M. Washington time, and when Dinitz told her he could not reach anyone at that hour, she raged: "I don't care what time it is. Call Kissinger now. In the middle of the night. We need the help today because tomorrow it may be too late."[37]

Finally, two events broke the logjam: Dinitz, weary of Kissinger's delay, threatened to go to Israel's friends in the Congress to force the Administration's hand; and the Soviets lauched their own large-scale shipment of military goods to the Arabs. American leaders now recognized that the Russian move doomed any hope of an Israeli victory without American aid. Within a matter of hours a decision was made, and the massive airlift was under way. Huge C-5 Galaxy transports flew around the clock to deliver vital arms to Israel. Within a matter of days, the tide of battle turned. Israel stopped the Arabs, and in a brilliant maneuver launched a surprise crosscanal invasion of its own, which led to the entrapment of a large part of the Egyptian army. Israeli units advanced on the roads to Cairo and Damascus.

On October 20, with their Arab clients in disarray, Russian leaders summoned Kissinger to an emergency meeting in Moscow. There they agreed on what would become UN Security Council resolution No. 338, calling upon all sides to cease firing. Israel accepted the resolution on October 22, despite objections from the military to Mrs. Meir, because of pressure from Nixon and Kissinger. The Secretary of State then began his famous rounds of shuttle diplomacy, which eventually led to the war's end. Kissinger succeeded in re-establishing American prestige in the Middle East and negating much of the Soviet influence there; the real question is whether he did so at Israel's expense.

Kissinger's critics, both in Israel and in the United States, believed that he played directly into Russian and Arab hands, that he snatched away an Israeli victory by forcing them to stop fighting before they could consolidate their gains. Tad Szalc refuted the claim that it had been Kissinger who overrode Defense Secretary James Schlesinger's objections to the resupply; to the contrary, Szalc wrote, Schlesinger had been ready to start the operation for days but had been waiting word from Nixon and Kissinger. Gil Carl AlRoy, in articles and a blistering book, charged that Kissinger undercut the Israelis at every step; moreover, if he had really been concerned with an Arab oil embargo, why did he give away the one effective tool he might have used to pressure the producing states, an Israel which was in an even stronger territorial position than before the war? The time to give back land would have been after the Arab states backed down, not before. Kissinger himself was reported as believing that Israel "has had it" unless it threw itself completely on his diplomacy, and at a White House meeting with Jewish leaders on October 9, he said, "I hope neither side wins—that will give me an opportunity to make peace." Kissinger also warned that Americans would blame the Jewish state for the oil problem; yet public-opinion polls showed just the opposite.[38]

The Secretary of State did, in fact, start a process, which at first gave some signs of hope that it might lead to meaningful negotiations. But Israel and the Arabs never negotiated. Israel talked to Kissinger; Kissinger talked to Sadat or Assad; then Kissinger returned to convey the contents of those talks to Mrs. Meir. Throughout this procedure the Israelis grew increasingly restive but were forced to give in on point after point because they saw no way to evade American pressure during

1974. The Jewish state desperately needed the arms and financial assistance being considered by the Congress, and could not risk antagonizing the Administration. As one Israeli official commented nearly a year after the war, "I feel we are being reduced from the status of a junior ally to the status of a junior client."

Israelis began to perceive of Kissinger as treating Egypt as a victorious ally, and Israel as a defeated nuisance. This pressure by the United States, a pressure that could not be resisted, according to Efraim Shmueli, put an end to the Zionist dream of normalizing Jewish life. The Kissinger experience shattered Israeli confidence and cast doubt on its very survival. Israelis became more and more hostile to Kissinger. By early 1975, he was being attacked daily in the Israeli press, and hardly any private conversations did not, at some time, come around to "Kissinger's betrayal."[39] Finally, in March 1975, Israel decided that it could not cede any more territory without receiving some firm commitment on the part of the Arabs to peace, and since neither Egypt nor Syria would give that, the Kissinger initiative came abruptly to an end.

Throughout this time, American Jewry played a relatively muted role, concentrating its efforts for the most part in Congress, where it hoped to build up the goodwill necessary to pass the massive aid bills and serve as a deterrent to any overtly anti-Israeli moves by the Administration. As long as the Meir and Rabin governments were willing to deal with Kissinger, American Jews remained silent (except for Rabbi Meir Kahane, who from the start accused Kissinger of selling Israel out and of being responsible for the twenty-seven hundred Israeli fatalities during the war).

But as Israeli resistance stiffened, so did that of American Jewry. At a meeting between Kissinger and several leading Jewish intellectuals, *Commentary* editor Norman Podhoretz told the Secretary that he joined with many Israelis in wondering whether Kissinger was "a Churchill disguised as a Chamberlain, or a Chamberlain disguised as a Churchill." Several months later Podhoretz evidently had made up his mind, and in a widely quoted article accused Kissinger of engineering an abandonment of Israel. Theodore Draper argued that the so-called guarantees to Israel were useless, since Israel had no means to ensure whether the United States would keep its word or not. As for the long-standing promise that the United States would never stand idly by and see Israel destroyed, Draper said he was no longer able to believe it. Hans J. Morgenthau, ever the gloomy critic of American policy, questioned how gullible Kissinger might have been in dealing with the Arabs. He recalled that Neville Chamberlain on his deathbed had remarked that everything would have turned out all right if Hitler had not lied to him. "Let us hope," Morgenthau concluded, "Henry Kissinger will not have occasion to assert that everything in the Middle East would have turned out all right if Sadat had not lied to him."[40]

Such charges had not been heard in American Jewish circles since before the establishment of the State of Israel, because in all those years no one had really believed that the United States would ever abandon Israel. Some of the pessimism undoubtedly resulted from the general depression of the war, but much of it reflected the realization that the United States and Israel could come into conflict over crucial questions of policy. No one knew how far the United States would push or Israel would retreat in an all-out clash of interests, but no one denied any more that such a conflict could ever arise. What many people lost sight of in those gloomy days of the war and afterward were the strong ties binding Israel and American Jewry and the widespread support for the Jewish state which existed in the Congress and among the American people as a whole. As long as those ties remained strong, domestic political pressures would exert a countervailing force within the government against any executive pursuing an overtly anti-Israeli policy. Indeed, when President Ford tried to pressure the Israelis into accepting the Kissinger proposal they found unacceptable, seventy-six senators, acting at the urging of the American-Israel Public Affairs Committee, signed a round-robin letter backing the Israeli position.[41] It was a clear signal to the Administration that Israel could be pushed only so far, that there was still much strength in that "historic and special" relationship between the two nations.

Chapter 18

"WE ARE ONE!"

In the years following Yom Kippur 1973, the Jewish people, both in Israel and in the Diaspora, were buffeted by numerous events. In the family of nations Israel found itself practically isolated, as the Arab states used their newly discovered economic powers with devastating results. The United Nations invited Yasir Arafat, the leader of the terrorist PLO, to address it as an honored guest; the world body also branded Zionism as racism, and under Arab pressure, tried to excommunicate Israel. An American President considered friendly to Israel resigned in disgrace, and his successor attempted to force Israel into accepting a settlement which its leaders saw as distinctly dangerous. Jimmy Carter, while reaffirming American support for Israel, also became the first American President to speak publicly about a "Palestinian homeland." Within the Jewish state a sense of aimlessness and despair grew, corruption within government and business mushroomed, thousands of Israelis emigrated, and finally the Labor Party, which had ruled first the *Yishuv* and then the State of Israel for nearly a half century, suffered a stunning electoral defeat. In the United States, criticism of conditions in Israel as well as of its foreign policy could be heard more openly and more frequently, and issues of friction between Israel and American Jewry, many of which had been kept under control for so many years, threatened to erupt with shrill intensity.

Yet despite all this, or because of it, the sense of Jewish unity grew stronger. Following the infamous UN resolution equating Zionism and racism, hundreds of thousands of Jews and non-Jews proudly donned lapel buttons or affixed bumper stickers to their cars proclaiming "I Am a Zionist." The United Jewish Appeal adopted as its slogan "We Are One!" and few Jews in the United States would deny this. In Israel, one sensed a growing appreciation of American Jewry and of its devotion to the Jewish state. The fights within the *mishpachah* went on, but as among brothers and sisters, not distant cousins.

And American Jews, reaching for a new maturity, began recognizing and exploring the maze of paradoxes in which they lived. They started to accept the fact that being a Jew in the United States in the last quarter of the twentieth century meant living amid possibly insoluble contradictions. Seeing themselves as Jews and as Americans, they realized that in certain areas of life these two roles would not mesh comfortably. As Conservative or Reform Jews who loved Israel, they would have to fight the Jewish state to break the Orthodox monopoly there. As American Zionists, they would not be able to accept an Israeli definition of Zionism, and prepared to develop and fight for a legitimate role within the movement. They acknowledged the centrality and importance of Israel in their Jewish lives, but continued to define themselves as Americans. They looked to the Jewish state for inspiration and were ready to make genuine sacrifices to preserve it, yet they became more willing to criticize Israel openly for its shortcomings and refused to see themselves as second-class Jews if they did not make *aliyah*. American Jewry began to understand that no matter how much at home they were in the United States, they would, at the same time, always be somewhat different and apart. And perhaps most important, despite all the differences among American Jews and those of Israel or Russia or Europe or South America, they fully accepted the notion of *Klal Yisrael* (the unity of the Jewish people).

*   *   *

The pace of world events since October 1973 has been such that it would be impossible to examine all of them in detail; one could write lengthy essays, for example, just on the reaction of the American Jewish community to the UN vote on racism or on the controversy surrounding Breira. The shock waves following Anwar el-Sadat's visit to Jerusalem in November 1977 have still not subsided. Instead, one must take a final look at some of the threads which have run continuously

through more than three decades of relations between American Jewry
and the Jewish state.

First of all, American support for Israel both in the political arena
and through financial aid remains high, although changing conditions
in American society may affect both areas. The "Israel lobby" is one of
the most effective in Washington. I. L. Kenen, and his successor,
Morris J. Amitai, have made the America-Israel Public Affairs Committee a respected voice in Washington. When necessary, AIPAC can also
call upon the national Jewish organizations for letter, telephone, and
telegram campaigns to impress Congress or the White House with just
how important Israel is to their constituents. Former Senator James
Buckley of New York, who enjoyed very little Jewish support, conceded wistfully: "The Jews are extremely effective in doing what the
Constitution encourages—that is, peaceful assembly and the right to
petition. I only wish others were as good at it as the Jews are."[1]

Yet, as Kenen and others have long been aware, the alleged power
of the Jewish voice is limited, restricted to the single question of Israel.
There is no Jewish voice on taxes, health care, defense, welfare reform,
or any of the other issues confronting American society today. On those
matters, Jews are just as divided and confused as are all Americans. But
on the survival and safety of Israel there is no ambiguity, and a good
part of American Jewry's success in lobbying for Israel derives from the
broad support which the Jewish state has enjoyed in this country since
its inception. Even at the height of the oil embargo, the Gallup poll
showed that only one out of a hundred Americans blamed Israel for the
energy crisis, and that three out of four believed the survival of Israel to
be important to the United States. Within Congress, senators and representatives have recognized that support of Israel extends far beyond
the 3 per cent of the electorate which is Jewish. A survey of the 94th
Congress found over 259 members in the House and 70 in the Senate
who could be counted on as friends of Israel; in one very specific test,
78 senators and 289 congressmen joined in cosponsoring the Jackson-
Vanik measure—although a majority of them had very few Jews in
their districts.

The "Israel lobby" has also benefited from the rise of a new generation of bureaucrats at the State Department. The old-line Arabists, who
saw the Zionist scheme as an attack on Great Britain's sphere of interest
or who viewed the Middle East as exclusively Arab territory, have either died or retired. In their places are relatively young men who have

almost always known Israel as a fact of Middle Eastern life, and to whom such a phrase as "British spheres of interest" belongs to history, not present reality. Moreover, within the State Department large numbers of experts see a strong Israel as a central factor in maintaining a balance of power in the Middle East, a counterweight to Arab regimes which would be less responsive to American initiatives if Israel did not exist. For the first time, the State Department has a pro-Israeli faction which can and does co-operate with leading pro-Israeli spokesmen in the Congress, such as Henry Jackson of Washington and Jacob Javits of New York.[2]

During these years, however, there have been far less encouraging signs. Israel became a pariah nation at the UN, more and more dependent upon the support of the United States. In this country, not only critics like William Fulbright were speaking of divided loyalties, but even friends like Senate majority leader Mike Mansfield of Montana, who publicly worried about the effects of "dual loyalty" on NBC's "Meet the Press." Newton Minow, former head of the Federal Communications Commission, and Marver Bernstein, president of Brandeis University, also expressed concern about a decline in pro-Israel sentiment. Rabbi Arthur Hertzberg, head of the American Jewish Congress, went even farther. If the Arab oil squeeze continued to hurt the American economy and accentuated the effects of the recession, not only Israel but also American Jewry would suffer. "When people are out of work and hungry," he warned, "they get angry, they start looking for scapegoats."[3]

The real question, one as yet unanswered, is whether American Jewry will be able to remain a "given" in American politics, whether it will be able to exert influence in the future comparable to its performances in the past. Some analysts believe that the recent campaign-spending law will hurt American Jewry by eliminating the clout of the big givers, while the congressional ethics codes will limit the honoraria paid so generously to senators and representatives speaking at Jewish functions. But it is doubtful whether either the big contributions or the honoraria have really had that much effect. The political influence of American Jews, so out of proportion to the 3 per cent of the population they constitute, is due to more than the mere fact of their demographic concentration in key electoral states. It has resulted from unity of purpose, organization, propaganda, and above all from the fact that they have been able to tap and channel widespread popular support for Israel and bring it to bear in the political arena. If that well should dry up, no amount of political contributions or overt pressure from a small ethnic minority would have much impact on American decision-makers.[4]

*   *   *

The second major area of pro-Israeli activity in the United States is fund-raising, and here American Jews have continued to be generous. Yet recent signs indicate that if the money well is not running dry, it may not, however, be spewing forth enough to meet Israeli demands. In November 1976, Finance Minister Yehoshua Rabinowitz presented a record $15 billion budget to the Israeli Cabinet, including a built-in $525 million deficit. A total of $4 billion was earmarked for defense, and obviously there could only be one source to help Israel meet its security needs. Efforts to influence the American Congress take on a new urgency when one realizes that tanks now cost $750,000 apiece, and fighter planes can run up to $15 million apiece. Social costs, to which the bulk of American money goes, are also on the rise. It takes more than $10,000 to settle a new immigrant, and the cost of medical care and equipment has also jumped sharply.[5]

The UJA still does an impressive job, working out a variety of ways to get more, and still more, money out of well-to-do American Jews.[6] Yet as Israel's needs grow, it is obvious that limits exist on American Jewish generosity. Moreover, with the recent discovery of large numbers of Jewish poor in America, there has been mounting pressure to use American Jewish money in the United States. Bertram H. Gold, the executive vice president of the American Jewish Committee, has condemned the "excessive" influence of Israel upon American Jewish life, and in an increasingly common refrain, asks: "Who is it that determines it is more important to provide funds for higher education in Israel than funds for Jewish education in the United States? Who is it that decides poor Jews in Tel-Aviv need improved housing and financial aid more urgently than do the poor Jews in Miami?"[7]

It should be plain, however, that the amounts of money raised for Israel give only a glimmering of the importance of the Jewish state in the life of American Jewry. Israel has become the dominant and central influence, and support for Israel has become the lowest common denominator of Jewish identity; opposition to Israel is seen by some to be an even greater deviation from communal norms than intermarriage. Israel, in the words of one writer, "is the ultimate reality in the life of every Jew living today. I believe that Israel surpasses in importance Jewish ritual. It is more than the Jewish tradition; and, in fact, it is more than the Mosaic law itself. . . . In dealing with those who oppose Israel, we are not reasonable and we are not rational. Nor should we be." The Jewish state is the chief source of pride and strength for the contemporary Jew; it has enabled him to cease being the victim of history, and to become an active and virile participant, to be a normal human being.[8] In this aspect, at least, the Zionist dream has succeeded.

Yet even while accepting Israel's importance, American Jewish leaders are also concerned about some of the implications of this relationship, and have pointed to a bewildering array of questions generated by the unique ties binding together Israel and the American Jewish community, questions which take on even greater urgency with the growing possibility of a peace settlement in the Middle East. Is Israel a part of the Jewish people, or is it the other way around? Are we truly equal partners in a dynamic Jewish peoplehood, or do we use each other? Do we exploit Israel as an "artificial kidney machine" to try to pump Jewish life into a moribund Jewish community? Is Israel our surrogate for a genuine Jewish life?

This last question in many ways is most troubling. Have we, as Daniel Elazar charged, developed a Judaism which is Israel-centered rather than God-centered? The Jewish state may be, as the Zionists have claimed, the pre-eminent expression of the Jewish people in modern times and is therefore the responsibility of the Jewish people, but it is not the end toward which Jewish history has tended. The real center of Jewish life must be Jewishness as a whole, not just its nationalistic aspects. Moreover, insofar as there is any hope of building an American Jewish life and culture in the United States, that life and culture must be based on American values and traditions. Israel can be a source of inspiration and pride, but it cannot sustain American Jewry vicariously, it cannot make American Jewry survive; only American Jews can accomplish these tasks.

A number of critics have also taken less than optimistic views of American Jewry's future. Robert Alter finds the community lacking in spiritual authenticity, and insulated from the necessity of "unflinching self-questioning" because the lives its members lead are only Jewish at one remove. David Sidorsky of Columbia University questions whether American Jews are even concerned about their long-term future in this country; indeed, any efforts to develop a particularistic cultural self-consciousness would probably be considered by most of them as a regression to ethnic parochialism and therefore opposed to the American spirit. "*The* issue for Jews in the 1970s," asserts Irving Horowitz, is "their survival as an ethnic group in their own right." And, according to both Milton Himmelfarb and Arthur Hertzberg, who agree on very little else, time is not on the side of American Jewry.[9]

While all this sounds dire indeed, one should bear in mind that forecasting doom is an old and honored Jewish tradition, honed by various prophets to a fine art; as Marshall Sklare has pointed out, "suffice it to say while American Jewry may be an ever-dying people, American Jewry still lives. The fact that American Jewry has survived the appeal of the New Left and the counterculture, the appeal of the Old Left to Eastern European Jews and of the Ethical Culture Movement to German Jews, the importunings of Christian missionaries (as well as dozens of other perils) will be taken by some as proof that the idea of *netzach yisrael* [eternal Israel] is valid and that its validity stems from a covenant between God and Israel." Moreover, Sklare recalls that Simon Rawidowicz noted that while Jews believe they are an ever-dying people, they have refused to hasten the end; to the contrary, they have undertaken heroic and extraordinary measures to prolong Jewish life.[10]

One can indeed find signs of life in the far from moribund corpus of American Judaism. For one thing, Orthodox Judaism, which observers in the 1950s and 1960s thought would die out in this country, has proven tenaciously durable, and the Lubovicher Hassidim, with considerable success, have actually set out to proselytize nonobservant Jews into fuller adherence to traditional customs. Younger Jews, disillusioned by the false hopes of the New Left, have flocked into Judaic Studies programs, which have mushroomed on campuses all across the country. Within the women's movement there have sprung up several groups attempting to synthesize traditional Jewish virtues and rituals with modern feminist demands for equality.

The old nineteenth-century saying of Y. L. Gordon, "Be a Jew in your home and a human being outside," has been turned around. The explosion of ethnicity in the 1960s made it possible for Jews of all classes and doctrinal persuasions to proudly proclaim their Jewishness. If black was beautiful, Jewish would be exquisite. Now it became fashionable to be Jewish outside one's home, to require that the greater society accept the right of Jews to be Jewish not only privately but also in public.

This is not to say that all is well with American Jewry. There are deepening differences among the three major religious branches, and even within them. In the past, Orthodox, Conservative, and Reform each conceded some measure of legitimacy to the other, a natural development in the light of the American pluralistic tradition. Now, due in no small measure to the strident militancy of the Israeli rabbinate, deviations from traditional practices are again becoming serious impediments to toleration and co-operation. American Jewry has, as a whole, tended to emphasize the ethnic bonds of Jewish peoplehood over the religious ties, thus allowing ritualistic and theological differences to be muted. But should there be a separation between ethnicity and religion, should one group of Jews deny legitimacy to another, schisms could easily occur, divisions which would weaken all of American Jewry in its struggle for survival and in its ability to support Israel.

Undoubtedly the greatest problem facing American Jewry results from its successful acceptance into American society. For the first time, Jews have been confronted with alternatives. Over thirty years ago, Jean-Paul Sartre, whose existentialist philosophy demanded that everyone choose how he or she would live life, declared: *"Ils ne peuvent pas choisir de ne pas être Juifs!"* Jews could not choose not to be Jews. But is this really true in America today? Jews, of course, could always opt out of Judaism completely, but in the United States they can select any number of points on a spectrum ranging from fully observant pietism to marginally cultural consciousness. The status of Jews in American society leaves individuals free to be whatever they choose, for better or for worse. It is the essence of a free society that this should be so. Such a condition, however, can either lead to a creative affirmation of Judaism, or to its rejection, or to total confusion. For all of the talk of ethnic and cultural pluralism and of triadic hegemony, American Jewry has still not found that delicate balance between Americanism and Judaism which will allow it to maintain its equilibrium. It is still seeking that ideal solution which allows paticularism to flourish in a pluralistic society.

*   *   *

There has been and continues to be hope that Israel will provide the ballast keeping Judaism in America stable, an anchor holding fast against the strong currents of assimilation. But can Israel, by itself, accomplish such tasks? For one thing, one can be a strong supporter of Israel yet only marginally attached to Judaism. Of greater difficulty, thirty years after the establishment of the Jewish state, relations between Israel and American Jewry are still in flux, with scarcely an outline apparent of what the ultimate set of relationships and responsibilities will look like. Unquestionably in times of crisis American Jewry will rally to Israel with political and financial support and do everything possible to sustain Israel's existence. But if the Middle East is about to enter a prolonged period of reduced tensions, what kind of ties will bind the two communities together? It is this question which concerns more and more Jewish leaders, both in Israel and in the United States.

Ideally, the Zionist movement might have become the chief instrument of communication and mediation between Israel and American Jewry, but the deliberate sabotage of the American organizations after 1948 practically destroyed this opportunity. David Polish and others still hope that Zionism might yet become "a measure by which the Jewish State and the *Galut* will test one another's achievements in terms transcending politics or immediacy." But whether Zionism can become, once again, a potent force in American Jewish life is debatable. David Sidorsky, noting the nonideological nature of American society as a whole, believes that it cannot; the dominant motif of American Jewry will be a generalized support of Israel, lacking both a philosophy of Jewish history and a coherent set of principles, although one with a high sense of moral purpose and a pragmatic political approach. In such a situation, he contends, "the distinction between a pro-Israeli consensus and a Zionist ideology is a distinction without a difference."[11]

But if Zionism cannot serve as the instrument of dialogue, neither can any other American or Israeli agency now in existence. The United Jewish Appeal is certainly striving to develop into that type of instrumentality, with an increasing part of its resources going toward Jewish education. Begun by the UJA Young Leadership Cabinet more than fifteen years ago, the program now has more than thirty-five thousand young Jewish men and women in development seminars, training sessions, and courses. Irving Bernstein, executive vice president of the UJA, believes that before the 1967 war, the campaign was used to raise funds; now it is used to raise Jews.[12] But while the UJA may be tending in the right direction, it still has a long way to go before it can or will be accepted as the major means of communication between Israel and American Jewry.

Such a conduit, however, is desperately needed, for a lasting and fruitful partnership between Israel and American Jewry cannot be built on support during crises alone. A partnership, and that is what American Jewry has always envisioned, needs stability, trust, and, above all, honest and at times critical dialogue. It also requires respect of the peculiar problems and traits of the other. And most important, there must be a willingness to recognize not only the ties that bind each to the other, but also the problems that separate them. Only then can partners begin to deal with their differences and, if possible, resolve them.

That there are problems no one denies. As Israel and American Jewry enter the fourth decade of their unique relationship, there is a certain sense of familiarity—one might almost say *déjà vu*—about some of these issues: the role of doctrine, acceptance of divergent religious practices, obligations of American Jews to Israel, *aliyah*, consultation, the influence of Israel upon American Jewish life. Some, such as the recognition of Conservative and Reform Judaism in Israel, are more pressing than others; the nature and importance of the relationship, however, may take decades to work out. But if there is to be any hope at all for the success of this partnership, it must be and always remain a relationship between equals. It is one thing for American Jewish life to be *Israelocentric*—that is, to have a vibrant, culturally creative Jewish homeland as a central feature of American life, to have it serve as a counterweight to the forces of assimilation. It is another to allow that relation to deteriorate into *Israelolotry*, the worship of the state without any critical or independent thinking or action by American Jews. All that can lead to is a feeling of inferiority and the ultimate demise of what has been an extraordinarily successful, creative, and free community.

An old Hebrew maxim holds that *Kol Yisrael arevim zeh lazeh*— All of Israel are responsible for one another—a statement which affirms the unity of the Jewish people, a sense of historical oneness transcending temporal or spatial differences of nationality, language, and customs. In the United States, this old saying has taken on a new form: "We Are One!" It does not mean that in all areas and on all issues American Jews and Israelis see eye to eye, or that they conform to an artificially imposed pattern. Rather it celebrates those ties that bind, those patterns which have emerged not only out of four thousand years of Jewish history and culture and tradition, but also out of the twentieth-century struggle for Jewish survival and for the re-creation of a Jewish state in its ancient homeland.

Key to Manuscript Citations

ACJ Coll. *American Council for Judaism Collection, American Jewish Archives, Cincinati, O.*

American Section Records *Records of the Jewish Agency for Palestine—American Section, Record Group Z5, Central Zionist Archives, Jerusalem, Israel*

AZEC Records *Files of the American Zionist Emergency Council and of the Emergency Council for Zionist Affairs, Zionist Archives and Library, New York, N.Y.*

Ben-Zvi MSS *Yitzhak Ben-Zvi Papers, Record Group A116, Central Zionist Archives, Jerusalem, Israel*

Berman MSS *Meyer Morton Berman Papers, privately held, Jerusalem, Israel*

Conference Records *American Jewish Conference Records, American Jewish Historical Society, Waltham, Mass.*

Ehrmann MSS *Herbert Brutus Ehrmann Papers, American Jewish Historical Society, Waltham, Mass.*

Feldmann MSS *Meyer Feldman Files, White House Staff Files, John F. Kennedy Library, Waltham, Mass.*

Frankfurter MSS *Felix Frankfurter Papers, Record Group A264, Central Zionist Archives, Jerusalem, Israel*

Friedenwald MSS *Harry Friedenwald Papers, Record Group A182, Central Zionist Archives, Jerusalem, Israel*

Goldstein MSS *Israel Goldstein Papers, Goldstein Collection, Jerusalem, Israel*

Hadassah Records *Minutes of Hadassah National Board, 1942–51, Hadassah Archives, New York, N.Y.*

Kaplan (Ageny) MSS *Papers of Eliezer Kaplan, as an officer of the Jewish Agency, Record Group S53, Central Zionist Archives, Jerusalem, Israel*

Kennedy MSS *John Fitzgerald Kennedy Papers, John F. Kennedy Library, Waltham, Mass.*

Landman MSS *Samuel Landman Papers, Record Group A226, Central Zionist Archives, Jerusalem, Israel*

Lehman MSS *Herbert Henry Lehman Papers, School of International Affairs Library, Columbia University, New York, N.Y.*

Levinthal MSS   *Louis Levinthal Papers, privately held, Philadelphia, Pa.*

London Office Files   *Records of the Zionist Organization/the Jewish Agency for Palestine—Central Office, London, Record Group Z4, Central Zionist Archives, Jerusalem, Israel*

Lowenthal MSS   *Marvin Lowenthal Papers, American Jewish Historical Society, Waltham, Mass.*

Magnes MSS   *Judah Leon Magnes Papers, Central Archives for the History of the Jewish People, The Hebrew University, Jerusalem, Israel*

Manson MSS   *Harold P. Manson Papers, Archives of Temple Tifereth Israel, Cleveland, O.*

Misc. Files, AJA   *Miscellaneous Files of the American Jewish Archives, Cincinnati, O.*

Near East Crisis Coll.   *Near East Crisis Collection, American Jewish Historical Society, Waltham, Mass.*

Non-Zionist Section Files   *Records of the Zionist Executive/Jewish Agency Section for the Organization of Non-Zionists, Record Group S29, Central Zionist Archives, Jerusalem, Israel*

Organization Dept. Files   *Records of the Zionist Executive/Jewish Agency Organization Department, Record Group S5, Central Zionist Archives, Jerusalem, Israel*

Political Dept. Files   *Records of the Zionist Executive/Jewish Agency Political Department, Record Group S25, Central Zionist Archives, Jerusalem, Israel*

Silver MSS   *Abba Hillel Silver Papers, Archives of Temple Tifereth Israel, Cleveland, O.*

Waldman MSS   *Morris D. Waldman Papers, American Jewish Archives, Cincinnati, O.*

Warburg MSS   *James Warburg Papers, John F. Kennedy Library, Waltham, Mass.*

Waskow MSS   *Arthur I. Waskow Papers, American Jewish Historical Society, Waltham, Mass.*

Weisgal MSS   *Meyer Weisgal Papers, privately held, Rehovot, Israel*

Weizmann MSS   *Chaim Weizmann Papers, Yad Chaim Weizmann, Rehovot, Israel*

Wise MSS   *Stephen Samuel Wise Papers, American Jewish Historical Society, Waltham, Mass.*

Notes to Prelude

1. The classic work on Arab nationalism is George Antonius, *The Arab Awakening* (London: Hamish Hamilton, 1938).

2. See Ehud Avriel, *Open the Gates!* (New York: Atheneum, 1975), *passim.*

3. Henry L. Feingold, *The Politics of Rescue: The Roosevelt Administration and the Holocaust, 1938–1945* (New Brunswick: Rutgers University Press, 1970), ch. 2; Golda Meir, *My Life* (New York: Putnam, 1975), p. 159; Chaim Weizmann to Stephen Wise, July 14, 1938, London Office Files, Z4/17198.

4. Melvin I. Urofsky, *American Zionism from Herzl to the Holocaust* (Garden City, N.Y.: Anchor Press, 1975), pp. 127–33.

5. *Congress Weekly,* January 17, 1941, quoted in Samuel Halperin, *The Political World of American Zionism* (Detroit: Wayne State University Press, 1961), p. 203; see also J. J. Schwartz and B. I. Vulcan, "Overseas Aid," *The American Jew: A Reappraisal,* ed. Oscar I. Janowsky (Philadelphia: Jewish Publication Society, 1967), pp. 289–90.

6. Halperin, *Political World of American Zionism,* p. 148; *Central Conference of American Rabbis Yearbook* 47 (1937): 98–99, hereafter cited as *CCAR Yearbook.*

7. Chaim Weizmann to Meyer Weisgal, May 1940, quoted in Meyer Weisgal, *. . . So Far, An Autobiography* (Jerusalem: Wiedenfeld and Nicolson, 1971), p. 165; see also Weizmann to Louis Levinthal, October 18, 1941, Levinthal MSS.

8. Urofsky, *American Zionism,* chs. 7, 9; Herbert Parzen, "American Zionism and the Quest for a Jewish State, 1939–43," *Herzl Year Book* 4 (1962): 348; Robert Szold, "The Issue Before the Convention," *New Palestine* 31 (July 18, 1941): 9; "The Proposed Zionist Commission," *ibid.* (Aug. 15, 1941): 4–5; "The Main Task of the Convention," *ibid.* (Sept. 5, 1941): 4.

9. Quoted in Robert Silverberg, *If I Forget Thee, O Jerusalem* (New York: Pyramid Books, 1972), pp. 183–84.

10. Halperin, *Political World of American Zionism,* p. 210; Felix Frankfurter, "The Palestine Situation Revisited," *Foreign Affairs* 9 (Apr. 1931): 409–34.

11. Ben Halpern, *The Idea of the Jewish State,* 2nd ed. (Cambridge, Mass.: Harvard University Press, 1969), p. 44.

12. Chaim Weizmann, "Palestine's Role in the Solution of the Jewish Problem," *Foreign Affairs* 20 (Jan. 1942): 324–38.

13. Shlomo Avineri, in Ehud Ben-Ezer, *Unease in Zion* (New York: Quadrangle, 1974), p. 37.

14. J. C. Hurewitz, *The Struggle for Palestine* (New York: Norton, 1950), pp. 156–57.

15. This and all other quotes from the meeting are taken from American Emergency Committee for Zionist Affairs, "Minutes of the Extraordinary Conference . . . at the Biltmore Hotel" (1942), typescript of stenographic record, Zionist Archives and Library, New York. See also New York *Times,* May 10–12, 1942.

16. See, for example, David Ben-Gurion, *Ben-Gurion Looks Back in Talks with Moshe Perlman* (New York: Simon & Schuster, 1965), p. 112; Weisgal, . . . *So Far,* pp. 173–77; interview with Weisgal, May 26, 1975. Revealingly, Weizmann does not mention the Biltmore conference in his memoirs.

17. Interview with Emanuel Neumann, Jan. 7, 1975.

18. Joseph M. Proskauer, *A Segment of My Times* (New York: Farrar, Straus, 1950), p. 237; Howard Morley Sachar, *Europe Leaves the Middle East, 1936–1954* (New York: Knopf, 1972), p. 443; Halpern, *Idea of the Jewish State,* pp. 40–47.

Notes to Chapter 1

1. An excellent history of the Committee is Naomi W. Cohen, *Not Free to Desist* (Philadelphia: Jewish Publication Society, 1972); for its relief efforts see Oscar Handlin, *A Continuing Task* (New York: Random House, 1964), and Zosa Szajkowski, "The Private and Organized American Jewish Overseas Relief, 1914–1938," published in six installments, *American Jewish Historical Quarterly,* beginning Sept. 1967. For the Jewish Agency, see Urofsky, *American Zionism from Herzl to the Holocaust,* ch. 8, and Zelig Chinitz, "The Jewish Agency and the Jewish Community in the United States," master's essay (Columbia University, 1959).

2. "Statement on the American Jewish Committee and Judge Louis Levinthal," Feb. 28, 1945, Silver MSS; Halperin, *Political World of American Zionism,* p. 121.

3. Arthur Lourie to J. Linton, Jan. 12, 1942, and to Leo Lauterbach, Feb. 12, 1942, Organization Department Records, S5/693.

4. Ben-Gurion, in effect, cut Weizmann out of the negotiations; see Meyer Weisgal to Gershon Agronsky, July 29, 1942, Weisgal MSS.

5. Minutes of Office Committee of Emergency Committee on Zionist Affairs, June 3, 1942, Kaplan (Agency) MSS, S53/469.

6. "Statement on American Jewish Committee . . . ," Silver MSS.

7. David Ben-Gurion to Maurice Wertheim, Apr. 18, 1942, Political Department Records, S25/41, and to Moshe Shertok, July 13, 1972, *ibid.*, S25/1458. For criticism regarding Ben-Gurion's actions, see Ben-Gurion to Shertok, July 8, 1942, Weizmann MSS, and to Louis E. Levinthal, July 9, 1942, Manson MSS.

8. Cohen, *Not Free to Desist*, p. 252; Selig Adler, "American Jewry and that Explosive Statehood Question, 1933–1945," *A Bicentennial Festschrift for Jacob Rader Marcus*, ed. Bertram Wallace Korn, (New York: KTAV, 1976), pp. 15–16.

9. Joseph M. Proskauer to Morris D. Waldman, Apr. 25, 1942, in Morris D. Waldman, *Nor by Power* (New York: International Universities Press, 1953), p. 240.

10. David Ben-Gurion to Louis E. Levinthal, Sept. 2, 1942, Political Department Records, S25/1458; Arthur Lourie to Leo Lauterbach, Sept. 4, 1942, Organization Department Records, S5/693.

11. For the basis of this attitude, see Moses Rischin, "The Early Attitude of the American Jewish Committee to Zionism," *Publications of the American Jewish Historical Society* 49 (1959): 188–201.

12. Daisy Monsky and Henry Bisgyer, *Henry Monsky: The Man and His Work* (New York: Crown, 1947), p. 86; Isaac Neustadt-Noy, "Toward Unity: Zionist and Non-Zionist Co-operation," *Herzl Year Book* 8 (1978): ch. 9.

13. Nahum Goldmann to Eliezer Kaplan, Dec. 21, 1942, Political Department Records, S25/469A.

14. Goldmann to Kaplan, Jan. 28, 1943; Arthur Lourie to Leo Lauterbach, Sept. 2, 1943, London Office Records, Z4/19948.

15. American Jewish Conference, *Organization and Proceedings of the First Session* (New York: AJC, 1944), pp. 15–17, hereafter cited as *Conference Proceedings*.

16. *Ibid.*, p. 23; Nahum Goldmann to Eliezer Kaplan, Jan. 28, 1943, Political Department Records, S25/469A.

17. *Conference Proceedings*, p. 39.

18. Goldmann to Eliezer Kaplan, Jan. 28, 1943, Political Department Records, S25/469A.

19. *Conference Proceedings*, p. 167; Proskauer, *A Segment of My Times*, p. 199.

20. Stephen S. Wise to Harry Friedenwald, Feb. 11, 1943, Friedenwald MSS, A182/20. Friedenwald had resigned from the Committee once before, in 1916, also in protest against its opposition to democracy in American Jewish life, and at that time was joined by Israel Friedlaender and Felix Frankfurter.

21. "Let the Majority Decide," *Congress Weekly* 10 (Feb. 5, 1943): 3.

22. Adler, "American Jewry and that Explosive Statehood Question," pp. 11–12.

23. Cohen, *Not Free to Desist*, p. 257; Waldman, *Nor by Power*, pp. 253–54.

24. Meyer Weisgal to Berl Locker, Feb. 7, 1943, Weizmann MSS; Stephen Wise to Harry Friedenwald, Feb. 11, 1943, Friedenwald MSS, A182/20; Waldman, *Nor by Power*, p. 253.

25. *Conference Proceedings*, pp. 40–41.

26. *Ibid.*, pp. 47–50; Proskauer, *Segment of My Times*, p. 200; Nahum Goldmann to Moshe Shertok, July 14, 1943, American Section Records, Z5/387.

27. *Conference Proceedings*, p. 67; Monsky and Bisgyer, *Henry Monsky*, pp. 92–93.

28. *Ibid.*, p. 93; see the criticism in Daniel Frisch, *On the Road to Zion* (New York: ZOA, 1950), pp. 118–19.

29. Zvi Ganin, "The Diplomacy of the Weak: American Zionist Leadership in the Truman Era, 1945–1958," doctoral dissertation (Brandeis University, 1974), pp. 27–28; Waldman, *Nor by Power*, p. 257; Abba Hillel Silver to Lazarus Goodman, Nov. 26, 1943, American Section Records, Z5/653; Monty N. Penkower, "The 1943 Joint Anglo-American Statement on Palestine," *Herzl Year Book* 8 (1978): ch. 13.

30. Minutes of Office Committee, Emergency Committee for Zionist Affairs, June 21, 1943, Organization Department Records, S5/693.

31. Emergency Committee for Zionist Affairs, Minutes, Apr. 29, 1943, AZEC Records; see also editorial in *New Palestine* 33 (June 11, 1943): 3.

32. Interview with Emanuel Neumann, July 1, 1975; Meyer Weisgal to Chaim Weizmann, Aug. 11, 1943, Weizmann MSS.

33. Halperin, *Political World of American Zionism*, p. 133; Waldman, *Nor by Power*, p. 258; Doreen Bierbrier, "The American Zionist Emergency Council: An Analysis of a Pressure Group," *American Jewish Historical Quarterly* 60 (Sept. 1970): 86–87; Abba Hillel Silver, *Vision and Victory* (New York: ZOA, 1949), pp. 13–14.

34. Interview with Emanuel Neumann, (July 1, 1975); Emanuel Neumann, *In the Arena: An Autobiographical Memoir* (New York: Herzl Press, 1976), p. 191.

35. *Conference Proceedings*, pp. 100–1.

36. *Ibid.*, pp. 177–78.

37. *Ibid.*, pp. 167–69; Arthur Lourie to Leo Lauterbach, Sept. 2, 1943, London Office Records, Z4/19948.

38. Address of Judge Morris Rothenberg to ZOA convention, Sept. 13, 1943, Organization Department Records, S5/777; *New Palestine* 34 (Nov. 12, 1943): 89; cable, Nahum Goldmann to Zionist executive, Jerusalem,

Sept. 3, 1943, Organization Department Records, S5/693; Stephen Wise's closing comments, *Conference Proceedings,* p. 178; Meyer Weisgal to Chaim Weizmann, Sept. 3, 1943, Weisgal MSS.

39. Cohen, *Not Free to Desist,* pp. 294–95; Emergency Committee for Zionist Affairs, Minutes of Sept. 27, 1943, AZEC Records; Halperin, *Political World of American Zionism,* pp. 245–46; *New Palestine* 34 (Oct. 29, 1943): 63.

40. Leo Lauterbach to Arthur Lourie, Nov. 4, 1943, Organization Department Records, S5/694; Joseph Seth Drew, "Elite Jews, Establishment Jews, and Zionism, 1943–1948: A Study of 'Leaders from the Periphery,'" doctoral dissertation (New School for Social Research, 1975), pp. 241–42; Bierbrier, "Zionist Emergency Council," pp. 101–2.

41. Louis E. Levinthal, *The Credo of an American Zionist* (Washington: ZOA, 1943), pp. 8–9.

42. 1942 speech, reprinted in Salo Wittmeyer Baron, *Steeled by Adversity: Essays and Addresses on American Jewish Life,* ed. Jeannette Meisel Baron (Philadelphia: Jewish Publication Society, 1971), p. 460; Philip M. Klutznik, *No Easy Answers* (New York: Farrar, Straus, and Cudahy, 1961), p. 74.

43. *New Palestine* 33 (Nov. 6, 1942): 4. Yiddish columnist Shmuel Margoshes agreed: "It is perfectly evident now that we shall either reach our aim by one bold stroke, or not at all."

44. Lionel Gelber, "American Jewry, Bethink Ye!" *Menorah Journal* 31 (Winter 1943): 1–14; also Emanuel Celler, *You Never Leave Brooklyn* (New York: John Day, 1953), pp. 113–14. Samuel Halperin notes that groups which would have preferred an independent course of action, such as the American Jewish Committee, were inundated by the pro-Palestine sentiment. He cites a memorandum from Morris Waldman in September 1943 regarding the "invulnerable position" of the Zionists, and contrasted it with "the weakness of opposition to the theory of a commonwealth or state on the ground that it would prove an embarrassment and danger to Jews outside Palestine." *Political World of American Zionism,* p. 188.

45. Roper poll, cited in Joseph L. Blau, *Judaism in America: From Curiosity to Third Faith* (Chicago: University of Chicago Press, 1976), p. 87; Handlin, *A Continuing Task,* p. 81; Naomi W. Cohen, *American Jews and the Zionist Idea* (New York: KTAV, 1975), p. 61.

46. Bierbrier, "Zionist Emergency Council," pp. 83–84; *New Palestine* 35 (Oct. 13, 1944): 13.

47. For yearly membership figures of the major Zionist organizations during this period, see Halperin, *Political World of American Zionism,* Appendix V, p. 327.

48. Alan R. Taylor, *Prelude to Israel: An Analysis of Zionist Diplo-*

macy, 1897–1947 (New York: Philosophical Library, 1959), p. 78; Silver, *Vision and Victory*, pp. 54–55; Halperin, *Political World of American Zionism*, pp. 185–86; Bierbrier, "Zionist Emergency Council," pp. 90–91. A good sampling of the favorable responses engendered by this effort can be found in American Zionist Emergency Council, *America Speaks on Palestine* (New York: AZEC, 1944); for day-to-day operations of the Council, see Arthur Lourie to Leo Lauterbach, Aug. 11, 1942.

49. Urofsky, *American Zionism*, p. 422.

50. Halperin, *Political World of American Zionism*, pp. 160–70.

51. Saul S. Friedman, *No Haven for the Oppressed: United States Policy Toward Jewish Refugees, 1938–1945* (Detroit: Wayne State University Press, 1973), pp. 31–32; *Christian Century*, May 3, 1933, quoted in Hertzel Fishman, *American Protestantism and a Jewish State* (Detroit: Wayne State University Press, 1973), p. 37.

52. Editorial, "The Christian World Must Act," *Jewish Frontier* 10 (Jan. 1943): 3.

53. Frank Talmage, "Christian Theology and the Holocaust," *Commentary* 60 (Oct. 1975): 72–75; Fishman, *American Protestantism and a Jewish State*, pp. 61–62.

54. *Biltmore Proceedings*, p. 464.

55. Joseph B. Schechtman, *The United States and the Jewish State Movement: The Crucial Decade, 1939–1949* (New York: Herzl Press, 1966), p. 65; Walter Laqueur, *A History of Zionism* (New York: 1972), pp. 550–51; Halperin, *Political World of American Zionism*, pp. 182–83.

56. Fishman, *American Protestantism and a Jewish State*, p. 73; interview with Carl Hermann Voss, Sept. 9, 1975.

57. *Palestine Year Book* 1 (5706/1945): 371–72.

58. Halperin, *Political World of American Zionism*, p. 185; Bierbrier, "Zionist Emergency Council," p. 95.

Notes to Chapter 2

1. Raul Hilberg, *The Destruction of the European Jews* (Chicago: Quadrangle, 1967), pp. 262–66; William L. Shirer, *The Rise and Fall of the Third Reich* (New York: Simon & Schuster, 1960), pp. 963–67.

2. Friedman, *No Haven for the Oppressed*, p. 141; interview with Louis E. Levinthal, Dec. 22, 1972.

3. Feingold, *Politics of Rescue*, pp. 168–71; Stephen S. Wise, *Chal-*

lenging Years (New York: Putnam, 1949), pp. 274–75; Silverberg, *If I Forget Thee,* pp. 224–25; interview with Gerhard Riegner, Feb. 23, 1978.

4. Justine Wise Polier and James Waterman Wise, eds., *The Personal Letters of Stephen Wise* (Boston: Beacon Press, 1956), p. 260.

5. Chaim Weizmann to Meyer Weisgal, Apr. 13, 1944, Weizmann MSS.

6. Baron, *Steeled by Adversity,* pp. 510–11; see the moving eulogy to this lost world, Abraham Joshua Heschel, *The Earth Is the Lord's* (New York: Harper, 1966), and also Mark Zborowski and Elizabeth Herzog, *Life Is with People* (New York: Schocken, 1962).

7. Speech in Madison Square Garden, New York, quoted in *Chaim Weizmann: A Biography by Several Hands,* eds. Meyer Weisgal and Joel Carmichael, (London: Wiedenfeld and Nicolson, 1962), pp. 265–66.

8. *Public Opinion Quarterly* 8 (1944): 588.

9. Richard L. Rubenstein, *The Cunning of History: Mass Death and the American Future* (New York: Scribner's, 1975), p. 18.

10. Originally published in *Yiddisher Kemfer,* Feb. 12, 1943, cited in Ganin, "Diplomacy of the Weak," p. 19.

11. Meir Kahane, *Democracy in Jewish Life* (New York: Jewish Defense League, 1975), pp. 2–3.

12. Elie Wiesel, *Two Images, One Destiny* (New York: United Jewish Appeal, 1974), pp. 4–5.

13. Friedman, *No Haven for the Oppressed,* p. 139; see also Kahane, *Democracy in Jewish Life,* p. 3.

14. Selig Adler, "The United States and the Holocaust," *American Jewish Historical Quarterly* 64 (Sept. 1974): 14–15.

15. Irwin Oder, "American Zionism and the Congressional Resolution of 1922 on Palestine," *Publications of the American Jewish Historical Society* 45 (1955): 35–47.

16. Morton Keller, "Jews and the Character of American Life since 1930," in Charles Herbert Stember et al., *Jews in the Mind of America* (New York: Basic Books, 1966), p. 265; *Public Opinion Quarterly* 7 (1943): 313; Joseph L. Blau, *Modern Varieties of Judaism* (New York: Columbia University Press, 1966), pp. 146–47.

17. Lucy S. Dawidowicz and Leon J. Goldstein, "The American Jewish Liberal Tradition," *The Jewish Community in America,* ed. Marshall Sklare (New York: Behrman House, 1974), p. 297; Max Kleiman, ed., *Franklin Delano Roosevelt: The Tribute of the Synagogue* (New York: Bloch, 1946), contains numerous eulogies of Roosevelt.

18. Urofsky, *American Zionism,* pp. 402–15.

19. David Ben-Gurion to Moshe Shertok, July 8, 1972, memorandum of meeting with Roosevelt, June 11, 1943, and Meyer Weisgal to Chaim

Weizmann, Mar. 13 and Apr. 20, 1945, all in Weizmann MSS; Weizmann, *Trial and Error,* p. 435; Stephen Wise to Eliezer Kaplan, Mar. 17, 1944, Political Department Records, S25/1010; *New Palestine* 34 (Feb. 4, 1944): 227; Schechtman, *United States and Jewish State,* p. 94.

20. The first sustained account was the popularized emotional volume by Arthur D. Morse, *While Six Million Died: A Chronicle of American Apathy* (New York: Random House, 1967); more scholarly works are David S. Wyman, *Paper Walls: America and the Refugee Crisis, 1938–1941* (Amherst: University of Massachusetts Press, 1968), and Saul S. Friedman, *No Haven for the Oppressed,* although I disagree with Friedman's interpretation that American Jews were willing collaborators in this process; the most balanced monograph is Feingold, *Politics of Rescue,* which takes into account institutional factors, and upon which I have relied heavily.

21. Cohen, *Amerian Jews and the Zionist Idea,* p. 47.

22. Wyman, *Paper Walls,* p. 210.

23. William E. Leuchtenburg, *Franklin D. Roosevelt and the New Deal, 1932–1940* (New York: Harper, 1963), pp. 101, 276; Arthur M. Schlesinger, Jr., *The Politics of Upheaval* (Boston: Houghton Mifflin, 1960), pp. 78–82.

24. Stember, *Jews in the Mind of America,* pp. 214–15; diary entry for Jan. 22, 1943, in Joseph P. Lash, ed., *From the Diaries of Felix Frankfurter* (New York: Norton, 1975), pp. 165–66.

25. Feingold, *Politics of Rescue,* pp. 141–42; Josiah E. Du Bois, Jr., *The Devil's Chemists* (New York, 1952), p. 189, cited in Schechtman, *United States and Jewish State,* p. 40n.

26. Feingold, *Politics of Rescue,* pp. 135–36; see also Fred L. Israel, ed., *The War Diary of Breckinridge Long: Selections from the Years 1939–1944* (Lincoln: University of Nebraska Press, 1966), although some of the entries regarding refugees were omitted.

27. See, for example, Hull to Louis E. Levinthal, Sept. 8, 1943, Levinthal MSS; *The Memoirs of Cordell Hull,* 2 vols. (New York: Macmillan, 1948) 2:1539.

28. Feingold, *Politics of Rescue,* p. 15; Silverberg, *If I Forget Thee,* pp. 226–27.

29. Israel Goldstein, *The Road Ahead: A Program for American Zionism* (Washington: ZOA, 1944), pp. 11–12.

30. George Backer oral history memoir, Oct. 20, 1966, Oral History Collection—ICJ; memorandum of interview between Nahum Goldmann and Sol Bloom, June 30, 1943, American Section Records, Z5/666; Feingold, *Politics of Rescue,* p. 265; see also James Heller to Paul Baerwald, Jan. 12, 1945, Goldstein MSS, file 841.

31. Wyman, *Paper Walls,* p. 209; see also David Brody, "American

Jewry, the Refugees, and Immigration Restriction," *Publications of the American Jewish Historical Society* 45 (June 1956): 222–25. There has been some dispute over the actual number of refugees admitted into the United States. In March 1943 Long asserted that 547,775 refugees from Nazism had entered this country since 1933; later in the year, before the House Foreign Affairs Committee, he set the figure at 580,000. Long did not distinguish between Jewish and non-Jewish refugees, and when the point was raised as to the specific number of Jewish refugees, he evaded a direct answer. Later research by various Jewish groups calculate the number of Jewish refugees at between 138,000 and 183,000. The Hebrew Immigrant Aid Society also disputed the number of visas available, claiming that of the 460,000 that could have been used between 1938 and 1942, only 228,964 had actually been issued.

32. See, for example, Silver, *Vision and Victory*, p. 66.

33. Celler, *You Never Leave Brooklyn*, pp. 88–89; editorial, "The Gentlemen at Bermuda," *Jewish Frontier* 10 (May 1943): 3.

34. John Morton Blum, ed., *From the Morgenthau Diaries: Years of War, 1941–1945* (Boston: Houghton Mifflin, 1967), pp. 220–24; editorial, *New Palestine* 34 (Feb. 4, 1944): 227.

35. Blum, *Morgenthau Diaries*, p. 226.

36. Stephen Wise to Felix Frankfurter (Oct. 14, 1942), quoted in Carl Hermann Voss, *Stephen S. Wise: Servant of the People* (Philadelphia: Jewish Publication Society, 1969), p. 252.

37. Hull, *Memoirs* 2: 1531–32.

38. Frank E. Manuel, *The Realities of American-Palestine Relations* (Washington: Public Affairs Press, 1949), pp. 310–11.

39. Memorandum of meeting, Mar. 3, 1943, American Section Records, Z5/1377.

40. Memorandum of conversation between Nahum Goldmann and A. A. Berle, Sept. 16, 1943, Weizmann MSS; see also memorandum of interview, Robert Szold, Nahum Goldmann, and Loy Henderson, July 6, 1943, American Section Records, Z5/666, and memorandum of conversation, Meyer Berlin and Henry Wallace, Feb. 24, 1943, Political Department Records, S25/10156.

41. Ganin, "Diplomacy of the Weak," pp. 27–28; memorandum, Apr. 11, 1944, *Foreign Relations of the United States, 1944* (Washington: Government Printing Office, 1965), 5: 602; hereafter cited as *FRUS*. A definitive study of the proposed Anglo-American document is Monty N. Penkower, "The 1943 Anglo-American Statement," *Herzl Year Book* 8 (1978): ch. 13.

42. Neumann, *In the Arena*, pp. 158–59; a similar conversation took place between Vice President Henry A. Wallace and Bernard Rosenblatt,

reported in Bernard Rosenblatt, *Two Generations of Zionism* (New York: Shengold, 1967), pp. 193–94.

43. AZEC Minutes, Jan. 7, 1943.

44. Memorandum of meeting with Cordell Hull, Sept. 18, 1943, American Section Records, Z5/666; *FRUS 1943*, 4: 757.

45. Chaim Weizmann to Blanche Dugdale, Jan. 8, 1943, Weizmann MSS; memorandum of conversation, Chaim Weizmann, Nahum Goldmann, and Sumner Welles, May 18, 1943, American Section Records, Z5/1377; entry for June 18, 1943, *Frankfurter Diaries*, p. 261; *FRUS 1943*, 4: 763.

46. *Biltmore Proceedings*, p. 463.

47. Weisgal, . . . *So Far*, p. 187.

48. Robert A. Divine, *Foreign Policy and U. S. Presidential Elections*, 2 vols. (New York: New Viewpoints, 1974), 2: 106–7; Leon I. Feuer, "Abba Hillel Silver: A Personal Memoir," *American Jewish Archives* 19 (Nov. 1967): 120.

49. Speech of May 2, 1943, in *Vision and Victory*, pp. 4–5.

50. Carl J. Friedrich, *American Policy Toward Palestine* (Washington: Public Affairs Press, 1944), pp. 45–46.

51. Manuel, *Realities of American-Palestine Relations*, p. 309; memorandum of conversation with Sol Bloom, Nahum Goldmann, and Henry Shulman, Dec. 8, 1943, American Section Records, Z5/666.

52. AZEC Minutes, Jan. 3, 1943; Christopher Sykes, *Crossroads to Israel, 1917–1948* (Bloomington: Indiana University Press, 1965), p. 272; *FRUS 1944*, 5: 560–62.

53. Hull, *Memoirs* 2: 1534–35; *FRUS 1944*, 5: 563–64.

54. AZEC Minutes, Feb. 7 and 28, 1944; Reuben Fink, *America and Palestine* (New York: Herald Square Press, 1945), *passim*; Emanuel Neumann to Abba Hillel Silver, Jan. 28, 1944, Manson MSS; Silver to Chaim Weizmann, Mar. 3, 1944, Weizmann MSS.

55. AZEC Minutes, March 13, 1944.

56. Silver, *Vision and Victory*, pp. 83–84.

57. AZEC Minutes, July 10, 1944; for details of the Republican platform, see Kirk H. Porter and Donald Bruce Johnson, eds., *National Party Platforms* (Urbana: University of Illinois Press, 1970), p. 413.

58. Stephen S. Wise to Morton Berman, July 5, 1944, Berman MSS; Wise to Harry Friedenwald, Aug. 1, 1944, Friedenwald MSS, A182/20; American Council for Judaism, *The American of Jewish Faith* (Philadelphia: ACJ, 1945), pp. 9–10.

59. Porter and Johnson, *National Party Platform*, p. 403.

60. Adler, "U.S. and Holocaust," p. 17; Celler, *You Never Leave Brooklyn*, p. 117.

61. Memorandum of interview, Abba Hillel Silver and Samuel I. Rosenman, Oct. 12, 1943, Weizmann MSS; *New Palestine* 32 (June 12, 1942): 4; Weizmann, *Trial and Error*, p. 435; Ben-Gurion, *Ben-Gurion Looks Back*, p. 111; Herbert Parzen, "The Roosevelt Palestine Policy, 1943–1945: An Exercise in Dual Diplomacy," *American Jewish Archives* 26 (April 1974): 35.

62. Friedman, *No Haven for the Oppressed*, p. 50.

63. Herbert Feis, *The Birth of Israel: The Tousled Diplomatic Bed* (New York: Norton, 1969), p. 16; Hull, *Memoirs* 2: 1517; Adler, "U.S. and Holocaust," p. 19; see also memorandum on interview, Chaim Weizmann and Franklin Roosevelt, July 7, 1942, Weizmann MSS.

64. See, for example, Roosevelt to Ibn Sa'ud, May 26, 1943, *FRUS 1943* 4: 786–87. *FRUS* volumes for 1943 (Vol. 4), 1944 (Vol. 5), and 1945 (Vol. 8) are replete with assurances to various Arab countries.

65. Parzen, "Roosevelt Palestine Policy," pp. 36–39; *FRUS 1943*, 4: 782–85; Hull, *Memoirs* 2: 1512–13, 1532; memorandum of conversation, Nahum Goldmann and Wallace Murray, Sept. 23, 1943, American Section Records, Z5/666.

66. Blum, *Morgenthau Diaries*, p. 208.

67. Weizmann, *Trial and Error*, p. 427; memorandum of meeting, Chaim Weizmann and Franklin Roosevelt, June 11, 1943, Weizmann MSS; Feis, *Birth of Israel*, pp. 16–17.

68. James F. Byrnes, *Speaking Frankly* (New York: Harper, 1947), p. 22; Charles E. Bohlen, *Witness to History, 1929–1969* (New York: Norton, 1973), p. 212. This conversation was omitted from the published record of the Yalta conference.

69. Manuel, *Realities of America-Palestine Relationship*, p. 313; Stephen Wise to Chaim Weizmann, Mar. 21, 1945, Weizmann MSS.

70. New York *Times*, Mar. 2, 1945.

71. Ganin, "Diplomacy of the Weak," p. 38; Schechtman, *United States and Jewish State*, pp. 110–11; Ben Hecht, *A Child of the Century* (New York: Simon & Schuster, 1954), p. 582.

72. Stephen Wise to Chaim Weizmann, Mar. 21, 1945, Weizmann MSS.

73. Meyer Weisgal to Chaim Weizmann, Apr. 20, 1945, *ibid.*; Schechtman, *United States and Jewish State*, p. 122; Sumner Welles, *We Need Not Fail* (Boston: Houghton Mifflin, 1948), pp. 30–31.

74. See, for example, Abba Silver's speech in May 1943 in *Vision and Victory*, p. 7.

75. James MacGregor Burns, *Roosevelt: The Soldier of Freedom* (New York: Harcourt Brace Jovanovich, 1970), p. 396.

76. Manuel, *Realities of America-Palestine Relationship*, pp. 314–15.

77. Feingold, *Politics of Rescue,* p. xiii; Selig Adler, "Franklin D. Roosevelt and Zionism—The Wartime Record," *Judaism* 21 (Summer 1972): 265–76, also shows the diverse pressures on the President.

Notes to Chapter 3

1. For criticism of the Conference, see minutes of Second Plenary Session, Silver MSS; Meyer Weisgal to Chaim Weizmann, Nov. 9, 1943, Weizmann MSS; *New Palestine* 35 (Nov. 17, 1944): 24; Frisch, *On the Road to Zion,* p. 118; (Indianapolis) *Jewish Post,* Jan. 21, 1944, in Waldman MSS; Hadassah National Board Minutes, Nov. 12, 1944.

2. Naomi Weiner, "Reform Judaism in America and Zionism, 1897–1922," master's essay (Columbia University, 1949); David Polish, *Renew Our Days: The Zionist Issue in Reform Judaism* (Jerusalem: World Union for Progressive Judaism and World Zionist Organization, 1976), ch. 2.

3. Herschel Levin, "The Other Side of the Coin," *Herzl Year Book* 5 (1963): 33–56; Arthur Gilbert, *A Jew in Christian America* (New York: Sheed and Ward, 1966), pp. 77–78; W. Gunther Plaut, ed., *The Growth of Reform Judaism: American and European Sources to 1948* (New York: World Union for Progressive Judaism, 1965), p. 97.

4. Ethan M. Fishman, "Reform: The Popularization and Politicalization of Judaism," doctoral dissertation (Duke University, 1974), pp. 99–100; Howard Robert Greenstein, "The Changing Attitudes Toward Zionism in Reform Judaism, 1937–1948," doctoral dissertation (The Ohio State University, 1973), pp. 68–69; Halperin, *Political World of American Zionism,* pp. 82–83.

5. Barry Silverberg, "Beyond the Communal Consensus: The American Council for Judaism," seminar paper (Brandeis University, 1974), p. 11; I am indebted to Mr. Silverberg for allowing me use of this paper as well as generously sharing the materials he has collected on the Council.

6. Greenstein, "Changing Attitudes Toward Zionism," pp. 77–78; Halperin, *Political World of American Zionism,* pp. 287–88; Louis Wolsey, "The Meaning of Reform Judaism," speech of Oct. 24, 1942, in *Sermons and Addresses* (Philadelphia: Congregation Rodeph Sholom, 1950), pp. 6–7.

7. Elmer Berger memorandum, Jan. 28, 1969, in possession of Mr. Silverberg; Silverberg, "Beyond the Communal Consensus," p. 15.

8. Myron Berman, "Rabbi Edward Nathan Calisch and the Debate

over Zionism in Richmond, Virginia," *American Jewish Historical Quarterly* 62 (Mar. 1973): 295–305; Esther Feldblum, "On the Eve of a Jewish State; American-Catholic Responses," *ibid.* 64 (Dec. 1974): 114–15.

9. Greenstein, "Changing Attitudes Toward Zionism," ch. 3; Eli N. Evans, *The Provincials: A Personal History of Jews in the South* (New York: Atheneum, 1973), p. 102.

10. Berman, "Edward Nathan Calisch," p. 302. One congregation, B'nai Israel of Baton Rouge, Louisiana, did follow Beth-Israel's example; see round-robin letter signed by the rabbi and officers of B'nai Israel, Apr. 25, 1945, in Silver MSS.

11. Greenstein, "Changing Attitudes Toward Zionism," pp. 110–13; *New Palestine* 34 (Dec. 10, 1943): 133.

12. Berger memorandum, Jan. 28, 1969.

13. Ben Halpern, "The Impact of Israel on Jewish Ideologies in the United States," *Jewish Social Studies* 21 (Jan. 1959): 67–68; interview with Louis Levinthal, Dec. 22, 1972.

14. Emanuel Neumann to Israel Goldstein, Sept. 15, 1942, Goldstein MSS, File 1614c; Bierbrier, "American Zionist Emergency Council," pp. 102–3.

15. See, for example, *New Palestine* 33 (Dec. 18, 1942): 5, 15; Oscar I. Janowsky, "Zionism Today: A Clarification," *Menorah Journal* 31 (Autumn 1943): 257; Israel Goldstein, *The Road Ahead* (Washington: ZOA, 1944), p. 19.

16. Nahum Goldmann to Eliezer Kaplan, Dec. 21, 1942, Political Department Records, S25/469A; see also Shlomo Grodzensky, "United Front Against Zionism," *Jewish Frontier* 10 (Jan. 1943): 10.

17. Alfred M. Lilienthal accuses the Zionists of using the Holocaust for their own purposes, but tellingly fails to mention any concern the Council might have had for European Jewry. *What Price Israel?* (Chicago: Henry Regnery, 1953), pp. 18–19.

18. *CCAR Yearbook* 53 (1943): 92–93; Michael A. Meyer, "A Centennial History," in Samuel E. Karff, *Hebrew Union College-Jewish Institute of Religion at One Hundred Years* (Cincinnati: HUC-JIR, 1976), pp. 131–32; for a rather bitter portrait of the college during the war years, see Richard L. Rubenstein, *Power Struggle: An Autobiographical Confession* (New York: Scribner's, 1974), pp. 57–60; Abba Hillel Silver to Stephen S. Wise, Jan. 6 and 20, 1944, Manson MSS.

19. Adler, "That Statehood Question," p. 15; Elmer Berger to George W. Maxey, July 31, 1944, and Maxey to Berger, Aug. 2, 1944, Organization Department Records, S5/694.

20. Louis Wolsey, "Why I Withdrew from the American Council for Judaism," *Sermons and Addresses*, pp. 13–16.

21. See also Lilienthal, *What Price Israel?*, p. 47.

22. See Herman (Chaim) Leiberman, *Strangers to Glory: An Appraisal of the American Council for Judaism* (New York: Rainbow Press, 1955), and Isaac Deutscher, "The Non-Jewish Jew," *The Non-Jewish Jew and Other Essays* (London: East West Press, 1968).

23. The following section on Revisionism is based primarily on Joseph Schechtman's two-volume biography of Jabotinsky (New York: Thomas Yoseloff, 1956 and 1961), and Schechtman and Yehuda Benari, *History of the Revisionist Movement* (Tel Aviv: Hadar, 1970).

24. Within the Irgun an even more extreme group of terrorists arose, the so-called Stern Gang, or *Lohame Herut Israel* (Fighters for the Freedom of Israel), which was responsible for the assassination of Lord Moyne, the British deputy minister of state, in Cairo in 1944; see J. Bowyer Bell, *Terror Out of Zion* (New York: St. Martin's Press, 1977), parts one and two.

25. Copy of circular letter from Jeremiah Halpern, n.d. [May 1942], in London Office Files, Z4/15297.

26. David Ben-Gurion to Berl Locker, Jan. 4, 1942, Eliezer Kaplan (Agency) MSS, S53/83C.

27. AZEC Minutes, Apr. 14, 1942; Meyer Weisgal to Gershon Agronsky, July 29, 1942, Weisgal MSS.

28. The New York *Times*, February 21, 1943.

29. Sol Liptzin, *The Jew in American Literature* (New York: Bloch, 1966), p. 188.

30. Hecht, *A Child of the Century*, p. 520.

31. Isaac Zaar, *Rescue and Liberation: America's Part in the Birth of Israel* (New York: Bloch, 1954), p. 39.

32. See, for example, Chaim Weizmann to Stephen Wise, May 29, 1943, Weizmann MSS; Hadassah National Board Minutes, Nov. 12, 1944.

33. Harry S. Truman to Stephen Wise, June 1, 1943, American Section Records, Z5/1216; memorandum of conversation, Meyer Weisgal and Henry Morgenthau, Aug. 4, 1943, *ibid.*, folder Z5/387; memoranda of interviews with Samuel Rosenman, Oct. 6 and 12, 1943, *ibid.*, folder Z5/666.

34. Judd L. Teller, *Strangers and Natives* (New York: Delta Books, 1970), p. 207; I. L. Kenen to Charles B. Kramer, Feb. 21, 1944, Waldman MSS.

35. Anglo-American Committee for a Jewish Army, memorandum, "The Jewish Army Project," n.d., Landman MSS, A226/39; Zaar, *Rescue and Liberation*, pp. 33–34.

36. Pierre Van Paassen to Kenneth Leslie [March 1944], copy in Waldman MSS.

37. Statement of Anglo-American Committee for a Jewish Army, n.d.,

Landman MSS, A226/39; Leon Lauterbach to Arthur Lourie, n.d. [1944], Organization Department Records, S5/694.

38. Press release of Jewish Agency, May 18, 1944, Kaplan (Agency) MSS, S53/471.

39. Statement by Leon Feuer, AZEC press release, May 18, 1944, *ibid.*; see also Stephen Wise to Eliezer Kaplan, Mar. 17, 1944, Wise MSS; *New Palestine* 34 (Jan. 7, 1944): 175; text of Hadassah resolution, Political Department Records, S25/6673; Hadassah National Board Minutes, Nov. 12, 1944.

40. AZEC Minutes, May 15, 1944.

41. Teller, *Strangers and Natives,* pp. 210–11; cables, Arthur Lourie to Moshe Shertok, May 10 and 26, 1944, Jewish Agency to Lourie, May 30, 1944, and Nahum Goldmann and Louis Lipsky to Jewish Agency, June 22, 1944, all in Political Department Records, S25/1971.

42. Feingold, *Politics of Rescue,* pp. 280–81.

43. Weisgal, . . . *So Far,* p. 167; Chaim Weizmann to Stephen Wise, Apr. 29, 1942, American Section Records, Z5/1216.

44. Yehuda Bauer, *From Diplomacy to Resistance: A History of Jewish Palestine* (Philadelphia: Jewish Publication Society, 1970), pp. 236–37; Laqueur, *Zionism,* pp. 544–45.

45. Interview with Louis Levinthal, Dec. 22, 1972.

46. Ben-Gurion to Weizmann, June 11, 1942, and Ben-Gurion to Stephen Wise, June 19, 1942, both in Weizmann MSS.

47. Wise to Ben-Gurion, June 22, 1942, and memorandum of meeting, June 27, 1942, *ibid.*; interview with Louis Levinthal, Dec. 22, 1972; Weisgal, . . . *So Far,* p. 175.

48. The sketch of Wise is drawn from a number of sources, but primarily from his autobiography, *Challenging Years,* and from interviews with Justine Wise Polier, James Waterman Wise, Nahum Goldmann, Emanuel Neumann, Morton Berman, Golda Meir, Israel Goldstein, and Meyer Weisgal.

49. Nahum Goldmann, *Sixty Years of Jewish Life,* tr. Helen Sebba (New York: Holt, Rinehart, and Winston, 1969), p. 124.

50. Unfortunately, there is no biography of Silver. I was fortunate to have read the manuscript of an autobiography he began, but which he did not live to finish, and also benefited from interviews with Jacques Torczyner, Emanuel Neumann, Daniel Jeremy Silver, and others; see also Leon I. Feuer, "Abba Hillel Silver: A Personal Memoir," *American Jewish Archives* 19 (Nov. 1967): 107–26.

51. Goldmann, *Sixty Years of Jewish Life,* pp. 227–28. A story that I heard from several sources reports that during the height of their controversy, Wise met Silver at a Zionist gathering and stopped him in the hall.

"Rabbi Silver," he reportedly said, "I am an old man, and have had my moment in the sun; you are a young man, and will have your proper share of fame. It is not necessary for you to attack me." Silver did not respond; he just turned on his heel and walked away.

52. Chaim Weizmann to Louis Namier, June 27, 1942, Weizmann MSS; ironically, Stephen Wise at this time also considered Silver a most able man, and wanted to involve him more in the Zionist leadership. Wise to Lavey Bakstansky, Sept. 29, 1942, Wise MSS.

53. Memorandum, David Petegorsky to Emergency Committee, Mar. 30, 1942, Manson MSS; AZEC Minutes, Apr. 14, 1942; Meyer Weisgal to Stephen Wise, Apr. 23, 1942, American Section Records, Z5/1216; Weizmann to Berl Locker, June 3, 1942, Weizmann MSS; Weizmann to Stephen Wise, June 20, 1942, Wise MSS; Wise to Ben-Gurion, and Weizmann to Wise, both July 6, 1942, Weizmann MSS.

54. Bierbrier, "Zionist Emergency Council," p. 85; Chaim Weizmann to Berl Locker, July 15, 1942, and to Blanche Dugdale, Jan. 8, 1943, Stephen Wise to Weizmann, Feb. 10, 1943, and Weizmann to Abba Hillel Silver, June 21, 1943, all in Weizmann MSS. Notes on meeting of Sept. 1, 1942, *ibid.*; Arthur Lourie to Leo Lauterbach, Apr. 13, 1942, Organization Department Records, S5/693.

55. Schechtman, *United States and Jewish State,* pp. 87–88; memorandum of meeting, Oct. 12, 1943, Manson MSS.

56. Abba Hillel Silver to Nahum Goldmann, Nov. 5, 1943, *ibid.*; Goldmann to Silver, Nov. 8, 1943, American Section Records, Z5/653.

57. Meyer Weisgal to Chaim Weizmann, Feb. 7, 1944, Weisgal MSS; Schechtman, *United and Jewish State,* pp. 87–88; Emanuel Neumann to Abba Hillel Silver, Jan. 18, 1944, Manson MSS.

58. Hadassah National Board Minutes, 1943–44, *passim.*

59. Israel Goldstein to Abba Hillel Silver, Aug. 2, 1943, Goldstein MSS; Stephen Wise to Nahum Goldmann, Aug. 4, 1943, Wise MSS; AZEC Minutes, Aug. 26, 1943; Arthur Lourie to Leo Lauterbach, Sept. 10, 1943, Organization Department Records, S5/693; Goldmann to Moshe Shertok, Sept. 16, 1943, Political Department Records, S25/237; interview with Israel Goldstein, Sept. 12, 1973.

60. AZEC Minutes, Oct. 5, 1943; Abba Hillel Silver to Chaim Weizmann, Mar. 3, 1944, Weizmann MSS.

61. Meyer Weisgal to Chaim Weizmann, Apr. 6, 1944, *ibid.*; Abba Hillel Silver to Emanuel Neumann, July 17, 1944, Manson MSS; AZEC Minutes, Aug. 14, 1944; Abba Hillel Silver to David Wertheim, Aug. 25, 1944, Manson MSS.

62. AZEC Minutes, August 28 and 31, 1944; David Wertheim to David Ben-Gurion, Sept. 1, 1944, Moshe Shertok to Ben-Gurion, Sept. 2,

1944, Nahum Goldmann and Louis Lipsky to Ben-Gurion Sept. 7, 1944, all in Political Department Records, S25/1971; Meyer Weisgal to Chaim Weizmann, Sept. 7, 1944, Weizmann MSS.

63. David Ben-Gurion to Abba Hillel Silver, Sept. 17, 1944, Political Department Records, S25/1971; Meyer Weisgal to Chaim Weizmann, Sept. 23, 1944, Weizmann MSS.

64. Emanuel Neumann to Chaim Weizmann, Sept. 28, 1944, Weizmann MSS.

65. AZEC Minutes, Oct. 12, 1944.

66. Maurice Boukstein to Meyer Weisgal, Dec. 5, 1944, Political Department Records, S25/1971; Sol Bloom to Israel Goldstein, Dec. 13, 1944, Goldstein MSS.

67. For a detailed, although biased, account and chronology of the events beginning at the end of October 1944 until their dénouement the following summer, see the draft of a proposed pamphlet, possibly written by Herman Shulman, in the Goldstein MSS, File 1614g (hereafter cited as Silver-Wise Memo); see also "Why Dr. Silver Resigned from the Zionist Emergency Council" and Marvin Lowenthal, "Backstairs to Nowhere," both pamphlets published in 1945 by the American Zionist Policy Committee.

68. See also "The Crisis in American Zionism," *Jewish Spectator*, Jan. 1945; *Jewish Morning Journal*, Dec. 28, 1944, and Jan. 1, 1945; *Der Tag*, Dec. 30 and 31, 1944; *American Jewish World* (Minneapolis), Jan. 5, 1945; and *Jewish Daily Forward*, Jan. 11, 1945.

69. Silver, *Vision and Victory*, pp. 72–73; *Jewish Morning Journal*, Jan. 8, 1945; Silver-Wise Memo; *New Palestine* 36 (January 19, 1945): 82–83.

70. Cable, Wise *et al.* to Weizmann, Jan. 9, 1945; Nahum Goldmann to Moshe Shertok, Jan. 31, 1945; Bernard Joseph and Goldmann to Shertok, [January] 1945; David Wertheim to Joseph, Feb. 5, 1945; and Shertok to Goldmann, Feb. 8, 1945, all in Political Department Records, S25/1971; Meyer Weisgal to Weizmann, Jan. 10, 1945, Weizmann MSS.

71. Meyer Weisgal to Chaim Weizmann, Mar. 9, 1945, *ibid.*; Israel Goldstein to Herman Shulman, Mar. 12, 1945, Goldstein MSS.

Notes to Chapter 4

1. Laqueur, *Zionism*, pp. 559–60.

2. "As for the new president, there has been little contact with him. Whatever contact there was, it has been friendly. . . . When some years

ago he was asked to join the American Palestine Committee, his answer was, 'Anything of which my friend Bob Wagner is chairman of, I can join without question.' Typically American." Meyer Weisgal to Chaim Weizmann, Apr. 20, 1945, Weizmann MSS.

3. Josef Cohen to Weizmann, Mar. 18, 1945, *ibid.*; Harry S. Truman, *Memoirs*, 2 vols. (Garden City, N.Y.: Doubleday, 1955, 1: 68–69; AZEC Minutes, Apr. 23, 1945.

4. Nahum Goldmann to David Ben-Gurion, Mar. 26, 1945, Weizmann MSS; E. R. Stettinius to Stephen Wise [Apr. 1945], American Section Records, Z5/934.

5. *New Palestine* 35 (May 18, 1945): 193; Silverberg, *If I Forget Thee*, pp. 285–86.

6. Eliahu Epstein to Zeev Sharef, May 30, 1945, Political Department Records, S25/5334; Epstein to Moshe Shertok, May 10, 1945, *ibid.*, file 5328. It looked for a while as if the Conference would also have problems with the Jewish Agency, which felt that it alone should represent the Jews on the Palestine question, and wanted to submit its own memorandum to the delegates. In the end, however, Nahum Goldmann backed down. See Goldmann to Shertok, Feb. 28, 1945, and Israel Mereminski to Ben-Gurion, Mar. 15, 1945, both *ibid.*, file 5330.

7. Max Hirshblum (executive vice president of American Mizrachi) to Moshe Shertok, May 23, 1945, *ibid.*, file 5328.

8. Monsky and Bisgyer, *Henry Monsky*, pp. 115–16; Nahum Goldmann to Moshe Shertok, May 29, 1945, Political Department Records, S25/5330; Jerald S. Auerbach, "Human Rights at San Francisco," *American Jewish Archives* 16 (Apr. 1964): 65; Cohen, *Not Free to Desist*, pp. 269–72.

9. Interview with Israel Goldstein, Sept. 12, 1973.

10. Bisgyer, *Challenge and Encounter*, pp. 180–81; Israel Goldstein to Herman Shulman, May 28, 1945, Goldstein MSS.

11. Nahum Goldmann, report on San Francisco, n.d., Political Department Records, S25/5334; American Jewish Conference, *The Jewish Position at the United Nations Conference* . . . (New York: AJC, 1945), pp. 8, 12, 36; Hadassah National Board Minutes, June 6, 1945; Maurice L. Perlzweig, "The World Jewish Congress at the United Nations," *Two Generations in Perspective*, ed. Harry Schneiderman, (New York, 1947), p. 277.

12. Richard H. S. Crossman, *Palestine Mission: A Personal Record* (London: Hamish Hamilton, 1947), p. 33; J. J. Schwartz and B. I. Vulcan, "Overseas Aid," in Janowsky, *The American Jew*, pp. 94–95.

13. Handlin, *A Continuing Task*, pp. 94–95.

14. Sachar, *Europe Leaves the Middle East, 1936–1954*, p. 462.

15. See, for example, Koppel S. Pinson, "Jewish Life in Liberated

Germany: A Study of the Jewish DP's," *Jewish Social Studies* 9 (Apr. 1947): 101–26, and Marie Syrkin, "The D. P. Schools," *Jewish Frontier* 15 (Mar. 1948): 14–19; Laqueur, *Zionism,* p. 568; Bartley C. Crum, *Behind the Silken Curtain* (New York: Simon & Schuster, 1947), pp. 84–85.

16. Crossman, *Palestine Mission,* pp. 85–86; Joseph P. Lash, *Eleanor: The Years Alone* (New York: Norton, 1972), p. 116.

17. *Public Opinion Quarterly* 10 (1946): 113; for examples of American Jewish attitudes, see Oscar Janowsky, "Zionism Today, a Clarification," *Menorah Journal,* 31 (Oct.–Dec. 1943): 254–55; Carl Hermann Voss, *Answers on the Palestine Question,* 3rd ed. (New York: American Christian Palestine Committee, 1948), pp. 33–34.

18. Sheldon Morris Neuringer, "American Jewry and United States Immigration Policy, 1881–1953," doctoral dissertation (University of Wisconsin, 1969), p. 274; Luke E. Ebersole, *Church Lobbying in the Nation's Capital* (New York: Macmillan, 1951), pp. 125, 157–58.

19. Stember, *Jews in the Mind of America,* pp. 174–76; Silverberg, *If I Forget Thee,* p. 335; AZEC Minutes, June 22, 1945.

20. Halperin, *Political World of American Zionism,* p. 70; Crum, *Behind the Silken Curtain,* pp. 97–98; *Hadassah Newsletter* 26 (Jan.–Feb. 1946): 31.

21. Cohen, *Not Free to Desist,* p. 265.

22. Meyer, "Centennial History," p. 132; Goldmann, *Sixty Years of Jewish Life,* p. 208.

23. See, for example, David Polish, *Centennial Papers: Israel* (New York: UAHC, 1974), p. 2; Cohen, *American Jews and the Zionist Idea,* p. 144; Alan T. Davies, *Anti-Semitism and the Christian Mind: The Crisis of Conscience After Auschwitz* (New York: Herder and Herder, 1969), p. 181; and Richard H. A. Crossman, *A Nation Reborn: The Israel of Weizmann, Bevin, and Ben-Gurion* (London: Hamish Hamilton, 1960), pp. 64–65.

24. Winston Churchill to Chaim Weizmann, June 9, 1945, Weizmann MSS.

25. Friedman, *No Haven for the Oppressed,* pp. 222–23; Truman *Memoirs,* 2:137.

26. Ganin, "Diplomacy of the Weak," pp. 74–75; Friedman, *No Haven for the Oppressed,* p. 223.

27. Alonzo L. Hamby, *Beyond the New Deal: Harry S. Truman and American Liberalism* (New York: Columbia University Press, 1973), p. 92; *Ben-Gurion Looks Back,* pp. 113–14.

28. Schechtman, *United States and Jewish State,* pp. 124–25.

29. *FRUS 1945* (Washington: Government Printing Office, 1969), 8: 782, 786.

30. Truman, *Memoirs,* 2: 142–44.

31. Loy Henderson to James Brynes, Nov. 13, 1945, cited in Ganin, "Diplomacy of the Weak."

32. For the workings of the Commission, and the pressures brought to bear on it, see the personal reminiscences of Bartley Crum, *Behind the Silken Curtain,* a Zionist sympathizer from the start, and of Richard Crossman, *Palestine Mission,* who became converted because of his experience on the Commission. A pro-Arab member representing the State Department was William Phillips, and his story can be found in *Ventures of Diplomacy* (Boston: Beacon, 1952), ch. 24. The best account of the Commission in action, and the Zionist pressures on it, is Ganin, "Diplomacy of the Weak," ch. 4.

33. Crum, *Behind the Silken Curtain,* pp. 126–27; Silverberg, *If I Forget Thee,* p. 315.

34. Crossman, *Palestine Mission,* p. 84.

35. Crum, *Behind the Silken Curtain,* pp. 195–96, 213.

36. Schechtman, *United States and Jewish State,* p. 151.

37. Tentative plan for presenting Zionist case, n.d., London Office Records, Z4/15440; Crossman, *Palestine Mission,* p. 133. Abba Hillel Silver, however, did boycott the hearings, and the Arabs refused to appear at the meetings in Palestine.

38. Memorandum from Arthur Lourie, Feb. 3, 1946, London Office Records, Z4/15440; AZEC Minutes, February 11, 1946; Bernard Joseph to Henry Montor, Mar. 28, 1946, Political Department Records, S25/1093; Ganin, "Diplomacy of the Weak," pp. 142–43; David Bernard Sachar, "David K. Niles and United States Policy Toward Palestine: A Case Study in American Foreign Policy," honors thesis (Harvard College, 1959), p. 25.

39. Anglo-American Committee of Inquiry on Palestine, *Admission of Jews into Palestine. Report . . . ,* Senate Document 182, 79th Cong., 2nd Sess. (Washington, 1946).

40. Neumann, *In the Arena,* pp. 221–22; Silver, Wise, Goldmann, Epstein, Lipsky, and Weisgal to Truman, May 2, 1946, Frankfurter MSS, A264/22.

41. Editorial, *New Palestine* 36 (May 17, 1946): 187; Schechtman, *United States and Jewish State,* pp. 155–56; Lessing Rosenwald to Harry Truman, May 14, 1946, in American Council for Judaism, *The Anglo-American Committee of Inquiry* (New York: ACJ, 1946); *Public Opinion Quarterly* 10 (1946): 124, 161.

42. Crossman, *Palestine Mission,* pp. 193–94.

43. Sachar, *Europe Leaves the Middle East,* p. 466.

44. Sykes, *Crossroads to Israel,* pp. 299–300.

45. Sachar, *Europe Leaves the Middle East,* pp. 475–76.

46. Nahum Goldmann to Henry F. Grady, July 24, 1946, London

Office Records, Z4/15440; AZEC Minutes, Aug. 1, 1946; Bisgyer, *Challenge and Encounter*, pp. 186–87; John Snetsinger, *Truman, The Jewish Vote, and the Creation of Israel* (Stanford: Hoover Institution Press, 1974), p. 31; see also Abba Hillel Silver to David Ben-Gurion, Oct. 9, 1946, Weizmann MSS.

47. Dean Acheson, *Present at the Creation: My Years in the State Department* (New York: Norton, 1969), pp. 169, 175.

48. Report of meeting, Harry Truman and James McDonald, AZEC Minutes; McDonald to Truman, July 27, 1946, London Office Records, Z4/15440; see also Stephen Wise to Harry Truman and David Ben-Gurion to Eliahu Epstein, July 29, 1946, Weizmann MSS.

49. Bernard Wasserstein, "Richard Crossman and the New Jerusalem," *Midstream* 21 (Apr. 1975): 51; Sykes, *Crossroads to Israel*, p. 297.

50. Chaim Weizmann to Meyer Weisgal, Apr. 13, 1944, Weizmann MSS.

51. Weizmann to Henry Morgenthau, Jr., July 26, 1945, *ibid.*; Ganin, "Diplomacy of the Weak," p. 84; "The Final Hour," *New Palestine* 35 (Aug. 17, 1945): 259.

52. Hadassah National Board Minutes, Aug. 22, 1945.

53. See, for example, *New Palestine* 35 (July 13, 1945): 235, and 36 (Dec. 14, 1945): 51; AZEC Minutes, June 22, Nov. 14, and Nov. 26, 1945.

54. Meyer Weisgal to Chaim Weizmann, June 8, 1945, Weisgal MSS; Stephen Wise to David Niles, June 18, 1946; Sachar, "Niles," p. 33n; *FRUS 1946* (Washington, 1969), 7: 722–23; AZEC Minutes, July 1, 1946.

55. *Ibid.*, July 15, 1946; Dr. David to Walter Eytan, Aug. 1, 1946, Political Department Records, S25/7498; Abba Hillel Silver to David Ben-Gurion, Oct. 9, 1946, Weizmann MSS.

56. Hadassah National Board Minutes, Mar. 13, Apr. 3, and May 2, 1946; *Hadassah Newsletter* 26 (May 1946): 7.

57. A. K. Epstein to Chaim Weizmann, Mar. 19, 1946; Weizmann to Epstein, Apr. 11, 1946; Meyer Weisgal to Eliezer Kaplan, Nov. 5, 1946; Weizmann to I. Linton, Apr. 5, 1946, all in Weizmann MSS; interview with Jacques Torczyner, Nov. 4, 1976.

58. Laqueur, *Zionism*, pp. 575–76; Neumann, *In the Arena*, pp. 231–32.

59. Silver, *Vision and Victory*, p. 121.

60. Hadassah National Board Minutes, Jan. 8 and Feb. 5, 1947; interview with Mrs. Rose Halprin, Mar. 23, 1973; Nahum Goldmann to Stephen Wise, Dec. 31, 1946, Weizmann MSS.

61. *New Palestine* 37 (Jan. 17, 1947): 47.

Notes to Chapter 5

1. Alfred O. Hero, Jr., *American Religious Groups View Foreign Policy: Trends in Rank-and-File Opinion, 1937–1969* (Durham, N.C.: Duke University Press, 1973), contains a table of relevant polls on pp. 360–63.

2. Fishman, *American Protestantism and Jewish State,* pp. 87–88, 92.

3. Virginia Gildersleeve, *Many a Good Crusade* (New York: Macmillan, 1954), p. 409; see also Kermit Roosevelt, *Partition of Palestine: A Lesson in Pressure Politics* (New York: Institute of Arab-American Affairs, 1948), pp. 1–2.

4. Hero, *Religious Groups View Foreign Policy,* p. 76; Esther Feldblum, "On the Eve of a Jewish State: American-Catholic Responses," *American Jewish Historical Quarterly* 64 (Dec. 1974): 105–6.

5. Quoted in Frank Talmage, "Christianity and the Jewish People," *Commentary* 59 (Feb. 1975): 60–61.

6. William L. Burton, "Protestant America and the Rebirth of Israel," *Jewish Social Studies* 26 (Oct. 1964): 205.

7. Arnold Gurin, "Impact of Israel on American Jewish Community Organization and Fund Raising," *Jewish Social Studies* 21 (Jan. 1959): 46–59; Schwartz and Vulcan, "Overseas Aid," pp. 292–93.

8. Abraham G. Duker, "On Religious Trends in American Jewish Life," *YIVO Annual of Jewish Social Science* 4 (1949): 56–57; Meyer Greenberg, "The Jewish Student at Yale: His Attitude Toward Judaism," *ibid.* 1 (1946): 229.

9. *Public Opinion Quarterly* 11 (1947): 655–56; Anti-Defamation League, *Anti-Semitism in the United States in 1947* (New York: ADL, 1948), p. 5; Arnold and Caroline Rose, *America Divided: Minority Group Relations in the United States* (New York: Harper, 1948), p. 323.

10. Kurt Lewin, *Resolving Social Conflicts: Selected Papers on Group Dynamics* (New York: Harper, 1948), chs. 11 and 12; Drew, "Elite Jews," pp. 19–20; Jacob Weinstein, "Anti-Semitism," *The American Jew: A Composite Portrait,* ed. Oscar Janowsky (New York: Harper, 1942), pp. 202–3.

11. Halperin, *Political World of American Zionism,* pp. 36–37, 327; *Palestine Year Book* 1 (5706/1945): 453–76.

12. Evans, *The Provincials,* p. 108; Abraham Tulin to Chaim Weizmann, Oct. 20, 1947, Weizmann MSS; see also memorandum of conver-

sation, Eliahu Epstein and Arthur Hays Sulzberger, Feb. 3, 1947, *ibid.*, for another example of an anti-Zionist changing his mind.

13. Robert Szold to Alice Goldman, Sept. 11, 1973, courtesy of Robert Szold.

14. Ernest Bevin, however, thought that the American Jews had caused all the delay; Norman and Helen Bentwich, *Mandate Memories* (London: Hogarth, 1965), p. 176.

15. Schechtman, *United States and Jewish State*, pp. 192–93; Silver, *Vision and Victory*, pp. 92–93; AZEC Minutes, June 21 and July 1, 1946.

16. *Opinion* 16 (Apr. 1946): 6–7; Wise, *Challenging Years*, p. 304; Wise to Lady Eva Reading, July 10, 1946, Wise MSS.

17. Meir, *My Life*, p. 135.

18. Truman, *Memoirs*, 2: 153.

19. Hadassah National Board Minutes, July 31, 1946; AZEC Minutes, Aug. 1, 1946.

20. David Golding, "United States Foreign Policy in Palestine and Israel, 1945–1949," doctoral dissertation (New York University, 1961), p. 418; James H. Rowe, quoted in Gregory William Sand, "Clifford and Truman: A Study in Foreign Policy and National Security, 1945–1949," doctoral dissertation (St. Louis University, 1973), p. 222.

21. Ganin, "Diplomacy of the Weak," pp. 240–41.

22. *Ibid.*, p. 245; AZEC Minutes, Oct. 1 and 14, 1946; Stephen Wise to Bernard Rosenblatt, Sept. 10, 1946, and to Nahum Goldmann, Sept. 11, 1946, Wise MSS.

23. According to Eliahu Epstein, Niles was the moving force behind Truman's message, and was a consistent friend to the Zionists. Epstein to Nahum Goldmann, Oct. 9, 1946, Weizmann MSS; interview with Eliahu (Epstein) Elath, June 5, 1975.

24. Abraham Feinberg, "The Anatomy of a Commitment," *Rehovot* 7 (Spring 1974): 19; Acheson, *Present at the Creation*, p. 176.

25. Abba Hillel Silver to David Ben-Gurion, Oct. 9, 1946, Weizmann MSS; AZEC Minutes, Oct. 14, 1946; Walter Millis, ed., *The Forrestal Diaries* (New York: Viking, 1951), pp. 309–10; Snetsinger, *Truman and the Creation of Israel*, p. 44.

26. Sachar, *Europe Leaves the Middle East*, p. 445; Crossman, *Palestine Mission*, p. 141; Hadassah National Board Minutes, June 20, 1945, and May 20, 1946.

27. Crossman, *A Nation Reborn*, p. 50; Malcolm Hays, *Thy Brother's Blood: The Roots of Christian Anti-Semitism* (New York: Hart, 1975), p. 204.

28. Bernard Postal and Henry Levy, *And the Hills Shouted for Joy: The Day Israel Was Born* (New York: McKay, 1973), p. 88; Jacob Leib

Talmon, *Israel Among the Nations* (London: Wiedenfeld and Nicolson, 1970), p. 152.

29. Not all Jews were happy about the Haganah's retaliatory policy. Judah Magnes, a lifelong pacifist and leader of Ichud, pleaded with Chaim Weizmann (who really had no control over Haganah) to have the organization revert to a solely defensive posture. Magnes to Weizmann, May 2, 1946, Magnes MSS.

30. Yehuda Bauer, *Flight and Rescue: Brichah* (New York: Random House, 1970), pp. 255–57; Goldmann, *Sixty Years of Jewish Life,* pp. 232–33.

31. Silver, *Vision and Victory,* pp. 100–1; AZEC Minutes, Aug. 7 and Sept. 10, 1946; Neumann, *In the Arena,* p. 224; Wise, *Personal Letters,* p. 276.

32. Goldmann, *Sixty Years of Jewish Life,* p. 234; Proskauer, *Segment of My Time,* pp. 242–43.

33. Bartley Crum to Nahum Goldmann, Aug. 26, 1946, Manson MSS; Ganin, "Diplomacy of the Weak," pp. 220–21; Chaim Weizmann to George Hall (Colonial Secretary), Sept. 12, 1946, Weizmann MSS; Abba Eban, "A New Look at Partition," *Jerusalem Post Weekly,* June 29, 1976; *Frankfurter Diaries,* entry for October 22, 1946, pp. 279–80; Snetsinger, *Truman and the Creation of Israel,* pp. 45–47.

34. Manuel, *Realities of American-Palestine Relations,* pp. 329–30; Halpern, *Idea of the Jewish State,* pp. 360–61.

35. Acheson, *Present at the Creation,* p. 180; Schechtman, *United States and Jewish States,* pp. 210–12; AZEC Minutes, June 4, 1947.

36. David Horowitz, *State in the Making,* tr. Julian Meltzer (New York: Knopf, 1953), p. 307.

37. Sachar, *Europe Leaves the Middle East,* pp. 490–91.

38. Schechtman, *United States and Jewish State,* pp. 214–17; AZEC Minutes, Aug. 29, 1947; editorial, *New Palestine* 38 (Sept. 12, 1947): 4.

39. Memorandum by Lionel Gelber, Sept. 3, 1947, Weizmann MSS; *New Palestine* 38 (Sept. 26, 1947): 7.

40. Truman, *Memoirs,* 2: 149, 162; Hull, *Memoirs,* 2: 1517; Welles, *We Need Not Fail,* p. 74; Loy Henderson to George C. Marshall, Sept. 22, 1947, *FRUS 1947.*

41. Arnold A. Rogow, *James Forrestal: A Study of Personality, Politics, and Policy* (New York: Macmillan, 1963), pp. 191–92; McDonald, *My Mission in Israel,* p. 13.

42. Niles to Truman, July 29, 1947, quoted in Sachar paper, p. 60; Lash, *Eleanor: The Years Alone,* pp. 122–23; Schechtman, *United States and Jewish State,* p. 412.

43. AZEC Minutes, Oct. 13, 1947; Silverberg, *If I Forget Thee,* pp. 359–60; Sand, "Clifford and Truman," pp. 222–23.

44. Interview with Emanuel Neumann, Jan. 7, 1975; Stalin said basically the same thing to Roosevelt at the Yalta conference.

45. Horowitz, *State in the Making,* p. 274.

46. Neumann, *In the Arena,* pp. 248–49.

47. Chaim Weizmann to Doris May, Oct. 18, 1947, and to Jan Smuts, Oct. 28, 1947, Weizmann MSS; Hadassah National Board Minutes, Oct. 23, 1947; Memorandum, Lionel Gelber to Jewish Agency Executive, Oct. 31, 1947, Weizmann MSS.

48. Weizmann to Henry Morgenthau, Jr., Nov. 20, 1947, *ibid.;* Weizmann, *Trial and Error,* pp. 457–59; Horowitz, *State in the Making,* pp. 269–70; Abba Eban in Weisgal and Carmichael, *Chaim Weizmann,* pp. 301–2.

49. Feis, *Birth of Israel,* pp. 45–46; Truman, *Memoirs,* 2: 158.

50. Jacob Arvey to Morton Berman, Dec. 13, 1947, Berman MSS; Welles, *We Need Not Fail,* p. 63; Feis, *Birth of Israel,* pp. 45–46; Snetsinger, *Truman and the Creation of Israel,* p. 68.

51. L. S. Linton to Jan Smuts, Nov. 27, 1947, Weizmann MSS; Larry Collins and Dominique LaPierre, *O Jerusalem!* (New York: Simon & Schuster, 1972), pp. 29–30; *Forrestal Diaries,* p. 246.

52. New York *Times,* Nov. 30 and Dec. 1, 1947.

53. Horowitz, *State in the Making,* p. 254.

54. Edwin M. Wright, introduction to American Jewish Alternatives to Zionism " 'Pentagon Papers'—1947: *The Origins of Our Problems with 'Arab Oil,' "* (New York: AJAZ, 1973), p. 5; Michael Arthur Dohse, "American Periodicals and the Palestine Triangle, April 1936 to February 1947," doctoral dissertation (Mississippi State University, 1966), p. 230; Ganin, "Diplomacy of the Weak," and Snetsinger, *Truman and the Creation of Israel, passim; Forrestal Diaries,* p. 361.

55. Silver, *Vision and Victory,* p. 158.

Notes to Chapter 6

1. Draft of letter, Chaim Weizmann to Moshe Shertok, June 23, 1946; Weizmann to Chaim Tchernowitz, Apr. 14, 1947, Weizmann MSS.

2. *New Palestine* 37 (Feb. 21, 1947): 69.

3. Memorandum of visit to British embassy, Oct. 12, 1943, Goldstein MSS.

4. Wise, *Personal Letters,* p. 271; Weisgal, . . . *So Far,* p. 229.

5. Boston *Traveler,* Aug. 27, 1946; Washington *Star,* Apr. 25, 1947.

6. Zaar, *Rescue and Liberation,* p. 200; Eliahu Epstein to Zeev Sharef, Sept. 23, 1946, Political Department Records, S25/2062.

7. Arthur Lurie to Jewish Agency Executive, Oct. 16, 1947, *ibid.,* S25/2071; Sykes, *Crossroads to Israel,* p. 201.

8. Hecht, *Child of the Century,* p. 615.

9. A. Joseph Heckleman, *American Volunteers and Israel's War for Independence* (New York: KTAV, 1974), pp. 78–79.

10. Schechtman, *United States and Jewish State,* pp. 338–39.

11. Zaar, *Rescue and Liberation,* pp. 221–22; New York *Times,* Apr. 19, 1947.

12. See Avriel, *Open the Gates!;* Bauer, *Flight and Rescue: Brichah;* Sykes, *Crossroads to Israel,* pp. 281–82; Pinhas E. Lapide, *A Century of U.S. Aliyah* (Jerusalem: AACI, 1961), pp. 90–91.

13. Marlin Levin, *Balm in Gilead: The Story of Hadassah* (New York: Schocken, 1973), p. 188.

14. Weisgal, . . . *So Far,* p. 231.

15. Leonard Slater, *The Pledge* (New York: Simon & Schuster, 1970), p. 18; I have relied heavily on Slater's book, which is the only complete work on the Sonneborn Institute and its operations.

16. *Ibid.,* pp. 114–15; Heckleman, *American Volunteers,* p. 73.

17. Weisgal, . . . *So Far,* p. 235.

18. Feinberg, "Anatomy of a Commitment," p. 20; Slater, *The Pledge,* pp. 66–67.

19. Silverberg, *If I Forget Thee,* pp. 497–98.

20. Slater, *The Pledge,* pp. 175–78.

21. Silverberg, *If I Forget Thee,* p. 389.

22. Henry Montor to Henry Berstein and Samuel Blitz, Mar. 16, 1948, and Blitz to Bernstein, Apr. 5, 1948, Goldstein MSS; Ganin, "Diplomacy of the Weak," p. 400.

23. Sharef, *Three Days,* pp. 219–21.

24. Meir, *My Life,* pp. 212–14; interview with Golda Meir, June 10, 1975.

25. Collins and LaPierre, *O Jerusalem!,* p. 167.

26. Statement of Jan. 28, 1948, cited in Schechtman, *United States and Jewish State,* p. 257; *Public Opinion Quarterly* 12 (1948): 160–61; Stember, *Jews in the Mind of America,* pp. 178–79.

27. Nahum Goldmann to Moshe Shertok, Dec. 18, 1947, and Chaim

Weizmann to A. Felix, Dec. 30, 1947, Weizmann MSS; AZEC Minutes, Dec. 11, 1947.

28. Schechtman, *United States and Jewish State*, p. 17; Sykes, *Crossroads to Israel*, pp. 344–45; Manuel, *Realities of American-Palestine Relations*, pp. 341–43.

29. *Public Opinion Quarterly* 10 (1946): 418, and 12 (1948): 161, 551.

30. Sharef, *Three Days*, p. 38; Washington *Post*, Feb. 9, 1948, cited in Ganin, "Diplomacy of the Weak," p. 359; Benjamin Akzin to Israel Goldstein, Jan. 19, 1948, Goldstein MSS.

31. Snetsinger, *Truman and the Creation of Israel*, pp. 5–6; Truman, *Memoirs*, 2: 160; George Marshall to Felix Frankfurter, Mar. 15, 1948, in *Frankfurter Diaries*, p. 350.

32. The Jacobson episode is based upon Jacobson to Josef Cohen, Mar. 30, 1952, later published as "Two Presidents and a Haberdasher—1948," *American Jewish Archives* 20 (Apr. 1968): 4–15; Truman, *Memoirs*, 2: 160–61; Bisgyer, *Challenge and Encounter*, pp. 190–91; and Frank J. Adler, *Roots in a Moving Stream* (Kansas City, Mo.: Congregation Bnai Jehudah, 1972), p. 209; Weizmann, *Trial and Error*, p. 472.

33. Divine, *Foreign Policy and U.S. Presidential Elections* 1: 187–88; Blau, *Judaism in America*, p. 88.

34. Hamby, *Beyond the New Deal*, pp. 220–21; Snetsinger, *Truman and the Creation of Israel*, pp. 98–99; Lash, *Eleanor: The Years Alone*, p. 130.

35. John Redding, *Inside the Democratic Party* (Indianapolis, Ind.: Bobbs-Merrill, 1958), p. 149; Ian J. Bickerton, "President Truman's Recognition of Israel," *American Jewish Historical Quarterly* 58 (Dec. 1968): 173–240, details many of the conflicting pressures besetting the President; Snetsinger, *Truman and the Creation of Israel*, p. 72; *Forrestal Diaries*, p. 362; Bohlen, *Witness to History*, pp. 283–84; Patrick Anderson, *The President's Men: The White House Assistants* . . . (Garden City, N.Y.: Doubleday, 1968), pp. 118–19.

36. Schechtman, *United States and Jewish State*, p. 424.

37. Weisgal and Carmichael, *Weizmann*, pp. 309–10; Sharef, *Three Days*, pp. 243–44.

38. Interview with Israel Goldstein, Sept. 12, 1973.

39. Sharef, *Three Days*, p. 80; Neumann, *In the Arena*, pp. 258–59; Shertok to Rusk, May 4, 1948, in Schechtman, *United States and Jewish State*, pp. 294–95. Schechtman, who was a member of the Political Committee, voted against delay.

40. Collins and LaPierre, *O Jerusalem!*, pp. 335–36; Sharef, *Three Days*, pp. 87–88.

41. Interview with Rose Halprin, Mar. 23, 1973; Emanuel Neumann sent a similar message to Ben-Gurion, interview with Neumann, Jan. 7, 1975.

42. Postal and Levy, *And the Hills Shouted for Joy*, p. 189; Collins and LaPierre, *O Jerusalem!*, pp. 378–79; speech by Meyer Weisgal, Oct. 11, 1972, Weizmann MSS; Sharef, *Three Days*, p. 244.

43. Chaim Weizmann to Harry S. Truman, May 13, 1948, Weizmann MSS.

44. "He said it all," Clifford reported, "in a righteous God-damned Baptist tone." Marshall was an Episcopalian. Alexander DeConde, "George Catlett Marshall," *An Uncertain Tradition: American Secretaries of State in the Twentieth Century*, ed. Norman A. Graebner (New York: McGraw-Hill, 1961), p. 257.

45. Jacob M. Arvey to Harry Truman, May 12, 1948, Berman MSS; Herbert Lehman to Truman, May 13, 1948, Lehman MSS; John S. Badeau oral history memoir, Feb. 25, 1969, Kennedy Library. The Arabs were convinced that the Jews dominated American media; see William Woodrow Haddad, "Arab Editorial Opinion Toward the Palestine Question, 1947–1958," doctoral dissertation (Ohio State University, 1970), p. 34.

46. Interview with Eliahu Elath, June 5, 1975.

47. Sachar, "Niles and United States Policy," p. 1.

48. Postal and Levy, *Hills Shouted for Joy*, pp. 274–75; Silverberg, *If I Forget Thee*, p. 425; Truman, *Memoirs*, 2: 164.

49. Meir, *My Life*, pp. 229–30; interview with Golda Meir, June 10, 1975; Collins and LaPierre, *O Jerusalem!*, p. 422; Postal and Levy, *And the Hills Shouted for Joy*, p. 223.

Notes to Chapter 7

1. Meir, *My Life*, pp. 214–20.

2. Collins and LaPierre, *O Jerusalem!*, p. 422; for the War of Independence, see Natanel Lorch, *The Edge of the Sword* (New York: Putnam, 1961).

3. Reuven Zaslani to Teddy Kollek, May 8, 1945, Political Department Records, S25/5334; New York *Times*, July 16, 1946.

4. Postal and Levy, *And the Hills Shouted for Joy*, p. 145.

5. Heckelman, *American Volunteers*, p. xv.

6. Harold R. Isaacs, *American Jews in Israel* (New York: John Day,

1966), pp. 82–83. According to a poll taken among them, 95 per cent were completely unaffiliated with any Zionist organization, 90 per cent knew no Yiddish either, and 83 per cent were American-born.

7. Heckelman, *American Volunteers*, p. 191.

8. *Ibid.*, pp. 169–70; Slater, *The Pledge*, pp. 92–94; Silverberg, *If I Forget Thee*, pp. 436–37; Ted Berkman, *Cast a Giant Shadow* (Garden City, N.Y.: Doubleday, 1962).

9. Heckelman, *American Volunteers*, pp. xxi, 191, 199.

10. Meir, *My Life*, pp. 234–35.

11. Interview with Mrs. Rose Halprin, Mar. 23, 1973.

12. Chaim Weizmann to Samuel Rosenman, May 17, 1948, Weizmann MSS.

13. Chaim Weizmann to Harry S. Truman, May 16 and 25, 1948, *ibid.*; Weizmann, *Trial and Error*, pp. 480–81.

14. Schechtman, *United States and Jewish State*, pp. 333–34.

15. Freda Kirchway to Ed Finn, June 18, 1948, Weizmann MSS.

16. McDonald, *My Mission in Israel*, pp. 4–5.

17. *Forrestal Diaries*, entry for June 23, 1948, pp. 440–41; Snetsinger, *Truman and the Creation of Israel*, p. 117.

18. AZEC Minutes, June 28, 1948.

19. Meyer Weisgal to Chaim Weizmann, June 23, 1948, Weizmann MSS; Adler, *Roots in a Moving Stream*, p. 213.

20. See Collins and LaPierre, *O Jerusalem!*, pp. 572–73; Meyer Weisgal to Chaim Weizmann, June 29, 1948, Weizmann MSS; Bell, *Terror Out of Zion*, pp. 318–27.

21. John C. Campbell, *The United States in World Affairs, 1948–1949* (New York: Council on Foreign Relations, 1949), pp. 392–93.

22. Adler, *Roots in a Moving Stream*, p. 217; Truman, *Memoirs*, 2: 166–67.

23. Divine, *Foreign Policy and Presidential Elections*, 2: 262–63; Louis L. Gerson, *The Hyphenate in Recent American Politics and Diplomacy* (Lawrence: University of Kansas Press, 1964), pp. 155–56; New York *Times*, Oct. 23 and 25, 1948.

24. This opinion was not shared by many other Zionist leaders; see, for example, David Ginsberg to Chaim Weizmann, July 1, 1948, Weizmann MSS.

25. Rosenblatt, *Two Generations of Zionism*, p. 202; Truman to Weizmann, Nov. 29, 1948, in Truman, *Memoirs*, 2: 169.

26. McDonald, *My Mission in Israel*, pp. 48–50, 116–17, 126, 182.

27. Michael Brecher, *The Foreign Policy System of Israel: Setting, Images, Process* (New Haven: Yale University Press, 1972) p. 171; McDonald, *My Mission in Israel*, pp. 88, 184–87, 256–57.

28. Divine, *Foreign Policy and Presidential Elections*, pp. 250–51;

memorandum of meeting, Josef Cohen and Samuel Rosenman to Chaim Weizmann, July 16, 1948, Weizmann MSS; Campbell, *United States in World Affairs*, pp. 400–1.

29. Teller, *Stranger and Natives*, p. 216.

30. Report of the president, Nov. 14, 1948, *UAHC Proceedings, 1946–1949*, p. 311. The Central Conference of American Rabbis at its first convention after May 1948 adopted a pro-Israel resolution, but the rabbinate was far more Zionist in outlook than the lay leadership. *CCAR Yearbook* 58 (1948): 93–95.

31. Elmer Berger, *Judaism or Jewish Nationalism: The Alternative to Zionism* (New York: Bookman Associates, 1957), p. 148; American Council for Judaism, statement of policy, May 21, 1948, *The Council News* 2 (May 1948): 1.

32. Cohen, *Not Free to Desist*, pp. 305–6; Proskauer, *Segment of My Times*, pp. 259–61; Voss, *Answers on the Palestine Question*, p. 35.

33. Cohen, *Not Free to Desist*, pp. 310–13; Nathaniel Weyl, *The Jew in American Politics* (New Rochelle: Arlington House, 1968), pp. 294–96; *Jewish Frontier* 17 (Oct. 1950): 6–7.

34. Handlin, *A Continuing Task*, pp. 102–3.

35. Michael Brecher, *Decisions in Israel's Foreign Policy* (New Haven: Yale University Press, 1975), pp. 59–60.

36. Handlin, *A Continuing Task*, pp. 104–5.

37. Meir, *My Life*, pp. 264–65.

38. Interview with Charlotte Jacobson, Mar. 23, 1973.

39. Interview with Rose Halprin, Mar. 23, 1973.

40. Levin, *Balm in Gilead*, p. 231.

41. Frisch, *On the Road to Zion*, p. 55.

42. Klutznik, *No Easy Answers*, pp. 101–2.

43. Eleanor Roosevelt, "My Day," June 12, 1951; George B. Sokolsky, "These Days," New York *Journal-American*, May 14, 1951; Hearst editorial, *ibid.*, May 10, 1951; for a sampling of nationwide editorial support of the American aid program to Israel, see American Zionist Council, *Public Opinion on America, Aid for Israel* (New York: AZC, 1951); Adler, *Roots in a Moving Stream*, p. 223.

44. *Palestine Reports*, Feb. 1949, quoted in Jacob A. Rubin, *Partners in State-Building: American Jewry and Israel* (New York: Diplomatic Press, 1969), pp. 217–18; Meir, *My Life*, p. 268.

45. *Ibid.*, pp. 268–69; Rubin, *Partners in State-Building*, pp. 206–7; *Encyclopedia of Zionism and Israel* (New York: Macmillan, 1971), 2: 1073–74. In addition, Israel redeemed more thn $200 million in bonds prior to their maturity through the use of bonds for tourist expenses in Israel, conversion into shares in approved business enterprises in Israel, and payments on death to the estates of registered bondholders.

46. Quoted in Joan Peters, "An Exchange of Populations," *Commentary* 62 (Aug. 1976): 39.

47. For a fuller discussion of the status of Jews in Muslim countries, see Gil Carl AlRoy, *Behind the Middle East Conflict: The Real Impasse Between Arab and Jew* (New York: Putman, 1975), especially ch. 8.

48. Hillel Halkin, "Driving Toward Jerusalem," *Commentary* 59 (Jan. 1975): 52.

49. *New Palestine* 34 (Mar. 3, 1944): 277; see also Weizmann, *Trial and Error*, pp. 461–62; Silver, *Vision and Victory*, p. 60; Bergmann, in Ben-Ezer, *Unease in Zion*, p. 83.

50. Sykes, *Crossroads to Israel*, p. 350.

51. Walter Eytan, *The First Ten Years: A Diplomatic History of Israel* (New York: Simon & Schuster, 1958), pp. 122–23; *Jewish Frontier* 15 (Nov. 1948): 31.

52. Sachar, *Europe Leaves the Middle East*, p. 551; Nafez Yousef Nazzal argues against the existence of any call to leave Palestine in "The Flight of the Palestinian Arabs from the Galilee, 1948: An Historical Analysis," doctoral dissertation (Georgetown University, 1974), ch. 5, but the thesis, written through the co-operation of the Palestinian Liberation Organization, is very biased.

53. On April 9, 1948, Irgun troops attacked the village of Deir Yassin on the road from Tel Aviv to Jerusalem, and when fired upon by Iraqi troops in the village started shooting madly into the houses and at fleeing civilians. Before the shooting ended, dozens of men, women, and children had been killed, and stories of other atrocities, some confirmed and some not, of rapes and mutilations and butcherings, have circulated to this day. See Bell, *Terror Out of Zion*, pp. 291–96.

54. Not until very recently have some Arab writers, and there have been only a handful of them, been willing to talk about the Jewish refugees. In 1975, Sabri Jiryis of the Institute for Palestine Studies, one of these isolated voices, wrote: "Actually what happened was a kind of 'population and property exchange,' and each party must bear the consequence. Israel is absorbing the Jews of the Arab states; the Arab states for their part must settle the Palestinians in their own midst and solve their problems." Quoted in Peters, "Exchange of Populations," p. 44. See also Terence Prittie and Bernard Dineen, *The Double Exodus: Study of Arab and Jewish Refugees in the Middle East* (London: n.p., n.d.).

Notes to Chapter 8

1. Weyl, *The Jew in American Politics*, p. 173; Erich Rosenthal, "Five Million American Jews," *Commentary* 26 (Dec. 1958): 499–506; William Attwood, "The Position of Jews in America Today," *Look* 19 (Nov. 29, 1955): 28.

2. Nathan Glazer, *American Judaism* (Chicago: University of Chicago Press, 1957), pp. 107–8; Glazer, "Social Characteristics of American Jews 1654–1954," *American Jewish Year Book* 56 (1955): 3–41; Herbert J. Gans, "American Jewry: Present and Future," *Commentary* 21 (May and June 1956): 422–30, 555–63. For the eastern European immigration and its life in America, see Irving Howe, *World of Our Fathers* (New York; Harcourt Brace Jovanovich, 1976). A similar study unfortunately does not exist for the earlier German migration, but a good popular study is Stephen Birmingham, *Our Crowd* (New York: Harper & Row, 1967).

3. Albert I. Gordon, *Jews in Suburbia* (Boston: Beacon, 1959), p. 217.

4. *Ibid.*, p. 16; Gordon, *Assimilation in American Life*, pp. 178–79.

5. Glazer, *American Judaism*, pp. 108–9.

6. Mordecai M. Kaplan, *Judaism as a Civilization: Toward a Reconstruction of American-Jewish Life* (New York: Macmillan, 1934), Part 3.

7. It should be noted that in the novella there is a strong undercurrent of affection for Jewishness, an affection that was totally absent from the movie version.

8. Marcus Lee Hansen, *The Problem of the Third Generation Immigrant* (Rock Island, Ill.: Augustana Historical Society, 1939) pp. 9–10.

9. Lewin, *Resolving Social Conflicts*, pp. 178–79. This complaint was not limited to just the young. Daniel Bell has noted that his generation, the second, had also struck out on its own, breaking its ties with the past, yet hungering for continuity. "Reflections on Jewish Identity," *Commentary* 31 (June 1961): 470–78.

10. See, for example, Maurice M. Shudofsky, "My People Are Destroyed by Lack of Knowledge," *Jewish Frontier* 18 (Apr. 1951): 8–11; Midge Decter, "The Fruits of Modern Jewish Education," *Commentary* 12 (Oct. 1951): 324–29.

11. Gans, "American Jewry," p. 428; Will Herberg, *Protestant-Catholic-Jew: An Essay in American Religious Sociology*, rev. ed. (Gar-

den City, N.Y.: Doubleday, 1960), p. 31. There were, of course, exceptions to this pattern. For one community where the more established and well-to-do families remained Orthodox, see Lucy S. Dawidowicz, "Middle-Class Judaism: A Case Study," *Commentary* 29 (June 1960): 492–503.

12. Immanuel Jakobovitz, "The Cost of Jewish Survival," *Judaism*, 15 (Fall 1966): 426; Jacob Neusner, "Freedom's Challenge to Judaism," *ibid.* 14 (Winter 1965): 3–4.

13. Marshall Sklare and Marc Vlosk, *The Riverton Study* (New York: American Jewish Committee, 1957).

14. C. Bezalel Sherman, "Demographic and Social Aspects," *The American Jew: A Reappraisal*, pp. 45–46.

15. Horace M. Kallen, *Of Them Which Say They Are Jews* (New York: Bloch, 1954), p. 9.

16. Hershel Shanks, "Jewish-Gentile Intermarriage. Facts and Trends," *Commentary* 16 (Oct. 1953): 37–75; Nathan Glazer and Daniel Patrick Moynihan, *Beyond the Melting Pot* (Cambridge, Mass.: MIT Press, 1963), pp. 160–61; Glazer, "What Sociology Knows About American Jews," *Commentary* 9 (March 1950): 275–84; Weyl, *Jew in American Politics*, pp. 302–3. Glazer noted that "Jews no longer take it for granted—as so many did (in the 1920s and 1930s)—that a natural concomitant of Americanization is the abandonment of the religious practices," and the reasons were simple—Hitler and Zionism. "The Jewish Revival in America: I," *Commentary* 20 (Dec. 1955): 493–99.

17. *Ibid.*, p. 303; Israel Goldstein, *Transition Years: New York-Jerusalem, 1960–1962* (Jerusalem: Rubin Maas, 1962), p. 170; Ludwig Lewisohn, "To the Young Jewish Intellectuals," *Jewish Frontier* 19 (Apr. 1952): 5; Irving Howe, "Mid-Century Turning Point: An Intellectual Memoir," *Midstream* 21 (June/July 1975): 25. See also Norman Podhoretz, *Making It* (New York: Random House, 1967) for one young Jewish intellectual's journey from Brooklyn.

18. Leslie A. Fiedler, "Plight of the Jewish Intellectual," *Congress Weekly* 18 (Apr. 9, 1951): 8–9; Will Herberg, "Is the Jewish Intellectual Really Alone?" *Jewish Frontier* 18 (July 1951): 7–9, agreed with most of Fielder's charges, but claimed they were affecting all American religions, and suggested that Fielder was not as alone as he thought he was. Marshall Sklare, however, agrees that in general the Jewish intellectuals of the late forties and fifties felt that the Jewish community had rejected them, and says that much of the background can be found in the keynote book, Judith R. Kramer and Seymour Leventman, *Children of the Gilded Ghetto* (New Haven: Yale University Press, 1961). See Sklare, "Problems in the Teaching of Contemporary Jewish Studies," *American Jewish Historical Quarterly* 63 (June 1974): 362–64.

19. Goldstein, *Transition Years*, p. 129.

20. Gordon, *Assimilation in American Life*, pp. 178–79. Again, the statistics varied sharply for Jewish intellectuals, who tended to associate primarily with other intellectuals, Jew or gentile. Gordon suggests that they belong more properly to an intellectual subsociety rather than to the Jewish subcommunity in their respective cities.

21. Gordon, *Jews in Suburbia*, p. 170.

22. Andrew Greeley, *That Most Distressful Nation* (Chicago: University of Chicago Press, 1972), p. 152.

23. Arnold and Caroline Rose, *America Divided: Minority Group Relations in the United States* (New York: Alfred A. Knopf, 1948), pp. 163–64. The Roses found that Negroes were the most discriminated-against group, followed by Jews and then Catholics.

24. Cohen, *Not Free to Desist*, p. 412; the annual editions of the *American Jewish Year Book* carried numerous articles on the status of American Jewry and the level of intolerance found; Stember, *Jews in the Mind of America*, p. 208.

25. Lois Waldman, "Employment Discrimination Against Jews in the United States—1955," *Jewish Social Studies* 18 (July 1956): 208; Milton Konvitz, "Inter-Group Relations," in Janowsky, *The American Jew*, pp. 79–80.

26. Arnold Forster and Benjamin R. Epstein, *The New Anti-Semitism* (New York: ADL, 1974), pp. 2–3.

27. John Higham, *Send These to Me: Jews and Other Immigrants in Urban America* (New York: Atheneum, 1975), pp. 168–69.

28. Herberg, *Protestant-Catholic-Jew, passim.* Herberg was not alone in viewing Jews as members of a triad. Rabbi Morris N. Kertzer reported a prominent Protestant church official as saying: "The Jews of the country . . . *psychologically* represent a third of the nation." Quoted in Irving Greenberg, "Adventure in Freedom—Or Escape from Freedom?" *American Jewish Historical Quarterly* 55 (Sept. 1965): 9.

29. Judd Teller, "A Critique of the New Jewish Theology," *Commentary* 25 (Mar. 1958): 243–52; Ben Halpern, *The American Jew* (New York: Herzl Press, 1956); Abraham G. Duker, "Impact of Zionism on American Jewish Life," *Jewish Life in America*, eds. Theodore Friedman and Robert Gordis (New York: Horizon Press, 1955), pp. 318–19.

30. Sherman, "Demographic and Social Aspects," p. 41. For the attitude of one "secular" Jew, see Ben Halpern, "Apologia Contra Rabbines," *Midstream* 2 (Spring 1956): 12–22.

31. Interviews with Moshe Kol (Minister of Tourism), Natanel Lorch (Secretary of the Knesset), Reuven Dafneh (head of the Foreign Ministry's North American desk). All of these men, who have widespread experience and knowledge of the United States, claim that whenever there is any

crisis, even a minor one, they are besieged with telephone calls to contact American Jewry, "as if we could push a button and the machinery would start."

32. Blau, *Judaism in America, passim.*

33. See Urofsky, *American Zionism,* ch. 5.

34. Mordecai M. Kaplan, *A New Zionism* (New York: Herzl Foundation, 1955), p. 124; see also Milton Himmelfarb, "Our Jewish Community Pattern and Its Critics, *Commentary* 16 (Aug. 1953): 115–31.

35. Meyer, "Hebrew Union College: A Centennial History," *passim.*

36. Bertram W. Korn, ed., *Retrospect and Prospect: Essays in Commemoration of the Seventy-fifth Anniversary of the Founding of the Central Conference of American Rabbis, 1889–1964* (New York: CCAR, 1965), *passim.*

37. Abraham Karp, *A History of the United Synagogue of America, 1913–1963* (New York: United Synagogue, 1964), *passim.*

38. Charles S. Liebman, "Orthodoxy in American Jewish Life," *American Jewish Year Book* 66 (1965): 21–97.

39. Amital Etzioni, "The National Religious Institutions of American Jewry," *Judaism* 11 (Spring 1962): 112–22.

40. Daniel J. Elazar, "Building Jewish Citizenship in the Emerging American Jewish Community," *Forum* 23 (Spring 1975): 9.

41. Quoted in Lilienthal, *What Price Israel?,* p. 190.

42. Hal Lehrman, "Turning Point in Jewish Philanthropy?," *Commentary* 10 (Sept. 1950): 205.

43. Silverberg, *If I Forget Thee,* p. 481.

44. Morris N. Kertzer, *Today's American Jew* (New York: McGraw-Hill, 1967), p. 91.

45. These donor books also were intended to be a roll call of honor as well. The Israel Bond Corporation, to mark its special sale on Israel's tenth anniversary, published *Who's Who: 1958 Trustees of Israel,* which consisted of pictures and brief biographies of 425 men and women who purchased more than $10,000 worth of bonds that year. The elaborate book carried the inscription "An Honor Roll of Leading Purchasers of State of Israel Bonds for Israel's Tenth Anniversary."

46. Kertzer, *Today's American Jew,* p. 102.

47. Arnauld G. Marts, *Generosity of Americans* (Englewood Cliffs, N.J.: Prentice-Hall, 1966).

48. Kertzer, *Today's American Jew,* pp. 92–93.

49. Cohen, *Not Free to Desist,* pp. 337–38.

50. David Petegorsky to Israel Goldstein, Dec. 31, 1951, Goldstein MSS, 1202a.

51. Will Herberg, "The Jewish Labor Movement in the United

States," *American Jewish Year Book* 53 (1952): 3–74, gives the best concise overview of the movement.

52. Robert M. MacIver, *Report on the Jewish Community Relations Agencies* (New York: NCRAC, 1951).

53. The most extensive analysis of the MacIver report, and especially of its theoretical aspects, is Abraham G. Duker, *Jewish Community Relations: An Analysis of the MacIver Report* (New York: Reconstructionist Foundation, 1952).

54. C. Bezalel Sherman, "The MacIver Report," *Jewish Frontier* 18 (Dec. 1951): 6–11; Selma G. Hirsh, "Jewish Community Relations," *American Jewish Year Book* 54 (1953): 162–77.

55. Knox, "Is America Exile or Home?," p. 486; Marshall Sklare, "American Jewry—The Ever-Dying People," *Midstream* 22 (June/July 1976): 18.

56. Eugene B. Borowitz, *A New Jewish Theology in the Making* (Philadelphia: Westminster Press, 1968), pp. 59–60.

57. Abba Eban, "The American Jewish Tercentenary," *Publications of the American Jewish Historical Society* 45 (Sept. 1955): 6–8.

Notes to Chapter 9

1. Arthur Hertzberg, *The Zionist Idea* (Garden City, N.Y.: Doubleday, 1959), p. 93.

2. Gen. 13:14–15; Amos 9:14–15; see also Jer. 46:27, Dan. 12:1, and Zech. 8:7–8.

3. I am indebted to Rabbi Jacob Kranz of Richmond for information regarding Talmudic views of *Eretz Yisrael;* see also Martin Buber, *Israel and Palestine* (London: East and West Library, 1952), pp. 47–52, and Abraham S. Halkin, ed., *Zion in Jewish Literature* (New York: Herzl Press, 1961), *passim.*

4. Harry Gersh and Sam Miller, "Satmar in Brooklyn," *Commentary* 28 (Nov. 1959): 389–99; David Sidorsky, "The End of Ideology and American Zionism," paper presented to the American Jewish Committee (Feb. 23, 1976), p. 14; S. Z. Abramov, *Perpetual Dilemma* (New York: World Union for Progressive Judaism, 1976), pp. 154ff.

5. Evans, *The Provincials*, p. 106; Lilienthal, *What Price Israel?*, pp. 190, 243.

6. Glazer, *American Judaism*, p. 115. Nearly two decades later, Rabbi Samuel Schafler echoed Glazer's judgment that, despite much pulpit rheto-

ric, "the impact of Israel on the inner workings of Jewish life on these shores has been negligible."

7. Elliot E. Cohen, "The Intellectuals and the Jewish Community," *Commentary* 8 (July 1949): 30.

8. Abba Lessing, "Jewish Impotence and Power," *Midstream* 22 (Oct. 1976): 52; Abraham Joshua Heschel, *Israel: An Echo of Eternity* (New York: Farrar, Straus, & Giroux, 1969), pp. 113–14.

9. Elie Wiesel, "A Plea for the Dead," in *Legends of Our Time* (New York: Holt, Rinehart, & Winston, 1968), p. 230; Rubenstein, *The Cunning of History, passim;* Jerome Eckstein, "The Holocaust and Jewish Theology," *Midstream* 23 (Apr. 1977): 36–45.

10. Rubenstein, *Power Struggle,* p. 13; Irving Howe, "Mid-Century Turning Point: An Intellectual Memoir," *Midstream* 21 (June/July 1975): 25.

11. Robert Alter, *After the Tradition: Essays on Modern Jewish Writing* (New York: Dutton, 1969), p. 163; Menachem Rosensaft, letter to editor, *Midstream* 21 (Feb. 1975): 3–4. Among the writings listed by Rosensaft as about or inspired by the Holocaust are: Saul Bellow, *Mr. Sammler's Planet* (1970); Bernard Malamud's short story "The German Jewish Refugee" (1963); Arthur Miller's play *Incident at Vichy* (1965); Daniel Stern, *Who Shall Live, Who Shall Die* (1973); Arthur A. Cohen, *In the Days of Simon Stern* (1973); Herman Wouk, *The Winds of War* (1971); Edward L. Wallant, *The Pawnbroker* (1961); Richard M. Elman, *The 28th Day of Elul* (1967), *Lilo's Diary* (1968), and *The Reckoning* (1969); Meyer Levin, *Eva* (1959), and *The Fanatic* (1964); and Leon Uris, *Mila 18* (1961) and *QB VII* (1970). It should be noted that the earliest fictional work about the Holocaust was written by a non-Jew, John Hersey's *The Wall* (1950).

12. Emil L. Fackenheim, *From Bergen-Belsen to Jerusalem: Contemporary Implications of the Holocaust* (Jerusalem: World Jewish Congress, 1975), p. 15, and in "Jewish Values in the Post-Holocaust Future: A Symposium," *Judaism* 16 (Summer 1967): 272.

13. Hilberg, *Destruction of the European Jews,* p. 666; see, however, Uri Suhl, ed., *They Fought Back* (New York: Schocken, 1972).

14. Jay Y. Gonen, *A Psychohistory of Zionism* (New York: Mason/Charter, 1975), p. 154.

15. Karl Shapiro, "Israel," *The New Yorker* 24 (June 12, 1948): 28.

16. *Ben-Gurion Looks Back,* pp. 241–42.

17. C. Bezalel Sherman, "Demographic and Social Aspects," pp. 49–50.

18. Arthur Koestler, *Promise and Fulfillment* (New York: Macmillan, 1949); Meyer Levin, *In Search* (New York: Horizon, 1950).

19. Liptzin, *Jew in American Literature,* p. 224; Philip Roth, "The

New Jewish Stereotypes," in Michael Selzer, *Zionism Reconsidered: The Rejection of Jewish Normalcy* (New York: Macmillan, 1970), pp. 107, 116.

20. Teller, *Strangers and Natives,* p. 260; Lawrence Francis York, "The Image of the Jew in Modern American Fiction," doctoral dissertation (University of Connecticut, 1966), p. 59. Despite the development of this new Jewish image, a number of critics suggest that in the 1950s American Jewish writers for the most part had not come to grips with Israel. York found little evidence of Israel influence, while Marie Syrkin and Harold Ribalow bemoaned the fact that American Jewish writers had avoided this most Jewish of subjects. Marie Syrkin, "Jewish Awareness in American Literature," in Janowsky, *The American Jew,* p. 226; Harold U. Ribalow, "Zion in Contemporary Fiction," *Mid-Century: An Anthology of Jewish Life and Culture in Our Times,* ed. Ribalow, (New York: Beechhurst, 1955), pp. 570–71. Bernard Cohen, on the other hand, believes that the existence of Israel definitely affected the tone and content of much Jewish writing in the United States. *Sociocultural Changes in American Jewish Life as Reflected in Selected Jewish Literature* (Rutherford: Fairleigh Dickinson University Press, 1972), pp. 218–19.

21. Milton R. Konvitz, "Individual Conscience and Group Consciousness: Religious Liberty in Israel and the United States," *Judaism* 20 (Spring 1971): 153–66.

22. Ludwig Lewisohn, *Israel* (New York: Boni and Livewright, 1925), pp. 158, 220: Meir, *My Life,* p. 459; Eytan, *The First Ten Years,* pp. 192–93.

23. Ahad Ha'am (Asher Ginzberg), *Ten Essays on Zionism and Judaism,* tr. Leon Simon (London: Routledge, 1922); Robert Alter, "Israeli Culture and the Jews," *Commentary* 62 (Nov. 1976): 59–60.

24. Abraham G. Duker, "Impact of Zionism on American Jewish Life," *Jewish Life in America,* eds. Friedman and Gordis, p. 316.

25. Eugene B. Borowitz, *The Masks Jews Wear: The Self-Deceptions of American Jewry* (New York: Simon & Schuster, 1973), pp. 151, 169; Stuart E. Rosenberg, *America Is Different: The Search for Jewish Identity* (New York: Thomas Nelson, 1964), p. 89; Borowitz, *A New Jewish Theology,* p. 31; E. Silberschlag, "Development and Decline of Hebrew Letters in the United States," in Janowsky, *The American Jew,* pp. 175–91.

26. Stephen Wise to Harry Friedenwald, Dec. 16, 1948, Friedenwald MSS, A182/20.

27. Kaplan, *Judaism as a Civilization, passim.*

28. Kaplan, *A New Zionism,* p. 42.

29. Mordecai M. Kaplan, "The Need for Diaspora Zionism," in

Ribalow, *Mid-Century*, p. 442; Borowitz, *A New Jewish Theology*, pp. 44–45; Kaplan, *A New Zionism*, p. 119.

30. Simon Rawidowicz, "Parashat Yohasin," *Bitzaron* (Dec. 1953/Jan. 1954), quoted in Henry Hurwitz, "Israel, What Now?" *Menorah Journal* 42 (Spring 1954): 28; David Polish, *Israel: Nation and People* (New York: KTAV, 1975), p. 136.

31. Maurice Friedman, "Martin Buber and the Social Problems of Our Time," *YIVO Annual of Jewish Social Science* 12 (1958/1959): 236–37.

32. David Ben-Gurion, "The Ingathering of the Exiles and an Exemplary Nation," *In the Time of Harvest: Essays in Honor of Abba Hillel Silver*, ed. Daniel Jeremy Silver (New York: Macmillan, 1963), pp. 121–23; Hurwitz, "Israel, What Now?," p. 2.

33. Leonard J. Fein, "Israel or Zion," *Judiasm* 22 (Winter 1973): 12; Louis Finkelstein, "The State of Israel as a Spiritual Force," in Moshe Davis, ed., *Israel: Its Role in Civilization* (New York: Harper/JTS, 1954), p. 16.

34. Rina Shapira, *Attitudes Toward Israel Among American Jewish Adolescents* (New York: Center for Urban Education, 1966), p. 8; Israel Knox, "American Judaism: ZOA Blueprint," *Commentary* 6 (Aug. 1948): 115; Norman L. Zucker, *The Coming Crisis in Israel: Private Faith and Public Policy* (Cambridge, Mass.: MIT Press, 1973), pp. 212–13; see also Abba Hillel Silver's attack on the Canaanites in *CCAR Yearbook* 68 (1958): 303.

35. Carey McWilliams, *A Mask for Privilege: Anti-Semitism in America* (Boston: Little, Brown, 1948), p. x; see the very negative comments not only about Israel, but also about their own feelings on Jewishness in "Jewishness and the Younger Intellectuals: A Symposium," *Commentary* 31 (Apr. 1961): 306–59.

36. Marshall Sklare and Benjamin B. Ringer, "A Study of Jewish Attitudes Toward the State of Israel," *The Jews: Social Patterns of an American Group*, ed. Marshall Sklare, (Glencoe, Ill.: The Free Press, 1958), p. 444; Abba Eban, "United States and Israel: Elements of a Common Tradition," in Davis, *Israel: Its Role in Civilization*, pp. 310–22; Eytan, *First Ten Years*, p. 194.

37. "State and Religion in Israel," *Jewish Frontier* 16 (Feb. 1949): 18–19; Zucker, *Coming Crisis in Israel*, pp. 51–52.

38. *Ibid.*, pp. 58–59; see also Ralph Simon, "Religion in Israel," *Judaism* 1 (Apr. 1952): 129–39.

39. Interview with Rami Carmi, June 1972.

40. This point is conceded by a large number of religious Israelis who believe that the rabbinic leadership has been shortsighted and reactionary;

see, for example, the criticism of Dr. Isaiah Liebowitz reported in Herbert Wiener, "Church and State in Israel," *Midstream* 8 (Winter 1962): 5–8.

41. Horace M. Kallen, "Whither Israel?," in Ribalow, *Mid-Century,* p. 507; Kaplan, *A New Zionism,* p. 92: Zvi Singer, "Israel's Religious Establishment and its Critics," *Midstream* 13 (Mar. 1967): 50–57.

42. *UAHC Proceedings* (1953): 231; *CCAR Yearbook* 67 (1957): 197; David Polish, *Renew Our Days: The Zionist Issue in Reform Judaism* (Jerusalem: World Zionist Organization, 1976), pp. 236ff.

43. *CCAR Yearbook* 60 (1950): 78–80; Zucker, *Coming Crisis in Israel,* pp. 91–92; Meyer, "Centennial History," pp. 208–11.

44. Interview with Yehudah Avner, June 5, 1975; Fackenheim, *From Bergen-Belsen to Jerusalem,* p. 17; Deutscher, *Non-Jewish Jew,* p. 111.

Notes to Chapter 10

1. Benno Weiser, "Ben-Gurion's Dispute with American Zionists," *Commentary* 18 (Aug. 1954): 98.

2. Robert Gordis, *Judaism for the Modern Age* (New York: Farrar, Straus & Cudahy, 1955), pp. 110–11.

3. Jakob J. Petuchowski, *Zion Reconsidered* (New York: Twayne, 1966), pp. 102–3.

4. J. K. Mikliszanski, "The Question of *Aliyah* in Jewish Law," *Judaism* 12 (Spring 1963): 131.

5. For an overview of the entire idea of exile, see Yitzhak F. Baer, *Galut* (New York: Schocken, 1947).

6. Quoted in Klutznik, *No Easy Answers,* p. 131.

7. See, for example, Ben Halpern, "Anti-Semitism in the Perspective of Jewish History," in Stember, *Jews in the Mind of America,* p. 283, and Polish, *Israel—Nation and People,* p. 132.

8. "Proceedings of the Jerusalem Ideological Conference," *Forum for the Problems of Zionism, Jewry, and the State of Israel* 4 (1959): 122–23; *Ben-Gurion Looks Back,* pp. 243–45.

9. Gordis, *Judaism for the Modern Age,* pp. 105–7; Marie Syrkin, "The Zionist Congress—A Post-Mortem," *Jewish Frontier* 18 (Oct. 1951): 21–23; Zvi Lurie, "Tests and Tasks," *In the Dispersion* 4 (1964/1965): 12–13.

10. "Jerusalem Ideological Conference," pp. 189, 199, 323–24, 362.

11. Israel Knox, "Is America Exile or Home?," *Commentary* 2 (Nov.

1946): 404; "Remarks by Mordecai Danzis," Sept. 1950, Ehrmann MSS.

12. Milton R. Konvitz, "Zionism: Homecoming or Homelessness?," *Judaism* 5 (Summer 1956): 206; Arthur Hertzberg, "America is *Galut*," *Jewish Frontier Anthology*, pp. 114–15; Polish, *Israel—Nation and People*, p. 134; Eliezer Berkovits, "The *Galut* of Judaism," *Judaism* 4 (Summer 1955): 226–27; Mordecai M. Kaplan, "Jewish Culture and Education in the Diaspora," in Ribalow, *Mid-Century*, p. 452.

13. "Ben-Gurion Against Diaspora," *Commentary* 31 (Mar. 1961): 199–200; Klutznik, *No Easy Answers*, p. 130.

14. Moshe Davis, "The Eretz Yisrael Dimension in American Jewish Life," *Proceedings of the Rabbinical Assembly* 34 (1970): 35; Immanuel Jakobovits, "The Cost of Jewish Survival," *Judaism* 15 (Fall 1966): 426–36; Margoshes quoted in Knox, "American Judaism: ZOA Blueprint," p. 115; Cynthia Ozick, "America: Toward Yavneh," *Judaism* 19 (Summer 1970): 265.

15. Ben Halpern, *The American Jew: A Zionist Analysis* (New York: Herzl Foundation, 1956).

16. Jacob B. Agus, *Guideposts in Modern Judaism* (New York: 1956), p. 189; Trude Weiss-Rosmarin, in Zionist Organization of America, *Re-Orienting Zionist Education* (New York: ZOA, 1948), p. 21.

17. Efraim Shmueli, "Israel, *Galut* and Zionism: The Changed Scene," *Judaism* 23 (Summer 1974): 266; Melvin M. Tumin, "Conservative Trends in American Jewish Life," *ibid.* 13 (Spring 1964): 133.

18. Hayim Greenberg, "Golus Jew," *Jewish Frontier*; see also, among many others, Horace M. Kallen, *Of Them Which Say They Are Jews*, pp. 189–90; Klutznik, *No Easy Answers*, p. 128; and Lewisohn, *The American Jew*, pp. 76–77. There was, however, a deep division between Orthodox rabbis and their Conservative and Reform colleagues on whether or not America was *galut*. Seven out of ten Orthodox respondents said America was *galut*, and this figure undoubtedly represented the traditional view that all nations were in exile until the coming of the messiah. Only three out of forty Conservative and one out of forty Reform rabbis viewed America as *galut*. However, 86 per cent of all respondents considered the Diaspora permanent. Eliezer Whartman, "Attitudes of American Rabbis on Zionism and Israel," *Jewish Social Studies* 17 (Apr. 1955): 125.

19. Arthur Hertzberg, "American Jews Through Israeli Eyes," *Commentary* 9 (Jan. 1950): 3.

20. Evron, in Ben-Ezer, *Unease in Zion*, pp. 151–52. Carried to its logical extreme, Evron noted, one could argue that "any Israeli loafer or pimp is quintessentially superior, as a Jew and as a human being (the distinction between the two concepts tends to become blurred) to Maimonides, Einstein, Kafka, Rabbi Nahman from Wroclaw, or the Gaon from Vilna."

21. Knox, "American Judaism: ZOA Blueprint," p. 114; Oscar Handlin, "Zionist Ideology and World Jewry," *Commentary* 25 (Feb. 1958): 105–9.

22. Whartman, "Attitudes of American Rabbis," p. 128; Petuchowski, *Zion Reconsidered*, p. 99.

23. Mati Meged, "The Jewish Intellectual in Israel," *Commentary* 31 (Jan. 1961): 28–33; Maurice Samuel, *Level Sunlight* (New York: Knopf, 1953), p. 266.

24. Konvitz, "Homeland or Homelessness?," pp. 206, 208.

25. Gordis, *Judaism for the Modern Age*, p. 108.

26. *Re-Orienting Zionist Education*, p. 29; Polish, *Israel—Nation and People*, pp. 62–63, 65. See also Ferdinand Zweig, "Israel and the Diaspora," *Judaism* 7 (Spring 1958): 147–50; Simon Greenberg, *Israel and Zionism: A Conservative Approach* (New York: United Synagogue, 1956), pp. 17ff.; Shlomo Avineri in Ben-Ezer, *Unease in Zion*, pp. 60–61.

27. Urofsky, *American Zionism*, pp. 131–32; Lewisohn, *The American Jew*, p. 5; Liptzin, *Jew in American Literature*, p. 176.

28. Morton Berman, "Zionist Reminiscences," p. 16; ms. courtesy of Rabbi Berman.

29. "Jerusalem Ideological Conference," pp. 189, 323; see also Nahum Goldmann's statement at p. 228.

30. Greenberg, "Education in the Diaspora," pp. 12–13; Maurice Samuel, "The Sundering of Israel and American Jewry," *Commentary* 16 (Sept. 1953): 200; see also Ezra Reichert, "Israel and the Diaspora," *Jewish Frontier* 15 (September 1948): 9; Halpern, *American Jew*, p. 26.

31. "Jerusalem Ideological Conference," pp. 122, 149, 199; see also Deutscher, *Non-Jewish Jew*, p. 92, reporting a conversation with Ben-Gurion.

32. Berger, *Who Knows Better*, p. 2; Eliezer Livneh, *State and Diaspora* (Jerusalem: WZO, 1953), p. 16.

33. Levi Eshkol, "Challenges of Today," *In the Dispersion* 4 (1964/1965): 9; Yigal Allon, "Israel's Economic Stability," in Zionist General Council, *The Challenge: Aliyah and Fighting Zionism* (Jerusalem: WZO, 1967), p. 27; Levin, *Balm in Gilead*, pp. 252–53; Samuel, *Level Sunlight*, pp. 198–99.

34. Weiser, "Ben-Gurion's Dispute," p. 94; "Jerusalem Ideological Conference," p. 203.

35. For one exception, see Shlomo Katz, "No Hope Except Exodus," *Commentary* 1 (Apr. 1946): 12–19.

36. Greenberg, "Education in the Diaspora," p. 13; Samuel, *Level Sunlight*, p. 204; Baron, *Steeled by Adversity*, p. 562; Hayim Greenberg, "Zionism and Diaspora," *Jewish Frontier* 18 (Sept. 1951): 8; Kaplan, *A*

New Zionism, p. 21; interview with Rose Halprin, Mar. 23, 1973; Louis Levinthal, address to twenty-fifth Zionist Congress, 1960, ms. courtesy of the late Judge Levinthal.

37. Hayim Greenberg, "On Dual Loyalties," in Ribalow, *Mid-Century,* p. 516; see also Ezra Shapiro, "A Zionist Movement Worthy of Its Name," *The Challenge,* pp. 33–34; Parzen, "Worksheet for American Zionism," p. 164.

38. Statement of American Jewish Committee in response to Prime Minister Ben-Gurion, Dec. 29, 1960; notes on AJC-Israel relations, Jan. 21, 1961; minutes of AJC executive board, Jan. 21, 1961, all in Ehrmann MSS; Jacob Blaustein to John F. Kennedy, May 23, 1961, Kennedy MSS, CO 126, Box 60.

39. Minutes of American Section of Jewish Agency, Sept. 28 and Oct. 5, 1951; Aug. 12, 1952, Goldstein MSS, 55b; Charles S. Liebman, "Does the Diaspora Influence Israel?: The Reconstituted Jewish Agency," *Forum* 23 (Spring 1975): 23.

40. Meyer Levin, "After All I Did for Israel," *Commentary* 12 (July 1951): 57–62.

41. Edwin Samuel, "On Fund-raising for Israel," *Menorah Journal* 43 (Spring 1955): 21; Maurice Samuel echoes this charge in *Level Sunlight,* p. 202; see also James Yaffe, *The American Jews* (New York: Random House, 1968), pp. 195–96; Borowitz, *Masks Jews Wear,* pp. 154–55; Samuel M. Blumenfield, "American Jewry—Reflections of Social, Communal, and Spiritual Trends," in Joseph L. Blau *et al., Essays of Jewish Life and Thought Presented in Honor of Salo Wittmayer Baron* (New York: Columbia University Press, 1959), pp. 135–36.

42. Nora Levin, "To an Israeli Friend," *Jewish Frontier* 19 (June 1952): 6–8; Handlin, "Ideology and World Jewry," p. 107; Israel Jefroykin, "Jewish State and Jewish Civilization," *Judaism* 1 (Oct. 1952): 340; Jacob Neusner, "A Stranger at Home: An American Jew Visits in Israel," *ibid.* 77 (Winter 1962): 30. Trude Weiss-Rosmarin, in a review editorial of *Level Sunlight* in *The Jewish Spectator,* wrote: "We Zionists know, all of us know . . . that our place is in Israel. . . . But, like Mr. Samuel, we have reached the conclusion that 'life in Israel is not for us.' Let us admit it, the real reason that keeps us here are the fleshpots of America."

43. Arthur Hertzberg, "American Zionism at an Impasse," *Commentary* 8 (Oct. 1949): 341; cf. Benno Weiser: "As time went on . . . the more conscious I became of the fact that despite my lifelong association with Zionism, I was as little an Israeli as I had been a Latin American." "Fall and Rise of a Zionist," *ibid.* 21 (Apr. 1956): 311.

44. Konvitz, "Homecoming or Homelessness," p. 209.

45. Kaplan, *A New Zionism,* p. 149; Polish, *Israel—Nation and Peo-*

ple, p. 173; Frisch, *On the Road to Zion*, p. 64; Ludwig Lewisohn, "Reflections on the Jewish Situation," *Jewish Frontier* 17 (Feb. 1950): 6.

46. Cohen, *American Jews and the Zionist Idea*, p. 116; Whartman, "Attitudes of American Rabbis," pp. 129–30; Chaim I. Waxman, "The Centrality of Israel in American Jewish Life: A Sociological Analysis," *Judaism* 25 (Spring 1976): 178.

47. Calvin Goldschneider, "American *Aliyah*—Sociological and Demographic Perspectives," in Sklare, *Jew in American Society*, pp. 351–54; Crossman, *Palestine Mission*, p. 39; Lapide, *A Century of U.S. Aliyah*, p. 129.

48. The best figures are in Goldschneider, "American *Aliyah*," Table 2, p. 353; Sklare, *America's Jews*, p. 213; *Time*, Mar. 10, 1975; Isaacs, *American Jews in Israel*, pp. 47–48.

49. Moshe Kerem, *Life in a Kibbutz* (New York: Reconstructionist Press, 1955), p. iv; interviews with faculty members at Bar-Ilan University, May 27, 1975; Isaacs, *American Jews in Israel*, p. 77; Lapide, *Century of U.S. Aliyah*, pp. 130–31; Diana Lerner, "*Aliyah* by Accident," *Israel Digest* 19 (Aug. 27, 1976): 12; Goldschneider, "American *Aliyah*," p. 376.

50. *Ibid.*, pp. 371–79.

51. Charles I. Glicksberg, "American Jews in Israel," *Judaism* 8 (Summer 1959): 248; Jacob Neusner, "A Stranger at Home: An American Jew Visits Israel," *ibid.* 11 (Winter 1962): 27–31; Isaacs, *American Jews in Israel*, p. 107.

52. Ernest Van Der Haag, *The Jewish Mystique* (New York: Stein & Day, 1969), pp. 241–42; Morris Yaacov, *On the Soil of Israel* (Tel Aviv: AACI, 1965), pp. 220–22; Ronald Sanders, "Settling in Israel?," *Commentary* 40 (Aug. 1965): 37–44.

53. Isaacs, *American Jews in Israel*, pp. 200–1; Neusner, "Stranger at Home," p. 28. In one group of 130 candidates for *aliyah* interviewed in New York, 106 declined to enter Israel on an immigrant visa, lest it jeopardize their American citizenship; Lapide, *Century of U.S. Aliyah*, pp. 105–6.

54. Isaacs, *American Jews in Israel*, pp. 98–99; AlRoy, *Behind the Middle East Conflict*, p. 96.

55. For two differing views of the problems of adjustment, one by a man who stayed in Israel, and the other who became an Israeli citizen, but then worked for the Zionists in New York, see Eliezer Whartman, "You Can't Go Home Again," in Ribalow, *Mid-Century*, pp. 548–55, and Weiser, "Rise and Fall of a Zionist."

56. Isaacs, *American Jews in Israel*, pp. 161, 205; Van Der Haag, *Jewish Mystique*, p. 246.

57. Cohen, *American Jews and the Zionist Idea*, p. 121; Lapide, *Century of U.S. Aliyah*, p. 111.

58. Jerusalem *Post Weekly,* Jan. 13, 1976.

59. Simon N. Herman, *American Students in Israel* (Ithaca, N.Y.: Cornell University Press, 1970), *passim;* see also a briefer study of ten youth groups involved in a summer program in Dan Ronen, "A Study of the Effect of a Summer in Israel on American Jewish Youth," *In the Dispersion,* 5/6 (1966): 210–80. For a personal view of how American students were treated, see Aliza Samuels, "I Listen Again to Joan Baez: Reflections of a New Israeli," *Midstream* 21 (May 1975): 33–43. Ms. Samuels, although an immigrant, was frequently mistaken as a visiting student.

60. Wiesel, *Two Images, One Destiny,* pp. 8–9.

61. See, for example, Gordis, *Judaism for the Modern Age,* pp. 120–21; Blumenfield, "American Jewry—Reflections," p. 136; Marie Syrkin, "Let Not the Work of a Great Creation Be Squandered," in *The Challenge,* pp. 77–78.

62. *Israeli Digest* 18 (Jan. 30, 1976): 11.

Notes to Chapter 11

1. "Foolish Talk," *New Palestine* 38 (Nov. 14, 1947): 4.

2. Halperin, *Political World of American Zionism,* p. 327.

3. Ben Halpern, "The Debate on Zionist Reorganization," *Jewish Frontier* 16 (Oct. 1949): 46–47.

4. Meyer Weisgal to Chaim Weizmann, July 13, 1948, Weisgal MSS; Abba Hillel Silver to Israel Goldstein, July 30, 1948, Goldstein MSS.

5. Neumann, *In the Arena,* pp. 272–73.

6. Brecher, *Foreign Policy System of Israel,* p. 143.

7. See, for example, digest of minutes of American Section of Jewish Agency, Dec. 21, 1951, and Feb. 8, 1952, and Berl Locker to American Section, Aug. 14, 1952, Goldstein MSS, 555b and c.

8. The texts of the Status Bill and the implementing covenant can be found in World Zionist Organization, *Zionism: The Force of Change* (Jerusalem: WZO, 1968), pp. 55–59.

9. Robert Szold to Harry Friedenwald, Nov. 18, 1948, Friedenwald MSS, A182/25; Rubin, *Partners in State-Building,* p. 203.

10. Minutes of meeting, American Section of Jewish Agency, Dec. 27, 1948, Silver MSS.

11. Telegrams to Joshua Trachtenberg from Berl Locker, Feb. 17, 1949; from Rudolph Sonneborn and others, Feb. 18, 1949; from Herman

Weisman, Feb. 19, 1949; and from Benjamin Brodie and others, Feb. 19, 1949, all in miscellaneous files, American Jewish Archives; Alfred Jacob Kutzik, "The Social Basis of American Jewish Philosophy," doctoral dissertation (Brandeis University, 1967), pp. 683–87.

12. See, for example, the editorial "Labor Zionist Turning Point," *Jewish Frontier* 19 (Aug. 1952): 4: "The Labor Zionist Organization in America thus finds itself in the enviable position of being able to speak to American Jews in the name of political colleagues [i.e., Mapai] with whose ideas they are in agreement."

13. Interviews with Jacques Torczyner, Nov. 4, 1976, and with Emanuel Neumann, Jan. 7, 1975; Leon I. Feuer, "Abba Hillel Silver: A Personal Memoir," *American Jewish Archives* 19 (Nov. 1967): 124–25.

14. Judd Teller, "Notes of a UJA Speaker," *Jewish Frontier* 18 (May 1951): 17; Shlomo Katz, "The Danger of Demobilization," *ibid.* 17 (Mar. 1950): 13; see also Daniel Frisch, "The ZOA at the Crossroads," *New Palestine* 39 (Jan. 13, 1949): 7; Zionist Organization of America, *Re-orienting Zionist Education Today: Proceedings . . .* (New York: ZOA, 1948), *passim*.

15. At the first Zionist Congress in 1897, the largest delegations had been from Russia (58), Austria, including Hungary and Galicia (49), and Germany (39); the United States had sent 4 people, and Palestine 3. In 1951, Israel had 210 representatives, and the United States 122; the next largest delegation was from Argentina, with 13.

16. Marie Syrkin, "The Zionist Congress—A Post-Mortem," *Jewish Frontier* 18 (Oct. 1951): 21–23; Judd Teller, "American Zionists Move Toward Clarity," *Commentary* 12 (Nov. 1951): 444–50; Ben Halpern, "The Impact of Israel on American Jewish Ideologies," *Jewish Social Studies* 21 (Jan. 1959): 78–79.

17. Arthur Hertzberg, ed., *The Zionist Idea* (New York: Herzl Press, 1959), p. 82n.; *Ben-Gurion Looks Back,* p. 238.

18. Ernest Stock, "Americans in Israel," *Midstream* 3 (Summer 1957): 39; Moshe Gurary, "Remembering Ben-Gurion," *Jerusalem Post* (Oct. 15, 1976). Although Ben-Gurion denied that he called American Zionism "bankrupt" (Ben-Gurion to Bernard Rosenblatt, Dec. 24, 1951, in Rosenblatt, *Two Generations of Zionism,* p. 241), the charge appears in several accounts; see, for example, *New Republic* 125 (Dec. 24, 1951): 6, and *Christian Century* 68 (Dec. 26, 1951): 1499. See also *Ben-Gurion Looks Back,* p. 239; David Ben-Gurion, "Israel and Zionism," *Jewish Frontier* 17 (Jan. 1950): 22.

19. *Ma'ariv* (Feb. 24, 1967), quoted in Meir Ben-Horin, "Judeo-Zionism: Meaning Old and New," *Judaism* 20 (Summer 1971): 295.

20. "Ben-Gurion Against the Diaspora," *Commentary* 31 (Mar.

1961): 194; Samuel, *Level Sunlight,* p. 206; Crossman, *A Nation Reborn,* p. 111.

21. Eliezer Livneh, "The Future of the Zionist Movement," *Jewish Frontier* 20 (July 1953): 5. See also Livneh's statement in *Davar,* May 29, 1953, quoted in Kaplan, *A New Zionism,* p. 17.

22. James G. Heller, "Confessions of an American Zionist," *Jewish Frontier* 21 (Mar. 1954): 16.

23. Zehava Epstein to Itzhak Ben-Zvi, Mar. 22, 1946, Ben-Zvi MSS, A116/85.

24. For discussions of the philanthropic basis of American Zionism, and the perverse effect it had on the movement, see Simon Halkin in *Reorienting Zionist Education,* p. 3; Israel Knox, "Is America Exile or Home?," p. 401; Petuchowski, *Zion Reconsidered,* pp. 60–65; Blau, *Judaism in America,* pp. 101–2; Livneh, *State and Diaspora,* p. 15; Agus, *Guideposts in Modern Judaism,* p. 155.

25. Cohen, *American Jews and Zionist Idea,* p. 95; Kaplan, *Future of American Jew,* p. 128; Leonard J. Fein, "Israel or Zion," *Judaism* 22 (Winter 1973): 12; Israel Goldstein to David Petegorsky, May 13, 1953, Goldstein MSS, 1202e.

26. Samuel, *Level Sunlight,* p. 206.

27. "Zionism," Jacob Petuchowski accused, "is a substitute religion, and it flourishes precisely because the real religion which it has come to replace is weak and colorless." *Zion Reconsidered,* p. 94; see also Borowitz, *Masks Jews Wear,* p. 173; Rosenberg, *America Is Different,* pp. 85–86; for a later statement of the same theme, see Martin Siegel, with Mel Ziegler, *Amen: The Diary of Rabbi Martin Siegel* (New York: World, 1971), p. 196.

28. Agus, *Guideposts in Modern Judaism,* pp. 177–78; Jacob Neusner, "Toward a Zion of Jewish Peoplehood," *Reconstructionist* 38 (Nov. 1972): 14–21; Neusner, "Zionism and the Jewish Problem," *Midstream* 15 (Nov. 1969): 34–45; Roland B. Gittelsohn, "American Jews and Israel," *ibid.* 18 (Feb. 1972): 58–59.

29. Halpern, *The American Jew,* p. 90; Sharrett, in *Zionism, The Force of Change,* pp. 41–42; Abba Eban, "Nationalism and Internationalism in Our Day," in Davis, *Israel: Its Role in Civilization,* pp. 124–25; Greenberg, "Jewish Education and Culture in the Diaspora," p. 85; Samuel, *Level Sunlight,* pp. 207–8; Kaplan, in "Jerusalem Ideological Conference," p. 31.

30. Ezra Reichert, "Israel and the Diaspora," *Jewish Frontier* 15 (Sept. 1948): 7; Ben Halpern, *The Idea of the Jewish State,* 2d ed. (Cambridge, Mass.: Harvard University Press, 1969), p. 215; Ben-Horin, "Judaeo-Zionism," pp. 296–97.

31. Buber, in Ben-Ezer, *Unease in Zion*, p. 117; Eliezer Livneh, "Is Israel a Zionist State?," *Midstream* 2 (Summer 1956): 19.

32. See Marie Syrkin, "Out of Zion: A Report on the Ideological Conference," *Midstream* 3 (Autumn 1957): 28–34; Oscar Handlin, "Zionist Ideology and World Jewry," *Commentary* 25 (Feb. 1958): 105–9.

33. Kallen, "Whither Israel?" in Ribalow, *Mid-Century*, p. 482.

34. For a listing of Zionist "tasks," but no comprehensive program, see Nahum Goldmann, Report to the American Section of the Jewish Agency, May 24, 1950, cited in Hurwitz, "Midcentury Inventory," p. 132; Hayim Greenberg, "Which Zionist Party?," *Jewish Frontier* 16 (Dec. 1949): 5; Lewisohn, *The American Jew*, p. 165; Lewisohn, "The Future of American Zionism," *Commentary* 10 (August 1950): 118; Louis Levinthal, "American Zionism in the Post-State Era," in Schneiderman, *Two Generations in Perspective*, p. 164; Eli Ginzberg, *Agenda for American Jews* (New York: King's Crown Press, 1950), pp. 62–63; Arthur Hertzberg, "American Zionism at an Impasse," *Commentary* 8 (Oct. 1949): 341; Leon Feuer, "Beyond Zionism," *CCAR Yearbook* 67 (1957): 129–38; Abba Hillel Silver to Zalman Shazar, Apr. 23, 1956, Silver MSS; Halkin, in *Reorienting Zionist Education*, p. 1; Samuel, *Level Sunlight*, p. 214.

35. Jacob Neusner, "Zionist Revival on the Campus?," *Commentary* 19 (Feb. 1955): 174–78; Shapiro, quoted in Gerald S. Strober, *American Jews: Community in Crisis* (Garden City, N.Y.: Doubleday, 1974), p. 21.

36. This section is derived primarily from Mordecai M. Kaplan, *A New Zionism* (New York: Herzl Press, 1955); see also Kaplan's speeches at the Jerusalem Ideological Conference, pp. 29–40, 102–6, 319–21, and "A Program for Labor Zionists," *Jewish Frontier* 16 (July 1949): 12–16.

Notes to Chapter 12

1. Minutes of executive committee, American Zionist Council, Sept. 9, 1952, Silver MSS. An example of the ZOA trying unsuccessfully to get itself involved with communal affairs can be found in the activities of the so-called Tannenbaum committee; see various documents in Goldstein MSS, 1202C.

2. "The First Zionist Assembly," *Jewish Frontier* 21 (Jan. 1954): 5–6.

3. Announcement of American Zionist Committee for Public Affairs, Mar. 22, 1954, Silver MSS; Benjamin Akzin to American members of Ac-

tions Committee, Mar. 30, 1948, Kaplan (Agency) MSS, S53/469; interview with I. L. Kenen, Nov. 13, 1975.

4. Yitzhak Yaron to Abba Hillel Silver, Apr. 8, 1953, Silver MSS.

5. Neumann, *In the Arena*, pp. 288–89; Charles S. Liebman, "Does the Diaspora Influence Israel: The Reconstituted Jewish Agency," *Forum* 23 (Spring 1975): 19; statement on Washington conference by Israel Goldstein, March 6, 1955, Goldstein MSS, 573.

6. Eugene D. Jaffee, *American Investment and Operations in Israel* (New York: St. John's University Press, 1969), *passim*.

7. Teller, *Strangers and Natives*, pp. 276–77.

8. Brecher, *Foreign Policy System*, pp. 502–3.

9. Robert St. John *Eban* (Garden City, N.Y.: Doubleday, 1972), ch. 16; Abba Hillel Silver to Eban, Sept. 14, 1952, and Eban to Silver, Sept. 19, 1952, Silver MSS.

10. Eytan, *First Ten Years*, pp. 200–1.

11. Brecher, *Foreign Policy System*, pp. 38, 231.

12. For German reparations, see Cohen, *Not Free to Desist*, pp. 268–79; Brecher, *Decisions in Israel's Foreign Policy*, pp. 72–73, 92; Bisgyer, *Challenge and Encounter*, pp. 118–19.

13. Abba Hillel Silver to Robert A. Taft and to I. L. Kenen, Feb. 9, 1951; Edward Martin to Robert J. Arthur, Mar. 19, 1951; Louis Lipksy to all local committees of American Zionist Council, Mar. 23, 1951; Abba Eban to Silver, Mar. 27, 1951, all in Silver MSS. Brecher, *Foreign Policy System*, p. 106, reports that altogether, Washington contributed $848 million to Israel from 1949 to 1965.

14. Talmon, *Israel Among the Nations*, p. 187.

15. Irving Louis Horowitz, *Israeli Ecstasies/Jewish Agonies* (New York: Oxford University Press, 1974), pp. 25–26; Brecher, *Foreign Policy System*, pp. 122–31.

16. James T. Patterson, *Mr. Republican: A Biography of Robert A. Taft* (Boston: Houghton Mifflin, 1972), p. 282.

17. I. L. Kenen to Abba Hillel Silver, June 17, 1952; David Ben-Gurion to Louis Lipsky, Aug. 31, 1952; Abba Eban to Silver, Nov. 8, 1952, all in Silver MSS.

18. Marvin C. Feuerwerger, "The Emergency Security Assistance Act of 1973 and American-Israeli Relations," *Midstream* 20 (Aug./Sept. 1974): 23–24.

19. Cohen, *Not Free to Desist*, pp. 371–72.

20. For a closer study of these issues, see Brecher, *Foreign Policy System*, pp. 43–44, and *Decisions in Israel's Foreign Policy*, pp. 34–35, 48, 116–18.

21. Cohen, *American Jews and the Zionist Idea*, p. 107.

22. Nadav Safran, *The United States and Israel* (Cambridge, Mass.: Harvard University Press, 1963), pp. 219–20.

23. Alan Richard Balboni, "A Study of the Efforts of the American Zionists to Influence the Formulation and Conduct of United States Foreign Policy During the Roosevelt, Truman, and Eisenhower Administrations," doctoral dissertation (Brown University, 1973), p. 191; *Der Tag*, Mar. 10, 1953; Abba Eban to Abba Hillel Silver, June 11, 1953, Silver MSS.

24. Henry A. Byraode, *The Middle East*, Department of State Publication 5469 (Washington: 1954), p. 11; see also Berger, *Who Knows Better*, p. 4, and Lieberman, *Strangers to Glory*, pp. 57–58

25. Halpern, *Idea of the Jewish State*, p. 425; for Dulles's convoluted and often contradictory policy in the Middle East, see Townsend Hoopes, *The Devil and John Foster Dulles* (Boston: Little, Brown, 1973), chs. 20–23.

26. Circular letter, Oct. 14, 1954, Silver MSS.

27. Memorandum submitted to Secretary of State by Jewish organizations, and summary of conference with Secretary of State, both Oct. 25, 1954, Goldstein MSS, 1246.

28. *CCAR Yearbook* 65 (1955): 7; excerpts of remarks, Mar. 6, 1955, Goldstein MSS, 573; Abba Hillel Silver to Sherman Adams, May 24, 1955, Silver MSS.

29. Dwight D. Eisenhower to Silver, Apr. 12, 1956; Silver to John Foster Dulles, Apr. 27, 1956, *ibid.*

30. I. L. Kenen, circular letter, Aug. 21, 1956, *ibid.*; Porter and Johnson, *National Party Platforms*, pp. 527, 557.

31. Theodore Draper, *Israel and World Politics: The Roots of the Third Arab-Israeli War* (New York: Viking, 1968), pp. 16–17.

32. Safran, *The United States and Israel*, pp. 232, 238; George Lenczowski, ed., *United States Interests in the Middle East* (Washington: American Enterprises Institute, 1968), p. 19.

33. See, for example, John F. Kennedy to John Foster Dulles, Apr. 15, 1956, in *John F. Kennedy on Israel, Zionism, and Jewish Issues*, ed. Earnest E. Barbaresh (New York: ZOA/Herzl Press, 1965), p. 15; *New York Herald Tribune* editorial of Sept. 23, 1956, deprecating the American policy as "Too Little, Too Late."

34. For the military history of the Sinai campaign, see Moshe Dayan, *Diary of the Sinai Campaign 1956* (London: Sphere Books, 1967); S. L. A. Marshall, *Sinai Victory* (New York: Morrow, 1958); and Edward Luttwak and Dan Horowitz, *The Israeli Army* (New York: Harper & Row, 1975), ch. 5.

35. Brecher, *Decisions in Israel's Foreign Policy*, pp. 239–40.

36. Emmet John Hughes, *The Ordeal of Power* (New York: Dell, 1964), pp. 183–85, 188–89; Hoopes, *Devil and John Foster Dulles*, ch. 21. For the context of American policy during the Suez crisis, see Eugene V. Rostow, "Israel in the Evolution of United States Foreign Policy," paper delivered at the joint meeting of the American Historical Association and American Jewish Historical Society, Dec. 28, 1976, Washington, D.C.

37. Brecher, *Decisions in Israel's Foreign Policy*, pp. 277–78; Neumann, *In the Arena*, p. 294.

38. Lucy Dawidowicz, "The United States, Israel and the Middle East," *American Jewish Year Book* 59 (1958): 203; Meir, *My Life*, p. 301.

39. New York *Times*, Nov. 1, 1956; Dawidowicz, "United States and Israel," p. 207; Cohen, *American Jews and Zionist Idea*, p. 101.

40. Stember, *Jews in the Mind of America*, p. 183; Nahum Goldmann to David Ben-Gurion, Nov. 7, 1956, in Brecher, *Decisions in Israel's Foreign Policy*, p. 287.

41. *American Jewish Year Book* 59 (1958): 174; George Steiner. "How U.S. Jews View Jewish State," *Life* 43 (Aug. 12, 1957): 112.

42. Stember, *Jews in the Mind of America*, pp. 189–91.

43. Hal Lehrman, "The United States and Israel," *Commentary* 23 (Mar. 1957): 208; New York *Times*, Feb. 6, 1957.

44. Lyndon B. Johnson to John Foster Dulles, Feb. 11, 1957, copy in Lehman MSS; Stephen D. Isaacs, *Jews and American Politics* (Garden City, N.Y.: Doubleday, 1974), pp. 250–51; Brecher, *Decisions in Israel's Foreign Policy*, p. 296.

45. Philadelphia *Inquirer*, Feb. 23, 1957, quoted in Bisgyer, *Challenge and Encounter*, pp. 220–21.

46. New York *Times*, Mar. 2, 1957; Meir, *My Life*, pp. 307–8; Dawidowicz, "United States and Israel," pp. 210–11.

47. American Assembly, *The United States and the Middle East* (Englewood Cliffs, N.J.: Prentice-Hall, 1964), p. 131.

48. Goldschneider, "American *Aliyah*," p. 353.

49. Isser Harel, *The House on Garibaldi Street* (New York: Viking, 1975), details the entire operation of the Eichmann capture.

50. Brecher, *Foreign Policy System*, pp. 239–40; Meir, *My Life*, pp. 178–79.

51. Gerd Korman, "The Holocaust in American Historical Writing," *Societas* 2 (Summer 1972): 260–62; interview with Gideon Hausner, Feb. 19, 1978.

52. "Jewishness and the Younger Intellectuals: A Symposium," *Commentary* 31 (Apr. 1961): 306–59.

53. Charles Y. Glock, Gertrude J. Selznick, and Joe L. Spaeth, *The Apathetic Majority: A Study Based on Public Responses to the Eichmann Trial* (New York: Harper & Row, 1966) *passim*.

Notes to Chapter 13

1. Higham, *Send These to Me*, p. 193.

2. Mark R. Levy and Michael S. Kramer, *The Ethnic Factor: How America's Minorities Decide Elections* (New York: Simon & Schuster, 1972), p. 99.

3. Interview with Shad Polier, Nov. 28, 1975; Israel Goldstein to David Petegorsky, reporting conversation with Bernard G. Richards, Jan. 22, 1952, Goldstein MSS, 1202a.

4. Leonard Dinnerstein, "Southern Jewry and the Desegregation Crisis, 1954–1970," *American Jewish Historical Quarterly* 62 (Mar. 1973): 234–35.

5. Cohen, *Not Free to Desist*, pp. 393–94.

6. Judd L. Teller, "The Negro and Jewish Diasporas," *Midstream* 5 (Summer 1959): 2–4; see also Ben Halpern, "Ethnic and Religious Minorities: Subcultures and Subcommunities," *Jewish Social Studies* 27 (January 1965): 44, regarding similarities between the two groups.

7. Horace Mann Bond, "Negro Attitudes Toward Jews," *ibid.*, p. 8.

8. "Negro-Jewish Relations in America: A Symposium," *Midstream* 12 (Dec. 1966): 3–91; Norman Podhoretz, "My Negro Problem—and Ours," *Commentary* 35 (Feb. 1963): 93–101; Weyl, *Jew in American Politics*, p. 286.

9. *Engel v. Vitale*, 370 U.S. 421 (1962).

10. "To Our Jewish Friends," *America* 107 (Sept. 1, 1962): 665–66.

11. Milton R. Konvitz, "Inter-Group Relations," in *The American Jew: A Reappraisal*, pp. 96–98; Arthur Hertzberg, "Church, State, and the Jews," *Commentary* 35 (Apr. 1963): 277–78.

12. Cohen, *American Jews and the Zionist Idea*, p. 106; Kertzer, *Today's American Jew*, p. 243.

13. *New York Times*, Apr. 29, 1960; Elmer Berger, *Problems of American Policy-makers in the Middle East* (New York: AJAZ, n.d.), p. 9.

14. Bernard C. Cohen, *The Influence of Non-governmental Groups on Foreign Policy-making* (Boston: World Peace Foundation, 1959), 2:8.

15. Levy and Kramer, *The Ethnic Factor*, p. 100.

16. "Politics in a Pluralistic Society," cited in Kertzer, *Today's American Jew*, p. 73.

17. Richard J. Whalen, *The Founding Father: The Story of Joseph P.*

Kennedy (New York: NAL/World, 1964), chs. 16, 17, 22: Meyer Feldman oral history interview, John Fitzgerald Kennedy Library, Waltham, Mass.

18. John McCormack oral history interview, *ibid.*

19. Saul Brenner, "Patterns of Jewish-Catholic Democratic Voting in the 1960 Presidential Election," *Jewish Social Studies* 26 (July 1964): 169–78; Theodore H. White, *The Making of the President 1960* (New York: Atheneum, 1961), pp. 259–62; Sanford T. Marcus, "John F. Kennedy and the Jews," term paper, HUC-JIR, on deposit at American Jewish Archives.

20. Barbaresh, *John F. Kennedy on Israel,* pp. 54, 60; Feldman interview.

21. *Ibid.;* Feinberg, "Anatomy of a Commitment," pp. 20–21.

22. Levy and Kramer, *The Ethnic Factor,* p. 104: Meyer Feldman to author, July 21, 1976; Cyrus L. Sulzberger, *An Age of Mediocrity: Memoirs and Diaries, 1963–1972* (New York: Macmillan, 1973), p. 448.

23. Oral history interviews of Meyer Feldman, John S. Badeau, and Francis Plimpton, all in Kennedy Library.

24. Feldman interview.

25. See, for example, I. L. Kenen to Meyer Feldman, Aug. 22, 1963, Feldman MSS, Box 18.

26. Memorandum of meeting, Apr. 30, 1962, Lehman MSS.

27. George A. Smathers to John F. Kennedy, Sept. 27, 1963; Meyer Feldman to John F. Kennedy, Oct. 7, 1963; memorandum, Benjamin H. Read to McGeorge Bundy, Oct. 29, 1963; all in Feldman MSS, Box 18.

28. L. D. Battle to McGeorge Bundy, July 17, 1961, and Bundy to Elmer Berger, June 24, 1961, Kennedy MSS, CO 126, Box 60; Berger, *Who Knows Better Must Say So!,* p. x.

29. Judah J. Shapiro, *Contemporary Jewish Community Life and the Zionist Movement: Dangers and Challenges* (Jerusalem: WZO, 1965), p. 3; Jacob Neusner, "Freedom's Challenge to Judaism," *Judaism* 14 (Winter 1965): 3–4.

30. Presidential address to World Jewish Congress in Brussels, 1966, quoted in Kertzer, *Today's American Jew,* p. 234.

31. Milton Himmelfarb, *The Jews of Modernity* (New York: Basic Books, 1973), pp. 229–30; see also Jacob Amit, "Dispersion and Redemption," *In the Dispersion* 5/6 (1966): 29.

32. Marshall Sklare, "Intermarriage and the Jewish Future," *Commentary* 37 (Apr. 1964): 41–52; Erich Rosenthal, "Studies of Jewish Intermarriage in the United States," *American Jewish Year Book* 64 (1963): 3–53.

33. Seymour Martin Lipset, "The Study of Jewish Communities in a Comparative Context," *Jewish Journal of Sociology* 5 (Dec. 1963): 163.

34. Emil Fackenheim, "Jewish Values in the Post-Holocaust Future: A Symposium," *Judaism* 16 (Summer 1967): 270.

35. Arthur Hertzberg, "The Changing American Rabbinate," *Midstream* 12 (Jan. 1966): 23; Shapiro, *Contemporary Jewish Community Life,* pp. 18–19; *The American Zionist* 51 (Sept. 1960): 1.

36. David Polish, *The Eternal Dissent: A Search for Meaning in Jewish History* (London: Abelard-Schuman, 1961), pp. 147–49 and *passim.* Rabbi Polish, though, never renounced the idea of *galut* or the obligation of *aliyah.* Rather, he has viewed them more in psychological terms, reflecting inward as well as outer pressures on Jewish existence, and thus generating tensions which he believes can be beneficial. One can recognize the Zionist obligation of *aliyah* and not act upon it; yet by conceding the ultimate logic of *galut,* one can become a better Jew. See also *Israel—Nation and People.*

37. Israel Goldstein, *Transition Years: New York-Jerusalem, 1960–1962* (Jerusalem: Rubin Maas, 1962), and *Israel at Home and Abroad* (Jerusalem: Rubin Maas, 1973).

38. James P. Warburg, "Israel and the American Jewish Community," copy of speech in Warburg MSS, Box 60.

39. Petuchowski, *Zion Reconsidered, passim.*

40. Ya'acov Tsur to Abba Hillel Silver, Dec. 8, 1958, Silver MSS; Mati Meged, "The Jewish Intellectual in Israel," *Commentary* 31 (Jan. 1961): 29.

41. Maurice Samuel, "Why Israel Misunderstands American Jewry," *ibid.* 16 (Oct. 1953): 300–10; Marc Lee Raphael, "The Image of American Jews and American Judaism in the Israeli daily, *Ha'aretz,* from March 1966 to January 1967," term paper, HUC-JIR, on deposit at American Jewish Archives.

42. Brecher, *Foreign Policy System of Israel,* p. 308; Levi Eshkol, "Building a Bridge," *In the Dispersion* 5/6 (1966): 7–8; Amit, "Dispersion and Redemption," p. 18; Crossman, *A Nation Reborn,* p. 109.

43. World Zionist Organization, *Zionist News: The 26th Zionist Congress* (Jerusalem: WZO, 1965), *passim.*

44. *Ibid.,* p. 29; Zvi Lurie, "Tests and Tasks," *In the Dispersion* 4 (1964/1965): 19.

45. A much more serious examination of these issues did, in fact, take place at the 29th Zionist Congress in February 1978.

Notes to Chapter 14

1. Quoted in Brecher, *Decisions in Israel's Foreign Policy*, p. 253.
2. Draper, *Israel and World Politics*, pp. 24–25.
3. Cohen, *American Jews and the Zionist Idea*, p. 108.
4. Brecher, *Foreign Policy System*, p. 44.
5. Feldman oral history interview.
6. Draper, *Israel and World Politics*, pp. 45–46.
7. The following account of the events preceding and during the war rely for the most part on Draper, *Israel and World Politics*; Randolph S. and Winston S. Churchill, *The Six Day War* (London: Heinemann, 1967); and the article by Misha Louvish on Israel and by George E. Gruen on the United States and United Nations during the 1967 crisis in *American Jewish Year Book* 69 (1968): 115–30 and 145–87.
8. Draper, *Israel and World Politics*, p. 67; *American Jewish Year Book* 69 (1968): 118.
9. Feinberg, "Anatomy of a Commitment," p. 21; Meir, *My Life*, p. 313.
10. Churchill and Churchill, *The Six Day War*, pp. 44–45; Draper, *Israel and World Politics*, p. 93; Lyndon Baines Johnson, *The Vantage Point* (New York: Holt, Rinehart & Winston, 1971).
11. Brecher, *Decisions in Israel's Foreign Policy*, p. 326.
12. Heschel, *Israel: An Echo of Eternity*, pp. 196–97.
13. American Histadrut Cultural Exchange Institute, *The Impact of Israel on American Jewry: A Symposium* (New York: Histadrut, 1969), p. 12.
14. Heschel, *Israel*, p. 197; David Polish, "The Tasks of Israel and Galut," *Judaism* 18 (Winter 1969): 3; Histadrut, *Symposium*, p. 72.
15. Rubenstein, *Power Struggle*, p. 178.
16. Herman, *American Students in Israel*, p. 136.
17. *Jerusalem Post Weekly*, May 26, 1967; this and most of the other newspaper articles cited in this chapter are to be found in the Near East Crisis Collection, American Jewish Historical Society.
18. Lucy S. Dawidowicz, "American Public Opinion," *American Jewish Year Book* 69 (1968): 211–12; this letter was read aloud by Carl Reiner at a Hollywood Bowl rally on June 11, 1967.
19. *Facts and Figures: Summary of Reports submitted to the 27th*

Zionist Congress, Jerusalem, Sivan 5728–June 1968 (Jerusalem: WZO, 1968), p. 45.

20. Meir, *My Life*, p. 361; for other reasons, see Dawidowicz, "American Public Opinion," pp. 212–16. An examination of questionnaires on Jewish background filled in by volunteer applicants at the Jewish Agency building showed that the early volunteers (in May 1967) had very strong Jewish and/or Zionist backgrounds and education; the later ones had never had any strong identification either with Israel or with Judaism. "What seemed to be happening to them," suggested Dr. Annulf M. Pins, who evaluated the questionnaires, "was that a dormant loyalty had suddenly been stirred up and had become at that moment an overriding passion."

21. Levin, *Balm in Gilead*, pp. 259–67; interview with Mrs. Charlotte Jacobson, March 23, 1973.

22. Teller, *Strangers and Natives*, pp. 284–85; Cohen, *American Jews and the Zionist Idea*, p. 137; Silverberg, *If I Forget Thee*, pp. 16–17.

23. *Ibid.*; Dawidowicz, "American Public Opinion," p. 208.

24. Ralph Simon, in Moshe Davis, ed., "The Eretz Yisrael Dimension in American Jewish Life: Presentation, Discussion, and Resolution," *Proceedings of the Rabbinical Assembly* 34 (1970): 49; Evans, *The Provincials*, p. 110.

25. *New York Times*, July 16 and 19, 1967; Elmer Berger to Barry Silverberg, Mar. 13 and Apr. 2, 1973, courtesy of Mr. Silverberg; Elmer Berger, *Prophecy, Zionism, and the State of Israel* (New York: AJAZ, 1968), pp. 9-10.

26. Marshall Sklare, "Lakeville and Israel: The Six Day War and Its Aftermath," *Midstream* 14 (Oct. 1968): 6.

27. Evans, *The Provincials*, p. 110; *Intermountain Jewish News* (Denver), June 9, 1967; Silverberg, *If I Forget Thee*, p. 21.

28. Norman L. Friedman, "Orientations of Jewish Professors to the Jewish Community," *Jewish Social Studies* 35 (July/Oct. 1973): 277–81; Yaffe, *The American Jew*, p. 181.

29. See, for example, editorial, "Never Again!" St. Louis *Jewish Light*, June 7, 1967, and Detroit *Jewish News*, June 9, 1967.

30. Quoted in Cohen, *American Jews and the Zionist Idea*, p. 140; Arthur I. Waskow, *The Bush Is Burning! Radical Judaism Faces the Pharaohs of the Modern Superstate* (New York: Macmillan, 1971), p. 85. See also Borowitz, *Masks Jews Wear*, p. 53.

31. Heschel, *Israel: An Echo of Eternity*, p. 5.

32. Polish, "Tasks of Israel and *Galut*," p. 6; Eliezer Schweid, *Israel at the Crossroads*, tr. Alton Meyer Winters (Philadelphia: Jewish Publication Society, 1973), p. 216.

33. *The American Zionist* 58 (Sept. 1967): 4ff.

34. Declaration of the 2nd of Tammuz, 5727 (July 10, 1967), in *Zionism—The Force of Change*, pp. 58–59.

35. Rubin, *Partners in State-Building*, p. 244; see also Talmon, *Israel Among the Nations*, pp. 175–76.

36. Goldschneider, "American *Aliyah*," p. 353.

37. Teddy Kollek to Joseph M. Furst, June 20, 1967, Near East Crisis Collection, Box 6; Brecher, *Foreign Policy System*, pp. 314–15; Herman, *American Students in Israel*, p. 140.

38. Interviews with Ben-Ami Scharfstein, Julian Meltzer, Meyer Weisgal, Col. Dov Shefi, Moshe Kol, Natanel Lorch, Reuven Dafneh, Daniel Elazar, Zelig Chinitz, Yehudah Avner, Eliahu Elath, Evyatar Friesel, Arthur Lourie, Moshe Davis, Golda Meir, and Charlotte Jacobson; all, with the exception of the last, took place in Israel between May 29 and June 10, 1975.

39. See also Shlomo Avineri in Ben Ezer, *Unease in Zion*, p. 64; Sklare, *America's Jews*, p. 217.

40. Sklare, "Lakeville and Israel," p. 8; Walter Kaufman in Histadrut, *Symposium*, pp. 52–53.

41. Siegel, *Amen*, pp. 37–38. In 1972 I witnessed a similar incident in Albany, New York, at the Yom Kippur services. Israel had just been involved in a series of bombing raids against Palestinian camps in Lebanon, and a number of civilians had been killed. When it came time for the annual appeal to purchase Israel bonds, Rabbi Bernard A. Bloom told the congregation of Beth Emeth that he was sure that the Israelis had good intelligence, and he felt constrained, in the light of all the pressures on Israel, not to try to second-guess the military decision. But he, too, wept for the innocent children, be they Arab or Jew. A number of people in the community active in the Israel bond drive were shocked at this sacrilege, and alleged that the rabbi's untimely speech had caused a drop in sales. My own reaction was that there were four groups in the congregation that afternoon: those who would have bought a bond no matter what, those who had no intention of buying a bond, those who did in fact change their minds and not buy because of the talk (a fairly small group), and a fourth group, in which I was included, that changed its mind and did buy a bond because of what he had said (an even smaller group).

42. Jerusalem *Post*, June 6, 1967; Fishman, *American Protestantism and the Jewish State*, p. 166. There were, of course, some Christians who supported Israel, but for questionable reasons. In Birmingham, Alabama, a member of a local Baptist church wrote a letter to the newspaper in praise of the Israelis who fought to "maintain their purity as a people." Jews in Georgia visited the governor's mansion, hoping to get some kind of statement from Lester Maddox, who was not considered friendly toward the lib-

eral Jewish community. He surprised everyone in the delegation by declaring that "everybody ought to be for Israel." When asked why, he winked and said, "Cause I ain't never seen a camel yet that could outrun a Cadillac." Evans, *The Provincials*, p. 109. A good sampling of Christian response can be found in Judith Banki, *Christian Reactions to the Middle East Crisis* (New York: American Jewish Committee, 1968).

43. Samuel Sandmel, *We Jews and You Christians* (Philadelphia: Lippincott, 1967), pp. 51–53.

44. New York *Times*, July 7, 1967; Strober, *American Jews*, pp. 79–80.

45. Michael Frayne, "Dear Israel," *Midstream* 13 (Aug./Sept. 1967): 46–47; the short piece originally appeared in *The Observer* (London).

46. Heschel, *Israel: An Echo of Eternity*, pp. 202–3; Tannenbaum, "Israel's Hour of Need," pp. 17–18.

47. Davies, *Anti-Semitism and the Christian Mind*, pp. 179–80; Polish, *Israel—Nation and People*, pp. 85–86.

48. Dawidowicz, "American Public Opinion," pp. 218–24.

49. New York *Times*, June 7, 1967; Silverberg, *If I Forget Thee*, p. 595; Draper, *Israel and World Politics*, pp. 118–19.

50. Henry Roth, "Kaddish," *Midstream* 23 (Jan. 1977): 54–55.

Notes to Chapter 15

1. Quoted by Seymour Siegal in Histadrut, *Symposium*, p. 27.

2. Nathan Glazer, "The New Left and the Jews," in Sklare, *The Jewish Community in America*, p. 306; Tom Milstein in Mordecai S. Chertoff, ed., *The New Left and the Jews* (New York: Pitman, 1971), pp. 299–300.

3. Arnold Forster and Benjamin R. Epstein, *The New Anti-Semitism* (New York: McGraw-Hill, 1974), pp. 11–12.

4. *The Militant*, Feb. 1969, quoted *ibid.*, p. 137; New York *Review of Books*, Aug. 3, 1967; see also the comments by Marie Syrkin, Joel Carmichael, and Lionel Abel in "I. F. Stone Reconsiders Israel," *Midstream* 13 (Oct. 1967): 3–17.

5. Jack Nusan Porter and Peter Dreier, *Jewish Radicalism: A Selected Anthology* (New York: Grove Press, 1973), p. xxxvii.

6. Jewish Peace Fellowship *Newsletter*, (Aug.–Nov. 1970), in Waskow MSS.

7. American Jewish Alternatives to Zionism, *Report No. 7* (July 1970): 6.

8. Waskow, *The Bush Is Burning*, pp. 64–65.

9. Aliza Samuel, "I Listen Again to Joan Baez," *Midstream* 21 (May 1975): 35.

10. Arthur Waskow, "Judaism and Revolution Today," in Porter and Dreier, *Jewish Radicalism*, p. 15.

11. Chertoff, *New Left and the Jews*, pp. 190–91; see also Rosenberg, "To Uncle Tom and Other Jews," in *Jewish Radicalism*, pp. 8–9.

12. *New Left and the Jews*, pp. 272–74.

13. Louis Henkin, ed., *World Politics and the Jewish Condition* (New York: Quadrangle, 1972), pp. 27–28; *New Left and the Jews*, p. 103.

14. See Cruse's *The Crisis of the Negro Intellectual* (New York: Morrow, 1967), where he attacked the "manipulation" of Negroes by Jewish communists in the thirties, and then generalized to a condemnation of Jews in the present.

15. Seymour Martin Lipset, "The Left, the Jews, and Israel," *Encounter* 33 (Dec. 1969): 24; Gary A. Glickstein, "Religion and the Jewish New Left—1960 to Date," *American Jewish Archives* 26 (Apr. 1974): 24–25.

16. *The New Jews*, p. 87.

17. Chertoff, *New Left and the Jews*, p. 143; Bill Novak, "The Failure of Jewish Radicalism," in Porter and Dreier, *Jewish Radicalism*, pp. 305–7.

18. Sol Stern, "My Jewish Problem—and Ours," *ibid.*, p. 361.

19. Joseph McCarty to Arthur Waskow, July 26, 1971; Arthur Lelyveld to Waskow, Sept. 26, 1972; A. Joseph Heckelman to Waskow, Sept. 11, 1972, all in Waskow MSS.

20. Porter and Dreier, "Introduction," *Jewish Radicalism*, pp. xxx–xxxi.

21. Kenneth B. Clark, "Candor About Negro-Jewish Relations," *Commentary* 1 (Feb. 1946): 8–14.

22. Lipset, in *New Left and the Jews*, pp. 120–21.

23. Max Geltman, *The Confrontation: Black Power, Anti-Semitism, and the Myth of Integration* (Englewood Cliffs, N.J.: Prentice-Hall, 1970), p. 181.

24. Strober, *American Jews*, pp. 119–20.

25. Fred V. Davidow, "Black Anti-Semitism, American Jewry, and Israel," term paper, HUC-JIR, 1971; Strober, *American Jews*, pp. 118–19; Robert G. Weisbord and Arthur Stein, *Bittersweet Encounter: The Afro-American and the American Jew* (Westport, Conn.: Negro Universities Press, 1970), p. 101.

26. *Ibid.*, pp. 77, 99; Geltman, *The Confrontation*, p. 233.

27. Weisbord and Stein, *Bittersweet Encounter*, p. 108.

28. For details of the strike, see Martin Meyer, *The Teachers Strike, New York, 1968* (New York: Harper & Row, 1969), which has a pro-union bias; Marilyn Gittell and Maurice Berube, *Confrontation at Ocean Hill* (New York: Praeger, 1969), favors the local governing board; Melvin I. Urofsky, *Why Teachers Strike: Teachers' Rights and Community Control* (Garden City, N.Y.: Anchor, 1970), provides interviews with many of the participants, and an interpretive essay.

29. New York *Times*, Aug. 16, 1967, and Sept. 13, 1968; Levy and Kraemer, *The Ethnic Factor*, p. 109.

30. Eugene Rothman, "Rome and Jerusalem: The Uncertain Voice of the American Catholic Press," *Midstream* 17 (Apr. 1971): 33; Frank Talmage, "Christianity and the Jewish People," *Commentary* 59 (Feb. 1975): 62; Fishman, *American Protestantism and the Jewish State*, p. 152.

31. Rothman, "Rome and Jerusalem," p. 33; Fishman, *American Protestantism*, p. 173; Malcolm L. Diamond, "Christian Silence on Israel: A End to Dialogue?," *Judaism* 16 (Fall 1967): 411. One example of this attitude can be found in the texts published by the Assemblies of God, a major pentecostal denomination, which after describing the Holocaust and the murder of millions of Jews, concluded that all Jewish suffering resulted from their "rejection" of Jesus. Strober, *American Jews*, p. 75.

32. Franklin H. Littell, *The Crucifixion of the Jews* (New York: Harper & Row, 1975), pp. 87–88.

33. Friedman, *No Haven for the Oppressed*, p. 232.

34. Interview with Louis Levinthal, Dec. 22, 1972; Isaacs, *Jews in American Politics*, p. 51; Borowitz, *Masks Jews Wear*, p. 56; Alan W. Miller, *The God of Daniel S.: In Search of the American Jew* (New York: Macmillan, 1969), p. 147.

35. Meir Kahane, *Never Again! A Program for Jewish Survival* (Los Angeles: Nash, 1971), p. 78.

36. Strober, *American Jews*, pp. 171–72.

37. Marvin Kalb and Bernard Kalb, *Kissinger* (Boston: Little, Brown, 1974), pp. 47, 217–18; Isaacs, *Jews in American Politics*, p. 69; Gil Carl AlRoy, *The Kissinger Experience: American Policy in the Middle East* (New York: Horizon, 1975), pp. 21–22. The Arabs were none too happy about Kissinger's appointment either. *Al Diyar*, a Lebanese paper, declared that "Kissinger's accession to the State Department can be interpreted only as a declaration of unofficial war against the Arabs." The Egyptian *Al Anwar* termed the appointment, an "Israeli victory over the Arabs, not only in America but in the Middle East." The Algerian embassy in London stated that "as far as we are concerned, there is no difference between a Jew and an Israeli," and that Algeria would act as if Israel had appointed the

American Secretary. Forster and Epstein, *The New Anti-Semitism*, pp. 315–16.

38. Bohlen, *Witness to History*, p. 461; Henkin, *World Politics and the Jewish Condition*, p. 18.

39. Marvin C. Feuerwerger, "The Emergency Security Assistance Act of 1973 and American-Israeli Relations," *Midstream* 20 (Aug./Sept. 1974): 26.

40. Sulzberger, *An Age of Mediocrity*, p. 754.

41. Kalb and Kalb, *Kissinger*, p. 240.

42. Strober, *American Jews*, pp. 192–95; Meir, *My Life*, pp. 387–93; Jewish Telegraphic Agency dispatch [July 1971] quoted in *JAZ Report No. 13* (Dec. 1971): 51.

43. Horowitz, *Israeli Ecstasies/Jewish Agonies*, pp. 102–3. Among the economic and political brokers who either openly supported Nixon in 1972 or abandoned the Democratic Party were Stanley Goldblum (president, Equities Funding Corporation), Davis Factor (president, Max Factor Cosmetics), Eugene V. Klein (chairman, National General Corporation), Irving Kristol (editor of *Public Interest*), Leo Cherne (director, Research Institute of America), William Wexler (chairman, World Conference of Jewish Organizations), and Leonard H. Marks (former director, United States Information Agency).

44. Lewis Coser and Irving Howe, eds., *The New Conservatives: A Critique from the Left* (New York: Quadrangle, 1974), p. 78; Isaacs, *Jews in American Politics*, p. 192; Strober, *American Jews*, pp. 198–99; *CCAR Yearbook* 82 (1972): 97.

45. Strober, *American Jews*, pp. 205–8.

46. Melvin Urofsky, "President Carter—A New Era?," *Midstream* 23 (Jan. 1977): 42–48.

Notes to Chapter 16

1. Neusner, *American Judaism*, p. 3; Borowitz, *A New Jewish Theology in the Making*, p. 19; Teller, *Strangers and Natives*, p. 225; Siegel, *Amen*, p. 67; Daniel Elazar, "Building Jewish Citizenship in the Emerging American Jewish Community," *Forum* 23 (Spring 1975): 8.

2. Milton Himmelfarb, "Comments on condition of the American Jewish community," at seminar sponsored by the Zionist Academic Council, Mar. 20, 1977, in New York.

3. Daniel J. Elazar, *Community and Polity: The Organizational Dynamics of American Jewry* (Philadelphia: Jewish Publication Society, 1976), *passim*.

4. Intermarriage, of course, is not restricted to Jew and non-Jew. The earliest Jews in the United States, the Sephardim, looked down upon the Ashkenazic German migrants of the midnineteenth century, and considered the marriage of one of their children to an Ashkenazi as an "intermarriage." By the late nineteenth century, the Germans had been fully accepted by the Sephardim, and marriages between the two groups lost their opprobrium. By then, however, the masses of eastern European Jewry from Poland and Russia had begun to arrive, and it would not be until the 1930s and 1940s that marriages between the Germans and the new groups became acceptable.

5. Miller, *The God of Daniel S.*, pp. 122–23; Jaffe, *American Jews*, pp. 74–75.

6. Van Der Haag, *The Jewish Mystique*, pp. 96–97; Alter, *After the Tradition*, p. 36.

7. Seymour Martin Lipset and Everett Carll Ladd, Jr., "Jewish Academics in the United States: Their Achievement, Culture, and Politics," *American Jewish Year Book* 72 (1971): 89–128; *Time*, Mar. 10, 1975.

8. Jaffe, *American Jews*, pp. 318–19; Goldstein, *Israel at Home and Abroad*, pp. 242–44; Borowitz, *New Jewish Theology in the Making*, p. 148; Elazar, "Building Jewish Citizenship," pp. 7–8.

9. Histadrut *Symposium*, p. 19; Strober, *American Jews*, p. 256.

10. Gary S. Schiff, "American Jews and Israel: A Study in Political Conduct," *Forum* 24 (1976): 22–23.

11. The most definitive and wide-ranging study of the problem of orthodoxy in Israel is S. Zalman Abramov, *Perpetual Dilemma: Jewish Religion in the Jewish State* (New York: World Union for Progressive Judaism, 1976).

12. *CCAR Year Book* 74 (1964): 21.

13. Abramov, *Perpetual Dilemma, passim*.

14. Actually, Mafdal, the religious Zionist political party, has been the most moderate of the Israeli Orthodox. But anytime they have been tempted to modernize Halachah, they have been attacked by the more militant Agudas Yisrael. Prior to the establishment of Israel, the Agudas were anti-Zionist and opposed to a state; they came around only because of the Holocaust and because it became obvious that, whether or not they liked it, a state would be established. In turn, Agudas is always looking over its shoulder at the fanatically pious Neture Karta, who continue to oppose the state and are accepted, implicitly, as the paragon of Torah-true Judaism.

15. Bertram Korn, "Reflections on My Trip to Israel, November 1967," miscellaneous files, American Jewish Archives.

16. Zucker, *The Coming Crisis in Israel*, pp. 94–95; Abramov, *Perpetual Dilemma*, pp. 37–74.

17. See, for example, "Open Letter to Prime Minister of Israel, May 1951," Lehman MSS, urging Ben-Gurion to support the demands of the Orthodox, and Eliezer Livneh, "Israel's Role in the Diaspora," *In the Dispersion* 8 (1968): 123.

18. Zucker, *The Coming Crisis in Israel*, pp. 90–91; Jakob J. Petuchowski, "The Shape of Israeli Judaism: Realities and Hopes," *Judaism* 20 (Spring 1971): 149.

19. Discussion, "Israel's Role in the Diaspora," *In the Dispersion* 8 (1968): 111.

20. *Ibid.*, p. 119; interview with Mrs. Charlotte Jacobson, Mar. 23, 1973; Sklare, *America's Jews*, pp. 220–21.

21. Chaim Adler, "Inside Israel," in *World Politics and the Jewish Condition*, pp. 175–76; Fred S. Sherrow and Paul Ritterband, "An Analysis of Migration to Israel," *Jewish Social Studies* 32 (July 1970): 216–19; see also Aharon Antonovsky, "Americans and Canadians in Israel," mimeographed Report No. 1, Israeli Institute of Applied Social Research (June 1968).

22. Harry Lieb Jubas, "The Adjustment Process of Americans and Canadians in Israel and their Integration into Israeli Society," doctoral dissertation (Michigan State University, 1974), p. 320. For the most severe criticism of the immigration and absorption process, see the Horev Report of 1976, discussed at length in the Jerusalem *Post* and other Israeli papers. For another firsthand account, see Avraham Ha-Yored [pseud.], "Broken Promises," *Jewish Spectator* 41 (Fall 1976): 52–54.

23. Siegal, *Amen*, p. 37; Borowitz in Histadrut *Symposium*, p. 4.

24. Jerome W. Grollman, "Our responsibility to reprove Israel," *Sh'ma* 3 (Mar. 30, 1973): 82.

25. Interview with Mrs. Meir, June 10, 1975; see also Saul Friedlander and Edward Luttwak, "War and Peace in the Middle East: An Israeli Perspective," in *World Politics and the Jewish Condition*, p. 132.

26. Horowitz, *Israeli Ecstasies*, p. 6; Ben Ezer, *Unease in Zion*, p. 42.

27. Yehuda Amichai, "My Father Fought Their War Four Years," tr. A. Gutman, *Encounter* 30 (Mar. 1968): 47, cited in Natan Rotenstreich, *Reflections on the Contemporary Jewish Condition* (Jerusalem: Institute for Contemporary Judaism, 1975), pp. 31–32.

28. Stanley Cooper, "Masada" (1972), in Samuel Hart Joseloff, *A Time to Seek* (New York: UAHC, 1975).

29. Horowitz, *Israeli Ecstasies,* p. 182; Alter, *After the Tradition,* pp. 205–6; see also Waskow, *The Bush Is Burning,* p. 127. In the spring of 1970, Meyer Weisgal wrote to Richard Crossman: "We didn't come to this country to shed blood or to shoot or to be shot at. The Zionist ideal was totally different. I am neither a dove nor a hawk, certainly not a vulture—just a very simple, sad Jew who has daily been working for the Zionist cause practically all his adult life. I ask myself all kinds of questions: When will the end come? Will there be an end? Will we ever be able to use our resources, our intelligence, our ability to work hard for the renaissance—not only of Israel itself but of the entire area? This, after all, was the essential idea of Zionism, and the motive force behind the re-establishment of the Jewish state." Weisgal, . . . *So Far,* pp. 369–70.

30. Polish, *Centennial Papers: Israel,* p. 10.

31. Albert Memni, *The Liberation of the Jew,* tr. Judy Hyun (New York: Orion Press, 1966); Schweid, *Israel at the Crossroads,* pp. 204–5; Julian Morgenstern memoir, Hebrew University Oral History Collection; David Schoenbrun with Robert and Lucy Szekely, *The New Israelis* (New York: Atheneum, 1973), p. 230.

32. Report of Ezra Spicehandler, *CCAR Year Book* 78 (1968): 228–29; personal observations from visits in 1971 and 1972.

33. Interview with Charlotte Jacobson, Mar. 23, 1973; Aliza Samuel, "I Listen Again to Joan Baez," *Midstream* 21 (May 1975): 38–39.

34. Reuven Sarkis, "What are the Israelis teaching their kids about us?" *interChange* 2 (October 1976): 1, 6–8; discussion on "Israel's Role in the Diaspora," *In the Dispersion* 8 (1968): 115.

35. Faye Schenk, "What Went Wrong at the Zionist Congress," *Hadassah Magazine* 53 (Mar. 1972): 2–3; interviews with Rose Halprin and Charlotte Jacobson, Mar. 23, 1973.

36. See, for example, Melvin Urofsky, "No *Aliyah* from America," and the responses by Moshe Kohn, Ephraim Tabory, and Michael Graetz, in *Forum* 25 (1976): 72–89.

37. Ben Halpern, "Zion in the Mind of American Jews," in *The Future of the Jewish Community in America,* ed. David Sidorsky (New York: Basic Books, 1973), p. 37; Samuel Sandmel Memoir, Oral History Collection, Hebrew University; Borowitz, *New Jewish Theology,* pp. 28–29; Goldstein, *Israel at Home and Abroad,* p. 39.

38. Information on the reconstituted Jewish Agency is drawn primarily from Charles S. Liebmann, *Pressure Without Sanctions: The Influence of World Jewry on Israeli Policy* (Rutherford, N.J.: Fairleigh Dickinson University Press, 1977), ch. 6; Ernest Stock, "The Reconstitution of the Jewish Agency: A Political Analysis," *American Jewish Year Book* 73 (1972):

178–93; Zelig Chinitz, "Weizmann and the Jewish Agency," paper delivered at Herzl Institute, May 4, 1975; interview with Zelig Chinitz, June 10, 1975.

Notes to Chapter 17

1. Robert O. Freedman, *Soviet Policy Toward the Middle East Since 1970* (New York: Praeger, 1975), p. 116.

2. Meir, *My Life,* pp. 248–52.

3. Abraham J. Bayer, "American Response to Soviet-Jewish Policies," *American Jewish Year Book* 74 (1973): 210–25.

4. Details on the Jackson amendment are drawn from three articles by William D. Korey: "The Struggle over Jackson-Mills-Vanik," *ibid.* 75 (1974–75): 199–234; "The Struggle over the Jackson Amendment," *ibid.* 76 (1976): 160–70; and "The Story of the Jackson Amendment, 1973–1975," *Midstream* 21 (Mar. 1975): 7–36.

5. New York *Times,* Apr. 20 and May 17, 1973.

6. Freedman, *Soviet Policy,* pp. 92–93; Sidney Liskofsky, "International Protection of Human Rights," in *World Politics and the Jewish Condition,* pp. 300–1.

7. Kalb and Kalb, *Kissinger,* p. 523; Jon Kimche, "Kissinger Diplomacy and the Art of Limited War," *Midstream* 20 (Nov. 1974): 3–12.

8. For an extremely critical view of Kissinger's efforts, see AlRoy, *The Kissinger Experience.*

9. Moshe Ma'oz, *The Image of the Jew in Official Arab Literature and Communications Media* (Jerusalem: Institute for Contemporary Jewry, 1976), pp. 9, 12–13, 20; AlRoy, *Behind the Middle East Conflict,* pp. 166, 176.

10. Marie Syrkin, "A Palestinian State?" *Midstream* 20 (Oct. 1974): 63; Oriana Fallaci, "An Interview with Yasir Arafat," *The New Republic* 171 (Nov. 16, 1974): 10–12; Ma'oz, *The Image of the Jew,* pp. 28–29.

11. Bauer, *From Diplomacy to Resistance,* p. 246.

12. AlRoy, *Behind the Middle East Conflict,* pp. 147–48.

13. Saul Bellow, *To Jerusalem and Back: A Personal Account* (New York: Viking, 1976), pp. 25–26.

14. Eytan, *The First Ten Years,* pp. 118–19.

15. Terence Prittie and Bernard Dineen, *The Double Exodus* (London, n.d.), pp. 1–2. Professor J. Coert Rylaarsdam of the University of

Chicago Divinity School has written: "The Jews of Yemen and of Iraq, the Jews of North Africa and of other Arab centers, were uprooted by the same Arab war on Israel that uprooted the Arabs of Palestine. . . . They too left their property behind them, they too suffered indignity, abuse, and death. Their rehabilitation, in contrast to their Arab counterparts, is due to the fact that their own cared for them. Isn't it ironical that this act of responsibility and compassion should have deprived Israel of a propaganda weapon so cleverly used by its neighbors?" Fishman, *American Protestantism and the Jewish State*, pp. 128–29.

16. Alter, *After the Tradition*, p. 224; Amos Perlmutter interview on National Public Radio, May 26, 1977.

17. Interview with Yehudah Avner, June 5, 1975; Leonard J. Fein, "Israel or Zion," *Judaism* 22 (Winter 1973): 8; David Polish, presidential address, *CCAR Year Book* 83 (1973): 5; Mordecai Waxman, "United States of America: Perspectives," in Moshe Davis, ed., *The Yom Kippur War: Israel and the Jewish People* (New York: Arno Press, 1974), pp. 72–73.

18. Daniel J. Elazar, "United States of America: Overview," *ibid.*, pp. 12–13; personal observations during Yom Kippur War of activities in Albany, New York.

19. Strober, *American Jews*, pp. 270–71; Alfred Gottschalk, "Perspectives," p. 41; Elazar, "Overview," p. 14; Arye L. Dulzin, "Perspectives," p. 268, all in Davis, *Yom Kippur War*.

20. Elazar, *ibid.*, p. 15.

21. Gary S. Schiff, "American Jews and Israel: A Study in Political Conduct," *Forum* 24 (1976): 28.

22. Samuel Rabinove, "Intergroup Relations and Tensions in the United States," *American Jewish Year Book* 75 (1974–75): 111–12.

23. Earl Raab, "Is Israel Losing Support?" *Commentary* 57 (Jan. 1974): 26; Forster and Epstein, *The New Anti-Semitism*, p. 321.

24. Frank Church, "Israel and International Concerns," *Congress Monthly* 42 (Mar. 1975): 6; *Christian Science Monitor*, Oct. 13, 1973.

25. Robert E. Cushman, "What Price Israel?" *The Christian Century* 90 (Nov. 7, 1973): 1,093–94; for an opposing Christian view, however, see A. Roy Eckhardt, "The Devil and Yom Kippur," *Midstream* 20 (Aug./Sept. 1974): 67–75; Strober, *American Jews*, p. 80.

26. Berrigan's talk was reprinted in several places, but first appeared in *American Report, the Journal of Clergy and Laity Concerned About Vietnam*, copy in Waskow MSS.

27. Arthur Waskow to Daniel Berrigan, Dec. 19, 1973, *ibid.*; Waskow to editor, *Village Voice*, Feb. 4, 1974, published in the *Voice*, Feb. 14, 1974.

28. Irving Howe, "Thinking the Unthinkable About Israel," *New York* 6 (Dec. 24, 1973): 44–52; Gottschalk, "Perspectives," in Davis, *Yom Kippur War*, p. 37.

29. Wiesel, *Two Images, One Destiny*, pp. 6, 11; Arnulf M. Pins, "Impact of the Yom Kippur War on American Jewry," *In the Diaspora* 21/22 (1973–74): 69; Union of American Hebrew Congregations, *Centennial Papers: Social Ethics* (New York: UAHC, 1974), p. 25.

30. Norman Lamm, "Perspectives," in Davis, *Yom Kippur War*, p. 54.

31. In August 1973, King Faisal of Saudi Arabia warned the American people that while he personally did not want to reduce oil exports, "America's complete support of Zionism makes it extremely difficult to continue to supply oil to the United States or even to maintain friendly relations with it." Freedman, *Soviet Policy Toward the Middle East*, p. 116.

32. Theodore Draper, "The United States and Israel: Tilt in the Middle East?" *Commentary* 59 (Apr. 1975): 34.

33. Schoenbrun, *The New Israelis*, pp. 196–97; AlRoy, *The Kissinger Experience*, pp. 59–60.

34. New York *Times*, Sept. 25, 1973; Kimche, "Kissinger Diplomacy," p. 7; Kalb and Kalb, *Kissinger*, pp. 514–15.

35. *Ibid.*, pp. 520, 523; Meir, *My Life*, pp. 421–27; Freedman, *Soviet Policy*, p. 120.

36. For the war, see Luttwak and Horowitz. *The Israeli Army*, ch. 10; Chaim Herzog, *The War of Atonement* (Boston: Little, Brown 1975); and London *Sunday Times*, *The Yom Kippur War* (Garden City, N.Y.: Doubleday, 1974).

37. Kalb and Kalb, *Kissinger*, p. 525; Meir, *My Life*, p. 430.

38. Marvin and Bernard Kalb, "Twenty Days in October," New York *Times* Magazine; June 23, 1974: Tad Szalc, "Is He Indispensable? Answers to the Kissinger Riddle," *New York* 7 (July 1, 1974): 33–39; AlRoy, *The Kissinger Experience, passim*; Draper, "United States and Israel," p. 35; Jacques Torczyner to author, Sept. 29, 1977.

39. Gil Carl AlRoy, "Kissinger Delivers Another Israeli Withdrawal," *Midstream* 21 (Nov. 1975): 13; Efraim Shmueli, "Israel, *Galut*, and Zionism," *Judaism* 23 (Summer 1974): 271; Walter Eytan, "A Time to Take Stock," *Israel Digest* (Apr. 25, 1975): 4–5; Bellow, *To Jerusalem and Back, passim*; personal observation and interviews in Israel, May and June 1975.

40. Kalb and Kalb, *Kissinger*, p. 593; Draper, "United States and Israel," pp. 41–42; Morgenthau quoted in *Reform Judaism* 2 (Apr. 1974): 8; Norman Podhoretz, "The Abandonment of Israel," *Commentary* 62 (July 1976): 23–31.

41. New York *Times*, May 22, 1975.

Notes to Chapter 18

1. Interview with I. L. Kenen, Nov. 13, 1975, and with Morris J. Amitai, Oct. 20, 1976; Aaron D. Rosenbaum, "The New Administration and Its Approach to Middle East Policy," briefing to National Board of American Zionist Federation, May 15, 1977; *Time*, Mar. 10, 1975.

2. Marvin C. Feuerwerger, "The Emergency Security Assistance Act of 1973 and American-Israeli Relations," *Midstream* 20 (Aug./Sept. 1974): 21–23; Horowitz, *Israeli Ecstasies/Jewish Agonies*, pp. 115–16.

3. Jerusalem *Post Weekly*, July 29 and Aug. 12, 1975, June 29, 1976; *Time*, Mar. 19, 1975.

4. Nathan Glazer, "The Exposed American Jew," *Commentary* 59 (June 1975): 28–29.

5. Milton Goldin, "Plaques and Flattery Will Get You Nowhere," *Present Tense* 4 (Spring 1977): 27; Schoenbrun, *New Israelis*, p. 210.

6. See, for example, Judy Siegel, "They Give to Israel Till It Hurts," Jerusalem *Post Weekly*, Oct. 14, 1975, and Avi Z. Binyamin, "Alan Rudy brings 'Koach' to Israel," *Israel Digest*, Oct. 21, 1975.

7. Goldin, "Plaques," pp. 25–26.

8. Sleeper and Mintz, *The New Jews*, p. 82; Chaim I. Waxman, "The Centrality of Israel in American Jewish Life: A Sociological Analysis," *Judaism* 25 (Spring 1976): 183–84; *Centennial Papers: Social Ethics*, p. 19; Rotenstreich, *Reflections on Contemporary Jewish Condition*, p. 28; Yitzhak Rabin, "Israel and American Jews," *Forum* 23 (Spring 1975): 70–71.

9. "An Exchange of Letters between Robert Alter and Shlomo Avineri," *Moment* 1 (May/June 1975): 10–23; Sidorsky, "End of Ideology," p. 20; Horowitz, *Israeli Ecstasies/Jewish Agonies*, pp. 109–10; comments by Milton Himmelfarb and Arthur Hertzberg at Zionist Academic Council conference, "Toward the Year 2000," New York, Mar. 20, 1977.

10. Sklare, "An Ever-Dying People," pp. 26–27.

11. Sidorsky, "End of Ideology," p. 29; see also Melvin I. Urofsky, "Zionism: Toward the Year 2000," *Midstream* 24 (Feb. 1978): 66–72.

12. Conversations with Ralph Stern and Irving Bernstein, Sept. 1977.

Index